Perictione in Colophon

Perictione in Colophon
Reflections on the Aesthetic Way of Life

Translated from the Arabic by
Roger Scruton

ST. AUGUSTINE'S PRESS
South Bend, Indiana
2000

Manufactured in the United States of America.

Library of Congress Cataloging in Publication Data
Scruton, Roger.
     Perictione in Colophon : reflections on the aesthetic way of life / translated from the Arabic by Roger Scruton.
        p.   cm.
     Sequel to: Xanthippic dialogues.
     ISBN 1-890318-59-0 (alk. paper)
     1. Plato—Parodies, imitations, etc. 2. Women—History—To 500—Humor. 3. Aesthetics, Ancient—Humor. 4. Philosophy, Ancient—Humor. 5. Imaginary conversations. 6. Dialogues, English. 7. Parodies. I. Title.
PR6069.C78 P47 1999
822'.914—dc21   99-050296

∞*The paper used in this publication meets the minimum requirements of the American National Standard for Information Sciences—Permanence of Paper for Printed Materials, ANSI Z39.48-1984.*

Contents

Contents

Preface

She was a Druze, daughter of a *sheikh al-'aql*, a holy man who had led his donkey from village to village in the Shouf, dressed in a white-turbaned fez and peddling his wares of aspirin, redemption and contraband whisky. After her father's death she lived alone in the little cottage of yellow stone, perched on the hillside below Souq-el-gharb – the 'Market in the West' where farmers and shepherds from the Shouf struck bargains with the Beiruti traders. She practised the art of concealment – which the Persians call *ketman*, and the Druze *taqiyya* or 'holiness.' She was friend to everyone and special friend to no-one; she belonged to all political parties and to none; and in the war which raged about her she was on the side of the person, whoever it might be, who asked her what she thought of it. She had pronounced the Two Testimonies and was recorded among the blessed; and, in consequence of a pre-war mission from Birmingham, she was a communicant member of the Church of England. Above her little porch was a verse from the Koran, whose ornate kufic calligraphy spanned the lintel: 'O ye who believe, be mindful of your duty to Allah and keep company with the righteous.' The door carried an icon of St Elias, patron saint of Lebanon, and another of the holy image known to Christians as St George, to the Druze as *al-khudr*, the green one, and to sceptical scholars as Attis, Adonis, Tammuz and Osiris – the god who dies each year and is born again in green, whose icon is a talisman against doubt, disease and mortar bombs.

Since her father's death, no-one but she had entered the little house. When the Syrians advanced to the escarpment half a mile from Souq-el-gharb, and the *Forces Libanaises* undertook to hold them there, the population of the battered town was evacuated; she alone refused to move. Now she stood each Thursday night in her downstairs window, her head wrapped in the Druze *mandil*, holding a candle to attract the water-tanker as it chugged over the hill-top out of the darkened valley, like a great black insect emerging from a cleft in the earth. And as the tanker approached over the broken cobbles, she would hold the candle above her head, her azure eyes narrowed in a sudden smile, and pointing with her free hand to the tar-caulked water-tub beside the doorway.

For reasons which have no bearing on what follows, I often drove that tanker. It was slow and dangerous work, crawling under cover of darkness, without lights but with the engine labouring up the steep incline so loudly, that no sniper could fail to hit his target. Each week new craters pitted the upper road, and the last few hundred yards, as the groaning lorry came within Syrian hearing, were especially hazardous. I was always glad to call a halt before the old woman's house, to receive her greeting as she stretched her elastic mouth into every shape of welcome, and to step for a moment into the shelter of her porch before resuming the journey to the sandbagged schoolhouse which was our headquarters.

It was a warm night when I stopped for the last time at her house. Overhead the sky was clear, Orion's sword hung motionless and beautiful, and also frightening in its changelessness, shining down equally on peace and war. An occasional rattle of machine-gun fire, the whine of ricocheting bullets, and the crash of mortar bombs in the orchard by the school did nothing to dilute the pious atmosphere of her house, with its outbuildings of amber stone, its carob tree hung with drying gourds, its wooden lintel painted with holy words and its candle now set down and flickering in the window, where she stood and watched me as I filled her tub. I turned to leave with a sense of departing from a sacred place, a place so invested with the spirit that the person who dwelt there could be moved from it by nothing save death.

Death came that night, in the form of a heavy shell from a new piece of Syrian artillery. It took us three hours to clear away the rubble of her house, which had been blown across the road like a house of matchsticks. The chimney had fallen in a heap upon her, but when we took out her body it was pale and unbloodied. I like to think she was killed at once by the shock.

In the room that only she had entered since the *sheikh* had died, the broken furniture and shards of Islamic pottery lay in confusion. A carpet smouldered beneath some stones, and we used our precious water to put out the fire. Books and papers were blown together in charred heaps, and scattered across the garden. It was the wreck of a scholar's library, and I grieved at the sight, secretly reproaching the old lady that she had hidden this treasure from the world until it was too late to save it. Then, rummaging in a corner which had been buried under falling stone, we came across two large boxes of steel. Assuming them to contain personal papers, I volunteered to take them in the tanker to Beirut, where they could be kept in safety while we looked for relatives.

No relatives were found. But one day, despairing over the fate of Lebanon, and preparing for the journey home, I happened to open one of the boxes. I was surprised to find a pile of old vellum, written all over in a stylish hand. The text is in classical Arabic, with vowels and nunation, the work of a conscientious grammarian. That it is the Arabic version of a hellenistic text I doubt: too many of the devices have been borrowed from Scheherazade. Nevertheless, I venture to suggest that it is the work of a medieval scholar thoroughly acquainted with the classical sources, and in particular with the *Xanthippic Dialogues*, the story of which he – or more likely she – purports to continue. The style is sometimes elevated, sometimes coarse, like the *Thousand and One Nights*. And except for the frequent references to '*aalam ul-hadith* –

which I have faithfully translated as 'the modern world' – the author was writing, like her great contemporary, not of Baghdad or Colophon, but of a Babylon of dreams.

Foreword

The speeches delivered at Phryne's Symposium, recorded in the *Xanthippic Dialogues*, reveal to us that Archeanassa of Colophon, then Plato's mistress (as attested also by Diogenes Laertius, *Lives of the Philosophers*, III, 31), had previously been the lover of Antimachus of Colophon, whom some credit with the invention of the new style of poetry. This new style, exemplified by the lost *Lyde* of Antimachus, was devoted to romantic love between man and woman. And if it was not invented by Antimachus, then, say the scholars, it was the work of Anaxandrides, a writer of middle comedy, who also came from Colophon (unless he came from Rhodes).

Plato is reputed to have been greatly interested in Antimachus and to have sent an emissary to Colophon on the poet's death, with the intention of retrieving his literary remains. There are many reasons why he might have done this, and many reasons why he might have burned the papers, had he succeeded in getting his hands on them. In any case, nothing of Antimachus survives, and almost everything of Plato. The *Lyde* was, however, famous in its day, and already the scholars of Alexandria debated its merits, and disputed whether Lyde, the subject of the work, were wife or mistress of the poet.

Plato's pupil Heraclides Ponticus claims (Fr. 91, Voss), that it was he who travelled to Colophon on the philosopher's behalf. But this story was surely invented to protect the reputation of the Academy. It would be the height of folly to expose this wealthy and high-born pupil to the risk of such a journey, and far more prudent to assign the task to an irritating and expendable novice, along with a discarded mistress whose presence in Athens had never ceased to be an embarrassment, and who, being intimate both with Antimachus and with Colophon, would have had a head-start over any competitor in the search for the manuscripts.

Present at Phryne's symposium was Plato's fastidious sister Potone, Potone's virgin daughter Perictione, and Xanthippe, widow of Socrates, old by then, and scraping a living as best she could from the tapestries which she wove, depicting the judgement of her husband. These tapestries (described in 'Xanthippe's Laws') became more important after the old lady's death, when means were discovered for their mass production. At the time they held little interest for the Athenians, and those who sought Xanthippe's company – who included most women of taste and education – frequented her for her brains. In fact, the old lady was bothered night and day for her philosophical opinions, and gave voice at last to the exasperated remarks which caused her downfall. She was ordered before the magistrates, probably at the behest of Philip of Macedon, who was reluctant to take possession of Athens while Xanthippe was still living in the city. In any case, her trial and execution on a charge of impiety occurred some years before Archeanassa's journey to Colophon, and I mention the fact only because it is the point from which the decline and fall of Greece began.

1

Concerning Archeanassa's return to Colophon

When Plato, old by then and frail, heard that Antimachus of Colophon had departed this life, he summoned Aristotle to his couch.

'You are familiar with the writings of Antimachus,' he said.

Aristotle responded by reciting the *Lyde,* to which his master listened with a troubled air. The boy had covered most of the first book, in which the town of Colophon is artfully compared, street by street, to Lyde's anatomy, and had embarked on the notorious passage which begins

> *As the golden sand brightens under the wavelet,*
> *So does my body shine to your caress . . .*

when Plato interrupted him.

'Those lines,' he said, 'are not in the edition that we have in the Academy.'

'No sir. But I have discovered another version, with curious marginalia and passages of considerable scientific interest.'

The old philosopher raised himself on his pillow with a gesture of mild alarm.

'And where did you find this version?' he asked.

'Well sir,' Aristotle replied, standing to attention and staring straight before him in that cocky way of his, 'a few years ago now, when I was a new boy, you had the kindness to introduce me to Xanthippe, wife of Socrates.'[1]

'I did no such thing,' said Plato indignantly.

'To be more accurate then, sir, I became acquainted with Xanthippe, having first met her in your company. And although I never knew her well, you understand, she did allow me to look through her library. A somewhat odd collection, sir, but with nothing, you will be pleased to know, that you would have burned.'

'So it was from Xanthippe's edition that you learned those indecent lines?'

'Not exactly, sir. She had borrowed the book from another lady, whom she described as an acquaintance of yours. So I assumed, perhaps wrongly sir, that you would have no objection to my reading it.'

'And who was this other lady?'

'I don't recall her name, sir, but I do remember that she came from Colophon, and had known Antimachus in her youth.'

Plato groaned.

'Was her name, by any chance, Archeanassa?'

Aristotle gave a sly sideways glance at his master.

'It could be, sir.'

After a silence, the old philosopher, who had become appreciably paler, spoke again.

'Listen boy. Do you have anything special planned for the next month or so?'

'It depends what you mean by special, sir.'

'I mean, are you free to travel?'

'Travel where, sir?'

'To Asia; Colophon to be precise. The sons of Apollodorus do a cheap fare – though of course your expenses would be covered. Up to a point, that is.'

'And what am I to do in Colophon, sir?'

'Well – this is just between you and me – I had rather set my heart on Antimachus's literary remains. For the library,

1 See the concluding pages of 'Xanthippe's Laws', in R. Scruton, ed., *Xanthippic Dialogues*, op. cit.

you understand. I gather he left most of his manuscripts behind when he came to Athens. There are some early versions of the *Lyde*, I am told, including the one from which you were quoting. I feel that, with letters of introduction and what have you, there should be no difficulty in obtaining them at rock bottom price.'

Aristotle pondered the suggestion for a moment.

'Would it be entirely safe?'

'Of course. Why, I'd go myself, if my legs would carry me. True, it is no longer a Greek city. But the Persians behave quite correctly towards visitors and they are tough on crime. Also the hotels are good – and cheap too. You'll enjoy yourself.'

'But, sir – how will I find Antimachus's writings? I mean, it is unlikely there is a box lying somewhere in a public place, with "Antimachus" written on it, and a guard waiting to hand over the keys to Plato's emissary. With respect, sir.'

'You will have a guide, if she can be persuaded. In fact . . .'

Plato coughed, and glanced at the bust of Socrates which stood at the foot of his couch.

'In fact the lady you mentioned, Miss Archeanassa, is the person I have in mind.'

'But, sir . . . I imagined that you and she, that . . . well, that you had ceased to be actively acquainted, so to speak. With respect, sir.'

'Exactly, boy. I should like you to be my emissary, first to Miss Archeanassa and then, through her, to the city of Colophon.'

'And how will I find Miss Archeanassa, sir?'

'I am told that she lives not far from the Stoa, in the street behind Apollo's temple.'

'And how will I persuade her to be my guide, sir?'

'Easy. She is hard up, and I will offer a useful fee.'

'Hmm,' said Aristotle.

'I would pay you too,' the philosopher hastily added, 'except that the arrangement between us forbids the exchange of money.'

3

'Of course, sir. Since you receive no fees, you can't be expected to pay them. To your pupils that is. Although I hardly count as a pupil.'

'Think of your education, boy. What an opportunity, to travel to Asia Minor, to see the famed city of Colophon, and to observe the ways of the Persians. You could write about it, become famous, another Xenophon. And all in the service of scholarship.'

'Yes, sir,' said Aristotle with a sigh. 'You are so right, sir.'

It was therefore agreed that Aristotle should take his master's request to Archeanassa and, on obtaining her consent, book two seats on the galley. According to Pamphila, however, who tells the story in her fifty-sixth chapter, Archeanassa travelled alone to Colophon as Plato's messenger, Aristotle having given her the slip in Piraeus and left her to fend for herself. Opinions differ as to why he did this. Pamphila suggests that Aristotle had already entered into negotiations with Philip of Macedon, who promised him far greater opportunities for travel in the very near future and without the risks attached to this reckless adventure. Hypatia (*Anecdotes*, 1004b) prefers to believe that Aristotle, concerned for his master's health, and not trusting Plato's judgement in the matter of Antimachus's papers, decided to stay behind to nurse the old philosopher; while Sosipatra, in her discourse on melancholy, is of the opinion that Aristotle, having stopped off on the way to Piraeus for a tutorial with Phryne, was so interested by her teachings that he missed the boat.[2]

---

2   The *Memorabilia* of Pamphila of Epidauros (1st century AD) have come down to us only in Favorinus's bowdlerised summary. Hypatia, last of the true (pagan) philosophers, was done to death by a Christian mob in fifth century Alexandria. Slight amends were made fourteen centuries later, when the Rev. Charles Kingsley wrote an idealising novel about her. Sosipatra is described by Eunapius, *Lives of the Philosophers*, 466–471. Phryne, the most famous courtesan in fourth-century Athens, is fully described in 'Phryne's Symposium', the last of *Xanthippic Dialogues*.

All commentators agree, however, that Archeanassa had few regrets at finding herself the sole passenger in a galley laden with mass-produced tapestries in the style of Xanthippe, depicting the corny old scene of Socrates' death and judgement, and destined for sale in the Persian markets. For several years now she had been alone with her thoughts, striving to cover with the ashes of a widow-like routine, the still warm embers of her love for Plato, and having lost, in Xanthippe, the only guide and counsellor that her years would trust. The thought of revisiting the scene of her first true love with the tiresome pupil of her second was far from agreeable; and she had accepted Plato's request largely because of certain letters, contained among Antimachus's papers, which she hoped to retrieve before the philosopher set eyes on them.

Thus it was that Archeanassa was borne by the summer breeze across the wide Aegean, pondering again her love for Antimachus, mourning with a shadow grief this man who had been a shade for her long before the gods recalled him. The winds were fair, the sea was calm, and the sailors good humoured, so that Archeanassa was left to her thoughts. And it was not until they entered the straits of Agrigentum and were ordered to land and declare their merchandise, that she formed any lively idea of the danger in which she had been placed by Plato's scheming.

No sooner had their galley, hemmed in by patrol boats, berthed against the wooden pier, than a Persian officer, in bright saffron robes and pearl-studded sandals, swept aboard, asking in imperious tones for the captain. This latter personage, with great presence of mind, pointed to a Sicilian galley slave who a moment before had been hauling the rope around the capstan. The slave, seeing only an advantage to himself in being received as so high a dignitary, quickly acquiesced in the deception, and stepped forward in the character of captain, expecting no doubt to be taken ashore, there to bargain for his freedom. The real captain, more familiar with Persian customs, busied himself with rope and sails, as the officer inspected the cargo.

Chapter 1

It was not so much the design of the tapestries that offended the Persian – although he noted that any attempt to represent the Deity as standing higher in the order of things than the Great King already amounted to a grave offence in law. Nor did he especially resent the fact that the scandalous Socrates was displayed in such favourable colours, despite the encouragement that he had offered through his example to subversive elements. The tapestries offended most of all in being designed by Xanthippe, a far greater criminal than her husband, notorious throughout the civilised world for her elitist opinions, and put to death as an enemy of the people, when her insolent contempt for the ideal of human equality had finally exceeded the patience of the Athenian courts. To mention such a woman was crime enough; to carry a cargo-load of her ideas to the innocent people of Persia amounted to the highest provocation, and a violation of the Treaty by which the Greeks were bound.[3] Having ordered the confiscation of the tapestries, therefore, the Persian decreed that the ship return forthwith to Athens. And because the Great King is merciful and requires no more suffering than is strictly necessary to enforce his just and benevolent laws, he would punish none of the crew save only the captain, whose hands and feet would be severed and who would be cast to the fish in the sea.

Having witnessed this terrible punishment, Archeanassa was of half a mind to return with the crew to Greece, despite the fact that provisions were low and the possibility of supplying them much reduced by the loss of cargo. However, she reflected on the poverty of her life in Greece, she remembered the loves which had exalted and ravaged her emotions, and was all of a sudden seized by so strong a desire to mourn her dear Antimachus at the scene of their

---

3 The King's Peace, effectively dictated to the warring cities of Greece by the Persian King Tiribazus, was concluded at Sardis in 387–386 BC; under the terms of this treaty (vigorously attacked as a shameful capitulation by Isocrates in his *Panegyricus*), the King assumed control of the entire Asiatic mainland, and also of Cyprus.

embraces, that she decided to make the journey to Colophon, appealing meanwhile to the Persian for protection. Besides, she knew the ways of the country, was fluent in the language, and although no longer in the full flower of her beauty, which was perhaps just as well, had retained enough of her attractions to win the heart of a man whose cruelty towards a helpless stranger only served to display his inward insecurity.

Her plan was successful and, while she felt towards the Persian nothing but contempt, she was able nevertheless, in the character of a Persian lady returning to her family in Colophon, to secure safe passage to her destination. The wagon in which she travelled was the Great King's property, guarded by two mounted soldiers, who rode to either side. The Persian officer did not neglect to load a good part of the cargo beside her, with instructions to the senior guard to auction it off in Colophon, and to return with the proceeds, which would be justly distributed among those who had taken part in the theft. And in a sudden access of pity, he pressed a bundle of the tapestries on Archeanassa, who reluctantly accepted them, conscious that she would need to supplement the meagre sums provided on account by Plato.

And so it was that, shaken but secure, Archeanassa proceeded to Colophon, bumping along the dusty road in the company of two taciturn soldiers, four horses, and a lewd but intimidated driver.

Once before she had travelled this road, in another and more solemn grief, as she left her homeland in pursuit of Antimachus. That was twenty years ago, when the road had been frequented only by peasants, driving mules loaded with produce for the markets. She recalled the great woods of oak and birch and cedar, the coastal pastures with their groves of olive trees, the clear streams bordered by tamarisks and the fields of artichokes and lupins, like blue-green jewels on the distant hillsides. Now the road was dense with traffic: wagons full of stones moved in trains or blocked the narrow junctions; soldiers marched in ranks, passing with unswerving eyes on the urgent missions of the King. Where there had been forests there were now only mutilated stumps. The groves had been felled, the streams were stagnant pools, and a few stunted trees stood amid the dying pastures like grieving women whose homes have been looted and burned. Ugly new houses of mud littered the roadside, and in the villages people, dressed in the grey uniform of the work-force, queued for bread at the King's official bakeries. And the landscape lay in a permanent indistinct shadow, as though by some royal decree the sun itself had been dimmed.

Strange though her surroundings were, yet stranger to Archeanassa's eyes were the people, who had a closed, forbidding, archaic appearance, like primitive idols, with square heads, obstinate square shoulders, and abbreviated necks. Their bodies were short and protuberant, and the hands which emerged from their worn and greasy tunics were gnarled and grasping like hooks. They moved slowly and cautiously, avoiding one another's eyes, and sniffing the air with their long shapeless noses as they made their way through the crowds. Often, as the wagon passed through a village, Archeanassa was startled to see the entire population gathered on the edge in an eerie silent throng, waiting for the convoy that would take them to their work. And as she passed they would look sideways at her from knobbly faces, their eyes haunted and uncertain under dark square brows. They seemed to belong to a dim and distant era, when human beings were inexpertly experimenting with the nature bestowed on them by some malicious god.

The temples of the Greeks had been sacked, their statuary broken, and their columns pillaged for lime. In their place were gaudy structures in blue and white ceramic, each carrying on its bright bronze door a giant portrait of the King. How ugly he was, with his cold grey eyes, his distended nostrils, his greased beard like the blade of an axe, his stone-coloured skin and the cruel commanding stare that captured your unwilling glance and told you, 'You are mine'! As they journeyed the long leagues to Colophon, Archeanassa's mourning grew to embrace not Antimachus only, but the world which had nurtured him and her – a world of light and grace and harmony, of modest appetites and pious deeds, of joyous festivals and rhapsodic poetry, which had vanished forever under the Great King's all-inclusive Plan. She recalled the little farms, with their stone houses and orchards, their pens of geese and chickens, and their herds of sheep and goats. In their place were acres of sterile ploughland, barns in which disconsolate cattle lowed in darkness, and what seemed like vast watchtowers, looming above the plains, and crowded with people who came and went like bees in a hive, their eyes and mouths rigid and expressionless, and with a strange new hopelessness – a hopelessness which comes not from losing hope, but from having never possessed it.

Except for the ceramic temples, which stood vigilant in each frequented corner, everything spoke of work. The buildings were machines for working in; the clothes were work-clothes; the faces, hands and postures were those of work, and the people seemed to meet only as work-mates, exchanging neither smiles nor glances, but only curt, mechanical nods. And yet nothing seemed to result from this work. The countryside appeared barren; no fruit or meat filled the lean, bare stalls in the markets, and everything had the drab look of a poverty from which all escape had been cut off. Most remarkable of all were the queues, which Archeanassa often had occasion to observe, being forced to provide for herself whenever the wagon stopped in some mutilated town. The queue arose out of nowhere, when some old woman, who had been wandering around the central square among ruined houses and heaps of rubbish, looking shiftily from side to side, and carrying what seemed to be a child wrapped in coarse blankets, would suddenly stop and allow her burden to unfurl to the ground. A few dried mushrooms, a string of onions, a bundle of wool, an old bronze instrument or two – nothing of any significance in Archeanassa's eyes, but at once the centre of that previously random crowd, which would rush towards these new exhibits from every corner of the square, to form a line of magnetised faces focussed on the things for sale. A special breed of people had arisen in modern Persia, with fixed, hard, ruthless manners, and an absolute precision of attack. They would await their turn without a word, conscious that every person in the queue was now their enemy. And having arrived at the head, they would hang on, badgering the vendor with their questions, asking what else was for sale, at what price and when, conducting as much business as possible in the time afforded, indifferent to those who still waited behind them. Words like 'please' and 'thank you' formed no part of their vocabulary, which was a kind of clipped, industrial jargon, more like a dialogue of machines than a human conversation.

Seeing the Persians like this, ugly, graceless and unyielding, Archeanassa experienced the sensation that they were made to be governed by an iron discipline, and that the rule of the Great King was exactly what they deserved – though at the same time, she knew, they were like this because the King required it. As to the question whether there really was a Great King, whether the Ten Year Plan had ever been conceived or written down, or whether there was perhaps nothing beyond the vast pictures of that gorgon face, frozen in a look of peremptory command, Archeanassa soon ceased to speculate. For in the end it was a matter of indifference whether the people were ruled by a tyrant, when they cooperated so willingly in their enslavement, and lived as though slavery were the natural lot of man. Indeed Archeanassa was tempted to agree with Xanthippe, that there are men who are slaves by nature, a view which had deeply shocked her when first she heard the philosopher defend it.[4]

For five days they journeyed. Archeanassa grieved the more, as she recalled the friends and cousins whom she had left behind, and who were now pegging out their days in this grey routine. On the morning of the sixth day, however, the prospect began to change. The watchtowers disap-

---

4   So *that* is where Aristotle got the most notorious of his political opinions!

peared from the fields, and neat little houses came in place of them. Some had orchards and vines, others lawns with neatly trimmed hedges of box and rosemary. The people were more brightly dressed, and something in their manner suggested a lightness and self-confidence that were more Greek than Persian. After a while she began to recognize the contours of her native Lydia, denuded now of trees and with crowded roads and villages, but nevertheless dear to her and wearing still beneath its Persian chains the serene soft smile of Greece.

And then at last, ascending to the top of the hill of Kunion, where the road passed the ruined sanctuary to which she had once brought flowers and myrrh in honour of the goddess of love, there, where the few untended plane trees still stood amid the ruins and the horses lingered for a moment in their shade, the city of Colophon came into view across the valley. Archeanassa's heart rose up to meet it, and she leaned over the driver, oblivious to the lewd remark with which he returned her courtesies, eager to gain the first and fullest view of her native city.

With a gasp she fell back into the wagon. Surely it was a vision in a dream, a mirage, a trick of the sun as it burned the barren landscape! Gone was the gentle slope crowned with the temple of Artemis; gone were the groves and terraces, the limestone houses arranged along their streets, the shrines and temples, and the beautiful library with its Ionic peristyle. In place of them she saw a regiment of towers fighting one another beneath the heavens, a cemetery of stone spreading for league upon league across the valley, vast still tombs piled each on each, with dirty fingers of rubble clawing out from them into the mutilated fields, like the hands of the suffocated dead! Surely it was a product of her fears and fantasies, this huge inhuman nothingness of slate-grey mortar and stone! Yet no, one of the taciturn soldiers assured her, this was Colophon and a commercial centre of such importance that the King himself had plans to visit it.

'You mean people *live* in those tombs?'

11

Chapter 1

The soldier gave her an uncomprehending glance.

'Why no, of course not. Nobody *lives* there. That is where they struggle.'

'Struggle?'

'For progress.'

'Struggle for progress.' She turned the words over in her mind. They had a faintly threatening air, like a muted curse. She could attach to them no definite meaning, but only a vague atmosphere of toil and hardship and machine-like discipline.

'What does this struggle involve?'

'Oh, business, administration, committee-work – papyrus.'

'And who is involved in it?'

'The people we passed on the road – the Colophonians.'

The soldier showing no further inclination to discuss the matter, Archeanassa ceased her questions and applied herself to the study of Colophon, which they were fast approaching down a road crowded with wagons carrying human cargo to and from the awe-inspiring cemetery that rose along the valley. How, in this great labyrinth of stone and mortar, would she come across the literary remains of Antimachus? Her few addresses referred to streets, temples and groves that must all have disappeared beneath the planned disorder of the King's new town. And the idea that the voice of a gentle poet, whose verses were like the whisper of a summer breeze in a grove of apricots, should still be heard in this great machine, such an idea could hardly be expressed in the Persian language. Besides, the Persian language had suffered the same pillaging as the Lydian towns and villages: only a limited vocabulary remained, a vocabulary of abstraction, as rock-like and immovable as the official cuneiform script. Her guards barely observed the world of human beings: when they spoke, it was of things and processes, of forces and struggles and abstract contests in which people were involved as it were by proxy, like blades of straw hardened into bricks.

Who could describe the feelings that invaded the heart

of Archeanassa as the wagon rumbled through those dreary streets, with their raw unfinished buildings, many of them taller than the highest trees and shored up by girders of wood and iron, with their ruined temples, whose shattered statuary lay on a sea of debris like mutilated sailors brought home by the tide, with their wide unfriendly avenues patrolled by soldiers, and their few Greek cottages crumbling now and boarded up, the occupants long since fled or murdered? What words could capture her anxieties as she stepped at last from the official wagon, exchanged cold farewells with her faceless escorts, and entered a pile of bricks over which the King's fierce head glowered in reprimand, and whose door was marked 'Official Visitors'? What sympathy could plumb the depths of her grief, as the uniformed warden with a parchment face buttoned down by jet-black eyes conducted her along half-lit corridors to the little cell which was to be her forbidding but temporary home? And what god of the Greeks, summoned by her tearful prayers, could move with her through those shattered precincts, and not partake of her awareness that the work of creation had here been all undone?

For several days Archeanassa searched for the traces of her former love. She had furnished herself with a few addresses: half-remembered uncles and a distant cousin of the poet's. But they named only vanished streets and ruined temples, and the Greeks whom she encountered had never heard of Antimachus. Soon, having lost hope of fulfilling her mission, Archeanassa turned her thoughts towards Athens, towards the boat that left each week from Notium, and towards the need to raise some money for her fare. She patrolled the ruined spaces of the city, stopping from time to time to unfurl her bag of merchandise on some pile of rubble, beneath the image of the all-seeing King displayed on a flimsy boarding. And straightway the silent faces, which had ignored her as they ignored everything save the inner voice which drove them on from tower to tower inscrutably, would diverge from their paths to form a queue. The tapestries, she declared, were medicinal bandages of an advanced design, and their figures were imbued with a magical restorative power. As they came forward one by one, throwing down coins and grabbing the cloth as though it existed only in the moment of its purchase, Archeanassa studied with amazement the residents of Colophon, whose expressions and gestures were so far from any human archetype. Their speech was abrupt and simplified, emerging from their mouths as though sent there by messenger from some distant zone. They did not look at her, as one soul looks at another, but targeted her with their eyes, guiding their faces like bits of machinery, from the same remote locality where they lurked out of sight. Courtesy had vanished entirely, and perhaps because of this the Colophonians seemed to avoid one another, veering away like animals at the scent of human flesh, and forming no groups other than the queue in daytime, and the mob at night.

Archeanassa wandered far and wide in the city, to discover beneath its monotonous sameness the subtle distinctions between the towers set aside for work, where her passage was barred by silent soldiers, and those on the outskirts where the people lived, and whose vandalized doorways belched their smell of rotting cabbage across tussocky wastes of rubble and couch grass. And in each place she heard the same sound – a noise of persistent drumming, which was in a strange way both rhythmical and rhythmless, as though a machine were trying in vain to dance to its own pulsation.

In Colophon there was no shouting, nor was there quiet, but always this strange swishing of the drums, which hung on the air like a nacreous skin, endlessly scratching the silence. Where the sound came from, and how it was produced, she did not know. But it inhabited each building, and in some peculiar way, she saw, the Colophonians depended on it for their meagre energy, and moved in time to its beat as though attached by invisible wires to a universal puppet-master.

There was another and more intermittent sound. In the squares and streets and vacant lots stood poles of timber, roughly hewn and often lop-sided, which bore the tangled cords of the royal communications network. If you pulled these cords at one end, she later learned, a bell would ring at the other, and by this means coded messages were sent to a central exchange, to be relayed to their destination. Every part of Colophon was in touch with every other part, and all day long the bells would ring with their urgent summons above the indolent swish and chunter of the drums.

In the wine shop where she ate her daily meal of bread flavoured with nasturtiums and a paste of anchovies, a table had been set aside for the Greek widows who still lingered in the neighbourhood, in hovels earmarked for demolition when Colophon's march into the future should demand it. The ladies retained only the vaguest idea of their national culture; no god or hero was remembered, and except for the occasional line of Homer, no poet recalled. But they gave a most extraordinary account of the life and leisure of the new Colophon, whose people, Archeanassa learned, imported in wagon-loads from the fertile crescent, were charged with the administration of Lydia and the imposition of the Great King's all-comprehending Plan. But what the Plan required, and what was its goal, nobody knew. For wherever the King's officials moved, they drove before them, like a stampede of bewildered animals, the desolation and destruction that were seen in Colophon.

The Greeks still lived in the countryside, though their numbers were much reduced, their temples desecrated, and their art and poetry forgotten. The culture of Colophon, Archeanassa discovered, was the mass-produced entertainment of Babylon – a ceaseless charivari of loud and artless music, of violent and obscene spectacles, and of carefully regimented propaganda designed to reinforce the message that everything was permitted save distinction, and that so long as people were equal in their accomplishments and talents, it did not matter if they had none. There were academies, but they were devoted not to philosophy or music or mathematics or any other subject once thought to be useful. The principal course, which lasted for five years and led to the coveted qualification required for any government post, was called 'communication studies,'[5] and was designed to remove any excessive vocabulary from the student's language, and to pare down his accomplishments to the point where nothing remained save a taciturn rejection of knowledge. The people busied themselves in the towers by day, on tasks which had no meaning save the consumption and distribution of papyrus. They appeared at night only to attend noisy festivals of song and dance in the old Greek theatre, to watch as slaves, pressed to bear arms in the arena, hacked at each other's limbs until death released them from their bondage, or to roam the streets in rowdy gangs, drinking in the wine-shops and clapping and cheering at the dancing girls, many of whom had come to the city from the Greek colonies, in order to enjoy the patronage of the Persian elite. For it is a curious fact that societies dedicated to the equality of their members very quickly give rise to a floating caste comprising those whose business it is to impose equality on the remainder. And this caste, being bound by no law save that which grants its privilege, is able to save or ruin whomsoever it pleases. To the destitute widow, or the betrayed fiancée, there may be no better hope, in such a society, than to become the mistress of some officer in the Royal Guard.

Of course, there were ordinary Persians. But they hid in the suburbs with their lovers and – where these could not be avoided – with their children too. And to ensure the continuing loyalty and invisibility of his subjects, the Great King had devised an ingenious form of home entertainment. Curious boxes had been distributed to the people, each containing puppets which were moved by turning a handle attached to the side. Every household had three of these boxes, devoted respectively to sex, torture and news. When the handles of the first two were turned the Colophonians could witness scenes of lust and violence, with simulated groans and cries and disembowellings and every ecstasy and agony that the mind of man could conceive; while in the box

---

5   Ar. *durus al-ikhbar:* not, certainly, the traditional study of rhetoric, but perhaps more like 'media studies' today.

marked 'news' would appear not sex or violence only, but a carefully adjusted mixture of the two, designed to inform the suburban audience of what was happening at that very moment in the city. And the news was always the same and always accurate, since, in the evenings, when the suburban visitors had retreated to their cells, life in the city was inspired by life in the box.

The crowds who stormed the city at night-time came from nowhere, and disappeared to nowhere, leaving behind them shards of broken pottery, pools of blood and vomit, and the occasional staring corpse. The residents of the city were few: the cooks, wine-merchants and dancing girls needed for the Persian entertainments, and the remnants and rejects who had survived the original purge of the Greeks. Most of the Greeks were poor, or, if raised to any eminence of fortune, it was because they had become the despised and avoided mistresses of Persian officers. But there was one exception, Archeanassa learned: a Greek girl of extraordinary beauty, who was famed throughout Persian Lydia for her dancing, and who was so much the object of contending desires, that no-one dared to touch her, lest implacable jealousy should put an end to his life. The girl lived in an old Greek house which she had lovingly restored and furnished with Greek antiquities, she having no family nearby and no better use for the quantities of Persian money that came her way each evening.

'Perhaps I should visit this girl,' said Archeanassa, who in truth had no great desire to see another face in Colophon, and was only waiting for the wagon that left in three days' time for Notium.

'That you should,' replied Callisto, the fading hetaera who dominated the table and who now turned for endorsement to her neighbour. 'Shouldn't she, Menia?'

Menia, the widow of a corn merchant, whose only interest was draughts and who had been distractedly pushing the counters around a board which lay always open in front of her, now looked up with a start.

'Shouldn't she what?'

Chapter 1

'Shouldn't she visit Perictione?'

Menia grunted non-commitally and returned to her game, while Archeanassa, suddenly alert, asked after the girl's origins and kin.

'Oh, that I'm not sure of,' said Callisto, 'except that she's an Athenian, and pretty upper crust I should say.'

Chloë, an eager young whore who joined the table when business was slack and who prided herself on her useful gossip, informed the company that Perictione was descended on her mother's side from Solon the Great, whose songs had been top of the charts for a hundred years in the ancient days, and who had written a best-selling autobiography. Also her uncle was a famous sophist, only she couldn't remember his name.

'There you are, you see,' said Callisto, as though some point had been proved. And the women returned to the topic of the day, a young Persian singer due to perform that night, whose name was Xerxes. Archeanassa, furnished with Perictione's address, set off without further ado along the boulevard which led to the empty centre of the town.

2

In which Archeanassa meets Perictione, grand-daughter of Perictione the Great

The house was of stone, with an Ionic portico above a flight of marble steps. The remains of a garden, with box and cypress, a pomegranate tree and a scorched brown lawn decorated with marble statuary, stretched out before the steps, though to either side the grey towers pressed close to the wall, casting their shadows over the roof of amber tiles, and polluting the air with the faint relentless sound of drumming. The city trembled in the brownish heat-haze; but the house of Perictione stood in its precinct, cool, silent and still.

In truth, the building had been beautifully restored, and was exactly as Archeanassa remembered from the day when Proteos, the pompous general, had rented it from Archolossos, in order to impress his visitors from Greece. Not far from here had stood the sanctuary of Demeter, and behind it, where a shaft of faceless mortar thrust its mute muzzle at the sky, had been the little cottage which Antimachus had rented for her in a street lined by orchards. It was the place of their first embraces, so dear in Archeanassa's memory that she averted her eyes from the hideous tower which had sprouted from its ruin, and hurried through the garden and up the steps.

She sounded the urn that stood in the portico, and after a moment an old servant – so old that Archeanassa could not tell whether it were man or woman – poked an enquiring

Chapter 2

nose around the door. On being addressed in Greek, the wrinkled face cracked into a smile, revealing two yellow fangs behind shrivelled lips. Yes, Archeanassa was informed, Mistress Perictione did indeed live here, and would surely welcome a visitor from Athens. But how did the visitor get past the guards?

'What guards?' she asked. The old servant pointed silently towards the garden gate. There, to Archeanassa's astonishment, stood two soldiers in uniform, with the golden greaves and shields of the royal infantry. How had she failed to notice them, and how had they failed to notice her? And why should Perictione be guarded – to protect her from the people? Or – uncanny thought – to protect the people from her? Archeanassa stood for a moment in bewilderment, and then said:

'Tell her that I come as an emissary from Plato the philosopher.'

The servant bowed low and gestured to the interior of the house. Archeanassa stepped through the door into a large hallway, fanned by a gentle breeze and lit from above by the sunlight that entered under the eves. The drums were suddenly inaudible; instead, a cithara sounded from somewhere in the back: a melancholy music which spoke of the pangs of love. And a gentle Greek decorum lingered between the columns of the hallway, like a frail and dignified old general waiting quietly for an audience. Seating herself on a wooden throne, Archeanassa allowed the music to spread its sadness through her thoughts; and when the cithara ceased, she started awake from a dream.

A tall woman with long black tresses and a robe of crimson silk came whispering across the flagstones towards her. Her face was still youthful but no longer fresh, and the eyes dark as pools seemed removed from the world, into a deep and self-communing quiet. The aquiline nose had a slightly haughty lift to it, and the ivory brow, as it moved in the dappled shadows of the rafters, had the beauty of celestial things – remote, impassive and all-knowing. Archeanassa hastily got to her feet and bowed to the approaching form.

20

In which Archeanassa meets Perictione

'Ah, but I know you,' said Perictione. Her voice was deeper now and slower, as though weighed down by the world.

'Indeed,' said Archeanassa, not a little embarrassed to recall their former meeting.

'Well, how very glad I am to see you,' said Perictione, 'and to hear news of old Athens. How is my Uncle Plato?'

Perictione accompanied her question with a cool and distant look, as though to emphasize that Athens was a long way away, and her uncle of no great significance to a girl who lived alone in Colophon. But Archeanassa was awash with nostalgia – with the sick longing for her two homes which were ever nearer in her thought and feeling. In her mind the home that she had left in Athens and the home to which she had tried to return, only to find it dead and buried, had begun to fuse, just as Antimachus and Plato were beginning to fuse in her grief, and just as she was uniting with her former selves, as they drifted together into the vale of regret and mourning. Perhaps it was an effect of the music; perhaps it was something in the proud still eyes that looked so curiously down on her; perhaps it was neither of these, but merely the sight and sound of this dreadful city, where she had wandered for two weeks in anguish, with no hope of finding the traces of her great affection – whatever the cause, Archeanassa fell back on to the marble throne where she had been seated and, burying her head in her hands, gave way to her misery.

The tears of a man come when all resources fail; those of a women are a resource in themselves. The very eyes that hotly weep may coolly observe the effect of their own weeping. And although Archeanassa was sincere in her distress, she did not neglect to take note of the other's reaction. Nor could she fail to observe that Perictione was rather repelled than endeared by this performance, and stood back in lofty isolation, like one who waits for a drunk to cease his tirade before dismissing him. She controlled herself, therefore, as best she could, and after a few more outbursts, offered a murmured apology.

'If you wish to rest here a while,' Perictione said, 'I can ask the servant to bring you some refreshment.'

'I had not meant to behave so shamefully,' said Archeanassa through her tears. 'I think it was the music that affected me.'

'The music?'

'The music that you were playing so beautifully.'

'You are too kind,' said Perictione. 'In fact it was the chamber-maid who played.'

Archeanassa felt the remark as a rebuff. Clearly it had been a mistake to intrude into this girl's privacy. Too much avoidance had shaped this aloofness, too much retreat from human affection.

'I always listen to music in the afternoon,' Perictione continued. 'And the sadder the music, the more serene do I feel. And if this were not the rule, why should there be such an abundance of sad music, and so many people eager to feast on it? So you must forgive me, if I doubt that your tears are musical.'

Perictione continued to observe her visitor, though a light of curiosity had now entered the girl's eye, a light that burned all the more strikingly against the great dim vistas of quotidian boredom that stretched behind it. Had this princess ever loved, Archeanassa wondered? Had she ever felt that fever of need which rushes like a fire through the furnishings of the mind, and leaves only ashes thereafter? Archeanassa doubted it. And this doubt gave her heart. She could match Perictione's disdain with a disdain of her own. This girl who had refused to become a woman, who stood forever on the threshold of life, was less to be admired than pitied. Thinking of this, Archeanassa raised herself up and said:

'These tears, my dear, are real tears. So much at least is true.'

'But real tears, honoured visitor, are about real things. And what in music is real?'

Archeanassa looked searchingly into those cool eyes, in which boredom and curiosity strove for dominion. And then, all of a sudden, her disdain and anxiety vanished. For this was Plato's face, the face that retreated into paradox, and made of every natural feeling a metaphysical mystery. Of course it was a mistake to weep before such a divine countenance, just as it had been a mistake – but how tempting a mistake – to show her love to the philosopher! Archeanassa recalled Xanthippe's description of Plato's character, during her speech at Phryne's long-ago symposium, when this very girl had danced in the dawn. And remembering the peace that came with Xanthippe's words, and all the consolation that she had afterwards received from that great philosopher, Archeanassa smiled on Perictione and said:

'You must forgive me, O most noble descendent of the divine Solon, if I do not understand your question.'

'Do you not?' asked Perictione, with a brightening glance. 'Then stay awhile, so that we may discuss the point.'

'I wish I were in the mood for philosophy.'

'Oh, as for that,' said the other breezily, 'philosophy creates its own mood. Come into the house, and we can make ourselves comfortable with a bowl of sweet grapes and juice of pomegranates.'

'You are most kind,' said Archeanassa, who rose to her feet and followed the graceful figure of her hostess as she swayed in stately rhythm across the hallway, clapping her hands and giving orders as she went. They entered a colonnade, fanned by a cool breeze from the dark rear of the house. Between statues of Pan and Dionysus (obtained, Perictione said, from a corrupt official at the royal lime-kilns) was a bronze door from a country temple, which opened on to a large and airy room.

Archeanassa's first impression on entering this, Perictione's private space, was that it was not private at all, but a kind of museum, dedicated to the perpetuation of the Greek idea. Everything in it, from the vast Cretan tapestries on the walls, to the tiny alabaster figurines from ancient Phrygia and Egypt, raised on silver tripods out of reach, was exquisite, eloquent and rare. Each object was placed to advantage, so that an irreproachable order filled the room. The couch of gilded limewood, with its carved frieze of centaurs, stood exactly across from another, on which lapiths prepared themselves for war. A magnificent urn from the Cyclades depicting the Muses stood on the porphyry chimney breast beneath an antique icon of Apollo. And the marble figure of Meleager surrounded by his hounds was matched by another of Atalanta. The bold chaste glance of the nymph sped like an arrow above polished jade lampstands and woven rugs depicting sylvan scenes, to plunge into the eyes of the hunter. Everything was exactly right, irreplaceable and emblematic – and also entirely wrong: cold, comfortless and symmetrical, like a tomb. The walls were decked in bold and vibrant colours – magenta and ox-blood, beneath a sea-green frieze of acanthus leaves, with borders of emerald and gold. But their splendour merely added to the sepulchral atmosphere, like the gaudy wrappings of a mummified king. When Perictione gestured her to one of the couches Archeanassa hesitated, and dusted her tunic before carefully lowering herself on to the embroidered tapestry. She feared to disturb the objects in the room lest she should wake them from eternal slumber. Perictione did not sit at first, but stood amid her exemplary possessions like another exhibit, aloof and untouchable as they. And then, gradually, with the exquisite slow movement of a dancer, she sank down opposite her guest and folded her body.

Perictione was smiling now. And the room smiled with her, a cold crystalline smile that registered its completeness.

'Of course, you did not come to talk philosophy,' said the girl, with an attempt at kindness.

'No,' Archeanassa replied, 'though perhaps, a little later, when I have got used to being here . . .'

'Do you think so? People never do.'

'Never talk philosophy with *you*?' expostulated Archeanassa.

'Never get used to being here.'

'Oh, you mean this room, these beautiful things, so ancient and stylish and – and superfluous.'

Perictione observed her coldly.

'I mean this town, and what it stands for.'

Archeanassa said nothing, but looked down at her tunic in embarrassment. A servant entered with a bowl of fruit and a silver pitcher brimming with golden juice.

'So how do *you* find this Colophon of ours?' Perictione asked.

Archeanassa looked up in surprise.

'This Colophon of *yours*?'

'Well, certainly not of yours, honoured Archeanassa – for you left here some years ago if I am not mistaken, and *your* Colophon is a memory.'

'Alas!' said Archeanassa with a sigh.

Perictione took a sprig of grapes from the bowl before passing it across to her guest.

'I take it you don't think much of our city.'

'Oh, I think a lot of it. But mostly bad things. I mean – it is so cruel, so cold, so inhuman.'

'You don't find it exciting?'

Archeanassa thought for a moment.

'Yes – perhaps. As madness and death are exciting.'

'Then why have you come to visit us?'

Perictione's steady gaze caused such awkwardness in her visitor, that Archeanassa began to choke on the grape that she was eating. It was some time before she could re-spond to the question.

'Well, I suppose madness and death have much to do with it. Your uncle's madness, in asking me to find Antimachus's papers; and Antimachus's death, which gave your uncle the idea to look for them.'

'And what makes you think they are here in Colophon?' asked Perictione.

'It is not what *I* think, but what your uncle thinks.'

'What do *you* think?'

'I am sure he left the bulk of them behind in Colophon. But as you say, that Colophon is just a memory. I shall be leaving for home soon, mission abandoned.'

'What a waste of a journey!'

Chapter 2

'Not at all,' said Archeanassa, with a hint of indignation. 'I have learned many things – things it is useful to know.'

'Such as?'

'I have learned how needful to men are cities, and how much is lost when the city loses its gods, its temples and its dwellings, so as to become an impersonal machine.'

'Is that your view of modern Colophon?'

'In a nutshell, yes.'

'And what else did you learn?'

'I learned that it is possible to live as a rational being, but with no knowledge of poetry, music or the arts, and without a trace of religion.'

'And that too is bad?'

'Do you not think so?'

'Well,' said Perictione, settling back on her couch with queenly decorum, 'it rather depends on the final balance.'

'The final balance?'

Perictione nodded.

'You see, honoured Archeanassa, it is not only the appearance of the city that has changed. The human soul has changed along with it. And as to which change is cause, and which effect, I warrant that neither you nor I nor anyone else could find the answer.'

'How can I dispute what you say? For everything I see in this new world is strange to me, and nothing stranger than you, most noble Perictione.'

'Really?' asked the girl, with a happy laugh. 'And what in me is so strange?'

'Is it not strange that a beautiful and well-born girl should live alone, in a monstrous foreign city, yet surrounded by these relics of her past?'

Perictione leaned forward suddenly and fixed Archeanassa with a penetrating stare.

'Do you want to know how Perictione, daughter of Potone and grand-daughter of Perictione the Great, removed herself from Athens, and settled nowhere until she came to Persian Lydia?'

Archeanassa's curiosity was so aroused by the girl's

urgent demeanour that she nodded her assent, though not without a tremor of anxiety, expecting by no means to like what she heard.

'Well then, honoured guest, let us strike a bargain. I will tell you my story. And in return you will explain to me how a city should be built, and why this Colophon of ours displeases you. For you cannot deny that your reasoning on this point has been somewhat shallow, a defect which may be overcome, when you reflect on what I now shall tell you.'

Archeanassa consented, wondering meanwhile whether the girl were mad, and if so, whether madness ran in the family. She recalled the way in which Plato, in the midst of some off-hand conversation, would interrupt his own lofty manner and fix you with an excited stare, as though noticing your existence for the first time. And then, veering with wild words towards philosophy, he would give you to understand that it was not *your* existence which had come to his notice, that you were just as irrelevant now as you ever were. It was his own existence that astonished him, and which prompted his crazy thoughts. Something of this, Archeanassa thought, had been passed to Perictione, who was now curled on the couch in a girlish and preening posture, staring through her visitor as though at a picture painted on the wall. And in that picture was the face of Perictione.

3

Concerning Perictione's meeting with Merope of Sardis

'When you first met me,' Perictione began, 'I was an innocent teenager. I grant you, not so innocent that I didn't understand the speeches at Phryne's symposium, or listen with relish to the story of you and Uncle Plato. But nothing had happened, and no feeling stirred in me, to suggest that my life would not follow the same course as my mother's life and her mother's before her – a comfortable marriage, with a quiverful of unhappy children, a fickle husband and dinner parties twice a week.

'But that was a decade ago, and in these ten years the world has changed more than it changed in all the centuries since Homer. The work of memory is now undone, the heroes forgotten and the old gods disowned. Oh, I grant you, we carried on in our family as though nothing were happening. Ours was a sophisticated household, in which the old religion of Greece was preserved along with the books and urns and tapestries that commemorate it. We sat among these things as among familiars; we honoured the gods, recited the liturgies and learned the poems. To all external appearances nothing had altered – and in our family external appearances were everything. To mention the vanishing of the gods would be like mentioning my father's mistresses. I did it once, with dire results. But that was at Phryne's symposium; it could never be done at home. A veil was drawn over everything that might disturb our ancient arrangements, and behind the veil a quiet machine was always at work, digesting the unpalatable fact and reducing it to nothing.

'So it was for my parents at least. But it was not so for me. True, Granny had given me the most elevated education, compelling me to read the classics, teaching me the old dances, bringing me up in the old religion, even initiating me into the mysteries. Not a day would pass without a speech from her on the Homeric virtues, on the sacred liturgies, on the noble characters of tragedy, on the imperatives of taste and the fine points of style in art and music. I was to carry the light of civilisation into the cave of the future – so she envisaged it, and all her instruction was devoted to this end. At the same time, however, I sensed that she inwardly withdrew from the things that she taught me, that her elenctic irony, as she called it, was a veil for inner doubts, and that her very sophistication had lifted her above the facts it fed on, so that her spirit floated free of them and judged them from afar. She was the highest point that our civilisation could reach, the point of supreme self-consciousness. And consciousness breeds doubt. Such self-knowledge could endure thereafter only for a generation, in the works of Uncle Plato and the rest of Phryne's circle. But to my generation it was already something theatrical – a set of costumes which lifted you for a moment on to the stage, but which were ridiculous if worn by the audience.

'Of course,' Perictione went on, 'Granny deeply influenced me. Thanks to her, I looked on Athens, in those days when still I thought of living there, with an ironical detachment. I saw the emptiness and vulgarity of popular art and music, the steady loss of knowledge, the decline in piety and virtue, the irreparable disorder that was spreading through the roots of society. I took pride in the good taste which led me to understand and scorn these things, and to set before myself those high examples which Granny had taught me to admire. At the same time I could not quite believe in the old gods. I knew the liturgies by heart, but to me they were more poetry than religion, and when I performed the act of worship, it was as a dancer – representing myself, but not being myself. And secretly I was tempted by that other and lower world which Granny had taught me to despise. I sought out young people for whom Aeschylus and Stesichorus meant nothing, who sneered at the gods and heroes while having only the vaguest acquaintance with their names, and whose idols were the singers and dancers of the day. I learned some of their songs, in Phrygian mode, and – while inwardly scoffing at their clumsy words and melodies – would sing along with the crowd of my cronies, sometimes wiggling obscenely as they did, and feeling my body within its crust of high culture like a moth striving to break from its chrysalis into light and air.

'With the change in my perception of religion came a change in my perception of marriage. For what is marriage if not a vow taken before an altar, and what remains of the vow if no god turns up to enforce it? Of course, a man and a woman can stand in front of a table and exchange promises. But I think you will agree, most honoured Archeanassa, that promises and vows are quite distinct?'

Archeanassa thought for a moment.

'Is it not a question of solemnity?' she suggested. 'I mean, the more solemn the promise, the more it approaches a vow.'

'By no means,' said Perictione, and she stared through her guest with evident satisfaction. 'The difference between a vow and a promise is profound and metaphysical. For a promise is fulfilled in time. And when the promise is fulfilled it is also finished. But a vow is never fulfilled in time: it is endless and changeless, and there is no point at which the account is closed. Those bound together by vows are bound eternally; which is why the immortals must be present, to seal the vow and endow it with a more than earthly power.

'Furthermore,' she went on, warming to her theme, 'promises and contracts can be undone by agreement, after which no obligation remains. Whereas a vow, once knit, can never be untied, but only dishonoured. Such it seems to me, is the real distinction. There is another difference too, and this deeply impressed me at the time of which I am speaking, because it helped me to understand the dilemma in which my poor mother had been placed by her husband's infidelity. Contracts, I hope you agree, are useful things. Without them, no society can endure, since there can be no security between strangers – and a modern society is a society of strangers, is it not?'

Archeanassa signified her assent to this, but could not forbear mentioning that she had heard the point argued by the great Xanthippe, whose ideas, she added, were so much more down-to-earth than those of Plato, and so much more in tune with the female temperament.

'Of course,' Perictione continued, with a slight frown, 'Granny introduced me, before she died, to her friend Xanthippe, and there was an exchange of ideas between us. But to return to the point. Contracts, you will admit, involve an exchange of goods and services. Nothing is given absolutely – all benefits offered depend upon benefits received. Hence the matter of a contract must be defined independently: a bag of horse-hair, say, or a wagon-load of beans. There cannot be a contract to be bound by a contract: such an agreement would be empty and senseless.'

'Indeed not,' said Archeanassa, who was by now firmly convinced that the girl had been driven mad by the solitude of Colophon. And the impression was oddly confirmed for Archeanassa as she looked through the window on to a slate-grey tower, behind which other towers stood in sombre ranks like a regiment assembled for battle. For although she could not hear the drums, Archeanassa was convinced that the towers visibly shook to their rhythm, that these monstrous creatures on stilts were quietly trampling the ground, pressing all human traces deeper and deeper into the soil until nothing remained of the past save Perictione's cluttered museum, where the girl in her madness parcelled out kingdoms and divided the skies. Perictione's face glowed in the light from the window, and as she talked her white cheeks seemed to fly down from celestial regions, converging on her moist sandy lips like swans on a strip of water. Truly it was the most beautiful face Archeanassa had ever seen, and at the same time untouchably remote like a face in a picture. Such a face in such a city must be protected by a veil of isolation.

'But the subject-matter of a marriage,' Perictione went on, as soon as she had recaptured Archeanassa's eyes, 'what is it, if not the marriage itself? What matrimony means, by way of cost and benefit, can never be foretold by those who create it through their vows. Cares and joys, rights and duties, failures and successes – all are in the lap of Fortune, and none can be known in advance. From which it follows, as I am sure you will concede, that marriage cannot be a contract.'

'Nor,' said Archeanassa, 'can the vow of love.' And she looked inwards, at the icon next to her heart. With a sudden stab of fear, however, she saw that the face of Antimachus had changed. For a brief moment the gentle poet was eclipsed by the eager seducer, and love was chased from those liquid eyes by calculation. Never before had she seen this version of Antimachus, and she paled, gripping the arm of her couch. The girl coldly observed her. Archeanassa imagined Perictione's gaze passing through some spiritual prism, so as to separate out its many hues, and to reveal the strands of experience which had been fused into this cold white glare.

'As for that,' the girl pursued, 'we must distinguish real institutions from unreal hopes. And in my father's case – since, after all, it is my father's case that we are discussing – love was no part of the deal. There was a marriage – the eternal vow which bound my mother and cut off her escape. And there was a contract – under the terms of which young Cholcis received rent and underwear, and my father expert caresses. As for the feelings – well, they take the shape of the institutions which channel them: stern duty in the one sphere, abject lust in the other. Do you follow me?'

'I wish I didn't,' said Archeanassa, 'for these are bitter things you speak.'

'Bitter no longer,' said the girl, 'and hardly bitter then.

For you know, I am like my uncle. When something troubles me I dissolve it in thought, and make of it an intellectual problem – which is what my parents' marriage became. I saw that marriage is not a contract but a vow, that men could not stay the course, and that in any case the immortals had faded away, leaving all vows to unravel like tapestries in which the binding thread is cut. Marriage ceased at once to be an option for me. Of course, I was intrigued by men, and tried a few experiments. But the fun occurred at a vast distance, so to speak, way below the place from which I studied it. The question came uppermost in my mind, how to live in this society of strangers – how to triumph, rather. For a descendent of Solon cannot merely live. And my first thought was this: I must replace vows by contracts, in which terms would be agreed in advance. Do you follow me still?'

'Yes,' said Archeanassa, 'and still, I think, your story is a sad one.'

'Let us see whether it is sadder than yours, honoured guest. For sadness, like happiness, comes in many forms; and what to the observer looks like the greatest misery, may be experienced from within with patience and joy.'

Archeanassa responded with a humble nod.

'After Granny died,' Perictione went on, 'I used to gather with certain friends in the Stoa, on those afternoons when the men vacated the place, and conversation could occur without their grabs and gurgles. Sometimes Xanthippe would join us, and, in hope of this great event, wise women from all over Hellas would attend our evenings. One of these women was Merope of Sardis, an itinerant sophist who had lived a shadowy life in her native Lydia before discovering philosophy and making the pilgrimage to Athens. Let me describe her, so that you may understand the effect she had on me.

'Merope was exactly forty years old when I met her, a tall strong woman, with azure eyes, a shapely nose and a reposeful, motherly smile. She wore always the clothes of her native Lydia – a cool tunic of yellow silk and a woollen head-dress in which she wrapped her bright auburn hair.

She had been a great beauty when young, and captured the hearts of many men. But she had been betrayed by the one whom most she loved, and had since wandered the towns of Hellas in search of inner tranquillity. After a while she took to exploring the libraries, and soon became so famed for her oratory and learning, that invitations to feasts would be extended to her whenever she entered a town. She directed her teachings to young women, and was always in their company. She liked to think of herself as an expositor of the Xanthippic philosophy, even though the great woman herself, who sometimes sat in on Merope's lectures, never expressed an opinion in the matter, and would always change the subject when asked about what she had heard.

'From the very first Merope made a huge impression on me. For she came into my life at a time when I was deeply troubled by my father's example, and curious, nevertheless, about the ways of men and how best to exploit them – for that we must always exploit them, honoured Archeanassa, I did not doubt. I needed a companion, an older woman, to whom I could confess my troubles, and who would comfort me with her advice. Now I would not say a word against my mother, who was the best reason I ever had to live in Athens. But my poor mum avoided the subject that concerned me, left me in all such matters to my own devices, and, when she found me sobbing one day on the couch, after a particularly dreadful encounter behind the Prytaneum, could think of nothing better to say than "it must have been the cutlets at lunch."

'Merope, by contrast, saw my need at once and did not hesitate to help me. It was during her first visit to our little circle, when she had given a lecture entitled "The soul in an age of nothingness." Often as she spoke her clear blue eyes sought me across the Stoa, and it seemed to me in those moments that she directed her words and her thoughts into my heart. And how inspired I was to hear her; how those ideas – famous later throughout Hellas, but then almost unknown – struck a chord in me! Her speech was a kind of funeral oration to the gods, a tender, grieving but resolute valediction to the old world, and a cautious acceptance of the new. The soul, she said, is like the human face, which is its only true image. It is constrained by nature, but shaped by art. There is no being behind the doing, any more than there is spirit behind the glance or lightning behind the flash. All that we are is what we make and do. Each generation must cast off the dead crust left by its predecessors, and begin again the task of self-creation. And sometimes, in these special periods of decay, when the old forms and ceremonies have lost their meaning, we stand still for a moment, take stock of our isolation, and listen to the great cisterns of the anonymous city. There, in the depths of civil order, we hear the last gasp of the past.

'Such were the words which rang in the Stoa, and my heart danced to the sound of them. Surely this woman would advise me. Surely she would know my trouble and be familiar with its cure! And when, after the lecture, Merope came with gentle step across the courtyard, how warm was my greeting, and how thrilling her touch! She took my arm and led me away from the crowd, to a small wooden bench in a distant corner, where sometimes Xanthippe would sit when she wished to be alone among her followers.

'No sooner were we seated side by side than Merope addressed me with honeyed words.

'"My dear young lady," she said, "for that you are a lady I see clearly from your robes: it is presumptuous in me to say that I know you. But I do. You may conceal your name from me, but you cannot conceal your soul."

'"I would not conceal it, even if I could," I said. "And my name, by the way, is Perictione."

'"Perictione, niece of Plato, grand-daughter of the great Perictione who danced before Parmenides?"[1]

'"The same," I answered proudly, and she beamed at me

---

1   That Plato's mother Perictione danced as a young girl before Parmenides is confirmed by 'Perictione's Parmenides', in *Xanthippic Dialogues*, op. cit.

for a long while, allowing her eyes to settle on my face as a heron settles by a lake.

'"Then," she said at last, "we must be friends. For I see in your face that your noble ancestry has shaped your character, and that you do not accept, as others accept, to live by half-measures."

'"You flatter me," I said.

'"On the contrary," she replied. "It is you who flatter me, by sitting here and showing your emotions. For I don't doubt that you would rather flee than be admired by someone whom you thought to be unworthy."

'She had placed a bait there, Archeanassa, and you won't be surprised that I was hooked by it. She took one of my hands and pressed it between her palms. How soft and womanly and full of help they were! A force of life seemed to pass into my blood-stream, and for the first time in months I was not alone. Oh, I grant you, I had enjoyed my talks with Xanthippe – as all of us did. But Xanthippe was remote, self-contained, a distant observer of the world which troubled us, whereas Merope revealed, in her youthful face and easy gestures, in her total absorption in the one whom she addressed, a kind of eager attachment to reality, a desire to live in this realm of common things without compunction. I asked her where she was staying.

'"I have found a barrel by the temple of Cybele, next to the barrel of Diogenes."[2]

'"How dreadful!" I cried, "You must come home with me. You can sleep in Granny's bed in the *gynaikaion*, and my father need never know."

'"Is that the way to begin our friendship, with an act of concealment?"

'"Does not all friendship begin in concealment?" I asked.

---

2   According to Diogenes Laertius (*Lives of the Philosophers*, VI, 23), Diogenes took up residence in a barrel in the Metroon – the temple dedicated to Cybele in the Athenian agora. It is clear from what follows, however, that the temple in question was another dedicated to the same goddess, on the outskirts of town, overlooking the Eleusian plain.

"For new friendships threaten old ones, and can show themselves only when they have gathered strength."

"'I am of another opinion," she replied, "and I welcome especially the opportunity to express it, since it will enable our friendship to begin as it should. You will admit that it is our nature to seek and love the truth?"

"'Certainly," I said, "unless the truth is painful, which it usually is."

"'Ah yes," she went on, "I see what is troubling you."

"'Then do tell me what you see, honoured Merope, since nothing more nearly concerns me."

"'You have had the great experience," she said confidingly, like a doctor revealing some fatal disease.

"'And what is that?" I asked, somewhat alarmed.

"'The experience from which there is no return."

'This did not enlighten me so much, that I felt it unnecessary to press for an explanation.

"'Of course you are right," she said, "that we distinguish comfortable from painful truths. Indeed, life turns on the distinction. And when truth is painful we take refuge in lies – I will not say holy lies, as your uncle does, since holiness, in my view, is a thing of the past."[3]

'She gave me an expectant look, as though trying out my responses. I nodded vigorously, and at once a mysterious beatific light glowed in her features.

"'Indeed," she went on, "holiness is itself a lie, the greatest lie of all, the lie that makes all other lies available. You have understood the matter. And this is the experience that has singled you out."

"'Not me only, but my whole generation."

"'No, most noble Perictione, you are mistaken. Of course, the young ignore the gods, look sceptically on the habits of worship and proceed in their daily business as though the moment were all. But they do not see through the

---

3   Merope uses the expression 'holy lie' (Ar. *ifku muqqadisah*), which is a serious distortion of Plato's 'noble lie' (γεννᾱῖον ψεῦδος) as expounded in *Republic*, 414B et seq. But it is clear from subsequent events that all Merope's targets are fictions.

lies. Theirs is a permitted scepticism, the scepticism that leaves everything in place. The world still divides for them into good and evil; and they describe as evil exactly what religion requires – everything that is stronger, larger, more noble and more interesting than themselves. All such things, which older generations described as *hubris* and which they saw as the call to divine revenge, young people now regard in more secular terms, as arrogant and elitist. But the effect is the same. Their morality does for them what piety did for their parents: it rearranges the world, with weakness ensconced and protected, and strength cast out in the wild.

'I don't need to tell you, honoured Archeanassa, how flattered I felt by these words, which singled me out as so precious a dissenter. Merope had not only endorsed my scepticism; she had consciously detached me from the herd. I begged her to continue, and again the beatific smile shone through her features.

'"Please understand me," she said. "I do not reject the modern world. On the contrary, I accept it. But I try to accept it from the standpoint of truth, and without those distorting veils which are called 'ideals.' For how are ideals manufactured? Here, most noble Perictione, is a cautionary tale. It seems to me that the strong live without ideals. What need have they of such illusions, when they have seized power and freedom, and thrown the leftovers to those who can win no battles for themselves? Ideals are manufactured out of weakness. I do not dare to strike my oppressor; so I call my cowardice forgiveness and make of it an ideal. I cannot match my neighbour's intellect or wealth, so I call my state humility, make of humility an ideal and castigate my neighbour for his pride. And the most pervasive of all ideals – the one that remains when all religion, all piety, all true striving has been subtracted – is that of equality, which makes distinction an offence against the moral order. It is in the name of equality that the life of indolence – life on the downhill slope – is justified."

'Here I made so bold as to interrupt her.

'"Surely, most wise Merope, there is a contradiction in

what you say. For you seem to dismiss the gods as mere illusions, and also to regret their passing, implying that religion and piety are obstacles to our modern indolence. What else do you mean by 'truly striving,' if not an assertion of strength?"

'Pride forbids that I should dwell on the compliments which greeted my interruption, honoured Archeanassa. But here is the gist of what Merope went on to say.

'"We no longer see anything that aspires to be greater – everything is becoming thinner, cosier, more equal and indifferent. We have lost the fear of humanity, and with it the love for humanity, and the will to be truly human. And what is it, to be truly human? It is to be *discontented* with what we are. Here is the paradox – that true human nature consists in the need to discard human nature. What were they, after all, those gods who so quietly departed in the night and left us grieving? Were they not the icons of ourselves, the higher forms to which we once aspired and could aspire no longer? There was a time when piety was a strength – when by worshipping the gods we amplified ourselves. But when faith becomes a refuge, and threatens those who strive for distinction, then is the time for truthfulness – the time to say aloud that the gods have gone home to their graves."

'How exhilarating it was to hear such words spoken from gentle lips! Merope came before me as a living paradox – the very paradox that she described, godless yet god-like, seeking, striving, restless, yet utterly serene and content.

'"Why," I asked, "is truthfulness so important?"

'"Because," she answered simply, "it is all that we have."

'"But you say that we should seek beyond what we have: that we should endeavour to transcend ourselves."

'"But that is just it!" she cried. "The same paradox runs through all things. We must be truthful, precisely at the moment when we recognize that there are no truths – that what a man calls truth is merely *his* truth, the lie which brings comfort to *him*. For this has become *our* truth, the truth that threatens theirs!"

'"Wow!" I said, and looked at her as Granny might have done, with an attempt at elenctic irony.

'"And that is what I meant about friendship," she went on more calmly. "Many things are called true, are they not? Statements, beliefs, feelings, inferences, what have you?"

'"Yes," I replied, "and I doubt truth means the same in all these cases."

'"Your doubt is premature. For when I call a statement true, is it not the case that I endorse it, that I make it *mine*?"

'"Yes," I said, for fear of preventing a Socratic dialogue.

'"And is it not likewise with a feeling – as when you say, 'How disgusting!' and I say 'True'?"

'"True," I echoed, rather neatly, I thought.

'"And so through all the cases that I mentioned. To call something true, be it words or thoughts or feelings, is to affirm it as one's own – to say, if you like, that *your* truth is *my* truth. In no case do we compare words or thoughts with something outside them, something which is neither thought nor word but the standard against which thought and word are measured."

'She pressed my hand and looked at me with a candid smile. And so free and kind and confident were the eyes that warmed me, that I consented without a murmur to her words.'

'Yet I cannot help feeling,' Archeanassa interrupted, 'that there is a dangerous fallacy in this view of truth. For if no standards remain to us, all is permitted – and it is then, surely, that we go downhill. With respect, most noble Perictione.'

The girl, who had been lost in memories, now focussed her visitor with a haughty stare.

'That, of course, is my uncle's view. And I daresay it has, intellectually speaking, much to recommend it. But there is also life, honoured Archeanassa, and what is dear to reason may be mocked by life. Reason is the resource of the individual, life the gift of the species; and the individual exists only so that the species may discard him. I don't deny that Merope's philosophy was full of paradox and that it led in time to disaster. But I shall come to that. As I sat with her in the Stoa I saw only the opening she had made in the crust of old authority, and I longed to escape through it and leave my inheritance behind.

'In any case, I nodded my assent to Merope's reasoning, and she promptly returned to her theme.

'"But it is not only thoughts and words that we call true," she went on. "There are also true friends. And the truth of friendship lies in trust, does it not?"

'I assented eagerly.

'"Moreover, if you really wish for a standard – something outside your truth in terms of which it to measure it – you have it here, in friendship. What we affirm together is larger than what we affirm alone, provided there is trust between us. True friends are therefore a *measure* of truth. My truth is fortified by yours, and as the friendship grows our thoughts and words gain an authority higher than the fact that you or I affirm them."

'Those were vertiginous thoughts, but I nodded my assent, keen to know where this Socratic path was leading.

'"Well then, let us assume that our friendship has advanced so far that I feel able to accept your invitation to sleep in the hallowed bed of your ancestor, the great Perictione. And then, next morning, after I have slipped away, your mother asks about the noise overnight in Granny's room, and you say it was the maid whom you sent to clean it. Then you must, of course, tell the maid to corroborate your story, and in response to her sarcastic smile you reply, O.K. then, someone *did* stay the night, a crony, if you must know, of my brother Speusippus. Speusippus is now part of the conspiracy and he too must be taught to spin a story. I meanwhile, who have returned to the house at a decent hour because there is no peace for my soul save in the ray of your glances, must pretend to your parents that I am visiting for the first time and feign astonishment at the noble furnishings which I had studied the night before, wondering whether they would be missed and how much they would fetch in the flea market. And I begin to debate in my mind what the official story now might be, and try to divine from your expression just who knows what about whom and how. What a tangled web we weave, you and I both victims of our own deception, and unable to establish the trust that would raise our words above the sea of falsehood and present them as truth – as *our* truth, which we will not deny before the world. I think you would agree, would you not, that this is no way to begin a friendship?"

'"No way," I said.

'"And there is another reason," she went on, "for beginning on a note of truthfulness. For if I am not mistaken, it is your parents who are the root of your problems, and it is their coldness that has put a stop to your heart."

'"How boldly you advance!" I exclaimed, with a laugh of protest.

'"So let me make a suggestion."

'"I should be honoured."

'"Let us go back to my place – O, I admit, it is no more than a barrel, but comfortable enough – and on the way we can talk. And if our talk is profitable, we can meet again to-morrow, and then the next day. And one day, perhaps, we shall know how best to make use of that room of Granny's."

'I looked at her askance.

'"And what shall we do at your place?"

'"We shall cook ourselves supper on an open fire. Come, you'll enjoy it."

'And there was in her face such a serene confidence that what she wanted was right, and right because she wanted it, that I needed little persuading. For I wished to be like Merope: willing my desire as a law for myself. I walked beside her to the temple of Cybele with a sense of embarking on a great adventure – the adventure which was to be my life.

'Merope had a cool, brisk walk, and her peripatetic lifestyle had made her fit and vigorous. I was as yet only an amateur dancer, and my body was limp and pampered. Rather than show my disgraceful state, I hurried along beside her, puffed and silent, while she calmly dictated her opinions to the air. She had a peculiar manner of passing in a flash from abstract thought to the most personal observations and back again, so that it was as impossible to know whether her theories about time, eternity and substance were not really about my eyes and cheeks and fingers, all of which she touched from time to time with her smiling lips, as it was to know whether her flattering remarks about my eyes and lips and fingers were not really about some transcendental reality. Not that she believed in transcendental realities. But for someone who disbelieved, she talked about them rather a lot. But I see you are bored, honoured Archeanassa.'

Archeanassa, who was not bored in the least, but whose revulsion at the vanity that sat enthroned before her had caused her to look away, quickly assumed a guest-like pose and vigorously affirmed her undying interest. Perictione responded with a haughty frown.

'I know what you are thinking,' she continued, 'and I accept that it is just. Much has happened since then to allay my childish vanity, but I remember these things as though I lived them again, and as though my distinguished social mask, so carefully imparted and so arrogantly guarded, were still the real me. Nor would it be seemly for a descendant of Solon to do otherwise, or to reveal to you, honoured guest, how much inner trouble has been caused by the pride which Merope encouraged and admired in me. But I digress.'

Archeanassa looked into those dark, still eyes and something fugitive appeared behind them, like a desperate creature at a window, dropping out of sight with stifled cries. And again she saw the eyes of Plato, eyes so needing love, which fled from love in bafflement.

'You do me honour, noble Perictione, in showing me your heart.'

'Well,' the girl continued, with a sigh, 'you must know that I have never told this story, and that it is you who prompt me to recall it. I had wanted to be immune to all regret, to shake off the past completely, to settle in this faceless city as cool, clear and ungraspable as a crystal fountain. But alas, since the death of Merope I have been very much alone. So, with your permission, I will return to the tale and give the reason for my being here. You can be the judge whether I was right to come, and right to stay. Drat that boy!'

The occasion of this sudden cry was a loud crash from the back of the house, followed by a peal of boyish laughter, and a brief toot on a hunting horn. A small spotted dog ran into the room, saw Perictione, who had meanwhile risen to her feet, and quickly escaped whence it had come. The girl swept into the peristyle and disappeared. Shortly afterwards Archeanassa heard her shouting orders in some distant corner of the building, the servants running to obey. When Perictione returned it was with a pale and serious face that forbade enquiries. She sat down slowly, with added dignity, like one who has suffered an affront.

4

Concerning the philosophy of Merope and the sale of Diogenes

'If ever I had doubts about Merope,' Perictione said, 'those doubts were dispelled by our walk that evening. Her ideas emerged so naturally, and were so much directed to my own experience, that I felt them on the tip of my tongue at the very moment she was about to give outward form to them. She spoke of the old morality – the morality that had been brought to us, fresh and believable, by the eager gods, but which now encumbered us like discarded costumes on the stage of life, from which the actors had departed. In these circumstances, she said, people give way to rancour and suspicion. They no longer believe in the gods, but dare not disbelieve either. Instead they dress themselves in those incongruous masks and roam the stage, hoarsely decreeing that nothing has changed, that the comedy continues, and that anyone who thinks otherwise, anyone who stands apart from the crowd and affirms the right to his own desire, should be forced once again into the ways of mediocrity. But why? It is a question they cannot answer. And she agreed with me that vows had become empty forms. Rather than pretend to be bound by them, she said, it would be better to find another and higher life. We should escape the tyranny of divine figments, and be ourselves our own divinities, living in friendship with those who can understand and accept our terms. She applauded my abhorrence of the married state, and listened patiently as I explained the catastrophe of our noble house, brought low by lies and subterfuge.

'"You think of your suffering as senseless," she said, as we passed the shrine of Hephaestus and came in sight of the rubbish dump beside Cybele's temple. "But it is not senseless at all. It is the source of the greatest satisfaction, not of course to you, but to those – your parents, for instance – who inflicted it, and could find no other way of imprinting upon you some indelible mark of their possession."

'I felt such a surge of joy and liberation at these words, that I did not notice, at first, the strange sight that had come into view as we left behind us the last half-finished houses which lined the road from the Acropolis. My eyes and ears were all for Merope, and if she had asked me in that moment to come away with her from Athens and never return, I should gladly have accepted, so much did her striding figure contain for me by way of hope and certitude. But my thoughts were interrupted by a long eerie cry, like the howl of a dog in pain, and my eyes were drawn from my guide and counsellor to a rotten barrel which lay, overgrown with ragwort and thistles, on the edge of the rubbish tip, where it must have been dumped some years before. A dark form was swaying in its aperture, and after a while I was able to make out a human face – or what once had been a human face, before the beard, clotted with slimy food and old saliva, had spread like a fungus over every inch of it, leaving only the dark brown eyes burning in their shadowy sockets and the little pink tongue flickering among black and broken teeth like a snake in some stinking cleft beneath the undergrowth. The creature howled again, cast a rabid glance in our direction, and then scampered back into the dark interior of the barrel and was lost to view.

'Of course I had heard of Diogenes, and had often been tempted to wander in these parts in the hope of seeing him. But even the wildest rumours had not prepared me for the appalling stench conveyed across our path by the vacillating breezes, for the raging sounds that now emerged from the belly of that cask, or for the diatribe into which those cries at last resolved themselves.

'"Athenians, arse-holes, what was it Pericles, the stuck-up old fart, said of you? 'In nobility of spirit we stand in contrast to most men' – amazing feat, which every pig achieves without instruction! And why? 'Because it is not by receiving but by giving that we acquire our friends.'[1] Cut the crap, Perry! What you mean is Athenians choose their friends from their inferiors. Virtue yes – *bourgeois* virtue, the power of leisure over labour! And you think those friends you purchase have any love for you? You've got to be joking! Snotgobblers! Insects! Donkey-cocks![2]

> *Hot snot and bogey pie*
> *All mixed in with a dead dog's eye,*
> *Mix it well and mix it thick,*
> *And wash it down with a cup of cold sick!*"'

'And with this he lapsed into howls of laughter, in the hollow depths of which you could hear the cry of a loneliness so absolute that only the gods could console it. And no sooner had I sensed this than Diogenes began again, a long string of abuse against those very gods he had brought to mind, informing his imaginary audience that, after all, no gods exist, so who could possibly be offended by his blasphemies against them?

'"So now you have heard it," said Merope, as we passed, "the sound of true resentment: the unbeliever who cannot accept his unbelief, the self-enslaved who cannot love his master. That is the *bad* way to go about it."'

---

1 Pericles' 'Funeral Oration,' in Thucydides, II, xi, 4.
2 Ar. *qaDaa'ib ul-Himar*. A strange insult, perhaps related to the belief, affirmed in the Bestiary of Tariq ibn al-Janoubi, that the penis of a donkey, boiled and pounded in a mortar, then smeared on the cheeks and forehead, would drive away djinns and demons, so repulsive is its smell. The children's street rhyme which follows is still in use in the backstreets of Alexandria: I have not attempted to translate, but used instead an equivalent chanted by Glasgow schoolchildren.

'"To go about what?"

'"Living in the here and now," she said. "But come, most noble Perictione, we have arrived at our destination, and I suspect you will enjoy what I have to offer far more than the lavish supper that awaits you in the house which you have ceased to regard as home."

'And she gestured to another barrel, a nicely coopered tun of Sicilian oak. Merope's home had been cleaned up and gentrified. The hoop of bronze which bound the rim had been lovingly polished, and shone in the declining sunlight with a warm red glow. There was a little garden of herbs beside the barrel, and two polished stones for sitting out in front. And in the shadowy interior I could see shelves bearing bowls and urns for cooking, neatly folded clothes and a roll of bedding, bound with a leather girdle and stowed away in the back. No sooner had we arrived than Merope took sticks of dry tinder from a store behind the tub, arranged them in the blackened hollow which was her fireplace, and lit them with a pair of flints.

'I had been brought up in the belief that cooking, cleaning, and serving are the work of slaves. Nobody in my family was ever seen taking care of the home, or ministering to the needs of others. My mother was not the fount of those comforts which our house provided, but merely another weary beneficiary, who took what she wished from the passing stream of nourishment, without thought or gratitude. And that is why our house was not a home. Food and drink arrived impersonally and unexplained like the weather. And nobody lifted a finger either to help another or to help himself.

'Imagine my feelings, therefore, as Merope prepared our simple meal – taking water from a tub with a wooden ladle, adding millet from an earthenware jar, salt from an olivewood box, and slices of marrow, cut with an old bronze knife that looked as though it had seen years of military service. Each gesture, as she poured and stirred and measured, was a giving, and the simple food was blessed by smiles as she shaped it for the table. And although Merope's barrel was only a temporary shelter, retrieved from the Cybelian rubbish-tip, it had more of home than our family mansion, and more of peace and refreshment, for all the cool breezes and susurrating slaves that haunted our inner peristyle. In our house I had reached into the stream of comforts and taken: everything there was take, take and take. But when Merope gave I did not take – I received. And my receiving was a giving, since something of myself flowed out to her as she set the bowl before me, inviting me to anoint it with oil.

'Never has any meal before or since tasted so wonderful, honoured Archeanassa! The fragrant oil, warmed by the millet, rose to my nostrils like nectar, and the soft strips of green marrow, which lay on the nut-brown mound like pastures on a hillside, were to me the sweetest fruit of the earth. And Merope's still smile shed its radiance over everything, including me among these wholesome things, burning away the years of fatuous fussiness, cleansing me of our household poisons and freeing me from our household gods. I was born anew in her carefree glances, and laughed and chattered like a child as we feasted in the sunlight.

'Here I should mention a curious fact, Archeanassa. During all the time that I spent with Merope, when nothing interested me more than her face and the words which sped from it, I could never quite decide whether she had a cast in one eye. Always, when I caught the glance from one of those pupils, I felt that the light of the other shone just to the side of me. And the strange thing is that it was the other eye, the one which pointed past me, which seemed to observe me most eagerly. Nor could I decide whether it was the right eye or the left eye that contained the most of her: for they took it in turns, the one to fix the target, the other to bathe it in a flood of interest. As a result of this Merope always seemed to watch me from a point beyond her face, a sun-drenched plateau where she gathered the rays of heaven and sped them downwards to the human world.

'During our supper Merope entertained me with stories

of her peripatetic life, of the sights she had seen and the people she had met. I was astonished by her erudition. No subject had escaped her notice, no curious fact eluded her. About everything she had thought her own thoughts and drawn her own conclusions. Her absolute confidence in the rightness of her views was soothing and contagious. I felt that, if I could but be honest with myself – which meant, of course, discarding the elenctic irony instilled by Granny – I would be as confident as she. I made up my mind to throw in my lot with Merope, and to join her, when the time came, on her pilgrimage. Side by side we would travel through a world whose beliefs and customs we discarded, free and insolent as the gods themselves.

'It was a warm summer evening, and as the light congealed along the far horizon I looked around me, seeing the world as though newly born, and astonished by its loveliness. The temple stood high on its crepidoma, the columns a rich indigo, their capitals picked out in gold. The building was a gift from Athens to the mother of all, and it bathed in the last rays of sunlight like a fine woman in the stream of the sea. The columns and entablature had gathered up all that there was of red and blue and gold. Beyond the temple peristyle, on the sloping hills of the suburb, there was only white and green: the whitewashed walls of the houses, and the green upon green of groves and gardens and wild vegetation. And because I was seeing all this for the first time, I became acutely aware of distinctions. How different, I noticed, was the yellow green of the poplars in the sacred grove from the brownish green of the wayside grass; how striking, before the green-edged blackness of the cypresses that made their mournful crenellations on the hillside, was the grey metallic green of a gnarled old olive. The blue-green skin of Merope's marrows spoke of growth and nourishment, while the enamel green underleaf of the neighuring laurel bush was like a warning, as though Daphne's desperate last cry still sounded from the wreath surrounding her. And along the feathery plain of Eleusis the folds of silken greenery lay on the river bank, soft and glowing with a silvery light as the sun stole away. A queer incumbent faintness came over me as I watched the lengthening shadows; it was as though the world were unwrapping itself in the twilight. The truth of things was revealed in the landscape, trembling and hardly visible.

'I rose to go. For I was not yet so brazen that I could spend a night away from the house of my ancestors. Merope too rose from her stone, and, taking my hands in both of hers, looked at me with a glow of frank affection.

'"You see how easy it is," she said.

'"Oh yes," I replied. "As flight is easy to a bird."

'And to quieten my fears, she walked back with me past that other barrel, whose occupant fell morosely silent as we disappeared into the twilight.

'That night I could not sleep, and many were the moments when I was about to rise from my bed and sally forth into the streets, seeking again my friend and protector. What bliss it would be to lie beside her, to smell again the oaken lining of that casket in which the jewel of a soul lay wrapped in its routine! Oh I know what you are thinking Archeanassa. You imagine that this passion was the flame of *eros*, the flame which burned so splendidly in Sappho, and which caused her to address the great goddess in accents that no poet so long as the world exists will ever equal. But I assure you, in the months and years we were together, not once did anything of that kind pass between us. Warm though our feelings were, spilling over at every moment into heartfelt hugs and kisses, never did we think of that compromising act, that melting of the flesh, of which you spoke at Phryne's symposium. My own experiments with men have confirmed my opinion of that ungrateful sex; but they have done nothing to turn me in the other direction, however fashionable it may be.'

'I had never for one moment entertained the thought –'

Archeanassa's words were waved aside impatiently.

'Be that as it may, honoured guest, my desire to rise from

my bed that night and join my new companion was as fervent as the desire of any lover. Only the lingering consciousness of my social position detained me. At the first light of dawn I was up and away, hurrying in scant clothes across the still sleeping city, to the dump on the outskirts where my hopes were stored. Merope was already busy with her domestic tasks, watering the herbs in her garden, and singing stanzas from the *Calyce*.[3] She greeted me quietly and without surprise, as though I had never been home, and offered me goat's milk in a wooden cup. I asked her where she had obtained this delicacy, and she mentioned a farm beyond the city wall, in a place of dereliction where no farm could be.

'"And if you are surprised," she added, "then let me tell you that there are two ways of knowing a city, the way of the resident and the way of the wanderer. And that place which is mapped out so exactly in your mind, by streets and temples and thoroughfares, and which seems the very image of permanence, is to me not permanent at all, but in a constant state of becoming. Everywhere I see new things growing and old things dying, and what for you is derelict land, lying beyond all human purpose since it has no place in the city, is for me a goat-herd's honoured field, destined to become a sanctuary or a theatre, or else to grow into a farm as the ruins of Athens succumb to the spreading pasture."

'And then, for the first but by no means the last time, she began to speak of cities and their meaning, of the styles and schools of architecture, of right proportions and fitting details, of public space and thresholds. And I will return to this, honoured Archeanassa, since, if you remember, you promised to favour me with your view of cities and to explain to me your adverse judgement of our Colophon. But before then I must allow my story to advance a little. For you will never understand what Colophon means to me if you do not first become acquainted with the person who

---

3   Lost poem by Stesichorus, which women were in the habit of singing while engaged in their domestic chores, and which is summarized by Athenaeus, *Deipnosophistae*, 14, 619D.

brought me here, my beloved Merope, now dead alas, but then the fountainhead of all my hopes.

'It did not surprise me that Merope began the day with a learned discourse: Granny was the same, and I was practised at the art of joining in, as though the day could wait on our conclusions. But I was surprised by my response to Merope – surprised by the extent to which I had changed in the hours of knowing her. For as she spoke, I took over her tasks – tasks which I had never dreamed of performing, but into which I threw myself joyfully, as into the preparations for a festival. I cleared away weeds, watered marrows, washed dishes from the night before, rolled up the bed and folded the linen. And these were like pious rituals, purifying the spirit as I completed them one by one.

'As I worked Merope spoke again of her travels. How lucky she thought herself, to live as she did in these sunset years, free to observe, to know, and to draw aside the veil of human deception. In her view there could be no future in democracy, which by according equal respect to every human type, forbade the hierarchy on which culture and glory – and therefore the will to live – depend. She was drawn to me by my origins and bearing, by the "pathos of distance"[4] as she described it, with which I viewed the world. But aristocracy was now an inner virtue, with no outward power. Only in friendship did it show itself – although friendship, she added, was enough.

'I was struck again by the paradox of Merope. Here was a woman who spoke as though her highest goal were the power and freedom of a ruling caste – a caste of proud heroes, scornful of the menial survivors beneath them. Yet she lived at the lowest and simplest level, humbly engaged in tasks with which no aristocrat could conceivably dirty his hands. And I took on those tasks, willingly throwing away my haughty habits, and living beside her as an equal. I loved her with a democratic love, in the very moments when I consciously joined her in scorning our democratic culture.

'Over the weeks that followed nothing caused in me

4   Ar. *ishfaaq ul-ba'ida*.

greater contentment than those hours of gardening and scrubbing and sewing that we put in together, or those meals of lentils and cress and unleavened bread that tasted to me of life itself, and for the sake of which I discarded all my society friends and all my upper-class pretensions. And I understood, for the first time, the rightness of those lines by Praxilla, which are so often mocked by the *cognoscenti*, but which will surely be on my lips when I leave this world:

> *Loveliest of what I leave behind is the sunlight*
> *And loveliest then the shining stars and the moon's face,*
> *But also ripe cucumbers and apples and pears . . .*[5]

For it is indeed true that vegetables, in their simplicity, and when offered to an invited guest, have an aura of holiness like the moon and the stars.

'Most evocative of all was the olive oil – the sole and sufficient sauce to all our feasts. Merope, who made no fuss about food except to insist that it be natural, and such as the gods themselves would eat were there no humans around to provide for them, the gods being in this case a suitable figment for our own deeper necessities, was nevertheless unbelievably fussy in the matter of oil, and kept an amphora of the very best – yellow-green, cloudy, with a fragrance of samphire and cloves. This she would replenish once a month from the shop in Piraeus owned by a crazy metic called Herpidos who, being an admirer of her philosophy, provided the stuff for free. I used to fetch it for her, and would glory in my new position as I swayed down the long walls to Piraeus, the amphora balanced on my head, to the astonished glances of the Athenians. Only once before,'

---

5   That the dying Adonis, having invoked the heavenly bodies, should suddenly remember his vegetable patch, struck ancient commentators as so ridiculous that the expression 'sillier than Praxilla's Adonis' became proverbial. Those who have read Sir James Frazer's volumes on Attis and Adonis will, however, credit Praxilla's anthropological insight, for Adonis was a god of vegetation whose death was required precisely so that cucumbers should reappear next season.

Perictione added with a mischievous toss of the head, 'had our family looked so ridiculous. But we won't go into that! And besides, you know, there is something infinitely ennobling in bearing ridicule from those you despise, and in knowing that the act which is shameful in their eyes, is a mark of the highest distinction in yours. Indeed, I was as distinguished by my love for Merope, as Uncle Plato was on that other occasion, by his love for you, honoured Archeanassa. And I am sure you know what I mean, when I say that, in such cases, the world sniggers precisely so that we can rise above and despise it.'

Archeanassa blushed, uncertain whether to feel insulted or exalted by the girl's remark. Then she saw the cool and measuring glance that Perictione bestowed on her, and decided to respond with a judicious nod of the head.

'I would come each day to our little home,' Perictione continued, 'where all was so clean and modest and free. Our meals were a foretaste of Elysium. To escape from those crowded social lunches at our house, where crusty generals rubbed shoulders with phoney poets, where high priests from competing temples pierced each other with deadly paradox, and where dish followed dish in weary succession, each smeared with an absurd sauce derived from some fashionable cookbook, but everything in the end having only one taste, which was the taste of death – to escape from this to our frugal campsite, to prepare with excited gestures our modest bowl of millet, and to sit on ox-hide cushions against the stones before our barrel, with all that was needed for life and joy and happiness stowed neatly away inside, everything tidy and hopeful and reflecting back to us the smiling life with which we placed it there – this to me was my first taste of liberation. And already my heart was journeying far from Athens, side by side with Merope on a reckless pilgrimage into the vast unknown. Our true desires, she told me, are also presentiments, harbingers of the action we are about to perform. So it was that I lived in a new way, confident of the future and contemptuous of the world.

'And I could not help noticing, since it so nearly

concerned my thoughts at this critical period, the contrast between our barrel and the barrel of our neighbour, who had stowed himself on the dump next to ours with a snarling, resentful determination to make his presence and his degradation known to the city he affected to despise. He scavenged in the neighbourhood for food and came home with his trophies between his teeth like a fox to his lair. He neither cleaned his hovel nor cleared away the droppings that he left outside. The opening was covered in slime and fungus, and he crawled in on all fours, obscenely waggling his encrusted buttocks as he went. And once inside he shouted and laughed like a madman, interrupting himself with farts and belches and periodically poking his clotted face into the sunlight to put out his tongue at the world. And though his behaviour was shameless, and deliberately so, in one particular he showed the most interesting spasms of shame – and that particular was us. He would not look in our direction, averted his eyes as though in fear from the sight of our quiet rituals, and projected his lewd remarks and gestures always in some other direction. But I could not help noticing the sly glances that he cast towards our tub when he thought we were unaware of him. In those glances I read a kind of baffled wonderment, a recognition that all he had failed to be, we were. And having rested his eyes for a moment on our happiness, he would retreat into his kennel and howl like a dog.

'We could have rolled downhill for four hundred yards on the north side with not so much as an obstacle once we had got the tub in motion – and often we thought of doing so. For when the wind was in the wrong direction the stench from our neighbour was quite revolting, and the noise of his antics as he sat under the rotting arch of pine-wood, scratching his armpits and rolling his eyes, often put a stop to our dialogue. But we decided to stay there, honoured Archeanassa, and I shall tell you why. Diogenes justified his way of life with philosophy. Like us, he had seen through the artifice of custom and morality, had repudiated the gods and heroes, and freed himself from the chains of law – so at least he said, to the crowds who would assemble for his Monday morning lectures. But he had done these things, as you might say, gracelessly, not taking comfort from his insights but, on the contrary, raging against the world for not endorsing them. And although he pretended that his stinking and puking and caterwauling were an act of defiance, a living proof of his indifference to the morality and conventions of the city, they were in a certain measure the opposite of this: a desperate appeal for attention, a desire for fame and even – yes – social recognition, as an integral but irritating part of the social order he hastened to condemn. I discussed his case with Merope, and as she enlightened me I noticed Diogenes looking across at us sadly and submissively, as though he caught every word.

'"He is doing everything possible," she said, "to persuade himself that he despises his fellows, whereas in fact he seeks nothing more than their good opinion. Just stick your tongue out at him and he will instantly cease his antics in astonishment and chagrin. Apply your foot to his posterior and he will wail with mortification at your contemptuous treatment and ask who told you that this was the last thing he could bear and how had you found him out? Indeed, he will even be surprised by his own reaction, since his continuous aping of contempt has taken him in. He has for so long disguised himself as a critic that he takes himself for the genuine article. In fact he is a child, a suitor for attention, a man whose very solitude is really a secret appeal for company, and who stinks and pukes and craps for others' benefit and in an acute anxiety to please."

'And of course the strategy worked. People came to our part of Athens expressly to observe him, often ignoring the temple, and behaving quite as though Cybele were as much a figment as Diogenes proclaimed her to be. And, although most would hurry past his tub and take care to avert their eyes from the philosopher, they would go home proudly to report the words that Diogenes had flung at them as they

Chapter 4

fled. For many people, to have been called "shit-faced bourgeois swine" by Diogenes was their highest claim to distinction, and at least one of our neighbours used to boast that he had earned a special recommendation as a "toad-eating piss-drinking Platonist."

'This universal attention directed to Diogenes cast around him a shadow of indifference. No other tub on the Cybelian rubbish dump was of any interest beside the barrel where he raved and screamed, and people would barely notice the two women quietly reading or conversing only a hundred yards away, in the polished hoop of their Sicilian wine-cask. Had we taken our home elsewhere – not that planning permission would have been obtained, for there was much overcrowding in Athens, and the new middle classes greatly resented the sight of improvised homes among their terra-cotta villas[6] – had we moved elsewhere, we should have attracted ten times as much attention. Besides, we found the sight and sound of Diogenes peculiarly edifying, and I shall tell you why, most honoured guest. The philosophy of Diogenes, precisely because it was so close to that of Merope, brought home the essential difference between them, and was the living proof of the rightness of our way of life. Like Merope, Diogenes had seen through the beautiful illusions – he knew that the gods are fictions, and that history too is a fiction, spun by those with power, in order to make their power more durable. He despised the culture of democracy, and the equal treatment which had removed every honour and distinction from the *polis*. And he laughed at the popular heroes – the crooning singers and spheromachs[7] who counted for more in the public affection than all the poets of antiquity. But there the resemblance

6   The difficulty of obtaining planning permission would of course be exacerbated by the fact that Merope was at best a 'metic' or resident alien. At about this time Xenophon vigorously advocated extending to metics the right to build houses within the city walls. See Xenophon, *Poroi*, ii, 6.
7   Ar. *la'iyoun ul-kurah*. I have used the nearest Greek word in translation, since football had not yet been invented.

ended. For Diogenes' rejection of the modern city was also a craving for it: his anger proceeded from loss and alienation, and in everything he did he was, as Merope had said, like a disappointed child, driven mad by the need for recognition. Merope's rejection of the city, by contrast, was also an acceptance. She had chosen to live outside the norms of modern life, and cheerfully conceded to others the space they needed for their degradation. And that is why, honoured Archeanassa, she lived in so orderly a way. Her life was conducted with a kind of piety – not the piety which spends itself upon the gods, but the other and more beautiful piety, which lies in a tenderness towards the earth, and a desire to leave the earth unchanged and undamaged by one's passage through towards extinction. And this piety was like a radiance around her, whenever she engaged in those homely tasks of cooking or cleaning for the sight of which I came each morning to her barrel.

'Well, perhaps I have said enough to explain my desire to be all day with Merope and to absorb her wisdom. I had broken free of my captive state, and for the brief summer months the barrel by the temple of Cybele was all that I sought, and all that I needed, of home. But the change in me could hardly go unnoticed, and moves were already afoot to end my emancipation. My trips to Piraeus were the last straw. That a descendent of Solon should sway down the street balancing an amphora of oil on her head – nothing like this had been spoken of since the rumours about you and Uncle Plato. Although your connection, if I may so describe it, with our family had somewhat dwindled, I am sure you too heard of the scandal, honoured guest, from this or that mischievous source. And perhaps you felt some flicker of sympathy for the poor mad girl who had been driven to distraction by the weight of her inheritance.'

'I did hear something of the sort,' said Archeanassa, with a dim smile. 'But you know, I paid no attention.'

'So people always say,' the girl went on. 'But I won't say it of your case, since nothing delighted me more at Phryne's symposium than your indiscretions concerning Plato. And when that scurrilous poem started to circulate a year or two later, I had a job, I can tell you, to feign surprise and to deny that it could possibly have been written by my uncle.'

'What scurrilous poem?' cried Archeanassa in alarm.

'Surely you know it – how did it go? Yes, that's it:

Archeanassa is my girl, she of Colophon,
Upon whose very wrinkles sits desire.
You bastards, you who boarded her upon
Her maiden trip, I bet she stoked your fire![8]

'Wrinkles! Why, the toad! Do you mean that this poem was put about for all to read and recite, and that your uncle had a hand in it?'

'Did you not know? Well, I suppose that is normal. It is the victim of a scurrilous rumour who is the last to hear of it.'

'Just wait till I get back to Athens! Wrinkles indeed! And this from a man with three folds of blubber round his stomach and a crinkled bum like hippo hide!'

'Don't worry, honoured guest. The whole story did you credit, and, had you been less of a recluse by then, you would have been invited to the best of parties on the strength of it. But let me return to my own case, which is even more instructive. My father decided to put a stop to my wayward habits, and he did this in the normal way, by presenting me with a fiancé. As you can imagine, there had been a queue of hopefuls – brains, class, looks and wealth telling so strongly in my favour. But for the business of the amphora, my father could have hitched me up with the richest and brightest of Athens. However, since the scandal, most candidates had discovered more urgent claims on their affections, and Dad was left in the end with a single choice – a moronic general called Heraclides, who had distinguished himself in some minor skirmish during the Sacred War, and

---

8   The poem is also attributed to Plato by Diogenes Laertius, *Lives of the Philosophers*, III, 31. But its authorship is hotly disputed: see A.S.F. Gow and Denys Page, *Hellenistic Epigrams*, pp 88 and 144–45, and the note in R. Scruton, ed., *Xanthippic Dialogues*, pp 269–70.

whose sole topic of conversation was the brilliant tactics with which he had confounded the enemy and defended his native city from destruction.

'Since I had resolved in any case not to marry, the announcement that I now had a fiancé merely hastened my plans. I went straight to Merope and asked if she intended to resume her peripatetic life.

'"Why yes," she said, "just as soon as you choose."

'"Then it depends on me?"

'"On what else? There's no money to be made here; the competition's too hot. Besides, I have an urge to show you some of the wonders of the world. We could leave tomorrow."

'I confess I was not really prepared for this instant decision. Could I really live as Merope lived? What clothes should I take? What books? Where would we stay and on what terms? What would we do for food and drink, and how would we keep ourselves clean and presentable? I plied her with anxious questions, in the course of which I discovered many interesting things about my darling. For instance, I discovered that she did not wash.

'"You don't wash?" I cried in amazement. "Then why don't you smell like Diogenes?"

'She laughed at this, and treated me to a discourse on odours.

'"Have you ever smelt a horse?" she asked.

'"Naturally," I replied, horses being a favourite animal.

'"Then you will recall the sweet aroma of fermenting hay, the discreet and vinous scent that hangs about them?"

'"Indeed."

'"And whatever the weather, however much they strain and sweat, you will notice that their coats are clean, fresh and fragrant?"

'"You are right Merope."

'"And do horses wash?"

'"By no means."

'"But suppose someone were to wash a horse – for of course this is done, since human vanity embraces every perversion. At once the fragrance disappears, and is replaced by a stale and lifeless cleanliness, which must be renewed each day with water and brush, much to the annoyance of everyone concerned, including the horse."

'"But does Diogenes wash?" I protested.

'"That's just it," she replied. "Once or twice he washed, and so removed from his flesh the sweet oils that protect it. And then the habit of neglect set in, with results that you smell and see. Had he never washed, however, even Diogenes might be presentable – provided the desire to wash did not occur to him."

'I begged her to explain these curious remarks.

'"You will admit that human beings differ from animals?"

'"From *other* animals, certainly."

'"Exactly. And how would you define the difference?"

'I recalled a discourse of Xanthippe's on this topic.

'"There are many ways of defining it," I answered. "You might say, for instance, that we are rational animals, or laughing animals, or animals with intentions, or speaking animals, or animals which wonder whether they are animals. All these seem to capture that strange thing which distinguishes us, but which is so hard to put into words."

'"Nevertheless, you might try."

'"Well then," I replied. "I should say that we are distinguished by our consciousness of self. The horse thinks and feels and sees: this much is undeniable. But there is no division in his world between self and other, between I and you. Or we could say that, for him, there is *only* I, that nothing enters his consciousness *except* the self. And that is another way of saying that in his case there *is* no self."

'Merope praised me for this speech, since it exactly fitted her purpose. The self-conscious being, she said, labours under a great disadvantage. Her world is fractured by a chasm, which runs through all things, dividing self from other. And the more she thinks, the wider the chasm becomes. One thing in particular puzzles her, since it seems to lie on both sides of the divide simultaneously, and that thing is her body. To the sleepy child and the urgent lover, self and body are one. To the philosopher seated at her meditations, self and body drift apart, and the body becomes a thing, an instrument, part of the world of others, impassably separated from the self that studies it. This division between self and body is part of the pathology of consciousness, and it is the origin, she added, of the human tendency to smell.

'"Do I smell?" I asked in alarm.

'"No, my dear. You are a special case. And I shall tell you why. Everything you are is the result of the most patient labour – your own labour and the labour of your ancestors. Not a day goes by without your studying to improve yourself in mind and body, and the result, by the way, is a masterpiece. You are the very opposite of the savage, who is at one with his body precisely because he has never perceived it as his – as something owned by him, and therefore other than him. His body is absorbed into the self, and the divide between self and other runs around its circumference. You are at one with your body for quite another reason. Both body and soul in you are artefacts. You have reached that high point of culture in which otherness has spread itself evenly over everything, including the self. Washing for you is like dancing – a shaping not of the body only, but also of the soul. And that is why I shall permit you to wash when we travel together, just as I shall permit you to dance.

'"The dreadful smell of Diogenes arises when the body is divided from the self and set outside it, so that its life becomes alien, thing-like and diseased. However much Diogenes may care for his alienated body, washing and scrubbing, anointing with unguents and oils, let him relax his labour only for a day, and the smell returns – for it is the smell of self-doubt.

'"Now it has been a precept with me to live according to nature's laws. And this has been the more necessary in that my great love, the love who betrayed me and took away from me all that I had of *eros*, would continue to haunt me, were I to regard my body as an offering, a gift, a thing to be prepared for my lover's embraces, and therefore washed and dressed and anointed as though it were other than me. Since that dreadful time, therefore, I have tried to possess my body anew, so that it becomes clean with the natural and unselfconscious cleanliness of a cat or a horse. And so, my dear Perictione, you may set your mind at ease on this topic. There are two ways not to smell – my way, and your way. And we shall travel side by side confident that neither of us gives offence to the other's nostrils."

'In this curious manner did Merope endeavour to reassure me. One by one she confronted my anxieties, and showed that those things which I imagined to be obstacles were not obstacles at all, but useful assets in the life of a philosophical vagrant. Youth and beauty, for example, which exposed stupid women to the greatest abuse, were, in intelligent hands, weapons equal to a battalion of hoplites. The scandal too would turn to my advantage, killing off the zeal of Heraclides and removing the last vestige of desire on my father's part to see me at the family table. Even poverty would be an asset, since now I should have to dance for a living, and so put myself heart and soul into the only thing which could ever make me famous.

'Briefly then, I resolved to join Merope on her travels. However, there were two obstacles, the first being my mother, or, to be more accurate, my feelings for my mother. For I don't mind confessing, honoured guest, that in this particular at least I had not yet transcended human nature. It is true that Mamma had only a limited interest in other people – unless they bore weighty titles of nobility, in which case they entered her conversation strategically, in the guise of intimate friends with whom she was out of touch only temporarily and for reasons that they too regretted. But she had preserved a soft spot for her only daughter and would often look at me askance, as though guessing my trouble and winding herself up to break the seal of silence. For several days I debated whether to inform her of my plans. But at last I decided against it, and this for a simple reason. It would be easier for her to live with my absence, I concluded, than to discuss with me or anyone else the reason for it. The unexplained disappearance of her daughter would leave the tissue of lies and illusions in place, and indeed add a flavour of tragic dignity to the reticence with which our household business was conducted. To have it out with her would be to destroy one way of life, without offering instructions for another. And I was not so heartless as to leave my mother without the consolation of an unbroken routine.

'But still, it wasn't easy. As I sneaked through the hall, carrying my bag of clothes and an anthology of poems, I bumped into her. I tried to hide my baggage, while she looked at me with wavering and embarrassed eyes. I could see her searching for words which would somehow hold me to my duty, while not suggesting the possibility of an alternative. "Well dear," she said eventually, "you'll soon be married, so run along and have your fun." And immediately she turned to one of the servants with instructions for lunch. I rushed out into the street, suffocated and gasping for air. How is she, by the way?'

'Oh,' said Archeanassa, with an uncomfortable shrug, 'I couldn't really say. Your mother and I don't move in the same circles.'

'No, I suppose not. But you must hear something from Uncle Plato.'

Archeanassa felt a rush of blood to her cheeks.

'Well, your uncle and I don't see each other now; except for business, I mean.'

'I see; like this trip to Colophon.' Then, after a pause, 'And you heard nothing at the time? About my disappearance, I mean?'

'There was a certain amount of speculation. But then your family put out an official story.'

'Oh,' said the girl nonchalantly. 'And what was that?'

'It was said that you had been abducted by some god or other – I can't remember which, though he was quite distinguished. Apollo maybe. On account of your beauty. And when the god accomplished his desire, they said, you were so stricken with shame that he took pity on you and agreed to hide you from men's eyes. So he turned you into a goose.'

Chapter 4

'A goose?' cried the outraged Perictione.

'Yes. And then they debated it in the Council and a resolution was passed to set you among the stars. Indeed, a
spare constellation was on offer at the time, which did have
the shape of a goose if you looked at it sympathetically.
Maybe that was why they invented the story; I was told your
father was lobbying night and day, since it is not often that
an Athenian family gets promoted to the skies. But nothing
came of it.'

'Why was that?'

'People weren't interested. Those stories of the gods and
their goings on were losing credibility by the day.'

'Poor Mamma,' said Perictione with a sigh. And she sat
for a moment in silence, a soft gauzy expression on her face,
like a child waiting to be kissed. Then abruptly she shook
herself and returned to her story.

'I need not remind you, honoured guest, of the immense
competition among the philosophers of Athens, and the
near impossibility of making so much as an obol without re-
sorting to the kind of eye-catching and stomach-turning
tricks engaged in by Diogenes. I had spent Granny's legacy
on clothes and poppy-sap and treats for Xanthippe, and
Merope was destitute. And although she was happy nevertheless to set out on our journey to nowhere, I thought it prudent to cushion my descent into reality, lest the routine of
hardship lead to cracks in my style.

'Well, as luck would have it, a minor Persian satrap was
staying at our house, having come with letters of introduction from some Phrygian tyrant. He had heard about this
thing called philosophy and was keen to acquire a philosopher of his own. I had therefore asked him to meet me outside the house, together with a couple of slaves, so that I
could take him to the temple of Cybele.

'As we walked through the city I gave him a lecture on
the consolations of philosophy, adding that philosophers
had the habit of sleeping in barrels on the rubbish dumps
which were their favourite haunt. And I mentioned Diogenes as the most famous of them and the one most esteemed

by those who sought after wisdom. As it happened, I added, Diogenes was coming to the end of his tenure at the temple, and must soon be replaced – as was the Athenian custom – by a newer model. For although wisdom is changeless as truth itself, the Athenians are a fickle people and ever ungrateful to the philosophers who seek to improve them. Anyone who purchased the barrel of Diogenes could take it away, contents included, and so obtain for his private use wisdom which the Athenians would bitterly regret once it had been removed from them, just as they regretted the death of Socrates.

'A lid of cedar wood had been dragged across the entrance to the tub, shutting in both the philosopher and his smell. The Persian studied the enigmatic cylinder excitedly, asking whether this were really the sacred casket in which wisdom was contained, and imploring me to reveal how much he should pay for the favour of possessing it. "That's easy," I said, "for over there stands the barrel of the priestess who is charged with disposing of unwanted doctrines. She is a friend of mine, and surely will oblige us with the lowest acceptable price. Just stay here while I open negotiations."

'Merope was already preparing for our journey and greeted me with a calm embrace, as though to impart the strength that I would need in the days ahead. She asked why I had brought so many friends along, and I explained my purpose. Certainly, she responded, Diogenes would be better off in a private collection than on public display, and when I suggested that it could be *her* truth, indeed *our* truth, if only for the moment, that she was the priestess of Cybele, entitled to auction off the discarded truths of others, she had no strong objection. Briefly then, honoured guest, I allowed the Persian to bargain us down to fifty drachmas – enough for a couple of months on the road – and to command his slaves to hoist the tub on to their shoulders and set off in the direction of Piraeus, from where Diogenes could be shipped to Phrygia. And the Persian skipped along behind his purchase, clapping his soft hands above his head, his beard glistening in the sunrise as he praised his great distinction as the owner of a real philosopher. Only when the lid fell away to bounce before them down the hill, did the owner of Diogenes show any misgiving. But by then we were ready to depart.[9]

'And here, honoured guest, is the point of my story. There was something prophetic in this beginning to our pilgrimage. For, as I watched the barrel approach the brow of the hill, I was surprised to discover that Diogenes had manoeuvred himself into the hoop and was looking round at his surroundings, the Persian now staring in amazement at his new possession, and pinching his nostrils with the thumb and forefinger of one hand. Diogenes put up no resistance. He did not howl or shake or shriek as was his custom, but simply hung there in the aperture, his hands clinging in childlike uncertainty to the rim, his head moving resignedly from side to side to obtain a last vision of the city that he scorned. It was as though life had suddenly been resolved for him – as though his willing exile in the midst of things had been translated into a real but unwilling exile far away, and as though he accepted this as the punishment that he had obscurely and unconsciously designed for himself. A wave of pity rose in my heart; and there came before my mind an image of Diogenes in Persia, cleaned up and restored to human shape, walking in a perfumed garden and surrounded by tinkling luxuries, meticulous in his Greek composure, silent and solemn with the memory of Greece.

'Merope waved to Diogenes, and as he disappeared below the hill he responded with a shy forgiving smile. We set off at once on the dusty road to Thebes.

'So there, most honoured Archeanassa, is the story of my departure from Athens, and I am sorry it took so long to tell that the sun has now begun to set, and I must prepare myself for work. For many questions must surely have occurred to

---

9   Among the lost works of Menippus the Cynic is one entitled 'The Sale of Diogenes'; Lucian also, a follower of Menippus, has a dialogue in which the philosophers, Diogenes among them, are sold off one by one by the gods. Perhaps Perictione's story was the archetype of these.

you, and the laws of hospitality require that I should do my best to answer them.'

The girl sat still, observing her visitor from inscrutable eyes.

'Many wonders have you told, O most noble Perictione, and I am flattered that you should recount them to me. But I would gladly learn how you came to Colophon, and yet more gladly how you decided to stay here, where the soul is so ill at ease, and every novelty a danger.'

'You do well to ask, honoured guest, and I fancy that my story will be of use to you.'

Suddenly, and without warning, Perictione was on her feet, moving with a dancer's light step towards her visitor, whom she raised from the couch with an imperious gesture.

'If you are free tomorrow morning,' she went on, 'you could return, and we will discuss the question that seemed to trouble you, and which interests me as well.'

'You mean, the whereabouts of Antimachus's papers?'

The girl gave a mischievous toss of the head.

'Ah, that's another matter. But you know, it is just possible that my story is relevant to your purpose – I should say, my uncle's purpose in sending you here. But I had in mind the great question of the city, concerning which you promised to enlighten me.'

As she spoke the girl discreetly guided her guest from the room and through the inner courtyard, so that, without making any decision in the matter, Archeanassa found herself on the steps of the portico, listening to the proud farewells of Perictione and barely able to reply to them as the door was shut from behind.

And then a curious thing happened. Turning to descend the steps, her mind buzzing with unanswered questions, and her eyes dazzled by the sudden light of the setting sun as it strode from behind a tower beyond the garden, Archeanassa felt a sharp blow to her side, and then another to her forehead. She raised a hand to defend herself, and the blow fell again, this time on her arm. As she staggered back into the porch there came a peal of laughter from the garden.

Chapter 4

Taking refuge behind the urn, she made out a figure, half hidden by the trunk of the pomegranate tree, its arm outstretched, and ready to assail her again with the small hard fruit that had been gathered in a heap on the ground. A large head, crowned with tousled red hair, and studded with blue enamel eyes came out from behind the tree, and stared insolently at Archeanassa. It belonged to a boy of some fifteen years, who now let the crab-apple drop from his hand and began to waggle his ears with his fingers, sticking out his tongue and inflating his cheeks so as to burble rudely at his victim. Behind the boy the gate to the street stood open, and she glimpsed the leather-clad arm of a Persian guard, standing motionless by the wall.

'Is it safe now?' Archeanassa enquired. 'Will you let me pass through the garden?'

By way of reply the boy spun round, raised his tunic, and dropped his head so as to peer up at her from between his thighs, shaking his scrawny buttocks from side to side as he did so.

The dog which had intruded into Perictione's drawing room came yapping out of a back door, and now danced in circles around its master. The boy joined in the barking, and rose up and down on his heels, all the time staring at Archeanassa from between his thighs with wide insolent eyes. Archeanassa was about to sound the urn for help, when a large female servant came hurrying across the garden, pulled the tunic over the offending bottom, and jerked the boy upright with a flick of her arm. Without looking in Archeanassa's direction, she dragged the miscreant across the lawn, and bundled him through a low door, kicking the dog in after him. There was a crash, a howl and a loud stream of curses, before silence reigned in the garden, and Archeanassa crossed with subdued step towards the gate.

5

In which Archeanassa gives a theory of the city and its meaning

Through the wide streets went Archeanassa, the buildings dark and silent above her. Long shadows lay across the roadway, and the day's heat, caught between the walls as in a gulley, pressed down with a weight of exhausted breath. It was Colophon's dead hour, after the work-force had been carted away, when the drums were briefly silent. A few sheets of papyrus rustled in a darkened alleyway; a dismal dog crept from a doorway and growled; a late worker hurried past, his face blank and staring, the grey tunic flapping around his body like the broken wings of a bird. An indescribable dreariness lay over everything, and no sound broke the stillness save the mournful buzzing of flies, which hung in black squadrons on the viscous air as though stuck there.

Archeanassa hastened on, her soul full to the brim with tormenting questions: about Perictione, about Merope, about Plato and Antimachus, about Colophon and Athens and Greece and the world. She feared the secret that surrounded Perictione. There was something familiar about the boy in the garden – as though he were related to herself, had been discarded and put out of mind, and was now come back to haunt her.

There was something vindictive too in Perictione's madness. Perhaps she had been waiting for this visit, certain that Archeanassa would stumble at last through her doorway –

that dreamlike threshold between nowhere and nowhere else – to receive a punishment that had been lovingly prepared. Maybe Perictione resented Archeanassa's affair with Plato; maybe she deplored the stain on her family's honour, had come to Colophon to escape the shame of it, and was merely pretending to be free from those old conventions, while not being free at all, but on the contrary totally guided by their grim imperatives.

As she thought of this, Archeanassa began to doubt the existence of Merope. What better way for Perictione to disguise her real identity than through this fiction of a free-thinking philosopher, a godless prophet of modernity, whose wicked ideas justified every perversion and every crime? She recalled Perictione's eyes, with their ironical detachment, which seemed to summon up and dwell on her visitor's failings. And then those strange and fugitive glances, as though the girl in her madness had withdrawn from her very self, as though she were hiding somewhere deep inside, a frightened malicious child locked in the statue of a woman.

As these doubts coursed through her mind, compounding the mystery of Perictione's presence here, in Colophon, Archeanassa felt a certain alarm. And when, on reaching the grey shuttered hostel for 'official visitors,' she found the doors barred against her, she was struck by panic, and called out tearfully to the guard. The parchment face waved in the aperture beside the door like a dead plant and for a long moment she stared at it, listening to the dry inhuman rustle of its movements and smelling the sour odour of inside that wafted into the street. The door opened with a growl and she went quickly into the building.

Silent figures sat beneath dingy pictures of the King, their grey tunics draped over the arms of drab grey chairs, and their dismal faces looking sightlessly into the drab grey twilight of the lobby. What these figures did she could not guess; but at every hour of the day and night they sat there, as though to emphasize with their vacant faces the utter desolation of the place in which they found themselves, or to which they had been allotted by the Great King's inscrutable Plan. In the darkened corner stood a plain desk, behind which sat another drab grey figure, who handed over the key to Archeanassa's room in silence. Down the long corridor she walked, past room after room where nothing stirred. She met no other guests, and hers was the only key that ever went missing from the board; yet from time to time strange crashes and howls would come from a distant part of the building, as though people had been walled in there, and now shrieked at each other in the dark.

She lay awake, listening to the revellers as they cascaded through the streets, tearing doors from their hinges, barging in and out of the foyer of the hostel and at one point letting out a chorus of screams into the very corridor where she lay sweating in the dark. Again there came before her mind the image of Perictione – haughty, cool and full of secrets – and that of the boy in the garden, whose upside-down head had been fixed to a string in her skull, and swung back and forth there like a sputtering lantern. And then she lapsed into fitful sleep.

She awoke in a calmer frame of mind. What after all had she to fear from the girl? And why not listen again to the story of Merope – that strange figment which Perictione had invented to replace the stories of the gods? Besides, had she not promised to return, and would it not seem equally haughty, equally ungracious, in a nutshell equally *Persian* in her, to retreat from their dialogue? Someone pushed against the door, and a grey withered hand came wavering like a curious animal round the crack. It held a chipped bowl of clay, and when Archeanassa took the vessel she discovered it to contain an infusion of mint and elderflower. She muttered her thanks, but the door had already closed. Footsteps shuffled quickly away along the corridor.

As she drank she began to think about cities and their meaning. She did so the more eagerly in that the city she summoned was the city of Antimachus, with the beloved poet still standing in its streets and groves and temples. She would persuade Perictione of this at least: that in architecture there are rules and conventions which must be obeyed.

It had been an ordinary night in Colophon, and mutilated corpses lay here and there across her path. The dustmen were clearing away the mess, their faces expressionless as they lifted the bodies on to the official carts. Wagonloads of workers were being crammed through the doorways, and high up in the towers she saw them, passing by open windows as they spiralled away to their desks. On the ugly lots between the towers, where rubble and ordure were piled in confusion, a few silent stragglers moved on enigmatic business beneath great hoardings bearing portraits of the King. The King watched from maniac eyes, and the people moved jerkily, nervously, as though in response to his whispered instructions. Whatever happened in the city, in however remote and useless and abandoned a corner, happened by royal command. As she hurried past those all-seeing eyes, Archeanassa wondered again at Perictione, that she should choose to settle in this place of tombs.

Again she found the house unguarded, and again, having opened the gate with a gentle push and entered the garden, she turned to discover two soldiers standing in the street outside, their leather-clad elbows just visible beyond the wall. These soldiers too formed part of the mystery. It was as though the space they guarded did not belong in the real world, and in stepping from the streets of Colophon into the domain of Perictione, she entered a dream. And so it seemed, as Archeanassa looked around at the musky, myrrh-scented garden, with its borders of asters and pale cyclamen, its lichen-stained statues, its medlar spreading on the brown dry lawn, and its carefully tended bushes that seemed to move and rustle like gently cropping animals. The house was still and closed as though in sleep. No sound came from behind the walls, and all the shutters were fastened. A spell lay over the place, and even the stones of the portico seemed to breathe quietly as though enchanted.

Archeanassa was on the point of turning away,

believing that she had arrived too early, when the front door swung open, revealing Perictione herself, who stood pale and majestic on the threshold, urgently beckoning her visitor forward.

'My dear Archeanassa,' she said, ushering her guest into the darkened hallway, 'I have been waiting for you impatiently, and I confess that I was not a little concerned that you might think twice about returning.'

'Oh no, most noble Perictione, I gave you my word. And I too have looked forward to this meeting, and to hearing again of the wondrous Merope of Sardis.'

'Ah Merope,' she said with a sigh. 'I fear I did not do justice to my darling, that I left you feeling somewhat ambivalent towards her.'

'Not ambivalent at all,' said Archeanassa, in a sudden rush of honesty. 'To tell you the truth, I found her quite repugnant.'

'I esteem you the more, honoured guest, that you should confess it. Come now quickly to my den, and let us endeavour not to wake the household.'

The girl sprang quickly out of reach, and Archeanassa followed her through the shuttered darkness into the parlour, where a tiny blade of light escaped between the shutters and lay glittering on the floor. In the half-light the room had another aspect – not sombre or majestic or frozen, but somehow expectant, like the stage of a theatre before the play begins. And when Archeanassa stumbled against one of the props and sent it crashing, it was as though she had set the drama in motion, and now must wait passively for its climax. Perictione moved slowly in her wake, picked up the fallen tripod, and shoved aside with her foot the fragments of an antique figurine.

'Don't apologize,' she said quietly. 'I rather hated the thing.'

Only when they were installed on their couches, facing each other across the artificial twilight, did Perictione look up. Her face was pale, drawn and hollow around the eyes. Evidently she had not slept, and she constantly raised her hands to her cheeks, as though to quieten some inner turmoil. Archeanassa's heart was softened, and she begged the girl to reveal her trouble.

'My trouble,' said Perictione, 'is you. For a year now I have been alone here, the long year since my darling died. And I have built up my defences: look around and you will see them. To be a civilised Greek in this city of barbarians, to live with irony among the incurably humourless, to be impassably remote from the modern world while absolutely immersed in it – these were my ambitions, and it is by clinging to them that I remained close to Merope. But my outward strength concealed an inner weakness. I should tell you, Archeanassa, that I have been very much afraid. Oh, not of physical things. I have made a lot of money here in Colophon – enough to bribe my way out of any trouble. And besides, the captain of the royal guard is, let us say, an admirer, which means that I am more protected here than ever I was in Athens. I expect you noticed the sentries which the poor dear has so thoughtfully provided.'

'I have indeed,' said Archeanassa. 'But the strange thing is that I see them only when I have entered your garden. Outside, in the street, they are invisible.'

'It takes some time,' the girl said with a dismissive wave, 'before the eyes become accustomed to Colophon. In any case, the guards cannot abolish the fear of which I am speaking. An inner voice calls constantly my name, softly and reproachfully, like the voice of a disappointed parent. Who are you? it asks, and what do you want? What justifies your being, and what good have you brought into the world? Of course, in my daily life I strive to ignore such questions. I live on the pinnacle of pleasure, and in this city of excitements I am celebrated, guarded, protected and invited like a queen. I enjoy myself in the night-club, where the select crowds roar out their applause at my dances, and when gloom is upon me I eat the sacred mushroom or suck the sacred poppy-sap and am transported to oblivion. But in the midst of all delights there is an emptiness – I will not conceal it – and often in the night I weep bitter tears, tears of loneliness and frustration, of longing for I don't know what, of despair at the futility of my own existence. And it is then that I am afraid, honoured Archeanassa, and cry out in my heart not for Merope but for my mother, for Athens, for the old gods that Merope taught me to despise.

'That is why I am troubled now. Until you came, I regarded this fear as nothing more than a weakness, to be ignored like some chronic ailment for which science knows no cure. And life, by the way, is such an ailment. Then you arrived, and put me in mind of what I had lost in being here: not Athens only, but all the ease and openness of our old democracy, that way we had of conversing freely, however much our talk might challenge the conventions or startle those in power. And you brought an air of safety – not the safety I have here, which is that of a wild thing held in a cage and bounding always against the bars with the same cries and gestures, but the safety of those Athenian manners, which permitted Merope to live happily in a barrel, and Uncle Plato to have a fling with you. And even so, as I survey these things which you bring to mind, I know that they are not the real cause of my emotion. What is it in you, honoured guest, that awakens me to myself, and tells me that the heart of my life is missing? It is the presence in everything you say and do of the other who is more important than yourself, be it Uncle Plato or that guy from hereabouts, what's his name? Antimachus. Yes, Antimachus! Whatever you do, you do for love. Whereas I . . . Enough! I am being most foolish!'

Perictione jumped to her feet with a sudden laugh and went across to the window, whose shutters she threw wide open. She wore the diaphanous tunic of a dancer, and the morning light, pouring abundantly through it, showed the contours of her body. She stood in the window for a moment, as though to give Archeanassa the chance to feast her eyes. Yes, thought the visitor, it really must be difficult for such a creature to love anything but herself. And that, she concluded, was the explanation of Merope, whose philosophy was a mirror for this vain princess, a mirror in which she perceived only her own studied perfections.

'Truly,' Archeanassa said, 'your story is as sad as mine.'

Perictione turned from the window with an enigmatic smile.

'You think so?' she said. 'Well, perhaps you are right. But another thing occurs to me, which is this. The difference between us is so profound that neither you nor I could remove it. That in me which prompts my fear, which causes me to awaken in the night with the cold sweat drenching my body and the hot tears pouring from my eyes, is not this or that emotion, this or that state of mind or body, but I myself, Perictione, daughter of Potone. To change in this respect I must cease to be, which is as much as to say that I cannot change. And there is something futile and irritating in those philosophies which tell us that our salvation consists in loving others, and not in the more arduous discipline of living with others whether we love them or not. But come, most honoured guest, for I have a great urge to tell you how my story concludes, and what brought me here to Colophon. And before I can do so, you must fulfil your promise and tell me what a city should be, and why you judge this place so harshly.'

So saying, she clapped her hands for the servant, and ordered a most sumptuous breakfast of pickled cuttle-fish, cream cheese, ground sesame, radishes and oil. Archeanassa marvelled at the food, having seen nothing in the shops save uniform slabs of fat, cheese and dried figs, all of them stamped with the royal insignia and changing hands without eagerness like some unwanted obligation. But Perictione, who was cheerful now and eating heartily, explained that in Persia there are two kinds of shop, just as there are two kinds of citizen and two kinds of house, and two kinds of culture and two kinds of everything. The shops which cater for the privileged caste, of which she was inevitably a member, were hidden from the general public and could be entered only with a special pass, issued by the royal office of privileges. And those who obtained this pass were themselves hidden from public view, and lived as she did, in houses that belonged elsewhere and elsewhen. Even their amusements were hidden from the general public, and she hastened to settle any doubts that Archeanassa might have entertained, by telling her that the nightclub where she worked was stowed high up in one of the towers, was frequented only by the highest officials of the King's ruling party, and was devoted exclusively to the classical dances of which the brutish multitude knew nothing.

'But now,' she went on, 'before you denounce this divided society and all its works, you are to expound the idea for which Greece will always be remembered, long after the gods of Greece have disappeared. And I am the more interested in the topic, honoured Archeanassa, in that my life with Merope, to which I shall shortly return, was a life outside the *polis*, and never more outside than in those days when, visiting some famous city, we took up residence and studied its beauties, its manners and its way of life.'

'Well then,' said Archeanassa nervously. 'Let me say, first of all, that I am not a philosopher, and have no gift to see the abstract truth of things. Nevertheless, I have listened to your uncle's tutorials from behind the curtain, and gained much, as surely you have done, from the conversation of Xanthippe. I hope, therefore, that my remarks will have a philosophical colouring.'

'And what exactly is that?' asked Perictione curiously.

'Well, I don't know *exactly*. But I should say that remarks become philosophical when they concern the essence of things – not how things are at a particular time and place, but how they must be, according to their inner nature.'

'And do cities have essences?'

'Not cities, if you mean cities taken one by one. But the city as such – yes, it does, I think, have an essence.'

'In which case,' the girl went on argumentatively, 'all cities partake of this essence, Colophon as much as Athens.'

'By no means, most noble Perictione. For as I see it, the essence of a kind is present only in the perfect instances. And I shall prove the point by a comparison. Lions, you admit, belong to a single kind?'

'Yes, I will admit that.'

'And there are essential features of this kind, and also inessential features – for example, lions are essentially four-legged mammals, but only accidentally the colour of stale mustard?'

'I will admit that too.'

'Yet, when the young lion is first conceived and begins to grow in the womb, does it have four legs?'

'By no means, honoured guest.'

'And when it is old and sick, and one by one its gangrenous legs fall off, yet is it still a lion?'

'Indeed.'

'And might there not be an entirely stunted, abnormal, monstrous lion – a lion with five legs and no eyes, for instance, which is yet from the same stock as normal instances?'

'Yes, but I doubt that it would survive.'

'Suppose, however, that such a lion is kept alive. Surely it is a genuine lion, but one that partakes only imperfectly of the leonine essence.'

'I grant the point.'

'Well, something similar is true, to my way of thinking, of this Colophon of yours. It is a city – I acknowledge that. But it is abnormal, diseased, far indeed from the perfect instances in which the essence of the city is revealed.'

'Name some perfect instances.'

'There are none. Not now. But let me describe ancient Colophon, and you will know what I mean.'

'I am all ears, Archeanassa.'

'On this hill, rising from a valley of orchards and pastures, with simple cottages of limestone, and neatly laid walls and terraces of the same material, the founders of Colophon built a temple to Artemis, and placed themselves under the goddess's protection, dedicating festivals to her honour, and teaching the Artemisian dances to their children.[1] The temple was of stone, with Ionic columns, for such was the style in Lydia. It was not large, but so perfect were its proportions that the Colophonians forbade all building next to it, and laid out a garden, with trees of limewood and hornbeam, to serve as a temple precinct. And it was from the dialogue between the temple and its garden that the city grew. Some brought precious gifts of furniture and statuary to the temple; others embellished the garden with shrubs and lawns and fountains. And each addition to the temple found some answering ornament outside, until the precinct became as much a work of architecture as if it had been built of stone, instead of grass and wood and growing things.

'Now there is much to be learned from gardens, noble Perictione, and especially from gardens of the kind I am describing. In such places the plants, buildings and furniture have no special use. There is a purpose to the farmer's fields and the merchant's storehouse, but not to the lawns and

---

1   Of course, Archeanassa is making this up. According to the early Colophonian poet Mimnermus (who flourished around 620 BC), the city was founded by settlers who came from Pylos in the Peloponnesus, shortly before the time when Mimnermus wrote. In early days Colophon was renowned for its navy which, operating out of nearby Notium, captured Smyrna and brought it from the Aeolian into the Ionian League. The Colophonian cavalry, which fought with fierce dogs, subdued the broad plain between the city and the sea. Famous children of Colophon include not only the fourth-century poets Antimachus and Anaxandrides, but also the fourth-century painter Apelles, and the pre-Socratic philosopher Xenophanes (born 570 BC), who criticised the decadence and luxury of his native city. Like all such criticisms, this of Xenophanes came too late. Colophon was subdued first by the Lydians and then by the Persians. It was freed, along with the other Ionian cities, in 479 BC, only to succumb again in 386 BC under the terms of the King's Peace. The final destruction of Persian rule by Alexander the Great in 334 BC liberated the city to a condition of indolent and insignificant decline. Nothing of Colophon is visible today.

statues in a garden. Each object is there for its own sake, not a means but an end. And we too, when we visit the precinct, leave our purposes behind. We wander in the cool shade, refresh our spirits with the sight of clear water sparkling over amber stones, and listen to the birds as they sing above us. And all for no other purpose than our delight in these things. Moreover, the garden is a social place. People cross each other's path, fall into conversation, perhaps play games together or sit side by side at peace. And these ways of being in a garden are of peculiar significance, Perictione; for they too are free from purpose. People in a garden are *beyond* purpose, in a side-by-sideness which is also an alertness to the world.'

'This reminds me,' said Perictione, 'of a conversation I once had with Xanthippe.'

'About gardens?'

'About dancing.'

'I would be grateful to hear, most noble Perictione, what Xanthippe had to say about dancing.'

'Really? Later then. Now you must fulfil your promise.'

Suddenly there arose in her mind the form of Antimachus, dressed in the patched old tunic that he sported on his 'literary' days. He was scratching behind one ear – and she could not help noticing how large and red and fleshy were his ears, like soft, glowing handles. She wanted to grip them and pull them, and shake that lovely head – though why it was lovely, with its over-wide brow, its uncertain eyes which might have been grey or green (she never knew which), its cheekbones so high and straight and the mouth that fell awkwardly open, she did not know – to shake it until the words (and he was never short of words) fell at her feet and she could pick them over and reassemble them, knowing that love was their cause. Archeanassa smiled at the thought, and all at once her spirits were restored to her, and she embarked on the task of inventing ancient Colophon. How often she had walked in its gardens – always thinking of Antimachus, though never, lest his wife should hear of it, in his company.

'Let me make another observation then about gardens,' she said. 'When walking in a garden we feel ourselves surrounded, do we not?'

'Yes. By eyes.'

'Maybe I should be more philosophical. The garden is a surrounding space, not an open space. And that which grows and stands in it, grows and stands *around* us. Trees, for instance. A tree in a garden is not like a tree in a forest or a field. It is not simply there, growing from some scattered seed, accidental. It stands and watches, as I stand and watch. And although it does not move, the tree converses, in a sense, with those who walk beneath it and who look up through its branches to the sky. In these circumstances we notice something very important. Trees standing in a garden join both earth and sky and also sunder them. At the base of the tree the trunk spreads out to grip the ground, while the upper branches brush the sky and fall away from it, leaving this most diaphanous of elements undamaged by their touch. I say we notice these things, but of course we do not consciously remark on them: they enter our feelings as we rest in the garden, and make us aware of standing between earth and sky. Between-ness is what we see all around us in the garden, in the trees and statues as much as the people who move among them. The kingdom of between is a kingdom of light and shade, of things which stand in repose, of objects gathered on the earth and beneath the sky, dwelling on the one and submitting to the other. In short it is a realm of consecrated space, in which people rest and are fulfilled because the god protects them.'

'And if no god exists?'

'Let us postpone that question, noble Perictione, since it was never raised in ancient Colophon.[2] There, in our municipal garden, we were at peace with each other and the world. And it is from peace that the city was built. Here is a curious fact. The column of a temple has often been compared to the trunk of a tree, has it not?'

2　Actually it was raised by Xenophanes, who concluded that yes, gods do exist, but there is only one of them.

Chapter 5

'Some say it *derives* from the tree-trunk. In fact there is a treatise in the library devoted to proving the point.'

'I would not go so far. Indeed, the comparison is in one sense highly misleading. The tree trunk is far higher than the column; it is covered in blemishes and irregularities, spreads into branches of every shape and size, culminates in no capital and rises from the ground directly and without a base. In short, it is unlike the column in every respect, save for the fact that it stands to attention – and even then, it does so only in gardens and parks. Why then do people dwell so much on this comparison? I will make a suggestion, most noble Perictione, and it is this. In the kingdom of between nothing matters more than the play of light and shade. The spangled sunbeams pierce the canopy of leaves, one thing casts its shade over another, and to each object that stands is given a shadow lying beside it. Shadow is the language of standing things, the foundation of their dialogue. And the trunk of the tree is the place of shadows, through which it reaches to the light. I wonder, noble hostess, whether you have ever observed the peculiar texture of bark – the bark of a hawthorn, say?'

'Yes,' said the girl with a burst of competitive zeal. 'It was a favourite theme of Merope's. And I should remind you that there is no such thing as the bark of a hawthorn: there is the bark of a young hawthorn, lightly lined and with a greyish mottled surface, and the bark of an old hawthorn, with streaks of reddish brown, folded into itself, and breaking away to reveal long stretches of polished wood. And in between these two there are so many varieties that to describe *the* bark of the hawthorn, honoured guest, would be the work of a morning. But such things are easier to draw than to speak about.'

Archeanassa, somewhat put off her stride by this attack, was silent for a second, before finding again the path to ancient Colophon.

'Well, that's as may be, noble hostess. But it is of columns that I wish to speak. Like the tree trunk, the column stands before us. And like the trunk, it is a place of light and shade.

Archeanassa gives a theory of the city and its meaning

It begins from a base, around which concave mouldings form a belt of darkness. It rises with a single gesture to the capital, where it flowers into carved volutes, and all kinds of delicate bands and ribs and flutings which I lack the language to describe but which are in any case more familiar to the eye than any words can make them. Sometimes, to enhance the effect, the architect will add flutes to the shaft, so that the column is transformed into long blades of golden light, laid on the fluffy shadow. And if you were to compare this fluting to the bark of a tree, which is the great gatherer and enfolder of shadows and the means whereby the tree steals and guards the light surrounding it, you would again be in error. For the bark of a tree is an outgrowth, its edges are relinquishings, and its shadows lie as do the shadows on a hillside, in valleys and crevasses among slopes that swell and rise. The fluting of a column, however, is an incision, something carved by exploring hands, a hollowing out and a sculpting of stone. Its edges are honed; they probe and question the air, and the light is not stolen by the channel but lives in it, like a smile in a face. And if I were to say what a column is *essentially*, what it is when judged in terms of its real meaning to the one who stands in its vicinity, I should not say that it is stone, or marble or wood. I should say that it is crystallised light. And by capturing light in this way we Greeks educated ourselves in the use of it. The temple column became the model for all other building, and rightly so, since by following this model we merely extend and furnish the kingdom of between.

'So that, most noble Perictione, was the beginning of Colophon. Soon there arose about the garden houses of stone, which followed in their simple way the principles of temple architecture. Each stood on its base like a column, and each bore a carved entablature beneath the roof, with string courses and mouldings dividing the wall, so that the junctures of a column were implied in it. And indeed, if you follow my definition of the column, as a kind of crystallized light, the column was as much present in those little houses as it was in the temple peristyle. Hence they had the posture and the dignity of standing things, and out of their dialogue came a kind of repose.

'Those old houses had an interesting feature which your modern towers lack. They faced in a certain direction, and this fact was emphasized by the design. You notice, I am sure, that the towers of modern Colophon have no orientation, no privileged approach, no gestures or expressions which conduct you into their vicinity. They face nothing, welcome nothing, smile and nod to no-one. Hence we cannot stand comfortably in their presence.

'Nor is that all, Perictione. The modern tower, which ignorant people might compare to the temple column, is in reality the very opposite. For the modern tower lacks everything that gives meaning to the column. It has neither base nor capital; it avoids mouldings, string-courses and ornaments as though they were crimes, and its surface is devoid of significant shadow and therefore devoid of light – for light needs shade if it is to be seen. The tower escapes upwards as though fleeing the ground; but it concludes in nothing – neither entablature nor pitched roof cushion the sky, which it wounds with blunt aggressive punches. The tower is like Diogenes, shaking a fist at the gods in which it disbelieves.

'And for those very reasons, although the tower is tall, vertical, and slim, it does not really stand before us. For it has no posture and no repose. Its vertical extent expresses no vertical order. On the contrary, its order is horizontal. The tower is composed as a ground-plan, which is then projected upwards through slab upon slab and floor upon floor, until the required number of desks or beds or prison cells can be accommodated. To make the design easy to execute, the ground-plan is regular – square or oblong. And this means that the tower must be constructed in a cleared site, and rises up surrounded by empty lots and destroyed streets.

'And perhaps this is what I most dislike, noble Perictione, in this Colophon of yours – that it has no streets. Oh, I grant you, there are thoroughfares and boulevards, carved through the city like swathes through a field of corn. But these thoroughfares are not lined by houses standing side by side and leaning against each other. They are not overseen by dwellings, and their borders are not thresholds between public and private space. Nothing stands along them in a posture of repose, and even the air above them is lashed and torn by wires.

'To my way of thinking a true street is like a garden – not a means but an end. It is a place where you linger and take stock; where you meet and converse; where you stand beside objects which stand beside you. The new thoroughfare is not an end but a means: it has only one purpose, which is to conduct the worker as quickly as possible to the tower where he slaves. It has no part in the kingdom of between, and the buildings that occur along its edges are merely dumped there, offending both earth and sky by their inability to connect to either.

'No sooner did houses arise in ancient Colophon, than streets arose along with them. For those old houses stood side by side, facing in the same direction. And people stood at the gates conversing. Soon, in front of each row of houses, a public space came into being, a space that was every bit as consecrated as the garden beside the temple. The citizens, in order to express their pride in the city, and to mark out the land not as mine or yours or his, but as ours, began to provide this public space with furnishings. They paved it with cobbles, lined it on each side with flagstones of polished slate, and erected little shrines of porphyry or marble, in order that the gods should feel at home there, which was the home of everyone. These streets stitched the town together, and provided arteries through which its life could flow. And so pleased were the Colophonians with their appearance, that they discussed in the assembly how best to conserve them, and how to ensure that this public space should remain always ours, and never his or hers. After much deliberation they passed a law, which decreed that in future all houses and shops built in Colophon must face on to a street, and that no building should be higher than those first houses by the garden of Artemis, save the temples of the gods, the assembly rooms and the public library, which was to be the symbol of their civic pride and through which they declared that what mattered most to them after the gods was the idea of Greece. And they decreed that whatever was built in Colophon, be it house or shop or temple, must be built in stone, and in a style set out in the Colophonian pattern-book.'

'The what?' asked Perictione.

'During this time of building several learned men of Colophon had travelled in Lydia and beyond, observing the temples, tombs and palaces, and acquiring a knowledge of the forms of architecture. And they noticed that, when an architect, working in stone, chooses as his unit of construction some particular style of column, then, by a kind of divine logic of which he himself is only half aware, he finds himself compelled to choose ornaments and details which match it and complement its life. There is, if you like, a grammar of ornament, which compels us, if we would build intelligibly, to combine the parts of a building in accordance with its rules. And this does not apply only to sacred architecture, or to the column and its entablature. It applies also to the house and the shop, whose doors and windows and cornices speak in muted accents of the same divine idea, and must be ordered accordingly. So, on their return to Colophon, these learned men composed a book, in which all the acceptable styles were set out, and their details made transparent. If a builder were to adopt a certain style of door, then the book told him that he must accompany it with the corresponding style of window and cornice. And the merchants in stone and wood assembled these parts in readiness, so that anyone who built in Colophon could, with the aid of the pattern-book, and without the slightest recourse to his own imaginative powers, construct a house that would be harmonious and pleasing to the passerby.'

'How boring,' said Perictione. 'Was there no place in Colophon for innovation? And is not architecture an art like any other, destined to progress and enrich itself as new styles are invented and old styles decay?'

'Those questions go to the heart of the matter, most noble Perictione. And let me say first that innovation is of two kinds: that which respects tradition, and that which defies it. And the liberty to defy tradition ought to be granted only to the genius, the man of vision who can understand what follows from his iconoclastic gesture. Now is the ordinary builder such a genius?'

'I suppose not,' returned the girl.

'Would it not be better, therefore, if his innovations were constrained by tradition?'

'What do you mean by tradition?'

'I don't exactly know. It's one of those ideas which are necessary but more or less impossible to define, so deep do they lie. But I suppose I would describe tradition as a form of knowledge – knowledge that is accumulated over time, inherited and enhanced, and which cannot be devised by a single person because one lifetime and one consciousness are not enough.'

'My uncle would be careful, in such cases, to distinguish true knowledge from mere opinion.'

'I am not as careful as your uncle, noble Perictione, which is why I am happier than he.'

'Fair enough. Just don't expect me to agree with you.'

'The pattern-book did not forbid innovation, but controlled it, on the assumption that the path-breaking gestures in architecture had already occurred, and that the city required a work of consolidation. But let me now turn to your second question, to which I reply immediately that, no, architecture is not an art like any other, and, no, it cannot progress as music or poetry progress, so as to conform solely to the needs of genius. Architecture is a public enterprise: the architect does not build for the private client, but for the city. All of us are compelled to live with the result, which must therefore be offensive to no-one. Originality should come second to good manners. The case is no different from clothing, which ought to be original only if it first conforms. The pattern-book resulted from a long process of trial and error, whereby the appearance of the city and the feelings of the citizen were gradually brought into harmony and an easy conversational relation established between buildings and their passersby.'

Archeanassa, surprised that the thoughts came so easily, attributed them not to herself but to Antimachus, whose dear old head shook up and down inside her, spilling out its gift of words. Not that they had ever discussed the city together – for they had met only on those love-logged afternoons, in a dream world bound by the walls of a rented cottage. But strangely the ancient Colophon that she invented was like an image cast by the flame of her love, a community grown from tenderness and dwelling and the peaceful trading not of goods only, but of words and laughter and kisses. She smiled at her hostess, a broad confident smile, as she took up the argument once more.

'And here I must again be more philosophical, most noble Perictione, for I see that I have not identified the real difference between ancient and modern Colophon, or the real way in which we shape and are shaped by our buildings. These things cannot be understood, it seems to me, in secular terms. Our architecture derives from the temple, for the reason that the city derives from its protecting god. The stone of the temple is the earthly translation of the god's immortality, which is in turn the symbol of a community and its will to live. The temple, like the liturgy, is forever, and the community contains not the living only, but also the dead and the unborn. And the dead are protected by the temple, which immortalizes them in stone. This is what you understand instinctively, when you see religious architecture. And it is the sentiment from which cities grow – the tribe's will to permanence.

'There is, it seems to me, a certain order and logic in the elements of architecture. The temple, surrounded by its peristyle, is permeable to the city, yet sacred and removed from it. This is something that we see: we do not think it explicitly, any more than we think a smile explicitly in order to see it as a smile. And from the permeable temple came the colonnade, and thence the column, as the unit of meaning and the principle of our architectural grammar. In ancient Colophon the buildings conformed to this grammar, but with such variety and humour as befits the members of a peaceful crowd. And in each of them, sensed but not seen, was a column, standing immovably as the spirit stands immovably and invisibly in us. The column was permanent in the midst of change, and endorsed our sense of belonging. In our streets and temples and gardens, therefore, we Colophonians perceived a visible licence to dwell, an affirmation of our right of occupation, and a reminder that we belonged to a community which included the living, the dead and the unborn. The civility of our buildings was a matter of manners and decency – for these are the virtues of the citizen, of the one who has settled in the land and renounced the habits of the nomad.

'And then the Persians came, driving new hordes of nomads before them, and the habit of dwelling was at once destroyed. A new architecture arose, and with it, as I have witnessed, a new human type, the one as dependent on the other as hills depend on valleys and valleys on hills. These bulks of lightless gypsum, these unarticulated verticals and blank screens of wall, these flattened deserts which once were streets, with the empty lots still grieving for their vanished houses – all speak of a flight from the city into some distant barricaded place, where neighbourliness expires and man lives for himself alone. Vast and overbearing though the buildings of new Colophon may be, they have no air of permanence. The town is like a frozen junkyard, and even if it remains like this forever, it will look forever temporary. The raw functionality of the buildings hurts both the eye and the soul, for it speaks not of *us* and our right of dwelling, but of *them*. It is *they* who built these things, for inscrutable purposes that lie beyond our sympathies. That is why these buildings are perceived as a desecration: nothing of the sacred remains in them. And the people who move in and around them are really in flight – in flight from themselves and their destiny, remaining only when coerced, and with purposes that are never their own.

'This, it seems to me, is what explains the peculiar horribleness of your modern architecture – which is not architecture at all, but a kind of assemblage of childish forms. The towers do not dwell in that "kingdom of between" as did the ancient buildings, which stood in the street like trees in a garden, parcelling out spaces with light and shade. And you will notice, noble Perictione, that shadows flee these new constructions, whose walls are stripped of mouldings, friezes, strings and ribs, so as to glare in the sunlight like the staring eyes of a corpse. And so it *must* be. For what remains of the border between light and dark, when no god inhabits it?

'And although I could say much more, about the grammar of our ancient architecture, and the relation between its liturgical and vernacular forms, I think I must rest my case, since I have reached bedrock. Colophon is no longer a city, but a new form of human life – life alienated from itself, and endured in collective solitude. And if you deny this, most noble Perictione, I shall ask you only to look around you at this room, this museum, into which you have retired, and ask yourself whether it really belongs to the man-made desert beyond your garden wall, and whether either it or you are really dwelling here in Colophon?'

Archeanassa would not have spoken so boldly, had she not noticed a gradual change in Perictione's manner, from a mute scepticism to lively nods of agreement. And although she mistrusted these, as she mistrusted all the girl's expressions, Archeanassa could not help responding to their theatrical appeal. Furthermore, she was persuaded by her own reasoning, which flowed with unwonted ease, as she went side by side with Antimachus on a tour of ancient Colophon.

'You have all but convinced me, honoured Archeanassa. But there is just one problem remaining.'

'What is that?'

'May I continue the story of Merope, and tell you how

we came to Colophon – not ancient Colophon, but the new town that you despise? For I can think of no better way to explain my meaning.'

'Of course you may, noble Perictione. However, you did say that you would relate Xanthippe's thoughts on dancing.'

'Later, later. Let's have lunch.'

'But we've only just had breakfast.'

'Thinking makes me hungry,' said the girl, who was on her feet and out of the room as though borne by the wind. During her absence Archeanassa rose and went to the window. The sun was high in the sky, and a dazzling light blazed on the tower beyond the garden. A man stood in an upper window, held motionless by the heat and dust and tedium of Colophon, in that moment of uncanny torpor which precedes calamities and which in retrospect seems like a warning sent from the gods. She tried to envisage the man's life, brought each morning to the office in a wagon-load of look-alikes, from a cell where he hid from his kind. Did love exist in that distant suburb? Or was everything there so atomised that people were housed together as strangers? Perhaps the new human type conducted itself as Perictione had wished, without vows, without marriage or love, each person joined even to his nearest partner by a contract which could be rescinded at a moment's notice. Yes, she thought, very probably it was like that, and as she sighed over the sadness of this modern world, a strange thing occurred. The man's face seemed to become larger and nearer, until she could clearly see the hollow eyes, set in blackened patches of gangrenous, vein-rippled skin, the white tuberous flesh of the cheeks, the limp, broken-down mouth, which munched the air slowly and lugubriously as though reciting some quiet dirge. And this weird face, carried on the stream of things, became huge and ponderous and accusing in her thoughts, as though it was lost beyond all hope of rescue and she was obscurely to blame. She wanted to call out to it, to send some message of hope and love and cheerfulness, a lifeline which would bring this drifting thing to shore. But the place where she stood, the place of love and comfort and community, was an imagined place, and she lived alone there with her ghosts. Even to attract the man's attention would be an act of senseless cruelty, a rousing of hope where no hope could be. Besides, he was lost in his vacancy, the enigmatic feelings running across his features like shadows over a barren landscape. His lips continued to move, with the secret intimate muttering of someone who thinks himself unobserved. And suddenly it seemed utterly wrong even to look at his defeated face, so that she abruptly turned from the window.

There, sitting on the couch, in the place which a moment before she had occupied, was the boy. He stared at her from large blue eyes, and in his cupped hands he held a toad, which was trying to free its suffocated head from the thumbs which squeezed it. Archeanassa uttered a cry, and the boy shook his large head in silent laughter, rocking back and forth on the couch, and lifting his sandalled feet high in the air. And then, without a word, he rose from the couch and came towards her, holding the toad near her face and waving it from side to side as though he would release it into her hair.

'Go away!' she screamed. 'Horrid thing!'

With a sudden, soundless movement, the boy dropped the creature into a large Attic vase that stood beside the window. He strode away with long quiet strides towards the door, spun round beneath the lintel, gave another burst of silent laughter, and sped from the room. And in that moment she recognized him.

When Perictione returned it was to find Archeanassa seated, pale and shaking, on a stool beneath the window.

'Is something the matter?' she asked, with a searching look.

'I've had a shock,' said Archeanassa, and her voice trembled.

'You sound as though you've seen a ghost.'

'I have.'

Perictione looked around her with a vexed expression.

'I don't doubt it was that boy, up to his tricks again.'

Archeanassa gives a theory of the city and its meaning

'Who is he?'

'Do you really want to know?'

'Indeed I do, noble Perictione, although I also dread to know it.'

'Then I shall proceed with my story, as I promised, since it is his story too. Hullo, here's Amphitryon.' She had been looking reprovingly at the vase beside the window, and now reached into it, fetched out the toad, and addressed the creature with scolding words. 'Haven't I told you to stay in the garden? Haven't I said time and again that you are not to intrude on visitors? Sometimes I think I waste my time with you, that I would be better off sacrificing you to some frail old buffer of a god. Well, since you smile so nicely, I shall grant you one more reprieve. Off you go.'

She set the toad on the window ledge, and laughed as it hopped down into the garden.

6

In which Perictione continues the story of Merope, while endeavouring to refute Archeanassa's theory of the city

Lunch was brought by the toothless old servant, who staggered under the weight of a silver tray, setting it down on a folding table between Perictione and her guest. Archeanassa was too troubled to eat with any appetite, and watched in silence as Perictione assembled the dishes around her bowl. The girl addressed the food with eager interest, tasting each dish with one finger, and making delighted sucking noises with half-closed eyes. But Archeanassa knew that she was being closely watched by those eyes, and therefore looked down at her bowl and toyed with a pickled lupin. With a loud 'yum yum!' Perictione helped herself to the saddle of hare and began to eat in silence.

The mid-day heat piled like crushed fruit through the window, covering Archeanassa with a sticky film of sweat. The food lay uneaten in her bowl, and her thoughts heaved and reeled as though on the hazy borderline of sleep. The image of the boy's face hung again inside her, swinging back and forth, and glowing with an eerie moon-like lustre. With an effort of will she dismissed it from her consciousness and focussed on some scraps of food.

Only when her bowl was empty did Perictione attend again to her guest, first wiping her pale lips on a damask napkin, then pouring straw-coloured wine from the cooler, sniffing it, and leaning back in her chair with one arm dangling to the floor at her side. She insisted on libations, offering one to Merope, another to Xanthippe, and a third to 'the geriatric ward on Mount Olympus,' in which blasphemous invocation Archeanassa refused to join, offering instead her own private prayers to Artemis and all-seeing Zeus.

'And now,' Perictione began, after she had drunk deeply from her bowl and set it down on the table between them, 'I shall speak again of Merope, and of our adventures together, so that you will know what brought us here to Colophon.

'For three years after leaving Athens we wandered in Attica, in the Peloponnesus and Thessaly, and in Thrace and Boeotia. Philip of Macedon was making trouble everywhere and Demosthenes was trying to persuade the decadent Athenians to resist him. At times we would be overtaken on the road by cohorts of tramping mercenaries, sent to besiege or relieve some strategic settlement, and prickling all over with the dust of war. Sometimes we would visit a town only to discover that it had been overrun and its inhabitants slaughtered. And once, having pitched our tent for the night in an Arcadian valley, we awoke to find Thebans charging from the north of us against Spartans chanting and stomping to the south. Only the timely appearance out of the fray of a riderless cavalry horse saved us from the general slaughter. We named the horse Phocis, and Phocis accompanied us thereafter on our travels, until the sad day when he fell from the pass at Thermopylae and whinnied out his last farewells.

'In each city we came to, educated people would invite us to stay. Merope was at the height of her fame, and I too was welcome, having made myself expert in the antique dances that were coming into fashion. I had also taught Phocis to dance, and we did an amusing double act for which I charged ten drachmas, to cover the cost of his feed. But all of us were happier outside the towns. Merope and I preferred to roam the country roads and temple precincts, filling roll after roll of papyrus with notes on what we saw, while Phocis could not keep still during lectures, and often drew attention with his farts and snorts to the weaker points in the argument. So we would leave each city just as soon as we had made enough money to fund the trip to the next one. Merope was the best of guides – erudite, but wearing her knowledge so lightly that to learn from her was like recalling something already known. She was well versed in the sacred stories, and delighted to explain them, putting allegorical truth in place of literal falsehood. And I should say, honoured Archeanassa, that this Greece of yours is the very image of holiness, and if one wished to believe again in gods and mysteries, it is in Greece that one should give the thing a try. Seeing my native country for the first time with open eyes, I felt the buoyancy of ancient things, the upsurge of spirit that comes from commerce, adventure and conquest and the inextinguishable interest in the really real. Every grove, every field, every tree and every river in Greece is owned, possessed, inhabited and brimming over with gods. There is not a hill or valley, not a grove or path or stream that does not have its story. Stop anywhere on your journey, be it by the sweeping gorge of Delphi or some lowly patch of nettles by a well, and you will hear in the rustling mid-day breeze the voice of the god or hero whose place it is, and whose visit transcribed this patch of earth into the book of eternity. Everywhere in Greece we found the memory of the same national spirit – the spirit of a people intent on immortalizing itself and by Zeus succeeding.

'And here I should mention some of Merope's virtues, honoured guest, lest you should leave this Colophon of ours with the bad opinion that you voiced this morning. Merope loved life, and loved life also in others. Her vagrancy was not a form of escape, but on the contrary, an exercise in curiosity. She wished to know the world as it is, unhindered by illusions. And to this end she wandered from place to place, observing all the mind-forged manacles of man, and teaching the ways of freedom. Unlike most tramps I have met she was a fount of knowledge. She would promptly answer any question of history or natural science, and her ability was the more remarkable in that she travelled without books and refreshed her mind only in the libraries of strangers.

'Nor was her knowledge of truths only. She had memorized the poems and liturgies, and was an expert in the "divine figments," knowing what the tribes believed of them and why. She was skilled in the arts, could play tunefully on the lyre and was an accomplished painter, having founded here in Colophon a school and style of her own – only to discover after she left that a guy called Apelles had grabbed her store of paintings and was selling them off as his own.'

'She was here before, in Colophon?' asked Archeanassa, astounded.

'Didn't I tell you? That was long ago, when she was a young woman, before she left on her travels. She came here from Sardis – on account of a man. You must have coincided,' the girl added with an innocent glance at the wall. 'But I am coming to that. I just want you to be aware of her virtues, since without them my story would be crazier than it is.

'Merope had what to my mind is the most precious knowledge of all, which is the knowledge of names, whether general names or proper names. Flowers and plants, birds and insects, stones and earths, all were known to her. Should we stop at a wayside shrine or watering place, she would not rhapsodise on the landscape, the beauty of trees and hills and streams, or the poignant nature of the light that held these things together. Such tourist chatter was repugnant to her, since it stood like a veil before the things themselves. For Merope the important matter was not the beauty or sublimity of those rocks that towered above us, but the fact that a thin slice of basalt was trapped there between layers of laminated granite, that pockets of ferruginous sandstone could be detected in the soft marl beneath our feet, that plates of glittering mica divided the rose-grey cliff-face, which was warmed here and there by spots of golden lichen, that a goshawk had made its nest on one of the ledges and was at that very moment hanging on the wind above a vole which was nibbling the asphodel – look there, don't you see it? – under a plume of tamarisks. And the further you look into the surface of this cliff, she might observe, the more it is troubled like waves, rippled as seas are rippled, trembling like harp-strings along its purple veins, all as if a great fear had brought the rock to a standstill and caused it to hold itself alert and wondering on the brink of some mighty fall, arrested in a sheaf of trembling towers above the gulley, its bastions poised with alarm as the stream rushed coldly over them.

'That was Merope's style, whatever the subject. No bird to her was merely bird: each was haloed with its name, and the call of wheatear, corncrake, kite or rock-thrush was echoed in the thousand chambers of her heart, where all the species dwelled in archetype.

'When she told me the name of a plant, it was always accompanied by some curious detail concerning the formation and distribution of its leaves, the shape of its stem, the bracts and toruses and codices and stamens and corollas and pistils of its flower, or the peculiar shape and tenacity of its root. As a vagrant she was particularly interested in roots, and her eyes often seemed to acknowledge and then discard all of the plant that ventured into the light of day, and to see into that darker and more beautiful part that lay beneath the surface. If a plant wanted only water, she said, it could spread in soft and senseless limbs like a sponge, as far down as it could; but to get the rocky, grainy, salty things it needed the plant must sift the earth, and taste and touch every grain of it with fine fibres. A root is not a sponge but a tongue. In such a way did Merope draw my attention to the deep and hidden likenesses of things, by first teaching me to marvel at their differences.

'To her culinary skills I have already referred. In truth she was Kore herself, a goddess of the vegetable kingdom, whose soul moved with the rhythm of the seasons, and rejoiced even in winter with the effervescence of fermenting fruit. She knew the names and uses of herbs – of chervil and caraway, of rampion and purslane and hyssop. She was an expert on mushrooms, and when it came to trees could have written a volume on each of them, in which botany, myth, religion, geography, history and medicine would each have had a chapter. How beautiful was her discourse on the laurel leaf: numerable, sequent, perfect in setting, divinely simple and serene. And when she told the story of Daphne, describing the flowing, watery rhythm of those incomparable leaves, and the eager pursuit of the sun as he touched and fingered their lustrous surface, the legend came alive for me. Pindar says it all: "beauty, which gives the myths acceptance, renders the incredible credible."[1] And the beauty lay not in her words only, but in her whole being, which melted into the myth and endowed it with life.

'In fact, if I were to capture what was distinctive about Merope, I would say that her words and her being were inseparable. And when she offered me each day my morning posy, it was also a posy of words: mullein, ravensleek and saxifrage; melilot, agrimony, vetch and chamomile. She addressed the world by name and knew how to capture colours, smells and atmospheres in speech, so that everything she touched and saw seemed in part her own creation.

'And although she lived outside society, and did not hide her disdain for its conventions, she was not, like Diogenes, a misanthropist. I should rather say that she was a *critic* – and by this I do not mean the kind of cavilling and negative soul who is never contented, and who hides his envy behind a mask of denigration. I mean one who searches in every human act and character for its meaning, who sees what people hide from themselves and others, and who strives to live honestly in a world of pretence. To my way of thinking, the life of the critic is the highest life on earth, and if few can manage it, and if the attempt to do so launches one on a path of unending vagrancy, this only confirms my low opinion of the others, who cannot abide in their midst the person who has seen through their menial subterfuge.

'Merope loved me with a mother's faithful love, asking nothing and giving all. Whatever hardship we encountered,

---

1   First Olympian.

she took it on herself to pay the price of it. I was the symbol of her aristocratic ideal, and her first concern was to protect me from defilement, even at the cost of being defiled herself. When the Euboeans took offence at my dancing, and sentenced me to be whipped, she stood calmly before them and said that it was she who should be punished since it was she who had ordered me to dance. And as the lashes fell across her back she smiled in gratitude that she could render me this service. When in Samothrace I was condemned to serve in a common brothel, she skillfully took my place and, by virtue of her strength and resolution, threw her first customer out of the window and made her escape. And all the while she cared for me both body and soul, teaching me to live in natural and healthy ways, and persuading me to be at one with my body so that I could please the world with my dance.

'She had the gift of healing too. How often did she cure me of stings and bites and scratches, or soothe my tired eyes with eyebright and yarrow water. And when once in Anthedon I slipped while dancing and twisted my ankle, she took me in her arms and carried me a whole league, to the field where Phocis was guarding our things. She laid me there beneath a hawthorn tree, and poulticed me with balm and comfrey and warm white clay. And for three days I basked in her love, which warmed me like a sun and made me whole as I had never been whole. For every moment with Merope was a kind of rebirth, a setting forth anew into the world.

'This too I admired in Merope, that she had no needs. If we ran out of food she would cheerfully go hungry, soothing her body's cries as one soothes a dog or a horse. If the weather turned foul and her tunic no longer protected her, she would cast it off and stand in the rain, an amphibian creature over whom water flows as unnoticeably as air. And when business required me to spend a few days in some rich man's villa, she did not pine in my absence nor did she secretly reproach me. Instead she set aside the loving Merope and replaced it with a practical alternative. She would depart on some frolic of her own, give impromptu lectures, sell phoney prophecies or visit the local tyrant with outrageous proposals for social reform. Always when I returned to her I found the same serene being, emerging from some new experience as from a refreshing bath. Not that she took baths, of course.

'And while we are on the subject let me say how beautiful she was, and how little marked by her forty years. It goes without saying that she used no artifice – no necklace, ear-rings, make-up, powder or hair oil. But her wide brow and strong profile, her straight noble nose which turned so boldly and surely towards the world, as though aiming the azure eyes that swam to either side of it, their odd squint always there but barely visible, her pale, sandy lips, the upper one long and fluted in repose, the fair arched eyebrows, always alert and quizzical, the flat, translucent ears just visible beneath the cascade of auburn hair – all these had such a painterly perfection that their very naturalness seemed like something artificial, as though some artist had set out to produce the image of natural beauty, of a woman whom no artifice could possibly improve, and had given us Merope. Although she was large and strong and definite in all her gestures, she moved with grace and discretion, her footsteps softer than falling petals, her breathing barely audible, however much she exerted herself. Her smile was never weak or hesitant, but untroubled and limpid as her name. A sheaf of fine wrinkles at the corner of each eye was the only sign she gave of middle age. And what, after all, is middle age, except the time of our greatest decision, the decision to be declining or thriving, obedient or obeyed?

'Alas, however, the vagrant life is hard, and it is hard to stand always apart from one's kind, in a posture of critical distance. In the evenings we would sometimes read from the poets, since I insisted on carrying them about with me. And how quick and just were her comments on their works, with what unfailing insight did she distinguish genuine feeling from unctuous sentiment and the true rhythm of life from the false sing-song of fantasy. But this exercise, which fully persuaded me of the truth of Merope's vision, and of the difference between the higher life of the spirit and life in the world below, did nothing to equip us for reality. As we wandered from city to city, avoiding every compromising routine, every indolent habit, every self-deceiving trick whereby people fit themselves to each other and learn to live side by side in mediocrity, we became increasingly strained. I won't say that I missed the life of the city, for I felt nothing but joy that I had escaped from my mother's meaningless routines. But I was often agitated, having no companion besides Merope and Phocis, the one demanding the highest and most scrupulous honesty of feeling, the other demanding nothing at all. And Merope too, I believe, suffered from the severity of her outlook. She knew in her heart that the modern world could make no place for her. Oh, she was calm and strong and glad: for such she was determined to be. But it is a small step from being without illusions to being disillusioned, and both Merope and I became steadily more aware of the danger.

'And here I should pause, most honoured guest, to take note of the new human type to which you yourself referred in discussing architecture. For it is true that the loss of the gods has brought about a momentous change in those who once believed in them. All formality, all aspiration to the higher life, all dignity have gone from their mutual dealings. And the very thing for which I hoped – the abolition of vows, and a life based purely in contract – has come about precisely among those least able to cope with it.

'But I would adjust your analysis in one particular, honoured guest. There is not one new type of humanity, but two – the first engineered by coercion, the second by laxity. Here in Persia you encounter the first kind: people whose gods have been violently smashed, who have been herded together by the Great Plan, which is to make them equal, and who in consequence exist together in a condition of mutual distrust, equal at least in those qualities like fear, resentment and ruthless calculation which make for survival. In Greece we encountered the second type. Their gods had been neither banished nor stolen; they had merely drifted away in the haze of new permissions. The new type that we met on our travels was permitted both to believe and to disbelieve – for what is liberty without the right to be who you are? But the result of this permission was to make everyone the same – different perhaps from the mass-produced slaves of Colophon, but equally disposable, and like the Colophonians, amusing only when viewed from outside, like monsters in a zoo.

'This new type (I speak of course of the uncultivated masses) is without the precious thing that Merope called "distance." When all is forbidden, people live behind barricades, as here in Colophon. When all is permitted, they stand on display, moronically awaiting the next excitement. As little as possible is held in reserve, and anyone who knows the name of the occupant can enter his space and examine the goods contained in it. Moral and social distinctions are discounted, and those things which must be held in reserve, if they are to exist at all – love and friendship, for example – are replaced by more saleable cloth-covered versions, which are as passionless and undemanding as dolls. The person who defends his territory, and who requires some moral or social qualification from those who seek to enter it, is condemned as "judgemental." She is the enemy of the liberal order, and her space must be invaded by force if need be, so as to ensure that she is concealing nothing dangerous within it. That is why Merope and I were often in trouble, and never more so than in those cities which called themselves democracies, and which regarded our critical posture as an offence to majority opinion. For sentimentality, vagueness, an easy-going indolence in which self replaces other as the object of concern – these had become necessary to the new routines and were the diet of popular culture. Indeed, it is only with the help of the gods that the common people could have avoided them without also losing their freedom. We, who openly denied the gods, were in a sense the last ones truly to honour them, the last to maintain in ourselves the high ideals of passion, and to live not for the self but for the self transcended.

'But steadily it came home to us, that neither Merope's philosophy nor my dancing could change the world, even if they excited its admiration. We were destined to be famous or not-so-famous eccentrics, but not to rid the world, as Merope sometimes put it, of "this disease called man." And Merope's lectures became increasingly shrill. She raged at her audience, denouncing their foolish morality, their impoverished emotions, their denial of the higher man who had once existed – Homer was the proof of it – but who existed no more. She stirred up the crowds. And they paid her handsomely for her speeches, so as to show that they were secretly just as virtuous as she hoped, while pressing her to depart at once to the neighbouring city, where people were in far greater need of her instruction.

'During this time we still clove to each other, but often sadly, lacking the social forum in which to display our love. For it is true even of the gods on the mountain tops, that their loves and hates cry out for some social endorsement, that they are true to themselves and their feelings only when they can display those feelings to the world. Of course, we had Phocis, and the poor beast was the recipient of much unwanted petting and coddling, as we strove to remodel him as a human multitude. But Thermopylae bereaved us of our last normal companion, and Merope was much affected, for the first time in my sight giving way to tears.

'But we were strong still, and we made up our mind to put Greece behind us, to start again in Persia, in the land of Merope's youth, from which the gods of Greece had been expelled and where another new human type was taking shape, unhampered by the past and its culture. And I especially welcomed this decision, having made up my mind to live as I now live, in the midst of barbarians, enjoying the fact that in everything of value I am immeasurably superior to those whom I meet, and able in a second to convince them of this. I except you from this judgement, honoured guest. But you are the first civilised being I have encountered since the death of Merope. And you won't deny that you owe your culture mostly to Uncle Plato – oh yes, and that other guy, what's his name? Antimachus.

'It was during our first weeks in Lydia that I noticed a change in Merope. We had come to Sardis, the place of her birth, and she had been light-headed and cheerful on the journey, like a child on holiday. I too was excited. For although I had qualms about travelling in Persian Lydia the very strangeness of the place, its mute indifference to judgement, struck a chord in me. I had made up my mind to embrace the modern world entirely, to live freely, pitilessly, burningly, beyond morality, with no "ought" but only "is" and "want" and "will be." And I imagined that in this I followed Merope. What better place to be than Persia, the laboratory of the new man, the land where all lives were of equal value since none was worth anything at all? And yes, I confess it, when first we came to Sardis and saw the great machine at work, smashing temples whose every stone had been the labour of a thousand hours and burning them for quicklime, laying waste the shrine-studded streets to make way for the convoys of wagons, building barracks of iron and mortar in the sacred groves, and turning over gardens, parks and precincts to the builders of towers, I was elated. Here at last I saw it happening – not the slow dwindling of an ancient culture that we had observed in Greece, but the rapid extermination of a conquered way of life. And when I discovered that the new Persian man exists in two varieties – the one manufactured for resentment, endowed with barbaric tastes and hidden away in places that can be visited only with a special pass, the other designed for enjoyment, endowed with a yearning for culture and the right of residence in all favoured spots – when I discovered this I saw my opportunity. I would be the darling of the new elite, and mistress, should I choose, of the Great King of Persia. O.K. I have grown up a bit since then. Still, had it not been for the catastrophe I am about to relate, I would have made a success of life in this place, as much of a success as my nature permits.

'To my surprise, Merope was depressed by her native city, and exchanged sharp words with me when I tried to defend it. It really *troubled* her, that the world she had known had been swept away, and the rootless hordes driven like dung-dropping cattle across the ruins. She began to denounce the new world in lectures full of irony, some of which – since she knew the language – she delivered in Persian. And the silent crowds which gathered before her, under the mistaken impression that this woman, standing so boldly in an open space, must have something useful or rare or at any rate rationed to sell, would, on discovering their mistake, ripple with menace, and even cry "shame" at her mockery of the Ten Year Plan.

'The situation couldn't last, of course, and we were soon accompanied everywhere by silent guards, busily gathering the evidence against us. And things would have ended badly, had it not been for a curious accident of fate which is worth recounting, honoured guest, since it was my lesson in how to live and prosper among the Persians.

'As you will have noticed, there is no official religion in Persia, apart from that devoted to the King himself. The priests and religious have been rounded up and sent down the mines, and the sacred literature destroyed. Schools and academies have courses in atheism, and blasphemies are routinely posted on the public billboards. The official hope has been that, without the gods, people would behave with a frenzied disregard for morality, a total devotion to the self, just as a drowning man permits himself everything as he beats down the competing bodies of his companions and pitilessly struggles for air. A society of suffocating men is not a society, but a tumult of atoms. And such a tumult is a paradigm of social equality, as well as being powerless against its ruler.

'Unfortunately, however, the religious urge survives these primitive measures, and even in Persia the need for community, for purpose and a common faith crystallizes from time to time around the memory of some god or prophet. And just occasionally a real prophet appears, surviving amid the official persecution on account of the fear or credulity or patronage of some local tyrant. It happened that our arrival in Sardis coincided with that of such a prophet – a long-haired freak from the fertile crescent, with the odd name of Sterbs.

'Now Sterbs had declared himself to be prophet of Mitra,[2] a goddess who had not yet been forgotten and the mention of whom caused shock-waves among the people of Sardis. He had long greasy hair, a cheesy complexion, and a large gap-toothed mouth, from which would issue howls and shrieks, as though he were possessed. He even managed to foam at the mouth. He accomplished this feat, some say, by chewing the root of a herb called soap wort, used in the dyeing trade. But the gullible people of Sardis were of another opinion, and interpreted the froth on their prophet's lips as the natal spume of the goddess, risen by secret channels from the sea. Each day Sterbs would stand in the streets of Sardis, wearing a purple and white robe with a white mantle over it, and brandishing a sickle in the style of Perseus. And the authorities hesitated to touch him, so great was his popular appeal: day and night the people would queue before him, to pass questions to the goddess on scraps of papyrus, and receive (on payment of a dinar) enigmatic answers that they would puzzle over for days and which elicited their faith precisely because they made no difference to anything.

'It so happened that Merope and Sterbs clashed one day in the centre of town, she lecturing on the absurdity of prophets and he prophesying the eternal punishment of sophists. In the riot that ensued we were saved from death by the governor of Sardis, a flabby sybarite called Mitridates, who happened to pass through the neighbourhood on a litter, accompanied by a troop of household guards. At the sight of the governor's convoy the people fled, leaving

2   The Persian name for Aphrodite: see Herodotus, Book 1, 131.

Merope, myself and Sterbs standing in attitudes of defiance amid torn scraps of prophecy and the votive offerings from the prophet's box, which Merope had jubilantly tipped across the street. Mitridates greeted Sterbs as a familiar, and the prophet began at once to complain of the ill-treatment he had received, demanding the extremes of punishment for the wanton female who had so insulted him. The governor consoled him with the promise that Merope would be flogged and beheaded for disturbing the King's Peace. My darling was led away, turning to me with a brave but comfortless smile.

'My efforts to gain admission to the governor's palace were not rewarded until the afternoon, when the morning guard, who were all queer as coots, gave way to a more normal, or at any rate, more susceptible contingent. I forced my way into the dining room just at the moment when the governor was ordering his adjutant to begin, by way of after-lunch entertainment, the punishment of Merope. Mitridates lolled across a groaning table, dressed in a tunic of camel hair dyed in the most startling colours, with the usual waxed beard, and that oily Persian skin which he caressed with slow rolling fingers as though gradually peeling off the outer layer. Hearing the commotion, he turned his neckless head in my direction, his eyes like dark half-risen moons on the ledge of his eyelids. Langorously he adjusted his position, until a look of quickening interest crossed his fleshy features. His moustache now began to quiver and his mouth to hang open in a moist lascivious smile. I begged permission to dance before him, and as luck would have it, he understood Greek. He sat silently, pondering my words. Then he held one arm in the air before him, and the adjutant responded by seizing the hilt of his sword. Everything hung by a thread. I mastered my looks and pierced that flabby face with the most accomplished dart in my extensive repertoire. And after a second or two, the arm collapsed in a languid gesture of acceptance.

'The adjutant retired to his place and Mitridates commanded me to astonish him. This I duly did, honoured

guest, so that when the dance was ended, and the last entic-
ing schemata had fluttered to a quietus in my robe like the
settling feathers of a bird, Mitridates fell drooling across the
table and asked me in a hoarse whisper to name my desire.
Naturally I said that my desire was Merope. He responded
with a gasp, saying that, while of course he must grant my
request, there was something degrading, perverted and
even insulting to his princely liberality, in demanding a miserable itinerant sophist. He snapped his fingers and, as
Merope was delivered to me, he rose from the table and
fixed me with a peculiar and penetrating look. The situation
was clearly turning nasty again, and I searched the eyes of
Merope for guidance. Then, with a sudden inspiration, I
asked for the head of Sterbs.

'The governor started, clapped a hand to his forehead
and paced about howling on the dais. "Aiee, aiee, aiee!" he
cried, "so I must destroy that innocent and holy man!" The
tears gushed from his eyes, the slobber flowed over his
fleshy lips, and a general ruin swept across his features as he
patrolled around the table, the portrait of the King staring
above him in evident satisfaction at this new turn of events. I
allowed Mitridates to enjoy his grief for a while before re-
peating my request, this time more firmly. The governor
stood still for a second, before collapsing on to his throne
with a sigh, and burying his face in his hands. He sobbed out
the order to fetch the prophet from his habitual abode,
which was a nearby cistern, chosen, I subsequently learned,
on account of the stupendous echo which added credibility
to his prophecies.

'As we waited for the arrival of Sterbs, the governor began to relax somewhat, toyed with a plate of figs and even
helped himself to a bowl of wine. We chatted a little about
Athens and Uncle Plato, although of course I did not reveal
the connection. And when the prophet was dragged in,
frothing at the mouth and prophesying terrible vengeance,
Mitridates had a certain difficulty in reassuming his tragic
expression. Still the job was done at last, and the governor
put on a credible performance, rising with one hand on the

table, his eyes bulging, and commanding me to leave the palace at once with my miserable companion, and to take that horrible thing with me. So saying, he turned away and began washing his hands, humming slightly, however, and sneaking another sip from his bowl.

'Nothing that I had been called upon to do for Merope had cost me so much as picking up that louse-infected brain-box, and making with it for the nearest exit, the blood smearing my hands and dripping in a trail along the palace floor. I don't suppose you have ever carried a severed head through the streets of a populous city, honoured guest, but I can tell you that there are few things more embarrassing. And if the head once belonged to a famous prophet, then you run the risk of serious inconveniences. Luckily, however, the adjutant had made such a botched job of the operation, requiring no less than three attempts, to the loud indignation of Sterbs himself, that the thing was recognisable as a human head only with the kind of close inspection that the Persian crowds were unlikely to bestow on it.

'And we had a further stroke of luck. Not far from the palace stood a butcher's stall, with nothing to sell beside a few lumps of yellowing sheep's fat. I was able to slip the thing on to the counter while the owner dozed in the back. Meat was already so scarce in Sardis that the sight of a blood-red oozing lump attracted an immediate queue of silent women anxious for a slice of it. Nor, standards of hygiene being what they were, did the customers mind the abundance of human hair that had got mixed up with the merchandise. We stationed ourselves at the back of the queue, composed our faces into looks of weary acquisitiveness, and then slipped quietly away when the screaming began.

'I mention this episode, honoured guest, since it gave me such a deep insight into the layer upon layer of pretence whereby the new Persian man is governed. I witnessed not only the helplessness of the people, but also the ease with which their rulers could be manipulated, provided one addressed their real interests, rather than their pretended duties. Mitridates could only gain credit from the King should the prophet be neutralized. At the same time, he could not be seen to do the job himself, or to be left holding the trophy. I came opportunely to his rescue, as I have come to the rescue of many a satrap since. And if it were not for the fact that Merope found this whole episode rather depressing, I think I might have offered my services as prophet-sweeper to the Great King himself.

'The encounter with Sterbs was Merope's last venture into the public arena. Thereafter she refused to give lectures, and wandered in baffled silence among the ruins. Now Sardis, as you know, was famous throughout the civilised world for its temple of Artemis, and Merope confided to me that she had been, in her youth, first among the worshippers there, chorus leader, verger, and in training for the priesthood. I was not surprised to learn this, honoured guest, since we all begin life in thrall to the superstitions of our parents. But I was surprised to discover that some of the superstition had remained – or rather that it had returned on our entering Sardis. For despite my eagerness to visit the ruins of this famous place, Merope resolutely refused, saying that it would hurt her to observe them, that she could not bear to witness the desecration of so holy a shrine, that every stone of the temple had been more precious than a thousand Persian lives, and other words to that effect.

'"But maybe it's still standing," I protested. "Maybe the wreckers are too busy elsewhere."

'"Is it likely?" she said. "Is it not part of the modern spirit to destroy the symbols of nobility, or at least stack them up in a museum where they can do no harm?"

'"At least we should go and have a look," I replied. "Imagine how embarrassed I would feel, when forced to say that I went to Sardis but missed the temple of Artemis."

'"Well, go if you must, but count me out."

'I protested at this, being of the view that solitary tourism is a kind of perversion, like getting drunk on your own.

And eventually I moved her so far as to agree to accompany me to the temple precinct, and to wait outside until I returned. When we arrived there, however, after picking our way through building sites and fields of rubble, her curiosity gradually got the better of her, and she tagged along behind. She surveyed the precinct with gasps of anger and astonishment, and stood mournfully among the broken columns of the pteron, discoursing, notwithstanding her grief, on the peculiar refinement of the capitals which lay shattered on the marble flagstones. Now Merope was an expert on architecture as on every subject, and she made me feel a measure of gratitude towards the Persian vandals who had wrecked the place, and who had thereby enabled us to kneel and study those unique designs. For you know, honoured Archeanassa, that the Ionic capitals of Sardis have carved floral ornaments of exquisite workmanship in the channel between echinus and abacus, and Merope pointed them out to me, blessing them with an immaculate description. One capital even has – unless of course it has gone to the lime-kilns[3] – palmettes carved on the eggs of the abacus, something that we never saw elsewhere on our travels, unless it were in the Ionic temple of Apollo Phanaios in Chios, from which, however, we had to flee before making a proper study of it, on account of an obnoxious priest with a positively Ionic erection, volutes and all.

'After a while, when Merope had settled into a more reflective frame of mind, she treated me to a discourse on architecture which I recall the more vividly, honoured guest, in that it relates to things that you were saying – which is why I nodded agreement with your words, even though, as I shall shortly mention, you seemed to overlook the fundamental problem.

'"Looking round at this desecrated place," she said, "I cannot deny the conflict in my feelings. For what was a city is here a city no longer, and a place once holy, whose every

---

3   No: it has been preserved, and is visible today on the columns that have been raised from the rubble in what is now the Turkish village of Sart.

contour was dedicated to a god or hero, is fast becoming a featureless nowhere. We must face up to the fact, my dear Perictione, that cities begin from a very special act – an act of consecration. A place is chosen, the gods endorse it, and the tribe is commanded to cease its wandering and defend the place as its own."

'I could not forebear reminding her, honoured guest, that the theory is Xanthippe's. Maybe I should have reminded you too. But I digress.

'"That's as may be," she said. "In many things, Xanthippe's truth and my truth coincide. How a city can be founded without religion I do not know. Of course, a pile of bricks and stones can be dumped in a field and people rounded up to live in it. But to call the result a city is to mistake the meaning of the term. Until the gods reside among us, how can we be still? And until we are still, how can we dwell? Oh, I grant you, we can stay put, shelter ourselves, as we did in the barrel by the temple of Cybele. But to stay in one place, to take refuge, to pull our coat around our shoulders or crawl into a hole – these are merely modes of vagrancy, variations of the wandering habit, which could never give birth to a city, but only to a camp. And if this camp remains from week to week and month to month and year to year, never will it become a city, for never will it have been attached to the land, as the city is attached, by that first rite of consecration, and never will the people who reside there learn also to dwell. The camp can remain for decades, retaining its air of stagnant impermanence, like a stream dammed by rotting branches, waiting for the burst that will sweep it away.

'"Now we should take notice of this temple, my dear Perictione. For it reminds us that man's greatest architectural efforts have been devoted to raising roofs over those who need no roofs to shelter them, and walls around those who could never be contained by a wall. What super-abundance of spirit is needed, if man is to build – the very super-abundance that spills over into gods! And conversely, if the stream of faith dies to a trickle, so that there are no gods but only doubts and rumours and stories, then building must cease, and something else must come in place of it, the something that you see in Sardis."

'And there you have the problem to which I referred, most honoured guest. Surely, if Merope was right, and she generally was, our godless world requires a new and godless architecture and a new and godless city. O.K., you may refuse the word "architecture" and the word "city" – but what's in a word? The things themselves must change. And I will tell you why, honoured Archeanassa. The old Colophon that you describe was built by faith – faith in Artemis and her redeeming love for us. This faith ran through all things, and provided not merely the motive to educate the next generation in the sacred rites and dances, but every smallest perception of the city and its meaning, right down to the sense that just this moulding or just this ornament or triglyph or modillion is the right one. Even those shadows of which you spoke so earnestly derive their significance from faith – for, as you yourself pointed out, what happens to the great divide between light and shade, when the gods have ceased to contend over it?

'And suppose that someone now, in this god-forsaken place, were to build in obedience to the Colophonian pattern-book. Could he really mean what he did – mean it as those original builders meant it, when every chiselling of a column base was an act of consecration? Of course not. He would be assailed by a sense of irony, by a knowledge that he was not building but playing at building, like an actor on the stage. For architecture, like any art, is liable to corruption, and the greatest corruption, in building as in poetry, is that of insincerity. Even if our new architect exactly reproduces the forms and styles of ancient Colophon, even if there is not a single detail in which his building could be distinguished from some ancient archetype, yet will it not look the same, any more than the mimic's perfect copy of my speech and accent sounds the same as I do. It will look what it is – an imitation, a sham, a gesture made but not meant.

And how such a thing could give meaning again to the city I do not know.

'Now I don't doubt that there could be a newer style of building, which used the old pattern-book, but as it were *against* itself. Since we cannot sincerely mean these gestures, the architect might say, why not *show* that we do not mean them? Why not stick a capital at the base of a column, a cornice upside down, a triglyph over a bare expanse of wall, picking the details up, so to speak, in quotation marks, as a surgeon picks things up with forceps for fear of contamination? But I am inclined to think, honoured Archeanassa, that the result will be not merely irritating but also, in the long run, deeply dispiriting. For we should be unceasingly reminded of how trivial human life becomes, when the gods flow out of it. Better, it seems to me, to build a new Colophon, adapted to the needs of modern life, in which those who dream of higher things can nevertheless select their precious nests and live apart, as I do. That, in brief, is my answer to your diatribe. And I cannot forebear mentioning that I have made this answer without denying a single thing you said, only drawing from your words the conclusions that you avoided. Like Merope, you see, I specialize in uncomfortable truths. By which I mean truths that make others uncomfortable.'

'Nothing that you have said makes me uncomfortable,' Archeanassa responded somewhat frostily. 'For as you say, the truths you utter are not mine but yours. And I wonder whether they are even yours, since you live apart from the habits you defend, in a capsule salvaged from antiquity.'

'How right you are,' said Perictione warmly, 'and this returns me to my story. For I could not help reflecting on Merope's words and the light that they cast on her philosophy. I was struck by the contrast between her cheerfulness as she wandered through Greece – a cheerfulness that she maintained even in the midst of war and devastation – and the melancholy with which she greeted her former city. And I began to see the matter thus, most honoured guest. When in Lydia Merope had been fully part of Sardis, a believer in its gods, a worshipper at its shrine, a dweller in a place and a time. And she had been happy, with the innocent happiness that comes from pious works. But then along comes the guy from Colophon and breaks her heart.'

Archeanassa gave a startled cry.

'What guy from Colophon?'

'I'm coming to that,' said Perictione, waving her limp hand with an autocratic gesture. 'How it happens, and on whose behalf, does not concern us. The fact is that Merope is of the temperament which can do nothing by half measures – neither love, nor hate, nor believe, nor feel, nor know save totally and passionately. So, losing her peace of mind she loses also her faith, her stillness, her piety, her ability to dwell. Because she does not believe in the city's gods, she cannot dwell about their temples. She wanders not by choice but by necessity – the very necessity by which she is what she is. And as she wanders, she frames a philosophy, a system of belief which matches her new lifestyle as exactly and as neatly as her old religion matched the life of the city. Hers is a philosophy of exile, a philosophy of the outsider, the wanderer, the one who *refuses to dwell.* Laws, conventions, morality for her are always the laws and morality of others. And she relates to these others not by obedience, still less by defiance, but by *diagnosis.* She sees through the customs and beliefs of everyone she meets, understands the weakness and fear of which they are the mask, and laughingly proceeds on her way, unaffected by their cries of outrage. She meets me, the embodiment of the aristocratic idea, and admires in me the life of culture and refinement and lofty disdain. But she re-makes this higher life in her own image – as a *vagrant* life, a homeless life, a life without commitment or duty or vows. And this is the nature of the liberation that she offers me – a liberation not from customs and codes only, but from the city itself. Like her I cease to dwell, and wander through the civilised world – the world of others – exploiting its otherness and disdaining it by turns.

'Then we come to Sardis, and her exile is over. Suddenly

it is clear to Merope that she has enjoyed no dispensation from her own humanity. Like all of us, she must belong – somewhere, somewhen, somehow. And the devastation of her dwelling place is also a revelation of her deep unrest. She has killed in herself the faith and humility that would enable her to dwell either here or anywhere. And seeing this, a great sadness overcomes her, and she feels a need to visit again, not Sardis which made her, but Colophon, where she was undone.

'However, the afternoon draws on, and see, on the great tower of Babylon Enterprises the sun's last rays trumpet their vulgar goodbyes. The night begins, and I have work to do. Shall we meet tomorrow? Do say yes, honoured guest, for I have a burning need to finish my story, and your time in Colophon is short.'

Perictione was already on her feet as Archeanassa, overcome with dread, nevertheless signalled her consent. The girl ushered her with expert gestures through the inner peristyle and out on to the steps. Before closing the door, however, she called Archeanassa back.

'Don't fear me,' she said, smiling distantly, 'for I am not what I seem.'

And with that she turned quickly away and pushed the door shut with her foot.

7

A dream of Diogenes, with the cynical philosophy explained

Archeanassa did not return to the hostel. Instead she walked behind the villa, looking for the place where her cottage had stood, the place where, except for those brief afternoons when Antimachus came, often unannounced and always breathless as though running between appointments, she had been alone with her thoughts. She found neither her cottage nor her street. A wide avenue of mud had obliterated the neighbourhood, and vast unfinished hulks lay among rubble beside it, like deep-sea monsters blown ashore in a storm. There was a distant noise of machinery, and a pall of acrid smoke lay over everything, so that she held her veil[1] across her face and breathed with difficulty. Some of the blocks were already operational, and in one of them the drums were throbbing as the last workers gathered up their bundles and were pumped in a sludge of bodies through the doors. They did not look at her, but flowed in silence into the wagons, their faces like masks. As the last wagonload trundled across the rutted wasteland towards the suburbs, the building fell silent, and an eerie stillness settled over the avenue.

The dusk was gathering, and it was some time before she

---

1   Ar. *lisaam*: the end of the *kufiyah* or headkerchief, used to veil the face and protect it from heat, cold, dust and contagion. It was quite common to carry a veil in addition to the tunic (*chiton*) which was the standard form of female attire.

discovered, built into the corner of an unfinished tower, a little fragment of stuccoed wall, with Grecian mouldings and a broken entablature. It was a piece from the gate of her garden, and she wept to behold it imprisoned there, crushed into the earth by mortar and granite and iron. And then, since this was the place of her love, she stood for a while in prayer.

Who knows to which gods Archeanassa prayed on that occasion or with what requests? But it is a curious fact about prayer, that we ask not only for future things and present things, but for past things too. 'Let it not be, great Poseidon, that my son has drowned.' But surely if he has drowned, it is too late to save him? 'Let it be, great Demeter, that my daughter is not with child.' But surely, either she is or she isn't, and a fat lot Demeter can do about it either way. To the pious, however, everything is in the lap of a god, and in that comforting lap they place their heads when world and time and fortune overcome them. And is not the world more beautiful and more bearable so? Archeanassa thought so, at any rate, and she lay down beside her vanquished garden with a temporary lull in her heart. And she was cheered to discover, in the ditch beside the tower, a patch of blood-red flowers, spore of the wounded Adonis, whose festival she had celebrated before leaving Athens, and whose spirit still haunted the land.[2]

---

2   '. . . the scarlet anemone is said to have sprung from the blood of Adonis,' writes Frazer (*The Golden Bow*, abridged edition, p. 336). And he goes on to add that the name of the flower is probably derived from 'Naaman', a Semitic word which, he tells us, means 'darling'. He adds that 'the Arabs still call the anemone "wounds of the Naaman."'

Let it be first said that, according to the OED, our name for the flower is simply the Greek *anemone*, meaning 'daughter of the wind' (in colloquial English the anemone is also the windflower). And let it be also said that the Arabic *shaqa'iq an-nu'amaan* (which also contains, for those unable to pronounce the *'ain*, the sound 'anemone') seems to mean 'drops of the blood,' though why *nu'amaan* should mean 'blood' the dictionaries (which agree on the meaning) do not reveal. The

Chapter 7

The air was purer at ground level, and the noise of machinery had ceased. Nobody save the gods visited this secret place, and the revelry sounded faint and far away. After a while Archeanassa judged it wiser to sleep here, hidden in the ditch beside the tower, her tunic drawn across her face and her sandals stowed beside her.

Into her troubled sleep came the boy, with the face of Amphitryon the toad, crowned in a brush of red hair. He stuck out a forked tongue and darted it towards her: she retreated, but something hard and unyielding pressed against her head. Ever closer came the tongue, and the lips in which it flickered were laughing and mocking and wriggling like worms. At last it was almost upon her; she shrank in terror but her head was held in a vice and her hands were trapped. The tongue brushed against her lips, and she awoke with a scream.

A blade of grass, weighed down by a grasshopper, lay bent across her mouth, touching her lips with its feathery seed-pod. She shook herself and stood up. The flowers had been crushed by her weight, and their pattern had the shape

---

root of the noun is the verb *na'ama* which means 'to be delighted,' and which provides the standard Arabic term of assent – *na'am*, 'yes.' Moreover, the usual word for 'blood' is *dam*, *nu'amaan*, seeming to occur in no other context. The Semitic name Naaman, familiar from the Bible, is from the same root, and means 'blessed.' Finally, it should be said that the 'adonis flower' of the Greeks, the blood red flower known in English as 'pheasant's eye' (*Adonis aestivalis*), is not an anemone at all.

The allusion to the festival of Adonis, together with other details of the story, indicate that Archeanassa's visit to Colophon took place in summer, when anemones would have finished flowering.

Incidentally, there seems to be no system among the Arabic names for wildflowers. Among those commonly called *shaqa'iq an-nu'amaan* are the anenome (also called *sakkir*), the large ranunculus or Persian crowfoot (also called, ridiculously, *shaqiqu shaqshaqiq*), and the ordinary field poppy (also known as *khishkhaash*).

of a boar. Had Adonis really visited this place, and was the dream his gift to her? Nonsense, she thought, and stared for a while at the long shadow of the tower, cast by the early sun across the cracked mud where thistles grew and half-formed buildings burst like giants from the ground. It was an unearthly scene, a scene from another planet. And the gods who haunted the ditches were as troubled as she.

Archeanassa bent down to retrieve her sandals. They were not where she had placed them. Nor were they any-where else. She contemplated this fact with a deep unease: who was it who had watched her sleep and why? She set out with painful steps for the house of Perictione. Away from the hardened avenue the ground was covered with spiny plants which pricked her skin and released their oily scent about her. There was myrrh and camphor, flax and bugloss, and a sticky thorn-covered stalk which she did not recog-nize, but which had a clean, flowery fragrance like beeswax. And because these plants were untouched by the world sur-rounding them, living and breathing as they had always done, possessing the land with the same shy tenacity as her memories and her gods, Archeanassa began to welcome the pain that they caused. It was a sign that she too belonged here, as these roads and buildings and wagons would never belong.

She stood with bruised and bleeding feet before the por-tico, reaching out for the baton with which to sound the urn. Suddenly the door opened, and the boy came running through. He stopped in front of her, his face split open in a grin like an over-ripe pumpkin. In his hands he held her san-dals, and with mock deference he placed them on the step at her feet, bowing slowly and obsequiously. Then he swung quickly around, lifted his tunic, farted, and scampered across the threshold, like a mouse disappearing into its hole. The door closed behind him, and she heard his howls of mad laughter as they dwindled in the back of the building. A moment later the old servant appeared, as though nothing had happened.

Archeanassa was shown into a room off the courtyard,

where a dim light filtered through closed wooden shutters and a long couch stood beside a table. The old servant went across to the couch, puffed up the cushions, shifted the table, swept the walls with an incurious glance, and then withdrew in silence. Something about this performance enhanced Archeanassa's weariness. Already her sore feet cried for rest, her eyes refused to stay open, and her spirit, unrefreshed by her night in the ditch, was lethargic and dull. She sat down, and the room turned about her; she noticed another couch, some chairs and far off, like an apparition in the mist, a pair of statues. Her eyes closed, sprang open and then closed again. With a long sad sigh, she sank on the cushions and slept.

And then it was as though Perictione were beside her, opening the shutters, and flooding the room with sunlight, a sunlight so intense that it seemed to burn away the furniture and leave only Perictione herself, standing in a golden pool of day.

'You know, Archeanassa,' she said, 'I have been thinking. You are right to be suspicious of this Colophon of ours. But I wonder whether you know an alternative – an alternative, I mean, for us, who are living now.'

'Am *I* not living now?'

'It is hard to say.'

Perictione cast a nonchalant glance in her guest's direction.

'Not far from here,' she continued, 'lies the town of Laodicea[3] – two hours by chariot. I go there for little luxuries – perfumes, preserves, erotica, tooth-picks, that kind of thing. In fact you can obtain more or less anything in Laodicea. The Persian army passed through once, and caught some embarrassing disease. Since then they avoid the place. Trade is free, and the Laodiceans are positively

---

3   A reference in the Revelation of St John the Divine has led to Laodicea being proverbial in English – a Laodicean is someone who is by nature incapable of making up his mind, as in Thomas Hardy's novel of that title. Clearly the town had not achieved this reputation in Perictione's day.

addicted to it: pepper, desire, wine, worship, silk, love, pickles – you name it, they sell it.'

'There is no such place,' Archeanassa protested.

'Curious,' said Perictione, with a secretive smile. 'Nobody believes in Laodicea. Yet everyone turns up there in the end. In any case, I have in mind to take you there today.'

'Today? I thought we were to talk about dancing?'

'On the way home, we'll talk about dancing. It'll make more sense after Laodicea.'

Perictione clapped her hands, and the old servant appeared with a basket. Soon they were hurrying across the lawn, Perictione issuing instructions and snatching the basket as they reached the gate. A gilded chariot stood in the street. Its motionless driver stared wide-eyed at the sun; two stock-still horses gleamed like polished statues in the shafts of the car. The air in the street was light, cool, as though wafted from mountain regions, and no traffic broke the morning calm. The driver, who wore a yellow livery so bright as to dim the golden flanks encasing him, and whose brown impassive face seemed to outshine the sun, made no sign of greeting as they mounted behind. He appeared to Archeanassa like a visitor from another world forbidden to take note of human things. The horses too stared away from their surroundings, as though their attention were fixed on the higher realm to which they would soon be recalled. Only the sight of Perictione's laughing face, as she tapped the driver on the shoulder and gave a girlish click of the tongue, dispelled Archeanassa's fear of this new contrivance. Clearly this too was theatre, and she would emerge from it, as she had emerged from all the other frolics of her hostess, like one awakening from a dream.

They hastened through streets without houses or trees or gardens, where walls of iron enclosed drastic angles above ramps of barren earth. Here and there some piece of inexplicable machinery scraped at a heap of dust, or lifted a metal cabin from which uniformed workmen stared at the sun. A strange murmuring sound hung in the air, like the voice of a mutinous crowd, growing louder as they approached each building, and then briefly fading away. At one point the street entered a kind of circus, into which sharp corners of metal pointed like daggers. In the centre stood a ruined temple of Apollo, the god fallen from his pedestal and lying in pieces among broken columns. His wide untroubled eyes followed them, and the eerie smile on his lips seemed to shift and settle as they passed.

The road climbed through scrub and wasteland, past groves of desultory poplars, where travellers had strung their tents between the trees, past ruined settlements destroyed by battle. Here and there an old Greek house, sealed up and covered with graffiti, crumbled into the dust. Half-built towers and industrial plants were scattered alongside the road, and the few people who wandered among them had a puzzled and provisional air, as though waiting for instructions. Perictione stood motionless, observing nothing and saying nothing. There was something uncanny in her posture: staring through things she seemed also to destroy them.

Then, without warning, the town fell away, and it was as though Colophon had never been, so unbroken was the landscape, so green the copses, and so mild and soothing the breeze.

'Here we are!' said Perictione with a sudden smile, 'the road to Laodicea!'

All hardness had at once retreated from her features; the eyes were gentle and full of laughter, the mouth supple, natural and bursting with girlish fun. The transfigured Perictione reached down for the basket, took out a terra-cotta vase and broke the waxen seal. The scent of honeyed wine mingled with the flowing air, and they drank libations to the gods of Greece. Perictione shouted gaily, and Archeanassa politely smiled, hearing nothing above the clatter of hooves and the rumble of wheels on the roadway. Trees, temples, streams and villages sped past them, and the few people whom she glimpsed in the fields seemed remote like memories, never looking up but sinking as it were still deeper into their pastness as the chariot hastened by.

A dream of Diogenes; the cynical philosophy explained

And then, as abruptly as it had begun, their passage ceased, and the chariot stood amid streets as though dropped there. People in brightly coloured costumes marched and danced on the pavements, some in animated groups, some woven together in pairs like lovers, some performing with monkeys or bears, others forging solitary paths through the sea of bodies like messengers. The buildings were new, not with the emergency newness of Colophon, but with a bright sheen of polished wood and painted plaster – white, dove-grey, pale pink or sandy yellow – and all crowded against the street in the cheerful sunlight with wide-open doors and windows. Banners waved in the breeze above the roof-tops, announcing goods for hire and goods for sale; and from every corner came the sound of music – cornets, citharas and castanets – plundering each ear for attention, and causing the crowd to ebb and flow like wine in the bowl of a drunkard. Never in her life had Archeanassa seen so many people, or heard so much light-hearted din. All of Greece and Asia seemed to have gathered in Laodicea, as though for the festival of a god. And, even as the thought occurred to her, what seemed like a religious procession rounded the corner of the street and made its way along the pavement. Two ranks of men in uniform marched to either side of a shoulder-high platform, on which they carried an assemblage of wooden statues. Behind them, following with uneven and erratic steps, came a group of children, who sang tunelessly at the top of their voices. The chant was constantly repeated, but she could not make out the words, which were neither Persian nor Greek. The procession attracted no notice from the crowds, and was soon disappearing round another corner. One of the statues wobbled as it passed them, and seemed to put out its tongue; it was a caricature of Socrates with a long flowing beard, from whose lower strands an enormous phallus protruded like a handle.

Two guards had approached, dressed in the same yellow livery as the charioteer, and were now handing the ladies down with deferential gestures, bowing low to Perictione as she nodded her thanks. How come they had been expected? The question, which briefly surfaced in the tumult of Archeanassa's wonder, was at once brushed aside. Perictione took Archeanassa's arm and hustled her forward towards an open door.

They were swept with the crowd through downstairs rooms and courtyards, pushed against tables laden with goods, shouted at, hawked at, smiled at and drooled over by salesmen with painted faces; cornered by bores, applauded by simpletons, petted and patted and generally discomposed by people who looked past them and through them as though they were air. Here were the masks and girdles which every woman needs, the belts and thongs and garters which lovers long for, the pictures of mating couples and rutting children which make every bedroom an adventure. Caressing voices, spoken from nowhere, urged them to pick up dolls and toys and miniatures, to touch and sniff and hold a thousand smooth and portable things whose only use was that they had none, to dress themselves in hilarious hats and underwear, to try on unfashionable gowns that transported their wearer, for a second or two, into the divine realm of farce. The air was thick with cries of desire and surfeit. Perictione looked about her with bird-like expressions, picking and discarding like some mad old woman on a rubbish dump. Everything elicited a grimace from her, and yet she carefully distinguished the possessible items from the rejects, sometimes going to the trouble of dividing the contents of a table into separate piles and offering a price – always ludicrously small – for the one that she preferred. She was particularly taken by a doll in some fibrous material, with flowing robes of an unspeakable orange, which could be fed and dressed and changed, and which uttered little erotic noises when pinched behind. For this she paid the full price, and then hid it in her tunic, telling Archeanassa that she would send it with her to Athens, as a present for Phryne.

They entered another street, where the crowds were thinner. 'A gift for all occasions,' said a sign; 'each comes with the seal of our resident expert, and a money-back guarantee should it fail to satisfy. With Philodoxa opinions, you will stay on the right side of every argument.' In the opinion shop you could buy acceptable views on any subject, neatly copied on to parchment and rolled up in a mock-leather case. Perictione purchased three – one on education, which held that children learn by expressing themselves; one on free speech, saying that all is permitted, unless it does harm; and a third which described wealth as the cause of poverty. She gave all three to a beggar, urging him to try out the words in other combinations and so make his fortune as a seer. She particularly recommended 'self- expression is permitted, unless it leads to wealth,' since it seemed to apply rigorously and without remainder to all the situations in which thoughtless people reach out helplessly for words.

Next to the opinion shop stood a large, windowless building. On the hoardings that composed its outer shell were displayed scenes of sensuality and violence, and banners on the rooftop declared that whoever entered would be horrified, shocked, outraged, scandalized, moved, troubled and challenged. Around the double doors of bronze a large and excited crowd was gathering, and a persistent drumming came from within, like the drumming of the towers of Colophon.

This, Perictione explained, was the market in emotions, which she had often passed but which she had never entered since it was always closed. On enquiring of the crowd, however, they discovered that there was to be an auction that very day. And when the double doors sprang wide, the two women had not a moment to think, but were swept resistless with the stream of bodies into the dark interior.

It took some moments for their eyes to become accustomed to the half-light, and the bustle of people caused Archeanassa to cling like a child to Perictione, lest she lose her one sure mode of transport back to Colophon. For, whatever the evils of that god-forsaken city, the sight that now dawned from the darkness troubled the soul of Archeanassa more deeply than all that she had witnessed since returning to her native land.

They were in a vast auditorium without seats. At the end was a stage, lit by oil-lamps that swung from the rafters. People were pushing and grunting and gesticulating as they struggled to clear a space from which to see. One was laying about him with a whip; another had a sword with which he threatened his neighbours, while a third, knocking down an old woman who obstructed his view, now stood on her unconscious form, staring with greedy eyes at the stage. Archeanassa turned away, tugging at the sleeve of Perictione and imploring her to leave. But, finding her hostess immovable, and following her eyes to the spectacle through which Perictione stared as though at some vision of sublime purity granted only to her, Archeanassa saw a knot of naked figures, each one coupled to its neighbours, all writhing together like some many-headed beast. No kisses or caresses, no tender words or loving glances – not even the face-to-faceness of desire. Only orifices, grossly entered, unsmiling grins, and a pig-like grunting which rose to a screaming climax and then lapsed into mutters and groans.

A man in a red cloak, who held a baton in one hand, leaped on to the stage. The figures sprang apart to form a chorus, the women showing their bottoms and wiggling their hips, the men shaking their now flaccid members and dancing back and forth from foot to foot. Cithara and drum sounded from the wings, and the crowd, cheering with delight, began to move to the music. Then, with a wave of his baton, the man in red commanded silence and the commotion ceased.

'Laodiceans!' he began. 'Today is a great day for this city, a great day for our business leaders, a great day for the entertainment industry, a great day for the children, a great day for us all. It is the day of care and love and community. First our team here' – he gestured to the chorus, who one by one were climbing into their clothes – 'will put the feelings on display. Then the auctioneer will enter, and you will have the chance to show how much feeling matters to you. Everyone is entitled to bid, and, because you have our complete confidence, we have set no reserves. You Laodiceans will put your money where your hearts are, and so prove to the world that this is a community of caring people. Spend and enjoy!'

With a twist and a twirl he danced into the wings. Stage-hands in black robes leaped up to extinguish the lights, and the chorus fled from the scene. The lamps were lit again, and the show began.

What prodigies did they then behold! All the feelings of mankind were summoned, prized loose from their circumstances, and melted down for sale. Fear, lust, anger, love, resentment, gratitude – each had its gilded tableau, through which the feeling could be conjured, packaged, and exchanged. Archeanassa watched in appalled fascination as one by one the highest gifts of passion were marketed as sweetmeats. First to be offered was shame, who stepped on to the stage in the guise of a sophist, holding a scroll of parchment from which he recited a list of crimes, the sacking of cities, the massacre of innocents, the enslavement of nomads, the rape of women and the sale of children, the torments of poverty, the unjust laws which protected the wealthy and punished the poor, the persecutions which drove whole peoples to despair and suicide. Every grievance that the mind of man could conceive was rehearsed before them, and each was illustrated by the chorus – slaying, raping and torturing with a loving attention to detail that elicited groans of excitement from the onlookers. Such, the sophist said, were the crimes of Laodicea, whose citizens, even as they relished the torments – crying 'yes! yes!' and 'more! more!' – beat their breasts in phoney recantation. To round off the tableau a platoon of hoplites, accompanied by priests, judges, knights, and other representatives of the city's past, marched in triumph across the stage, to loud boos and cat-calls from the audience.

Wondrous too was fear: a rotund man in armour, whose stomach jutted upwards to his breastplate, and whose thick legs clanked in their grieves. As he strode about the stage, sword and dagger at the ready, life-like dummies were thrown in his path, to be slashed, torn and disembowlled while blood-curdling screams sounded from the wings. The screams were quickly taken up by the audience, until the house was one great hullabaloo of pain and terror, and Archeanassa stopped up her ears.

Anger was a little girl, dressed in a tattered tunic and with cuts and bruises painted on her face. She addressed the crowd in a lisping monotone: 'It wasn't daddy did this to me; my daddy loves me and it's not his fault there's no money so he's had to go down the mines in Susa only why didn't he come back when he said he would so he could stop them killing little Euphorbus who hadn't done nothing wrong hardly except bark when Timon was beating me . . .' and more in the same vein, unfolding the story of Hecuba and her cruel mother, whose lovers drive the little girl at last to lonely suicide. The audience, stamping their feet and crying for justice, began to rush forward to offer their protection, and were prevented only when the master-of- ceremonies stepped from the wings and spirited the girl away. She was replaced at once by love, in the form of two boy-lovers, one dying of a mortal disease, the other plan- gently mourning him. As they rocked in each other's arms, the sick boy recalled his former loves, one for each day of the year, and tried to attach a name, a face, or at any rate a penis, to the one who had fatally infected him – not in order to accuse or condemn, but to forgive and commiserate, as his friend forgave and commiserated in a speech so unctuous that Archeanassa once again put her fingers in her ears. When the sick boy finally died in his lover's arms, his melodious sigh was echoed throughout the theatre, where sniffs and snivels bore witness to the copious tears.

But this performance was nothing beside the final act, devoted to compassion. The hero is a boy from a poor family, whose parents have disappeared, and who has learned to survive by stealing and cheating. He becomes addicted to poppy sap, which he takes with his street companions, and under the influence of which he commits spectacular and profitable crimes. All human beings for him have but one significance – which is their utility. If they have money, then steal from them; if they want sex, then sell it to them; if they impede you, then strike them down; if they are a threat, then kill them – such are our hero's rules of thumb. In one horrible scene after another these principles are enacted, but so cleverly that the hero always escapes the adverse judgement of the crowd. The old man whom he rips open with a kitchen knife has only himself to blame: for did he not snatch the drug away from our hero, who had to retrieve it by force or die for lack of it? The girl whom he captures and hands over to his playmates to be raped, was it not bad luck on our hero's part that he should have been so high on poppy-sap as to take her for Medusa? And when his girlfriend swallows the drug that he needs, and he jumps time and again on her stomach, afterwards lapping up the bloody vomit with trembling mouth, does he not deserve our compassion? Heartless people condemn him; but those with sympathy see him for what he is – the victim of a heartless world. It is as such, at least, that the actor portrays him, and the audience concurs. Archeanassa too feels the force of what she sees, like a long-drawn-out flutter of the stomach, as though she were melting inwardly, as though at any moment she would lose all power to keep herself upright and aloof and would collapse in a heap, among the bodies of those who had succumbed to the force that spread from the stage. She too is tempted to cheer with relief at the hero's escape from punishment; and when finally he is seized by soldiers, she inwardly joins in the loud 'boo!' of protest that fills the auditorium. Many of the onlookers rush forward to defend him, and are held back only by the sudden re-appearance of the master-of-ceremonies.

'And so, Laodiceans,' he shouted, gesturing with his baton for quiet, 'we come to the end of our exhibits. I hand you over to the auctioneer. Bid him welcome!'

A roll on the drums crescendoed to a climax. And then all was breathlessly silent, as a small round figure emerged from the wings and moved with ponderous gait across the stage, his tunic held close to his body and his face turned from the crowd. Archeanassa was suddenly aware of

Perictione, who had stood unmoved throughout the show, staring through the actors, and seeming hardly to notice what they did. Now she was straining forwards, an expression of unbelief on her face, her mouth fallen open in astonishment. As the auctioneer turned to face the crowd she let out a gasp.

'Great Zeus, it *is* him!' she cried.

'Who?'

'Diogenes!'

'Diogenes!' echoed Archeanassa. And she studied with amazement the philosopher of whom she had heard so much, but who had clearly been transformed so far by his Persian experience that nobody except those who had been his intimate neighbours could recognize Diogenes the dog, whom Perictione had sold with his kennel. Clean shaven now, and with pink and polished features, only a studied untidiness of the hair betrayed the philosopher. His eyes were of a deep and penetrating brown, and flashed into the darkened auditorium like darts from a bow. The flesh of his neck was furrowed with wrinkles; but the mouth was even and smooth like a boy's. On his cheeks was a bloom of artificial youth suggesting hours of attention before a mirror. His smart tunic, decorated with the purple sash of a royal companion, gave witness to his new-found social status, while his gestures, as he commanded the crowd to silence, were imperious and genial, emanating confidence and ease.

'Laodiceans!' he began. 'It gives me great pleasure to see so many of you here today, practising the sympathy for which you are famous. In the Greek cities, let me tell you, kindness of heart is a rarity; the old habits persist everywhere: indifference, coldness, hardness, punishment. Of course, these habits are known by other names: temperance, fortitude, wisdom, justice. Philosophers have written reams of nonsense in praise of the virtues, as they call them. But don't believe them. There is only one way to happiness, and that is feeling.'

There was a burst of applause, which Diogenes stretched out a hand to extinguish.

'Before we get down to business, I must remind you of an awkward truth. Not all feelings are equally good. Some are downright horrible. Fear, for instance. Fear of dogs, strangers, mice, failure. Some people eat and sleep with fear, drink jars of it twenty times a day. Fear waits for us in unexpected places. You sit down for a rest and fear comes quickly from the shade and sits beside you. Fear lingers in a smile or a kiss; comes running after you down country lanes; looks at you from the eyes of children. Fear is bad news. It ought to be sold cheap, if it is to be sold at all.

'But I'm going to ask you to bid as eagerly for fear and grief and anger as you will bid for love, compassion and hope. And I'll tell you why. The feelings we are selling off today have been properly packaged. They will not spill out or overflow but remain fresh and self-contained. You can entertain them at leisure, and they won't invade you or poison you or become part of yourself. You can sell them on for the same price or higher. Or you can store them somewhere safe and take them out from time to time to show your visitors.

'This, Laodiceans, is the triumph of our city. We have made feelings safe. Our emotions are spectacles, which can be staged whenever we desire. We feel them, of course. But at one remove: they are the work of sympathy. Fear may be horrible; but sympathy for fear is sweet. It comes in handy packages, tied with ribbons of self-love. A perfect gift for that special occasion, worth its own weight in gold.

'So now, Laodiceans, I shall proceed without further delay to our business. And what better way to begin than with fear itself?'

So saying he swung round and gestured to the wings. Drums rolled and flutes screamed while the audience murmured in anticipation. And then out rushed the paunchy man in armour, bowing and smiling and blowing kisses to the crowd. Ten obols, twenty, fifty, a drachma – at each offer he squealed like a whore with mock indignation. One drachma, two, two drachmas fifty, and then, at three drachmas Diogenes closed the sale with a clap of his hands, to loud cheering from the crowd.

Chapter 7

'Androcles, son of Ischion,' cried a voice from the back.

Diogenes summoned a slave to take down the purchaser's name, while the men of the chorus invaded the stage. To the accompaniment of flutes and drums, Fear was lifted into the air, and taken squeaking and squirming into the wings, to be replaced by Anger, who pouted most winsomely as her price began to soar. Diogenes rolled his eyes and slobbered, his lips writhing around the stream of patter, while his hands majestically carved the air.

'What am I bid now for this delicious morsel, three drachmas, four, a picture of wounded innocence, trembling like a bird, eyes begging for protection, five, five-fifty, five seventy at the back, surely you can do better than that Ladocieans, where is your heart? six I'm bid, six for this packet of helpless suffering, six-fifty . . .'

The crowd began first to murmur, and then to shout, as two large men pushed their way to the front and began to call out their bids. The price was pushed up to ten, then eleven, then twelve drachmas, the two men spitting out their bids in rage. The crowd set up a rhythmical chanting, above which the high tenor of Diogenes soared like the voice of an ecstatic priest. Before long the two bidders were locked in combat, one gripping the other's neck in a wrestler's hold, and squeezing with his arm until all breathing had stopped. Only when Diogenes accepted his bid of thirteen fifty, did he let his rival fall unconscious to the floor.

'Proteus, son of Hymion,' he said with a snarl, and strode from the hall.

Archeanassa began to tug again at Perictione's sleeve, beseeching her to come away from the degrading spectacle. But Perictione stood rooted to the spot, watching Diogenes with a cool scientific interest, and ignoring Archeanassa's pleas. It was several minutes before she could turn to her guest, and by then the hall was in uproar. Compassion was on offer, bidding had reached fifteen drachmas, and the crowd was waving frantically, each trying to jump higher than his neighbours in the effort to appeal to the stage. Diogenes seemed to snatch new numbers from the air, letting them fly from his fist like birds. As for Compassion, he was being contested over by furious women, each of whom had seized some portion of his anatomy and was pulling at it, relishing his agonised screams.

Without warning Diogenes turned and waddled into the wings. At that moment the crowd surged forward, rushing at the knot of bodies from which the now feeble cries of Compassion emerged in sobbing monotones. Archeanassa was swept off her feet, kicked and trampled. A sandalled foot came down on her outstretched hand. Then the tip of a sword, swinging from a belt above her head, caught in her hair and untied the tresses. The lights went out on the stage, and a scream of horror greeted the darkness. There was a rushing and stamping all around, and Archeanassa curled herself into a ball, breathing the dust and praying to the gods for protection.

And then she noticed a little ribbon of light, not far away, separating the floor from the darkness above it. She crawled across to discover a small door, set in the wall, which opened inwards. A figure was leaning against it, breathing heavily and groaning. Archeanassa gave him a sharp push and he sank down in a heap, leaving just enough room for her to turn the handle and squeeze past him into daylight. She shut the door behind her, and the noise of shouting and stamping was at once extinguished.

She found herself alone in a quiet courtyard, where a cistern stood amid flagstones, and an oleander bush with soft pink flowers grew in an old stone jar. The walls were pierced by scrubbed doors of walnut, and beside one of them stood a cage, in which a few brightly coloured birds were hopping from perch to perch. The quiet of this inner space astounded her. Not a murmur intruded from the auction room; the only sounds were those of the courtyard itself – small, muted, listening noises: a frog croaking in the cistern, a bird ruffling its wings, a soft exploring breeze passing through on its way from nowhere to nowhere.

She stood breathing the sweet air. A lizard poked its golden head from a shadow in the cistern, flashed in the sunlight, and was gone, leaving an intenser shadow behind him. A sound of running water briefly veneered the silence. From somewhere behind a wall came a soft patter of footsteps. And then all was still.

This was the Lydia she remembered: a place of inner tranquillity, governed by gentle and domestic gods. She went across to the bird-cage. The door beside it stood slightly ajar, showing a crack of darkness in the wall and a blade of light on the flagstones beneath it. She pushed the handle gently.

Light from the doorway fell across a table on which books were piled, roll upon roll, each in its protective sheath of leather. The walls too were lined with books, packed into shelves that reached the ceiling, where an opening, through which Archeanassa could see a lozenge of sky, let daylight into the room. Stools and boxes were scattered here and there, and they too were piled with books. Some had rolled on to the floor, which had the appearance of a battlefield strewn with corpses; others were shovelled up against the skirting. Archeanassa picked her way across in trepidation, as though entering the temple of some unknown god.

There were voices in an adjacent room: a man and a woman. It sounded at first like an argument. Approaching the door, however, Archeanassa recognized the unmistakeable rhythm of a philosophical dialogue. 'Yes,' then 'no,' then 'it would seem so,' punctuating dark but rhythmical questions. The speakers, she discovered to her astonishment, were Diogenes and Perictione. Standing behind the door, she could make out their words.

'So,' Diogenes was saying, 'when the tragic hero suffers some terrible misfortune, and we see and hear his distress, you will admit that we, the audience, feel pity and fear – knowing what will happen and also hoping absurdly that it won't?'

'Yes,' said Perictione, and Archeanassa was surprised by the meekness of her tone.

'And you will admit that this pity and fear dominate our feelings?'

'It would seem so.'

'Yet we go willingly to the theatre, eager to witness suffering, and feasting afterwards among our friends?'

'How can it be denied?'

'Tragedy, then, is one of our greatest pleasures?'

'Yes.'

'Which seems to imply that fear, for example, which we condemn as a form of pain, can also be a form of pleasure?'

'It would seem so, yes.'

'So, my dear, er . . .'

'Perictione.'

'So, my dear Perictione, that is the secret of Laodicea – to turn feelings into fictions. To exchange every emotion for its equivalent in thrills. Odd name, Perictione. You're not related to that old fraud Plato?'

'He is my uncle.'

'So it was his idea, was it, to sell me to Mitrobates, and ship me off to Lydia?'

'Actually no. You see, I needed the money. I'm sorry.'

'Oh, no need to apologize. You did me a favour. You started me on my journey, not only from Athens to Lydia, but from Diogenes the dog to Diogenes the poodle.'[4]

'I have certainly noticed a few cosmetic changes,' said Perictione.

'Not cosmetic at all. Changes in the very essence of the beast.'

There was a pause, during which Archeanassa pondered the mystery of Laodicea. Definitely, she concluded, Colophon was not so very bad. Yet this place where she stood, amid Greek books and Greek tranquillity, existed, like Perictione's villa, in another world, cut off from the surrounding madness. With a queer feeling, as though the ground had fallen away beneath her feet, she saw herself as a fiction – exchanged, as Diogenes described, for her imaginary equivalent in thrills.

---

4   Because of his disgusting habits, Diogenes was known as *to kuon* – the dog. From this word is derived the general label ('cynic') for Diogenes' school of philosophy.

'I don't suppose you will be surprised to learn,' the philosopher was saying, 'that I was not happy in my old kennel on the Cybelian rubbish-dump.'

'I did sometimes wonder why you snarled so much.'

'The fact is that the old cynical philosophy was a failure. I had tried to hide this failure from myself. But gradually it was brought home to me, as I raged against the illusions of the Athenians, that I was myself a victim of them. The old gods, the old virtues, the old ideas of beauty still held me in their grip. My rantings were an admission of weakness. I sneered at the gods out of respect for them – because I hoped against hope that they existed, or at least that I could provoke them into doing so. What my followers called the cynical philosophy was not a denial of the gods but an inverted affirmation of them.'

'We suspected as much,' said Perictione gently.

'But that is not all, Perictione. I scoffed at religion, defied morality and when it came to personal hygiene I was, you may have noticed, far from conventional. The real target of my rage, however, was not god but man – or, to be more precise, the divine in man, the thing which had perverted man from his nature as a sneaking, dealing, exploiting thing. I am referring, you understand, to love, the source and goal of our illusions, and especially of those illusions about the soul which your uncle specialised in. This ludicrous idea that we can attach ourselves to the pure individual, eternally and completely, and accept no substitute, no exchange – as though the laws governing the rest of nature were to be suspended for our sake, so that we could look into another's eyes and witness absolute freedom only to throw that freedom away in the self-sacrifice of love – this idea haunted and disgusted me. Why am I telling you this?'

'It's time you told *someone*.'

'You're right. Because every now and then I fall victim to it still, tempted into illusion by innocent eyes – as though innocence were not a fault, and in any case a fiction. At the time, however – and you may as well hear this confession – I had suffered a deep disappointment. Her name was Chloë, and her father was warden of the Erechtheum – a distinguished position which meant that in any case I could not hope to marry her. I used to meet her behind the Stoa, under the lime trees there. She would follow in silence wherever I beckoned, sit down modestly beside me on some promontory of stone, and then raise her still eyes to mine. I gazed for hours into those lovely eyes, not daring to touch her or even to speak, but just feeding my illusions. The Chloë who looked at me so meltingly was not, I believed, this lovely body, which could be matched by any number of equivalents. Nor was it the demure posture, the exquisite modesty, the graceful movement – all of which she shared with others who had taken my fancy. It was she herself, that unique, mysterious, irreplaceable thing, the inner essence, the soul – incarnate in that body and yet gazing from it as from another world. I was in the grip of the soul-illusion, and all desire in me was diverted through this celestial channel, as though I could unite with Chloë only in some higher realm. It was three weeks before I discovered that she was an imbecile.'

'Was that all?'

'It was enough – enough to persuade me that there is no safety in illusions, least of all in this one, of erotic love. Only a woofter like your uncle can examine such junk and still believe in it.'

Archeanassa, by now beside herself with indignation, seized the handle of the door and pushed her way into the room. Perictione and Diogenes, who were sitting opposite each other, separated by a table bearing fruit and wine, looked up in astonishment.

'What on earth has happened to you?' cried Perictione.

'Nothing, apart from hearing my life and loves insulted. You can take it from me, Diogenes, that there *is* such a thing as erotic love, that it is not an illusion, and that Plato, thanks to me, knows the experience well.'

'Well,' said the philosopher, not visibly perturbed, 'that

hardly explains your appearance, unless you have Plato too behind that door.'

'My appearance? What on earth do you mean?'

'Most honoured Archeanassa,' put in Perictione, 'you do look a sight: your hair undone, your face all smudged and your tunic in shreds at the bottom.'

'That is hardly surprising. Much more strange that you should have escaped without a blemish.'

'Do you think so?' Perictione gave a pert little smile. 'Still, I'm glad you made it. I *was* a little worried.'

Diogenes, who had lapsed into a musing state, his smooth hands folded on his pudgy stomach, suddenly smiled and sat up.

'Archeanassa! Of course – she of Colophon! How did it go? "Upon whose very wrinkles sits desire." You've got to give it to Plato: he could try his hand at anything. And not only his hand.'

'Most noble Perictione,' said Archeanassa, 'I am astonished that you should seek the company of so coarse a person as this Diogenes, and only hope that you have made suitable arrangements for my speedy return to Colophon, now that my tutorial in Laodicean manners has been accomplished.'

'Relax, my dear,' said Perictione. 'Think of him as a dream. I really can't tell you how much he has *improved* since first I knew him. And even then, he meant no harm.'

'She's right there,' added Diogenes, 'only I could never admit it at the time. Do take a seat, honoured Archeanassa. It is so rare that I am able to entertain a lady celebrated in a work of literature, however marginal.'

The studied ambiguity of this remark momentarily silenced her. Diogenes, however, gave what was clearly intended to be a welcoming smile, of a slightly theatrical kind, gesturing the while to a vacant stool beside Perictione.

'Well,' Archeanassa said at last, 'since I must wait for my transport to Colophon, and Perictione is obviously not yet in a mood to provide it, I suppose the choice is between sitting and standing.'

A dream of Diogenes; the cynical philosophy explained

'Make yourself at home,' Diogenes pursued. 'There are plenty of books if you want to browse.'

He waved to the room which was, like the one through which Archeanassa had entered, piled high with scrolls. Light from a window in the corner fell across an antique table, on which styluses and inkwells were neatly arranged beside a roll of fresh papyrus. Diogenes leaned forward and pushed the bowl of wine across to Archeanassa. Following a slight show of reluctance, she drank as deeply as she dared.

'I was explaining,' Diogenes said, 'the new cynical philosophy. When, in my old character as Diogenes the dog, I railed against the official illusions, it was, as I was saying to Perictione, because I secretly subscribed to them. Only here, in Laodicea, have I found true freedom. Now those old illusions – God, the soul, love, loyalty – found a powerful advocate in Plato. I'm sorry ladies, but I can't forebear speaking disrespectfully of that old fraud. You would feel the same, if you had tried to earn your keep as a philosopher in Athens, and been forced to try every damned trick in the trade, even living in a barrel and eating vermin, in order to create some faint reputation that would cut into Plato's monopoly of the market. I was much better off out of it, I can tell you. And though I was worried when they shipped me over to Lydia, I discovered that Mitrobates was rather a decent sort of satrap. Unlike the Athenians, he didn't regard me as a second-rate example of the philosophical way of life, but as his own unique possession, which he couldn't wait to show off to his friends.

'To be frank, it was a relief to find myself on Persian soil, without need for the old disguise. My first bath in years, barber and masseuse, robes and perfumes, magnificent feasts, dancing girls – and paid for by Mitrobates. All I had to do in exchange was to stage some philosophy once a week, for the benefit of Mitrobates' cronies. I did little one-man shows, take-offs of Plato and Socrates, tongue-in-cheek stories about the soul and its eternal destiny, about love and beauty and the divine spark in man. Of course they were far too thick to rumble me. For all they could guess, I actually believed the gibberish I spouted. And in fact it was precisely by spouting it, rather than railing against it, that I at last freed myself from its grip.

'Here is how I came to see things, ladies. The old stories of God and the soul had not been believed because of the arguments that weighed in their favour, for there were none – or none that could stand up to a moment's examination. No. They had been believed because of the feelings grafted on to them. These feelings owed their strength and persistence to forces which had nothing to do with the individual at all – forces rooted in the old forms of human society. The sacred stories limited the sphere of human choice. Under their influence feelings ceased to be temporary states which we could discard and exchange, and became instead part of our very selves. Of no feeling is this more true than sex. Sex was reforged as love – the eternal bond between individuals, from which, once contracted, they could never be free – the bond that I had once imagined between myself and a moron called Chloë. By linking all our feelings to virtues and vices, the philosophers had made emotion into a part of human character. Accident had become essence, and humanity had been enslaved by its own passing appetites.

'But we are not such creatures as the philosophers describe. We live by strife; we pursue the things that attract us and discard the things with which we are bored. And this is as true of emotions as it is of everything else. In this sphere too, what people really want is a market. Morality is there to prevent the market from forming, just as Plato had prevented the market in philosophy by dictating from his Academy.

'Now the old illusions attach us forever to things which we would rather discard – feelings that have outlasted their charm, opinions that nobody needs, habits that lead us to failure. The person brought up on illusions therefore lives in a state of disillusion – unless he learns to buy and sell on the open market, as they do in Laodicea.'

Here Archeanassa, who had reapplied herself to the bowl of wine, suddenly put it down with a bang on the table.

A dream of Diogenes; the cynical philosophy explained

'This is preposterous!' she cried. 'Real love cannot be bought and sold. The very suggestion is nonsense.'

'Precisely,' Diogenes pursued. 'That is what led me to my great discovery. What we call "real" love, "real" compassion, "real" grief and so on are fictions. Each of them looks to the soul, as unique, individual, indivisible, unexchangeable, eternal, and similar nonsense. While in the grip of real love we follow an impossible path – a path whose impossibility is not just practical but metaphysical. Our very language, built over centuries, condemns us to repeat the old lies, so that each generation automatically enslaves itself, just by learning to speak.

'But then, I said to myself, these feelings which destroy us in life, leave us quite undamaged in the theatre. Love, anger, hatred, grief, desire – all rush through us as we watch and listen, and all are enjoyed. Nothing harms us, nothing poisons us, nothing becomes part of us, as those "real" emotions are part of us. And if on one day it is grief that we find interesting, and on another day love, we have but to choose the most suitable performance, and the emotion is offered on a plate.

'If we could transport into real life the principles that govern the theatre, I concluded, we could finally break the old monopoly on human feeling. We could market love, grief and the rest, as *fakes*. Teach people to live their lives as part of a drama – though not, I admit, a drama of the highest quality – and you will give them freedom. Emotions can now be purchased over the counter. And as with any market, the goods become cheaper and cheaper until, as here in Laodicea, they are worth nothing at all.'

Diogenes rocked backwards and forwards in his chair, without the faintest suggestion of a smile.

'And of course,' said Archeanassa, 'this philosophy of yours is also a fake.'

Diogenes thought for a moment.

'When I first came to Laodicea,' he said, 'five years ago, it was to bid for a collection of books left by an old Greek, priest of Apollo, whose library had come to the attention of

145

Mitrobates. Now for a long time I had been wanting to try out my new philosophy, and what better place than a free city, run on market principles? I sent word to Mitrobates that I had travelled on to Susa, having heard of another and better library for sale. With the money he had entrusted to me, I set up an experimental theatre here in Laodicea. Only small-scale stuff, and with just a few second-hand actors. But with live sex on stage, and gushings of love, compassion and what have you, I began to pull in the crowds. Of course, it all had to be done rather discretely: religion still fought its hopeless battle with the market; there was a prejudice against obscenity, as it was quaintly called, and a council of old buffoons still laid down the law. Little by little, however, word got around, and soon the theatre was packed each evening. The Laodiceans quickly came to accept my product, which fitted in so well with their way of life. I was able to expand the business, set up a proper auction house, and mount spectacles like the one you saw today. And success breeds success. Thanks to my business, the Laodiceans began to change. They rapidly lost their illusions, ceased to see the world in religious terms, forgot all the crap about real loyalty and real love, and began for the first time to enjoy themselves. My philosophy was vindicated.

'But you are right, Archeanassa. My philosophy is also a kind of fake. I don't regard this as a criticism, mind. An enjoyable fake is much to be preferred to a miserable reality. If there were such a thing as real philosophy, it would involve a restless pursuit of truth, an avid questioning and doubting, a general accusation against the world, and a troubled call on God to stop dithering and begin existing instead. My fake philosophy leads in a contrary direction. Truth, to me, is unattainable; thinking leads nowhere; and our best hope is to turn our back on God and his fastidious requirements and to make no judgements at all. Do have some more wine.'

Diogenes was smiling now, but it was not a smile of triumph. The new cynicism may have worked its magic on the people of Laodicea, but its inventor was clearly disappointed with it – such was the impression that he made on

Archeanassa. Nor did Perictione seem persuaded. Having sat in silence through the philosopher's apology, she now pushed her bowl to one side and began to question him.

'What exactly do you do?' she asked.

'What do I do?'

'Yes. What do you do here, in Laodicea, when you are not engaged in an auction?'

'Well, that's easy. I retire to my kennel.'

He gestured to the room.

'But what do you do in your kennel?'

'I read. Sometimes I write.'

'So these books are all yours?'

Diogenes looked at Perictione for a long moment.

'I have made a hobby of books, certainly,' he said. 'Though whether they are exactly mine is a moot point. People just throw them out. Or else they use them to wrap up fish and meat, paste them over cracks, feed them to pigs and burn them instead of firewood. It would break your uncle's heart to see how books are treated over here. So I have done exactly what Mitrobates intended, and acquired as much as I can of the Laodicean libraries. Not that Mitrobates will ever see the result.'

'And why have you done this?'

Diogenes gave her a melancholy smile.

'Well yes, I admit it, I cannot enjoy life as the Laodiceans do. Once a philosopher, always a philosopher, if only a fake. When I am not working, I read. To be quite frank, Perictione, people disgust me.'

'Yes,' put in Archeanassa, 'since you have made them disgusting.'

'Oh it was not my doing, I assure you. I provide the goods: the market does the rest. And markets are blameless. No, Archeanassa, people make *themselves* disgusting. And it is their right. Who are we to forbid them?'

'I would rather say: who are we to permit them?' retorted Archeanassa.

'But there you have it,' Diogenes went on. 'The new philosophy, unlike the old, is a philosophy of permission. All I ask of the world is that it should allow me what I want. If other people want something else, so be it. The only desideratum is space. And my space, you see,' he went on, with a strange look in his eye, 'is an inner space – the space of this undiscovered courtyard, where I sit alone with the dead.'

'With all those,' said Perictione, 'whose illusions you despise.'

'You are wrong, my dear. I am irresistibly drawn to those illusions. They are the symbolic framework for great works of art – works like those of Homer or Pindar or Aeschylus which so far surpass in imagination and understanding anything that could be sold off next door, that I can regard them as my exclusive and private possession, the thing that inwardly distinguishes me, the thing that justifies the burning contempt I feel for every human being that I see.'

He paused to take another mouthful of wine.

'Present company excepted, of course.'

Diogenes' voice had lost its self-confident sheen, and he now spoke quietly and hoarsely, staring down as he did so into his bowl. He himself seemed visibly to have shrunk, his chin collapsed on to his chest and his arms held tight against his sides. The crust of pomade had broken away from his cheeks, showing patches of cheesy skin which trembled as he spoke.

'And there it is, ladies. Diogenes the realist is also a fake. Having killed off the old illusions, he now resurrects them – as things imagined, rather than things believed. But the distinction between imagination and belief has no real meaning for him. He might as well believe in the old gods, therefore, and have done with it. And, to tell you the truth, when the evening shadows fill the courtyard, and one by one the stars appear, I often sing to myself the old hymns, offering my thanks to beings who are more real, in that moment, than I am.'

He shook his head sadly, and Archeanassa felt a wave of pity. Yet she could not help thinking that the loneliness of

Diogenes in his book-lined kennel was a fitting punishment for his sinful trade.

There was a silence, during which Perictione glanced at Archeanassa and nodded to the door, quietly unfolding her body and reaching with one foot for her sandals.

'Yes,' Diogenes went on in a whisper, 'the cynical philosophy is a great success. It shows people as they are, with all the sacred nonsense wiped away. And for the same reason it is a catastrophic failure. People as they are don't compare with people as they might be, or as they would be if the gods existed. The true cynic, therefore, must take refuge in the very illusions that his thinking destroyed, living, as I do, an imaginary life among imaginary people. People, my dears, like you.'

By this time the two women had tip-toed to the door. Archeanassa turned to take a last glance at the drunken Diogenes. He was slumped over his bowl of wine, and beginning to snore, his hand clawing at the table like an infant's. She turned and followed Perictione through the outer library into the courtyard, and then, by a passage between two stone cottages, out into the sunlit street.

'What a bore he has become!' said Perictione. 'I much preferred the disgusting old dog. At least he had a sense of humour.'

Then, putting two fingers in her mouth and blowing hard, she made an ear-splitting whistle, which caused the shoppers in the street to turn in amazement. At once the chariot appeared from behind the opinion shop, coming towards them at a brisk canter, and skidding to a halt where they stood. A uniformed guard, appearing from nowhere, handed them up into the car, behind the impassive driver and his polished horses. Before Archeanassa could collect her thoughts, they were cantering back to Colophon, the sun sinking rapidly before them and Perictione, a faint smile playing along her lips, humming the sweet old hymn to Aphrodite.

8

A memory of Xanthippe, with her views on dancing

Archeanassa started awake to discover Perictione, who stood by the open window through which morning sunlight streamed into the room.

'Sorry for the delay,'she said, 'but you looked as though you needed the sleep.'

'Most noble Perictione, I have had the strangest dream.'

'Yes. That tends to happen in this room. About Diogenes was it? Or Merope?'

'Diogenes,' she replied with astonishment.

'Then don't believe a word of it,' Perictione said. 'What were we supposed to talk about today?'

'I believe it was dancing.'

Perictione stood for a while in thought, and then turned with a faint smile towards her visitor.

'Good. I propose to fill our day with the memory of Xanthippe. I have not convinced you, I know, of my darling's virtues, nor have I justified my love for her – if love is what it was. But about Xanthippe we are probably in agreement, and since what she said to me bears directly on our discussions, I propose to recall it now.'

'I shall listen the more eagerly, most noble Perictione, in that my heart has greatly softened towards poor Merope, and no doubt will soften more.'

'You are too kind,' said Perictione coldly, 'though I

should point out that Merope hated nothing more than a softened heart – unless it was a softened head.'

So saying she clapped her hands for the servant and ordered octopus and lupins, calves' brains, beetroot and fillet of mule – to be delivered in three hours time, when, by her calculations, her appetite would be restored.

'You must understand,' she began, 'that this discussion took place a year or two before I had met Merope, when I was far more prim and proper than I subsequently became.'

Archeanassa's polite protests were waved impatiently aside.

'I happened to be walking with Xanthippe one afternoon in the Agora,' Perictione went on, 'when we were overtaken by a gang of young men hurrying in a state of excitement. Stopping one of them, Xanthippe enquired into the cause of their haste, and was told that Xylophantes and his Screaming Corybants were about to perform at the Odeion.'

'"And why is that so interesting?" she asked.

'The young man looked confused.

'"Why," he replied, "the music is wonderful. We listen and jig about. Sometimes we throw up our arms, and there are those who scream."

'"And what is the point of doing that?"

'"It's not something you *do*," the young man said, after a moment's hesitation; "it's something that happens."

'"But still, there must be a point to it," she persisted.

'"Yes. It's therapeutic. Gets it out of your system."

'Being impatient to join his companions, he cut the conversation short and hurried after them. Xanthippe pondered the young man's words for a while, and then turned to me.

'"Have you ever noticed," she asked, "that when people wish to deny responsibility for their actions, they will describe them in medical terms?"

'I asked her to explain.

'"I mean, when asked the point of doing something, they refer to its effect on the organism. Just as this young man believes that the purpose of listening to Xylophantes is to rid his system of some poison, in the same way, you notice, people justify obscene pictures, and lewdness in the theatre. It rids us of our base desires, they say, and so makes for a healthier community. Without it, people would put into practice what otherwise they are content to see merely represented on the stage. Have you not heard this defence?"

'Indeed I had, and I begged Xanthippe to explain what is wrong with it.

'"Had our young man stayed awhile, I should have asked him what he meant, when he told us that his jigging and screaming 'gets it out of the system.' Maybe this frenzy puts it *into* the system. For have you not noticed how those who poison themselves with wine, like my poor Socrates, will always tell you that by drinking they rid themselves of something worse?"

'"Yes," I said, "and they assume the right to say things and do things which decency forbids, on the assumption that they thereby rescue us all from the threat that they might say or do these things when sober."

'"I see that you understand my point," she replied. "It is with wine as with other drugs that we take when our bodies have no need of them. It fills the soul with emotions that seem of the greatest importance, as though our very essence were distilled in them, and yet which, once released into the air of rational discourse, vanish at once, insubstantial as dreams. And while these feelings live in us, we remain convinced that we are fulfilling a long-delayed duty to our psyche, and that our more sober companions are repressing their nature in a dangerous way."

'"But surely, Xanthippe, there are forces in the psyche which we barely understand, which operate, as it were, without our consent, and which we must strive to release if we are not to succumb to them."

'"Do you think so?" she replied, and fell silent.

'As you know, the philosopher had the habit of dawdling, and would sometimes come to a complete standstill, oblivious to her companions, awaking with a start after several minutes as though surprised by her surroundings. Witnessing the admiration that this conduct excited, I am told, Socrates had tried to copy it, but with patchy success. I was not surprised, therefore, when Xanthippe drifted to one side of the road and, without so much as a sign that the conversation had ended, began to stare into the horse-pond by the temple of Demeter.

'I came to her side, and for several minutes stood to watch two ducks, male and female, which had settled in the middle of the pond and were circling each other with bright and expectant eyes. A kind of rhythmic dance began, the female weaving in a double loop and the male imitating her, so as to remain alongside. It was a charming sight, and I became so absorbed by it as almost to forget that the greatest philosopher in Hellas, the teacher of Socrates, was standing dumbstruck next to me. The female duck took sudden fright, and rose in the air with a rush of wings and water, her mate in hot pursuit. Xanthippe, jolted from her stupor, seized me by the arm and resumed her speech.

'"Often you hear tell, do you not, of courtship among the animals. How many poets have delighted us with their descriptions of the birds, who seem to approach each other with such shame-clad interest, who dance as those two did, fleeing to another place only to dance and delay again. And this behaviour, so like that of human lovers, invites us to describe it as we should our own. These birds, we say, are driven by love and desire, they pay court to each other, dance in anticipation, and finally join in a bond of love, as though the vow of marriage awaited at the end of all their agitation. Do you not see an error in this?"

'"A charming error, Xanthippe."

'"Precisely. And you know that there are two kinds of charm: the charm of enchantment, and its opposite, the charm of disenchantment, the charm which compels us to take all charm away."

'I asked her to explain this paradox.

'"Just as a man can be delighted by the behaviour of a

dog, when he sees it as he would the conduct of his human friend, so can he be delighted by the conduct of a human being, when he sees it as he would the behaviour of a dog. There, he tells himself, is the truth of our condition! And like as not he laughs. I think you know this state of mind?"

"'Surely I do, Xanthippe," I answered. For already Diogenes was making a name for himself with this kind of propaganda.

"'Alone among the works of nature," she went on, "the rational being is subject to illusions. Only the rational being has an interest in falsehood. His world is not given but created, and he himself draws up the plan. It is a world made in his own image, and in making it he makes himself. When we observe the natural order, we do not confront impersonal forces or a blind machine. We look into a mirror, and our own face returns our gaze. For us, the wind does not make a sound only: it howls, moans and sings to us. The sun smiles on us, and when we walk along the shore on a summer night, the sea sleeps for us beneath the moon. Truly 'all things are full of gods,'[1] and all happenings are doings – though we don't know whose. We coax nature from her mute detachment with our prayers, and bring her into the human community. We dress her as a person, make her a partner in our dialogue, and endow her with will, freedom and an immortal soul. When we describe the mating of birds as though it were the courtship of man and woman, we merely continue the story, seeing all that lives and moves in human terms.

"'Illusions are necessary. But they are never secure. And this, my dear Perictione, is our modern destiny. We knew the world of our ancestors, and we knew how full and beautiful it was. But we saw that its beauty depended on a false idea. The cynics and sceptics expelled the poets and priests. We had given nature a face, they told us, but the face was ours and moved only with our own emotions – like the mask of the actor which lives and changes with the spectator's mood. Unmasked at last, nature is mute, impassive,

---

1   Thales.

governed not by will or reason but by the iron laws of physics. The gods, we have discovered, are no more lasting than the temples built to worship them, and if the world endures for us, it endures without a soul."

'I could not help remarking, as Xanthippe spoke these words, that she glanced towards the temple of Demeter and then lowered her eyes, as though to ask that the goddess forgive her. I should add, honoured guest, that this all took place pre-Merope, when I had not worked out as clearly as I should that Demeter had just as much and just as little power as people had the will to believe in her.

'"But this is only one half of our predicament," Xanthippe went on. "The disenchanted world is one in which our projects and desires find no endorsement. All around us we encounter cold, unyielding and metallic things. Our methods of enquiry, the philosophers tell us, show the world as it really is, and it is a godless world – a world in which every change is explained by causes and in which nothing has a goal, not even those things like the mating of ducks, which seem so full of purpose. And we ourselves are part of this world, offspring of the natural order, animals like any other, who differ from the rest of creation only in our need to tell ourselves consoling stories – including the story of creation itself.

'"Our efforts to live in such a world, while safeguarding all that has been most dear to us, are attended by grief of a kind which only a rational being can know. And thence arises the charm of disenchantment. Knowing that we cannot stand against the force of science, we decide instead to join it. We pull down our dear illusions, hurry impatiently onwards, to the point where nature will be stripped of her moral clothing, and stand before us as she really is – not a she but an it. In this way we take revenge on the hopes which disappointed us.

'"And then we invent for ourselves another story, the story to end all stories. The old illusions, we tell ourselves, were the enemies of happiness. It was they which set us against our fellow men, which bound us in chains, and which cheated us of love and life and freedom. We have nothing to fear from science; on the contrary, only when the cloud of illusion has been dispelled will we know what it is to be free. And we begin to hunt the world for illusions, in order to expose the imposture by which the mind of man was governed. Every attempt to clothe the world in will and personality is derided, and bit by bit the face is scratched from the world's cold surface, until nothing of our image remains.

'"Nor does the process end when the gods have been driven from their sanctuaries and dispelled into air. For amid the ruined temples unhappy faces linger, uncertain of their destiny, forsaken and forsworn. These, we persuade ourselves, are the victims, who suffer, not from the loss of their convictions, but from the fact of having once possessed them. Better to be born with no illusions, than to see our world destroyed."

'"Naturally," I answered the great philosopher, "this state of mind is familiar to me, for I was brought up in the midst of it. No other joy has been offered to my generation, than the joy of pulling things down. Nevertheless, the charm of disenchantment seems only a thin reward. The cynics tell us to distrust the old illusions as the enemies of freedom. But they also tell us that greatest among our illusions is that of freedom itself. In which case we shall emerge from our illusions only to know the full extent of our bondage. We will know ourselves as parts of the great machine, our life no more significant than the life of the animals, and blameless as theirs. Indeed, this is now happening, and even explains the feelings of that young man, as he joined in the stampede to hear the songs of Xylophantes. For such young people there are no gods, but only human idols."

'Xanthippe stood for a while in thought.

'"But are these idols not illusions too?"

'"I think not," I replied, "and I shall tell you why, O most revered Xanthippe. When Xylophantes gets up on stage it is for two purposes – first to sing a tuneless song, the words of which are full of a cynical distaste. The second is to shake and writhe and squawk – to become animal, or lower still than animal, a part of the machine. And in this way his followers, led by the charm of disenchantment, find their idol converted, in the very act of worship, into something spiritless and strange. Here before them is the very truth of their condition – the world as it is in itself, free from all enchantment, free even from freedom itself. And in worshipping this thing, the followers of Xylophantes throw in their lot with emptiness, acknowledge that nothing matters, since mattering is a mere illusion, and glory in the nothingness of human hopes."

'"Well," said Xanthippe, "this is grim indeed. But you do not imply, I hope, that you share the feelings which you describe? Or am I to infer that no-one in your generation can escape them?"

'I found it hard to answer her. For as I said the other day, most honoured guest, I had made my own ventures into the sordid world of my contemporaries. I knew their music and their dances, their drugs and drinks and boorish language, had been charmed by the tantalising dresses which they had made for brute stupidity, and had joined with them in mocking the high culture in which I had been raised, and to which I have since returned, though at a higher and more conscious level.

'Not that I had the remotest desire to live in their lower world even then. Far from it; my ambition was to be a lyric poet, a dancer in the high tradition to which Granny belonged and perhaps one day tyrant of some small but distinguished city somewhere in the Aegean. Still, I was young, and needed to share what others of my age were feeling. Hence I had come to experience this "charm of disenchantment" from inside. And I held the feeling as it were suspended within me, turning it over and over in the withering light of consciousness, knowing that it belonged to the lowest part of me and was, in truth, a rank betrayal of my inheritance. Only later, when Merope had shown me the way, was

I able to betray my inheritance willingly and gladly. But by then I knew that I was betraying my betrayer.

'In any case, my reply was to shrug my shoulders, as though to shake off Xanthippe's question. She suggested that we sit for a while, since her bones were weary, and finding a hospitable table by the sanctuary of Delphic Apollo, I called out for fruit and water to refresh us. After we had eaten, and gossipped about matters of no philosophical importance, Xanthippe returned to her theme.

'"Tell me," she inquired, "do they really dance to the music of Xylophantes – if music it is?"

'"Well, as the young man said, they sway and jig about."

'"Would you call it dancing?" she asked.

'"What's in a word?"

'"Nothing," she answered, "short of everything. Words rightly used and to good effect show the truth of things. And here I see an answer to our great dilemma."

'"What great dilemma?"

'"Well, we did not express it quite so drastically. But our problem, you recall, was this. If we follow the philosophers, and look for the truth of things, then one by one the gods and heroes vanish, religion, morality, beauty and freedom follow them in disarray, and nothing remains save the meaningless machinery of nature. If, on the other hand, we follow the priests and the poets, and try to live in an enchanted world, we are haunted by the knowledge that this world is our creation. What can be made can also be unmade, and bears no authority greater than our own desire. Moreover, whatever I make is a lesser being than I. Hence the gods lose their power over me. I cease to stand in awe of them and piety, far from being restored to us, receives a mortal blow. The dilemma is that we seem to have no path before us save these two, and the end of each is disillusion."

'"So what is your answer?"

'"Let us take a retreating step. I asked you whether you would describe those movements, prompted by the noise of Xylophantes, as dancing."

'"Yes. And I still wonder why we should avoid the word."

'"You remember the ducks on the horse-pond? Well, were *they* dancing?"

'"Their movements were like a dance, certainly."

'"But not really a dance."

'"I agree with you, Xanthippe, but for the life of me I cannot say why."

'"Then you have forgotten your grandmother's lessons. Few things were more important to her, as I recall, than rules – the rules of etiquette and morality, as well as those of harmony and style. And dancing is governed by rules."

'"The ducks too appeared to follow a rule, as they swam in loops together."

'"Appeared to follow a rule, yes. But we must distinguish rule from regularity. The heart which beats in steady rhythm obeys no rule in doing so. Rules exist only where there is the possibility of disobedience, and only where we can distinguish the right way from the wrong way to proceed."

'"Perhaps, then, it is only rational beings who can obey a rule."

'"And are ducks rational?"

'"I suppose not," I said, 'though I could not prove the point.'

'"Let's delay the proof, for we do not need it. Imagine Calliope, a nervous woman who claps her hands involuntarily whenever she enters a room. And imagine Pasariste, a bold egoist who has formed the policy of entering any room with a clap of the hands, as though to announce herself. To outward appearances these women behave in the same way, do they not?"

'"I suppose so."

'"Yet they are doing different things. Their movements are identical, but their actions distinct. Calliope's clap is a habit, Pasariste's a policy. The first is a regularity, the second a rule."

Chapter 8

'"So far I accept your argument," I said.

'"Could we make such a distinction in the case of a duck? Could we distinguish a duck which regularly quacked on taking flight, from a duck which quacked as a matter of policy?"

'"What conceivable grounds could there be, for making such a distinction?"

'"I think we could generalize the point, could we not? Animals are creatures of habit, as we are. But their habits are not chosen. When a bird meets a female and struts before her, we do not think of this as a custom – as though the bird had learned these manners and now took pleasure in displaying them. Such movements come into being as the heart-beat comes into being: they belong to the repertoire of instinct. If they look like a dance, it is only in the way that regularities sometimes look like rules. But where we cannot distinguish rule from regularity, we cannot speak of rule."

'"And, therefore," I put in, "we cannot speak of dancing."

'"I assume not," she said.

'"But perhaps there are dances that have no rules."

'"No rules," she added, "save this one: that there should be no rules."

'"Which permits me to say," I replied, "that the followers of Xylophantes are, in their own way, dancing."

'"Let me make another distinction," she said, ignoring me. "Many of our actions have a purpose, have they not?"

'"Indeed they have."

'"For instance, my purpose on going out today was to set up shop by the tomb of old Socks[2] and sell my tapestries. And this I should now be doing, had I not fallen in with my friend Perictione and, for the sake of philosophy, cancelled my resolve."

'"You are too kind," I said.

---

2 Xanthippe's habit of referring to her husband by the nickname given to him by Aristophanes dated from the earliest days of her marriage. See 'Xanthippe's Republic', in *Xanthippic Dialogues*.

A memory of Xanthippe, with her views on dancing

'"But do all our actions have a purpose?"

'"Surely they do – for purpose is the mark of a rational being, who does nothing without a reason, and is answerable before god and man for all that she does."

'"To act without purpose," Xanthippe said, "is not to act without reason. Consider this conversation: does it have a purpose?"

'"No single purpose," I conceded.

'"Surely," she insisted, "no purpose at all. Else why should we find it so agreeable?"

'"But do we not aim at the truth?"

'"Speak for yourself," she said. "Even if truth is my long-term hope, it is not my aim in speaking now. So far as I can see, I am enjoying myself. And it is the conversation that I enjoy, wherever it may lead, and even if it turns in some quite frivolous direction, or takes the form of my chats with your grandmother, in which only irony and paradox were welcome."

'"Are you saying that conversation is purposeless?" I asked.

'"Not purposeless, but not purposeful either. Or rather say that it is purposeful without purpose. And the same is true of much that we most esteem."

'I seemed to recall this idea from another context. Maybe it was one of Granny's sayings, though she had so many, since, for her at any rate, conversation did have a purpose, which was to lift the mask of common sense – not in order to expose the bare reality, but so as to replace the mask with a more amusing one of her own. But I digress.

'"And since we are in a mood for distinctions," Xanthippe went on, "let me make another: that between purpose and function. When we enquire into the nature of dancing, we ought surely to consider the broader category to which it belongs – the category of play. It is obvious, is it not, that play has a function: it is the safest way to explore the world, and to prepare the child for action. But this function is not the purpose. The child plays because she wants to play: play is its *own* purpose. Indeed, if you make the

161

function into a purpose – playing for the sake of learning, say – then you cease to play. You are now merely in earnest, as some barbarian philosopher once expressed it."[3]

'"Let me take another example. Friendship has a function: it binds people together, making communities strong and durable; it brings advantages to those who are joined by it, and fortifies them in all their works. But make those advantages into your purpose, and the friendship vanishes – for the motive of friendship has been undermined. Friendship is a means to advantage, but only when not treated as a means. The same is true of everything worthwhile – education, for instance, sport, hunting, oh yes, and dancing. You might say that all time that is not spent in such pursuits is wasted time. I think it was Xenophon who said as much, in his book on hunting."[4]

'"But surely people often dance for a purpose," I protested. "For example, they dance at the festivals so as to honour the gods. I have heard of people who dance in order to summon the rain, and when *I* dance it is with a view to shaming those who imagine they could dance as well as a grand-daughter of the great Perictione."

'Xanthippe thought for a while, and then answered:

'"Consider the game of draughts. This too may be played 'for a purpose.' There are those who play draughts with their neighbours, for the purpose of friendship. There

---

3   It is well known that Perictione the Great, mother of Plato and grandmother of Perictione, was influenced by Shakespeare, Hegel and Oscar Wilde, and that this retrospective influence made a real contribution to the development of Athenian culture. See 'Perictione's Parmenides', in *Xanthippic Dialogues*. However, there is no evidence that Xanthippe had such a talent, and therefore we must assume that the barbarian philosopher to whom she refers is not Schiller but some now forgotten precursor.

4   Xenophon, *Kynergetikos*. Although Xenophon implies this, he never explicitly says it. A much later, post-Xanthippic, philosopher tells us that 'all time wot is not spent in 'unting is wasted time' (Jorrocks, as reported by R.S. Surtees in *Handley Cross*).

are those who play in order to relax, or to demonstrate their skills. But all these purposes must be set aside, the moment we begin to play. The player has one purpose only – which is to play as best he can, and according to the rules. If his purpose were to make friends, who knows whether this might not be more effectively achieved by disobeying the rules, by fooling about, by deliberately losing or by exchanging draughts for some other game? When playing we are purposeful: but there is no purpose which animates our actions, beyond the aim of playing draughts."

'"And you say the same of dancing?"

'"Not exactly. For I admit that dancing is complex, and I am describing only a part of it – although a central part, I think, and the one which explains the high esteem in which this art is held."

'"And do you distinguish the purpose of dancing – which for you is dancing itself – from its function?"

'"I do," she replied. "But I should say that dancing has many functions. It teaches us to make graceful gestures, to move in a pleasing way. Through dancing we learn charm and cheerfulness, and come to know the life within us and its inexhaustible flowing. None of these are *why* we dance: think of these things while dancing and you will quickly tie yourself in knots. But there is also a deeper function to dancing, and one of which we Athenians know less, I think, than our Aeolian cousins."[5]

'"You mean the erotic?" I said, recalling the experience with Parmenides which Granny was so fond of relating.[6]

'"If you insist. But the erotic is only part of it; and let us be under no illusions – the erotic exists in many forms and is

---

5 Xanthippe may be referring to the choirs of young girls, for whom Sappho wrote many songs, and which formed little domestic clubs suffused by a quasi-erotic tenderness. It was to such a club that Merope belonged in her early days in Sardis. See Claude Calame, *Les Choeurs de jeunes filles en Grèce archaïque*, two vols., Rome, 1977.

6 The experience is recounted by the elder Perictione in 'Perictione's Parmenides,' *Xanthippic Dialogues*, op. cit.

shaped by its expression. And this too is a function of the dance – not to release our erotic feelings, but to give them discipline and form. Rather than describe this function as erotic, I should prefer the word 'nuptial.' For it captures the strange phenomenon I have in mind."

'"And what is that?"

'"Let us return to the ducks. What tempted us to describe them as dancing was not the rhythm of their movements so much as their moving together in time: they were fitting their motion to a common pattern. Now it seems to me that there are two forms of dancing. There is that of which you are so skilled a practitioner, which you can dance alone as much as in company, and which is in some way addressed to the spectator. And this I should number among the theatrical arts, since it is not so much an action performed as an action represented. In this kind of dancing you become a mask, and that is why your grandmother was so good at it. But there is also the dancing which is available to the rest of us, and this kind of dancing is a human action, performed in company, and addressed to the others with whom we dance.

'"And here is the deep reason, as it seems to me, why animals cannot dance. For consider what it means when we 'dance with' another – how much is captured in the little word 'with'! It is as though the music became an intermediary between you and me, giving to my feet not only a cause of movement, but a just reason, a reason that lies in you. The 'why' of my step lies in that step of yours, and over my feet and yours there lies the charm of music, so that we move not only with each other, but with that purely spiritual thing, the music, whose motion is not of the body at all. Thus rightly does Pindar say 'the footstep hears, as the dance begins.'[7] The footstep of a person who dances is no longer the step of an animal – for no animal is so completely without purpose as this, and at the same time so fully guided by reason."

'"And yet," I put in, "is this not the music's doing?"

7   *Pythian* Odes, no. 1.

'"Music," she replied, "lives in the one who listens. Music is not sound, any more than sculpture is bronze. It is the living order that we hear in sound, when we hear it as music. To hear this order is to move with the music, which becomes a voice for us, the voice of the other with whom we dance."

'I sensed in Xanthippe's words so vast a weight of theory, honoured guest, that I refrained from asking her to explain them, lest we should lose the thread of our conversation. So I gently reminded her that she had promised to describe the deeper function of the dance.

'"Yes," she said, "I was coming to that. For it is this little word 'with' that leads us to our goal. It is a word upon which I have often meditated, since it describes my own condition. I am with old Socks, and have been with him, moving with him, talking with him, singing with him, in all the long years since he died. 'Being with' is a state of the soul, a direction outwards to the other. Even if the other is dead or unborn, even if he is merely imaginary, the 'withness,' if I may invent a word, remains, and gives form and direction to our feelings. If you ask me what we really learn from dance, then withness would be my reply. Indeed, were it not for dancing I fear that we should never learn this precious thing. I even sense in this an explanation of our modern sadness."

'Not caring for explanations of our "modern sadness," I asked Xanthippe to be a little more precise about this withness business. "You do not solve a philosophical problem," I said, "merely by inventing a word – a word, moreover, that is grammatically impossible. It is as though a philosopher were to answer the problem of contingent existence by saying that things have 'thrown-ness.' Not," I hastened to add, "that a civilized thinker could be quite so self-indulgent." And I might have added, honoured guest, that you do not explain the mystery of gardens by invoking their "between-ness."'

'"You are right, Perictione," the old philosopher said, "and I owe you an explanation of this peculiar word which, however much I push it from my consciousness, obstinately returns to pester me. Suppose, then, that the city fathers were to announce a public holiday, and declare that wine would be distributed free of charge in the Prytaneum. And suppose that Clerophon, or some other thug, in his impatience to receive yet another dose of public charity, runs to the place, not stopping to talk to those who address him, pushing aside those who obstruct him, thrusting to the front of the queue, and seizing the largest share on offer. Such a man is not *with* the others whom he meets, but decidedly against them, as I am sure you will concede. And something similar should be said of anyone whose purposes are so urgent that others do not count for him. Nowhere is this lack of withness more troubling than in love and desire. For are we not repelled by the one who makes his purpose too plain, who cannot hesitate, who brushes aside our protests and regards decency, shame and courtship as a waste of time?"

'"We are indeed," I replied, and my sigh made clear to her that, in this matter at least, I needed no instruction.

'"More," she added: "do we not require of a lover that he hesitate even to acknowledge love as his purpose, that he approach us as though all purposes were still to be acquired?"

'I nodded.

'"And is this not the meaning of courtship, she went on, that it is not so much a postponement of purpose, as a period in which purpose is set aside, so that man and woman can be truly free in each other's presence? That is how it seems to me, at least. And anything else, to my way of thinking, is shameful. The period of courtship is like an extended dance – lasting for months or even years – as the partners move with each other, sometimes conversing, sometimes in silence, purposeful but without purpose, and all the while shaping their desires through the idea of union. This is not a preparation for love, but a creation of love. For love is the child of hesitation, and courtship the godparent who bestows its name."

'The world that the old philosopher invoked with those

words had already vanished. But who was I to tell her so? I nodded in silence.

'"The withness of courtship survives and grows through marriage, lives on beyond death, and changes the very features of those who are schooled in it. For have you not remarked in old portraits, the peculiar mellow certainty that comes, when a face is shaped by others and not, as today, by the self?"

'I nodded again.

'"So now let us define this thing more generally. Withness is the state of being which leads us to hesitate before others, to jettison our purposes, to rest for a while in conversation, courtesy or ceremonial gestures. It is something more than respect, something more than obedience to the moral law, something more than good manners or good will. And it extends to all who have an interest in our being – to the dead and the unborn as much as the living. And that is why we should value dancing – and no dancing more than that which permits us to dance with strangers, to change partners as we move in formation, and to step with those whom we shall never love or desire."

'I could contain my cynical thoughts no longer. "I fear you are describing a vanished world," I said. "If that is what you mean by dancing, then young people of my generation have ceased to dance, and would pour scorn on those who offered to teach them."

'"True enough," said the philosopher. "Hence we must bear witness to this thing which will shortly disappear. Dreadful would the future be, were the stories no longer told of what it might have been, had the gods looked on us more kindly."

'After giving voice to this strange remark, Xanthippe sat for a while, humming a tune beneath her breath. The day was drawing to a close, and I had nothing much to do until later in the evening, when Xylophantes would have left the stage, the crowd of his admirers would be released on to the streets, and a particular young man, who I am ashamed to say was always one of their number, would be waiting for me in the precinct of Aphrodite Pandemos. I suggested to Xanthippe that we order wine from the nearby tavern, and when I produced the necessary obols and explained how well provisioned I had been since Granny's journey across the Styx, she readily assented to the idea. I suggested we pour a libation to Granny, and she, concurring, insisted that we drink to Socrates too.

'A few bowls later, honoured guest, when the shadows lay like drunken guests across the table, the philosopher started tapping her fingers on her thigh. To my enquiry she replied that all her life there was a matter she had failed to understand, and which words seemed unable to encompass.

'"And what is that?" I asked.

'"I mean rhythm," she said, "on which melody hangs like the fruit on a bough."

'She swallowed from her bowl, lent back on her stool, and uttered a loud laugh.

'"I am reminded," she said, "of my last dance with old Socks. It was the evening before his trial; we had just read the indictment and were in fits of laughter at the pompous language of this Meletus, 'good man and patriot' as he called himself, trying to put into legal language the accusation that I myself had made against old Socks and which all of Athens knew already – that he was a corrupter of the youth.[8] We had no idea that such a charge could hold up in court, or that Socks would be condemned and executed. It all seemed too wondrously absurd, and such anxieties as we felt we happily drowned in wine. I had prepared a few speeches, in case he needed them, and they did, in the event, turn out rather handy. It was great fun to rehearse them in the kitchen, myself trying to keep a straight face in the role of Meletus, and Socks standing on the table, booming on about the honour of the city and how he will not stoop to defend himself as cra-

---

8   Plato's *Apology* gives a (biased) account of Socrates' speech at his trial, and confirms the role of Meletus in laying charges against the philosopher.

ven cowards do, dragging his wife and children into the courtroom to beg in tears for their protector's life.

'"And then, after a bowl or two, he started to sing, a number by Stesichorus with a catchy iambic rhythm, and invited me to join him on the kitchen table. Now, despite his clumsy build and somewhat pudgy legs, old Socks was an agile dancer, and could stay on his toes for hours at a time, dancing to his own song, clapping his hands above his head and often releasing whoops of joy as he turned and leapt in time to the music. And such a prodigy of energy was he, that he could interrupt his singing with dialogue and still maintain the rhythm in his feet, which seemed to dance to a soundless music of their own. And it is those bare feet of Socrates that I recall, dancing among crumbs and peelings on our kitchen table, when I wish to remind myself of joy. For those feet had been lifted from their animal nature. They were no longer flesh and bone, no longer a mere adjunct to the mind that governed them, an instrument of motion. They were Socrates himself, and moved in dialogue with my feet, for all the world as though our words and smiles were theirs. And as I watched them – rough, horny, encrusted with dirt, and with those yellowing toenails hard as conchshells, absolutely lethal beneath the blankets – I had a vision of something that I can only describe as immortality. In some way those feet, having lifted themselves and all their earthy essence into the realm of spirit, broke free of earth entirely and danced on forever, leaving infinite footprints, so to speak, in some other dimension of being.

'"Now I don't say that there is any literal truth in that. But the metaphor forced itself upon me. No other words could quite capture my experience on that happy evening. And it was Socks himself who explained the matter.

'"'You see, Xanthippe,' he said between snatches of song, puffing a little and his face aglow, 'we do not live only here and now. Eternal shadows are cast by our movements, and eternal echoes follow our words.'

'"'And yet,' I replied, 'it is very much here and now that we are dancing.'

'"'Socks whooped and spun round in a most fetching way.

'"'That is exactly what I mean. For what animal lives in the present?'

'"'Do not all animals live in the present? Indeed, should we not say that, lacking reason, they have no vision of anything *except* the present?'

'"'Precisely,' he replied; 'they are so full of the present that they have no concept of it. Here and now make sense only by contrast with there and then. Unlike the animals, we experience the present as the tip of hidden time, and for us the present is 'always.' It contains the meaning of those hidden times – not past times only, but possible times, times that might have been. What has been and what might have been point to one end, you might say, which is always present.'

'"'And here he resumed his song, changing to anapests so that at first I had difficulty in keeping time. But again those feet of his, which smiled and sang across to mine, led me into their orbit and we danced in harmony. Watching him, I began to understand what Socks had said. Only sometimes, and only in certain frames of mind, do we live in the present moment. This happens by an act of will, which is also a renunciation of purpose. The here and the now come before us only when the veil of purpose has been drawn aside, and we confront the present moment, a lone wave on the sea of possibilities. The moment then resounds in us, and this resounding is what we mean by eternity.

'"'I was inclined, therefore, to agree with my husband, that animals know nothing of this, that just as it is only a rational being who can visit the past or dream of possibilities, so is it only a rational being who can live in the present. And I saw that this existence in the present moment is not an ordinary or easy thing, but a rare achievement. Just as I thought I had worked out for myself what kind of achievement it is, old Socks again interrupted my thoughts with a whoop and a clapping of hands, and began to punctuate his song with dialogue.

A memory of Xanthippe, with her views on dancing

'''So you see, my dear Xanthippe, that we should study how to enter the present, which is not, as the vulgar think, a house of ill-fame whose door stands ever open, but the holiest of temples, into the precinct of which only the initiate can find their way. And here is the strangest part – do please attend to my feet, your cross-rhythms are distracting me – yes, the strangest part: that we encounter the here and now only when our purposes are cancelled.'

'''I told him I had already figured this out.

'''Of course you had, by the dog. But do you see what light this casts on human conduct?'

'''I confessed that I had not thought this far. After a few more bars of his song, and having danced off the table to swallow a bowl of wine and danced back again, Socks continued his breathless instructions.

'''A man driven by a purpose,' he said, 'eats up time. Each moment is thrown like a sacrificial offering into the machinery of his desire, and expires without a trace. There are those who say that life has a meaning only for the man with a purpose. I say rather the opposite, that meaning comes to us when purpose is set aside. But not any renunciation of purpose will produce this effect: for purpose is rightly overcome only in company and only through the encounter with another soul, in conversation, music or some other thing that approximates to dance.'

'''But do we not set our purpose aside when we contemplate a picture or a sculpture or when we read a work of poetry? And are such arts not also passages to meaning?'

'''All art,' he shouted, 'has its origin in dance. Those who read or sing or watch alone are not really alone: another soul speaks to them through the words, the forms or the music. They are like the solitary dancer, who dances not alone, but with himself. All dancing, as I remember you saying the other day, is dancing with . . .'

'''With that he re-applied himself to the dance so vigorously that I stumbled from the table and fell in a heap against the wall. For half an hour more he danced and sang, until his feet were glowing through their veil of dirt, and his tunic was soaked in sweat. And I smiled as I watched him, my soul dancing along with him, and a calm joy filling my senses."

'Xanthippe sighed, and turned to me with a smile.

'"So there, my dear Perictione," she said, "we have a kind of answer to our dilemma, and I can only wonder at my stupidity for not having thought of it before."

'I confessed that I did not follow her.

'"Our dilemma was this: either we embrace the way of disenchantment which the cynics recommend, in which case we believe ourselves to be no better than parts of the great machine. Or else we succumb once again to enchantment, but in full knowledge that the gods and nymphs are our own invention, with no more power than a dream. But do you not see in this a grave simplification?"

'"Many," I said, for it is true that words always seem simpler to me that the things they describe.

'"I mean," said Xanthippe, "our dilemma leaves out the most important fact, which is that human beings create *themselves*, and they do so, not alone, but through dialogue and dancing. And although that which I create is of necessity a lesser being than I, that which I create in company with others may be greater – perhaps indefinitely greater. And here, in dancing, we have the proof.

'"When two people dance together they are doing something which is its own motive: dance and dancer are one, and the reason for placing your foot just here, your hand just there, is given only in and through the dance. There is no purpose governing these movements, nothing that enables us to say that this or this is the most efficient way to the goal. Each movement is a response to another, which is its sole and sufficient reason. What I do, when I dance, I do only because this purposeless practice exists. But it is a practice that transforms the world. It releases me from the tyranny of purpose and allows me to enter the present moment and to be wholly at one with it – so much at one that I can hear in these footfalls the echo that spreads before and after through infinite time.

A memory of Xanthippe, with her views on dancing

'"Now it is true that when people cease to dance something goes from the world, something man-made, yet irreplaceable. But we should no more question the reality or power of this thing than we should question the reality and power of a temple, just because it was built by human hands. In bringing this purposeless thing into being we propagate neither myths nor stories; we tell no lies about the gods, and invent no concepts beyond the one which describes this very action – the concept of dance. Yet we also change the world and give it meaning.

'"Return for a moment to our ducks. Ask yourself now why they were, and why they were not dancing. They were dancing because their behaviour so closely resembled ours when we dance. But they were not dancing, because they were not acting with the *reason* that inspires the dancer. Only those creatures dance who possess the concept of dancing. Only they can lift themselves free from the world of purpose, to converse with another in a dialogue of movement."

'"So far as that goes," I remarked, "the followers of Xylophantes might as well be dancing. For they too have the concept, and they too respond to the rhythm that they hear, and which comes to them from the lyres and tambours of the Screaming Corybants."

'"But there you have it," she said. "The rhythm comes to them from elsewhere, but is not *theirs*. Why else should Xylophantes require so much noise, such a crude and emphatic beat, which compels even the stones of the theatre to vibrate in time? Often, when Socks danced after dinner, there was no sound save the squeak of his leathery feet on the table and the occasional stanza of a song. Yet rhythm was in those feet, and magnetized the air surrounding them. Say, if you like, that the followers of Xylophantes dance; but be aware of all that is missing here from the old way of dancing. Be aware that to move in time to a beat is not yet to dance with another, nor even to dance with oneself. Indeed, I suspect that if we were to inquire into the matter, we should find ourselves obliged to make a distinction between rhythm and beat, and to question much that now passes for music.

'"Although I am in deep water here, and find myself at a loss to say what rhythm is, or why rational beings alone respond to it, I will venture nevertheless a criticism of Xylophantes and his followers. For between them they have devised a substitute for dance which more thoroughly destroys the art than any legal prohibition. Let us take a parallel example. Just as animals are unable to dance, so are they unable to fall in love, to plight their troth, or to do any other of the things which humans do, on the long troubled journey from virginity to marriage. But we could imagine Diogenes, or some other cynic, saying: 'take away the myths, look with a dispassionate eye on our acts and feelings, strip everything bare of the vain ornaments with which we disguise it, and we find that humans are prompted by the very same force as compels the animals. Deep down we are the same as them: in essence love and courtship are but sex.'"

'"But this again," I said, "is the charm of disenchantment."

'"Indeed it is," she replied; "but the charm is a deception. For when a philosopher say that the deep-down source of love is sex, and sex a thing that we share with the animals; and when he adds in the peculiar tone of voice which the expression demands, that therefore sex is the *essence* of love, and all those 'higher' things like courtship mere accretions: not only does he confuse the nature of a thing with its explanation; he puts before us an entirely false idea of essence. He has fallen victim to the greatest of modern illusions, a myth, as Socks used to describe it, of the half-educated. He has imagined that the essence of a thing is the part which is hidden from us, the part which we discover only by delving deep beneath the surface until a chance similarity with some other and simpler thing so vividly strikes us, that we believe we have at last struck truth. Love and desire are reduced to unconscious forces, which work in us we know not how, and we ourselves are conceived as passive victims in those very enterprises into which we put all our highest motives and desires."

"'Now you are speaking like Granny," I said, and such a vivid image came before me of my relative that I laughed aloud and sipped from my bowl with the same flourish of high-born contempt that she affected.

"'Yes," Xanthippe concurred, "I am indeed speaking like my dear dead friend. For did she not famously say that it is only a shallow person who does not judge by appearances? And here, I believe, is what she meant. We imagine that we discover the essence of things only by tearing down what we have contributed – showing the world as it might have been, had we done nothing to alter it. Human labour, the cynics say, builds paper castles in the world of seeming; the world of being remains always remote from us and unchanged. But there is a hole in their argument. For that which we create is created for our uses, for our senses, and for our thoughts. Such a thing can *only* be appearance: not *mere* appearance, but appearance in its final flowering, when essence and appearance are one. You no more reach the essence of the human world by delving beneath appearances than you reach the essence of a picture by scraping away the paint.

"'And when the cynic tells us that love is nothing but sex, and sex nothing but the clamorous instinct that we share with the animals, he does not describe reality. He alters it. To the extent that we believe him, we set about to transform the human world, to dig in the garden of courtship a cesspool of lust. This new garden is not less real than the one it destroys; but it is not more real either. It is built to another and uglier design, and we live in it as they live in the Babylonian towers of Persia, estranged and uncomforted, preying on each other, and deprived of the precious gift of withness."

"'But why should we wish to do such a thing?" I asked. (You must remember my pre-Meropian naiveté, honoured guest, when assessing my part in this dialogue.)

Chapter 8

'"There lies the appeal of the cynical philosophy," she answered. "It is the philosophy of those who have lost the art of setting their purposes aside, who are hurrying on-wards like leaves on the wind of desire, and who recognize no hesitations. The charm of disenchantment lies in the infi-nite permission that it bestows. Desire erupts unhindered into the disenchanted mind, fills every corner with its liquid urgency, and presses on to its satisfaction, diverted neither by shame nor by courtesy. The cynical philosophy is one with the new style of dancing – if dancing it must be called. Xylophantes shows his followers the way of purpose: there is, in their movements, neither withness nor shame. The noise from the stage endorses their desires, and holds desire aloft as sovereign. The new kind of dancing is therefore no longer a dancing with – not even with oneself. It is lonely, with the loneliness of a purpose that will not suffer its own extinction.

'"And now you see why the cynical philosophy is so widely believed – not because it is true, but because it so per-fectly describes the world of the human being who is now striving to create himself. By believing it, we help to realize that world, just as, by moving to the sound of Xylophantes, we destroy the old world which wars against it."

'"But is there any hope for that old world?" I asked her.

'"Oh," she replied with a yawn, "there is always hope, provided we do not make the supreme mistake."

'"And what is that?"

'"The mistake of hoping for the impossible."

'"So what is possible?" I asked. And truly I wished to discover. For what rational being, who knows what it is to be with her fellows, to set her purposes aside, and to enter the eternity of a present moment, could live with the belief that never again will this experience be hers or anyone's? Alas, Xanthippe, who had finished the amphora, lay slumped across the table, in a sleep from which I tried in vain to wake her. Shaking the last drops into the dust, and with a hasty prayer to the muses, I hurried off to my date.'

9

The story of Merope continued, with further thoughts on dancing

So much had passed before Archeanassa's mind during this recital that, when it was over, she sat in silence, reflecting on the mysteries of life, and on the charm of disenchantment that removes them. Perictione meanwhile strode about the room in a state of high excitement, shouted for the lunch that she had ordered, and began to chatter about Colophonian politics, about the nightclub where she worked, and about some Persian general – a cut above the average, although of course in this new world the average was set rather low – who hoped to dine with her that night.

'But you see, my dear Archeanassa, I am not going to.'

Archeanassa awoke from her thoughts with a start.

'Not going to what?'

'Not going to have dinner with Pharnabazus.'

'I see.'

'No, I have other plans. For today is my day off, tomorrow you will be leaving for Notium, and I wanted to spend the time with you.'

'I am most flattered, noble Perictione.'

'Don't be. Let's go in to lunch.'

'Go in?'

'Yes. I thought that, today being the special day it is, we ought to lunch *en famille*.'

'*En famille*?'

'I'll lead the way,' said Perictione, who went quickly to

the far end of the room and stood between two grim statues, the one depicting Achilles, his heel pierced by an arrow, the other showing Philoctetes clutching his foot in pain. Perictione touched a spot on the wall, which instantly swung away from her, revealing a sumptuous dining room, where a long table of rose-wood laden with silver vessels stood on a floor of polished agate. Around the table were arranged gold-lacquered chairs, their arms adorned by the heads of curious beasts, and at the far end of the room stood a marble figure of an athlete, wearing the Olympian crown, and supported in front and behind by the three Graces and the four Seasons. The ceiling was embossed with plaster medallions, in which scenes from Homer and the tragedians were etched by an exquisite hand. Frescoes adorned the walls, and Archeanassa gasped with pleasure as she studied them, for the artist had depicted the groves and streets of ancient Colophon, with a religious procession winding its way to the temple of Apollo. And the faces of the chorus as they danced in the wake of the holy emblems were like the faces of old friends, warm, familiar, glowing with the corporate life that had also been hers. The eyes of the priest looked out at her with a glance full of reverence and holy laughter, and the crimson velvet of his mantle was so alive with delicate highlights and trapped shadows as to appear to fan the air. All kinds of curious and familiar details had been captured by the artist's brush: the fountain in the grove of Artemis, which winked and glistened over steps of amber stone; the wooden stalls of the fish market, with their canvas awnings flapping to the rhythm of a morning breeze, and their silvery burdens glittering in the sunlight. In the bottom corner stood the sun-drenched chalice of a courtyard, where the poets congregated to read from long yellow scrolls, their solemn faces all aglow with civic pride. And she could almost believe that the one who stood with his back to her, heaving his broad shoulders as though lifting the burden of his song, was her own Antimachus: for certainly it was the same patched tunic that he wore, and his outstretched hand had the commanding softness of a hand that was kissed every day by some foolish woman. Her eyes wandered along the streets, recognizing shrines and gates and doorways, and arriving at last at the little cottage – she could hardly believe it! – where she had waited each morning for her love.

'These frescoes must have been here when you bought the house,' she said, and then instantly regretted it. Perictione was not the kind of person who bought or sold.

'No, I had them done by an old guy who has lived here for ever, and who remembers ancient Colophon. Apelles in fact, the very one who stole Merope's paintings. He has a line in imitation antiques.'

'How is it, most noble Perictione, that you can live with them? For by your standard they are hardly sincere.'

'Not sincere, certainly. But with no quotation marks either – the guy was too old for that. Besides, they are decoration, not art.'

'Perhaps you will explain the difference.'

'Easy,' said the girl with a wave of the hand. 'Art is an end, decoration a means.'

'A means to what?'

'In this case, a means to showing me to advantage.'

Perictione spun round on her toes and, lifting a silver canopy from one of the dishes, revealed a brick-red stew of octopus. 'Yum! yum!' she cried, and her alabaster nostrils flared in the steam.

'I don't mean that, of course. It is the guests that need to be shown to advantage, lest I should die of boredom. Do sit down.'

She took her place at the head of the table, and gestured to the chair on her right. A third place had been laid further down, and Archeanassa looked at it enquiringly.

'You mustn't mind the boy,' Perictione said, as she picked up a silver bell that stood beside her bowl and shook it. 'He doesn't speak, and he behaves himself. In his own way.'

The subject of those remarks promptly entered the room. He did not look at Archeanassa as she intently studied his features. No, she said to herself, it can't be, not with that wide brow, those blue eyes, those coarse rubbery nostrils which distend with every breath like the nostrils of a horse, those long sensuous lips which lie side by side like sleeping boats at a quay, to be suddenly dashed apart by a storm of cackles. She pondered with amazement his bush of red hair, which sprouted everywhere, even pushing in coarse clumps from the ears like artichokes. It might have been a handsome face, had it actually *been* a face, rather than a stage-set for a drama. But wave after wave of mad expressions swept across it, seizing the features and wrestling with them as an infant wrestles with a toy. She settled in her chair and waited for her hostess to introduce her.

Perictione, however, was not of a mind to favour her with an introduction. Instead she ignored the boy, who sat in his place like a dog, rested his hands on the table, twitched and grunted and muttered, and then let his mouth hang open in an idiotic gape. Archeanassa began to think that he must be mentally defective – some unhappy creature who had been left by his parents at a cross-roads, and who had wandered the streets until Perictione took pity on him. But then, she reflected, how likely is it that Perictione would take pity on anyone, let alone this embarrassing monster?

'I do hope you like the octopus,' said the girl. 'I have it brought in by special courier from Ephesus – five hours, allowing for a change of horse.'

'Truly it is delicious, noble Perictione. But I am surprised at this luxury after the simple meals you once preferred.'

'Oh I still prefer them. But you see, honoured guest, I had to make a decision. Do I live as a vagrant still, but alone and unprotected? Or do I settle here, and make a go of it? I took the second option. And when I settle, I must settle in style, in a private Athens of my own. Am I making myself clear?'

'Up to a point,' said Archeanassa. And then, noticing that the boy had taken no food, she whispered, 'what is the boy called?'

'There is some dispute about his name. I call him "Boy."'

'And you say he doesn't speak?'

'No, but he listens. Eat boy!' she added, pushing the octopus across to him.

The boy chewed on the air for a moment, stretching his long lips into a grotesque coil around his mouth. And then, with a sudden grab, he filled his hands with octopus, dropped it into the bowl before him and began greedily licking his fingers.

'Disgusting!' said Perictione, with a nonchalant shake of the head.

'Is he – is he quite all right?' whispered Archeanassa.

'Quite all right?'

'In the head, I mean.'

'Oh yes, he is very clever, quick to learn, and widely read.'

'Widely read?'

'I'll show you,' said Perictione. 'Listen boy:

Lo, word becomes deed
And the earth rocks beneath me.

Sophocles?'

The boy shook his head violently.

'Euripides?'

He shook his head again.

'Aeschyl . .'

Before she had completed the name the boy was nodding, not with his head only but with his whole upper body, spitting octopus from his lips, and clapping his hands in self-applause. Instead of resting after this performance, he seemed to take inspiration from it, to respond to himself as a crowd responds to a corybantic dancer. He began to snake his head from side to side, with level eyes glaring in front of him, his lower lip slipping now to the left, now to the right as though trying to catch something – a butterfly perhaps – from the air. Then he picked up an imaginary cithara and strummed it with one hand, while running the fingers of the other in a wild dance across the strings, his head all the time moving from side to side in excited agitation. And at the climax his face took on an ecstatic glow; he threw back his head, barked triumphantly, and from half-closed eyes shot a quick glance at Archeanassa. Finally, casting the instrument from him, he wiped his hands together, snorted, and abruptly sat still, letting his damp mouth hang open as before. Archeanassa turned to her hostess in amazement.

'Try him,' said Perictione.

'On what?'

'Oh, anything: philosophy if you like.'

'Really?'

'Boy,' said Perictione. 'Listen to our guest, Miss Archeanassa of Colophon, upon whose very wrinkles . . . whoops!'

'Well, young man,' said Archeanassa. 'Who was it said "the examined life is not a life for a human being?" Plato?'

The boy shook his head.

'Socrates?'

Another shake of the head.

'Xanthi . . .'

With a shriek and a clap the boy cut her short. This time he played a more soothing tune on his imaginary instrument, and pointed his smiling head to the ceiling, so that it swayed like a heavy flower on his long pale stalk of a neck.

'Astonishing,' said Archeanassa, when the commotion had ceased. 'And how was he trained?'

'Wait a while, and I shall tell you his story. But first, let us refresh ourselves with wine. And perhaps, as we do so, you can give me your opinion, honoured guest, on Xanthippe's theory of the dance. For if I am not mistaken, there are some important similarities to your own thoughts about the city.'

'Indeed there are,' said Archeanassa. 'And one in particular strikes me.'

Perictione rose to pour sweet wine into Archeanassa's bowl. The boy darted a mocking glance at the visitor, and instantly averted his eyes, assuming an expression of wounded innocence. With a sigh and a shrug Archeanassa poured a libation to Artemis, and then drank deeply from the bowl.

'Boy,' said Perictione, after she too had drunk. 'Assuming you have had enough to eat you may retire to your cage. You will read *Oedipus at Colonnus* and memorize the speech which begins at line nine hundred and sixty. Off you go.'

The boy rose to his feet with subdued and rigid features. As he marched through the door, Archeanassa followed him with her eyes. The face, the manner and the soul: all these were original. But the posture, the way of walking – so easy and fluent and self-contained – these rushed like a wind into the chamber of memory, making the ghosts roll over in their semi-sleep. With an effort of will she turned her attention to the wine, and swallowed a long, cool draught of sweetness.

'Cyprus,' Perictione commented. 'The year of Xanthippe's execution. A good year for brown wine, if for nothing else.'

'When I spoke of the city,' Archeanassa began, 'I described the side-by-sideness of its residents. And this recalls Xanthippe's "withness" business. And when I meditated on gardens I was struck by the very thing that Xanthippe mentioned. As she put it, there is a higher purposefulness in things, a purposefulness beyond purpose, and in achieving this, in transcending temporary goals, we cease to be "merely in earnest" and achieve another and truer fulfilment. Is that right?'

'More or less,' said Perictione.

'And the "withness" or "side-by-sideness" goes hand in hand with the emancipation from purpose, does it not – both for her and for me?'

'So it seems.'

'That is to say, it is only in society that we can really free ourselves from the chain of means, and so attain the end.'

'Why do you always put things in a loaded way?'

'It saves time,' said Archeanassa.

'True, and we haven't much of it. When does the wagon leave?'

'At dawn, from the hostel.'

'You know something, Archeanassa? I really am going

to cancel that Pharnabazus. We'll have dinner together here. And if you want to stay the night I should be most honoured.'

Archeanassa was so taken aback by the invitation that she could not muster the excuses necessary to refuse it. Yet her inner qualms returned, and she accepted with a hesitating murmur.

'Don't worry,' the girl went on. 'I'll send the servant to the hostel for your things, and you can pick up the wagon here. We'll tell the driver.'

'I am deeply obliged, noble hostess.'

Perictione clapped her hands, and the servant came at once to receive her instructions. And then, with a relaxed and eager smile, the girl waved away the dishes, took the wine cooler from the table, and ushered her guest into the parlour, sipping from her bowl as she went.

'I'm as bad as Granny,' she remarked, as she replenished Archeanassa's bowl. 'But you only live once, and most people not even that much. You were saying about society.'

'Yes,' said Archeanassa, as she sat on the couch to face her hostess. 'But it is not a word I like.'

'I'm not surprised. There is no word more tricky in the whole language than "about." Just try to define it.'

'The word I had in mind was "society."'

'Oh, I see,' said the girl with a frown. 'I bet there is more philosophy to be got from aboutness than ever we could squeeze out of withness.'

'But surely our purpose is not to squeeze philosophy out of things, but to understand them?'

'Do you think so? Well, I suppose it's a possible view.'

'The reason I dislike the word "society,"' Archeanassa went on, 'is that it obliterates distinctions. People speak of society when they mean the state; but they also use the word to describe families, tribes, choruses or schools. From every relevant standpoint, those things are far from the same.'

'True enough, honoured guest. So let's not use the word.'

'Let us use it with caution. A city is a society, so too is a dance. And we have noticed similarities between them. But there are enormous differences, and here is one of them: a city is a substance,[1] whereas a dance is not.'

'A substance?'

'It's a word I picked up from Xanthippe. Substances are individuals, which endure through time and change, but which remain one and the same at every moment of their existence.'

'How boring.'

'I mean *numerically* the same, as you are from day to day.'

'It's a possible view of me.'

'But substances are of many kinds, and it is important to understand the distinctions between them.'

'Distinctions of class?'

'No: distinctions of category – also one of Xanthippe's words. In particular, we must distinguish those substances which are persons from those which are things.'

'That's pretty loaded, Archeanassa. What was Phocis – person or thing?'

'I should say he was a problem case.'

'Too true,' said Perictione with a sigh. 'And that reminds me . . . but I mustn't interrupt.'

'Well then,' Archeanassa went on, 'what of the city: is it a person or a thing?'

'I should say neither, but containing both.'

'There you are wrong, most noble Perictione. A city is a person, just as you are. It makes choices, commitments, contracts – even vows, where vows are permitted. It is praised and blamed for its actions; it is resented, hated, loved and forgiven, just as people are. And each generation of citizens must honour the debts and enforce the credits of its predecessors. They do these things not for themselves, but for their city, whose representatives they are. Now what are the defining marks of persons? Surely, that they make choices,

---

1   Ar. *jism*. The Greek *ousia*, Latin *substantia*, is implied by the ensuing reference to Xanthippe, from whom Aristotle would have derived the term which he made so famous.

that they are free and responsible in their actions, that they are praised and blamed, as cities are. Yet nothing like that is true of a mere thing. And this is why, my dear Perictione, cities are to be respected, and not to be used. The city, like the human being, is an end and not a means.'

'Clearly, honoured guest, you don't know many human beings.'

'Oh, I grant you, human beings can *become* things. As here in Colophon.'

'Not here, in this house, unless you are thinking of that boy.'

'No, I mean out there, in the great machine. And now I should like to return to those remarks of Xanthippe's, since they help me to understand my meaning. The philosopher distinguished two kinds of dancing, did she not – the dancing of Socrates, which was, to paraphrase, a purposeless withness, and the dancing of Xylophantes and his fans, which was frenzied, full of purpose, and yet, in a peculiar way, alone?'

'Loaded, as always. And anyway, she wouldn't admit that those ghastly adolescents, who sometimes counted me among their number, were really dancing.'

'Just so. And you will recall that I distinguished two kinds of city, the old Colophon and the new, and that I would not admit that the new Colophon was really entitled to the name of city?'

'I see where this is going.'

'Do you? Then perhaps you will agree that the dance and the city are corrupted in similar ways. The dance loses its consoling peacefulness when it lapses into mechanical movement, in which the dialogue between self and other is extinguished, since every dancer has become other to himself. Likewise the city loses its meaning when it becomes a machine, a means for the production of human beings, who live together not side by side, but in a state of otherness.'

'What's wrong with otherness? I find it rather suits me to be other. You should try it some time.'

A becoming wine-flush glowed in Perictione's face as

she wriggled slightly on the couch and tucked her toes beneath her.

'You can afford to be other, noble hostess, because you are so fully yourself. Your otherness is a game, a mask, one of your many disguises.'

Perictione threw back her head with a glad laugh.

'Don't you think it might be the real me?'

'Well,' observed Archeanassa, in some confusion, 'I can hardly pronounce on that.'

'A pity,' said Perictione, who smiled across at her guest. The girl's face was briefly inundated by the eyes, in the depths of which a vast teeming life of imagination showed itself. 'I always hope that my guests will tell me who I am. Still,' she went on, 'we have the afternoon ahead of us. You were saying about Colophon, the machine city, the city of otherness, the city without a meaning, and such tourist-brochure stuff.'

'I wished to say that the corrupted city has no personality. It is no longer to be respected, for it is now a thing. The new Colophon makes no choices, takes no responsibility for itself, is answerable to no-one, and respectful of no-one. And that is why it has no face, no smile, no way of greeting the citizens, if citizens they can be called.'

'You are talking of government, not architecture.'

'But government and architecture are one and the same. Buildings are built for others, for strangers, for passersby. Their appearance expresses an attitude to the stranger, to the one who shares with you nothing save his citizenship. Citizenship exists where strangers live side by side, achieving a repose beyond purpose. In the new Colophon there is no citizenship. Here the government of men has given way to the administration of things. And the buildings show this, just as clearly as the faces of the people who go in and out of them. Here, in Colophon, men have *become* things.'

'Neat, Archeanassa. But you have strayed a long way from dancing.'

'Not so. For I believe I can see a little further into this withness business.'

'Good, because it is the weakest point in Xanthippe's argument.'

'You deny that to dance is to dance with another?'

'I have never danced with another in my life!' said Perictione indignantly. 'Except Phocis, of course. And he, as you say, was a problem case.'

'But so too is your dancing, most noble Perictione, as Xanthippe argued. These classical *schemata*, this ordered exhibition on a stage – this is not so much dancing as the representation of dancing, as in a picture. Representation summons a thing in its absence; in just that way, you summon the withness of the dance, while dancing alone.'

'Except that I don't. For who is there to summon? Who else, I mean?'

'I shall tell you, noble Perictione. When I compared dancing to the city, I argued that the second is a substance, but not the first, did I not?'

'Indeed,' said Perictione.

'But when I discussed the word "society," so loosely and ignorantly used, I mentioned among the things called societies not the city only, but also the chorus.'[2]

'I believe you did. And now you are going to say that choruses are substances, and I shall forestall you by asking whether they are persons or things, and replying that they are persons, just like cities.'

'That's cheating,' said Archeanassa, not a little put out by the girl's arrogance.

'But it saves time,' she replied with a toss of the head.

'O.K., that *is* what I wanted to say. In their own manner, which of course is not the manner of the city, choruses are persons. They have an identity; they make decisions, are answerable for their doings and their dancings, and those who belong to them are bound by ties of membership every bit as strong as the duties of the citizen. And it is through belong-

---

2   Ar: *jami'ah ar-raaqisaat*. It is obvious from the context that the author is referring to the choruses, often attached to temples, which were fundamental to the education of young girls. See above, p. 163, note 5.

ing to a chorus that girls learn to move with one another, to converse politely, to give and to yield, to demand and to charm, and to achieve a kind of collective purposelessness which sets them above the stress of daily life. The chorus is our best example of withness, and it shows that we achieve this state most effectively when we are bound together as members of a single person.'

'Thank Zeus I've always stayed out of that kind of thing.'

'Yes, but you are the problem case. And I shall tell you why, noble Perictione. The chorus does in fact have a purpose of sorts, which is to perform the dances in honour of the god, to uphold his divine reputation, and to set a model of holy conduct.'

'Which is why I would be a hopeless member.'

'But it is why the chorus is so important to those who belong to it. For this holy purpose lies *beyond* purpose. It cannot be fulfilled in time, nor can it be renounced or exchanged or contracted away. It is a purpose to which you must dedicate your life, with a vow and not a contract, as you would say. And having done this, you live in another way – the way of piety.'

'Until some person comes from Colophon and steals away your heart.'

'Leaving that possibility to one side, let me draw a conclusion. The peculiar thing of which Xanthippe spoke – the purposefulness without purpose which she attributed, if I remember rightly, to dancing and poetry and music, does it not have its archetype here, in the religious community? For although the chorus is bound by duty, this duty lies so far beyond mere purpose as to merit just the description that she employed. Moreover, all those things of which she spoke come together in this community of souls, and if we wanted a word with which to summarize and contain the consoling ways of life – the side-by-sideness of the citizen-stranger, the withness of the dancer, the tie of membership which turns groups into persons, and the dedicated rhythm of the chorus-dancer – then the word I should choose would be "piety." And if I understand her rightly, Xanthippe is raising the question whether piety can exist without the belief in gods. For if it cannot, then what charm is left to us, save the charm of disenchantment?'

'You put the point rather well, honoured guest. And I am especially glad that you have mentioned the life of the chorus, because it returns me to the subject of Merope. And once again the best way of answering you is through the tale of my adventures.'

Perictione stretched one hand across the table to toy with a vase of yellow roses, twirling the stems in her fingers and shaking the blooms apart. Then she slipped silently from the couch on to her knees and leaned her elbows on the table, her fingertips gently buttressed beneath her chin. The reflected sunbeams danced on the nape of her neck, where the hair had been tied in a crown, and the skin of her hands shone like mother of pearl. For a moment she seemed strangely at peace, and Archeanassa looked down on her in troubled sympathy. There was no sound in the room save the moth-soft dropping of rose-petals, which fell around that lovely face like the gold that rained on Danaë. When Perictione began to speak, it was in a voice at once quiet and resolute, as though beginning a confession.

'Merope, though. Why did she set her heart on returning to Colophon? Was it, as she said, because the free being is the one with the least choice – the one who has only *one* path down which to go, which is the path of now? And if so, was Colophon that path – Colophon the experimental city, in which the new order – the order beyond morality – had been conjured from the void? Or was it because she had a premonition of the fame and wealth that I could earn in this dump of mass-produced morons, where a classical dancer is as rare and precious a sight as a pea-shooter in Plato's Academy? Or was it another and deeper cause, a cause to which she would not confess, so much did it reveal the fatal re-enchantment of her feelings?

'Well yes, I incline to the third explanation. For although

there is a joy in understanding what has been lost forever, and although it is also a religious joy, focussing on what has gone from the world and therefore sits eternally in judgement, this joy arises only when the loss is not yours or mine but everyone's – an impersonal loss, which adds distinction to the one who senses it. Merope's loss, however, which became impersonal during those years of wandering, had suddenly come home in the form of a private catastrophe. Returning to Sardis the old pieties had stirred in her. She remembered the orderly rituals, the noble songs and dances, the trivial, hilarious secrets which bound the chorus together, and she regretted her innocent life as a temple virgin. And hot behind these holy things came the love which had defeated them, the love which brought her here to Colophon, and which had here been betrayed. As we left the temple of Artemis I saw a great change in her. Her eyes were downcast and melancholy, she walked with slow and shambling gait, and when I mentioned the possibility of a nightclub, where I could dance and earn a slap-up dinner, she shook her head as though dancing were never to be thought of again. All she said, in response to my anxious questioning, was "Colophon, to Colophon," and when I cheerfully consented to the journey she looked at me long and sadly, as though I could not possibly know the meaning of what she proposed.

'Of course, we had to leave Sardis in any case. The decapitation of Sterbs had not done our reputation any good, and although the governor had impaled a few slaves, flogged the butcher, and placed a rival prophet under house-arrest – for which actions he had been ennobled by a Great King rejoicing in his new condition of Sterbslessness – the general feeling in Sardis was that itinerant Greek sophists were superfluous to Persian requirements. Had it been left to me I should have counselled a long holiday by the sea, maybe searching for the ruins of Troy. But Merope was bent on Colophon, and I foresaw that much would be asked of me if my darling were to survive the experience.

Chapter 9

'We left the town by the south gate, which led, Merope assured me, to the Royal Road to Susa. But it was no Royal Road that we stumbled across: only a tract of half-derelict land where burdock and bladderwort grew in the dust, and derelict cottages crumbled between unfinished blocks of slate. Roads of crushed brick and rubble had been driven through the gorse, and here and there along the parched ditches tamarisks hid in their pinkish tresses, like ageing harlots behind veils of coloured hair. The place was dreary, god-forsaken, hostile, and it did not help that Merope – who had been aiming for a sacred grove where we might sleep on our way to Colophon – was by now completely lost. However far we walked, the open country seemed no nearer, and roads which promised to stride away from Sardis had the habit of abruptly ceasing, or turning through two right-angles and heading back in the direction from which we had come.

'After we had walked for three hours, the encroaching darkness forced us to take stock of our situation. It was too late now to return to Sardis, and unsafe to remain where we were. I suggested that we abandon the road, and make for a ruined cottage which stood half a league away, and which caught the even light on the upper slopes. Merope, whose face had assumed a glazed expression, followed me meekly like a child. We crossed fields of coarse grass, tripping over ant-heaps, falling into ditches, pushing our way through gorse and nettles and wild artichoke, plagued all the while by flies and mosquitoes. We stumbled into a patch of marshy ground where bullfrogs croaked, and had to leap from one clump of tangled couch-grass to the next, the light continually diminishing, so that we hardly saw the ground. And then, with wet legs and bruised hands, we encountered a wall of vegetation: entanglements of biting spray, black as a bird's nest, spindly birches strangling one another, knotted stumps of blackthorn and choked stragglings of acanthus, all laced and tethered round with a thatch of bramble. It was as though we were struggling free of Persian Lydia, pushing against the hostile edge of things. We emerged at last at the foot of the hill where the cottage stood, raw with bites and stings and scratches.

'As we climbed the slope, however, the atmosphere began to change. The land was ribbed with terraces, on which medlars, mulberry trees and a few straggling vines survived amid the thorns. A goat-track zig-zagged between the narrow plantations, and by the side of it we came across a shrine, with a broken statue of Apollo. We had risen out of Persia into a memory of Greece, and Merope's face was restored to something like its old expression. She looked about her with enquiring glances, became distinctly more cheerful as we passed a ruined sty with a bas-relief of Circe, and smiled at the sight of the cottage, whose sagging roof of stone tiles, supported by a half-rotted beam running the length of one wall, still glowed in the shards of dwindling daylight.

'One wall of the cottage had fallen away, and the interior was exposed to view. In the dusk we could make out a bed, with a mattress of straw, and next to it an old chestnut table. This was all that remained of furniture, but it was enough, and after dropping our bags on the table, and examining the place for rats and snakes and scorpions, we shook out the mattress, replaced it on the bed, and threw ourselves down to rest. We were sheltered on three sides, and the roof was still intact. From our bed we looked out through the broken wall across the valley. Hesperus burned brightly on the far horizon, lighting the way for the sickle-shaped moon, and one by one the stars appeared – those stars to which the Greeks had given names and stories, and through the unchanging face of which they had eternalised themselves. And yes, as we lay there, two Grecian women in this Grecian cottage, looking over Grecian fields, I felt an intimation of my immortality; for I was a small but distinguished part of that incomparable work of art – that Hellas of the imagination which would last forever in the mind of man. I could not forebear conveying this to Merope, as she lay there in silence, holding my hand.

'"Don't you think we're lucky?" I asked.

Chapter 9

'"Lucky?"

'"Lucky to be Greeks, with a place among the gods. So to speak."

'She squeezed my hand and I felt a wave of emotion pass through her in the darkness. Spontaneously we whispered that line of the poetess:

Men will remember us, I think, even hereafter[3]

and suddenly the world assumed a glorious symmetry as though shaken in a kaleidoscope. I sensed the stars above us, stacked up in layer upon layer at every imaginable distance, some still and staring vigilantly down at us, others trembling and dancing in their orbits, yet others shooting out of nowhere, burning bright like startled eyes and at once extinguished in the wide untroubled ocean of the night. From horizon to horizon this vast crepitation, changeless epitome of change, eternal image of the fleeting moment, spread its dome upon dome above us, visible but unimaginable. A dog barked in the distance, breaking the silence like a tiny sparkle on a lake of darkness. And then all was still, with the soft, attentive stillness of a lover who lies in wait for his love.

'I put my arms around Merope and hugged her. The life was coming back to her body, which was firm again and strong. She took my hands and gently pushed them aside. Then she rose from the bed and walked into the corner of our little room, where a wooden cover lay on a platform of stone. The moon was bright enough to see by, and its light reached through the branches of a cedar tree, to lay a brocade of shadow on the flagstone floor. I watched as Merope removed the cover and reached down into the platform. There was a distant splashing sound, a clatter of wood on stone, and then, with long breaths and a firm flexing of the shoulders, Merope pulled a glistening rope from the dark-

---

3 Sappho, Fragment 30 in E.M. Cox, ed., *The Poems of Sappho*, New York 1925. There is no rendering of this line in English which can explain why Dio Chrysostom, writing about 100 AD, should describe it as 'said with perfect beauty.' It is not much good in Arabic either.

ness. At the end of it was a wooden bucket, which she grappled on to the top of the stone and then carried across to the table. It was full of cool clear water, and we drank eagerly, laughing like children. I even took soap from my bag, to wash away the stains of our journey. We were aloft now on the edge of things, and had death come I should have looked on him with the same stylish unconcern as I look on those Persian generals who compete for my favours. I reached into my bag for the amphora of coarse wine that I had brought from Sardis. We drank to the end of things, and then sat still on the bed, all will and desire arrested. An owl tore the silence, which magically repaired itself. And then Merope took the amphora, drank from it, passed it back to me with a kiss, and began to speak.

'"Look there," she said. "Do you not see the seven Pleiades, daughters of Atlas, fast by the blue horizon?"

'She pointed to a cluster of stars, which had come up behind Perseus, the hero who had turned Atlas to stone; and as I watched them twinkle in the clear Lydian sky, she recalled their sacred story. Their mother was one of the Oceanides, and they too – Alcyone, Maia, Electra, Taygeta, Sterope, Celeno and Merope, my darling's namesake – were granted immortality and placed in the heavens. And all of them had gods for husbands, save only one, the unfortunate Merope, who in consequence glowed less brightly, and was indeed all but invisible to our moon-struck eyes as we scanned the far horizon. And Merope's husband was Sisyphus, king of Corinth, a thief and a cheat and a seducer, who after death was punished for his crimes, being condemned by the gods to roll a great stone to the top of a hill in Hades, only to have it tumble back again, renewing his punishment forever. And even today in Hellas, to be of the blood of Sisyphus is a matter of disgrace.

'Nor had the other Merope, who nestled against me in the darkness, been luckier. For although she had freed herself from men and wandered the world, gaining her own kind of immortality, which is the eternal recurrence of the moment, she could not hide the fact that the moment is not enough – no, not even if it occurs again and again forever. Something else is needed, and that something else is one-ness through time. It was this that she had lost in Colophon, when she had been compelled to cut away her former self, to send it drifting backwards into darkness, and to plough her lonely skiff out over the uncharted sea, scorning the mortal certainties of those who do not accompany each belief with its refutation. And yet she longed to be joined again to that former self, so that her life should be whole and entire, even if this wholeness were a cause of suffering. For it is only as a unified work of art that a person achieves completeness, and it is only for such a work that recurrence has a meaning. If I could make use of your Xanthippic term, honoured guest, my darling wanted to be of one substance with the Merope who had led the Artemisian chorus. But how could this be achieved, without re-living the period between, when she had been in thrall to another Sisyphus? So it happened that she told me her story. And she told it the more easily, she said, in that this very cottage where we sat side by side had been part of the background scenery.

'When Merope was a young girl, esteemed for her beauty throughout the region of Sardis, she had a friend called Archidameia, who danced and sang with her in the chorus, and who clung to her with a canine affection. Archidameia was an only child, whose mother had borne her late in life, and whose father farmed this land, producing fruit and chickens and pigs for the Sardian market. He lived here in justice towards his neighbours and piety towards the gods. And when his old wife died, he grieved for three long years, before advertising in the local temples for a replace-ment. During this time Archidameia became attached to the chorus, acquired sophisticated city manners, and, lacking a mother, clung the more closely to Merope. And she became ever more reluctant to visit her father, with whom she had nothing in common besides a coarse and insatiable appetite for crispy sucking-pig.

'Now it so happened that there came to Sardis at this time an itinerant philosopher called Hermione who, after a disastrous entanglement in Colophon, was looking for a quiet place in the country where she could settle down for a year and write her memoirs. One day this Hermione visited the temple of Demeter which stood down there in the valley, wishing to refresh her weary limbs and to pray to the goddess for the peace of mind that had so far eluded her. Being of curious disposition, she soon discovered the papyrus that Archidameia's father – whose name, by the way, was Phorbas – had pinned to the public notice-board. And it occurred to her that marriage to a mild and undemanding farmer might be just as good a way of regaining her peace of mind as a period of solitary meditation. And she was additionally charmed by the quaint spelling, and by the list of Phorbas's requirements, which included pickling, jam-making, Homer, pig-rearing, geography, water-divining, Aeschylus, hen-plucking and theology. She went at once to the cottage, fearing only lest some equally enterprising professional had got there first.

'Hermione was young, attractive and with a quick intelligence, while Phorbas was a simple person, unused to the ways of the world. Nevertheless, he was immensely proud of his daughter, and in despair as to how he might learn to converse with her. When Hermione – who presented herself as a poor widow, with no knowledge of pigs and chickens but an ability, nevertheless, to cook them – revealed that she was also a philosopher, that she had once visited Athens, that she knew the classics, and that her dowry consisted of nothing but a wagonload of books, Phorbas was overjoyed. He proposed at once, on condition that Hermione would teach him philosophy, which she did to such effect that his daughter began to prolong her visits home, and was no longer ashamed to invite her friends, Merope in particular. By degrees Merope became part of the household, learning about the great philosophers of Athens, whose names, according to Hermione, were Philip, Amphion and Polyprocrastines. Unfortunately Hermione's library cast little light on their teachings, since most of the volumes dated from the time of Aspasia, and concerned gardening, hunting and patent medicines. Still, it was a mind-broadening experience, and Hermione's lively and open manner ensured that the girls were fully at their ease in this novel company, and Phorbas rejoiced to see his home restored. And many were the lovely days that Merope spent in this place, with its refreshing breezes and its farmyard smells, with Hermione's wholesome cooking, and the quiet soporific conversation in the evenings, as they discussed the cosmology of Amphion, who argued that everything is water, and the rival view of Philip, for whom everything is piss.

'So matters proceeded for several years, during which Merope completed her education and was chosen for a priestess. And all would have been well, and Merope's intended career a reality, had it not been for a peculiar accident. It happened one day that Hermione went again to pray at the temple of Demeter. There, to her astonishment, she encountered the man from Colophon, the man with whom she had been so disastrously entangled. When Hermione, who could not suppress the gasp with which she beheld his familiar gait and features – for he was a man of singular charm – had unavoidably attracted his attention, he smiled and came across to her, with that seductive ease of manner which certain men have when encountering a woman they have ruined.

'Now this man, my dear Archeanassa, was a poet of sorts, and had captured her heart with a long encomium, written in her honour, which he was hoping to publish. He explained to her that he was journeying to Sardis with this end in view and had paused to refresh his weary spirits at the temple, although of course his true intention, Hermione divined, was to take a good look at the women there.'

At this point Archeanassa, who had been gripping the edge of her couch and looking with pale face and open mouth intently into the face of Perictione, could no longer suppress her agitation.

'Most noble Perictione,' she said, 'you must tell me the name of this would-be poet.'

Perictione looked up at her curiously.

'He went by the name of Anaxandrides,' she said.

'What do you mean, "went by the name of?"'

'That, honoured Archeanassa, was the name that he gave out as his own.'

'I see,' said Archeanassa, who shifted a little on her couch and then lapsed into a meditative silence.

'Shall I go on with the story?'

Receiving Archeanassa's silent nod, Perictione returned to her theme.

'Well,' she said, 'the reference to the poem, and the quiet, attentive concern with which this Anaxandrides addressed her, could not fail to awaken in poor Hermione the recollection of her former entanglement. And it must be said that, in comparison to this handsome poet, the ageing and half-educated Phorbas cut a poor figure indeed, even though immeasurably superior in all those qualities that make a reliable husband. Nor did the poet conceal the warm desire that Hermione still awoke in him, or refrain from suggesting that her departure from Colophon had been far too precipitate, and that she hadn't given him a chance to patch up their quarrel or to explain that the other girl had meant nothing to him, nothing at all. The cottage, he said, was standing empty, and he could redeem it from the landlord just as soon as he returned to his native city. And when the poem was published Hermione would become famous all over Lydia, all over Hellas, and would live in Colophon as his uncrowned queen and consort.

'To cut the usual story as short as it deserves to be, Hermione fell into the trap, and there the matter would have ended, my dear Archeanassa, had not Hermione been possessed of the spirit, if not the education, of a true philosopher. And here is what she did. Leaving her former lover to make his own way to Sardis, with a promise to see him in Colophon just as soon as the travel arrangements could be made, she went straight to her husband and addressed him thus:

'"My dear good Phorbas, who has done me no wrong and to whom I shall always feel the deepest gratitude, I beg you to listen to my confession with as much understanding as you have shown in all our days together. I came to you as a widow, believing my husband to have died in a shipwreck off the coast of Cyprus. And now, having gone to pray in the temple of Demeter, whom should I meet but this very husband, Anaxandrides, who looks on me in astonishment, having returned from his trip to find the house locked up and his wife departed. It seems that he did not travel, as he had given me to understand, to sell musk-pods in Cyprus, but went off with some floozy to the Bosphorus, though how he could have the cheek to tell me this I do not know. In any case, my dear good husband, you are not my husband at all, and now I must return to Colophon, departing from you and the gentle Archidameia, whom I love as a daughter, and bereaving you for the second time."

'Phorbas cried out and wept and tore his hair, but there occurred to him no remedy for this dire predicament, and when Hermione assured him that Anaxandrides was ready to take her away by force if necessary, he gave way to despair. And then, bethinking himself of his daughter, he set off for Sardis to obtain her counsels, enjoining his wife meanwhile to do nothing until his return, in which she solemnly promised to obey him, knowing that Anaxandrides, who was always in debt, would in any case need a week or two to redeem the cottage.

'Now this Anaxandrides, honoured guest, had not wasted time since taking leave of his mistress, and had gone straight to the temple of Artemis, to catch sight of the chorus girls as they went to their morning duties across the precinct. And his roving eye fell on Merope and was instantly entranced by her beauty. He waited in the sacred grove beside the temple until the liturgies had been sung, when Merope and Archidameia, being always first to emerge from the peristyle, came tripping hand in hand across the sandy soil, laughing their tender laughter and smiling their tender smiles. And without further ado he accosted them, asking whether they would be interested in some new songbooks which he brought with him from Cyprus and in which the goddess is praised more worthily than ever she had been praised before, and for which he asked no payment, provided only that they would allow him thereafter to send further samples of his wares as they were published. And when they hesitated, he mentioned other goods which he could offer, including philosophical dialogues in the style of Aeschines and a batch of stylish sandals from Corinth which had just arrived in his warehouse at Ephesus but which he could dispatch within the week on a sale or return basis.

'Soon the girls were hooked, and he was sitting between them on a bench in the shade of an artemisia, the sacred fountain making a filigree border to his velvet words, and the manuscript of his unpublished poem lying open on his knees. And what beautiful knees they were, Merope said, smooth as polished ivory, round, strong and reposeful like the knees of a god. Not that they were his only attraction. On the contrary. But to a bashful girl with down-turned eyes knees assume an importance that no other part of the body can yet acquire, and the sound of the salesman's voice, as it slipped at ease between every subject that had ever awoken her curiosity or ever touched her heart, was enough to incline the poor girl quite hopelessly in the speaker's direction. Anaxandrides had discovered their two names, and was about to reveal his own, when Phorbas came running into the precinct, his face still wet with tears, and his arms outstretched towards his daughter – who, it must be confessed, recoiled from him at first, ashamed to admit to such a father. But when Phorbas, ignoring the stranger's presence, delivered his story, saying that he had come at once to his only friend and counsellor, and that without his daughter's wisdom he was surely destroyed, Archidameia's heart was softened, and she held her poor father in her arms and mingled her tears with his.

'The stranger coughed, and wondered aloud whether he were not perhaps *de trop* in this new situation, even suggesting to Merope that they slope off somewhere where they would not be in the way. But Merope was a pious girl, and resolved to offer what help she could. And the first step was to ask the name of Hermione's other husband. 'Anaxandrides,' Phorbas said between his sobs. 'Anaxandrides of Colophon.' On hearing which the stranger suddenly pushed the manuscripts back into his bag and exclaimed:

'"Anaxandrides of Colophon! Why, I know the rascal!"

'At which everyone turned to him in surprise, and Merope took advantage of the general mood to take a long, cool look at the stranger's face. It was a look from which she never recovered, and a look that he instantly and expertly returned.

'"Yes," the stranger went on. "And I know exactly how to rescue you from the predicament in which you find yourself, my good . . ."

'"Phorbas."

'"My good Phorbas. My name's Antimachus, by the way."'

At which Archeanassa gave a shriek.

'Antimachus?'

'Well, he couldn't give his real name, could he?' said Perictione with a pert little frown. 'Can I go on with the story?'

'If you must,' said Archeanassa, and she raised her hands to her face, which felt as though veiled in cobwebs.

'Well, this is what the stranger, Antimachus as he called himself, unless it was some other borrowed name, it hardly matters, proposed. The villain, he said, may very well have married Hermione: who knows? In any case, it would be better not to test the matter in a court of law. But it was also true that Anaxandrides – who was, the stranger informed his audience, an undistinguished poet with a side-line in brocades – had long been seeking an excuse to divorce his absent wife, in the hope of acquiring a new one. This the stranger knew, since all Colophon knew it.'

'*I* didn't know it,' said Archeanassa.

'But you, my dear, led the life of a recluse.'

'True,' said Archeanassa with a sorrowful sigh.

'And, the stranger went on, the principal obstacle to this design was the absence from Colophon of any young woman beautiful enough, and well-bred enough, to satisfy the would-be poet's vanity. If, however, such a young woman could be found, and introduced to Anaxandrides as a possible fiancée, their troubles would of a certainty be over. All they needed to do, therefore, was to present Anaxandrides with a suitable candidate, and demand that he divorce Hermione as the condition for proceeding with his courtship.

'"But where might such a candidate be found?" asked Merope, believing that no-one of her sex could stoop to so shameful a stratagem.

'At this the stranger turned to Archidameia.

'"Who," he asked her, "is the most beautiful girl you know?"

'"Merope," came the unhesitating answer.

'"Who is the most well-bred girl you know?"

'"Merope."

'"Who, among the girls you know, has the greatest wisdom, courage, resourcefulness and will?"

'And always the answer was "Merope."

'"And who would have the supreme goodness to help her friend and her friend's poor father in this dire emergency – provided of course that she need go no further than to *pretend* to an interest in this rascal, and that she would emerge from the ordeal, which would not really be an ordeal but only an amusing prank played on a knave who deserves far worse, without damage to her prospects or her reputation?"

'Although this question was greeted merely by gulps of astonishment, the stranger continued to speak.

'"And who would wish to augment still further the admiration of a man whose esteem for her will in any case never die?"

'"Merope?" said Archidameia, with a sullen frown.

'"I will do it," said Merope, and with a cry of joy Phorbas embraced her, calling her his daughter, his guardian spirit, his goddess, and so on and so forth, and beginning to shake the stranger by the hand as if everything were already signed and sealed and Hermione were back to square one or at any rate square two where she belonged.

'But now,' said Perictione, rising of a sudden to her feet and filling her bowl, 'I need to interrupt this story, in order to reply to your argument. For you will see that a great difference has arisen between Archidameia and Merope, in the matter of the handsome stranger.'

'On the contrary,' said Archeanassa. 'They feel the same about him.'

'Sameness in some things causes difference in others,' Perictione observed, as she settled again on the couch, and neatly stowed her feet beneath her tunic. 'The fact of the matter is that Merope and Archidameia were for the moment quite estranged, and while they danced and sang together that afternoon according to their sacred duties, they did so with wrath in their hearts.'

'O.K. So what follows?'

'You will recall your description of the chorus: not just a thing, but a person, with a will and an answerability of its own.'

'Yes, most noble Perictione. And what I said of choruses could be said of schools and families and teams and clubs and even of your uncle's Academy – indeed, of any institution through which the soul of man acquires its . . . its . . .'

'Its aboutness?'

'Well yes, let's say "aboutness," so long as we don't get distracted by the word.'

'But here, you see, is a great difficulty for your philosophy, honoured guest. I would believe the more readily in this collective person of yours, if it took charge of its members, as my soul takes charge of my limbs. But I ask you to envisage that dance in the temple of Artemis on the afternoon in question, Archidameia and Merope moving side by side as the formation requires, each expertly shuffling and leaping and pirouetting in accordance with the liturgy, reaching arsis and thesis together, and extending the anacrusis in titillating counterpoint as only the Artemisians can – and all the while their hearts set each against the other in a burning indignation. In what way has the collective soul of the chorus ordered the affairs of its limbs? To my thinking, in no way at all. For there is no such soul, no self which is the chorus, over and above the twenty selves who inhabit those twenty dancing bodies, and who may have nothing in common apart from the fact that, just for this one moment, they are obeying the same set of rules.

'And I would go further, honoured guest, and question whether this chorus is even – what was the word you used? – a substance. For a substance, as I understood it, is an individual thing, which is one and the same at different times. But by what right do we say that the chorus in which Archidameia and Merope danced is one and the same as the chorus fifty years before, when neither of them existed, or ten years later, when the Persians put a stop to the thing, or on that day soon after when Merope left the Artemisian order, never to return? The fact is that these collectives have no real identity through time, but only a fiction of identity, just as they have only a fictional soul and a fictional power of choice.'

Archeanassa thought for a while, and then spoke as follows:

'What you say is persuasive, noble Perictione. But I refer you to your grandmother's wise remark, that it is only a very shallow person who does not judge by appearances. Consider the painting by Apelles on the wall next door. In it we see old Colophon, its streets crowded with people, and a procession in honour of Phoebus Apollo making its way to the temple. Of course, none of these things are really present, here and now. This is a fictional procession, with fictional people and fictional horses. Yet, if someone were to look at the wall, and see nothing there – no procession, no street, no temple, but only a wall smeared with colours – would we say that he perceived things correctly?'

'By no means, honoured guest.'

'To see the wall correctly is to see the fictions, is it not?'

'Indeed.'

'In which case the fictions are real – real, that is, for us, who have eyes, imagination and rational intelligence. And so it is with many other things in our world, noble Perictione – things which might be dismissed by Diogenes as mere appearances, but which are just as real as you are.'

'And how real is that, I wonder?'

'Things which are appearances, but not *mere*. And yes, we too are such things. For what is Perictione – the face that I admire and fear, or the skull beneath it?'

'Let's leave that question, honoured guest, for some future committee of experts. But I have already told you not to fear me, for I am not what I seem. And as for this collective person of yours, the chorus, the city, the school or whatever, I should describe it as a sequence of appearances, all of which are mere. And I would add a diagnosis in the style of Merope. For when people look around the modern world for something in which to believe, something that is larger and fruitier and less lonely than the self, invariably they end up with one of your collectives, honoured guest, a group identity in which to dissolve the mere individual who seems so frighteningly alone. And these collective persons are fictions of the same kind as the gods – we have painted them on the backcloth of our world, just as Apelles painted the procession on the wall next door. People search in them for the traces of a vanished holiness, as an animal sniffs for the scent of a companion who has departed forever from the scene. And it always befalls that those who need gods, and who have lost their faith by the way of disenchantment, endeavour, honoured guest, to re-enchant the world, by inventing collective persons and beseeching them to give us what the gods once gave – a more than human willing and a more than human love. And you might say, to put the matter bluntly, that such collective persons are like the ghosts of the gods, lingering just a little after their interment, but soon to be blown away by our thinking as mist is blown by the wind.

'And whence comes this desire to re-enchant the world, honoured Archeanassa? To my way of thinking it is the child of solitude, and of the insufficiency of solitude. True, you have had lovers, and two of them, Uncle Plato and the one you call Antimachus, have been of some importance – or so you believe. But the very intensity of your passion has kept you apart from the world, in a secret place of waiting and watching and doubting. I say this not as a criticism. I have the greatest respect for the path of love, and envy those who follow it. But she who walks that path loses sight of society, and erects in place of it a sentimental fantasy, an image of harmony and order and enchanted congregations. She consoles herself with the thought that society will one day welcome her back, with its ancient consolations, its innocent ceremonies and its pious day-to-day rituals. And then her isolation becomes bearable. For it seems more like a decision, more like a sacrificial offering, and a preparation for the time when she will be once again included and redeemed.'

As she spoke the expression changed on Perictione's face. In place of her haughty irony came a solemn and priest-like wakefulness, and when she turned to her guest, her eyes shone with compassion.

Or could it be that she was drunk? Certainly she had been downing bowl after bowl that afternoon, and a high flush now enflamed her cheeks. But Archeanassa had no time to come to a conclusion before the girl was on her feet, and clapping her hands for the servant.

'With your permission, honoured guest, we shall have some music. And if I snore you are to wake me.'

'Certainly, noble Perictione. And if the music is sad, you are to lend me a handkerchief.'

'I am beginning to wonder whether you understand music,' said Perictione. 'But we shall see. You will not object if the boy sits with us. For music is the cornerstone of education, not least because it teaches us to be still. And I think you will agree with me, honoured guest, that the inability to sit still in one place is the cause of all our calamities.'

10

A discourse on music and the death of Merope

As the servants were re-arranging the furniture and setting up the lyre, Perictione led her guest into the courtyard, to enjoy the refreshing breezes there. And taking Archeanassa confidingly by the arm, she began to speak with strange solemnity, and in a low tone as though she were afraid of being overheard.

'Much has become clear in my mind, honoured guest, in the course of our discussions. And one thing I beg to tell you now, before the wine goes dead in me.'

'To what do you refer, noble Perictione?'

'That although I have no solution to the problem that has troubled us . . .'

'What problem?'

'The problem of life in the modern world. Although I have no solution, I recognize a third way – a way that depends neither on disenchantment, like the way of Diogenes, nor on re-enchantment, which is your way, and perhaps Xanthippe's too. This third way is the one that Merope chose, and forever am I in her debt for showing it.'

'And what is this third way?' asked Archeanassa, who in truth liked this Merope less, the more she heard of her, and could barely contain a sneer.

'Neither disenchantment nor re-enchantment nor any enchantment at all. For these look for the solution outside the self, hoping to find it painted on the walls of other lives, or scribbled there like rude graffiti. No, the third way involves a turning inwards, a truthfulness to the one thing of which we can be certain, which is our own will to power. Oh, I don't mean political power, or brute force or anything like that. I mean the power to move, to dominate, to persuade, to impress the world with one's image and to leave it to recover from the blow. I mean the sense of style, both amused and amusing, which never stoops and never compromises, but openly competes and wins.

'And this, my dear Archeanassa, was the tragedy of Merope, that her life had been split in two. As I said before, she could not live by half measures. As a member of the temple chorus she had been wholly and sincerely an Artemisian, rejoicing in the ceremonies of the religious life. And later, as a wandering scholar, she had been wholly and sincerely a wandering scholar, casting down idols and laughingly purging the world of its gods – blowing away, as she put it, the stink of divine putrefaction. But the two didn't connect. Each of her lives was, from the point of view of the other, a fake. And the thing which sundered them, the third life of which you know so much since it was your life too, the life of the mistress, estranged her from herself: it cruelly abolished the pious maiden, and was itself abolished and denied by the impious tramp. It was this act of denial that tormented her. She could not heal the breach between the first and the final Merope, even though nothing else would enable her to create the work of art which was to be its own redemption. This is what led her at last to Colophon, the vain and tragic attempt to examine her life here, to re-assume it and re-incorporate it, to make herself whole. Her philosophy, which was one of intransigeant success, led her inexorably to failure.'

'So why do you say there is a third way, noble Perictione?'

'Because not everyone is Merope, and not everyone is doomed by love.'

'You are speaking of yourself, and proudly.'

'No, honoured guest. I am speaking of the new world,

and the art of survival. But come, let us listen to the music, and afterwards, with your permission, I will finish my story.'

So saying, she led her guest back into the parlour, where a fair-haired girl sat by the window in a gown of flesh-coloured samite, looking for all the world as though she had just flown in from Mount Helicon. She was intently tuning the lyre with ivory fingers; music moved in the drift of her limbs and the folds of her costume; melody shone in her brow, and her clear cheeks, pale lips and Grecian profile were harmony re-made as flesh. Yet this, Perictione explained, was the chamber-maid, a girl quite devoid of culture, who, like so many musical people, had not an inkling of the higher life to which her own music pointed. Next to the maid stood the old servant with a flute, while tambourine, castanets and what looked like a string of little bells had been set on a table beside them. A steaming infusion of dried fruit stood in the fireplace.

'Boy!' shouted Perictione, and at once he appeared from behind the door. He stood to attention and looked past her ear at the wall.

'For this was I doomed to sin, against myself and mine. Nine hundred and eighty?'

The boy shook his head.

'Later?'

A shake of the head.

'Nine hundred and sixty eight?'

The boy shrieked and danced, beating the air with imaginary hammers, his lips pursed and eyes narrowed, like a soldier sounding the alarm for battle. And then he promptly sat down on a stool that had been set beside the musicians. Perictione, having poured the infusion for herself and her guest, held up a hand for silence, and the music began.

How new and strange and wonderful were the sounds which filled Perictione's parlour! And with what attentive rapture did Archeanassa listen to them! Never before had she heard the lyre played like this, with cascading runs that left the strings sounding together, or with a delicate plucking that seemed to hang on the air like stars. Never before had she heard such sounds from the flute – and surely, Archeanassa thought, this must be a new kind of flute, so high and sweet and fluent was its wandering melody, so full and poignant its tone. And when flute and lyre combined, she gasped with delight to hear their tunes together, the one soaring and tumbling and darting, the other softly flowing beneath it, like a stream beneath the flight of a bird.

How strange and moving was the sight of the two performers: the one so graceful, her perfect child's face the very personification of music, the other ancient, hoary and sexless, the mere husk of a human being – and both of them domestics, who owed their living to a mistress who soared above them on wings of pride. Music rose from them like the fragrance from a flower; yet neither could say whence it came or what it meant. Did this not point to a mystery in the human soul, which we can glimpse here and there, but invariably in some place where we least expect it?

The music quickened to a dance, and to Archeanassa's surprise the boy rose to his feet. Taking castanets and tambourine from the table, he began to emphasize the rhythm – tap-tap, tap; tap-tap, tap. He rocked back and forth in time to the music, and a look of total absorption came into his face, eyes bulging, cheeks puffing, forehead frowning and lips pursed, the features clustered like a bunch of radishes. Archeanassa found herself smiling at him, but the boy was so absorbed in his task that he did not return her glance.

The music ceased, and Perictione announced that the band was now to play one of her own compositions, in a style that she herself had developed. She clapped her hands and there entered into the room two more musicians, a man and a woman, the first carrying a cithara, and the second an instrument that Archeanassa had never seen before and which she begged to examine. She discovered it to be a kind of lute, but small, without frets, and held on the shoulder. The strings were not plucked, but sounded with a bow of horse-hair, stretched on a wooden frame. And when the music began she thought that no more exquisite sound could be imagined than the voice of this lovely instrument, which sobbed in the empyrean like a lark in summer.

Equally astonishing was the music itself. The four instruments played together, but not in unison. Rather they conversed, discussed, presented topics and digressions, and commented on each other's arguments. A melody would be introduced by the cithara, to be at once taken up by the lyre, expounding the theme at one pitch while the cithara developed it at another. The flute entered in the same way, and then the strange new instrument, but in another key now, and doubling the notes, so that the theme burst open and poured its rich tunefulness through the whole musical structure. To Archeanassa's ears it was more like thought than sound, and seemed to echo within her as though she herself were producing it. But the music was beautiful too, with a strange, remote, abstract beauty that recalled the sky and the sea. And when it worked its way to a gentle climax, the strange instrument holding a high trembling note while the others slowly rose towards it through glistening harmonies, and the boy getting quickly and quietly to his feet to take the string of bells and suddenly, at the very apex of the melody, shaking from it a shivering cascade of silver sound, Archeanassa could barely contain her tears, so limpid and serene and accepting did the music seem. When it was over she looked at Perictione with admiration and astonishment.

'Did you like it?' asked the girl with a pleased smile.

'It's lovely. What is it called?'

'Oh, it has no name.'

'No name? Surely a piece of music must have a name?'

'If you say so. Let's call it Plutarch.'

The boy uttered a high-pitched laugh, but fell instantly silent on receiving a frown from Perictione.

'Why Plutarch?' asked Archeanassa.

'Why not? After all, one name's as good as another.'

'Surely not, noble Perictione. Suppose Homer had called his poem "A florilegium of helmets," or "Bad times for Priam." Would those names really be as good as the *Iliad?*'

A discourse on music and the death of Merope

Perictione thanked the musicians and asked them to refresh themselves next door. When only the boy remained, staring motionlessly before him, she turned again to Archeanassa.

'Your question,' she said, 'is an interesting one, and it relates to something you said yesterday, when discussing the city.'

Archeanassa asked her to explain.

'Architecture, you said, is not like the other arts. For it is public. It does not take place, like this little concert of ours, between consenting adults in private. Therefore, you said, in distinction from music or poetry or painting, architecture is not free to innovate and experiment and give itself airs.'

'And do you not agree?'

'I neither agree nor disagree, honoured guest. But this much at least we can accept, which is that music progresses, is always surpassing itself, always looking for new forms, new melodies, new harmonies, new ways and means of expression.'

'You have given us a splendid example, noble Perictione.'

'I do my best. But although, in this as in everything, I am slightly ahead of my time, you cannot deny that music has a history, that originality and innovation are of its essence, and that, as music changes, so does the ear, the mind and the soul of the audience, with the result that nothing ever sounds quite the same from one year to the next.'

'For the moment let us grant the point,' said Archeanassa.

'Well then, honoured guest, there was a time when music was the province of the human voice, when all melodies were sung, and all songs had words. And this was the origin, no doubt, of poetry and dance, maybe even of tragedy, comedy and the minor arts. I imagine a great festival, and the people coming together as a chorus, singing their praises to the gods. Then one by one the arts of the chorus take on a life of their own – song breaking away from dance, and

213

poetry from music. Art as we know it is the final distillation of religion, the clear residue which is left, when no trace of a god remains.'

'It is a possible theory.'

'And for that reason melodies always had names, just as poems do. So that in referring to the "Calyce," for instance, I instantly remind you of a tune.'

The boy nodded vigorously at this, but continued to look away, as though to show that he took no part in the dialogue. And to emphasize the effect he seized from the air an imaginary flute which he played with the fingers of one hand, while blowing through his lips and shaking his head in concentration. Then, with a gesture that took the breath away from Archeanassa, so intimate and careful and creative did it seem, he lifted an imaginary puppet on to his free arm. And by some peculiar magic, he made the puppet dance to the music, so that Archeanassa saw as clearly as though they had been real the long flowing scarf about its head, the graceful upturned hands and flexing knees, and the sudden twirl upon the toes as the music ended. Imagining the music and the dance together, Archeanassa understood that, in some strange way, music and dance are one.

'But now, music has freed itself from words, has become purely instrumental, and in losing the words it loses – what shall we say?'

'Its aboutness?'

'You see how the word comes back to us? But I should rather say that this new music is about nothing in particular, than that it has no aboutness at all. For that is the peculiar thing, is it not? The music describes nothing, tells no story, paints no picture, and yet a kind of aboutness permeates through it, as though it were pointing, but we know not where. And of course, that is precisely why "Plutarch" is not a good name for it, any more than "Fate" or "Seascape" or "Indigestion." Indeed, it refuses every name save the one that describes its form, which is why I call it – if you must know – "Four Part Fantasy in the Lydian mode, number 3."'

'What you say, noble Perictione, seems entirely

reasonable. Yet is there not a mystery in this instrumental music of yours? It seems to speak to us, as it were from soul to soul, and to have a meaning which is every bit as real as the meaning of poetry. But when I try to put the meaning into words, how inadequate and irrelevant they seem, and how far from explaining the mystery!'

'Boy!' said Perictione, turning to him. 'Go and fetch the flute and the lyre.'

The boy went off without a glance, skipping and dancing as he went, his sandalled feet light and soundless as they fluttered above the floor. Archeanassa could hardly believe that this was the very oaf who had tormented her, and was beginning to excuse his former failings when the boy, returning through the doorway with the instruments, surreptitiously turned in her direction and put out his tongue.

'I think I can cast light on this mystery, honoured guest,' the girl continued, 'not by solving it, but by showing it to be a mystery of a more general kind. But first we must consider what happened in this room a short while ago, and why it is so remarkable.'

'What happened? Why – music was played, and we listened to it.'

'And which of those two, the music or the listening, is the more mysterious?'

'The music, of course; for listening follows naturally, when music occurs.'

'Now there I disagree with you, honoured guest, and would rather say the opposite: that music follows naturally, when listening occurs. Sit down, boy, and wait for your instructions. Suppose someone were to strike a note on the lyre – the forefinger[1], say. Boy!'

The note sounded in the room.

'Is that music?' Perictione asked.

'It is a sound certainly. But perhaps not music – not yet.'

---

1   Ar: *asbu' as-sabaabah*. Because the author is translating the ancient Greek names for the notes of a standard melodic mode, I have followed her example. The names are explained by M. L. West, *Ancient Greek Music*, Oxford 1992, pp 218–28.

'So let us try to turn this sound to music. We shall follow it with another: first forefinger on the lyre, and then the tone above – the *parhypate* – on the flute. Boy!'

One note sounded, and then the other.

'Is that music?'

'Well, it could be music, if . . .'

'If what?'

'If someone heard it as such.'

At this the boy jigged up and down on his stool. Then, with a weird smile, he began to play with the imaginary puppet, holding it in one hand and gently smoothing its hair.

'Well then, honoured guest, what must you hear, in order to hear those two sounds as music? Presumably it is not enough to hear the sounds.'

'Why no. For often in the street we overhear such noises, and they never strike the ear as music. But maybe if you *listened* to the sounds . . .'

'Ah! We are getting warmer. Play the notes again, boy! Now, if you listen, what exactly do you hear? One sound, yes? followed by another. And what else?'

'I hear the beginning of something – a melody – that moves from the first note to the second.'

'And what kind of movement is this?'

'Well, I cannot describe it, except to say that it is a movement upwards. Yes, that's what I hear. Something begins on the first note, and rises to the second.'

The boy clapped his hands in approval at this speech, and played the two notes again and again as though in proof of her words.

'Enough, boy,' said Perictione. At once he set down the instruments and began to try out imaginary alternatives, preferring an enormous version of the flute which required him to puff with inflated cheeks and to reach below his knees with his fingers. Perictione watched him distractedly, and then returned to her theme.

'And what is this thing that rises? Is it the string of the lyre?'

'Why no. For the second note is sounded on the flute.'
'Is it the note itself then?'

'No,' Archeanassa responded after a moment's thought. 'For how can the first note move to the place occupied by the second? The note cannot change pitch without becoming other than it is.'

The frenzied clapping that greeted this remark confused her, and only when Perictione had put a stop to it with a frown was Archeanassa able to pick up the thread of her thoughts.

'And here I am tempted to conclude, noble Perictione, that, although we hear movement in music, there is nothing in music that moves.'

'Good, honoured guest. But this nothing that moves, in which direction does it move?'

'Well, upwards, of course.'

'So there is a kind of space in music, an up-and-down space, with places and distances?'

'I am tempted to say so.'

'But where is this space? Boy! *Encore!* You just heard the movement, honoured guest. But where did it occur? Where was the place from which it began, and where the place in which it ended?'

'Not in this room certainly. But not out of it either.'

'Nowhere then?'

'It seems so, noble Perictione.'

'So when we hear music we hear a nothing which moves in a space that is nowhere?'

'Not a nothing, but not a something either.'

'Come now, a nothing will do as well as a something about which nothing can be said. Boy, improvise!'

Playing the lyre with one hand and the flute with the other, the boy filled the room with a wild torrent of sound. Rushing arpeggios on the lyre raged like a wounded animal, and the flute descanted above them with screams of terror and foreboding. Mad ecstasy had seized the boy's face, which was wrapped and knotted like a dishcloth, the eyes closed and the red hair standing on end. His fingers moved on the instruments like packs of charging soldiers, stabbing and wrestling and clattering as though clothed in armour. The sobs and screams of the flute seemed to rise up through his body, and he shook and danced with the force of them. Soon he was thumping the floor with his feet and trembling the length of his body as though giving birth; and great gusts of sound flapped against the faces of the listening women like stinging sheets of rain. Louder and louder did the music sound and wilder and wilder came the tremors of his body, until Archeanassa, in fear and alarm, suddenly put her hands to her ears.

'Stop boy! Enough!'

He stopped at once, lowered the instruments and stared expressionlessly at the wall.

'Plenty of movement there, I should say,' Perictione went on. 'And feeling too, of a kind. But not something you should want to listen to for long. But let us return to our simple example, with a slight addition. Boy! Add the final note – the *hypate* – on lyre or flute, it matters not which.'

The notes were dutifully played.

'Do you not notice something else, honoured guest, in this new example?'

'Certainly, noble Perictione. For now the movement is completed, it has come home to rest. And I see that the movement that we hear in music is not merely a movement up and down, but a movement *towards*, and *away*.'

'Let's put it slightly differently. This nothing that moves – it moves with a purpose, does it not?'

'Indeed.'

'Whose purpose?'

'Why, the purpose of the composer or the player or whoever is in charge.'

'Is that what you heard when the boy was improvising – his purpose to produce those sounds?'

'Not exactly, for the boy is inscrutable. But the sounds themselves had purpose – they moved towards and away from each other and when you told him to stop they hung in the air as though frustrated.'

'So this nothing that moves through nowhere, it moves with a purpose that is no-one's?'

Archeanassa would have signalled her assent, had the boy not forestalled her with a round of applause. Once again he was cradling the imaginary puppet, smiling into its face with an idiot smile, and pinching its nose and ears with little gestures of affection.

'But when the boy improvised, what else did we hear?'

'Well, this is what bewilders me most, noble Perictione. I heard movement certainly, and purpose of a kind. But the purpose was *in* the movement, and as it were running through it like a thread.'

'Just as in dancing?'

'Well yes, as in dancing. But there is something else. In this purpose, which is not a purpose at all but a kind of purposeful parody of purpose, I heard terror, foreboding, and a kind of disorder of the sentiments which was one with the disorder in the music.'

'And whose was this terror, and whose this foreboding?'

'Well, the boy's, I suppose.'

She said it in a whisper, hoping that he would not hear. But he shook his head, nevertheless, and then raised the puppet high in the air, pointing to the place which it occupied and making it dance from side to side.

'In this household,' said Perictione with a haughty frown, 'there is neither terror nor foreboding, and you greatly mistake the boy's circumstances if you believe anything else.'

As she watched the puppet, a light dawned in Archeanassa.

'Then the terror and the foreboding which I heard in the music were also no-one's?'

'No-one's, my dear Archeanassa. But are they the meaning of this music nevertheless?'

The boy shook his head and so did Archeanassa.

'I think not,' she said, 'for, with all respect to the boy, whose talents are by no means to be disparaged, the music that he played was meaningless.'

219

The applause that greeted this remark again prevented speech, and the boy folded the imaginary puppet and put it away in the breast of his tunic. Then he shifted to the edge of his stool, looking keenly at the two disputants as though taking a ringside seat at a wrestling match.

'And if I may continue the thought, noble Perictione, your Fantasy in the Lydian mode was the very opposite of this, brimful of meaning. There was feeling too. But if someone were to ask me *what* feeling, I should say, let them play the piece again. For no form of words can capture the emotion as the music captures it.'

The boy gripped his stool and nodded.

'And another thought occurs to me. It is the very disorder, the arbitrariness of the boy's improvisation that makes it so easy to identify its mood; and it is this same disorder that cancels the meaning. Whereas in the Fantasy mood and meaning are one, and the discipline of the music conveys them. It is as though a state of mind that we know in ourselves but only intuitively, so to speak, had entered the music, had been taken up, refined and made conscious of itself through the musical dialogue, and so translated itself from feeling into thought.'

'Wow!' said Perictione when the applause had died down. 'You are rushing ahead of me. Let us at least say this, that there is a meaning in music, that it is like an argument, and that its subject-matter is feeling – feeling which achieves consciousness of itself in this musical form. Would you agree?'

'Yes.'

'And it is only through musical discipline, and the rigours of style, that this consciousness is granted?'

'Yes, noble Perictione.'

'But then, I ask you again, whose is this feeling? And what is it about?'

The boy pulled the puppet from his tunic, dusted it, and set it to perform a slow dance, waving the fingers of his free hand in its face, as though to charm it to life.

'Well,' Archeanassa replied after a pause. 'The feeling,

as we said, is no-one's. And it is about nothing – for about-ness needs an object, does it not, and music gives no picture of the world?'

'Correct, honoured guest. So now we have a statement of the mystery, do we not? Music is a movement of nothing in a space that is nowhere, with a purpose that is no-one's, in which we hear a non-existent feeling the object of which is a nobody. And that is the meaning of music.'

The boy looked at Archeanassa, who fancied that the puppet also looked at her. And the strange thing was that this non-existent glance was more intense and meaningful than any glance she had encountered, passing through her like a sword and startling the life within.

'In which case,' she said, 'we are back where we started: music is a pure aboutness, without subject or object. And the mystery is contained in the word "about."'

The boy shook his head gently, and the puppet renewed its glance, prompting her towards the right reply.

'Not quite, Archeanassa. For the aboutness we are talk-ing of is aboutness of a certain kind – the aboutness that we know in love and fear and anger.'

'Got it!' cried Archeanassa. 'We are talking, are we not, of the refinement, or better say, the liberation of the passions – the lifting free of passion from the subject who suffers and the object who wounds? Is this not what happens in music – true music, I mean, music whose arduous discipline refines away the debris of our dreams? And is that not why sad mu-sic pleases us?'

Here both Perictione and the boy applauded.

'But what makes this possible, honoured guest?'

'Now I think I understand, noble Perictione, why you said that listening is the mystery, and music the result of it. For let us return to Xanthippe's example. Those fans of Xylophantes, do they listen to the music that excites them?'

'Up to a point.'

'Would it not be better to say that they hear, but that they do not listen?'

'Better for whom?'

Chapter 10

'Better for us,' Archeanassa continued eagerly, 'who are squeezing philosophy out of withness, betweenness and aboutness. The music is played so loudly precisely because it is to be heard but not listened to. If it were not so, the empty repetitions would begin to weary the fans and the purpose of divine stupefaction would fail. Listening, however, comes at the end of movement – it is what remains when the frenzy is restrained, and the mind itself engages. Now, noble Perictione, do animals listen?'

'Certainly.'

'But their listening is always, is it not, a listening *out* – searching the world for information, being alert to danger, food, companions and so forth?'

'When I taught Phocis to dance – but we agree, he was a problem case.'

'It does not occur to a horse – since it cannot occur to him, however talented he may be – to listen to a sound for its own sake, to listen to how it sounds. Certainly, he can *hear* how it sounds, but to *listen* to the how of it, is this a real possibility for a horse?'

'So "musical animal" replaces "featherless biped" as the definition of man?'

'If you like, but I prefer to see the matter as you did, in your first talks with Merope. The consciousness of self distinguishes us from all other creatures. It is this which fills our thoughts with aboutness – the mystical link between inner and outer, between self and other, between soul and the world, which we look for and listen to in everything we see or hear. And it is this which prompts us, on hearing sounds, to pause for a while in our daily tasks and listen. And then, perhaps, in the presence of such a wonder as your Fantasy, the imaginary space opens to our ears, and fills with the image of aboutness, as note summons note out of nothing, striving towards nowhere, and reaching its goal.'

'Hurray!' shouted the boy, who threw the puppet high in the air above him and clapped his hands. Perictione leaped to her feet in astonishment.

'Great Zeus!' she cried. 'He speaks!'

A discourse on music and the death of Merope

The boy stood to attention, with the slope of the shoulders and the stiffening of the legs which Archeanassa knew so well. And it is true, she thought, that his knees are beautiful, smooth, white and delicate as polished eggs. With a prayer to Artemis, she made herself ready for his story.

'Help!' said the boy, as he fled from the room. Perictione stared after his vanished form. Then she clapped her hands for the servant, ordered hot towels and finger bowls, and gave instructions that the boy be returned to his cage at the back of the house and watched closely until bed-time.

'And so,' she said, when the howling and rattling had dwindled to an occasional chortle, and the women were settled on their couches, with hot towels around their heads and a cooler of Lemnian wine upon the table, 'I must return to the story of Merope. And I am grateful to you, honoured guest, for this discourse on the art of music. For it teaches a lesson that we both must learn.'

'And what is that, noble Perictione?'

'We must work upon our loves and griefs as music does, so as to create a pure aboutness in their stead. And already you have ceased, I think, to fear me, knowing that this Merope of whom I speak is not the woman who trudged beside me along the muddy lanes of Hellas, but a refined and reconstituted Merope, yes, a figment, as your Antimachus soon will be a figment. And this translation of our loves into a realm where there is no disappointment redeems both us and them.'

'Do you think so?'

And again that fugitive thing, that other, secret Perictione, made itself known for a moment in the window of her eyes.

'I think so, my dear Archeanassa. And you will be the more convinced of this when you have heard my story.'

'I am willing to hear it.'

'Anaxandrides of Colophon was not slow to see the effect that he had on Merope, since women and his effect on them had been his principal study since birth. (You must understand, honoured guest, that he was the spoiled child of a doting mother.) He therefore anticipated no resistance to his plan. As luck would have it, he said, he was renting a little cottage in the hope of providing a roof over the head of his poor old mamma. As a temporary measure Merope could be installed there, and introduced to this rascal Anaxandrides as his – that is to say Antimachus's – cousin, visiting from Sardis. Beauty and virtue would have their effect, there being in any case no competition in Colophon –'

'No competition in Colophon?' cried Archeanassa in outrage.

'– there being no competition in Colophon, and the handsome stranger would himself play a minor part, by withholding permission for the courtship until proof of divorce.

'The plan was greeted with enthusiasm by Phorbas, who was to put it about that Merope was staying with Archidameia and her family for a long weekend. On the next day, therefore, they agreed that Antimachus, as they called him, should travel with Merope to Colophon, while Archidameia and her father returned to the farm, to take to Hermione the good news of her impending divorce. Archidameia was in two minds whether to spill the beans to Merope's parents, so painful were her baffled emotions. But here is what put an end to her scheming, honoured guest, and henceforth removed her from the drama.

'No sooner had they arrived at the farm than Phorbas poured out his story to Hermione, unable to contain his joy at the good deed undertaken by this stranger called Antimachus. Archidameia watched her step-mother become paler and paler as she listened. And when Hermione learned that Anaxandrides was to be tempted with the peerless Merope, she uttered a little scream of vexation – of which Phorbas in his innocent good nature took no notice. Archidameia saw then how matters stood, and realised that her father was the victim of a scandalous deception. She did not understand everything, but she understood enough to heed the warning which Merope had scorned. So she held her peace, and tearfully embraced her step-mother, showing every affection. And in due course Hermione was reconciled to the rustic life from which she had been tempted to stray, and took no lover until . . . but that's another story.

'Meanwhile Anaxandrides had hired a chariot and set off with his prize at a spanking pace for Colophon, knowing that in so risky a venture time was not on his side. And no sooner was Merope installed in the cottage, and a slave appointed for her needs, than Anaxandrides bowed his head before her and confessed to his great deception.

'"Most virtuous Merope," he began, "I am Anaxandrides of Colophon, the very one whom you were to confuse with your beauty, and who has indeed been confused. Before scorning me as I deserve, listen, O fairest creature, to my story and take pity, if you can, on a wretch who etc., etc."

'And here is the story he told. For years he had led an honourable life in Colophon, a respected merchant and poet, looking after his poor old mother and bearing as best he could the provincial dreariness of the Colophonians. Although bashful and retiring by nature, he felt duty-bound to enter society, if only to add grace and intelligence to what would otherwise be a garbage-can of human rejects. (His opinion, honoured guest, not mine.) He came to the notice of Hermione, who, starved of intelligent company, began to bother him with her attentions, to wait for him at literary gatherings, to seize hold of him as he passed her in the street, and in short to do everything in her power to tempt him from the chaste and honourable life which he had chosen.

'At last he was forced to complain, though in the kindest and most forgiving terms, to Hermione's father, who, as the best remedy for her obsession, dedicated the girl to Demeter, and sent her across to Chios to train in the chorus there. Now as you know, honoured guest, the Demetrian order has an itinerant branch. It was this branch, Anaxandrides said, that Hermione chose in time to enter, travelling to Athens and other places in the hope of meeting a suitable philosopher. And that is how she came, he said, to the temple near Sardis where, having discovered the advert placed by Phorbas, and being bored out of her mind with the life of the temple, she decided to try her hand at marriage. So it came to pass that one day, pausing to offer a prayer to the goddess, Anaxandrides had stumbled across her and re-awoken those old desires.

'Having escaped in fear and trembling from Hermione's clutches, whom should he encounter but the only girl he could ever love, whose virtue and intelligence equalled her beauty, and who caused him to waver, for the first time, from the honourable goal of a dedicated chastity. And, having suffered one temptation, he then suffered another, which was to practise the deception that would bring Merope to Colophon, not for any base purpose, he hastened to add, but to pour out his heart to her and solicit her help in devising a final solution to the Hermione problem.

'Furthermore, he said, while there were certain technical difficulties which he wouldn't go into, but which stood in the way of an entirely instantaneous marriage, his happiness and peace of mind now depended on the hope that she might see him as a possible husband. And when Merope asked why he had not been more forthright in explaining all this to Phorbas, Anaxandrides threw her the tenderest look and indicated that he would not for all the world jeopardise poor Phorbas's chance of happiness, by revealing to him the true character of his wife. Surely, he added, the plan that I devised has saved this innocent farmer's peace of mind, and that, Anaxandrides implied, was its primary purpose.

'Men like Anaxandrides, honoured guest, have many skills, and the greatest is the ability to act for the noblest of motives while fulfilling their lowest desires. Merope, whose trademark was commitment, made up her mind there and then that this was the man for her. All at once, and without a moment's hesitation, the life of the temple fell away, and she stepped towards her chosen hero new and unencumbered, like Aphrodite from the waves. And she was the more enamoured to discover that Anaxandrides would take no advantage of her desire, but enjoined her to wait and consider the consequences, so as to give herself to him when the moment came with a clear and happy conscience.

A discourse on music and the death of Merope

'On the next day he maintained the same stance of regretful chastity and cautious desire, and on the next day too. And so it went on until Merope, who by now had foresworn any intention of returning to Sardis, was beside herself with passion. That was the moment when he chose to enjoy his prize, being careful, as he did so, to murmur "are you sure we're doing the right thing?," "I feel really bad about this," and other such ready-made disclaimers. In consequence, Merope awoke to her new condition feeling that it was she and not he who had caused it.

'Of course it was not long before she raised the question of the technical hitch that prevented their marriage. And when Anaxandrides revealed that he already had a wife and that he could not, in all decency, abandon her, this was explained to the girl as further proof of his virtue. This wife of Anaxandrides' was old and infirm; he had married her in a burst of compassion. *Eros* had never been part of the deal, and if he felt obliged by decency to see the thing through, this did not prevent him, he confided, from feeling the occasional burst of relief that the old woman's chronic lumbago would soon put an end to her days. Of course, he paid for this feeling with agonies of guilt; and these would often keep him awake in his separate bed far into the night. Nevertheless this was the reason why he could never visit Merope in the afternoons, when he sat with his wife and read to her from the classics. He begged the girl to understand that his love could only be increased by this minor irritation, and that she was of such surpassing value to him that he would never, for her sake, do anything reprehensible lest he should tarnish his love. And more to that effect.

'In short, the true impediment to marriage was Anaxandrides' virtue. And in proof of his love he offered to Merope a poem, which he claimed to have written and which he hoped one day to publish. It told the story of his passion, using the city of Colophon as an extended metaphor. He was looking forward to the day when he could lay public claim to both the poem and its subject. Meanwhile, however, he would probably produce a limited edition under a

227

pseudonym, out of regard for his wife and with a view to protecting Merope.

'Whether such a poem existed, honoured guest, and whether Anaxandrides had written it or stolen it, are questions that need not concern us. The fact is that Merope had set her heart on the man, and resolved to live out her passion completely, doing everything to ensure that those morning visits were the fullest proof of her devotion. And she turned her back on Artemis, wrote not a word to her parents, and gradually forgot the rituals and the dances that had occupied her virgin days.

'So things proceeded for a year or more, and they were times of happiness. True, Merope sometimes wished to ask the gods to advance her marriage plans. But which god specialised in lumbago? In any case her moments of doubt were drowned in the ever-renewing flood of her emotion. And that was when, in her joy and self-confidence, she took up painting. The little cottage which Anaxandrides had rented soon became a studio, littered with brushes and boards and pigments. Had it not been for the enforced privacy of her life, many more would have come to sit at her feet besides the wretched Apelles.[2] For it was Merope, honoured guest, who discovered the laws of perspective, together with the art of realistic portraiture. And precisely because she was so private a person, cut off from public life and devoted to her passion, she began to paint the portraits of ordinary, humble people, discovering in their hands and clothes and faces the secret folds of human happiness and those mysterious shadows and flesh-tints which tell the story of our lives and redeem us from time.

'Merope said farewell to Artemis with a picture of the goddess, for which she used a baker's assistant as model, dedicating the girl to the goddess by incarnating the

---

2   Apelles of Colophon was generally credited in the ancient world with the major advances which were rediscovered by the painters of the Renaissance. He was born in Colophon during the fourth century BC, but is thought to have worked in Ephesus.

goddess in the girl. You can see this picture today in the house of Pharnabazus, to whom Apelles sold it as his own. The goddess stands forward on the canvas. Her column-like thighs are enlaced by skirts of sky-blue, which hang across them like garlands, enhancing their everlastingness. Her head is bowed and slanting like the head of one who listens with loving patience, and a pale silk scarf blows out flairing from her gathered hair. The right arm stretches across the picture to pluck a wild anemone: this arm is strong, determined, but also relaxed, untroubled, pointing to its own pointing, as it were, and making of this gesture an imperishable sign of itself. The background is sparse, symbolic – bare green hillocks, with a lake, blue hills, and a fortified bridge linking nowhere to nowhere. And although this figure is a portrait of the baker's girl, you do not see it so. No questions gather around the gentle face: no "who were you?," no "what became of you?" Nor is she a type or symbol. Something quite different was achieved by Merope, and achieved, honoured guest, for the first time – a sense of the human form settling into its eternal meaning. Everything about the figure is outside time and change. Her clear brow and soft, concentrated eyes, the pursed readiness of natural sentiment in her lips – these suggest an astonishing freedom from the sensual world, a freedom that is nevertheless entirely human and always with us, an object of thought, emotion and prayer. Never has a goddess received so fitting a farewell.

'Here I should return to your own rhetorical question, honoured guest. What remains of the border between light and shade, when no god inhabits it? Nothing, and everything, is my reply. It was only when she had laid the divinity to rest that Merope understood shadow. To the cynic and the believer shadows are imperceivable – to the one because he can conceive no living mystery, to the other because mystery for him lies hidden in the depths of things. The person who can see light within light and shade within shade, who discerns a border between them only to erase it with fine strokes of the mind and the eye, who observes divisions and gradations and barely perceptible highlights within the quivering film of shadow, such a person must first have loved a god, and then rejected him. For to see the meaning of shadow you must transfer to the surface the awe and piety which were once reserved for the depths. You must do this because you know that, in a real sense, there *are* no depths, and that all that we are and fear and hope must somehow live for us in the shimmering skin of things. And Merope, who passed from the purest religion to the most passionate refusal to be duped, was the first artist to understand this. Hence those extraordinary portraits, in which faces and flowers and humble jars and bowls seem like the shadows cast by darkness in a sphere of illumination.

'Only one subject seemed to defeat Merope's brush, and that was Anaxandrides. Whenever she came to paint his portrait the features seemed to melt away before her view. No sooner had she captured the peculiar grey of his eyes, than she saw that they were not grey at all but a muddy green. And just as soon as it had been mixed on her palette, this colour too seemed wrong. His ears, which seemed so large and fleshy when first she came to paint them, were pinned back and taut when she glanced up from her work. The nose had all shapes and none, and the cheeks seemed to smear beneath her brush like discoloured fat, lifeless, rancid and unwholesome. The human face, she discovered, is not separable from its portrait. We build our face as a painter does, and in building the face we build also the soul. It was through her brush, therefore, that she began to discover the falsehood of her lover, and the unreality of his golden promises. After a while she would paint him only from behind, standing to address imaginary admirers, while her eyes explored the sinewy nape of his neck – a neck in which she discovered, by degrees, the inner rhythm of self-centredness.

'One day Anaxandrides came to Merope in a solemn frame of mind. Business was not too good, he said, and his poor wife was ailing. The doctor had recommended sea air, which would raise her spirits and ensure that her last months were peaceful. Anaxandrides therefore proposed to kill two birds with one stone, and take the old woman with him on a trip to Athens which his bankers insisted to be necessary in any case. Oh, he would be back as soon as he could. And never would there be anything in his heart but the thought of Merope. However, he couldn't see what other course was open to a man of honour, and he begged Merope to understand the problem. And, lest anything should befall him on the journey, he proposed to leave with her his manuscripts, including early drafts of his amorous elegy, the final version of which he intended to publish in Athens, though whether under his own name or another he could not yet say. At any rate, he would send her a copy as soon as it was published. And he enjoined Merope most urgently not to try to contact him during his absence, and to wait patiently and prayerfully upon his return.

'As you can imagine, honoured guest, Merope was stunned by this announcement, and all the more so when she discovered that Anaxandrides had slipped out of the cottage by the back door as she wept in the parlour. Her state of mind was worsened by the knowledge that she was with child. She had intended to announce this fact to her lover that very morning, and had grasped at it through her tears as the means of retaining him in Colophon. When she had recovered her composure, she saw that there was but one course remaining to her, which was to set off in search of Anaxandrides, and persuade him to remain for the sake of his child. But no sooner was she out of the house than she realised that he had neglected to give her his address. Too ashamed to ask information of passersby, she retreated to the cottage, where she collapsed as though dead on the floor. It was three hours before she awoke, to find Apelles standing over her with a box full of papers.

'"These are from Anaxandrides," he said, putting them down on the floor. "He's gone to Athens, and asked me to drop them off. I say, you look as though you've had a bit of a turn. Maybe we should postpone our lesson till tomorrow."

'Well, you will not be surprised to learn, honoured Archeanassa, that Apelles had no more lessons in painting, and was able to complete his education only later, when Merope had departed on her travels. Merope, meanwhile, gave way to her emotions. It was not so much the grief itself that mattered as the fact that there seemed to be no part of her in which the feeling could be cornered and destroyed. Grief was nowhere and everywhere, like the air she breathed; and if she expelled it with one breath it was only to take it in again with the next. For seven months she sat motionless before the hearth. She paid off the landlord with paintings, and thereafter opened the door to no-one. Nothing stirred in her heart or mind, and when at last something stirred in her body, she went at night to the midwife and gave birth without a cry. Then it was that the great change occurred in her. By casting off the child she would cast off Anaxandrides; by setting out from Colophon she would walk away from the past; and by denying the gods she would deny the weakness of the heart which leads us to believe in them. And because Merope was Merope, and lived always with the finality of purpose that I adored, these thoughts were no sooner formulated than acted upon. The child and the box of papers were left with her neighbours, together with a painting or two by way of compensation. And to complete the gesture, she called the boy – for it was a boy – Anaxandrides, and thrust him from her with a flourish of disgust.

'So there, honoured guest, you have the gist of Merope's tale – recounted in that cottage where the tale had begun. When she had finished speaking she rose on the bed to stare at the all-seeing stars. I came beside her, raised my hand to her face, and her tears fell on my fingers like the warm rain of summer storms. This molten, pliable Merope followed me like a child through Lydia, her firmness of purpose dissolved, her moods vacillating and her thoughts confused. Often, as we rested by the way, she would sit beside me in silence, clutching my hand with hooked and anxious fingers, like a child clinging to its mother for fear that she might suddenly be snatched away. At other times she would indulge in cheerful reminiscences, recalling people, places and gods of a happier age. But as soon as she had done so, she would lapse into a sombre silence from which no sight or sound could recall her, and I sensed the swelling wound of emotion that would not be healed. As we journeyed onwards the conflict in her feelings grew. She would laugh for a while at the Persian automata as they worked in the fields; and then rage against this world without cities or dancing. She would pause by some mossy stream to paint in words its teeming abundance, and then turn aside with a contemptuous gesture, as though pierced by the senselessness of concrete things. And when we came at last to Colophon she was distressed by my excitement, making a feeble attempt to forbid me from visiting the night-clubs in search of a job. However, she hadn't given a lecture since her encounter with the late Sterbs, and by now we were completely broke.

'We found a barrel by the ruined temple of Artemis, and as she tidied our temporary home and made plans for supper Merope cheered up a little. My Persian was still fairly basic; but I fell in with a Greek whore who told me that the Babylon club was looking for a classical dancer. I left the interview with a cash advance for clothing. Joining first one queue and then another, I was able to obtain firewood, millet, a marrow and even sunflower oil, with which to prepare a simulacrum of our first supper together. And as I cooked it for her, the old serene smile reclaimed her features.

'For some months, honoured guest, we lived in this way, and I was relieved to discover that a calm had settled over Merope's spirits. Life was not easy at first: we were strangers, Greeks, aliens, and our eccentric habits caused the workers to gather near our barrel and stare in silent amazement before scampering home to the suburbs. But I began to make my mark. The Babylon Club was soon more popular with the Colophonian elite than impalings, and I was given a pass to the royal shops, where you could get soap (I still needed soap), papyrus and real olive oil. I perfected my Persian, and became sufficiently well off that, when this site came up for re-development, we were able to buy it and make essential repairs. We lived in the garden, and Merope felt more secure there, not because of the wall only, but because everything she saw, provided she did not raise her eyes too high, was old, and sacrosanct, and Greek.

'And here is a peculiar thing, honoured guest. Merope, who had wanted at all costs to be modern, and to shake off the old traditions which had died around our necks, could no longer abide the sight of modern things. If she came with me into the town it was to wander with a quizzical expression on her face around the ruined temples, or to stare vacantly at some piece of marble cornicing built into a modern wall. She was calm now, but also melancholy, and was never happier than when sitting in our garden and reading the tales of the gods.

'Then one morning she reverted to her story.

'"It is time for me to find him," she announced.

'"Find whom?"

'"Anaxandrides."

'My heart sank at the idea of such a futile search among the ruins.

'"I doubt that he returned from Athens," I said. "And if he did return, he would surely have been arrested by now and sent down the mines."

'"I mean the other Anaxandrides," she replied. "His son. And mine."

'Well, honoured guest, you know this son of hers, and it remains to tell the tale of his discovery. Holding my hand and in fear and trembling, Merope set out towards the street, not far from here, where her cottage had stood among orchards. Of course, we found nothing – only waste-land, a few slate-grey towers and a factory for making hair-oil out of horse manure. We enquired of the passersby but they stared at us blankly, bewildered by our reference to streets and temples and cottages, all of which were so much things of the past that a kind of obscenity attached to naming them.

'Then, after searching all morning, we stumbled on a dank passageway near the central plaza, between a ruined shop and a disused temple that had been boarded up for demolition. My curiosity was aroused as it is always aroused by dereliction, and we made our way to the blank façade of mud bricks which sealed the bottom of the passage, and from which a confused murmur of voices emerged into the pestiferous air outside. We stood at the battered door listening, and were astonished to hear the sound of Greek, spoken softly by old and lifeless voices, as though a group of dying actors were painfully re-learning a text. Pushing open the door we found ourselves in a long corridor which sank into the channelled darkness of the building, with tables arranged along its sides. Light, of a meagre kind, issued from coloured lamps in the wall, and fell over the unsmiling faces of the people, many of whom were sitting alone, clutching bowls of wine and staring fiercely before them into space. Others were talking quietly, or raising their voices in a sudden bark as drunkards do. Grim-faced waitresses plied between the tables, receiving orders as though they were insults, and putting down drinks like farm-hands throwing pigswill into a trough. The place had no decoration save a lurid picture on the right-hand wall, in which naked women stood in absurd poses against an impossible view of the Egyptian Nile, their pink nipples pointing provocatively, their pasty haunches smeared with violet highlights. Merope turned to flee, but I held her by the sleeve and asked the waitress for a table and an amphora.

'We were sitting in the Pericles Taverna, named, we were told, after some politician who had been important in the Trojan war. A few Greeks gathered here each day to while away the hours in protected silence. Every now and then one of them would get up and lift his chair high in the air, to break it over the head of his neighbour, who would collapse for a while on the table, and then rouse himself to return the compliment. But, aside from this amusement, it was clear that the customers had nothing much to do, and had more or less lost the art of conversation. Both men and women sat at the tables, but their behaviour was of a uniform coarseness, meaninglessly affectionate by spasms, and then morose and blank. Laughter occurred rarely among them, and only as a kind of mad outrush of air, used like the ink of the cuttlefish, to render the atmosphere turbid and impenetrable. After buying three rounds of drinks, however, we managed to elicit a few words from our new companions. And after three more rounds, one of the old whores responded to our questions by saying that she remembered Merope's neighbour. She directed us towards a compound on the edge of town, where the Greeks from Merope's street had been piled up for sifting and sorting when the King got round to it.

'The Pericles Taverna was depressing enough. But it was nothing beside the experiences that followed as we made our way, guided by our permeable resolve, towards the edge of town. It was a wet autumn, and we were obliged to cross a desolate waste of mud where wagons lay broken and abandoned, some with the skeletons of horses still fixed in their shafts. A dismal, lightless sky pressed down on the city, like the lid of a coffin, and sheets of rain slashed at our faces as we went. The rain was part of the unrectifiable disorder – wearying, enervating and relentless like the cry of an infant lying discarded out of reach; dirty, smearing, a stream of wet over everything, as though all objects melted at our touch and ran in a cold film through our fingers.

'Our vision was fractured by the raindrops that hung from our lashes, and at first we could not distinguish the contours of the place to which we came, or separate the buildings where people lived from the those where sodden archers stood motionless on high, aiming from time to time at a door or a window. The towers had been built close together, with long balconies at every level, on to which doors opened out of dark interiors. There were no streets, only muddy pathways between the vast unlettered tombstones of the living. Nothing bore a sign: neither path, nor building, nor balcony: in everything the claim to "me" and "mine" was visibly negated, to the point where, had someone ventured to attach a name to his door, it would be like a lunatic laugh, from which one turns in shame and embarrassment. Although we had been given an address it was no more than a number, and we went from block to block and stairway to stairway, peering through the semi-darkness for room 3065, our hair dripping into our faces, and our feet congealed in the unwholesome mud which flowed across the lobbies. It was an hour before we found the door for which we were searching, high up on the twentieth storey of a tower. Rain poured in long strings down the stairwell, and a dreary sound of running water came from deep within; I imagined the place to have been built above an underground river, from which evil spirits arose to haunt its corridors. The door on which we knocked had been many times broken and many times repaired, and the face which peered from the crack was of a similar cast, as though it had been smashed up regularly with a hammer, and then restored with a poultice of mud. The half-closed cunning eyes looked long and hard at Merope, and when the woman recognised her visitor and gaped, a peculiar noise emerged from deep within her, like the clanking of chains in a dungeon. The lines and ridges which criss-crossed her face spoke not of age only, but of suffering and fear and the pitiless ruses of a survivor. She ushered us in, and closed the door quickly and quietly, glancing nervously along the balcony as she did so.

'We found ourselves in a lightless room, which seemed at first to contain no furniture, but in which I made out the dim forms of boxes stacked against the walls. A figure moved in one corner, but I could not tell whether it was man or woman. It seemed to be rocking up and down on one of the boxes, clutching its feet and with its head pointed to the ceiling. The old woman spoke in whispers, and expressed her astonishment that Merope had returned. Her husband, she explained, had been forced to pull one of the wagons in which the Greeks and their possessions were transported to their modern quarters. After a league, he had collapsed in the shafts and died. His widow and their protégé were therefore slightly better off for space than most of the residents. Mention of the boy caused Merope to tremble, and I held her hand as the creature was brought forward to peer at his mother.

'"So this is Anaxandrides," Merope said at last, looking

intently into his cretinous face. He lolled his tongue and rolled his eyes and shook his shoulders in a kind of twitching, solitary dance.

'"Yes," said the old woman, "this is Antimachus."

'"Antimachus?"

'"We kept the name you gave him, for fear of offending the gods."

'"But I called him Anaxandrides!" Merope cried. "After his father."

'The woman looked puzzled.

'"I could have sworn . . . ," she began. "But then, it all happened in such a hurry, and what with me being hard of hearing, and the poor husband having no memory. . . . Still, that's what we call him, and what's in a name?"

'Merope was so shaken by this dialogue that she ceased to speak, and merely looked at the boy, who returned her stare with a kind of vagrant interest. Then, reaching out a hand towards her face he began to explore its features, pulling with gentle tugs at ears, cheeks and nostrils, and beginning as he did so to grin and then to laugh, and then to clap his hands in a fit of merriment.

'"Well," Merope said at last, "aren't you going to greet me?"

'The old lady coughed and fidgeted.

'"Beg pardon, your honour," she said, "but he doesn't speak."

'"Doesn't speak? You mean never?"

'"Never ma'am."

'"In the name of Zeus, why?"

'"I don't rightly know, ma'am. But bearing in mind as there's nothing much to speak about, and bearing in mind as my husband was stone deaf towards the end, and bearing in mind as he's cooped up alone here with no companions of his age, and bearing in mind as they wouldn't take him when we was hard up and tried to sell him as a slave, so that he come back from the market with a pretty low opinion of hisself I daresay, and bearing in mind all the troubles as I've had on his account, and the great burden as must weigh on his little soul whenever he's minded to think of the debt what can never be repaid, and – well, bearing all this in mind I think you'd be surprised to find that he *did* speak, your honour. Not that he doesn't read, though."

"'He reads?'"

"'I can't stop him, ma'am. Of course, we're not in the way of cluttering the place with books. But there's that box of papyrus you left along of him, and he is in it every day."

'The boy, as you can envisage, honoured guest, was dancing up and down through all this, chuckling out his agreement, and looking eagerly into his mother's face. And on being told that this was indeed his mother he gave a shriek, somersaulted backwards, raised his tunic, and stuck his head between his legs to look at her. Fortunately the light was too dim to give a clear vista of his masculine credentials, and the old woman quickly pulled back the tunic, leaving him stuck in that awkward pose for several minutes like a vase beneath a dustcloth.

'To cut a long story short, honoured guest, it was no easy matter rescuing that boy, and I would not have done it had Merope not set her heart on giving him a Greek education, and making of him what Granny made of me, an exercise in *anamnesis*, a memory of culture in a world of organised forgetting. It didn't seem to bother her that the raw material was less than promising. In any case, such was her plan, and what with the bill for milk, another for bread, a truly exorbitant one for laxatives, an amazing sum for haircuts and what have you and another to pay for his transportation, including damages for the death of the husband – what with all this I found myself obliged to part with six months of savings before the old crone would let the creature and his box of manuscripts out of the door. Luckily I had bought the house, and there was room for him in the kennel behind the kitchen, which I was just beginning to restore. So now we were settled in Colophon as a family, and I could devote myself to the cause of Perictione's fame.

'Alas, however, things were not well with Merope. Whether she was afflicted with guilt over the boy I do not know, since she never mentioned him. But whenever he emerged from his kennel to fetch another book from the library, she would rise from her stool and go out into the city. (I should say, honoured guest, that those early years of modern Colophon were a splendid opportunity to acquire second-hand editions of the classics, and the library, under my stewardship, was growing fast.) Merope's days were spent either in the garden, where she sat staring into the void, or in the precincts of the temples, where she recited the liturgies and seemed to search for something lost among the ruins. Her mind wandered, and during dinner she would converse with people faraway or non-existent. If ever you needed a lesson in why not to commit yourself to a man, honoured guest, that lesson was Merope. She came undone before my eyes, and the impudent heroine of our travels shrivelled to a helpless girl.

'Not that she believed again in the gods. But she wrote them letters, which she gave me to deliver, and it was obvious that she was getting ready to join them in their common grave. She thanked Artemis for her education, and complained at length to Apollo of his influence, and of the chilling effect he had on the art of tragedy. She wrote also to the dead, composed a lengthy refutation of Parmenides which she sent to Elea with a basket of apricots and the compliments of Dionysus, and dropped a line to Xanthippe, addressed from Mount Olympus and promising to intercede with Zeus on the old philosopher's behalf.

'That letter to Xanthippe was almost the last thing she did. Having dropped the papyrus into my hand she ran from the house, and because there was foreboding in her eyes I anxiously followed her. In the street a horse was being cruelly beaten by a wagoner. Merope ran towards it, crying "Phocis! Phocis!" and indeed, there was an uncanny resemblance to our dear lost friend. The horse even seemed to recognise her, and although staggering under the blows across its back, whickered at her approach and reached out its head towards her. With a gasp and a sob Merope fell on the poor creature's neck and slid to the ground. The horse too collapsed, breaking the shafts of the wagon as it fell. And they lay there side by side, the horse shuddering and panting in its death-throes, and Merope staring fixedly into the sky. I raised her in my arms, and my useless tears watered her face like rain on a place of stones. I called out her name, but she did not hear me. I shook her and squeezed her and kissed her; I promised the gods I would believe if only my Merope came back to me. But it was not to be, honoured guest. The vacant stare on my darling's face never left it thereafter, and Merope died a month later, her sightless eyes fixed on the wall of the garden, her speechless mouth set firm as though set in stone.

'But there, I have been boring you, and it is time for our supper.'

Perictione rose swiftly, and hid her face as she went with rapid strides to give orders for the meal.

11

In which Archeanassa discovers many things, including (perhaps) the papers of Antimachus

They sat in silence as the food was set upon the table: a bowl of millet decorated with strips of green marrow, and an amphora of fragrant oil. The servant departed and her shuffling steps dwindled across the hall. The boy howled once in the back of the building and then was quiet. Only the crickets in the garden made a sound, ushering in the twilight with a monotonous scraping of the legs, as though to rid themselves of the viscous day that clung to them. At last Archeanassa broke the silence.

'So what happened to the papers, noble Perictione?'

'What papers?'

'The papers of Anaxandrides.'

'Oh those! They are down in the cellar somewhere. Merope asked me to burn them. But I never got round to it. I'm glad you reminded me.'

'And you, Perictione. Why have you told me this story?'

The girl was silent for a moment. And then she turned her beautiful eyes upon her guest, and looked steadily into her soul.

'Do you not know?'

'I have tried to guess, but there is too much mystery.'

'The mystery, Archeanassa, lies in you. Like the votary who dedicates her life, you have lived in thrall to a figment.

And even if this figment is as real as Merope's cottage, painted there by Apelles, it is nevertheless you who devised it, you who embellished it, you who made it, in your imaginings, an object of love.'

'But that cottage!' Archeanassa cried. 'It was mine. I would know it anywhere!'

'That cottage, honoured guest, is yours or hers or anyone's. For when the moment is past, what is there but the work of memory? And when the painter takes up his brush he remakes the world as a thing remembered.'

'And Merope,' Archeanassa asked after a pause. 'Was she a figment too?'

'She became one, alas. And in telling her story I have tried my hardest to learn from you. For I wished to cast credit on my darling, while taking revenge on the one who destroyed her.'

'Oh yes, you have taken revenge. And not only on Anaxandrides. You have sown great doubt in my heart, Perictione, so much that I cannot rest until we have gone through those papers.'

'That we shall shortly do, my dear. And perhaps by then you will see things more clearly. Let us meanwhile eat this sacred food while I tell a story.'

Archeanassa took millet from the bowl and anointed it; and the scent that arose to her nostrils was the scent of Greece, the Greece of her childhood, the Greece that once was here in Colophon. And was that a figment too?

'A girl was born to a family of respectable ghosts,' said Perictione. 'Their faces had the frozen look of immortality, and their words were polite, impersonal and meaningless, addressed to the eternal void. They passed the girl with silent nods, or walked straight through her, failing to notice that she was a thing of flesh and blood. Once or twice they looked askance when she spoke, for even a phantom has doubts. But they reassured themselves with ancient texts, and returned each evening to Elysium, congratulating themselves on their well-run establishment.

'The girl was dedicated to a goddess, but secretly, since

the ghosts thought it shameful that one of their number should need to be redeemed. And the goddess lifted the girl from her illusions, and showed her a world of anarchy and dread, in which the hordes stampede from place to place, fearing what treads behind them, and fearing what goes before. But when she sought for those things that the multitude feared, the girl found nothing but rumours and myths and fairy-tales. Bewildered, she left the service of the goddess, and wandered by the sea of love. The stretch of shore on which she walked was stony and desolate, and the waters were cold. The girl removed herself, and lo – another walked beside her, dressed like the goddess, but in mortal guise. And they went together, laughing at the tales of the gods. To be entire, to live entirely, and to receive each moment as an eternity – such, she decided, was her destiny.

'But a cloud descended, and the light went from the world. For mortal things are fragile, honoured guest, and nothing is proof against corruption save the figment. And then at last the girl saw the meaning of the gods, and the wisdom of the old belief in them. When the friend had been taken from her, the girl re-made her as an icon, an image in the sky of her desiring. As she refined the picture, taking away the dross and corruption, slowly her friend dissolved into the ether, and what remained was no longer the object of love, but love alone, redeemed from all attachment. And the girl too was redeemed. Her darling had wished to express this in words, to announce to the world that each life is its own salvation. But words could not encompass what had happened. So the girl turned to music, and, devising a style in which sound became thought and thought became sound, she composed her Fantasy in the Lydian mode – her sacred song of thanksgiving from the convalescent to the goddess, to give the piece its actual name. And with this gift to the world she rested for a while, waiting for the one who would understand it.

'There came a visitor, one who knew the path of love on which her darling had stumbled. And this visitor grieved for the past and its ruin, was hounded by sorrow, and wished the world to conform to her memory and her deep desire. The visitor too, the girl resolved, must tread the other and more sacred path, must look with sombre feelings on the beloved who betrays, so as to rescue the love which is ever faithful. So the girl took the visitor's love from her, and returned it as a figment. And she did this for the sake of the goddess, knowing that figments feed on figments, and that phantoms are made real by the blood of living things.'

Once again Perictione's face had become imbued with that solemn and sacerdotal air, and once again, as she turned to her guest, a light of compassion shone about her. Archeanassa took those pearl-white hands and kissed them, saying

'Let me now see the papers, and I will accept what they prove.'

'Yes, by Zeus, the papers,' said the girl, shaking herself from her dream. 'I'll go and fetch them.'

And she went swiftly from the room as though in embarrassment. Her footsteps scuttled through the hall. With a grinding of keys and a squealing of hinges, a door opened somewhere on the other side. The sandals slapped on steps with a hollow echo, and then the house fell silent as the sound dwindled away.

Archeanassa stared in wonder at the picture of her cottage, and turned over and over in her mind the story of its other occupant. Without doubt Archeanassa had fallen into a mystery. And it was a mystery like music, bound by an inner logic to before and after, aimed straight at the heart – yet god-like, ineffable, beyond the reach of human words. A shudder passed through her body, and she quietened herself with a prayer.

Perictione's absence began to weigh on Archeanassa. It was dark outside, and a servant quietly entered, placed a lamp upon the table, and retreated with a bow. But the effect was to fill the room with shadows, which sped away from the light and danced against the wall. Arrows of darkness quivered on the painting, and the cottage glowed faintly behind them like a face behind a veil of feathers. Whose face was it? The boy howled in the reaches of the house; a woman's voice sounded somewhere, footsteps pattered, and then everything was still. Again a shudder passed through her body, and again she stilled it with a prayer.

And then it seemed to her that the door of the cottage was suddenly ajar, and that someone stood beneath the lintel. It was a woman – tall, majestic, serenely smiling. She beckoned to Archeanassa. And from her open lips there came the sound of music, lifting a silken robe of meaning as virgins bear the temple veil. The penetrating sound of that strange new instrument soared ever higher as though in search of the gods. And the eerie woman looked at Archeanassa, waving her arm as though in valediction.

Archeanassa jumped to her feet and fled into the hall. On one side of the peristyle a door stood ajar, with stone steps leading downwards and the flickering light of a candle falling across a vault of yellow stone. She ran across to it, pulling her tunic close around her body. A narrow stairwell led down towards the light, and Archeanassa stumbled on the moss-covered steps, slipping here and there and bumping her head on a projecting stone at the bottom. She arrived in a passage, at the distant end of which another candle burned uncertainly. And thinking to find Perictione busy with the box of papers, or perhaps lost in dreams, as happens when people make the mistake of unearthing memories, Archeanassa felt her way along the narrow tunnel towards the light which beckoned from afar. There was no sound save a distant dripping noise. She stood for a moment to listen, thinking she heard the murmur of a human voice. But the murmur resolved itself to the steady drip of water, and she continued down the passage-way. Then something touched the crown of her head, and she turned round, startled. Blade-like sea-shells hung from the vault above her, and tinkled quietly as she freed her hair.

She walked on, and the distance un-nerved her. Surely this was no ordinary cellar, that reached so far under the garden, and must indeed already have passed beyond the outer wall? The vault pressed closely, and a chill draft went suddenly past her body, like a flock of ghosts rushing to their place of punishment. And still the light glowed in the distance, and still the passage echoed with her tread. She was about to cry out for Perictione when close by there sounded a rhythmical whisper.

> *Goddess whose footsteps glow on this stone, Demeter, O hear me!*
> *Who in my wandering, ever near to me, altered my fortune,*
> *Took from my hands the gifts that I offered, warmed by affection,*
> *Lifted my soul to you, spoke to me, loved me, called me your daughter . . .*

The hexameters hung on the air like the scent of a temple, fragrant and changeless. And a great peace came over Archeanassa as she listened. She ceased to think of Merope, of Antimachus, of Anaxandrides and the other figments; she forgot the little cottage, and the woman who stood in its door; she thought no more of the boy and his antics, and in place of all these things there came a great emptiness like the emptiness of a far horizon – dwindling beyond thought and feeling and harm. She joined the whispering voice in prayer, and the story of Demeter's wanderings passed before her mind and moved her to love and pity.

Then she looked about her and discovered that the tunnel branched off into a vaulted crypt, where a lamp was burning and a priestess robed in the veil of Kore stood before an altar of polished stone. Archeanassa was drawn by an unseen hand, which plucked at her sleeve with a familiar urgency. And the priestess turned to face her, revealing the golden insignia of the mysteries, glowing like truth itself in the lamplight.

For a long time the two women faced each other in silence. Then the priestess returned the holy objects to their casket, and placed it in a cavity hewn into the wall. Turning to Archeanassa, she murmured something inaudible before lifting her veil.

'Then you really are a priestess!' cried Archeanassa.

'Oh you know,' Perictione replied, 'I like dressing up. And I brought these things with me from Athens. I wouldn't be parted with them for the world, they're such fun. But I thought you were upstairs, having supper?'

'And I thought you had come down here to find the papers.'

'What papers?'

'The papers of Antimachus.'

'Who?'

'Anaxandrides.'

Perictione clapped a hand to her brow.

'Zeus! What's wrong with me? As soon as I am down here I forget everything except the mysteries. By the way, honoured guest, you will be interested by this crypt. Originally it lay beneath the temple of Demeter, near the cottage we were talking about. There are some inscriptions on the altar stone which suggest that the story of Demeter was told differently here in Colophon. Nothing is more sensitive to climate than a god. But let's find those papers.'

So saying she led her guest along the passageway, to the place where the distant candle guttered in the draught. A recess at the end contained a pile of bric-à-brac: two leather satchels, some copper urns for cooking, an oil-jar, a roll of bedding and a large bronze knife in a pig-skin sheath.

'These are the things with which we travelled,' the girl explained. 'I couldn't bear to throw them away. Now, papers, papers, where were they?'

Some wooden boxes had been stacked behind the bric-à-brac, and she looked into each in turn. Broken amphorae, alabaster statuettes, paintings on boards, and pieces of a bronze tripod were taken out and replaced with a frown.

'I really don't know why I collect these things. The trouble is they are too old to be useful, and not old enough to be antiques. And while we're on this subject, honoured guest, I should say that nothing is more modern than an antique.

In which Archeanassa discovers many things

When an object becomes antique it falls out of history, and changes from a thing to a sign. It ceases to be itself, and becomes the representation of itself. It is no longer used but only *interpreted*. And this change from innocent signified to guilty signifier is what we mean, or ought to mean, by modernity. Or does that sound a trifle too pretentious, too Xanthippic? Here they are!'

She pulled a box from beneath the stack and set it down before her visitor.

Archeanassa lifted the lid with hands that trembled.

'I expect that boy has left them in a dreadful mess. How do they look?'

'Damp, slightly foxed, some mildew too. You really should have been more careful.'

'I know. I should have burned them as she asked.'

The ink had faded from the papyrus that Archeanassa held. But here and there a line was legible. At last she made out a couplet:

As the golden sand brightens under the wavelet,
So does my body shine to your caress . . .

'The Lyde!' she cried.

'Wasn't that written by Antimachus?'

'Yes, by my Antimachus.'

'Then I was right: that lying Anaxandrides stole his poems, just as he stole his women. Here, what's this?'

A little fragment of papyrus had been pinned to the manuscript, and the girl detached it and held it to the light.

'If my eyes are not deceiving me, this is Merope's script. Or at least one of her scripts. Or a script very like one of hers. It's a poem. Shall I read it?'

'I can take it,' Archeanassa murmured. At which Perictione declaimed the following verses, lifting the veil from her shoulders and glancing with sparkling eyes towards her guest.

Lyde was his name for me, the name too of my race,
And mine the noble figure which his lines are meant to trace.
Who has not sung of Lyde, the girl of Antimachus,

249

Or read the things he wrote of me – with help, it's true, from Bacchus?[1]

'Well, my dear Archeanassa, what do we make of that? It looks as though Anaxandrides did publish under a pseudonym after all. But then, I don't get it. Why does Merope – if it is indeed Merope, though looking at the writing I have my doubts – why does Merope insist that it is *she* who is Lyde? Was she afraid of competition?'

'It hardly matters, noble Perictione. For, as you say, they are all figments, the real Lyde, if ever there was a real Lyde, and the other girls who claim the title.'

Perictione looked at her thoughtfully.

'And do you really want to take this junk to Uncle Plato?' she asked.

'I think you should burn it, as you promised.'

Perictione seemed to approve these words, for she took Archeanassa in her arms, and begged her to dry her tears.

'And now, I think, you must get some sleep. For the wagon leaves at dawn, and your journey home will be long and troublesome. And if you could take the boy with you, I should be most grateful, honoured guest. He could be exhibited profitably at Athens and he is wasted here; besides he likes you. Perhaps, in the course of time, you might invent some parents for him. They come in handy, even when dead – especially when dead.'

Perictione paused, and then took Archeanassa by the hand.

'Follow the lights and you will find the way to your room. I shall say goodbye now, since I have some thinking to do, and it is here, with Demeter, that I think most calmly.'

Archeanassa made her way slowly along the passage.

---

1   If Merope were really the author of this poem, then it must be dated a century earlier than the version contained in the Greek Anthology (III.63) and there attributed to Asclepiades. However, there is a slight discrepancy between the two: Antimachus gained assistance, according to the Anthology, not from Bacchus but from the Muses. Surely Merope was more honest?

But, as she placed one foot on the steps, she turned back to her hostess.

'Perictione,' she said. 'What are you?'

'What am I?' asked the girl, who had donned again the veil of the goddess. 'I thought you knew. *I am the last gasp of the past.*'

Epilogue

Archeanassa awoke to a soft pink light, framed in the window like the background to some entrancing portrait. Peace hovered between the walls, as though a loving parent had watched over her through the night, and tiptoed away in the dawn. The room was large, airy, and uncluttered, with a bed of rosewood and a gilded table supporting a bowl of dried flowers. Through the window she could see a group of towers and beyond them a distant hill, covered in grey buildings and criss-crossed by wires. Had Merope slept in this bed? Had she stared from this window at the nothingness of Colophon? Was this the table at which she had written those troubled letters? And did Perictione come to this room to comfort her, to hold those hooked and anxious fingers, and to coax them open with a smile? Archeanassa thought so; and as she dressed she said a prayer for Merope and another for herself.

A breakfast of baked eggs, dried fruit and unleavened bread had been set down in the hall. As Archeanassa rose from the table the old servant came forward with a basket of provisions for the journey, and a beautiful amphora of enamelled terra-cotta, brimming with Cyprus wine.

It was not the public wagon that stood by the gate, but a private chariot, hired for the journey. Archeanassa's few belongings had been neatly stowed behind – even the last few tapestries, which had been carefully wrapped in papyrus and tied with a leather strap. The two Persian guards saluted at her approach, and handed her carefully into the vehicle, like something precious and rare. And as she sat down on the leather seat and turned to take a last glance at the house of Perictione, the boy came quickly through the gate and jumped up beside her. In one hand he held a wooden box, with air-holes drilled in its top, in the other a sheaf of papyrus. A hunting horn hung around his neck and, setting down his burdens, he lifted it to his lips and gave a quick toot. The dog scampered from the back door of the house, and leaped over the wall of the chariot on to its master's knees.

'She said we are to come.'

The boy spoke slowly and carefully, practising each word with his lips before pronouncing it. He looked past her, as though addressing someone far more important who sat on her other side. And when he had finished his speech, he stretched his lips in a comic parody of a smile.

'Oh,' was all Archeanassa could think of.

'Yes. Me, Teuchon, who is a dog, as I expect you have noticed, and Amphitryon. I have already introduced you to Amphitryon.'

Archeanassa nodded.

'I apologize,' said the boy, and immediately began a grotesque pantomime, illustrating the idea of apology with fawnings and scrapings, raised eyebrows and half-open arms, and beginning to search around himself for imaginary gifts with which to propitiate Archeanassa, while indicating with his sagging mouth that there was nothing to hand that could conceivably suffice to make amends.

Then the charioteer called to the horses, and with a jerk of the reins they were away, moving at a brisk trot towards the southern suburbs. The boy ceased his display, and settled down to read. But not for long was he still. Soon he began to snort and shake, slapping his hand on the papers and staring upwards with an astonished expression. Astonishment turned to anger, which in turn gave way to grief, then hilarity, then wide-eyed dismay. He laughed and was sad in such rapid succession that his face had the look of a clinging elastic mask which some unseen hand was struggling to pull across his features. Tears and slobber fell across the page, and at one point he howled so loudly that the horses took fright and started forward at a canter. At last Archeanassa asked him what it was that so excited him. He looked up blankly, his mouth drooping open like a great moist cave, and she repeated her question.

'This book?' he said. 'I found it. In a box downstairs, where she keeps her – her clothes for dressing up. It's about a girl called Lyd . . .'

'Oh no!' Archeanassa cried, and without a second thought she seized the papers from his hands and tossed them from the chariot.

'What did you do that for? When I have nothing to read I am a dreadful bore.'

The boy's reproach was mild. Within minutes he had consoled himself with the imaginary flute, which he played while rolling his eyes at Archeanassa in a parody of courtship, moving his head from side to side, and seeming to suck the film of air from around her face and turn it into music. So grotesque was the performance that she found herself laughing, and the boy too laughed, setting aside the flute and clapping his hands above his head in self-applause.

'What *shall* I call you?' she asked as she caught at the air for breath.

'Me? My name's Apelles.'

'*Apelles*?'

'Yes. After my father.'

'But she told me – she told me you were the son of Antimachus, I mean Anaxandrides.'

The boy laughed again, and pinched the face of the puppet until it was surely black and blue and squealing in protest.

'The stories she tells! Like her uncle in that book of his! And do you know, she has the cheek to call them holy lies?'

Migrant Marketplaces

Migrant Marketplaces

Food and Italians in North and South America

ELIZABETH ZANONI

UNIVERSITY OF ILLINOIS PRESS
Urbana, Chicago, and Springfield

Library of Congress Cataloging-in-Publication Data
Names: Zanoni, Elizabeth, author.
Title: Migrant marketplaces : food and Italians in North and South
    America / Elizabeth Zanoni.
Description: [Urbana] : University of Illinois Press, [2018] | Includes
    bibliographical references and index.
Identifiers: LCCN 2017031761| ISBN 9780252041655 (hardcover : alk.
    paper) | ISBN 9780252083297 (pbk. : alk. paper)
Subjects: LCSH: Italians—Food—United States—History. |
    Italians—Food—Argentina—History. | Italy—Emigration and
    immigration. | Consumers' preferences—United States—History.
    | Consumers' preferences—Argentina—History. | Emigration and
    immigration—Economic aspects—History.
Classification: LCC GT2850 .Z36 2018 | DDC 641.59/251073—dc23
LC record available at https://lccn.loc.gov/2017031761

To Leo, Cathy, and Dominic Zanoni

Contents

Acknowledgments

While writing this book, I have learned from and relied on numerous individuals and institutions. First, my deepest gratitude goes to Donna Gabaccia for her endless intellectual and personal generosity during my doctoral work at the University of Minnesota and beyond. Her knowledge of transnational, migration, and gender history and her moral support were indispensable tools for seeing this project through from inception to completion. Erika Lee also offered her guidance, providing me critical feedback and encouragement all along the way. In Donna Gabaccia and Erika Lee I found unparalleled mentors, inspiring me through their scholarship and professional and personal lives. I also want to thank Mary Jo Maynes, Sarah Chambers, and Jennifer Pierce for their careful readings and keen insights.

Several fellowships and institutions at the University of Minnesota (UMN) furnished essential support for this book. The James W. Nelson Graduate Fellowship in Immigration Studies and the UNICO National Graduate Fellowship in Italian American Studies allowed me to conduct research at the Immigration History Research Center (IHRC). As it has been for generations of scholars, the IHRC was for me a vibrant intellectual home, a productive space for interdisciplinary and international exchanges about human mobility. I am grateful for these exchanges, for they indelibly shaped my research agenda. I want to thank in particular IHRC staff and friends, especially Daniel Necas, Halyna Myroniuk, and Haven Hawley. Also, the Hella Mears Graduate Fellowship for German and European Studies at the Center for German and European Studies sent me to Italy for research, and a Graduate School Research Grant from the UMN Graduate School supported four months of archival work in Argentina. Finally, the UMN Graduate School's Doctoral Dissertation Fellowship gave me invaluable, uninterrupted time to finish my work.

In Italy, helpful archivists and personnel at the Archivio Centrale dello Stato, the Biblioteca Storica Nazionale dell'Agricoltura, the Istituto Nazionale di Statistica, and the Biblioteca Nazionale Centrale di Roma lent assistance in navigating their rich collections. In Rome, Stefano Luconi and Matteo Sanfilippo granted me helpful encouragement and research advice. While I was not in the archive, I enjoyed the wonderful company of my roommate, Giuliana Candia, whose own work on immigration inspired great conversation. A very special thank you goes to my family in Rome, especially Nadia, Valeria, and Aris Marches, who wholeheartedly welcomed me into their home, families, and lives. Due to their kindness, Via Pietro Paolo Rubens served as my second home, a place of relaxation, company, and delicious meals, and a jumping-off point for our numerous adventures across the Italian peninsula. Trips to Cloz, Trentino-Alto Adige, the hometown of my grandparents Oreste and Annetta Zanoni, permitted me time to explore my own family's migration story; there, Maria Pia Zuech served as a gracious host, lovely companion, and expert cook. I thank her and all the Zanonis and Zuechs in Cloz for embracing their distant *cugina americana* from Michigan.

In Buenos Aires, Argentina, I benefited from the guidance of staff and archivists at the Centro de Estudios Migratorios Latinoamericanos (CEMLA), the Biblioteca Nacional de la República Argentina, and the Centro de Documentación e Información at the Ministerio de Hacienda y Finanzas Públicas. Alicia Bernasconi and Mónica López at CEMLA were particularly friendly and helpful, as was the staff of Biblioteca's Hemeroteca, where I spent countless hours poring over *La Patria degli Italiani*. I also want to thank Alejandro Fernández for kindly taking the time to share his research and sources with me.

Old Dominion University (ODU) generously supported the completion of this book through a Summer Research Fellowship Program Grant, which allowed me to visit the David M. Rubenstein Rare Book and Manuscript Library at Duke University and the Hagley Museum and Library in Wilmington, Delaware. I am indebted to the staff and archivists at these two libraries for their expertise and assistance. Over the last six years, ODU's Department of History has provided me financial help to attend conferences while serving as an intellectually spirited space for revising the manuscript. I wish to especially thank members of the Junior Faculty Writing Group—John Weber, Brett Bebber, Erin Jordan, Timothy Orr, Jelmer Vos, Anna Mirkova, and Megan Nutzman—for reading multiple iterations of manuscript chapters and providing smart feedback. I had the good fortune to find in this group and their families not only excellent and dedicated colleagues but giving and caring friends as well. I also want to thank Maura Hametz, who read and commented on grant applications and manuscript chapters, and our past department chair, Douglas Greene, and current chair, Austin Jersild, for their constant support of my project. During my third year at ODU, a National Endowment for the Humanities summer stipend gave me the precious time and support to reframe my manuscript and complete a key chapter, making it overall a much stronger work.

Finally, a postdoctoral fellowship at the Culinaria Research Centre in the Department of Historical and Cultural Studies at the University of Toronto Scarborough challenged me to push my intellectual comfort zone and see my project in a new light. Culinaria's dynamic and interdisciplinary group of faculty and students encouraged me to more fully flesh out links between mobile people and the movements in foods and culinary traditions that their migrations produce. It would be impossible to overstate my appreciation for the mentorship and friendship of Jeffery Pilcher, Donna Gabaccia, Dan Bender, and Jo Sharma. Whether shucking oysters or attending operas with Dan and Jo, or visiting Montreal, Niagara Falls, and Muskoka (thanks to the warm hospitality of Franca Iacovetta and Ian Radforth) with Donna and Jeffrey, my time in Toronto was one of the most intellectually and personally enriching moment of my academic career. I also want to extend my gratitude to Simone Cinotto, Mike Innis-Jiménez, and Glen Goodman, whose participation in the Migrant Marketplaces Workshop helped me sharpen my analysis and contemplate the larger significance of my project. The friends and colleagues I met in Toronto, especially Jean Duruz, Irina Mihalache, Camille Bégin, Sanchia DeSouza, Nick Tošaj, Lesley Davis, and Matt White, offered me support and much fun.

I could not have found a more enthusiastic and capable editor than Marika Christofides at the University of Illinois Press. I thank her along with Jill R. Hughes and all those at the press who made this book possible. Since both of my readers have revealed their names, I am delighted to provide my gratitude to Linda Reeder and Simone Cinotto for the tremendous amount of time and consideration they put into their readers' reports and for the many ways they helped me refine the manuscript. Jeffrey Pilcher also gave me key feedback during one of the project's most crucial phases. My ODU colleague David Shields very graciously resized and adjusted the images that appear in the book. I claim any mistakes or shortcomings as my own.

This book owes a great deal to dear family and friends. While a student at Minnesota, I was lucky to acquire lifelong friends in Sonia Cancian, Melanie Huska, Trent Olson, Johanna Leinonen, and Pascal Gauthier. They have been pillars of support through academic and personal highs and lows, and their friendship is the only thing better than the book to come out of this work. Since I moved to Norfolk, Emily Moore, John Weber, Lisa Horth, Sonia Yaco, Erin Jordan, and Elizabeth and

Michael Carhart have been especially supportive of my professional and personal endeavors, and for this I am very grateful. Kerri Bakker and Maggie Powers and their respective families provided much-needed diversion and complete encouragement over the last ten years. My academic and life journey would not have been possible without the constant love and companionship of Katie Zemlick, whose friendship means the world to me. Between writing, researching, and teaching, trips home to Kalamazoo, Michigan, to spend time with family and friends, especially my grandmother Linda Markham and my godparents, Rene and Joan Adrian, revitalized my soul and reminded me of who I am. Finally, I want to thank my parents, Leo and Cathy Zanoni, and my brother, Dominic Zanoni, for their unconditional love and unwavering support. It was no surprise to me (or to them) that I opted to write on food, for it has been at the heart of our beautiful family culture as it has evolved over the years in Kalamazoo and in Bucerias, Mexico. It is their love and goofiness that keeps me going. I dedicate this book to them.

Migrant Marketplaces

Introduction

In November and December 1925, Cella's, a New York importer and seller of Italian food and wine, published a set of consecutive advertisements in the Italian-language newspaper *Il Progresso Italo-Americano*. Each advertisement presented a snapshot of Italian people and imports in the United States for 1895, 1910, and 1925 and did so in the changing figure of a stylishly dressed woman. The first advertisement, "1895," highlighted the masses of Italian newcomers at the turn of the twentieth century who joined established Italian communities in cities like San Francisco and New York (see fig. 1). "Italian-American trade follows hand in hand intensifying from our immigration," the advertisement read.[1] While the publicity makes no textual reference to women or female consumers, it is dominated visually by an illustration of a well-dressed Victorian lady in a long, corseted dress with puffy sleeves and with an elaborate bonnet fixed to her head. Two weeks later Cella's "1925" advertisement presented an image of a lean woman in a shorter, tubular tunic, playfully fidgeting with a long pearl necklace (see fig. 2). "Italians are now a living and active part of American greatness and civilization," the advertisement began, a civilization, it implied, that Cella's helped create by providing its customers with olive oil, canned tomatoes, wine, and other foods from Italy for over seventy years.[2]

As the series of Cella's advertisements suggest, migrants frequently discussed and represented global connections between trade and migration in Italian-language newspapers like *Il Progresso*. In major cities of the Americas, where transatlantic commercial and migratory flows converged, Italians formed their consumer experiences and identities based on an awareness and exploitation of the inherently global nature of migration and trade. They sold, bought, and consumed in

Figure 1. Cella's Inc., *Il Progresso Italo-Americano* (New York), November 29, 1925.

"migrant marketplaces," urban spaces defined by material and imagined transnational links between mobile people and mobile goods. As migrant marketplaces, cities like New York were global and gendered sites where male and female sellers and buyers interacted with products from their home and host countries in ways that shaped migrants' consumer identities and practices, the consumer cultures in which they were enmeshed, and wider transatlantic commodity networks.

The history of Italian migration to North and South America illuminates the historical formation of migrant marketplaces. Italians were one of the most mobile ethnic groups during the age of mass proletarian migration, and in the late nineteenth and early twentieth centuries their transnational labor paths opened and sustained global networks of trade in Italian products.[3] During these decades the United States and Argentina were the two most popular overseas destinations for Italian people and trade goods. Between 1880 and the beginning of World War II over four million Italians migrated to the United States and over two million mi-

Figure 2. Cella's Inc., *Il Progresso Italo-Americano* (New York), December 13, 1925.

grated to Argentina.[4] On average, during those same years, the United States and Argentina received annually around 80 percent of all Italian products exported to the western hemisphere.[5] The port cities of New York and Buenos Aires served as principal gateways for Italian migrants and trade goods entering the Americas through the North and South Atlantic. Merchants and business leaders connected migrants in New York and Buenos Aires to Italy and to each other by facilitating the flow of Italian goods, especially foodstuff, including cheeses, macaroni, fruit, wine, and olive oil, but also nonedible items, such as clothing, textiles, and industrial products. In migrant marketplaces of those two cities, Italian migrants constructed changing and competing connections between gender, nationality, and ethnicity through the consumption of these global imports. *Migrant Marketplaces* argues that the formation of Italian migrants' consumer habits and identities was transnational and gendered, connected to food goods and to ideas about masculinity and femininity circulating in the Atlantic economy.

Theoretical and Methodological Framing

The migrant marketplace framework encourages a global perspective that encompasses transnational and comparative approaches to the study of people and products on the move. It builds on a rich interdisciplinary body of literature by scholars who have used transnational perspectives to study cross-border migratory activities and identities.[6] Historians of Italian migration have offered some of the best examples of work that explores enduring cultural, political, economic, and familial links between migrants and the regions and towns from which they left.[7] Scholars of Italian migrants, like scholars who study other transnational people, have employed the term "migrant" because it moderates the role of the nation-state in defining the experiences of people as they enter (*im*migrant) or exit (*em*igrant) borders, while highlighting the multidirectional and circular movements that characterize the complex reality of migrants' lives.[8] The term "trans-local" perhaps best describes the ties Italians' maintained with their home country; as part of migration chains that linked one small *paese,* or village, in Italy to a community of its villagers abroad, Italy's disparate peoples identified with the traditions and values of their local *paesi* rather than with an idea of Italy as a unified nation or with other people from their homeland as "Italians."[9]

Despite labor migrants' tenuous connections or loyalty to the Italian government, Italy and other nation-states exerted real power over migrants' lives by managing and inhibiting transnational movements. As Mark Choate has shown, the Italian government sought to control the transnational movements of both Italians and products and incorporate them into nation- and empire-building projects.[10] Indeed, the migration and diplomatic practices of Italy, the United States, and Argentina often interacted and sometimes clashed with migrants' short- and long-term strategies. Furthermore, it is the varying geopolitical priorities of nation-states that generate variances in the way migration unfolds across the globe. The comparative and diasporic approaches used by both Samuel Baily and Donna Gabaccia show that while migrants' experiences and movements transcended national borders, Italian people and trade goods also remained entrenched in the economies, cultures, politics, and migration histories of particular nation-states.[11] By incorporating both transnational and comparative approaches, this study of New York and Buenos Aires as migrant marketplaces reveals how transnational linkages and nation-specific processes transformed migrant consumption. Furthermore, by treating North and South America as a single analytical site within the field of transnational history, it also exposes north-south hemispheric connections between migrant marketplaces in the Americas, connections fostered in large part through the United States' increasing presence in South America over the twentieth century.[12]

Until fairly recently scholars have examined migrants and the products they consumed separately, and within the context of a single nation, detached from other migrant-receiving countries and from the larger Atlantic world of commerce and migration.[13] Historians of global migration have focused mainly on the movement of people rather than on commerce, while economic histories of global trade have largely overlooked the role of labor migrants in shaping commercial flows.[14] And yet connections between the circulations of migrants and consumer markets were vitally important to the history of globalization in the late nineteenth and early twentieth centuries. By exploring Italian migrants as facilitators of global goods, and by drawing from historical work on both migration and trade, migrant marketplaces characterize everyday exchanges between migrant buyers and sellers as critical to the history of global integration.

The migrant marketplace paradigm also provides a methodological meeting ground where questions about ethnic enclaves and entrepreneurship that have traditionally interested social scientists can be combined with insights about identity, consumption, and representation from consumer theorists, cultural historians, and food studies scholars. Social scientists interested in ethnic enclaves have focused mainly on evaluating whether and to what extent these enclaves create opportunities for social and economic mobility and for eventual incorporation into the host society.[15] This literature has largely overlooked migrants' consumer experiences and how consumption produces practices, meanings, and ideologies that structure ethnic enclaves while connecting them to expanded national and global spaces.[16] Conversely, cultural historians and food studies scholars, while attentive to discourses that structure identity formation and culinary practices in migrant communities, have been less interested in exploring how meanings about and connections between gender, race, ethnicity, and nationhood evolved through and shaped commodity paths.[17]

One field in particular that has separated and continues to separate scholars interested in migrant economies is gender. An interdisciplinary group of scholars has analyzed the gendered nature of human mobility and how men and women experience the migration process in different ways.[18] Gender, however, does not figure centrally in dominant narratives of the history of migrant entrepreneurship or global capitalism, even though ideas about masculinity and femininity intersected with nationalism, race, and ethnicity to influence the formation of migratory and commodity links.[19] Migrant marketplaces redirect attention to consumption and retailing to incorporate scholarship on gender, identity, and consumerism into histories of enclave markets. This scholarship has identified consumption as a key factor in the development of capitalism and in the formation of national identities, especially for white middle-class women in Western societies.[20] However, aside from a small number of histories focused on migrant consumption—some of which have employed both gendered and transnational approaches—many questions remain about how consumption affected the creation of identities and practices among mobile people.[21] That Cella's utilized images of a demure Victorian lady and a flirty flapper from the Roaring Twenties to illustrate change over time in bonds between Italian migrants and food imports points to the role gender played in the establishment of migrant marketplaces. It also illuminates migrant women's evolving position in a larger, global consumer society that increasingly viewed consumption and femininity as interconnected.[22] In New York and Buenos Aires gender functioned concomitantly with ethnicity and nationality to organize transnational connections between trade and migration and to affect the consumer experiences of Italians living abroad.

In the migrant marketplaces analyzed for this book, food served as the central commodity around which migrants defined and redefined themselves as gendered and global consumers. While this study at times brings in discussion of nonfood items, such as textiles, another lucrative Italian export, it concentrates predominantly on foodstuff. Food-related enterprises, both small and large—import houses, grocery stores, restaurants, and industrial food enterprises—were the most numerous of the Italian-owned and -operated businesses in migrant marketplaces. Cheese; canned tomatoes; bottled wines, spirits, and olive oils; packaged pastas and tobacco products; and agricultural staples, including lemons, hazelnuts, and rice, counted among Italy's most profitable exports during the late nineteenth and early twentieth centuries. Quantitative trade and migration data make clear that migrant sellers, buyers, and consumers moved food merchandise across the Atlantic, and they did so to very specific locations. It is no surprise that the Italian government distinguished the "direct influence" that migrants abroad exerted on Italy's food export market through their desire for familiar homeland tastes from the "indirect influence" they had over other Italian exports, which were consumed by migrants and nonmigrants alike.[23] The Italian government therefore meticulously tracked the flow of foodstuff across the Atlantic and confidently celebrated the powerful influence that migrant consumer demand wielded over Italy's food trade.

Italian politicians and economists proved correct in assuming that perhaps more than any other commodity, foods intimately tethered migrants abroad to their pre-migration lives. Homeland foods went way beyond offering material nourishment to migrant bodies. Food products, rituals, and traditions also served as symbols through which migrants formed and maintained collective but changing transnational identities and practices, as well as power relations based on gender, race, class, and nationality.[24] Hasia Diner, Simone Cinotto, Donna Gabaccia, and Vito Teti, among others, have described the transformation of Italian migrants' diets over the early twentieth century and with it meanings about what *eating* Italian, and subsequently *being* Italian, signified to migrants, their children, and members of their host countries. Poor Italian day laborers, peasants, and *contadini* (farmers), accustomed to monotonous diets based on regional staples back home, found in the Americas new and more abundant ingredients, which they incorporated into traditional dishes, creating new, more varied and nutritious iterations of what they had eaten in Italy. Migrants clung to regional gastronomic customs from back home, seeing in them symbols of comfort and stability as well as the material means for solidifying familial bonds and communal identities. And yet Italian migrants, even poor laborers, used a profusion of cheap, new, and more abundant ingredients, especially meat, to build on their traditional foodways.[25] Indeed, in both the United States and Argentina, two of the world's largest meat-producing countries, cheap access to beef, pork, and other animal proteins slowly transfigured Italian food cultures abroad.[26] Moreover, migrant remittances and food products sent back to families in Italy, as well as new food knowledge and experiences carried home by returning Italians, altered the diets of Italians in Italy, evidencing how mass migration produced changes in food cultures on both sides of the Atlantic.

Focusing on food especially accentuates the gendered nature of consumption in migrant marketplaces, since Italian women, like women in other ethnic groups, held the responsibility of food production, purchase, and preparation both before and after migration. Gendered conceptions of labor division charged women abroad with combining the old and the new, a task that became particularly critical, and sometimes contentious, as mothers navigated the changing tastes and desires of their U.S.- and Argentine-born children, whose palates were less moored to the regional foodways of their parents.[27] Women's public and private interactions with foodstuff not only influenced the local economies of migrant communities and the wider global networks in which they were situated, but they also conveyed the complicated and often contested values and meanings associated with foods and eating.

The Archive of Migrant Marketplaces

Migrant newspapers like *Il Progresso*, in which the Cella's advertisements appeared, make a thorough discussion of migrant marketplaces possible because they ground migratory and commercial flows in specific cities, reminding us that global processes take shape in and depend on localized social relations. A 1916 advertisement for imported Turin-based Cinzano vermouth, appearing in Buenos Aires' *La Patria degli Italiani*, features a rotund, bespectacled gentleman lounging in a comfy armchair, reading the very paper in which the ad appears (see fig. 3). This intertextual strategy employed by Cinzano functions to wed the product and its consumers specifically to readers of *La Patria*. Cinzano's brand recognition derives just as

Figure 3. Ad for Cinzano vermouth, *La Patria degli Italiani* (Buenos Aires), September 20, 1916, 63.
Courtesy of the Hemeroteca, Biblioteca Nacional de la República Argentina.

much from its placement in and reference to Italian-language readers in Buenos Aires as it does from the actual vermouth, which is conspicuously absent from the publicity; *La Patria* itself, as well as its readership, becomes an integral part of the Cinzano brand. Furthermore, Cinzano vermouth did not appear in Italian-language newspapers in the United States, which instead advertised other popular brands such as Cora and Martini & Rossi, demonstrating how the two diasporas supported particular transatlantic commodity paths.

The Cinzano ad demonstrates the vital role the foreign-language press played in shaping migrants' evolving consumer habits and identities.[28] Migrant print culture offers indispensable source material for the study of migrant consumption from a transnational perspective because it reveals material and discursive links between people and products and between home and host country. Italian-language newspapers include statistical data such as weekly ship manifests, information on national and international markets, and demographic details about migrant communities, institutions, and businesses. But they also contain discourse and representations about consumption in the form of op-ed pieces, articles, advertisements, and photographs. This quantitative and qualitative evidence together demonstrates that Italians did not encounter goods merely as economic actors but also as cultural mediators who produced new spaces and meanings about gender, ethnicity, race, and nationhood in their host countries. They depict migrants not only as laborers but also as serious consumers who took advantage of new opportunities to buy and consume Italian as well as Argentine and U.S. foods. And they paint a picture of migrant marketplaces that anchored Italians and products to specific locales while extending beyond them to connect migrants to Italians in Italy and to nonmigrants and other migrant groups in the United States and Argentina. Migrant print culture reveals migrant marketplaces as simultaneously bordered and permeable spaces, bounded by the communities and cities in which they developed, while equally influenced by urban, national, and transnational webs of commerce and migration.

This study focuses specifically on the Italian-language commercial press and on publications of Italian chambers of commerce in New York and Buenos Aires. I concentrate mainly on the two most popular Italian-language commercial newspapers during the late nineteenth and early twentieth centuries: *La Patria degli Italiani*, published in Buenos Aires, and *Il Progresso Italo-Americano*, published in New York.[29] Similarly, I focus primarily on monthly bulletins published by the Italian chambers of commerce in New York and Buenos Aires: *Rivista Commerciale* (New York) and *Bollettino Mensile* (Buenos Aires).[30] Members of Italian chambers of commerce shared with the owners and editors of *Il Progresso* and *La Patria* elite, or *prominenti*, status as middle-class community leaders. Their publications reflected a shared desire to unify Italy's migrants around a common *Italianità*, a sense of Italianness, which they believed would strengthen migrants' loyalty to their homeland and Italy's global repute. Migrant newspapers and business publications served as the principal channels through which Italian government representatives and merchants, as well as migrant business owners and retailers, made economic and cultural demands on migrants. But they were also sites where migrant entrepreneurs in New York and Buenos Aires, as well as U.S. and Argentine businesses, championed their own products and used them to fashion alternative identities, habits, and geographies for Italians abroad. In their desire to craft national identities around commodities, and to profit from these linkages, prominenti journalists and merchants struggled to manage working-class migrants' spending and consuming practices.

The experiences of migrants in New York and Buenos Aires, both of them urban, commercial, and global cities, hardly reflects the experiences of Italians migrating to and living in other parts of the United States and Argentina. However, as the two cities with the largest number and concentration of Italian migrants in the western hemisphere, Buenos Aires and New York were the principal nodes in a triangular geography connecting Italy, Argentina, and the United States. They were the cities where the large majority of Italian migrants and trade goods entered their respective countries and therefore served as locations where linkages between people and products had an especially visible and powerful impact. While there are limits to what migrant marketplaces of these two cities can reveal about migrants in other cities of the Americas, as the most important access points, the connections between migration and trade and the meanings and practices these connections produced influenced Italian communities in other urban areas. Moreover, *Il Progresso*, *La Patria*, and the chamber of commerce bulletins circulated way beyond New York and Buenos Aires, and they regularly discussed larger U.S. and Argentine economic, political, and cultural issues, as well as communities of Italians throughout their respective countries. As such, they provide insight about migrant consumption in other cities where Italians settled in large numbers, such as San Francisco, Boston, and Chicago in the United States, and Rosario and Mendoza in Argentina.

The Structure of the Book

While the Cella's advertisements joined migrant consumption to women during the 1920s, it was laboring migrant men who first dominated migrant marketplaces in New York and Buenos Aires. The first three chapters of this book concentrate on the late nineteenth and early twentieth centuries, a period characterized by the Italian government's official support of Italians abroad and by relatively low restrictions on mobile people and goods entering North and South America. The voracious demand for mainly unskilled manual labor in the United States and Argentina produced heavily male, temporary migrations from Italy to the Americas before World War I. Chapter 1 establishes a foundation for the study by mapping links between Italian migration and trade between Italy, the United States, and Argentina, and by discussing endeavors by Italian elites to exploit these links as part of larger nation- and empire-building projects. It compares trade and migration statistics to representations of Italian people and products in political tracks and export iconography to show how those elites masculinized migrant marketplaces at the turn of the twentieth century.

Chapters 2 and 3 consider differences and similarities in the migrant marketplaces of New York and Buenos Aires before World War I. Chapter 2 explains how assumed similarities between Italians and Argentines—racial, familial, linguistic, and cultural—generated shared consumer experiences in Buenos Aires for migrants and nonmigrants in relation to Italian foods in ways that they did not in New York. Furthermore, differences in the ethno-racial, economic, and political landscapes of the United States and Argentina allowed Italians in Buenos Aires, but not in New York, to assert their ability to influence Argentine trade policies in order to access homeland foods. Chapter 3 compares the development of *tipo italiano* products—Italian-style goods manufactured by entrepreneurs in the United States, Argentina, and Europe—to explore changing meanings of nationality and authenticity applied to foodstuff. Because they were cheaper than Italian imports, tipo italiano goods better met the financial goals of Italian male consumers in transnational family economies who strove to save money to send home. Italians in New York took advantage of their host country's robust industrial capacities and protectionist economic policies to manufacture domestically made wines, cheeses, and pastas on a mass scale. Together, these chapters show that while Italian elites sometimes treated migrant marketplaces in New York and Buenos Aires as interchangeable, and as inextricably linked to Italy, differences in how the United States and Argentina were integrated into the global economy produced varying opportunities and challenges for migrant sellers, buyers, and producers.

Chapter 4 describes World War I as a major turning point in the history of New York and Buenos Aires as gendered and transnational migrant marketplaces. It shows how migrants' involvement in wartime campaigns to buy Italian products abroad and to redirect trade to Italy normalized consumption as a "duty" to the homeland among a people who were more used to saving than spending and largely unfamiliar with nationalist feelings toward a unified Italy. In both countries, temporary gender-balanced and even female-dominant migrations brought on by the war, along with a growing, more gender-balanced second generation, made women central to these campaigns. During the interwar years, migrant marketplaces in the two countries feminized as advertisements for and discussion about Italian products, as well as the national identities they generated, became increasingly moored to women.

The final two chapters turn to the interwar years, when a worldwide depression, intensifying restrictions against mobile people and products, and rising nationalisms globally politicized migrant consumption in especially controversial ways. It is also a time when U.S. businesses' increased interest in Argentina as a site for consumer goods and investment changed the global geography of migrant marketplace connections. Chapter 5 shows that during and after World War I, U.S. food conglomerates began actively employing the Italian-language press to target Italian consumers in both New York and Buenos Aires as distinct consumer groups within their respective national marketplaces. As explored in chapter 6, ties between Italian consumers in these two major cities became particularly visible and politicized with the rise of fascism in Italy. Ironically, as Prime Minister Benito Mussolini tried to divorce Italian women from U.S.-style consumerism at home, migrant print culture employed links between women and consumer goods to generate Italian identities abroad. And yet while migrant consumerism emerged out of transnational ties to Italy during World War I, migrant marketplaces became less grounded within the national boundaries of either Italy or migrants' host countries by the interwar years. By the late 1930s, Italy, the United States, and Argentina all competed for the attention of Italian consumers, especially female migrants, who after the war became ubiquitous in advertisements for both Italian imports and domestically produced goods.

The book's epilogue ponders the fate of Italian transnational migrant marketplaces after World War II. Migrant marketplaces in New York and Buenos Aires came to exist increasingly in the imaginary and in commodified form rather than in the actual embodied movements of Italians and trade goods from Italy. Nevertheless imagined and deterritorialized ties between mobile Italians and foods continued to play a vital role in the performance of ethnicity for the descendants of Italians and in the consumption of Italianità for nonmigrants in the United States and Argentina.

CHAPTER 1

Manly Markets in
le due Americhe, 1880–1914

In 1888 a manual published in Genoa for Argentina-bound Italians included a dictionary of useful phrases in Italian with their Spanish translations. Among the many practical phrases designed to help Italian newcomers in Buenos Aires was "I do not like this wine. Bring me a bottle of Barbera or Barolo."[1] In providing Italians abroad with the vocabulary necessary for demanding homeland goods, the guide promoted a vision of the ideal migrant consumer, one whose preferences for the Piedmont wines traveling with him across the Atlantic heralded a new, imperial age for the Italian nation. While there is no way to know if and how migrants used the guide to manage their purchases, trade and migration data suggest that Italians stimulated international trade in Italian wine: Italians made up 63 percent of all migrants arriving in Argentina during the 1880s, and in the five years after the guide appeared, Italy rose from third in the quantity of wine exported to Argentina—behind France and Spain—to first place, surpassing its European competitors.[2] The guide anticipated that migrants' purchases of wine and other Italian edible goods would bind mass migration to mass exportation in building a *più grande Italia*, a "Greater Italy," a nation constructed in large part abroad by its peoples scattered across the globe.

Like the authors of the manual, Italians in positions of political and economic power during the late nineteenth and early twentieth centuries sought to capitalize on the consumer activities of the more than 16 million Italians who left Italy from 1870 to 1915. Italian politicians, economists, businessmen, and merchants desired to intensify transatlantic links between migrants and exports and to incorporate them into nation- and empire-building projects. Debates over migrant consumption focused particularly on the United States and Argentina in *le due Americhe* (the two Americas), which, as the two most popular overseas destinations for both Italian people and products, held the greatest promise as commercial colonies abroad. Elites enthusiastically pointed to trade and migration data as proof of migrants' potential to bolster Italian commercial flows and the economic power and prestige of Italy more generally. Unlike its European neighbors, Italy's future lay not so much in formal imperial rule, but in its unrelenting export of men and markets. Italian leaders assured themselves and the world that Italian-style expansion via men and markets was just as manly as state-dominated colonial pursuits in Africa and East Asia led by England, France, and Germany. Under the guidance of Italian merchant princes, and with the blessing of notable Italian men, past and present, transatlantic labor migrants transformed into armies of commercial explorers, warriors, and defenders of *la patria*.

Emerging from elite representations of Italian people and products abroad before World War I is a gendered geography of migration and trade that masculinized migrant marketplaces and the transatlantic spaces in which they were embedded. While labor migrations made up of predominantly male workers opened and sustained commercial routes for Italian goods to the Americas, these idealized man-centered depictions of overseas nation and empire building reflected the aspirations of Italian leaders rather than the more troublesome social problems and diplomatic realities facing the newly united nation-state. Furthermore, gendered representations of migration, trade, and consumption overlooked how labor migrants' commitments to families left behind restrained their purchases of Italian exports.

Elite Fantasies of Italian Migration and Empire Building in the Americas

In 1900 Italian economist and future president Luigi Einaudi popularized elite dreams of Italian empire building through emigration and trade with the publication of *The Merchant Prince: A Study in Colonial Expansion*. Einaudi described and praised what he called Italian "merchant princes"—migrant entrepreneurs who transplanted the country's capital, products, and culture to Italian communities or "colonies" abroad. These merchant princes, he predicted, would supply a growing class of Italian consumers overseas who, "used to consuming objects from their homeland, prefer among all, the wines and oils of their country because they better satisfy their tastes, and Italian furniture and clothes because they have the form and color that they like."[3] Einaudi focused especially on Enrico Dell'Acqua as a contemporary merchant prince, whose exportation of almost 50 million lire worth of yarn and textiles to South America won him high honors at the "Italians Abroad" section of Italy's 1898 National Exposition in Turin.[4]

Einaudi was one of a number of leaders at the turn of the twentieth century who debated the most effective means of dealing with the country's colossal emigration. In an effort to enhance Italy's international reputation as a great imperial power, Italian politicians and economists implemented a program for its citizens abroad that envisioned migration and colonialism as inextricably connected. Italian nationalists such as Prime Minister Francesco Crispi imagined state-sponsored migrant settler colonies in East Africa—where Italy had established its first African colony, Eritrea, in 1890—as the foundation for a reborn Roman empire characterized by conquest and territorial gain. However, after Ethiopia's defeat of Italian forces in 1895 frustrated nationalists' plans for expansion in Africa, liberals transferred the conception of colonies as demographic settlements to the Americas. Einaudi and his liberal supporters conceived of migrants in North and South America as modern incarnations of Genovese and Venetian medieval merchant princes whose peaceful commercial pursuits created voluntary emigrant colonies tied patriotically and economically to Italy. Migrant entrepreneurs in free settlements of the Americas, liberals agreed, represented a more sophisticated and less violent form of colonialism than expensive European conquests in Africa and Asia where commerce forcibly followed the flag.[5] While Italian political leaders—liberals and nationalists alike—continued to pursue African settlement, liberals contended that Italian commercial expansion was best achieved when Italian commodities followed the footpaths of Italian migrants to the Americas.[6] Advocating for a type of free-market imperialism in which migrants like Dell'Acqua formed Italian colonies abroad to absorb Italian goods and disseminate Italian culture, Einaudi hoped to transfer the glory and wealth of medieval Italy to the western hemisphere.

A year after the publication of Einaudi's manifesto, liberals in the Italian government passed the country's historic 1901 emigration law, the first piece of national legislation, globally, to actively guide, protect, and profit from its migrants. Its passage signaled a shift in many lawmakers' attitudes; rather than conceive of migration negatively, as an embarrassing hemorrhage of labor power, capital, and military resources, the law's architects depicted migrants as political and economic instruments to enlarge and secure international prestige and colonial terrain, and to assist Italy domestically through remittances and new markets for Italian exports.[7] The law was one of many progressive steps taken by the Italian government during the Giolittian era, named after Giovanni Giolitti, who as prime minister oversaw much of Italy's arduous path toward industrialization from 1900 to World War I.[8] Unlike Western European countries such as Germany, France, and Britain,

Italy's colossal migration, combined with a weak industrial sector and fledgling consumer market, necessitated a worldview that envisioned migrant consumption in the Americas as central to economic growth at home as well as to imperial pursuits abroad.

The wide-sweeping 1901 law established the Emigration Commissariat, an independent agency under the foreign ministry to oversee emigration, and the *Bollettino dell'emigrazione* (hereafter *Bollettino*), a monthly, voluminous bulletin dedicated to the documentation and study of Italian emigration.[9] National and local commissariat agents reporting on transatlantic migration in the *Bollettino* ruminated positively on ties between Italian migrants and trade. As a 1904 report confidently stated, "The links between emigration and commercial flows are many. Our emigrants take with them their lifestyles and their tastes, and they continue to consume products from Italy, which sustains an active exportation of our market." By requesting Italian articles of popular consumption, especially foodstuff such as wine, olive oil, pasta, cheese, and tobacco products, migrants exerted a powerful influence over trade routes. Pointing to large annual increases in the amount of such items to the United States, the report urged Italian businesses to continue catering to migrant demand. "And it is our hope that our exporters follow, with a shrewd eye, migration, and know how to respond to the needs of our colonies abroad."[10] The 1901 law, the Emigration Commissariat, and the *Bollettino* represented new mechanisms through which migrants' links to Italy's export markets were described, measured, and analyzed.

While the commissariat and its *Bollettino* gave Italy unprecedented bureaucratic authority to connect emigrants and exports, it was not the first governmental attempt to capitalize commercially on its citizens' purchases abroad. In the late nineteenth century, the Italian Ministry of Foreign Affairs set up chambers of commerce abroad in order to promote trade between Italy and the rest of the world. The chambers, run by prominenti migrants, worked assiduously to arm Italian merchants with the resources and information needed to boost Italy's export market. From major cities outside of Italy, they produced for their members regular publications that discussed trade and migration legislation, local and international consumer prices, current and potential markets for Italian exports, emigrant communities and their commercial activities, and national and international trade exhibitions and meetings.[11] And they looked specifically to migrant consumers as outlets for Italy's exports. As Mark Choate explains, Italian chambers of commerce as well as nongovernmental and private organizations that were focused on expansion, such as the Dante Alighieri Society and the Italian Colonial Institute, promoted a cohesive Italianità, a national identity that would use Italian exports, language, religion, and ethnicity to unite Italy's heterogeneous migrants.[12]

In the late nineteenth century, as increasing numbers of government officials, economists, and businessmen turned away from Africa and toward the Americas, they focused specifically on the United States and Argentina as the two most particularly fruitful locations for Italy's overseas colonies. In 1893 lawyer and emigration promoter Guglielmo Godio described the United States and Argentina as the prototype countries of *le due Americhe* (the two Americas) in *America and Its First Factors: Colonization and Emigration*. He justified his focus on those two countries because of their "greater vitality and pronounced character, for the vastness of territory and for the splendor of destinies," and because they represented what he articulated to be distinctly different histories based on contrasting modes of European colonization by the Spanish and English.[13] Presaging Einaudi's study and the 1901 law by almost a decade, Godio wrote his comparative history of colonization in order to encourage the Italian government to protect its migrants and the export markets they developed. He anticipated that if and when Italy woke up to the importance of its emigrants, "Oh! Then, yes, the other exporting nations would have reason to be alarmed."[14]

Almost twenty years later Aldo Visconti, then a student at the Institute of Advanced Studies in Trade in Turin, also focused on the United States and Argentina as the two destinations that were exceptionally suitable for wedding men and markets. Visconti began his 1912 thesis, *Emigration and Exportation: A Study on the Relationship between Italian Emigration and Exportation to the United States of North America and the Republic of Argentina*, arguing that Italian overseas migration made these two countries the most important outlets for Italian exports. While geographical proximity accounted for Italian commercial success in France, Germany, Austria, and Switzerland, migrant demand for Italian products explained why outside of Europe, Italian exports did so well in these two faraway countries.[15] By constantly comparing and linking le due Americhe, Italian trade experts like Visconti suggested that the commercial achievements of one of the two countries reinforced the potential of the other. Economist Luigi Fontana-Russo, who also devoted his 1906 article "The Emigration of Men and the Exportation of Goods" to the United States and Argentina, introduced his section on Argentina by writing, "That which we said about the U.S. finds ample confirmation in our relationship with Argentina."[16] Italy's commercial triumph in the United States and Argentina promised future achievement in other countries of le due Americhe with growing Italian populations, especially Brazil, Uruguay, and Canada. Elites envisioned the United States and Argentina as the principal gates through which Italian migrants and exports would disseminate throughout the western hemisphere.

While Italian leaders disagreed over whether the United States or Argentina offered more promise for linking migrants and exports, together they provided optimal locations for building a Greater Italy from the commercial activities of Italians abroad. Trade and migration statistics bolstered their faith that Italian commerce followed the footpaths of migrants across the Atlantic. Figure 4, based on Italian government migration and trade data, represents the percentage of all

Italian people and products headed to the western hemisphere that arrived in the United States and Argentina from 1880 to 1913. This figure shows that the dynamics of export trade did closely follow the dynamics of migration in both countries. With few exceptions, when Argentina's and the United States' share of arriving migrants increased, so too did both countries' share of exports. In part this is because people and goods traveled together on the same ships across the Atlantic; transporting both people and goods made passenger traffic a more profitable business for steamship companies.[17] During downswings in the global economy, when fewer Italians migrated and when higher numbers of migrants repatriated back to Italy, exports decreased as the primary consumers of Italian products either dwindled or returned home. A focus on the two dotted lines representing exports also shows that migration to the United States and Argentina fluctuated considerably more than did exports to these two destinations; unlike migrants, who often returned home or made multiple trips back and forth across the Atlantic, Italian products did not repatriate.

Representing Italian migration and trade to the United States and Argentina as percentages of the total made to the western hemisphere also reveals the importance of focusing on both countries within a single analytical frame, since they constituted the two overseas countries that received the largest number of Italian people and goods. Almost every year between 1880 and 1913, the United States and Argentina received over 80 percent of all Italian goods and 60 percent of all Italian migrants headed to the Americas. Increases in the percentage of exports and migrants in one country almost always meant a decrease in exports and migrants to the other. This is reflected in the way the lines for people and products to the two countries appear in figure 4 as almost mirror opposites of each other. The figure also shows how booms and busts in the global economy influenced migration patterns to the Americas, and in turn how migrants' decisions affected national and international labor and trade markets.[18] A major depression in Argentina in 1890 and 1891 created a temporary break in what was until then a steady increase in Italian migration to the country. Italians responded to the Argentine downturn by reorienting their voyagers northward, where unskilled labor was in high demand; after 1890 more Italians migrated to the United States than to Argentina until the early 1920s, when restrictive immigration legislation in the United States made Argentina once again the preferred destination. Similarly, when the Panic of 1907 dealt a heavy blow to the U.S. economy, Argentina's share of Italian exports increased slightly the following year, as did Argentina's share of Italian migrants, who most likely responded to unemployment in the United States by turning their journey southward. Clearly, a symbiotic relationship existed between Italian people and products on the move, and between Argentina and the United States as the two most important receiving countries in the western hemisphere.

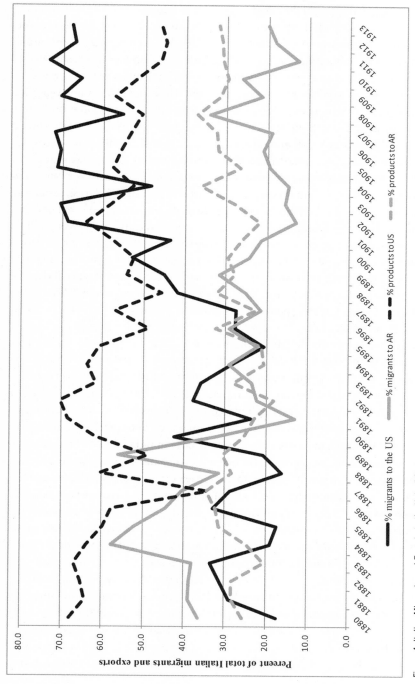

Figure 4. Italian Migrants and Exports to the United States and Argentina as a Percent of the Total of the Western Hemisphere, 1880–1913. Sources: Exports—*Movimento commerciale del Regno d'Italia* (1880–1902) and *Annuario statistico italiano* (1903–1913), publishers vary. Migrants—Commissariato Generale dell'Emigrazione, *Annuario statistico della emigrazione italiana dal 1876 al 1925* (Rome: Edizione del Commissariato Generale dell'Emigrazione, 1926).

Although elites lauded the beneficial effects of migration on all Italian exports, they noted the particularly strong correlation between the joined increases of migrants and food exports. The *Bollettino* differentiated between exports like cotton and silk, over which migrants exerted an "indirect influence"—indirect because migrants and nonmigrants alike consumed such goods—and foodstuff, over which migrants' "direct influence" stimulated commercial flows.[19] The United States and Argentina absorbed by far the bulk of Italy's western hemisphere–bound food exports and, for certain food items, the majority of Italy's total global exports. In 1907 the United States and Argentina together received over 90 percent of all Italians headed to the Americas; that same year the United States was the leading importer worldwide of Italian cheese, pasta, canned tomatoes, hazelnuts, lemons, and citrus extract, and Argentina was Italy's number one global importer of olive oil, wine, rice, vermouth, and spirits. Argentina and the United States together imported 75 percent of Italy's global exports of vermouth, 76 percent of Italy's bottled spirits, 60 percent of Italian tomato preserves, 44 percent of Italy's exported oil olive, 37 percent of Italian cheese, and 34 percent of Italian wine.[20] Demand for these foods and beverages by emigrants drove the transformation of Italian agricultural processing and industrial food production at home. By 1911 food manufacturing was one of Italy's most industrialized sectors, with 14 percent of industrial workers employed in the industry, third behind textiles (22.9 percent) and engineering (16.7 percent).[21]

Trade and migration statistics demonstrate that migrants moved merchandise, especially the products of Italy's developing commercial food and agricultural industries, and to very specific transatlantic locations with large Italian populations. Quantitative data justified elites' initiatives and attached measurable monetary values to the consequences of migrants' consumer decisions. That both countries exhibited such strong correlations between migration and trade, elites surmised, confirmed that such links were not a coincidence but rather a particular ability or asset of the Italian nation-state. Italian merchants and business leaders abroad agreed; given the large number of Italians and exports in the United States and Argentina, it is no surprise that Italian chambers of commerce in these two countries became powerful migrant institutions. In Argentina the government founded the Italian Chamber of Commerce and Arts in Buenos Aires in 1884; the following year an Italian chamber of commerce opened in Rosario, capital of the province of Santa Fe. In the United States the Italian government created the San Francisco Italian Chamber of Commerce in 1885; two years later, the Ministry of Foreign Affairs established a sister chamber in New York City.[22] These chambers drew attention to migrant consumption in order to depict the United States and Argentina as exceptional among Italy's diasporas. "Only in *le due Americhe*," wrote Guido Rossati, head of Italy's wine department in New York, in an article appearing in the New York Italian Chamber of Commerce's bulletin, "has the exportation of national wine continued to progress," while exports to European countries decreased. This trend, Rossati concluded, proved "the truth of the axiom that trade follows emigration."[23]

Prominent Italians like Rossati built their dreams about trade and migration in le due Americhe on a number of assumptions. Economists, politicians, and academics confidently proclaimed that Italian migrants served as loyal consumers. As the image of the Barbera-drinking migrant in the 1888 guide suggests, emigration promoters largely presumed that Italians abroad would request Italian imports and reject domestically made alternatives. "The emigrant is the most loyal consumer of merchandise from the homeland," Fontana-Russo asserted. "He demands it even from far away, he pays more because it is better, he gives to homeland production a force that it did not have previously."[24] A publication prepared for the "Italians Abroad" display at the 1906 Milan International exhibition described Italians' diets in the United States as unsusceptible to Americanizing influences: "All that arrives on his table must be imported from Italy, or, when his finances do not allow it, made in the Italian way by producers in the colony."[25] Elites described migrants in the Americas as having discriminating tastes: they refused to drink weak wines made from grape varieties grown in the Americas and avoided bitter U.S. American and Argentine beers; they turned up their noses at cooking oils diluted with peanut and cotton oil, preferring the more costly but pure olive oils from Genoa and Lucca; and they purchased dried pasta manufactured in Italy from 100 percent *semola,* or semolina, flour.[26] At the first Congress of Italian Ethnography in Rome, in 1911, Italian social reformer Amy Bernardy, in her discourse on Little Italies abroad, noted, "Above all, it is in the kitchen where [migrants] conserve Italian habits, because it is very difficult for an adult emigrant to adopt, after many years, the cooking of the [host] country." "The Genoese do not renounce the *taglierini* with pesto, and the Neapolitans remain loyal to *maccheroni*," she reported.[27]

While Italian food exports offered the most obvious evidence of migrants' direct influence on Italian commerce, preference for Italian exports extended beyond edibles. Fontana-Russo, reflecting with wonder on the remarkable success of Italian textiles in the United States, noted that such growth could only be explained by migration. In an industrially sophisticated country like the United States, with a well-developed textile and clothing industry, Fontana-Russo surmised, "The fact has to be the emigrant, who does not change his taste and therefore abandon homeland goods; rather he spreads them among the people with whom he has contact."[28] Migrants' consumer tastes and habits were immutable and unchanging, preserving their character as they moved across the Atlantic and materialized in migrants' everyday lives. Visconti agreed, suggesting that Italian commerce to le due Americhe defied the natural laws of economic competition; commercial flows responded to a different, more powerful pull: the insatiable demand for homeland goods by Italians in migrant marketplaces like New York and Buenos Aires.[29]

In their optimistic predictions, the ultimate focus of much elite discourse was not on le due Americhe but on la patria. Liberal migrant supporters were particularly confident that migrants' purchases abroad would eventually turn Italians in Italy into consumers. They surmised that profits from the sale of exports, combined with migrant remittances, would stimulate Italian industry, developing a broader domestic consumer base and emancipating Italian consumers from foreign imports. Godio argued that migrants' achievements were best gauged by observing the changing spending patterns of *reduci* (returnees) and the enlarged consumer opportunities of Italians left behind by their migrant relatives.[30] While insisting that migrants maintained traditional consumer habits in the Americas, officials also conceded that reduci brought home new desires and dietary standards. A 1908 *Bollettino* report on meal service aboard Italian passenger ships proposed a new food regime with increased meat rations to better harmonize with the "habits and tastes" of migrants. Migrants who returned with savings "demand steak, and when they cannot get it, they buy it at an exaggerated price from first-class service, and in this habit acquired in the new world is the explanation of their success."[31] Success, as evidenced by the report, involved eating steak and other foods that were unavailable to most poor farmers and day laborers before migration. Migration and Italian commercial expansion, acknowledged a group of Italian businessmen in South America, increased the standard of living among Italian peasants, indicated by access to better-quality clothing, furniture, tobacco products, and especially nutritional and varied foods. As a consequence of migration and trade, they boasted, "Nearly every farmer [in southern Italy] is permitted the luxury of eating at cafes and taverns."[32] Italian government officials also directly attributed the improved diets of Italians to better economic conditions created by migration and trade.[33] Reporting from Basilicata and Calabria for the commissariat, Adolfo Rossi similarly commented that while at one time day laborers were content with a modest meal, "now they want instead food of the highest quality."[34]

These confident projections countered vocal opponents of emigration, who pointed to the perceived moral, economic, and social consequences of mass male migration. Rather than drain the country of workers and the consumer base necessary for stimulating domestic industries, liberal leaders predicted that migrants would not only activate consumption at home but would also eventually discourage emigration altogether.[35] Migrant demand for Italian goods triggered higher production levels and the expansion of Italian industry; the resulting economic development created better-paying jobs, which allowed workers to buy more Italian products, while curbing migration. "Therefore, an almost invisible force, born under the impulse of emigration, begins to work against emigration," Fontana-Russo predicted.[36] Until Italian transnational migration decreased, it would continue to encourage the growth of Italian consumer societies on both sides of the Atlantic.[37]

Finally, Italian elites assumed that migrant consumers would serve as conduits for enlarging consumption among non-Italians in the United States and Argentina. Luigi Einaudi confidently stated in 1900 that Italians abroad were "the most enthusiastic apostles of our worldwide expansion."[38] A decade later Visconti agreed; migrants, he acknowledged, "represent a bond between two countries," who, by demanding products from their homeland, "are truly the most effective and precious agents of international trade."[39] Italian chambers of commerce abroad often reported on the diffusion of Italian exports in the larger Argentine and U.S. marketplaces. Migrants not only served a "direct commercial function" by favoring Italian products, but "they become without even having realized, free traveling salesmen of trade for the Italian export houses." Their consumer habits and Italians' increasing interactions with non-Italians, especially around foodstuff, developed among the people of their host countries the desire to buy Italian olive oil, pasta, and wine.[40] The Italian Chamber of Commerce in New York gloated, "It can be asserted, in fact, without exaggeration, that the Italian emigrant to the U.S. was and is still the major salesman for projecting Italian articles among American consumers."[41] Italian migrants would serve as the primary medium for introducing U.S. Americans and Argentines to new consumer practices around Italian products, practices that advanced Italy's economy and global repute.[42]

Although their inflated confidence in Italy's transatlantic transfers of men and markets would wane over the course of the twentieth century, prominent Italian men had high expectations for Italian consumers in migrant marketplaces abroad. They surveyed the growing amount of government data from both sides of the Atlantic confirming that Italian mass migration fostered overseas trade routes and revolutionized agricultural and industrial production at home. In the face of broader economic and social insecurities confronting the newly unified nation-state, such high expectations would be met only by turning Italy's male labor migrants in le due Americhe into merchant princes and commercial warriors for the homeland. In the hands of Italian business, economic, and political leaders, the exportation of men and markets became manly markets.

Gendered Representations of Migrants, Markets, and the Italian Nation

An 1895 trademark for Lombardy-based Enrico Candiani, one of the largest manufacturers and exporters of Italian cotton fabrics, captured Italian elites' hopes of capitalizing on Italian migration, trade, and consumption (see fig. 5). Candiani's trademark features a crowned image of a classically robed "Italia," female embodiment of the Italian nation, being propelled eastward across the Atlantic on her chariot of exports by small *golondrine* (birds of passage), the Italian word given to the thousands of male laborers who migrated abroad during the winter harvest

Figure 5. Trademark for Enrico Candiani cotton fabrics, Archivio Centrale dello Stato, Ministero dell'Industria, del Commercio e dell'Artigianato, Ufficio Italiano Brevetti e Marchi, fasc. 3098, 1895. Courtesy of the Archivio Centrale dello Stato.

seasons and then returned to Italy.[43] While Italia floats celestially in the heavens, she is being pulled along well-established routes linking cities of departure and arrival for both emigrant golondrine and the exports they convey.[44] A commercial expression of Einaudi's axiom "the flow of commerce must follow the flow of Italian emigration," the image produced and then compressed space and time to articulate a triangular geography between Italy, North America, and South America.[45]

Candiani represents one of many turn-of-the-century businesses that employed a complex repertoire of symbols and images in their packaging and marketing to project gendered meanings about the Italian nation and about the global commercial and migratory links connecting Italy, the United States, and Argentina.

That Italia holds the reins attached to the golondrine's wings suggests she exerts a degree of influence over migration and trade; yet she is also being escorted by male migrants, who carefully guide both her and the purchase orders nestled in their beaks. As detailed above, in political and economic tracts, government reports, and publications issued by chambers of commerce in the United States and Argentina, Italian elites detailed and promoted the formal commercial routes created and maintained by migrants. These discussions echoed trademarks for Italian exports such as Candiani's in projecting gendered messages equating exports, migrants, and consumption with Italian notable male personas, industrial power, imperial pursuits, and military dominance.

In accordance with Italian laws governing trademark registration and protec-tion, Italian businesses registered their trademarks with Italy's Office of Intellectual Property within the Ministry of Agriculture, Industry, and Commerce.[46] Italian firms typically commissioned trademark art from Italian lithography and printing companies, who in turn hired artists to create the graphics. While little is known about the relationship between Italian manufacturers and the printing establish-ments that produced the images, before the advent of professional advertising firms after World War I, Italian business owners played an active role in the creation of trademarks.[47] The varied messages about Italian migration, trade, and consump-tion in visual representations did not mirror economic and political realities, nor can they provide insight into how migrants as viewers and consumers in New York and Buenos Aires responded to such depictions. However, exploring commercial and discursive depictions of Italian migration and trade reveals recurring patterns in the gendered ways Italian elites presented people and products to themselves, to migrants, and to other nations as they struggled to secure Italy's location in the competitive world of commerce, diplomacy, and imperialism. Rather than reflect consumers' actual interests, these trademarks projected their creators' gendered worldview, a worldview colored by their own positioning as elites who saw their personal goals and the progress of the Italian nation intimately tied to manly mar-kets of migration and trade.

Trademarks for Italian exports before World War I often used images of well-known men to associate the production and consumption of products abroad with Italian notables. Chief among these were the monarchs of the House of Savoy, the dynastic family who ruled the Kingdom of Italy from 1861 to the end of World War II. Garofalo's pasta factory, founded by Alfonso Garofalo, was one of the many small pasta factories in Italy that began exporting macaroni during the late nine-teenth and early twentieth centuries.[48] In the Garofalo trademark, Italia balances a shield with the red and white crest of the House of Savoy while overlooking the smoke-billowing Garofalo pasta factory in Gragnano near Naples (see fig. 6). At the bottom of the trademark is a series of medallions featuring almost identical-looking busts of whiskered Italian leaders. One pictures Vittorio Emanuele II,

Figure 6. Trademark for A. Garofalo macaroni, Archivio Centrale dello Stato, Ministero dell'Industria, del Commercio e dell'Artigianato, Ufficio Italiano Brevetti e Marchi, fasc. 6976, 1905. Courtesy of the Archivio Centrale dello Stato.

the first king of a united Italy and emblem of the Risorgimento, the Italian unification movement; the other two are less recognizable figures—although one labeled "empereur" suggests links between Garofalo and the legacy of imperial Rome, while the medallion of the merchant marine in Naples ties the product to Italy's contemporary commercial fleet. Although the trade and migration routes in this trademark are less explicit than Candiani's westward-bound golondrine, the intertwined U.S. and Italian flags in the lower left-hand corner, along with the writing in English, symbolize transatlantic routes between producers in Italy and consumers in the United States. The regular use of monarchs and other royal imagery gave trademarks like Candiani's an official quality by featuring Italian kings as product endorsers.

Internationally renowned spiritual and cultural leaders joined Italian kings as masculine bearers of Italian civilization. A number of trademarks for exported Italian food products used the image and name of Italian poet and statesman Dante Alighieri. A 1907 trademark for Dante-brand olive oil, produced by Giacomo Costa, one of the largest exporters of olive oil to the United States, featured an illustration of the laurel wreath–crowned Dante in profile.[49] Depictions of the winged and often nude Mercury, the Roman god of commerce and protector of merchants, appeared regularly in trademarks for Italian exports.[50] These real and mythological male luminaries meshed well with liberals' articulation of Italian migration and colonization as a commercial conquest secured not only through trade, emigration, and consumption but also through the spread of Italianità embodied in Italian history, civilization, and culture.

Trademarks also employed well-known Italian migrants, especially Giuseppe Garibaldi and Christopher Columbus, to market their wares for consumers in the Americas. Numerous companies, especially those exporting to Argentina and other parts of Latin America, featured nationalist leader Giuseppe Garibaldi in the packaging of their products. Before fighting in the Risorgimento, Garibaldi led the Italian Volunteer Legion, which fought to defend Uruguay against forces led by Juan Manuel de Rosas, the dictatorial governor of the Province of Buenos Aires, and the ex-Uruguayan president Manuel Oribe.[51] An 1899 trademark for Milan-based Brancaleoni and Company, a manufacturer and exporter of *fernet* (an *amaro,* or bitter herbal liqueur), linked Garibaldi to Vittorio Emanuele II, the principal architects and symbols of Italy's independence struggles (see fig. 7).

Explorer and merchant Christopher Columbus, the most famous Italian transatlantic voyager, served as a key emblem of Italian commercial and demographic expansion in trademarks.[52] As the original medieval merchant prince and real-life Mercury, depictions of Columbus served as symbolic devices for communicating a new era of Italian economic and cultural imperialism made possible by Italy's abundant migration. These commercial images of Columbus complemented the writings of Italian elites who constantly compared Italian merchants and migrants

Figure 7. Trademark for Fernet Brancaleoni *amaro,* Archivio Centrale dello Stato, Ministero dell'Industria, del Commercio e dell'Artigianato, Ufficio Italiano Brevetti e Marchi, fasc. 4217, 1899. Courtesy of the Archivio Centrale dello Stato.

in the Americas to medieval and early modern explorers. In 1904 Edoardo Pantano, a member of parliament and future head of the Ministry of Agriculture, Industry, and Commerce, described Italian merchants abroad as "enterprising and determined, with an astute intuition, with unceasingly activity, unsettled and bold wanderers, reminiscent of our medieval merchants."[53] A *Bollettino* report that same year equated early twentieth-century Italian exporters with the "audacious merchants from Lombardy, Genoa, Naples and Sicily, that, in the Middle Ages, traveled all the known world." These contemporary Columbuses, the report concluded, "contributed to maintaining the tastes of our emigrants for national products, enjoying therefore an impulse to Italian exports."[54]

Other trademarks glorified modern incarnations of Columbus-like men who moved abroad. Silvano Venchi, founder of the S. Venchi & Company in Turin, began his chocolate and confectionary factory in 1878; by 1906 Venchi manufactured more than two thousand different types of candy, chocolate, and caramel and exported his confections within Europe, as well as to North and South America.[55] The company's 1901 trademark for *Stella Polare Cioccolato* (Polar Star Chocolate) shows a snowy scene from the North Pole, where men hoist the Italian flag at a campsite surrounded by boxes of Venchi chocolate (see fig. 8). Suspended above the landscape are pictures of Luigi Amedeo of Savoy-Aosta (the Duke of Abruzzi), grandson of Vittorio Emanuele II, and Captain Umberto Cagni of the Italian Royal Navy. The Duke of Abruzzi, an Italian prince and explorer, became internationally esteemed for his Arctic explorations, especially in Alaska, and later served as an Italian admiral during World War I. The trademark reenacts his expedition with

Figure 8. Trademark for S. Venchi & Company chocolate, Archivio Centrale dello Stato, Ministero dell'Industria, del Commercio e dell'Artigianato, Ufficio Italiano Brevetti e Marchi, fasc. 5126, 1901. Courtesy of the Archivio Centrale dello Stato.

Cagni to the North Pole in 1899 on the steam whaler *Stella Polare*, from which the brand derived its name.[56] The duke, a turn-of-the- century Columbus and real-life prince affiliated with geographical surveys, heroic adventures, and the Italian military, represented the model migrant envisioned by elites.

Export iconography featuring male notables also functioned as geographic and diplomatic bridges between Italy and le due Americhe. Trademarks paired famous Italian male persona, including Italian royalty, not only with generic U.S. and Argentine emblems, such as national flags and the Statue of Liberty, but also with specific male political leaders from these two countries. Such trademarks condensed transatlantic space for buyers and sellers to create imaginary forums where well-known men from Italy, the United States, and Argentina were joined together through Italian oils, liquors, pastas, chocolates, tobacco, and other exports. Moreover, these trademarks presented a set of layered yet interlocking pasts—from ancient Rome to the Age of Exploration, to colonial and early U.S. and Argentine history—in ways that inserted Italy into the political traditions and foundational myths of le due Americhe. A 1902 trademark for Fernet-Branca from Milan, one of the most popular Italian exported bitters in North and South America, for example, included illustrations of the busts of both Christopher Columbus and George Washington.[57] A 1907 trademark for Emanuele Gianolio's America-brand Italian vinegar, manufactured in Genoa, exhibited a most bewildering mixture of manly geopolitical links (see fig. 9). The trademark displayed Columbus flanked by major nineteenth-century Latin American revolutionary figures, including Simón Bolívar, Domingo Faustino Sarmiento, José de San Martín, and José María Paz y Haedo.[58] A robed woman embellishes the leaders' portraits with laurel wreaths while attending to a *fasce*, the ancient Roman symbol of the Roman Republic representing strength and unity.[59] Trademarks made transnational and transhistorical links between nations by associating Italian migrant explorers and military heroes with Argentine and U.S. American male political figures. Appearing on cans, boxes, and bottles, commercial iconography eliminated real temporal and geographical divides in gendered ways to create and display relationships between prominent men who personified their countries' past, present, and future accomplishments.

Trademarks, like the one for Garofalo's pasta (see fig. 6), regularly paired portraits of Italian monarchs and other male notables to illustrations of factories in order to associate Italy's industrial successes and export capacities with male political leaders. Expressions of progress and abundance tied to industrial production became standards in advertising during the late nineteenth century when Western industrialists began emphasizing their material and cultural contributions to modern civilization by relying on popular representations of productivity and efficiency, including factories, locomotives, railroads, and electricity.[60] Italian companies' glorification of science, technology, and modernity in factory-centered trademarks

Figure 9. Trademark for Emanuele Gianolio vinegar, Archivio Centrale dello Stato, Ministero dell'Industria, del Commercio e dell'Artigianato, Ufficio Italiano Brevetti e Marchi, fasc. 8593, 1907. Courtesy of the Archivio Centrale dello Stato.

for exports tapped into global discourses of progress to present an Italian nation on par with other major manufacturing powers.

Trademarks frequently coupled effigies of well-known male personas and industrial settings with images of the medals companies received at Italian and international expositions.[61] A 1909 trademark for Martini & Rossi vermouth displayed its steam-powered, sprawling factory in Turin under text reading "awarded with 40 medals," including "a gold medal at the Paris World's Fair in 1876" (see fig. 10). The factory is flanked not only by two figures—one, a crowned female, her arm resting on a map of Europe, and the other a male, wearing a headdress and indig-

Figure 10. Trademark for Martini & Rossi vermouth, Archivio Centrale dello Stato, Ministero dell'Industria, del Commercio e dell'Artigianato, Ufficio Italiano Brevetti e Marchi, fasc. 9408, 1909. Courtesy of the Archivio Centrale dello Stato.

enous attire, next to a map of the Americas—but also by a colorful assemblage of national flags and gold exposition medals.

Italy's dependency on Italians abroad as economic resources required international platforms for intensifying migrants' loyalty to their homeland. As the Martini & Rossi trademark illustrates, international exhibitions offered Italian companies' optimal sites for such international nation- and empire-building ventures around men and markets. Italy hosted the world's fair twice in the early twentieth century: the Milan International in 1906 and the Turin International in 1911. Like other nations, Italy used these occasions to affirm its place among expansionist countries; however, in contrast to other participating powers, Italy employed fairs to showcase migrants as the instruments upon which Italy's industrialization, modernization, and empire building would be built. Prominenti

Italian migrants with political and business clout participated in such venues, staging special exhibitions of "Italians Abroad," sponsored by the Commissariat of Emigration, to highlight their contributions to Italy.[62] During both expos the commissariat awarded a number of medals specifically to Italians who established new markets for Italian products abroad and who built Italian industries outside of Italy that employed Italian workers. The Italian Chamber of Commerce in Buenos Aries, reporting on its support for the "Italians Abroad" display at the Turin International, professed, "There is probably not a region of the world where the Italian—encouraged by a thousands of years of migratory traditions—has not reached everywhere demonstrating his admirable habit of colonization, his brilliance in industrial work, in scientific investigation, in artistic creation, the robustness of his arm like the quick agility of his mind."[63] Trademarks that tied Italian royalty to award-winning exports affiliated Italy with other industrialized exporting nations, who also incorporated exhibition medals into their marketing campaigns, while projecting positive messages about migrants and the transnational markets they nourished.

The ubiquity of industrial scenes also suggests the gendering of work and space accompanying Western industrialization throughout much of Europe, a process that slowly, unevenly, and not without challenge legitimized factories as male-dominated public establishments built on the wage work of men and the rational, scientific, and mass production methods fostered by their owners and overseers. While there was much regional variation in how industrialization, urbanization, and land reform affected divisions of labor between men and women throughout Italy, the transition from a subsistence economy to a market economy redefined wage earning in industry and agriculture as male, even in regions where women continued to work as agriculturalists.[64] Unsurprisingly, then, when women did appear in trademarks for exports, they were used exclusively as either allegorical representations of the Italian nation or as representatives of an idealized peasant past untouched by the forces of global capitalism. Artists and advertisers have frequently employed women to represent traditional values, a romanticized homeland, nature's abundance, or a sense of timelessness.[65] Such trademarks for industrialized food goods featuring female agriculturalists offered a sharp contrast to the modernist and masculine images of factories and industry common during this period. A 1904 trademark for Sasso-brand olive oil, one of the most common brands of olive oil exported abroad, especially to Argentina, included a barefooted woman in classical robes collecting olives (see fig. 11). Trademarks for olive oil, canned tomatoes, pasta, and dairy products displayed women as rural harvesters dressed in traditional folk clothing contentedly collecting fruit or wheat, or milking cows in rural bucolic settings.[66]

Ironically, while such trademarks referenced a gendered trope that associated women's labor with a precapitalist past, the commercialized agricultural and pro-

Figure 11. Trademark for P. Sasso e Figli olive oil, Archivio Centrale dello Stato, Ministero dell'Industria, del Commercio e dell'Artigianato, Ufficio Italiano Brevetti e Marchi, fasc. 6676, 1904. Courtesy of the Archivio Centrale dello Stato.

duction methods that produced the foods destined for mass consumption and export were part of larger gendered processes in which women were gradually disappearing from the agricultural work force. Turn-of-the-century trademarks for exports projected gendered versions of Italian productivity: one tied women to agricultural labor portrayed as exclusively female and outside the industrialized economy; the other associated Italian men with migration, industrial development and commercial expansion, and well-known political leaders.

Italian monarchs, medieval and contemporary merchant princes, and Italian cultural figures mirrored liberals' vision of migrant colonialism modeled after the medieval maritime republics—one that was built on trade, consumption, culture, and industrial productivity—as an alternative to nationalists' more costly and bloody forms of expansion based on the rejuvenation of an ancient Roman empire.[67] And yet while liberals often publicly eschewed this alternative model, references to and images of war-making and conquest, and to ancient Rome, also appeared frequently in trademarks. National leader and general Giuseppe Garibaldi surfaced often in export iconography, as did more generic images of Italian soldiers or combat troops, such as in a 1906 trademark for the Società per l'esportazione e per l'industria Italo-Americana (Society for Exportation and for Italian-American Industry) (see fig. 12). The society included a partnership between a number of successful textile firms led by Enrico Dell'Acqua, the "merchant prince" protagonist of Einaudi's 1900 manifesto.[68] The trademark portrays an armored Italian cavalryman bent forward on lookout with a flag in hand. Ready for action, he gazes at a railroad and steamship, the modern transportation marvels that made mass migration and exportation possible. The word *vedetta* (sentry) underneath him characterizes the scout as a commercial warrior and protector of the society's economic activities.

A number of trademarks also utilized the specific military figure of the Italian Bersagliere, a special corps of the Italian Royal Army that fought for Italian unification and is still in existence today. Images of *bersaglieri*, identified by their unique helmets adorned with black capercaillie feathers, associated Italian migrants and exports with virile and belligerent methods of national defense while harking back to the grandeur of the Risorgimento past. A trademark for canned olive oil produced by Raffaello and Pietro Fortuna from Lucca showcased a war

Figure 12. Trademark for the Societá per l'esportazione e per l'industria Italo-Americana, Archivio Centrale dello Stato, Ministero dell'Industria, del Commercio e dell'Artigianato, Ufficio Italiano Brevetti e Marchi, fasc. 7730, 1906. Courtesy of the Archivio Centrale dello Stato.

monument commemorating fallen soldiers in Lucca's Piazza XX Settembre, a city square dedicated to the final event culminating in the unification in Italy: bersaglieri's capture of Rome from the Papal States in 1870.[69] Depictions of armed men and military leaders like Garibaldi tied Italian migration and commerce to a nation-state in competition with other industrialized countries looking to expand their markets and influence abroad.

These commercial images matched the masculinist and militarist language used by Italian business and economic elites to describe Italy and Italian migrants in commercial battles with other imperial powers. Italian businessmen who published the trade guide *Italy in Latin America* proudly described Italian migrants in Argentina—"our faraway brothers"—as an "army of our children always enlarged with new troops. They are, in our mind, the pioneers of a radiant civilization rising on the horizon."[70] Einaudi himself dubbed Dell'Acqua and other exporters as "army generals," and "captains of industry" and referred to Italian migrants as "a disciplined army which moves as one, under the leadership of captains and generals in the conquest of a continent." Emigrants, Einaudi and others asserted, were vital assets in competing against other nations in "a fertile economic and social war."[71] Similarly, economist Visconti discussed the entry of Italian people and products in the Americas as an "invasion" and the competition between Italian and other countries for markets as "battles" won victoriously because of Italy's migrants.[72] In 1900 the Italian Chamber of Commerce in Buenos Aires described its "noble scope" of helping Italian trade surmount difficulties in the "fight" against its "rivals."[73] This martial language matched trademarks featuring commercial explorers and warriors who moved abroad to open up trade routes and guide and protect them.

Multiple temporal landscapes—ancient imperial Rome, medieval Italian city-states, and the more recent Risorgimento—and the different versions of migrant colonialism they implied served as gendered symbolic tools for Italian elites. Together they projected confident and positive messages about Italy as a great European power and expansionist country, one that could vie with other industrialized nations by relying on the past glories and future successes of its male migrants. This was especially critical as Italy, "the least of the great powers" of Europe, battled to maintain international standing. As Richard Bosworth argues, Italian liberal policy makers constantly fought to maintain prestige among the country's European neighbors, even though they lacked the resources to do so.[74] While commercial imagery and elite discourse emphasized Italy's role in fueling the commercial revolution of the Middle Ages and Early Modern period, in reality the Italy of the late nineteenth and early twentieth centuries had a less glorious reputation as a major supplier of cheap human labor and agricultural staples. Critics pointed to Italy's failed colonial adventures in East Africa, its regional divisiveness and inability to control peasant revolts and socialist uprisings, and its inadequate spending on military and naval buildup as proof of its junior status in the league of European power players. Despite the real economic and social achievements during the Giolittian era, on the eve of World War I Italy continued to lag industrially behind Western Europe; the country suffered from a frail banking system, depended heavily on foreign investment, and relied almost entirely on Great Britain for its coal supply, which slowed Italy's industrial and transportation revolutions.[75] Only the colossal remittances sent home by migrants abroad kept Italy's balance of payments positive during the country's volatile industrial takeoff.[76] Furthermore, while migration helped make Italian exports as a percentage of the country's total gross domestic product double from 6.2 percent in 1861 to 12.4 percent on the eve of the war, Italy's European competitors far exceeded Italy in terms of total exports, despite economists' boastful language about Italy's commercial capacities.[77]

Italian elites' martial discourse and commercial imagery also offered a rebuttal to the feminized language often used by Italy's European competitors to describe the country's people, culture, and economy. Leaders of Germany, Britain, France, and Austria, as well as some Italian politicians, viewed Italy with condescension, addressing the nation and its people using gendered stereotypes, as, for example, a "Young Italy" of emasculated and powerless children, or an effeminate country with *un popolo donna* (a womanly people).[78] Demographically speaking, mass male emigration did leave Italians as un popolo donna. The nation came to be depicted as such by Italian and non-Italian writers, both critics and supporters of emigration, who all agreed that emigration was strictly a masculine undertaking. Professor Giovanni Lorenzoni described migration from southern Italy and Sicily not only as a modernizing process in which the old farmer is carried into the "larger world of modern industrial life," but also as a process through which he "becomes a real man" by finding wealth and being adequately compensated for his work.[79] As Linda Reeder writes, "In the cultural imaginings, the migrant and the act of migration became identified with characteristic male traits (strength, virility, and action), whereas the people who chose to remain behind became imbued with female qualities (weakness, passivity and dependence)."[80]

Elites countered such feminized portrayals of the Italian nation by depicting Greater Italy as being built largely from without, through manly markets of migrants and exports. By linking male migrants' purchases abroad to Italian nation and empire building, Italy differed from its Western European neighbors in its gendering of consumption. While Britain, France, and Germany made increasing distinctions between the masculine realm of production and politics and the feminine sphere of consumption and family life, Italian leaders tied consumption to its male citizens abroad.[81] Italy was not entirely immune to trends that were prevalent in industrialized countries such as Britain, France, and the United States, where middle-class ideals of gendered divisions of space framed women's emergence as consumers and connected them to the nation-state.[82] However, this model was not wholly practical for migrant-sending nations like Italy that relied largely on consumerism and remittances of male migrants outside its borders to construct a più grande Italia. Instead, Italian leaders focused much of their effort on the country's migrants abroad, rather than middle-class women at home, as the major consumers of Italian goods and as one of the principal protagonists in fueling Italian global expansion.

Migrant consumption was instrumental in carrying out and legitimizing male-centered Italian-style expansionism. Elite representations of manly markets showcasing famed political leaders, factories and industry, merchant princes, and war and imperial Rome all employed images and discourses of masculinity to associate the consumption of Italian commodities overseas with manliness and to assert Italy's position as a great power in the Atlantic political economy.

Reluctant Consumers in Transnational Family Economies

Man-centered descriptions factored so centrally into elite depictions of migratory and commercial links between Italy, the United States, and Argentina in part because Italian worldwide migration during the age of mass migration remained overwhelmingly male, particularly for the years before World War I.[83] Male-predominant migrations were even more pronounced in transatlantic flows to le due Americhe. The percentage of migrating males from Italy hovered between 69 and 78 percent for the United States and 65 to 74 percent for Argentina from 1880 to 1914.[84] However, male migrants did not travel undetached from homeland social and familial networks nor from the obligations those networks carried. Italian political and economic leaders, in their fervor to make manly markets abroad, overlooked how transnational familial and economic arrangements influenced Italians' consumer decisions in migrant marketplaces.

Italian liberals' plans for linking Italian people and products would function effectively and profitably only if migrants conceived of themselves as consumers rather than primarily as producers and savers. However, while migration introduced Italians at home and abroad to novel consumer items, practices, and values, transatlantic migration did not fully nor abruptly wrench them out of the subsistence economies and cultures in which they were embedded. In nineteenth-century Italy, subsistence production was organized around family economies in which all members contributed to the survival and well-being of the household and where little cash was earned or used. With some regional variation, most rural families in Italy made almost everything they ate and wore, with women largely in charge of producing food, clothing, and other consumable goods.[85]

In the late nineteenth century new taxes instituted by the Italian state, the intensification of commercial agriculture, and failed land reform schemes forced more

Italians, especially in the south, to search for wage work. Family economies in rural areas adjusted by sending men to earn money as laborers on faraway estates or northern cities, leaving women and dependent children to cultivate food, without wages, in fields closer to their villages.[86] Women also continued to produce cloth for family consumption and as part of a disappearing cottage industry in the south, where cheap cloth imported from abroad was slower to affect women's traditional work.[87] As it became increasingly impossible for peasants to work and possess their own land, they responded to the growing needs of a global economy by sending mainly male family members abroad for agricultural, mining, construction, and factory work and by extending family economies across national borders. These transnational family economies functioned best when male wages earned outside of Italy combined with the continuation of mainly female semi-subsistence production of food and clothing at home. The ultimate, but usually unrealized, goal for most rural families was to use male wage earnings abroad to buy land back home and live off the profits from rents, thereby freeing themselves from low-status, dependent, and poorly paid wage work. Excessive consumption in the Americas, therefore, was not conducive to the success of transnational family economies. Migrant laborers tended to spend the higher salaries they earned abroad not in their host countries, where the cost of living was high, but back in Italy, where the cost of living was low and where their earnings helped strengthen families' position in the extant social and economic hierarchy of rural Italy.[88] Despite elites' dreams, migrants sought to enhance the material security of their individual families in transnational economies, with little regard for the economic well-being and reputation of the Italian nation itself.

Indeed, most migrants lived thriftily in le due Americhe, choosing to forgo rich diets, high rents, expensive consumer items, and entertainment in order to create the savings necessary for the purchase or improvement of their homes and social standing in Italy. Male labor migrants in New York and Buenos Aires saved money by boarding with families or relatives from their home villages or in larger boardinghouses. Lodging expenses included laundry and meal service, often provided by an Italian woman, or sometimes by the padrone, the gang boss. There, workers were served mainly inexpensive meals consisting of pasta dishes; bean-, vegetable-, and rice-based soups and stews; and coffee with bread, which they supplemented with cheese, wine, produce, and other foods purchased from street vendors, restaurants, and grocery stores or raised in small urban gardens.[89] And although living thriftily may have prevented Italians from buying imports regularly, they reported eating well because food was more abundant and cheaper than back home. After migrating to Argentina in 1902, Oreste Sola wrote to his parents in Biella, Piedmont, about the plentiful "fruit of all sorts," especially peaches and pears, which, he wrote in amazement, were so numerous "they are used to fatten pigs." Argentina's booming cattle industry gave migrants like himself consistent access to meat. "We eat steaks and grilled meat every meal just like eating potatoes at home." He assured his mother, "Here I lack for nothing. We are in America, and so everything is available here."[90]

While overseas Italian migration remained predominantly male, women in Italy played central roles in transnational family economies, financing and sustaining the migration networks in which Italians operated. Women and their work were not unaffected by the larger forces that sent their husbands, fathers, and brothers abroad. These commercial images of subsistence economies—recalling unchanging and idealized worlds of peasant families, hermetically sealed off from the larger forces of capitalism—belied the world of motion affecting Italian women. Linda Reeder has demonstrated how mass male emigration transformed Italian women's lives, especially for Sicily's *vedove bianche* (white widows), women left behind by their migrant husbands. In contrast to contemporary depictions of such women as abandoned victims of male migration, and, in their removal from male supervision, as threatening to traditional familial arrangements and gender roles, most migrants' wives actively invested in migration as a strategy to enhance their family's standing. Women's handling of remittances—invested in house improvements, property, small businesses, educational opportunities, and dowries—represented an extension of rural women's long-standing role as managers of family resources and money.[91] Within a larger patriarchal system limiting female autonomy and authority, women held substantial power over the domestic sphere, including control of the family's finances. Mass male migration enlarged these responsibilities for women, who employed them to make demands on the state on behalf of their families and faraway husbands even while traditional power relations between men and women remained relatively unchanged.

Male migrant frugality allowed for an increasing number of rural women and men in Italy, as well as returnees, to help build and participate in the country's embryonic consumer society. Using remittances sent home, migrants' wives purchased food, furnishings, and cloth for their homes, families, and businesses. Like their male relatives abroad, women left behind also moved merchandise from faraway places into small agro-towns and rural villages throughout Italy in ways that transformed Italy's relationship to global markets. When elites acknowledged rural women's increased consumer activities, they usually did so with skepticism and disapproval, identifying women's spending power with immorality, indolence, and a reversal of proper class hierarchies. Reporting for the government from Molise and Abruzzi in southern and central Italy, Cesare Jarach noted that emigration produced *"la donnicciuola"* (a gossipy woman) who "comes to the city on Sundays to shop, handling with great arrogance large bank notes."[92] One affluent *molisano* (a person from the southern Italian region of Molise) lamented to a government investigator that "the wives of the Americans arrive at the marketplace and buy up all the fresh fish newly arrived from Termoli, regardless of price."[93] Another official proclaimed that in the southeast region of Campania, "remittances from abroad allowed women to live in complete idleness."[94] Such reports portray women as inimical to Italy's economic and cultural progress as a nation. However, they also disclose how rural women, like male migrants, shaped and were shaped by the forces of globalization—migration, trade, industrialization, imperialism, and commodity culture—which in turn transformed Italy and Italy's relationship to the world.[95] While it would be unwise to exaggerate the diffusion of consumerist activities in early twentieth-century Italy, especially in rural areas of the south, by putting cash in the hands of women, male migration linked Italy's inchoate consumer society just as much to women left behind as it did to male migrants abroad.[96]

Despite elites' predictions of a più grande Italia built on migration, trade, and consumption abroad, male labor migrants remained reluctant consumers. Mass migration stimulated Italy's export market, especially in foodstuff, while helping to slowly revolutionize Italy's agricultural, manufacturing, and commercial sectors. However, to the frustration of Italian leaders, migrants' transnational familial strategies constrained migrant spending on Italian products in le due Americhe and on the consumer goods of their host countries. While trademark iconography relegated women to a precapitalist, rural, and idealized past, the same modernizing forces motivating global migration and exportation altered women's activities in transnational family economies and ultimately hindered elites' plans to construct manly markets abroad.

*   *   *

In December 1912 the magazine of the Italian Colonial Institute, formed in the early twentieth century to promote Italian colonial expansion, published "Ten Commandments for Italians Abroad," iterations of which would appear in migrant papers across the Atlantic. Together, the final two commandments evidenced the unstated links between transnational family economies and the manly markets they fostered. The institute's ninth commandment instructed Italians abroad to sell, buy, and consume Italian products and to reject foreign goods. The tenth and final commandment read, "You shall marry only an Italian woman. Only with this and by this woman shall you be able to preserve in your children the blood, language, and feelings of your fathers and of your Italy."[97]

By exhorting Italian labor migrants to accept Italian wines and Italian wives exclusively, the country's leaders hinted at gendered and transnational connections between migration, trade, and consumption, connections represented in political tracts and export iconography. To elites, trademarks for Italian exports connoting industrial, commercial, and cultural superiority and national defense served as transnational and sometimes transhistorical commercial sites for linking Italian nation and empire building abroad almost entirely to men. Equating migrants and exports with warriors, weaponry, industrialization, and colonialism confronted stereotypes depicting Italy as a politically, economically, and militarily weak and effeminate nation. Rather than un popolo donna, migrant merchants and consumers, and the trade paths they sustained, would yield a nation of producers and consumers led by migrant "merchant princes" worthy of respect from other industrialized, imperial powers.

As the twentieth century progressed, however, the strong faith elites had in migrants as loyal consumers of Italian exports would begin to wane. In remarkable ways, consumer demand from overseas facilitated trade in Italian goods, especially foodstuff, to le due Americhe. But to elites' consternation, Italians in migrant marketplaces abroad often prioritized their own economic and familial interests over a commitment to constructing a Greater Italy through manly markets. The Italian Colonial Institute's tenth commandment, directing migrants to "marry only an Italian woman," stifled migrants' ability to follow the ninth commandment, to buy Italian exports, as migrant consumption detracted from laborers' obligations to wives and children back home. It would take a world war, a slow but significant reconfiguration of gender ratios in migrant marketplaces, and intensifying ties between women and consumption globally to turn migrants toward consumption for the homeland.

CHAPTER 2

Race and Trade Policies in Migrant Marketplaces, 1880–1914

U.S. tariff policy, claimed Italian food importer C. A. Mariani in 1911, turned Italian migrants toward crime. In an article for the *Rivista*, the New York Italian Chamber of Commerce's bulletin, Mariani articulated a link between the racialization of Italian migrants and the recently passed Payne-Aldrich Tariff Act. Higher tariffs on Italian imports imposed by the act prohibited migrants from purchasing the olive oils, tomato products, cheeses, and pasta that were so characteristic of Italians' "mode of living." By forcing migrants to consume U.S. foods exclusively, the U.S. tariff policy compelled the Italian "to get a new stomach, which is only within the power of the Almighty." Even more nefariously, it tempted consumers toward whiskey, a product unknown to Italians back home. Excessively high taxes on the Italian wines that migrants had consumed without drunkenness in Italy drove them to drink whiskey and other less expensive, domestically produced beverages, leading to moral decay. "Many crimes are charged to the Italian emigrant which should be charged to American whiskey and the American form and habit of drinking," Mariani concluded.[1] While nativists pointed to Italians' inborn tendencies toward criminal behavior to explain high crime rates and incidences of public intoxication, Mariani blamed prejudicial tariff policy.

A year before the publication of Mariani's article, an ad for Luigi Bosca and Sons' Piedmont wines in Buenos Aires' Italian-language daily *La Patria* boasted that despite elevated tariffs, consumers in Argentina preferred Bosca wines over all others. While in New York, Italians' wine-drinking habits linked migrants to criminal activity, the Bosca ad characterized Italian consumers as a civilizing force in Europe and in the Americas. Bosca wines produced in the "ancient" Piedmont winery were known "throughout the civilized world," the ad explained. Starting with references to Virgil's *Aeneid*, the publicity recalled Italy's illustrious history from the Roman Empire to the proclamation of Rome as capital of the Kingdom of Italy in 1871. Popular throughout Europe by the mid-nineteenth century, Bosca's sparking white wines reached South America with Ligurian migrants in the 1860s. The same high tariffs that in the United States seduced Italians toward a life of illegality and depravity proved innocuous to Italians in Argentina, where Bosca wines had conquered the Argentine and South American markets.[2]

As these examples attest, migration and exportation were not unrelated to each other and to notions about race and ethnicity; instead, they collided in migrant marketplaces to shape migrants' consumer options and host societies' perceptions of newcomers and their foodways. Italian elites' optimistic proclamations of transoceanic empire building through men and markets often disregarded on-the-ground differences in le due Americhe. But clearly these differences generated distinct experiences relating to Italian foodstuff for migrants in the United States and Argentina. In New York perceived racial dissimilarities between Italians and Anglo-Americans and the foods they ate inhibited migrants' ability to use consumption to forge ties with non-Italians. Instead, Italians used food to articulate differences between Italian and Anglo-American eaters. Migrant merchants, however, resisted racialization by arguing that anti-Italian prejudices could be bridged as more native-born U.S. Americans consumed high-quality Italian imports. In Buenos Aires, on the other hand, migrants used connections between migrants and markets to construct bonds between Italians and Argentines as members of the "Latin race," rooted in assumptions about the superiority of Italian and European civilization. The real and invented solidarities between the people and food products of Italy and Argentina opened up opportunities for shared consumer identities and experiences involving Italian imports between newcomers and natives in Argentina.

Imported foods in migrant marketplaces provided Italians an opportunity to shape racial boundaries but also to comment on their host countries' economic policies vis-à-vis Italy. In Buenos Aires, Italians used their prominent place in the larger Argentine social and economic landscape, and the often-discussed commonalities between Italians and Argentines, to position themselves as commanding players in the nation's economy with the power to affect Argentine trade legislation. Conversely, as only one of many foreign-born groups in a much more multicultural, industrially mature nation, Italians in New York struggled to portray themselves as having the ability to influence U.S. economic policy. However, they too denounced tariff increases as biased detriments to Italian consumption and inextricably linked to corporate trusts. In both countries, migrants employed connections between mobile people and mobile foods to represent themselves to their communities, to Italy, and to their host countries as formidable consumers in the larger transatlantic political economy.

Nation-Specific Differences Shaping Consumption in Migrant Marketplaces

Italian migrants' locations within the ethno-racial and socioeconomic structures of the United States and Argentina produced different foundations for assembling and challenging racial identities as food consumers and for arguing against protectionist legislation. Late nineteenth- and early twentieth-century industrial transformations in both countries relied enormously on a steady supply of international migrants as sources of cheap labor and, increasingly, as consumers. However, while more than twice as many Italians went to the United States than to Argentina from 1880 to 1914, they represented a much smaller percentage of the United States' total foreign-born population. Argentina, on the other hand, attracted Italians disproportionately as compared to other migrant groups.[3] Italians made up 59 percent of Argentina's total migrant population but only 6 percent of the United States' between 1881 and 1890. During the first decade of the twentieth century, Italians constituted 29 percent of the United States' total migrants, whereas in Argentina, Italians counted as 45 percent. In New York, which by 1910 had a larger population of Italians than any other city in the western hemisphere, Italians made up just 7.1 percent of the city's foreign-born residents, whereas in Buenos Aires, Italians more than tripled that, at 23 percent.[4]

Given Italians' demographic dominance in Argentina, it is no surprise that Italians made up the largest percentage of the foreign-born in almost every occupational category. Yet it was their overwhelming presence in Argentine commerce and industry—especially in the importing, manufacturing, and selling of foodstuff—that made Italians exceptionally powerful protagonists in shaping the country's consuming patterns and identities around imported edibles. This ascendancy can be traced back to Italians' earlier presence in Argentina; among the diverse group of exiles, laborers, and elites arriving in Argentina starting in the 1820s were groups of Ligurian merchants and commercial elites who by the 1870s counted among la Plata's leading families, setting the foundation for subsequent migrations and Italian commercial activity.[5] By 1901, when the Italian Ministry of Commerce requested a list of all Italian-owned commercial firms in Buenos Aires, Eduardo Bergamo, president of the Italian Chamber of Commerce in Buenos Aires, stated that the list could include only major Italian establishments. "Otherwise," he noted, "it would be materially impossible to make a complete list of the millions of Italian firms that specialize especially in the sale of edibles and drinks."[6]

Argentina's two-class system, which was divided into a small group of mainly native-born elites and a large non-elite population, explained the prominent location held by Italians in the nation's food trade. The Argentine upper class focused predominantly on law, politics, and land ownership—especially before 1912, when federal electoral reforms began to draw more migrants into politics—allowing the foreign-born and their children to almost completely control commerce and small-scale manufacturing, as both employers and employees. The Buenos Aires Chamber of Commerce reported in 1898 that Italians made up 58 percent of all merchants in Argentina, with the Spanish coming in second at 9 percent.[7] In 1914 the Argentine government found that foreigners, predominantly Italian, operated 70 percent of the country's total food-related commercial establishments. Of the 3,409 bodegas, retail shops, and warehouses enumerated in the 1910 Argentine census, Argentine nationals owned 28 percent, compared to the 47 percent owned by foreigners. Migrants also owned a large majority (71 percent) of the nation's liquor shops.[8] These Italians joined an emerging middle class of merchants, retailers, artisans, manufacturers, white-collar workers, and bureaucrats that grew as the country expanded economically and demographically.[9]

While small-scale migrant merchants and retailers predominated, not a few developed their businesses into some of the largest commercial houses in the country. One of the most prominent was Sicilian Francesco Jannello, former sea captain in the merchant marine and Italian Royal Navy. After overseeing the transatlantic shipping of Palermo-based winemaker I. V. Florio, Jannello opened a branch of the company in Buenos Aires in 1891 with exclusive rights to sell Florio products in the city. From his store on San Martín Street in the city's financial center, Jannello sold Florio wines and cognacs, especially the company's famed Marsala dessert wine. By 1910 Florio Marsala represented 90 percent of all imported Marsala in Argentina, helping make it more popular than similar dessert wines from France, Spain, and Greece. In 1908 Jannello also became the sole representative of another widely popular Italian liquor, Martini & Rossi vermouth, from Turin, and he aggressively marketed both imports in *La Patria*.[10] Jannello's association with the city's leading commercial and fraternal organizations provided him with access to the personal connections, ethnic networks, and financial resources necessary for building his successful import and retail business. He was vice president of the Italian Chamber of Commerce in Buenos Aires from 1901 to 1906 and was involved in several Italian fraternal organizations; he also served as a board member of the New Italian Bank from 1893 to 1907 and as an officer of the Bank of Italia y Río de la Plata, two important financial institutions in Argentina for migrant *prominenti*.[11]

In the United States, Italians faced a different set of economic, social, and cultural challenges that prevented migrants from competing as successfully as their counterparts in Argentina for control over their host country's commercial food sectors. In New York, Italians encountered a middle class that was already dominated by native-born whites and older migrant groups, such as second-generation Germans, Scandinavians, and Irish. With some regional variation, Italians settling in urban areas were relegated to the working class in construction and factory jobs with less opportunity for social and economic advancement than their counterparts in Buenos Aires.[12] Furthermore, while industrialization and the development of commercial agriculture in both countries required, above all, semi-skilled and unskilled workers, the United States' more rapid transformations starting in the late nineteenth century attracted larger numbers of seasonal and unskilled workers from Italy. Using census samples, Samuel Baily estimated that at the turn of the twentieth century almost twice as many Italians in Buenos Aires worked in nonmanual, white-collar positions—mainly commerce—than in unskilled jobs as laborers or servants. In New York the opposite pattern reigned: twice as many Italians worked in manual laborer positions than in white-collar work.[13]

With less opportunity for socioeconomic mobility in a country where they counted as only one of many migrant groups, Italians made up a smaller percentage of the United States' total number of food merchants and retailers. Although Italians came to dominate the importation of select bulk agricultural products, such as lemons, most Italian food businesses prospered chiefly within Italian urban enclaves like the Mulberry District south of Fourteenth Street and East Harlem on the Upper East Side in Manhattan, where they sold their wares to other Italians.[14] Observers characterized Italian neighbors in New York as isolated from the larger city, culturally, socially, and commercially. Social worker Louise Odencrantz wrote in her study of Italian families in New York, "They form small communities in themselves, almost independent of the life of the great city. Here the people may follow the customs and ways of their forefathers. They speak their own language, trade in stores kept by countrymen, and put their savings into Italian banks. . . . The stores all bear Italian names, the special bargains and souvenirs of the day are advertised in Italian, and they offer for sale the wines and olive oils, 'pasta,' and other favorite foods of the people."[15]

Despite Italians' smaller presence in the United States' import and food industry sector, as in Argentina, a number of migrant-owned businesses evolved into sizable firms. Among the biggest was L. Gandolfi and Company, established in New York City in 1883 by Luigi Gandolfi and Ettore Grassi, migrants from the northwest Italian province of Lombardy. The company offered consumers a wide variety of Italian foods at their store on West Broadway in the Mulberry District, such as cheeses from Milan and Parma, olive oil from Lucca, and dried pastas from Genoa and Naples. They also represented Fernet-Branca, a Milan-based maker of an amaro, and Florio-brand Marsala wine, making them Francesco Jannello's North American counterpart. Like other large and prosperous migrant importers, Gandolfi joined Italian associations; he was a longtime member of New York's Italian Chamber of Commerce and served as vice president of the Italian American Trust Company, a major credit-granting institution.[16]

Nation-based differences in the two countries' ethno-racial makeup and socioeconomic hierarchy produced different opportunities for interactions between Italians and non-Italians involving imports. While Italian merchants in both places dominated the Italian import market, those in Buenos Aires benefited from entering an economic and class sector that was not dominated by native-born Argentines. Italians' command of the nation's food-related commerce—as well as other industrial sectors—meant an expanded consumer base beyond Italians to include Argentines. In New York, Italian merchants, who made up a small percentage of the nation's total food-related establishments, had a less extensive market reach beyond Italian communities.

Commercial newspapers depict Buenos Aires' migrant marketplace as a permeable location where migrants and Argentines forged shared consumer experiences. Ads for Italian foodstuff had a more formidable presence in the Argentine Spanish-language dailies than in nationally circulated English-language newspapers such as the *New York Times*, where publicity for Italian goods did not show up with regularity until after 1920. As early as 1900, for example, both Buenos Aires' *La Prensa* and *La Nación*, the nation's chief Spanish dailies, included ads for Italian imports, especially liqueurs, wines, and sparkling water.[17] Italian retailers also ran ads for various Italian goods in *Caras y Caretas*, Argentina's popular Spanish-language magazine.[18] In 1910 a full-page ad for Cora-brand vermouth sold by José (Giuseppe) Peretti featured two well-dressed ladies lounging on a sofa, enjoying a glass of the vermouth, "the father of Turin vermouths."[19] By the early twentieth century, large department stores in major cities like Buenos Aires and Rosario, which attracted a wide range of consumers from different national backgrounds, sold Italian imports. An ad for La Gran Ciudad de Chicago in Rosario reminded readers of *La Patria* that it had "the most complete assortment of Italian articles."[20] These department stores, products and emblems of an emerging urban modernity built on merchant capital and mass consumerism, clearly sought out the pesos of Italians, the largest foreign-born consumer base in the country.[21] Conversely, department stores in New York, such as Wanamaker's and Macy's, which stocked a wider range of both domestically produced goods and imports, advertised regularly in New York's *Il Progresso* only after World War I. Spanish-language dailies also more regularly covered stories related to Italy and to the Italian migrant community than did English-language newspapers in New York. As early as 1900, Argentina's *La Nación* ran a regular column titled "Vida Italiana" (Italian Life) that focused on Italian politics and economics and on Italian migrant fraternal organizations.[22] Ads and articles in the Spanish-language press reveal a shared print culture that promoted the consumption of Italian imports among Italian and Spanish speakers in Buenos Aires.

That the consumption of imports both reflected and helped forge connections between Italians and Argentines is also evidenced by the large number of ads in

Spanish for Italian foods that appeared in the Italian-language *La Patria*. From the late nineteenth century through the 1930s, a quarter to a half of these ads ran in Spanish rather than in Italian. Conversely, publicity for Italian imports in New York's Italian-language *Il Progresso* remained almost exclusively in Italian; ads for Italian foodstuff rarely appeared in English.[23] And while the bulk of articles in both *La Patria* and *Il Progresso* ran in Italian for the entire period of Italian mass migration, information dealing with international trade often appeared in Spanish in Buenos Aires but remained in Italian in New York. In *La Patria*, detailed *manifesti* (ship manifests) listing the importer, quantity, and often brand name of Italian imports entering Argentine port cities were consistently published in Spanish.[24] New York's *Il Progresso* issued a regular column called "The Commercial Bulletin" in Italian beginning in the early twentieth century, but the column included a very limited list of the local market prices of mainly food items. It evolved to include some international commerce, but only regularly after World War I, and they remained in Italian, not English.[25] The widespread use of Spanish in ads for and information about Italian imports in Argentina's Italian-language press indicates not only linguistic similarities between the two romance languages but also a readership and consumer market that included both Italians and Argentines, increasing numbers of whom were the children of migrants. Linguistic anthropologists might argue that *La Patria* was a language contact zone, where Italians' dominance in commerce combined with linguistic similarities to produce a mixed-speech community of buyers and sellers who facilitated the consumption of Italian imports by both Argentines and Italians.[26]

Italians in Buenos Aires had a more formidable presence as food merchants, retailers, and consumers in Argentina than did New York–based Italians. The greater scale and scope of the U.S. economy and its more heterogeneous foreign-born population limited the reach and influence of Italian imports beyond Italian consumers in New York. Italians' prominent place in the nation's food sectors made Buenos Aires' migrant marketplace a more commercially fluid site that engaged both Italians and Argentines. These nation-specific differences provided migrant food purveyors and consumers with dissimilar foundations for constructing ideas about race.

Constructing Race in Migrant Marketplaces

In 1909 the Italian Chamber of Commerce in New York set out to debunk the myth that in South America, particularly Argentina, Italian migrants and the trade in Italian imports they opened had a more promising future than they did in the United States. As an example, the chamber argued that the derogatory term "gringo" used by Argentines to describe Italians equated to the pejorative terms "dago" and "guinea" used by U.S. Americans. According to the chamber, "The Argentine government, always hospitable and courteous, hides under the promise of fraternity." And yet, "It is useless to deceive oneself. Latin America follows *il programma yankee*" (the Yankee way). Argentina, the chamber concluded, "does not give a damn about their and our *Latinità*" (Latinity).[27]

Italian-language newspapers and business publications in Buenos Aires, however, suggest that migrants employed the "promise of fraternity," suggested in the concept Latinità, to account for their acceptance and commercial success in Argentina. In New York the "Yankee way" frustrated Italians' attempts to attract food consumers; in Buenos Aires, Italians argued that Latinità elevated Italian foods and their consumers as "forces of civilization."[28] They suggested that migration, the "foundation of commercial relations between Italy and Argentina"—a foundation built on the wine, oil, cheese, rice, and "hundreds of other Italian articles" in Buenos Aires—could not occur in the less racially hospitable United States, where the Italian "finds himself among people who seem to be another race, which has diverse customs."[29] Ideas about race shaped, and in turn were shaped by, migrant marketplaces of New York and Buenos Aires, making the two cities radically different locations for identity building and racial formation.

Global conversations about race circulating among academics, physicians, and politicians in the mid-nineteenth century shaped U.S. and Argentine attitudes and policies toward Italians and other migrant groups. During this period, racial thinkers in Europe and the Americas began categorizing humankind in a system of castes, with the assumption that racial characteristics were the most important societal indicators. Using allegedly scientific methods to study and typologize populations, eugenicists blamed social problems, such as illiteracy, poverty, and immorality, on the supposedly inherited and unchanging character traits of degenerate groups. Eugenicists joined Social Darwinists in applying evolutionary principles to society in order to justify actions and inactions by nation-states that were increasingly worried about protecting superior racial stocks and the higher levels of civilization they represented. Against the backdrop of massive global migrations, migrant-receiving nations responded anxiously by using pseudoscientific thinking to judge the racial fitness of the people entering and exiting their borders.[30]

Italians held an ambiguous position within these developing racial typologies. By the late nineteenth century, experts concurred that northern and southern Italians belonged to two biologically different and unequal races. Italian criminal anthropologists, led by Cesare Lombroso, characterized southern Italians—who by the early 1900s made up the majority of overseas migrants—as racially inferior and innate criminal types, "barbarians" associated with organized crime and immorality. He joined other racial scientists in blaming the social and economic problems of the *mezzogiorno* (southern Italy) on southern Italians' inborn racialized traits. And yet there remained a number of academics who counted Italians as part of the civilizing "Mediterranean race"; they were reluctant to completely deny Europe's and modern Italy's links to the Roman Empire, the Renaissance, and the Age of Exploration, although they increasingly connected that illustrious history to northern Italians exclusively.[31]

Notwithstanding shared dialogues about race among elites in Europe and North and South America, differences in the U.S. and Argentine racial landscapes affected Italians' wherewithal to practice racial inclusion through imports and the foodways they helped create.[32] In the viceroyalties of Peru and of the Río de la Plata, a system of castes, a hierarchical socio-racial classification used by Spanish colonial elites to categorize mixed-race people, privileged Catholic, Spanish-born *peninsulares* and *criollos*, those born in the colonies of Spanish ancestry.[33] After Argentina declared independence in 1816, a leading group of liberals—many of them wealthy criollo landowners—strove to eradicate the nation's allegedly barbaric and savage elements. These elements included indigenous populations and the then significant number of people with African ancestry, along with *caudillos* (rural warlords) and their gaucho (cowboys of the pampas plains, often of mixed race) followers in the countryside.[34] European modernity and civilization, professed future president and leading liberal Domingo Faustino Sarmiento in his 1856 opus *Facundo*, offered the best model for Argentine nation building.[35] His ideas manifested in the Argentine Constitution of 1853, which included a special clause encouraging European migration. The government recruited and subsidized transatlantic migration, especially through largely unsuccessful programs to settle migrant farmers in Argentina's interior.[36] Europeans were encouraged to populate and civilize an allegedly empty and wild pampas frontier and to "whiten" indigenous and mestizo populations through intermarriage. European migrants helped Argentine elites to construct Argentina as a "white" nation, especially in comparison to Latin America's other most populous countries, Mexico and Brazil.[37]

While Argentine immigration policy did facilitate Italian migration, over time eugenicist ideas, social and political agitation, and financial woes led Argentina's liberal oligarchy to rethink whether Italians posed a possible threat to Argentine national and racial identity.[38] The majority of Italian migrants were poor, uneducated, and assumed radicals. Elites' claims that left-leaning foreigners brought about social unrest and working-class protest in cities like Buenos Aires resulted in the passage of the Law of Residence in 1902, which allowed for the exclusion and deportation of radical and criminal migrants, as well as the comparable 1910 Law of Social Defense, which banned anarchists from the country.[39] However, Argentine elites also reluctantly admitted that their country depended on Italians as the largest foreign-born group. As Nancy Leys Stepan argues, Argentines could not deny the country's obvious Latin roots as a Hispanic nation, even while not fully accepting that Argentina's racial identity would be Latin rather than Anglo-Saxon.[40]

It would be the United States, not Argentina, that would eventually exclude migrants based on racial and class categories.[41] While Anglo-American founders in the United States shared with Argentine elites an antipathy toward native peoples and strategies for removal, the country's long history of slavery concretized naturalization laws and citizenship rights based on a black-white binary, a more rigid and less complex—if equally oppressive—racial system than that which developed in colonial Latin America.[42] Whiteness in itself, however, did not guarantee Italians entry or inclusion.[43] The popularity of Social Darwinism and eugenics, the end of slavery, U.S. and global imperialism, and the arrival of millions of non-Protestant migrants from Europe, Asia, and Latin America created a cauldron of racial anxieties directed at foreigners. In 1882, when the U.S. Congress passed the Chinese Exclusion Act, which barred all Chinese laborers from entering the country, it became the first major piece of legislation to exclude a group based on racial selection.[44] By the 1920s nationalism brought on by the war and the ensuing "red scare" made increasing numbers of migrants fall under suspicion as inferior and excludable. The resulting Immigration Act of 1924 used a racially prejudicial quota system to drastically reduce the number of Southern and Eastern Europeans from migrating to the United States.[45] Racial discrimination, combined with elites' continued fear of national degeneracy through miscegenation, encouraged Italians to locate ethnicity as the centerpiece of their hyphenated identities, particularly among the second generation. This was different from Argentina, where eugenicists viewed racial mixing, albeit of superior blood types, as conducive to positive nation building, an approach that encouraged Italians and their children over time to identify simply as Argentines.[46]

The distinct ethno-racial histories of the two countries provided different contexts within which Italians in New York and Buenos Aires constructed race through trade and consumer experiences. In Buenos Aires, Italians associated their foods with both Latinness and Europeanness to explain Argentina's acceptance of and demand for Italian imports and people. In New York, where migrants confronted a dominant culinary culture that largely disdained Italian foods, merchants maintained that racial divides between Italians and non-Italians could be overcome as more Anglo-Americans appreciated high-quality Italian imports. Food practices, food studies scholars have shown, serve as a central arena around which unequal social hierarchies based on race are inscribed materially in bodily practices.[47] Imported "foreign" foods, because they arrive from the outside, often at the behest of the "foreign" migrant consumer, held the potential not only to racialize migrants as unpatriotic, perpetual outsiders but also to challenge notions of national sov-

ereignty and racial purity. Imported olive oil, wine, pasta, cigarettes, canned tomatoes, and other foodstuff offered migrants the wherewithal to produce, as well
as object to, racialized linkages between race, nation, and commerce.

When Ernesto Nathan, mayor of Rome, stated in honor of Argentina's centennial in 1910 that Argentina and Italy were "the two branches of the Latin race
that populate the old and the new world, and shake hands across space because
they move toward the conquest of human progress," he expressed a common assumption articulated by sellers and buyers of Italian imports in Buenos Aires.[48]
In a country where skin color, socioeconomic status, and descent combined with
a belief in the superiority of European culture to define race, Italians regularly referred to migrants and goods arriving from Italy as important civilization builders
in Argentina. Civilization and race collided in Italians' repeated use of Latinità, a
category employed to construct shared racial similarities between Argentines and
Italians and to explain and enforce ties between Italian migrants and exports.[49]
La Patria called attention to "the intimate relations of interests and sentiments
that unite Italy to the great country [Argentina] where its children find, as is said,
a second homeland and carry in exchange a continuous, precious contribution of
the vigorous and refined Latin blood, of commercial and industrial genius and of
honest work."[50] Basilio Cittadini, editor of *La Patria*, cited Argentina's immigration
and trade policies as proof that the country welcomed Italians and encouraged
them "to assume its share of partnership in the common work of civilization, of
intellectual and economic evaluation of the Nation as it marches toward its highest destiny."[51] As both "children of the Latin race," Italians and Argentines worked
harmoniously in migrant marketplaces toward the modernization of Argentina.[52]
Migrant publications often claimed that Italians essentially *made* Argentina, hinting at the deep debt the country owed migrants for their commercial, economic,
and cultural successes. In 1910 the Italian Chamber of Commerce in Buenos Aires
reminded readers of its bulletin that the Italian community had been and continued
to be "the principle factor of development and progress in this country in every
area of human activity."[53]

Given the predominance of men in Italian migration to Argentina, it is no surprise that expressions of Latinità overwhelmingly characterized relationships between Italians and Argentines as brotherly rather than as sisterly. Italian-language
newspapers and business publications in Buenos Aires described Argentines and
Italians as "brotherly people" and were filled with emotional declarations of fraternal love for their Argentine "brothers."[54] Argentines, too, often discussed relations between themselves and Italian migrants using sentiments of fraternity.
The Argentine daily *La Nación*, in an article titled "Genuine Fraternity," claimed,
"Italian-Argentine brotherhood is not limited to the exchange of international
politeness or to the pretense of official state sentiments; this fraternity is a fact; it

is in the heart that loves as it is in the brain that thinks."[55] Migrants and Argentines alike constructed Latinità through the gendered language of brotherly affection.

While migrants used the narrative of Latinità to cement cultural and commercial bonds between host and home country, they sometimes asserted their superiority over Argentines within this larger transnational Latin family. They echoed Italian elites like Luigi Einaudi, who insisted that in South America "there lives a similar race to ours at a level of civilization not superior to ours and sometimes inferior to the level of Italians."[56] Latinità allowed Italians to position themselves and their trade goods as harbingers of European civilization, with the potential to *italianizzano* (Italianize) Argentines. In 1908 the Italian Chamber of Commerce in Buenos Aires ran an article that described Argentina as a "second Italy," while claiming that a third of the nation's population had Italian blood in their veins—proof that Argentina had been Italianized.[57] Italian judges awarding Italian importers and industrialists for their commercial success in Argentina noted that Italians there (as opposed to in the United States) transplanted Italian pasta, wine, sweets, and olive oil easily and with success because of Argentina's "weaker population," and because "almost all the industrial fields are formed by Italians."[58] Latinità and Italians' demographic and commercial authority made Buenos Aires' migrant marketplace a permeable site where both Italians and Argentines consumed Italian imports, and where through such interactions migrants Italianized a "civilization in formation."[59] Economist Aldo Visconti agreed that similarities between the two populations made this process inevitable and imperceptible: "Despite its contrary will, despite all its efforts to avoid and continue to avoid it, the Argentine population had too many similarities with the Italian element to not be in part Italianized."[60] He saw this occurring most visibly around the consumption of Italian food imports; Argentines, as well as Italians, desired Italian products; by simply following their own preferences, Argentines favored the growth of Italian imports without even realizing it.

The Italianization of Argentines also occurred through women's reproductive labor. Visconti pointed to the large number of Italian families formed by Italian men who called their wives over from Italy and by Italian men who married Argentine women. Citing statistics showing that Italians had the highest birthrates in the country, he wrote, "In this way, the Italian population in Argentina continues to increase in intensity, not only due to continued immigration, but because they rapidly multiply, so that in innumerous families one can verify the infiltration of the Italian element."[61] City-level demographic data confirms that Italian migrants did have many more children than Argentines in the late nineteenth and early twentieth centuries. In 1900, for example, 11,468 babies born in Buenos Aires were born to Italian parents, compared to only 3,926 born to Argentine parents. The racial and cultural similarities embodied in the concept of Latinità also produced families constituted through mixed marriages between Italian men and Argentine women. In that same year, 2,190 children were born to an Italian father and an Argentine mother, far more children than those resulting from unions between Argentine mothers and migrants from other countries, including Spain.[62] By 1917 half of Italian men and a quarter of Italian women in Buenos Aires married either Argentine or migrants from other countries.[63]

While migrant newspapers and business journals most often emphasized fraternity or brotherhood as the foundation for Italy and Argentina's common Latin origins, Latinità was not a wholly masculine construct. The presence of women—Italian women, their daughters born on Argentine soil, and to a lesser extent the Argentine wives of Italian men—provided further means for asserting Italians' demographic dominance and for constructing racial connections between Argentines and Italians. Italians in the United States were harder pressed to conscript women into race making in migrant marketplaces. Despite the heavily male migrations to both countries before World War I, Italian migration to Argentina was slightly more gender-balanced than it was to the United States. Furthermore, because Italians migrated earlier and over a longer period of time to Argentina, by 1910 a larger second generation and more gender-balanced community formed in Argentina than in the United States.[64] And while the Italian government admonished male migrants to marry Italian women exclusively, commonalities in familial arrangements, language, and religious beliefs between Italians and Argentines seem to have facilitated couplings, however limited, between Italian men and Argentine women in ways that did not occur in the United States, where Italians were slightly more likely to marry other Italians.[65] In theory these mixed marriages furthered the goals of Argentine liberals, who anticipated that intermarriage between Europeans and the country's local population, and the improved offspring such intermarriages produced, would push Argentines up the civilization hierarchy. Conversely, in the United States, racists' fears about the fecundity of migrant women and about the "racial suicide" of the Anglo-Saxon race discouraged unions between Anglos and Italians.[66]

The large numbers of Italian children born in Buenos Aires, as compared to other nationalities, and mixed marriages between Italians and Argentines provide clues as to how women's presence strengthened the consumption of Italian foods in Argentina. As food buyers and meal preparers, women who cooked for Italian husbands and children literally and figuratively reproduced Italian food preferences, habits, and rituals. In discussions of Latinità, Italian print culture employed family metaphors that included, at least discursively, feminine depictions of Italy and Argentina as a rhetorical strategy for strengthening connections between the two countries. Tapping into the well-established trope of the feminized nation-state, in 1898 the Italian Chamber of Commerce in Buenos Aires defined the "demonstration of fraternity" between Italians and Argentines as "that sentiment of fraternity and affection that comes from a commonality in origin, aspiration, needs, and that makes this young Nation more than a friend, but our sister."[67] As "sister nations" Italy and Argentina were portrayed as members of a Latin family that extended beyond the Atlantic and included the sons and daughters of Italians born in Argentina, children counted as "Argentine" by Argentina and "Italian" by Italy.

In arguing for Italians' superior positioning within the larger Latinità hierarchy that included Argentines, migrants echoed the often-stated attitudes espoused by Argentine elites who saw European migration as a vital ingredient in Argentine nation building. And yet Argentine liberals questioned whether "Latin" migrants—especially poor, seasonal, and working-class migrants from Italy—represented the quality European civilization necessary for Argentine modernization, turning instead to Northern and Western Europeans, "Anglo Saxons" and "Nordics" from countries like Britain and Germany. At the very moment when Argentine elites increasingly dissociated Italian migrants from desirable forms of Europeanness, Italians used imports to characterize themselves and their foodways as both Latin and European. Insisting on both the Latinity and Europeanness of Italians and their trade goods inserted Italians into Argentina's obvious Latin heritage, rooted in Spanish colonization, while concomitantly connecting them to a desirable European imaginary.

The simultaneous Europeanization and Italianization of Argentines occurred most visibly around the consumption of imported Italian foodstuff, especially beverages. In 1910 *La Patria* praised a speech by Italian criminologist Enrico Ferri in which Ferri called on the Italian government to favor exportation toward Argentina and other Latin American countries. "There are millions and millions, between edible and industrial products, that pour out of European countries toward these overlooked lands," boasted Ferri, "lands one can consider still virgin, barely marked with the invasive murmur of our civilization."[68] Ads conflated Italian imports with refined European-style consumer practices. Luigi Bosca assured consumers that his imported Italian wines were "known throughout all the civilized world."[69] Florio-brand Marsala, publicity proclaimed, was the only Marsala "allowed on the tables of the European courts."[70] The Italian Chamber of Commerce in Buenos Aires pointed to Italy's export market, especially the market for wine and liquors, as proof that Italy was winning in the global commercial battle to dominate the "young" Argentine market. Martini & Rossi vermouth was enjoyed "in Italy and beyond, in all the European nations, in those of new and old continents that deserve fame that comes from incomparable exquisiteness of the product." The vermouth's reputation as a refined European and Italian *aperitivo* accounted for continued consumer demand in Argentina. "It's evident that in all these stores, in the numerous bars, in the cafes, the exquisite product from the renowned Turin firm is demanded by all consumers of good taste."[71]

Discursive constructions of Latinità in articles and publicity served as powerful vehicles for assembling meanings about race through imports due to real similarities in the food cultures of Italians and Argentines. These similarities are rooted in Spain's long-standing presence in the Italian peninsula during the medieval and early modern period, including the Kingdom of the Two Sicilies of southern Italy and Sicily, which for most of the fifteenth century though 1860 fell under the control of rulers with ties to the Spanish crown. Furthermore, the Spanish empire forged connections with Ligurian merchants and explorers from Italy's northern city-states who sailed in service of Spain. Spanish colonization of the Americas and Spanish rule in Italy produced commonalities between Italian and Spanish foodways and eventually a receptive platform for Italian foods in Argentina. Already by the seventeenth century, Spain, as well as Portugal, introduced "New World" foods such as tomatoes, potatoes, corn, and chili peppers to Italy, eventually manifesting in typical regional dishes like polenta, potato gnocchi, and tomato- and pepper-based sauces, stews, and condiments by the time of mass Italian emigration.[72] These early modern Atlantic circulations of foods and culinary knowledge between Spain, Italy, and the viceroyalty of the Río de la Plata influenced the culinary repertoires of all three regions and, without homogenizing them, created overlap in their cuisines as they evolved over three centuries.[73] Notwithstanding local traditions that influenced the creation of Argentine cuisine—making it distinct from both Spanish and Italian foodways—Spanish expansion in the Mediterranean and Atlantic meant that Italians arriving in Argentina found food staples such as maize, tomatoes, and peppers that many would have recognized from back home.[74]

Latinity, Italian migrants' dominating presence in the country's food sectors, and Argentine elites' emulation of European culture produced an emerging Argentine national cuisine and public dining culture in which Italian foods, chefs, and consumers loomed large. As in the United States, Argentina's landed elites looked to France in particular as the epitome of culinary sophistication. As Argentine food scholar Rebekah Pite has noted, affluent *porteños* (Buenos Aires residents) expressed their racial superiority over the country's local indigenous and mestizo populations by having their cooks prepare French meals and by eating out in fine French and European restaurants. And while wealthy Argentines may not have considered Italian cuisine on par with French, neither was it linked to the foods consumed by Argentina's poorest, mixed-race eaters. A book published by the commission in charge of Argentina's centennial celebrations in 1910 associated Italian food with national progress and cosmopolitanism. The modest and monotonous meals of yerba mate (a caffeinated beverage made from the leaves of a tree in the holly family), empanadas, and the various meat and vegetable stews such as *locro*, *puchero*, and *carbonada* of the colonial era, the authors claimed, had been "almost completely banished for . . . the modern cosmopolitan cuisine," listing as examples the popularity of *tallarines* (*tagliatelle* pasta), *ravioles* (ravioli), and *milanesas* (a thin cut of beef, breaded and fried, that originated in Italy as *cotolette alla milanesa*). While the book's authors identified French cuisine with the eating patterns of the rich, they wrote, "The Italian cuisine, with its famous macaroni and risotto, is the one that has been popularized in all the homes of the middle classes, for the reason of the preponderant number of the immigrant element from the Italian peninsula." The poor, instead, ate Spanish food, and the "purely *criolla* cuisine has passed its final end, and more than a characteristic [of Argentine cuisine], is a memory."[75] While local criollo dishes like *asado* (grilled meat), the Hispanic pucheros, and the African-influenced squash dishes increasingly found inclusion in Argentine cookbooks and were enjoyed privately by Argentines, it would not be until the ascent of nationalist Juan Domingo Perón in 1946 that native criollo foods would take center stage as "national" dishes.[76] Clearly, Argentine elites' emulation of European culture produced a hierarchy of cuisines in which Italian foods were perceived as part of Argentina's "modern cosmopolitan cuisines," above local criollo, indigenous, and even Spanish traditions, an attitude that aided Italian migrants in depicting their imports as civilization makers.

Despite Argentines' Francophile tendencies, Italians helped construct an Argentine national cuisine as it developed, and Italian migrants worked hard, with much success, to associate Italian foods with fine European cuisine. Argentine food scholar Aníbal Arcondo found that Italian food writer Pellegrino Artusi's 1891 *La scienza in cucina e l'arte del mangiar bene* (Science in the kitchen and the art of good eating), considered the first Italian cookbook for the middle classes, was well received in Argentina; Arcondo cites a print run of forty million copies of its twelfth edition in 1908 as evidence of its wide diffusion.[77] Italians owned some of the most notable Argentine restaurants. In a special supplement in honor of Argentina's centennial in 1910, the Spanish-language daily *La Nación* featured the Londres Hotel in Buenos Aires and the Gran Hotel Italia in Rosario, as well as the hotels' restaurants, run by Italian chefs. *La Nación* wrote that the Genoese cooking at La Sonambula restaurant in the Londres Hotel attracted the nation's "gourmands," among which counted the country's most notable people in politics, finance, commerce, and ranching.[78] When Le Cordon Bleu, the prestigious French culinary institution, opened in Buenos Aires in 1914, it came under the leadership of an Italian migrant chef, Angel Baldi. And cookbook writer and food personality Doña Petrona, whom Pite shows was instrumental in building a national Argentine cuisine, was the granddaughter of an Italian migrant.[79] Italians as well as Argentines constructed Italian dishes as part of both a European cuisine and an emblem of Argentine social and cultural progress.

Similarities between Italians and Argentines and the foods they ate appeared more prominent when compared to the supposed racial and cultural incompatibilities between Italians and non-Italians in North America. Whereas Italians in Buenos Aires talked constantly about similarities that bound migrants to Argentines as "brotherly people," Italians in New York reflected regularly on the "total difference" between Italians and Anglo-Americans.[80] Noting the wide disconnect between Italians and U.S. Americans, E. Mayor des Planches, the Italian ambassador in New York, wrote that despite better economic opportunities in the United States, it was understandable that Italians preferred countries like Argentina in South America, which, he said, were "more alike in language, in race, in customs, climates, religious beliefs."[81] Buenos Aires' *La Patria* often referred to migrant and nonmigrant populations as sharing the same Latin roots; New York's *Il Progresso,* on the other hand, often described Italians and U.S. Americans as a "community of two people, of two races" and criticized Anglo-American attitudes toward Italian migrants.[82]

Despite apparent racial differences, Italian prominenti in New York, like their counterparts in Buenos Aires, argued for full membership in U.S. society based on a racial construction of Italianness that used the magnificence of ancient Rome and the Renaissance to link whiteness to Western civilization.[83] And yet the United States' more rigid racial hierarchy, in which working-class migrants from Italy, especially southern Italy, were seen as racially inferior to Anglo-Americans, as well as to migrants from Northern and Western Europe, made the country a less productive site for forging affinities between Italians and U.S. Americans through imported foods. Many U.S. political leaders viewed their country's heritage as tied to Anglo-Saxon and Nordic settlers in ways that marginalized the role that Spanish and French, or "Latin," colonization played in the nation's history. While U.S. Americans had been "crossing the boundaries of taste" since the colonial era by mixing regional staples and ethnic foods, as nativist and xenophobic sentiments increased, middle-class Anglo-American culinary nationalists reached back to an imagined New England cuisine with its roots in Northern Europe for what it meant to eat U.S. American.[84] In this context, self-proclaimed guardians of the country's culinary borders racialized working-class Italians though the foods they insisted on eating—foods that, in their eyes, were irrational, unsanitary, and lacking in nutrition.[85] In 1904 settlement house founder Robert A. Woods suggested that the foods eaten by Italian migrants ill-prepared them for life in the United States. "Their over-stimulating and innutritious diet," he wrote, "is precisely the opposite sort of feeding from that demanded by our exhilarating and taxing atmospheric conditions."[86] An 1888 *New York Times* article equated Italian and African American foodways and poked fun at the culture of poverty the writer saw informing Italian food culture, a culture in which Italians "dine royally upon four olives and a chuck of sunburnt bread" and rarely enjoy meat.[87] Italians like Baptist minister Antonio Mangano protested such characterizations. He argued in his 1912 thesis on Italians in New York, "The fact that an Irishman or a German gorges himself with a pound of steak at each meal does not make him superior to or a more desirable citizen than the Italian who is satisfied with a plate of macaroni or a plate of beans."[88]

This perception of migrants and their food traditions meant that Italian cuisine held a marginal place in the public restaurant cultures associated with fine dining that emerged in U.S. cities, even as Italian food entrepreneurs played a role in forging that culture. While Buenos Aires' La Sonambula advertised its cooking as Italian and associated it with desirable fancy European cuisine, its North American counterpart, Delmonico's in New York, founded by the Italian Swiss Giovanni Del-Monico, served mainly a version of French cuisine and trivialized foods associated with the founder's home region.[89] And while elite tastemakers in the late nineteenth century may have accepted a few, mainly French-style Italian dishes—like the macaroni *au Parmesan*, *à l'Italienne*, and *au gratin* served at fine-dining restaurants, such as at the Fifth Avenue Hotel in New York—the middle class remained largely disinterested in and even hostile to the foods eaten by Italian migrants.[90] This was quite different in Buenos Aires, where risotto and pasta had become associated with middle-class cuisine.

These perceived racial differences and Italians' less ubiquitous presence in the nation's food trade prevented migrants from exerting a commanding influence over consumers outside Italian quarters, making New York's migrant marketplace a less gastronomically porous site. And yet Italians insisted that racial divides could be bridged as more non-Italians came to develop a taste and appreciation for Italian foods. Given the small percentage of Italian consumers, as compared to the total number of U.S. consumers, it is no surprise that migrant merchants and retailers viewed their monetary success and prestige as wrapped up in tapping a consumer market beyond Italians. "Few of our products succeed in permanently penetrating the American consumer market," lamented wine merchant Emilio Perera. He admonished readers of New York's *Rivista* for boasting that Italy had conquered the U.S. market for foodstuff and drink when in reality "the consumption of our principal edible products and our wine in the United States . . . is almost exclusively due to our Italians."[91] While exerting a powerful pull on Italy's export market, working-class migrants who were bent on saving, merchants admitted reluctantly, did not always have the money to buy imported foods, which were usually more expensive than domestic alternatives. Given this reality, sellers turned their attention with fervor to non-Italian consumers. U.S. Americans' increasing interest in and admiration for Italian olive oil, canned tomatoes, wine, and other foods, merchants hoped, would challenge characterizations of Italian imports and their eaters as undesirable.

Challenging racial stereotypes related to Italian foods required, above all, educating U.S. consumers about Italian products and cuisine. Although growing numbers of U.S. Americans were coming to understand and value Italian foods—especially through their experiences in Italian restaurants in cities like New York and San Francisco, and during holiday tours through Italy—most U.S. Americans, migrant merchants declared, were largely ignorant about Italy's gastronomic contribution to high-class eating.[92] Merchants were particularly annoyed with U.S. consumers' lack of basic knowledge about some of Italy's most cherished exports, especially olive oil, which many U.S. Americans thought of as "a drink of fishermen" and for medicinal use only.[93] They had to be taught the various ways olive oil could be used in cooking and about its superiority to other cooking oils. Importer C. A. Mariani, for example, expressed frustration at a group of "American ladies, of unimpeachable standing in the community," who mistakenly thought "Virgin" referred to the brand name rather than the quality of the olive oil.[94] Similarly, consumers did not understand that the potentially toxic sulfate rind on gorgonzola cheese needed to be removed before consumption; their unfamiliarity with such high-quality imported cheese led to burdensome regulations that inhibited trade.[95] Equally irksome were narrow-minded "puritan" temperance advocates, who, blinded by prejudice and ignorance, likened wine to whiskey-based "patent medicines."[96] U.S. retailers needed instruction on how to handle, store, and display Italian imported foods so as not to damage, spoil, or misinform consumers about the items.[97]

In educating U.S. Americans about imports, Italians often denounced the palates of Anglo-American food consumers as bland, unrefined, and crude in a way that reversed the hierarchy of racialized tastes in which migrant food cultures stood toward the bottom. In an article on brined Sicilian olives—more bitter than the olives with which most U.S. consumers were familiar—Guido Rossati noted with disdain, "It is obvious that this article will never adapt to the American consumer, educated to dull and bland flavors."[98] In a piece on food fraud, the *Rivista* bemoaned that U.S. consumers with "defective palates" could not tell the difference between genuine olive oil and cottonseed oil.[99] The haughty tone with which the bulletin began an article directed at non-Italian retailers of Italian imports is emblematic of the way migrant merchants challenged taste hierarchies: "As a general rule, imported articles are superior to the domestic of the same class, as it stands to reason that superiority only can justify the higher price."[100] From this perspective, if high-quality imports did not bridge racial divides between Italians and non-Italians, the failure rested on U.S. Americans' unsophisticated palates rather than on Italian foods or their eaters. After the passage of the Pure Food and Drug Act of 1906, which set new, stringent standards in food production and inspection on imports, merchants regularly criticized U.S. Americans' nationalist attitudes for dampening the popularity of Italian imports.[101] In 1911 the *Rivista* pointed out that most edible goods that failed to pass federal inspection were domestically made rather than imported. Using Shakespearean English, the *Rivista* chided the U.S. consumer "who allowest thy patriotism to poke its nose into the business of thy taste" and who believed "the liking for imported articles is simply a fad."[102] In a follow-up article the paper again accused the U.S. consumer of thinking "he would commit a crime if he should happen to purchase something which is not a product of, or manufactured in, the United States."[103] Migrant sellers challenged the racialization of foreign foods as un-American, unclean, and unsafe by pointing out the popularity of quality Italian goods and their superiority over local items.

While migrants often portrayed non-Italian consumers as ignorant, they simultaneously worked hard to appeal to them. They believed that increased trade between the United States and Italy would "tone down the *angolosità* [Anglo-ness] and diminish the racial prejudice."[104] The *Rivista* debated how best to attract more U.S. buyers, especially after the passage of the Pure Food and Drug Act of 1906. Merchants increasingly insisted that tapping U.S. consumer markets required assuring consumers of their products' purity and that this was best accomplished by pressuring one another to import only the highest-quality foods, even if they were more expensive. Only the most excellent, uncontaminated, and safe edibles would preserve Italy's reputation and tempt U.S. Americans away from, for example, domestically manufactured canned tomatoes and toward Italian imported ones.[105] Another strategy for reaching U.S. eaters was to insist that manufacturers and retailers take great care in labeling their products; not only did packaging have to be aesthetically pleasing, but also, in order to comply with U.S. food regulations, labels had to clearly indicate the product's contents, origins, and weight.[106] New York's Italian Chamber of Commerce posited these specific strategies as part of larger organizational overhaul in the financing and regulation of the Italian-American trade. Without these reforms, Emilio Perera wrote, Italy's trade in food products and wine would remain "enslaved" by the consumer demands of Italian migrants exclusively.[107] To entice U.S. consumers and challenge the stigmatization of Italian foods, merchant prominenti at times distanced Italy's export market from the working-class migrant eaters who sustained it.

In their attempts to reach a non-Italian market, merchants often targeted middle-class Anglo-American women as holding the best potential for bridging racial differences between Italians and non-Italians. Chicago's Italian Chamber of Commerce noted that Italian Moscato champagne was "preferred to the dry and extra-dry French by ladies and gentlemen of the best societies."[108] Migrant trade promoters frequently talked about Italian imports in the context of U.S. homes and kitchens, where an item like Sicilian tomato paste "has become absolutely indispensable even in the American kitchen."[109] New York's *Rivista* insisted, "There is not an American family who does not consume canned tomatoes, and it is universally recognized that there does not exist better canned tomatoes than Italian ones."[110] As these affluent women came to value Italian foods and incorporate them into their family meals and dinner parties, a rising number of U.S. consumers would come to cherish Italian foods.

That merchant migrants focused their attention on Anglo-American female consumers made sense. They recognized the gendering of consumption, including food provisioning and preparation, as increasingly linked to white, middle-class women. Their interest in Anglo-American women also reflected the unbalanced gender ratios of Italian migration, as well as its working-class character. Italian women made up a small percentage of the total female population, and exogenous marriages between Italian men and American women were uncommon.[111] While Italian migration was heavily male in both the United States and Argentina, Anglo-Americans in the United States more often characterized the homosocial worlds created by male migration as abnormal, threatening to middle-class gender arrangements and to the increasingly consumerist function middle-class families served in the United States' industrializing society. Merchants, therefore, dissociated themselves from Italian women and the working-class consumption they represented, instead hoping to affiliate their wares with middle-class Anglo-American female consumers and their families.

Ironically, as merchants looked specifically to white, middle-class female buyers of Italian edibles to overcome gastronomic boundaries, Anglo-American women associated with Progressive Era reform organizations pressured migrant women to change their families' diets and eating rituals and to avoid imported goods, which were considered too expensive for working-class families. As one anonymous social worker reported after a visit to an Italian family, "Not yet Americanized, still eating Italian food."[112] A dietary study of working-class families in New York blamed the high rates of rickets among Italian children on Italian mothers, who bought small amounts of expensive imported cheese rather than cheaper and easily available milk.[113] Laboring hard to rationalize migrant foodways, social workers and domestic science practitioners viewed the migrant table as chaotic, filthy, and morally circumspect sites where the meals they served were unsanitary, repulsive, and nutrient-deficient.[114]

By the early twentieth century merchants measured their commercial success not so much by migrant consumption, but by the extent to which non-Italians in the United States purchased Italian imports. Merchants took migrant consumers for granted, believing that Italians "were used to using them [Italian products] since infancy and they know them and demand them," an assumption that migrant food entrepreneurs and their clientele in New York and elsewhere would challenge.[115] In 1909 the New York Italian Chamber of Commerce congratulated itself when Italian imports increased during a time of attenuating migration, attributing the sustained trade to U.S. consumers' increasing demand for Italian foods.[116] On the eve of World War I, migrant sellers were regularly depicting their products as popular items among U.S. consumers. As Emilio Longhi of Chicago's Italian Chamber of Commerce announced, "It is a well-established fact that the great American department stores, the large grocery stores, the clubs, the hotels now keep Italian goods; these are preferred, and the customers have the habit of calling for them, and one hears insistent requests for Italian macaroni, Sicilian tomato paste, Parmesan or Gorgonzola cheese, etc. not mentioning olive oil."[117] Like their counterparts in Buenos Aires, merchants in New York associated their products with the refined dinning and consumer practices of the well-to-do. But they did so with less success. Notwithstanding Longhi's confident projections, the continued stigmatization of Italy's migrants and food practices inhibited both the widespread diffusion of migrant culinary practices and migrants' ability to craft shared consumer experiences between Italians and Anglo-Americans in New York. As Simone Cinotto, Donna Gabaccia, and others have shown, although Italian food restaurants in New York's Little Italy attracted a small number of curious native-born Anglo-American eaters, many of whom went "slumming" in ethnic neighborhoods as a temporary exotic thrill, the widespread adoption of Italian foods by Anglo-Americans occurred only after World War II.[118]

While migrants in New York discussed differences between Italian and non-Italian consumers and their food preferences and debated how best to bridge such differences, in Buenos Aires there was a conspicuous absence of strategizing over how best to attract non-Italian eaters. Migrant newspapers and business publications in Buenos Aires certainly praised migrant demand for facilitating transatlantic commercial flows in Italian imports; however, Latinità, built in part on a transatlantic and Mediterranean history of food trade, made educating Argentines about foods from Italy seem unnecessary. Furthermore, as Argentina's dominant foreign-born group, and at the helm of the nation's food sectors, Italians' economic livelihood in Buenos Aires did not depend as much on reaching beyond the city's already gastronomically porous migrant marketplace, where migrants and Argentines both purchased and consumed Italian imported foods.

The ethno-racial landscapes of the United States and Argentina, and Italians' place within them, affected identity building and consumer experiences in migrant marketplaces. The selling and buying of Italian imported foodstuff offered a platform for migrants to shape racial understandings in ways they hoped would strengthen commercial and migratory ties between Italy and the Americas. In Argentina perceptions of a shared Latinità between Italians and Argentines allowed Italians to better position themselves and their products as harbingers of European progress than Italians in the United States. The people and foods of Argentina and

Italy shared affinities—both real and imagined—that shaped Italians' perceptions of themselves and the foods they consumed. These similarities made Buenos Aires a permeable migrant marketplace, one that was flexible enough to brand imports and their multinational eaters positively as Italian, Latin, and European. In New York, where migrants entered a more rigid system that viewed Italians and their foodways as racially inferior to Anglo-Americans, merchant migrants expressed contradictory impulses in their attempts to overcome racial prejudice; they both denounced and sought to change the palates of U.S. eaters while adjusting their trade to win them over. In the United States the low status of Italian foods and the working-class migrants who ate them, as well as the absence of a colonial past conceived of by U.S. elites as "Latin," produced a more culturally and gastronomically contained migrant marketplace, where less food exchange occurred between Italians and non-Italians.

"A chi giova? [Who benefits?]": Making Trade Policy from the Diaspora

In February 1902 the Italian Chamber of Commerce in Buenos Aires noted that imported Italian olive oil, cigars, cheeses, vermouths, fernet, and wine were flying off the shelves in response to an anticipated hike in the import duties on these items. Migrant consumers responded to the impending increase by stocking up on the lower-cost foods that had already cleared through customs.[119] Two years later, retailers could not get customers to buy Italian wine, even in December, a month that usually saw sharp increases in sales for the Christmas and New Year's holidays. The cause of the slowdown, the chamber noted, was the imminent abolition of a 10 percent internal tax on wine, which would make these items cheaper. The following month, after the tax went into effect, most retailers saw their stocks completely liquidated.[120] Tariffs and taxes were not disconnected from migrants' everyday consumer decisions and identity making in migrant marketplaces. In fact, the often-discussed links between men and markets relied squarely on the ability of products and people to move together across borders relatively unimpeded.

Most nations' migration policies began as an inextricable element of international trade strategies; until well into the twentieth century, political elites considered migration a part of diplomacy to be determined though commercial treaties with other countries rather than through governmental legislation. Diplomats assumed that the freedom to trade internationally rested on the rights of migrants to traverse national borders without restraints.[121] And yet as the labor-abundant economies of Europe interacted with the land-abundant countries of the western hemisphere, and as nations attempted to manage the often jarring effects of an emerging global economy on their nation-building ventures, the regulation of trade as well as migration become contentious issues.[122] Indeed, over the course of the late nineteenth and early twentieth centuries, "the tariff question" emerged as a key debate among lawmakers and economists in exporting and industrialized nations. Businesses also attempted to mitigate the fluctuating boom-and-bust cycles brought on by global integration through economic concentration. Created in part by high tariffs, business trusts became vehicles used by industrialists to control market share, labor costs, foreign competition, and access to raw materials. Such monopolist practices drew increasing criticism from labor unions, consumer advocates, and government officials concerned with capitalists' growing political influence.[123] A growing number of political economists argued that while free trade remained the ideal, temporary protection in the form of trade barriers and large-scale corporate trusts could advance industrial development at home and economic progress globally.

Migrants, both merchant prominenti and everyday consumers, expressed passionate interest in how debates over tariff legislation and monopolies among diplomats, economists, and politicians affected migrant marketplaces. "The tariff is always the order of the day," wrote New York's *Rivista* in 1911, noting the ubiquity with which the issue was discussed in political and trade journals.[124] Rather than passively react to top-down decisions, Italians abroad attempted to influence the commercial and economic policies of their host countries. "A chi giova il protezionismo?" (Who benefits from protectionism?), the title of an opinion piece in Buenos Aires' *La Patria*, became an important question for migrants, one that provided them with an opportunity to insert themselves into discussions about commerce and migration.[125] And while tariffs joined trusts in remaining the order of the day in New York and Buenos Aires, nation-specific differences emerged in migrants' arguments against economic protection. In Buenos Aires migrants perceived themselves as more powerfully affecting the policies of their host country and as exerting more control over their consumer options. Italians cited their dominant presence in Argentina and solidarities based on Latinità as affecting international trade policy. Italians in New York—a much smaller, segregated market in a more consumerist, protectionist country—struggled to portray themselves as influencing legislation, although they used anti-Italian prejudices to describe both tariffs and migration restriction as excessive and unjust. By objecting to tariffs on imported food items and to high-priced domestic foods protected by corporate trusts, Italians in both cities mobilized migrant marketplaces as transnational consumers.

Migrants in Buenos Aires exploited Argentina's dependency on Italian migration to protest against tariffs and trusts. *La Patria* regularly asserted that increased tariffs on imports discouraged transatlantic migration. Italians would stop migrating to Argentina and those in Argentina would repatriate if higher tariffs made the cost of living too high for migrant consumers. In articles discouraging Argentina from approving tariff hikes, Italians echoed the civilizing discourse inherent in expressions of Latinità by describing migrants as "the richest contingent to the vivacious force of this country" while touting the threat of migrant reduction and its impact on the Argentine economy.[126] They marshaled government statistics showing a decrease in Italian migration to lobby against tariff hikes. The Argentine government, *La Patria* argued, should do everything possible to reactivate migration, "without which all aspirations of greatness and prosperity for Argentina is a fallacious dream."[127] Noting the way Italian migration to the United States far outpaced migration to Argentina, the Italian Chamber of Commerce in Buenos Aries argued that the United States was threatening to "absorb, in a period not far away, almost the totality of our [Italy's] excess population."[128] The "big secret" behind migrants' repatriation or migration to the United States was the increasingly high cost of living, including food prices, a condition that protectionism exacerbated. According to the newspaper, if Argentina increased tariffs on imports in an effort to protect domestic industries, migrants would not be able to pay the higher, inflated cost of domestically made Argentine products.[129] Exaggerated protectionism, warned *La Patria* in 1900, made Argentina "uninhabitable for the working classes of Europe that emigrate in search of a good life."[130] Taxes were so high that migrants were "forced to consume items infinitesimally small but still very expensive." The exaggerated costs of food and other items in Argentina would no longer entice "the foreigner to abandon his homeland and transfer to a country that does not offer him an easy life and plentiful sources of nutrition."[131]

Migrants used tariff debates to position Italians as consumers of both imported products and Argentine goods. They argued that any attenuation in migration would have disastrous effects on the country's budding manufacturing economy. Argentine industries, *La Patria* stated, suffered from an "exaggerated confidence in the progress of the country"; protecting fledging Argentine manufacturing with high tariffs did not make sense, because the country had not yet attracted a large enough consumer market capable of absorbing factory products.[132] The United States became protectionist and industrial, the paper reminded readers, only after an internal market expanded to absorb industrial goods. "First work to populate the country and then we will talk about protectionism," the paper concluded.[133] The Italian Chamber of Commerce agreed, pointing out that Argentina "does not export industrial products in the strict sense of the word, with very few exceptions; it is still not an industrial country . . . it relies almost exclusively on importations for its needs."[134] The anti-tariff stance taken by the Italian-language press and the Italian Chamber of Commerce became a pro-migration and pro-importation position that lauded Italians' consuming potential and importance in Argentine nation building. The future prosperity of the Argentine economy depended on an increase in Italian migrants as both a "consuming and producing population."[135]

It is difficult to assess migrants' actual impact on Argentine tariff legislation. Argentine elites' liberal economic policies, combined with the nation's slower path toward industrialization, are probably most responsible for the relatively low duties on imports before World War I. Tariff policy commanded much debate between government officials and industry supporters starting in the late nineteenth century when Argentine lawmakers first considered tariffs as a way to foster industrialization.[136] Migrants' anti-tariff stance paralleled the position of Argentina's powerful landed interests, which pressured the government to maintain low tariffs to preserve cheap access to imported machinery and to keep European markets open to Argentine wheat, beef, wool, and leather. Manufacturers, on the other hand, blamed the nation's weak industrial sector on the government's favoring of this agro-export sector and its unwillingness to pass higher tariffs. Nevertheless, industry did receive some protection: Argentina increased duties on imports starting in the 1870s, mainly in response to the 1873 and 1890 depressions, with tariff valuation set in law in 1905; furthermore, the Argentine legislature repeatedly revised the tariff schedule on select items in response to the concerns of wealthy industrialists.[137] Tariffs on many imported Italian goods actually decreased through the early twentieth century; duties on foodstuff and alcoholic beverages went down, although after the takeoff of the Argentine wine industry in the late nineteenth century, the country did increase tariffs on European wines.[138] In 1899 the Italian Chamber of Commerce in Buenos Aires expressed satisfaction with recent adjustments to the Argentine tariff schedule, which secured slight tariff reductions for most imported foods, including pasta, tomatoes, preserves, cheese, and spirits. By the early twentieth century, however, the chamber increasingly treated Argentine tariff hikes as one of the principal threats to Italian goods.[139] In 1905 *La Patria* lauded the work of the League of Commercial Defense, made up of a multinational group of merchants, whose lobbying resulted in the Argentine 1905 tariff legislation that maintained low tariffs for most Italian imports, tariffs "that burden importation making life more expensive for the worker."[140] Objections to tariffs tended to unite prominenti merchant importers and journalists with left- and radical-leaning socialists, two groups that were sometimes hostile toward each other but joined in their desire to keep the cost of consumer goods low for migrant laborers.

Migrants in Buenos Aires lobbied hard to maintain Argentine trade policies favorable to Italian imports. But they also attempted to influence the trade policies of their home country, arguing that Argentina's continued acceptance of both Italian products and migrants depended on Italy's willingness to accept Argentine goods. In 1908 the Italian Chamber of Commerce pointed out, "Italy enjoys special circumstances that allow trade between the two countries to prosper," referring to Italian migration.[141] The chamber regularly urged Italy to take Argentina seriously as a trade partner. It denounced Italy for favoring imports from Europe over those from Argentina and accused Italy of being a poor consumer of Argentine agricultural goods.[142] "Why," the chamber asked, "should Italian industry import items like wool and leather from European markets when it can get them from Argentina?" Illustrating migrants' awareness of ties between tariffs and immigration restriction as forms of protectionism, the chamber cited intensifying xenophobic sentiments against migrants in the United States to spur the Italian government to open its markets to Argentine products. "Perhaps the day is not far off in which European immigration will find serious obstacles to be welcomed where now it is directed," as has occurred in the United States, the chamber noted ominously. If Italy refused to strengthen its commercial relationship with Argentina, Argentina, in turn, might restrict Italian migration and most certainly enter into more favorable treaties with other countries.[143] The chamber employed increasingly discriminatory immigration policy in the United States as a threat in order to prod Italy into cultivating a stronger trade relationship with its migrants' host country.

Although Italians in Buenos Aires insinuated that some form of tariff protection seemed appropriate for its more industrialized and populated neighbors to the north, Italians in New York argued the opposite. And yet in their objection to tariffs, migrants in the United States faced a varied set of powerful obstacles. Compared to Argentina, the United States had a more diverse economy, a much stronger industrial base, a vibrant consumer society, and a larger and growing middle class of mainly native-born Anglo-Americans who consumed many of the manufactured goods produced in urban factories. In the United States industrialization sparked fierce debates between Democrats and Republicans over tariff reform, especially before 1912, when power over commercial diplomacy transferred from the partisan bickering of the legislative halls to the executive branch. Republicans and northern industrialists typically called for higher tariffs, in part to protect industries and U.S. labor against competition from abroad. Conversely, Democrats, mainly representing the South and Southwest, argued against tariffs out of fear that higher tariffs would encourage Europe to increase tariffs on U.S. agricultural staples and raw materials.[144] However, whereas in Argentina migrants' low tariff position paralleled the stance of influential leaders in the export sector, in the United States migrants campaigning against tariffs stood in conflict with a powerful coalition of pro-tariff Republican politicians who lobbied to keep import duties relatively high. Although the overall tariff values of the United States and Argentina were comparable, rates on some of Italy's most popular exports, such as canned tomatoes, bottled wines, cheeses, pasta, and olive oil, were slightly higher in the United States. Italians in New York were also disadvantaged demographically in their arguments against tariffs, as they made up a small percentage of the United States' total consumer market. Moreover, Italians in both countries naturalized in low numbers, and their delayed entry in U.S. and Argentine politics further diminished their impact on tariff debates. Even so, Argentina's disproportionate reliance on migrants from a smaller number of countries gave Italians in Argentina more real and perceived political clout. In the United States, where Italian imports faced major competition from domestically made goods, which received protection in the form of tariffs and corporate trusts, migrants had a weaker voice as transnational consumers in nationwide tariff debates.

Despite these obstacles, migrants in New York condemned tariffs and used such objections to characterize themselves as global food consumers. They echoed their Argentine counterparts in blaming tariffs for "promoting monarchial tendencies" by "concentrating large fortunes in a few hands."[145] *Il Progresso* described tariffs such as the "unfortunate" Payne-Aldrich Tariff Act of 1909 as "a direct cause for the high cost of living."[146] Migrant trade promoters viewed U.S. commercial and migration policies as nationalist manifestations of U.S. American "egoism." Luigi Solari, president of the Italian Chamber of Commerce in New York, argued that the United States—a country that was formed as a rebellion against the "political and economic impositions of Europe"—was now hypocritically espousing "egotistical principles of exaggerated financial, industrial and social protectionism." Solari rejected U.S. isolationism as conservative, an ultimately futile stance against the inevitable march of progress toward internationalism. "The epoch in which one state was able to nearly isolate itself from others and operate only and exclusively in their own interest is over," he concluded. "Men can get worked up about erecting barriers, but these fall to the powerful blow of civilization that advances."[147] In 1912 the *Rivista* again denounced U.S. movements, organizations, and legislation that promoted tariffs as "stick-to-a-protective-tariff-or-nation-will-bust associations, that rely on the tariff to keep the dreaded foreign food out of the land."[148]

Merchants in particular, who relied on migrants as consumers of their imported foodstuff, viewed tariff and migration policy as linked, and they associated both with xenophobic sentiment. Journalist and lawyer Gino Speranza, writing on Italian-U.S. diplomatic relations for the *Rivista* in 1905, announced, "the emigrant is a type of international citizen." Connecting migration and trade, he continued, "The movement of a population from one state to another is a question eminently international. It will be a delicate question, if one wants, but not impossible to deal with and resolve. If nations have been able to make international agreements regarding commerce, can they not make them with respect to men?" Not only did the United States need to treat migration as an international rather than domestic issue, but it also had to stop treating Italian migrants as if they were "a population of misers" and Italy as if it a were a South American nation.[149] It seemed that an equitable diplomatic relationship between the United States and Italy rested on the racialization of South American countries like Argentina, whose low status within the hierarchy of nation-states apparently called for a less egalitarian and more unilateral approach to trade and migration policy. In his crusade against tariffs, olive oil importer C. A. Mariani offered the most poignant condemnation of tariffs as forms of racial discrimination against working-class migrant bodies. The United States, he wrote, reserved for Italians the most physically arduous work, work that required laborers to replenish their bodies with foods, and yet tariffs essentially starved migrants by denying them homeland olive oil, pasta, cured meat, and cheese, the only foods that truly replenished Italians physically and psychologically.[150]

Unlike their co-nationals in Argentina, migrants in the United States directed some of their most trenchant criticism not at tariffs, but at corporate food trusts. They treated trusts and tariffs as interrelated, since powerful corporations pressured Congress to raise tariffs while using monopolistic practices to increase prices on consumer items.[151] Armed with both trusts—the "imperialism of American capital"—and protectionism, U.S. capitalists "oppressed consumers who are forced to pay exaggerated prices," wrote *Il Progresso* in 1905.[152] The *Rivista* called trusts a form of "commercial feudalism" while arguing that all consumers, regardless of nationality, were "tired of everyday paying greater for life's comforts."[153] In 1910 *Il Progresso* criticized "meat king" Jonathan Armour, head of the Chicago-based Armour and Company meatpacking plant, for blaming the exorbitant cost of meat and other foods on migrant congestion in cities, where high demand elevated prices. Instead, the paper claimed it was "fat cat" industrialists like Armour who promoted that very congestion and accompanying price hikes by building factories in high-density urban areas.[154] *Il Progresso* attacked monopolies and tariffs as iniquitously connected and injurious to consumers, and regularly supported Democratic presidential candidates whose platforms called for low tariffs and corporate regulation.[155] Buenos Aires' *La Patria* also called attention to the power of trusts, especially in the bread and meat industries, trusts that "starve poor people" by raising the price of foods for working-class families.[156] In response to insufficient demand and periodic depressions, already by the late nineteenth century Argentine industrialists, including those in the food, cigarette, and beverage industries, moved toward economic concentration.[157] However, before World War I Argentina's weaker industrial base—the nation's inability to fully substitute imports with domestically made goods—largely shielded corporate trusts from severe criticism by Italians in Buenos Aires.

Italians in New York and Buenos Aires who denounced economic protectionism called attention to links between the movement of people and foodstuff produced by their transnational migrations. Migrants in both countries positioned themselves as global buyers of Italian imports and of U.S. and Argentine foods, buyers whose purchases affected and were affected by the trade policies of their host countries. In debates over economic protectionism, Italians in Buenos Aires used migrant print culture to more effectively position themselves as consumers with the ability to influence trade and migration patterns, in part because they made up a larger, more united consumer base in what was, perhaps ironically, a less consumerist society. Migrants in New York—facing more severe economic protectionism in the form of both trusts and tariffs, which they viewed as linked—connected and condemned restrictions on and prejudices against both Italian people and goods.

* * *

Differences in the migration histories and socioeconomic structures of the United States and Argentina helped Italians in Argentina generate shared food experiences for migrants and nonmigrants in Buenos Aires' permeable migrant marketplace. While merchants in the United States endeavored to extend the cultural, racial, and gastronomic borders of New York's migrant marketplace by attracting a non-Italian clientele, they struggled to engage U.S. Americans. Italian-language newspapers and business publications disclose New York and Buenos Aires as important sites where connections between migration and trade allowed migrants to produce and challenge racial identities linked to their consumer habits and food traditions. The consumption of imports also provided migrants with a tool for positioning themselves as powerful protagonists shaping their host nation's commercial networks and economic development. In this aspect as well, Italians' overwhelming presence in Argentina advantaged migrants in their efforts to secure access to homeland foods. Discussion about ties between trade and migration before World War I reminds us that migrants in le due Americhe labored and consumed at a time when nation-states increasingly expressed their wariness about the world through both tariff and immigration policy. As the next chapter explains, one way migrants responded to these restrictions was by producing *tipo italiano* (Italian-style) foods in the diasporas, which, while satisfying working-class migrant consumers with limited budgets, threatened Italy's profitable export market.

CHAPTER 3

Tipo Italiano: The Production and Sale of Italian-Style Goods, 1880–1914

A 1902 Italian consular report from Philadelphia echoed the pessimistic sentiments of an increasing number of Italian government officials stationed in major urban centers across the United States. Rather than advantaging Italian trade, transatlantic migration, the report concluded, was sometimes having the opposite effect: the report described a weakening of the Italian import market brought on by increased migration. Ambitious migrants in U.S. cities posed a danger to Italy's valuable food trade "in that they [migrants] successfully produce and counterfeit the articles most desired" by migrant consumers. The report noted that local pasta factories in and around Philadelphia, all owned by Italian migrants, "operate on a large scale, and with perfected American machines have expelled similar [imported] articles from Italy." The report concluded, ominously, that a similar process was occurring with "counterfeit" Italian olive oil and salami, which were slowly crowding out genuine Italian imports.[1]

The burgeoning number of pasta factories in Philadelphia and other cities with sizable Italian migrant communities was an outcome of the increasingly globalized world in which workers labored and consumed in countries thousands of miles away from their homelands. Italian elites in Italy and abroad were not alone in attempting to profit from manly markets of trade and migration. As Italian leaders predicted, migration created and sustained trade paths in Italian goods. But it also generated new opportunities for migrants who used their social and cultural capital to secure employees and consumers and to craft new food experiences in migrant marketplaces. As the products demanded most by migrants, food imports were also the most susceptible to substitution. By effectively competing with Italian imports, these substitution tipo italiano products—"Italian-style" goods like the domestically made pasta maligned in the consular report—created a rupture in Italian commodity chains linking Italian food producers in Italy to migrant consumers in le due Americhe. That transnational commodity chains, and not transnational family economies, fractured explains the success of tipo italiano industries. Because they were less expensive than imported products, Italian-style foods made abroad allowed hungry male migrants to maximize their savings to send home to family; driven by homeland obligations, migrant eaters experimented with new foods to save, survive, and create meaning in their everyday lives. The entrepreneurs, merchants, and retailers who supplied them successfully navigated their often awkward, liminal positions at the interstices of national and transnational economies, and migrant and nonmigrant consumers, all the while enlarging their own economic and social standing in diasporic communities.

Comparing the development and popularization of tipo italiano products in New York and Buenos Aires sheds light on the varied meanings of nationality, ethnicity, and authenticity in migrant marketplaces. While in both cities the presence of tipo italiano foods grew rapidly in the years before World War I, in New York migrant entrepreneurs took advantage of economic and market conditions that were distinct to the United States' more industrialized society in order to popularize a wider variety of lower-priced tipo italiano food products. Unlike importers who sought out Anglo-American consumers, specifically Anglo-American women, in hopes of raising the status of themselves and their foods, tipo italiano manufacturers used their ethnic backgrounds to secure a labor force of migrant workers who in turn bought the lower-priced foods they produced. Manufacturers used migrant print culture to publicize their domestically made pasta, wines, and other foods as transnational products in ways that reflected consumers' continuing links to homeland culinary traditions and their evolving identities and tastes in a society that continued to mark them as inferior.

While a vibrant tipo italiano industry of domestically made foodstuff also developed in Buenos Aires, the country's weaker industrial structures kept the industry limited in size and scope; before World War I, consumer demand outstripped local production and migrants continued to rely heavily on imports to satisfy their desire for homeland foods. In Argentina tipo italiano became associated not as much with domestically made alternatives, but with products originating outside Argentina, especially Spain and France. In their depictions of the competition between Italian imports and similar foods arriving from European competitors, Italians once again used masculinist language of war, diplomacy, and expansion to describe Argentina as a key overseas site upon which Italy would win "battles" by "conquering" markets. Migrants had used commerce and consumption to construct the people and products of Argentina and Italy as "Latin" while simultaneously depicting Italians and their foods as "European" to advantage Italian imports. These racial and cultural similarities, however, proved expansive enough to include the peoples and food cultures of other Mediterranean nations—Spain, France, and Greece—that were also understood by migrants as "Latin" and to the detriment of Italian trade.

Migrant Entrepreneurs and the Growth of *Tipo Italiano* Industries in *le due Americhe*

In 1909 the New York Italian Chamber of Commerce featured an article in their bulletin on the De Nobili Italian Cigar and Tobacco factory, established in 1905 by Prospero De Nobili, ex-deputy to the Italian Parliament. The three-story, thirty-thousand-square-foot building in Long Island City rivaled other modern enterprises in its manufacturing technology and managerial sophistication. De Nobili recruited technical and managerial personnel directly from tobacco-processing plants in Italy, plants owned and operated by the Italian government. And like the government-run plants in Italy, De Nobili received his tobacco from Kentucky and Turkey. Modestly paid, mainly female Italian migrants working for piece-rate pay composed the majority of its labor force; for every one hundred cigars these workers earned twenty-three cents, with a medium income of about twelve dollars a week. By 1910 the De Nobili factory produced close to 180 million *sigari di tipo italiano* (Italian-style cigars) daily and had begun to export its products to Argentina. The article underscored especially the centrality of migrant consumers to De Nobili's success. "It is the consumption of our innumerable emigrants," the article closed, "that, above all else, justifies and fortifies the factory."[2]

Migrant entrepreneurs like De Nobili creatively responded to the labor and consumer needs of Italians in migrant marketplaces of the Americas. Employing food knowledge, expertise, and workers from Italy, but using raw materials, industrial technologies, and distribution networks in the United States, large-scale manufacturers of tipo italiano foodstuff successfully competed with popular Italian commodities for migrants' attention. Celebratory articles about tipo italiano manufacturers by the migrant press and by Italian chambers of commerce also reveal the intermediary positions held by producers and sellers of Italian-style products as they navigated between the demands of Italian business and government leaders in Italy and the everyday necessities of working-class migrants. Publicly, Italian chambers of commerce often looked askance at products like De Nobili's sigari di tipo italiano for competing with Italian imports sold by migrant merchants and retailers, whose interests the chamber represented. And yet this public posturing against such items did not prevent merchants from simultaneously embracing their makers as intrepid "self-made men," as New York migrant

businessmen did during their annual banquet in 1907, where they called De Nobili's factory an "act of audaciousness," a model to be followed by other migrants
who were "still afraid of courageous initiatives."[3] In their praise for De Nobili and
other emerging tipo italiano industrialists, Italians linked men to migrant capitalism abroad, even while migrant food production and consumption in migrant
marketplaces was increasingly being done by women.

Starting in the late nineteenth century, an increasing number of Italian-style
goods such as the lauded De Nobili tobacco products and the disparaged Philadelphia pasta appeared in migrant marketplaces throughout the United States and
Argentina. Whether made abroad or imported as "Italian" from other European
nations, these products challenged Italian elites' faith in the "indissoluble chains"
between Italy and its diasporas abroad, those unbreakable links upon which dreams
of nation and empire building rested.[4] Notwithstanding importers' efforts to attract
U.S. and Argentine consumers—efforts met with more success in Buenos Aires'
permeable migrant marketplace—Italians remained the foremost consumers of
Italian foodstuff during the entire era of mass migration. Italian economists and
politicians predicted that if migrant consumers opted to buy cheaper, more easily
available tipo italiano foods, and developed a taste for and reliance on them, Italy's
commerce would weaken considerably. In 1912 economist Aldo Visconti pointed
to tipo italiano businesses as proof that the commercial advantages created by
transatlantic migrants could only be transitory. In his discussion of "on-site imitation" Italian foods in Argentina, for example, Visconti anticipated that in time
Italy's export market "would be damaged by our same emigrants that in Argentina
work and produce, or try to produce, our most sought after goods."[5] Migrants created a major demand for Italian goods, but once they improved their conditions
economically, they became Italy's biggest competitors.

Italian leaders clearly viewed consumption in migrant marketplaces with am-
bivalence. Ideally, ties between migration and commerce functioned to advantage Italian imports; however, if managed improperly, migrant consumers proved
damaging if not ruinous to Italian transatlantic trade. While regularly asserting
migrants' preference for genuine Italian cheese, canned tomatoes, and other foods
over alternatives, Italian elites also implied that migrants' consumer desires were
menacing in their unrestrained voraciousness; their needs were so robust that if
not met though imports, Italians would inevitably turn to substitutes. "When our
colonies grow and the demand for Italian products becomes more active," explained
the *Bollettino* in 1904, "industries for the production of articles demanded by Italian consumers appear abroad," pointing to the large number of pasta factories in
North America as proof.[6] Italian trade promoters worried about migrants whose
undisciplined food consumption prompted the growth of domestic food industries.
Given the perceived detriment such goods posed to links between emigrants and

exports, Italian consulates and Italian chambers of commerce regularly reported on the growth of Italian-style industries abroad and often expressed concern over their effects on Italy's export markets.[7]

To the consternation of Italian businesses, the markets for Italian imports and tipo italiano food products did indeed grow simultaneously in the United States and Argentina. The two countries possessed abundant fertile land for the cultivation of raw materials used in many of Italy's most profitable food exports. By the turn of the twentieth century, both countries were among the world's most productive breadbaskets and meat suppliers; the grains grown and cattle raised, slaughtered, and processed in the U.S. Midwest and mid-Atlantic regions and on the Argentine pampas fed their inhabitants and much of Europe.[8] The United States and Argentina both cultivated the *triticum* species of wheat, better known as durum wheat, which produced the semolina flour used in most commercial dried pasta in Italy by 1900.[9] Many of the fruits and vegetables in popular Italian exports, such as tomatoes (a "New World" crop) and grapes (an "Old World" crop), were cultivated in the Americas, allowing for the expansion of the canned tomato and wine industries. The burgeoning large-scale dairy, beef, and pork sectors provided migrants with the raw materials for producing various Italian cured meats, such as prosciutto and mortadella, and cheeses that approximated the asiago, gorgonzola, and parmigiano-reggiano varieties from Italy. Migrants building tipo italiano businesses relied on raw materials similar to those found back home, materials that could often be produced in larger quantities and at cheaper prices in their host countries, albeit with changes in quality and taste.

The availability of staple ingredients, access to manufacturing technologies, and minimal taxes, tariffs, and transportation costs combined to make most tipo italiano foods less expensive than imported versions. The lower price perhaps best explains the growing popularity of these foods, as they satisfied working-class migrants' simultaneous desires to nourish themselves with homeland foods and save money to send home. Producers and sellers of such foods better understood migrants' enduring ties to wives, parents, and children left behind than did importers and Italian business promoters who disregarded the way transnational family commitments restrained migrant consumption. Domestically made substitutes almost always cost less than imported products from the same food categories. For example, the *Bollettino* reported that in the United States in 1902, a pound of imported *maccheroni* cost nine to ten cents a pound, whereas "domestic" maccheroni cost six to seven cents; similarly, Italian rice cost eight to nine cents a pound while U.S. rice cost five to six cents.[10] In migrant newspapers, ads for Italian imports often linked their foods to the affluent consumption patterns of European aristocrats; manufacturers of tipo italiano goods made the modest cost of their products an integral part of their advertising campaigns while assuring consumers that their items equaled imports in excellence. The United States Macaroni Factory in Pennsylvania accentuated the "economic convenience that renders it [their pasta] more preferable to imported pasta" in a 1905 advertisement in New York's *Il Progresso*.[11] That same year Domingo Tomba advertised his Mendoza wine, "the best table wine in Argentina," in Buenos Aires' *La Patria* as having "modest prices convenient for all families."[12] Tipo italiano industrialists responded to the economic constraints of migrant consumers, who often made better buyers of cheaper products fabricated in the diaspora.

While the high demand for lower-cost tipo italiano products certainly encouraged the growth of such industries, so too did migrants' employment needs. A steady source of working-class laborers made tipo italiano businesses possible, because they supplied the industry's labor and consumer market. The informal small-scale domestic production of various foodstuff usually relied on the unpaid labor of migrant wives and daughters.[13] However, already by World War I, not a few of these food businesses had grown into great industrial establishments that employed large numbers of workers from Italy. As Simone Cinotto has shown, especially in his work on the California wine industry, Italian migrant entrepreneurs used their ethnic backgrounds as social and cultural capital to secure a cheap migrant workforce and to guarantee a loyal consumer base. Similarly in urban migrant marketplaces, manufacturers producing Italian-style foods exploited ethnic bonds between themselves and their employees to procure workers who frequently toiled under poor conditions for minimal pay.[14] Migrant print culture reported, often with pride, on the number of Italians employed at various larger-scale tipo italiano businesses.[15] Rocca, Terrarossa, and Company, founded by Giacomo Rocca from Genoa and based in Buenos Aires, became one of the country's leading meat-processing plants, where some 250 Italians slaughtered 50,000 cattle and pigs annually and produced Italian-style cured and smoked meats.[16] The California Fruit Canners' Association in Sacramento, founded by Ligurian migrant Marco Fontana in the late nineteenth century, employed hundreds of Italian migrants, many of them female, to can California-grown fruits and vegetables.[17]

Although Italian men outnumbered women in the United States and Argentina, tipo italiano food businesses employed increasing numbers of Italian women by the early twentieth century. By the end of the first decade, continuous migrations from Italy had pushed up the number of Italian women in the United States and Argentina; these new migrants, and a growing second generation of Italian women born abroad, provided migrant food industrialists with an expanded labor market. Female migrant workers made up a large portion of laborers in urban centers like New York and Buenos Aires, where some became active in radical labor movements.[18] In the Italian households of New York studied in 1911 by the U.S. Immigration Commission, 47 percent of family members were female; 38 percent of the 544

Italian-born women for which the commission collected data reported working in manufacturing.[19] Industrialists desired these female workers because they could pay them less than men and because they assumed women were more controllable and less radical employees. Textile work, tobacco production, confectionary manufacturing, and fruit and vegetable canning, as not entirely mechanized "light industries," were deemed especially appropriate for female workers. In Buenos Aires, for example, there were over twice as many foreign-born women employed in the city's bakeries than Argentine women in 1895; in the cigar business, migrant women more than tripled the number of Argentine women.[20] By 1919 Louise Odencrantz found that in the over three thousand Italian families in New York she studied, 91 percent of all daughters above the age of fourteen contributed to the family income, mainly through work outside the home in nearby factories, including those producing foodstuff such as candy and tobacco.[21] The Italian American Cigar Company in San Francisco, founded in 1910 by Edoardo Cerruti, employed sixty *sigaraie*, most of whom had worked previously in cigar factories in Lucca and Naples. These young, female cigar rollers helped turn ten tons of tobacco per month into Tuscan- and Napoli-style cigars.[22] Similarly in New York, Giovanni Battista Raffetto's confectionary factory, which specialized in candied fruit and chestnuts in syrup, hired almost exclusively female laborers.[23]

Such entrepreneurs built social and cultural capital in part through their understanding of how migration and industrial capitalism challenged the division of labor and gender and sexuality norms that had governed families in Italy; to a certain extent, these norms rested on patriarchal fears about the dangers of unwatched female sexuality. In order to meet their social and housing goals, rural peasant families who unified in cities abroad adjusted their work patterns. When possible, families kept mothers and wives at home, where they often "turned their kitchens into factories," mainly as garment finishers doing homework for subcontractors in the textile industry.[24] But other mothers and wives—and, increasingly children, both female and male—worked outside the home to earn wages in support of the family. As Jennifer Guglielmo and other historians have shown, Italian families relocating to New York greatly depended on the wages of these women for survival.[25] In textile manufacturing, owners and workers did not always share the same ethnic background, but this was more often the case in the tipo italiano food industries, where entrepreneurs commercialized culinary specialties that were specific to regions in Italy. The rising number of women in tipo italiano food establishments suggests that the Italian background of employers helped ease the movement of wives and daughters out of the home and into large Italian-style industrial pasta, canning, confectionary, and tobacco businesses. As Italian employers did with male laborers, they used their shared ethnic background, as well as the networks that female workers themselves cultivated, to obtain inexpensive feminized labor.

While access to cheap, increasingly feminized migrant labor contributed to manufacturers' success, so too did access to Italian working-class consumers in migrant marketplaces, consumers who were attracted to lower-cost alternatives. The *Bollettino* reported in 1906 that tipo italiano businesses "employ Italian workers and they find in our colonies their market." Such firms grew from migrants' "impressions of needs, real and imagined," hinting at the way exposure to new foods and expectations abroad moved migrants' eating concerns beyond material and nutritional considerations only.[26] Owners of tipo italiano factories carried production and consumption together across the Atlantic to migrant marketplaces; they domesticated what had once been a transatlantic commodity chain, but their success continued to depend on material and cultural connections to Italy.

As global spaces, migrant marketplaces also disclose how migration and trade together complicated attempts to mark foods by their national origins. Most emblematic of this were tipo italiano items made from imported Italian ingredients. In 1880 Angelo and Antonio Pini, Italian migrants from Lombardy, turned the modest liqueur factory started by their father into a four-thousand-square-meter factory in Buenos Aires while opening a second distillery in the northeastern province of Corrientes. Yet they produced their Pineral-brand aperitivo from imported Italian herbs, red and white wine, almonds, saffron, and orange and lemon rinds; the product itself, therefore, embodied the actual trade routes in Italian foods opened up by migrants like the Pini brothers and sustained by migrant demand for homeland flavors.[27] Similarly, the award-winning Canale-brand biscotti made by the Vedova Canale company, founded by the Canale family from Genoa in the late nineteenth century, employed ninety-five workers, mainly Italians or their children, in their Buenos Aires factory. While the flour, butter, eggs, and sugar used in the biscotti came from Argentina, every month the company used about one hundred kilograms of lemon extract imported from Sicily.[28] After migrating to New York from Liguria in the late nineteenth century, Giovanni Battista Raffetto began preserving imported Italian chestnuts and domestically produced fruits such as strawberries and peaches. Relying predominantly on female workers, his firm churned out its famous chestnuts in syrup and cognac using machines that he invented and patented in the United States and Europe.[29] The wine industry especially muddled demarcations between italiano and tipo italiano; early twentieth-century wine entrepreneurs in the United States and Argentina often blended heartier and stronger imported wines with the more "anemic" or light wines made in California and Mendoza.[30] At a time when merchants shipped much of their foodstuff in bulk rather than in small containers with clear labeling, the drawing of neat boundaries around what counted as tipo italiano and what counted as imported proved difficult. Migratory and commercial flows together produced hybrid foods and beverages that reflected in some ways the transnational lives of their migrant producers and consumers.

Despite their regular denouncement of tipo italiano products, importers and retailers affiliated with Italian chambers of commerce acknowledged these blurred lines between domestically made and imported foods and often sold both in order to maximize their profits and satisfy their customers. In 1900 New York importer Ernesto Petrucci advertised his store as a "grand deposit of California wines" while also lauding his Italian olive oils and pastas from Genoa and Naples.[31] In Chicago, Emilio Longhi sold numerous Italian-brand macaroni, olive oil, liquors, *antipasti*, and tuna, but also Cavalleria-brand cigarettes made in the United States with "tanning and tobacco identical to the Italian manufacturing."[32] Even Francesco Jannello, seller of the renowned Florio-brand Marsala and Malvasia wines in Buenos Aires, traded in Mendoza wines.[33] Selling both imported and domestic foodstuff allowed food purveyors to appeal to a wide variety of preferences among Italian migrants as well as their transforming palates. While *piedmontese* Oreste Sola lauded Mendoza wine as "one of the best products" in Argentina, his wife, Corinna, complained not only about Mendoza wine but all tipo italiano foods that crossed her path in Buenos Aires. In a letter home, she urged her in-laws back in Biella to drink a bottle of Piedmont wine, pointing out, "Here you can't do that since there isn't any good wine. Not only that, but in everything you don't get satisfaction, like cheese, salami; none of the food we eat here is satisfactory."[34]

Likewise, tipo italiano food and beverage manufacturers often sold imported food items along with their domestically made products. G. B. Matelli in Buenos Aires produced the noted Margherita-brand Argentine vermouth while simultaneously selling imported Barbera, Grignolino, and Moscato wines from Italy.[35] The Savarese V. and Brothers pasta factory in Brooklyn, which employed some one hundred workers, sold its domestically made pasta along with imported Italian cheeses, wine, and olive oil, and even pasta.[36] A number of tipo italiano food manufacturers began their businesses as importers, opening up enterprises only after acquiring a critical mass of capital, business contacts, and clientele. Upon migrating from Liguria, Antonio Cuneo opened a small grocery store in the Italian quarter of Mulberry Street in New York and soon began importing a variety of foods directly from Italy. After accumulating money and experience, he founded the Atlantic Macaroni Company in Long Island, which under his son's direction became one of the largest pasta producers in the United States.[37] Similarly, in 1891 importer Luigi Gandolfi opened a bottling plant in New York where his Italian employees treated imported wine to a natural fermentation process. Using better technology available to him in the United States, the sparkling wine he produced and sold under his own label, he claimed, rivaled the imported bubbly wines he continued to sell in his shop.[38] The global economic integration that allowed ingredients, technologies, and laborers to move back and forth across the Atlantic made ascribing national labels to both food products and the people that produced them increasingly difficult.

The evolution and growth of tipo italiano industries in the United States and Argentina reveals the intermediary position of migrant producers, importers, and sellers. Rather than serve as mouthpieces of the Italian government or Italian food businesses, migrants in food sectors knew that it was in their best interest economically to represent and sell both tipo italiano and Italian imports. They navigated their own sometimes delicate place as unofficial commercial attachés of the Italian government from their positions in Italian chambers of commerce and as migrant prominenti interested in bolstering their status among consumers. Migrant merchants showed off their expertise and Italy's dependence on them as commercial interlocutors by sending back advice and instruction to Italian manufacturers. In 1900 the Buenos Aires–based Italian Chamber of Commerce encouraged Italian businesses to send representatives to Argentina in order to better understand changing consumer needs. Their experience buying and selling in the Buenos Aires migrant marketplace revealed to them that Italian consumers' desires were not immutable and constant, concluding, "Our workers and our citizens acquire in America a marked tendency to change taste."[39] They chastised Italian exporters for making assumptions about migrant preferences rather than basing their decisions and advertising strategies on calculated investigations of specific consumer preferences. In response to a proposed Argentine law regulating the wine trade, the Buenos Aires *Bollettino Mensile* noted, "Our exporters must persuade themselves that in the modern battle of trade it is not the market that must conquer the product, but the product [that] must conquer the market."[40] Similarly, in 1910 the Italian Chamber of Commerce in Chicago advised the Italian Ministry of Agriculture, Industry, and Commerce to follow U.S. pasta manufacturers' lead by boxing Italian pasta intended for sale in the United States in small, rectangular, elegantly designed cartons. "It now lies with the manufacturers in Italy to follow their example," concluded the chamber.[41] By using the tipo italiano industry to show off their marketing and business acumen, migrants positioned themselves as indispensable trade experts with knowledge of both their host country and migrants' changing consumer expectations.

The growth of tipo italiano goods provides an example of migrant merchants' intermediary position between national and global markets of people and products and between Italian and non-Italian consumers. They understood and capitalized on migrants' long-term plans and economic restraints, as well as their desire for familiar, if transforming, tastes, by offering them a way to consume in an ethnically distinct manner but at a cheaper price. Migrant food entrepreneurs did not, as critics often stated, simply imitate or emulate Italian goods; rather, they appropriated links between migrants and exports and creatively and profitably responded to migrant laborers' economic exigencies, changing appetites, and shifting relationships to their host countries.

Comparing *Tipo Italiano* Industries in New York and Buenos Aires

Ernesto Bisi, with his United States Macaroni Factory, was one of many migrant entrepreneurs in the late nineteenth and early twentieth centuries who capitalized on the growing demand for foodstuff and for employment among Italian migrants and on the technologies and resources of his adopted country (see fig. 13). Associating his product with industrial modernity, Bisi advertised his pasta factory in Carnegie, Pennsylvania, as "the most perfect, the most modern and among the largest that exist in the United States."[42] He employed a diverse set of symbols that reflected the transnational worlds in which his migrant consumers lived. A large illustration of the Statue of Liberty tied the production and consumption of a popular tipo italiano food to a U.S. emblem of freedom and migration, as the statue stood near Ellis Island, the migrant processing station through which thousands of Italians arrived.[43] Bisi, like other migrant food entrepreneurs, used the migrant press to invent new meanings about the consumption of Italian foods.

Figure 13. Ad for United States Macaroni Factory, *Il Progresso Italo-Americano* (New York), December 1, 1905, 3.

The Bisi advertisement also suggests how nation-specific differences characterizing le due Americhe influenced the growth of tipo italiano goods in New York
and Buenos Aires, creating various consumer experiences and notions of Italianness in migrant marketplaces. That Bisi produced pasta by the "carload" for buyers in the United States, Canada, and Mexico, and presented his establishment as
an "Emporium of Foodstuff," hints at the industrial resources available to him in
the United States but inaccessible to migrants in Argentine cities.[44] While pasta
importers in both countries worried about the competition that entrepreneurs like
Bisi represented, in the less industrially developed Argentina, importers fretted
more about tipo italiano foods arriving from European countries such as Spain,
France, and Greece.

Tipo italiano industries in the United States and Argentina relied equally on
migrant laborers and consumers, as well as on the raw materials (fruits, vegetables,
wheat, meat, and tobacco) used in Italy's most profitable food exports. However,
migrant entrepreneurs like Bisi took advantage of the United States' more mature
manufacturing sector and transportation and communication networks to produce, market, and distribute their domestically produced foods on a mass scale.
The first tipo italiano businesses in both countries depended on mainly imported,
hand-cranked machinery for making pasta, sausage, wine, and other products.[45]
However, the industrial food system developed much earlier in the United States
than in Argentina.[46] Already by the late 1800s food constituted the United States'
foremost manufacturing sector; by the turn of the century food made up one-fifth
of the country's total industrial output, and the nation moved from small-scale food
production for local markets to large-scale, mechanized production for an increasingly integrated, national market. New fuel sources; advances in transportation,
distribution, refrigeration, canning, and bottling; and novel advertising techniques
helped birth several large-scale agribusinesses, milling giants, meatpacking plants,
and industrial food corporations that fundamentally changed the eating patterns
and food cultures of U.S. Americans. Italian migrants remained hesitant to embrace
the standardized factory foods they encountered, even while industrialization offered migrants access to their traditional foods—coffee, sugar, wheat bread and
pasta, and meat—available only to the well-off back home.[47] But the United States'
sturdy industrial infrastructure also provided the resources used by migrant food
entrepreneurs to begin manufacturing Italian industrialized food for co-nationals
in migrant marketplaces. By the early twentieth century, the United States' more
extensive manufacturing base meant that migrants with capital and connections
had at their disposal much of the machinery used for processing, bottling, canning,
and packaging industrialized, domestically made foods.[48]

Migrants in Argentina did not have access to the same range of industrial capabilities and technical resources to fabricate large quantities of tipo italiano goods.

Fernando Rocchi describes Argentina's industrial takeoff in the 1880s and 1890s when the state implemented policies, such as taking the peso off the gold standard and tariff protection, that helped jump-start the country's manufacturing sectors, including food processing. Migrant entrepreneurs began turning modest pasta and biscotti factories, vegetable and fruit canning operations, and wineries into larger establishments.[49] However, Argentina's food businesses remained slow to mechanize: handicraft labor continued to be used extensively in factory production; its restrictive banking system made it difficult for migrants to secure long-term loans; its small stock market limited businesses' wherewithal to raise capital; and many businesses continued to rely on imported machinery.[50] A book on Argentina at the 1906 International exhibition in Milan listed none of the 4,377 small-scale food manufacturers in the country (86 percent of which were owned by migrants) as mechanized.[51] Finally, Argentina's overall population was much smaller than that of the United States and had a difficult time supporting economies of scale.[52] As in the United States, migrants in Argentina used their family, kinship, and cultural ties to overcome financing, administration, and legal obstacles, and to capture consumer markets. However, with some important exceptions, such as wine, spirits, and meat production, tipo italiano industries in Argentina remained small-scale before World War I while still meeting the basic needs of migrant laborers for lower-cost foods. Argentina's weaker manufacturing economy forced consumers to rely heavily on imports until after World War I.

Tipo italiano migrant businesses in the United States also benefited from the country's more protective economic policies and food safety legislation, legislation criticized by *Il Progresso* and the Italian Chamber of Commerce in New York. Higher tariffs encouraged the establishment of tipo italiano industries, as they could produce locally made foods cheaper than imported versions, which even without high duties were disadvantaged by the higher costs of transportation and storage. Trade promoters in the United States lashed out at migrant entrepreneurs, claiming that as soon as migrants in the States established tipo italiano businesses, they lobbied politicians to increase tariffs on Italian products. New York's chamber explained that once migrants, especially those in California, cultivated agricultural produce typically imported from Italy, such as citrus fruits, hazelnuts, vegetables, and tomatoes, they "ask, implore, demand protective measures, which they almost always obtained for their products, to the harm of those imported."[53] While praising Italian winemakers in California for their hard work and determination, victories "that make us think of the Genoese and Venetians of the middle ages," New York's *Rivista* reminded readers, "Do not talk to them about solidarity with the mother country regarding custom taxes." "Free traders at home became protectionist in the United States!" the article continued. "Regarding all else they are Italian, the most Italian, ready to sacrifice for the mother country . . . but don't touch the protective duties!"[54] Conversely, Italians in Argentina before World War I enjoyed relatively low import duties on major Italian imported products, and with some success they lobbied their host government to keep tariffs on imported foods relatively low.[55] While tipo italiano migrant entrepreneurs in Buenos Aires may have campaigned for tariff hikes to benefit their locally produced foods, their voices were drowned out by the more unified stance of migrant merchants, consumers, and workers who wanted, above all, access to cheap foods and other consumer goods.

Importers of Italian foodstuff also saw U.S. food safety laws, especially the Pure Food and Drug Act of 1906, as unfairly handicapping imports while advantaging tipo italiano industries. U.S. government inspectors, claimed the New York chamber, applied laws regulating food purity more stringently to foreign foods arriving at major U.S. port cities than to products made in the country. Authorities applied these laws "in a manner that suggests almost that these provisions were imposed with hate on particular products," especially imported Italian cheeses.[56] The act, for example, did not apply to products that moved within states, and migrants in the United States could more easily defend their tipo italiano foods against sanctions than could Italian businesses located across the ocean.[57] Argentina also had strict sanitary requirements in place for imported food goods. Legislation called for food inspections, the labeling of food, and the prohibition of spoiled and toxic substances.[58] However, while described as a nuisance to international trade, migrants did not discuss food safety legislation as prejudicially disadvantaging imports.[59] Unlike migrants in the United States, those in Buenos Aires wasted little discussion on the deleterious effects of food sanitation measures on the import market, probably because imports faced less competition from these domestic industries.

A good example of how industrial, economic, and legal factors advantaged tipo italiano industries in the United States is the evolution of pasta production in le due Americhe. The great demand for pasta among the United States' large Italian population fueled the wildfire-like growth of pasta factories in cities throughout the country. By 1906 in greater New York alone there were more than a dozen large-scale pasta factories employing over two million workers.[60] The economist Aldo Visconti complained of the United States, "Wherever there are nuclei of Italians of some importance, factories of pasta develop and, having owners and training almost all Italian, function perfectly well from the beginning."[61] Even in small towns outside of the Northeast and Midwest, migrants established pasta factories. In 1903 the *Bollettino* reported that in Texas five pasta factories had appeared in cities with sizable Italian migrant populations, including two in Houston and one each in Galveston, San Antonio, and Fort Worth.[62] Ads in New York's *Il Progresso* further reveal the generous number of medium and large-scale pasta factories by the early twentieth century. By 1905 pasta manufactured by A. Castruccio and Sons in Brooklyn, New York, and B. Piccardo in Pittsburgh regularly publicized their *paste domestiche* in *Il Progresso*.[63] In cities with large migrant marketplaces like New York, San Francisco, and Philadelphia, a number of pasta factories grew into vast establishments with wide distribution networks. Rivaling Ernesto Bisi's United States Macaroni Factory was the Atlantic Macaroni Company, established and managed by Andrea Cuneo, which produced thirty thousand kilograms of pasta daily by 1906 in its Long Island factory.[64] A tax of five cents per kilogram on imported pasta helped stimulate this growth, as did the 1906 Pure Food and Drug Act, which, New York's chamber claimed, "produced grand inconvenience to importers," as imported pasta remained in dock warehouses, sometimes for days, waiting for inspection after being unloaded from ships.[65]

While producing obstacles for importers, such tipo italiano pasta factories in and around New York thrived because their modest prices allowed poor migrants to regularly enjoy the foods that back home had been reserved only for the wealthy. As a Sicilian woman living in New York said to Italian American educator Leonard Covello, "Who could afford to eat spaghetti more than once a week [in Italy]? In America no one starved, though a family earned no more than five or six dollars a week. . . . Don't you remember how our *paesani* here in America ate to their heart's delight till they were belching like pigs and how they dumped mountains of uneaten food out the window?"[66] The ability to overeat Italian-style spaghetti and even to waste food symbolized to working-class migrants a reversal of class hierarchies in Italy, a hierarchy that had kept their meals modest and unvaried.

In Argentina a substantial number of pasta factories, mainly operated by Italians, also flourished by the end of the first decade of the twentieth century. In 1910 the Argentine Industrial Census counted 177 pasta factories, employing a total of 794 people, 88 percent of which were owned by migrants.[67] While much fewer in number, several pasta factories in Buenos Aires evolved into major producers that supplied urban consumers and those in the interior provinces. Giovanni Casaretto opened his Buenos Aires pasta factory in 1895 after migrating from Liguria; just five years later, 50 Italian laborers produced more than 4,000,000 kilograms of pasta daily in his 1,200-square-meter, two-story factory.[68] Canessa, Pegassano, and Company also counted among the country's oldest and largest pasta manufacturers, making 15,000 kilograms of pasta a day by 1906 and employing over 150 workers, almost all Italian.[69] Despite these Italian pasta tycoons and despite the low tariffs on pasta imports, obstacles and limitations embedded in the country's weaker industrial base and consumer market kept most pasta establishments modest before World War I. Indeed, few ads for pasta factories appeared in *Il Progresso* during the first two decades of the twentieth century. In Argentina demand for pasta and other Italian-style food items outstripped local production capabilities, ensuring a continued market for imports. In 1909 the value of Italian pasta imports to the United States was almost 150 times greater than the value of such exports to

Argentina. Just six years later, in 1915, however, the value of pasta exports to the United States had decreased by almost half while imports to Argentina continued to rise. In 1916 Italy exported almost four times more pasta to Argentina than to the United States.[70]

The more rapid development of domestically made pasta in the United States mirrored the growth of other tipo italiano foodstuff in the two countries. Migrant newspapers help evidence this difference, as a wider array of products and a larger number of medium- to large-scale tipo italiano businesses appeared in New York's *Il Progresso* than in Buenos Aires' *La Patria*. Readers of *Il Progresso* viewed publicity for a growing variety of Italian-style wine, liquors, cigars and cigarettes, canned fruits and vegetables, candies, cheeses, and cured meats by the early twentieth century, whereas in *La Patria* ads for tipo italiano foods remained limited. Ads for such products in *Il Progresso* often referred directly to imports, assuring consumers that their products simulated and perhaps surpassed Italian foodstuff, certainly in price but also in quality. Ernesto Bisi assured readers that his pasta was "guaranteed to compete victoriously with imported pasta."[71] In 1900 the Italian Cigar & Tobacco Company of New York stressed that their Tuscan- and Neapolitan-style cigars were "fermented in perfect imitation of form and taste to the Italian ones."[72] In a country that, notwithstanding a revolution in the fields of marketing and mass advertising, depicted the mainstream U.S. consumer as homogenously white and middle-class, migrant entrepreneurs employed an assortment of national and regional symbols to appeal to migrant consumers' transnational livelihood, as well as their changing tastes.[73] Like Italian businessmen in their trademarks for popular Italian exports, they used the names and images of notable Italian men in their branding to emphasize the Italianità of the product. In New York the Razzetti Brothers manufactured and sold "Garibaldi" cigars, while the firm of G. B. Lobravico produced Dante-brand Italian-style cigars.[74] References to various national and regional identities and geographical indicators often merged together, as in the American Chianti Wine Company of Brocton, New York, which produced 12 million gallons of wine annually, wine made not from the Sangiovese grape, as the winery's name suggests, but from Concord grapes cultivated in New York State.[75] Likewise, De Nobili cigars, "vastly superior to any other Italian cigar manufactured abroad," used both U.S. and Italian flags in publicity for the company's products in ways that reflected the transnational experiences of De Nobili's workers and consumers.[76]

Entrepreneurs like De Nobili who called their goods "Italian" also pioneered in crafting national rather than solely regional identities for their products and clientele. Ads for imports in both New York's *Il Progresso* and Buenos Aires' *La Patria* tended to accentuate the local or regional origins of their products and brands— Ligurian olive oil, tomato sauce from Naples, Marsala from Sicily, Chianti wine, vermouth from Turin, candy from Siena, and so on. Ads for tipo italiano foods, however, more often referred to their foods simply as "Italian" while sometimes continuing to also employ regional labels. Despite Italian elites' hopes that their country's heterogeneous peoples scattered abroad would unite as "Italians," in part through the consumption of imports, migrants continued to identify with the regional traditions of their local paese well into the twentieth century.[77] And yet publicity for and articles about tipo italiano goods indicate that the formation of a more unified national identity among migrant consumers began already in the early twentieth century and around tipo italiano wine, cigars, pasta, and other foodstuff rather than in relation to Italian imports, which continued to be marketed as regional specialties. Migrants' identities became consolidated and commodified in migrant marketplaces through interaction with tipo italiano foods just as much as, if not more so, than through imported goods.[78]

As Simone Cinotto has found in his research on Italian foodways in New York during the interwar years, migrant food entrepreneurs constructed an Italianità based less on provenance or notions of authenticity as it relates to a primordial fixed past and more on the need to forge identities that helped migrants grapple symbolically and materially with their daily existence as low-wage transnational workers.[79] While tipo italiano producers viewed the mingling and merging of national and regional symbols as a key element in their marketing strategies, importers described such practices as consumer fraud. Indeed, the growing presence of tipo italiano foods in the United States unleashed a wave of concern over issues of food authenticity. The Italian Chamber of Commerce in New York regularly associated tipo italiano foods with "counterfeiting," "manipulation," "imitation," and "falsification," labels connoting poor sanitation, low quality, and illegality.[80] They took particular aim at manufacturers and vendors who mislabeled their products or used confusing and misleading wording. At the 1906 "Italians Abroad" exhibit, the jury awarded the Italian Swiss Colony in Sonoma County, California, for the quantity and quality of their wine but used the occasion to admonish the winery for using flasks similar to those in Tuscany and for including the word "Chianti" on their labels. This disingenuous practice made the California wine an "illegitimate" and "fearsome" competition to "true Chianti."[81] Similarly, Luigi Solari, president of the Italian New York chamber, rallied against tipo italiano businesses that used the adjective "yellow" to describe foods and oils that were just barely greenish in color and who pronounced their products "sweet" even when they were bitter. While he described these misleading words as "venial sins," he saved his most vociferous condemnation for store owners who passed off locally made products as Italian. Such retailers, he claimed, strategically employed phrases such as "oil from Lucca," "Romano cheese," and "Aged Chianti wine," instead of the more direct "guaranteed pure olive oil from Lucca or guaranteed real Romano." Fighting against this "parasitic commerce," Solari concluded, was one the most important obligations of Italian chambers of commerce abroad.[82]

Moreover, by focusing its efforts on imported foods, the New York chamber claimed that the 1906 Pure Food and Drug Act did not regulate the arenas where real harm was enacted on food consumers: U.S. factories, warehouses, and retail outlets, where migrants made Italian-style foods in unregulated, unhygienic tenement buildings, and where greedy merchants and grocers mixed genuine Italian goods that had just passed rigorous inspection with domestically made inferior ingredients. They counted as the worst offenders dishonest migrant importers and retailers who combined genuine Italian oils and wines with domestically made, inferior products such as cotton and peanut oil or grape varieties grown in California or New York. "It is an incontrovertible fact," an article in the *Rivista* claimed, "that many imported Italian products like olive oil, in passing from places of production to this grand consumer market, are often altered or artificial, adulterated or counterfeited."[83] To importers seeking to popularize their products among Anglo-Americans, who often held prejudicial stereotypes about Italian food, such fraud threatened the high reputation of Italian products that importers worked so hard to cultivate. This threat arrived just as the quality of many Italian food exports, especially wine and olive oil, was greatly improving. In Italy advances in knowledge about grape and olive cultivation, investment in new machinery and bottling facilities, the commercialization of monocrop wine and olive regions, and a growing national and international consumer market modernized these industries, as well as others such as pasta, tomato preserves, spirits, and cheese manufacturing.[84]

In response to the real and perceived dangers represented by tipo italiano foods, the Italian Chamber of Commerce in New York intensified its policing of boundaries between imported and domestically made items. Starting in 1909 the chamber began a program of inspection and certification in which importers and retailers could voluntarily submit to an examination by experts affiliated with the chamber—usually other reputable importers—in order to obtain a certificate of origin that guaranteed the authenticity and purity of imports.[85] In 1910 a short column in the *Rivista* called "Commercial Fraud" provided information on lawsuits against merchants accused of food falsification and imitation. In what amounted to a public shaming, the column included the details of the case: the name of the defendant, the products and brands in question, and the outcome. In October 1910 the *Rivista* reported that the Board of Food and Drug Inspection had arrested Giuseppe Rindone of New York for five accounts of counterfeiting, including the forging of Ferro China Bisleri and Fernet-Branca spirits. He was declared guilty, sentenced to five months in jail, and fined five hundred dollars.[86] In 1911 A. Fiore & Company in New York admitted to passing off their cottonseed oil as "olive oil," and the Board of Trade found that macaroni sold as imported by the Ceravolo Brothers of Philadelphia was actually made in the United States.[87] Migrants wielded U.S. food legislation that they felt had so damaged the import trade against co-nationals to monitor the boundaries of authenticity in migrant marketplaces. While merchants hoped this self-policing would ultimately boost the sales of imports, the tipo italiano industry continued to grow unabated. The chamber failed to understand that migrant consumers cared less about the origins of the foods they ate and more about whether those ingredients, meals, dishes, and brand names satisfied their everyday nutritional and cultural needs as transnational eaters.

Italian business leaders in Buenos Aires also reported on the growth of domestically made tipo italiano edibles and denounced migrants who passed off their goods as Italian imports, selling them under the most accredited Italian brand names.[88] However, the most perilous menace to Italian commerce in Argentina was perceived as originating abroad rather than from within Buenos Aires' migrant marketplace. Argentina's weaker industrial structure meant that the country's tipo italiano industries developed more slowly than in the United States. Migrant consumers in Buenos Aires continued to demand and rely on imported European goods; as such, Italian-style foods brought about less notice or sanction from trade promoters, who sometimes condescended to local industries attempting to compete with Italian imports. Despite the extraordinary increase in the local production of cheese in Argentina, the Buenos Aires Italian Chamber of Commerce declared, "Among all the countries that furnish this article to Argentina, Italy will probably be least disadvantaged by the 'indigenous industry,' because manufacturers here have not succeeded yet in imitating with success the Italian product."[89] Therefore, in Argentina merchants came to associate tipo italiano not so much with ambitious and sometimes unscrupulous migrant entrepreneurs, but with threatening competitors abroad in countries such as Spain, France, Greece, and Portugal.[90] It is no wonder that these countries competed aggressively with Italy for the pesos of Argentine consumers, and Italians specifically, as the largest consumer block in the country. While the Argentine population comprised only 8 percent of the total Latin American population, it constituted one-third of all imports into the region in the early twentieth century.[91] Argentina, more so than other Latin American countries, represented a lucrative site for European manufacturers, and to the exasperation of Italian importers, Italy's neighbors also reached out to migrant consumers there.

These countries, it turned out, produced similar products for export to Argentina, products so similar that they could substitute for Italian goods. Italian trade promoters obsessively compared the quality, quantity, price, and style of Italian imports from similar items arriving from other countries: Italian preserved fish, canned goods, wines, and spirits found fierce competition in comparable products from Spain and France; cheese from Switzerland rivaled Italian parmigiana-reggiano and gorgonzola in flavor and cost; Italy and Germany competed to be

Argentina's number one supplier of rice; and Portugal did the same with their exports of dried fruit.[92] In such discussions the Italian Chamber of Commerce in Buenos Aires portrayed Argentina as a critical site upon which modern commercial battles between European powers played out. Italian cheeses, noted a 1908 article in the *Bollettino Mensile*, competed with the products of "all other nations anxious to conquer a market such as this one, where all high-quality articles find easy and profitable positioning."[93] They echoed the language used by Italian business and political leaders in Italy by employing martial discourse to project masculinized images of combative commercial transactions in Buenos Aires. The "numerous armies" of Italian workers served as the "direct consumers of Italian products."[94] In this grand "fight for commercial expansion," Italy proved victorious, succeeding in the "conquest of the markets of *la Plata*"; importers sustained, "with praiseworthy tenacity, a loyal battle of competition with other similar products that are imported from Spain, France, Greece and other countries of the old world."[95]

In the United States merchants focused their ire on the Italian-style foods made, sold, and consumed in migrant marketplaces; in Argentina most of these foods were tipo italiano on arrival. In 1899 the Italian Chamber of Commerce in Buenos Aires wrote a letter to the Italian government expressing concern over Greek wine imported to Argentina under the guise of Italian wine. Imported Greek wine, entering as "Italian" but of inferior quality, the chamber claimed, was causing major damage to the good reputation of Italian wines.[96] Two years later the chamber noted with alarm the increase in the number of consumers buying "Swiss cigars imitated in Italian style" because they were less expensive than imported Italian tobacco products.[97] Merchants' constant fear of products arriving as "Italian" from Italy's competitors in Europe suggests that industrialists across the Atlantic were aware of Italian emigration patterns and looked to tap into Argentina's multinational consumer base.

Tipo italiano items arrived in the Americas not only from countries like Switzerland, Greece, and France but also from Italy itself. As the twentieth century progressed, Italians in Argentina became more vocal in their condemnation of dishonest Italian manufacturers and of the Italian government for not exercising sufficient vigilance on the producing end of Italian commodity chains. Merchants accused unscrupulous Italians of exporting foodstuff to Argentina that were labeled "Italian" but actually contained only a small portion of real Italian ingredients or none at all. These adulterated "Italian" products, migrant merchants complained, irrevocably damaged Italian commerce; fake "Italian" goods lost consumers' trust while destroying the good name of quality Italian foods.[98] In 1902 the Buenos Aires chamber began engaging in a series of heated discussions about Italian industrialists who had been exporting "guaranteed pure" Italian rice to Argentina that proved to be Italian rice mixed with Japanese and Burmese rice, allegedly of a much inferior quality. Two years later the chamber continued to rail against industrialists selling "Italian" rice made from a mix of Italian and Asian varieties, claiming that 75 percent of all Italian exporters involved themselves in this "work of demolition."[99] Similarly, in 1908 the chamber argued that most abuses to the Italian olive oil market were made in Italy, in places like Genoa, where companies mixed Italian oil with cottonseed oil from Tunisia and other places but then sent them abroad under the label "Lucca" or "Riviera."[100] Crooked Italian manufacturers in Italy proved just as threatening to Italian-Argentine trade and consumption in Buenos Aires' migrant marketplace as did industrialists in other European nations.

Rather than direct their policing efforts toward the production and sale of tipo italiano products internally, within migrant marketplaces—as did merchants in the United States—migrants in Argentina directed their patrolling outward, toward Italy and other European countries. In 1900 *La Patria* urged their Italian Chamber of Commerce to support a measure that would require every barrel of wine imported from Italy to contain a certificate of origin, the brand name, the number of the barrel, and its weight and quality as had been done with wines from the northwest Piedmont region of Asti. *La Patria* noted that better labeling and identification would help eliminate "falsification on a vast scale," which the paper estimated amounted to 75 percent of the "Italian" wine entering la Plata. Requiring certificates of origin for all Italian wines would "render a valuable service to our country and our numerous Italian communities in the Río de la Plata who long, in vain until now—with some honorable exceptions—to taste Italian wine that is truly authentically Italian."[101] This lobbying may have played a role in the Italian government's passage of a law later that year designed to combat fraud in the preparation and commerce of Italy's wine.[102] Merchants used the passage of this law to urge the Italian government to adopt similar measures for other goods in order "to protect the true Italian industry."[103] They pointed fingers at Italy, at times blaming the commercial policies of the government for the growth of tipo italiano industries both in European counties outside of Italy and locally in Argentina. In 1901 importer Francesco Jannello complained when the Italian government granted a monopoly to only one cigarette and cigar importer and retailer in Argentina. Jannello argued that the monopoly damaged Italy's tobacco market in Buenos Aires by keeping the price of Italian tobacco high, forcing migrants to buy alternatives arriving from other countries.[104] Four years later the chamber used the looming specter of tipo italiano businesses within Argentina to again denounce Italy for the monopoly; by inhibiting competition, concessionaries' high prices provoked not only the continued importation of Italian-style cigars arriving from countries like Switzerland but also the local production of tipo italiano cigars, evidenced by a new cigarette factory opening in Buenos Aires. In a spiteful letter to the Italian Ministry of Commerce, the chamber noted, "It had always seemed that the privilege of the concession on the importation of our tobacco would surely be a damage to the interests of Italian finance."[105]

U.S.-based merchants also made appeals to the Italian government to regulate and foster Italian trade, especially in the production of wine for export. In 1909 New York's *Rivista* published a report by Guido Rossati, head of the Italian Wine Station, to the Italian minister of Agriculture, Industry, and Commerce in which he blamed poorly enforced Italian laws governing wine production and labeling for compromising the reputation of Italian wine among U.S. consumers. Discussing abuses in the geographical designations, he wrote, "In this way Chianti has never seen its namesake region, Marsala has never seen the provinces of Trapani or Palermo, Barbera has never seen Piedmont."[106] He joined the members of the chamber in pressing the Italian government to pass new, more stringent and punitive laws regulating the classification and regulation of wine. However, aside from the wine trade, most of the chamber's efforts remained fixated on patrolling food authenticity within U.S. migrant marketplaces.

Tipo italiano Greek wine, Swiss cigars, Tunisian olive oil, and Japanese rice arriving from across the Atlantic reveal that in an industrially weak Argentina, threats to Italian commerce came less from savvy migrants in Buenos Aires and more from industrialists across the Atlantic. Of all European nations, Spain represented the most dangerous menace to Italian products in la Plata. In 1901 the chamber noted that Spanish food imports such as wine, oil, olives, and dried citrus fruits gave "serious competition to similar Italian goods" in Argentina.[107] Merchants felt threatened by the presence of Spanish migrants, the second-largest foreign-born group in Argentina, whose demands for homeland goods also sustained transnational commodity chains in Spanish foods. Migrants' boasts about the consumption of Italian imports often accompanied cautious warnings about what decreases in migration would do to Italian-Argentine trade. In 1901 the chamber assured themselves that Spain, a "population poor" country, could not provide the same large number of *braccia* (migrant manual workers) to justify the type of privileged trade status Argentina continued to have with Italy. And yet, the chamber concluded, Italy should not rest easily: Italy produced the same products as Spain and must turn to the same markets; therefore Spain remained a threat to Italian commerce in Argentina.[108] In 1908, the first year in over half a century when more Spanish migrants arrived in Argentina than Italians, Italians linked the dwindling of Italian migrants, who are "naturally consumers of the products of the mother country," to a slowdown of Italian commerce and a simultaneous increase in Spanish trade.[109] "As you see, the diminution is a continuous advantage to the Spanish element and can already be seen in many warehouses that sell edibles—in which the trade had been almost an Italian monopoly."[110]

A history of Spanish empire building in Latin America also led Italian migrants to view Spain as the most harmful threat to Italian commerce. Foods similar to Italian exports—olive oil, wine, and dried fruits, for example—proved popular not only because of the competing presence of Spanish migrants but also because of Spain's colonial legacy. Spanish products, the chamber claimed, "find complete acceptance by the public, maybe in homage to the ancient ties that unite the two nations as one community of race and interest, and for the bonds of tight solidarity that represent in one man all those who, abandoning Iberian soil, came in search of better fortune in this country of emigration."[111] The chamber worried about consumers in Latin American countries like Argentina who, "forgetting the bloody battles in support for their independence, respond with enthusiasm to the call of the country of origin."[112] Italian migrants used consumption to help construct Latinità, shared cultural and racial traits between Argentines and Italians that supported Argentina's continued acceptance of Italian people and goods and promoted Italian foods among Argentines. However, as a racialized category associated with ideas of European civilization, Latinità proved broad enough to also unite Argentines and Spaniards as "one community of race." That is, notions of Latinness were perceived as advantaging the foods and migrants of Europe's other "Latin" countries, especially Spain and France. Italian migrants built ties between Argentines and Italians based on a shared culinary tradition linked to Spanish colonization. The past Mediterranean orientations and imperial forays in Latin America by Spain, Portugal, and France, however, also affected the food traditions of these nations, of Latin American countries, and of Argentina's other "Latin" migrants."[113]

While migrant prominenti asserted that Italians' strong demographic presence, combined with cultural commonalities between Italians and Argentines, allowed for the "Italianizing" of Argentines, they simultaneously worried that such similarities could conversely "Argentize" or "Europeanize" Italian migrants. As increasing numbers of Italians remained in Argentina, learned Spanish, raised families, and bought tipo italiano products arriving from Spain, Greece, and France, Latinità threatened to absorb Italians into Argentine society and endanger Italian commerce.[114] The chamber did not always trust that Italian migrants could distinguish between the olive oils, canned goods, wines, and tobacco products arriving from Italy and those arriving from Europe's other "Latin" countries. In 1904 merchants in Buenos Aires urged the Union of Chambers of Commerce in Rome to hold an exhibition of Italian products in Buenos Aires. "The goal," their proposal read, "is to familiarize consumers, and to show that there is a difference between Italy's goods and those of other countries who have similar products."[115] While merchants often assumed that Italian migrants were duped into buying goods from other countries because of deceptive labeling, discussions also hinted at a larger fear that Italians, and especially their children, were voluntarily buying non-Italian products because of their lower prices and migrants' evolving tastes.

Italians dominated not only much of the international commerce in food imports but also the emerging domestically produced tipo italiano industries, which, while smaller and less varied than in the United States, made up an important, if not the most important, manufacturing sector in Argentina's slow process toward industrialization. Italians often pointed to migrants' contributions to Argentine industrial life, contributions so great that Argentine manufacturing was marked with an "Italian stamp." Pointing to Italians in the nation's food processing sectors—pasta, biscotti, bread, wine, beer, liquor, and the fishing and dairy industries—a 1906 report concluded, "How could Italians in Argentina demonstrate a more admirable industrial development?"[116] In their debates over whether to participate in the "Italians Abroad" exhibit for the 1911 International exposition in Turin, members of the Buenos Aires chamber haughtily asserted that even if the chamber opted out, Italians would be present at the fair because the items displayed at the Argentine pavilion were essentially the "product of the work of Italians."[117] Italian industrialists in Argentina, including producers of tipo italiano pasta, liqueurs, wines, chocolates, and cured meats, they complained, could not count in the "Italians Abroad" exhibit, "since their products are considered national [Argentine] production," revealing again ongoing fears that Italians and the "Italian" foods they made in Buenos Aires were being claimed by Argentina on the world stage.[118]

Italian migrants' predominance in both domestic and international food sectors meant that Argentines bought not only Italian imports but also domestically made Italian-style goods. And yet, unlike in the United States, where tipo italiano foods, like Italian imports, marked their consumers as distinct from Anglo-Americans, the commonalities upon which Latinità was forged in Argentina defied attempts to tie many local foodstuff to one nation exclusively. The production of panettoni— the cylindrical sweetened breads with candied fruits, originally from Milan and consumed especially during the Christmas holiday season—reveals how migration complicated efforts to affix particular national culinary traditions to foods in Buenos Aires. By the turn of the century, ads for the holiday bread, called panettone in Italian and pan dulce in Spanish, appeared regularly in both the Italian-language La Patria and in Argentina's Spanish daily La Prensa, suggesting that both migrants and Argentines ate the holiday treat. For example, Italian Chamber of Commerce member Carlo Gontaretti, owner of the Two Chinese bakery in Buenos Aires, advertised his pan dulce a la Genovesa, Milanesa o Veneciana (Genoa-style, Milan-style, or Venetian-style sweet bread) in La Prensa and La Patria.[119] Panettone's widespread consumption in Argentina signaled not only migrants' overwhelming presence in Argentina's bakeries but also culinary similarities that made the production and consumption of sweetened bread made from wheat flour a long-standing tradition in Italy, as well as in Spain and France.[120] In a country where cultural foundations— including culinary traditions—were linked, in perception more than in reality, to Northern Europe, it is no surprise that panettone, imported or domestically made, rarely appear for sale in New York's *Il Progresso* until the 1930s, nor was it absorbed into the U.S. culinary mainstream. While today "pan dulce" in other parts of Latin America, such as Mexico, refers to a larger category encompassing many variations of sweetened breads and pastries, such as *conchas, orejas,* and *roscas de reyes,* in Argentina "pan dulce" has come to refer mainly if not exclusively to the Italian panettone rather than to a wide variety of pastries.[121] By World War I what began as a food item imported from Italy and made in Argentina by Italians had been absorbed into Argentina's national cuisine.[122] Buenos Aires' migrant marketplaces allowed Argentines and Italians shared consumer experiences around Italian imports, tipo italiano goods arriving from European countries, and tipo italiano goods like panettone made in Argentina by migrant entrepreneurs.

Whereas Italian imports and tipo italiano goods arriving from Europe and made in Argentina helped migrants construct commonalities between Italians and Argentines, in the United States the consumption of these same goods racialized Italians as inferior, "foreign," and "illegal." This is evident most poignantly in the production and consumption of tipo italiano wine. Italians in both countries led the way in establishing the first large-scale wineries in the western hemisphere. Starting in the late nineteenth century, Italian migrants in the state of California, United States, and in the provinces of Mendoza and San Juan, Argentina, pioneered in experimenting with imported and domestically grown grape varietals, eventually dominating one of their host country's most essential agricultural sectors.[123] In 1882 Venetians Antonio and Domingo Tomba founded the Domingo Tomba winery in the central western province of Mendoza. The winery became the largest and most important in Argentina, producing 254,000 hectoliters (6.7 million gallons) of wine on their 59,000-square-meter establishment by 1909.[124] Their U.S. counterpart was the Italian Swiss Colony in Sonoma County, California, founded in 1881 by Ligurian merchant Andrea Sbarboro along with a group of migrant businessmen from Piedmont. By 1911, under the leadership of Pietro Carlo Rossi, the Italian Swiss Colony owned 5,000 acres of vineyards and a wine cellar with the capacity to hold some 4 million gallons of wine.[125]

As they had done with Italian imported goods, migrants in Argentina used tipo italiano wine as proof that migrants brought European civilization to Argentina's uncultivated frontier. Describing Argentina as a "young" nation, a publication of the Buenos Aires chamber cited the success of Domingo Tomba winery as evidence that "Argentina in every way wants to emulate the ancient nations." The book associated the winery with similar establishments in Italy and France in terms of size, modernity of machinery, and quality of product. Linking Argentine wine cultivation to ancient Rome, the book described the Tomba wine cellar as an "enormous warehouse, suspended by a long line from arches that look like those of a Roman aqueduct."[126] Ads in the Italian-language press also played up wine entrepreneurs' links to western civilization and the Age of Exploration. The *Bollettino Mensile* asserted that Italians saved Argentina's wine industry from Spanish colonists, who had abandoned colonial-era vineyards.[127] A full-page ad for the Domingo Tomba winery from 1910 featured an image of Christopher Columbus on a ship with two shirtless indigenous men genuflecting before him. The ad included a list of all the awards the winery had won at mainly European international exhibitions.[128] In the hands of Italian businessmen, tipo italiano wine entrepreneurs represented migrants' entrepreneurial genius and Italy's contributions to Argentine industrialization and progress. However, the long-standing tradition of wine production and consumption in Argentina also allowed Italian wine entrepreneurs to be subsumed in Argentine nation-building endeavors. In the Spanish-language *La Nación*'s special centennial issue, the paper included a feature story on the Domingo Tomba winery, in which the founders' nationality was not mentioned. Instead, the celebratory article, which described Tomba wine as "being admired as a true wonder in all the wine producing countries of Europe," praised the winery as representative of Argentine industrial and agricultural virtuosity.[129] While Italian prominenti called attention to the winery's Italian roots, the ads for the winery more frequently left out the nationality of its founders; publicity in Spanish and Italian by the early twentieth century described Tomba as "genuine product of the Mendoza winery, the best Argentine table wine."[130]

In the United States, conversely, migrants' desires to employ wine production as a covetable symbol of civilization ran up against racist attitudes toward Italians and a powerful temperance movement that increasingly saw migrants' drinking cultures as threatening to white, Protestant, middle-class notions of respectability.[131] As the stigmatization of wine and wine drinkers as "criminal," "immoral," and "foreign" intensified, migrants from France, Austria, and Germany exited California's nascent wine industry, leaving it in the hands of Italians. The racialization of migrant wine producers and consumers, therefore, presented business and market opportunities to savvy Italian entrepreneurs, who came to dominate wine production and distribution, mainly to Italian consumers in cities on the East Coast.[132]

While the U.S. temperance movement would not triumph nationwide until the passage of the Eighteenth Amendment in 1919, Italian winemakers battled prohibitionists intent on shutting down their operations by challenging unfavorable depictions of wine producers. In 1911 Ettore Patrizi, director of San Francisco's *L'Italia*, characterized the Italian Swiss Colony in Asti as an idyllic site of upstanding morality, where the company's one thousand workers found steady employment and lived healthy, virtuous lives. Patrizi described the colony as a "picturesque scene of happiness, of vitality and of health" with beautiful houses and a Catholic church "creating pleasant Italian settings with all the most beautiful and brilliant

characteristics of our race and our customs." He emphasized the modern ameni-
ties of the colony, which included an electric plant, a doctor, and a pharmacy, a
colony that painted a "most pleasing moral image."[133]But, unlike in Argentina,
Italian entrepreneurs struggled to position themselves and their businesses as
civilization builders. Merchants used the Prohibition movement to identify and
attack Anglo-American ignorance, suggesting that most U.S. Americans did not
understand wine as a high-class symbol of sophisticated European culture. They
expressed particular frustration and dismay when temperance advocates placed
wine in the category of "intoxicating drinks" and "patent medicines" made largely
of whiskey, accusing them of foolishly mixing "sacred and profane things."[134] Italians in Argentina also reflected on how wine consumption produced divide rather
than unity between Italians and U.S. American consumers. A 1910 article in Buenos
Aires' *La Patria* explained that while Argentines drank wine, U.S. Americans did not,
preferring beer; because U.S. Americans considered the drinking of wine "vulgar,"
the children of "Latin" migrants, especially Italians, adopted the habits of their host
country and abandoned wine to avoid stigmatization.[135] Argentine reformers in
the early twentieth century also expressed increasing concern over excessive alcohol consumption and linked the social problems it created to migrants. However,
wine's long-standing place as a regular component of the Argentine diet already
in colonial Argentina combined with Argentine leaders' continued gaze toward
Europe as a model civilization to work against successful campaigns to eliminate
the importation, production, and consumption of wine there.[136]

*   *   *

While entrepreneurs in both the United States and Argentina used their host nations' agricultural and industrial resources, as well as consumer and labor markets,
to jump-start tipo italiano food industries, migrants in the United States exploited
the country's mature manufacturing base and distribution networks to produce
and sell a richer variety of commercial foodstuff by the early twentieth century.
Migrants affiliated with the Italian Chamber of Commerce in New York feared
that the mushrooming tipo italiano sector would damage trade between Italy and
the United States, and they directed the bulk of their policing efforts within New
York's migrant marketplace. In Argentina tipo italiano came to be associated not
so much with migrant entrepreneurs in Argentina, but with unprincipled European
and even Italian industrialists across the Atlantic who produced and exported food
items that were similar in taste, appearance, and quality to Italian imports. As a
racial and cultural category, Latinità proved expansive enough to facilitate not only
the purchase of Italian imports and tipo italiano foods like panettone and wine but
also the consumption of foods arriving from other "Latin" countries in Europe,
such as Spain, France, and Greece. The growth of tipo italiano industries in the

United States and Argentina discloses how early twentieth-century globalization complicated rather than clarified attempts to attach national labels to global foods and notions of food authenticity.

Clever entrepreneurs on both sides of the Atlantic took advantage of ethnic connections and migrants' desire for homeland tastes in order to produce new foods as well as work and consuming experiences for migrants in New York and Buenos Aires. They capitalized on their intimate, firsthand knowledge of migrants' economic restraints, employment needs, and gastronomical traditions to satisfy migrant consumers, and often they did so in better ways than did importers. Even while increasing numbers of Italian women and their daughters labored in the food industries of the host countries, migrant prominenti only rarely acknowledged how women in Italy or abroad influenced migrants' consumer practices. This oversight continued despite the reality that male migrants' contributions to transnational economies—perhaps more than any other factor—explained the consumption of lower-cost tipo italiano foods. Migrants desired foods from home, but buying expensive imports regularly detracted from their ability to make good on familial responsibilities. Because consuming tipo italiano foods allowed migrants to more quickly achieve their long-term objectives, they frequently proved more meaningful than imported foods, whose sellers fixated on provenance and purity. As events in Europe mobilized women and men in migrant marketplaces in le due Americhe, however, provenance would come to matter as migrants organized around commodities in Italy and abroad as resources for their homeland in need.

"Pro Patria": Women and the Normalization of Migrant Consumption during World War I

It was no one's business how Italian migrants chose to spend their money, New York's *Rivista* asserted in 1911. After reminding readers of the extraordinary contributions Italians made to their host countries' economies as manual laborers, the author pointed to a double standard by which migrants' spending patterns were scrutinized: "When I go to buy a pack of cigarettes, do I ask the tobacco seller how he will spend the 20 cents that I gave him in exchange for the cigarettes? And then why would this same cigar seller, when he gives me a dollar in exchange for my day of work in his tobacco factory, ask me where and how I will spend that dollar, or insist I spend that dollar on a miss in America rather than send it to my family in Italy?"[1] Italian elites expected that laboring male migrants would sustain Italian trade paths through their robust, patriotic consumption of imported foods. Nevertheless, reports such as these suggested that the transnational family economies in which migrants were enmeshed constrained migrant consumption in the United States and Argentina. Indeed, by associating consumerism abroad with spending money on a "miss in America," the report represented male migrant consumption as paramount to marital and family disloyalty. Overseas migrants, with their wives, parents, and children at home, held tight to their hard-earned cash.

Italy's entrance into World War I in 1915, however, turned migrants in New York and Buenos Aires toward consumption and Italy simultaneously. In doing so, the war served as a turning point in the history of migrant marketplaces in le due Americhe. While prominenti migrants and Italian leaders had attempted to cultivate a national identity among its disparate peoples across the world, and partly in relation to Italian products, most labor migrants continued to identify with the local traditions and values of their small *paesi*. At the same time, labor migrants' enduring commitments to family back home curbed migrants' consumer behavior. World War I, however, created an unprecedented opportunity to mobilize migrants as Italians and as consumers around a common cause and enemy. Italian merchants, businessmen, and journalists in New York and Buenos Aires used the war to cultivate a more powerful commercial and cultural relationship between migrants and their homeland in need.

In May 1915, as soon as Italy entered the war to take back from Austria-Hungary its "unredeemed" territories in the Adriatic Sea region, migrants in the United States and Argentina organized national and local war committees to raise money, goods, and support for Italy. That same month, Italians in Buenos Aires formed a national Italian War Committee with numerous regionally based branches; similarly, in New York the Italian General Relief Committee ran a variety of "pro patria" fund-raising campaigns.[2] As the main publishing outlet for their communities' diverse wartime activities, the migrant press proved instrumental in intensifying bonds between migrants abroad and Italy. *Il Progresso* in New York and *La Patria* in Buenos Aires supported war committees' initiatives in almost daily reminders to assist Italy by, for example, donating money to the Italian Red Cross and investing in Italian government bonds. In addition to running their own fund-raising projects, the press meticulously reported on community events, regularly listing the names of donors and the exact amount of money donated by each individual, business, or fraternal organization. The regular logging of donors' names and contributions provided a public forum for attaching specific monetary values to the patriotic redirecting of migrants' resources to Italy. The newspapers reported on major fund-raising galas at important cultural venues such as the Teatro Colón and Teatro Verdi in Buenos Aires and Carnegie Hall and the Century Theatre in New York City as lavish, elegant affairs, during which migrants conspicuously consumed and donated for the homeland.[3]

These fund-raising campaigns, which characterized migrants' spending and saving as a *dovere* (duty) to Italy, politicized migrant marketplaces in ways that disclose consumption's role in national and ethnic identity formation. As members of transnational families linked to subsistence production in villages back home, migrants were reluctant consumers as well as reluctant "Italians," preferring to save their money and to preserve their local or regional identities. While tariff debates in the late nineteenth and early twentieth centuries first offered migrants a vehicle for presenting themselves as transnational consumers, it would be fund-raising campaigns during World War I that would ultimately turn migrants toward consumption. From Buenos Aires and New York, Italians vocalized their ability to affect the outcome of the war, in part by influencing the international commodity chains that they helped generate and sustain through a history of transoceanic migration. Furthermore, unlike turn-of-the-century tariff debates in which migrants focused on securing access to low-cost homeland foods for mainly male laborers, migrant women's active involvement in a variety of initiatives called public attention to their spending power. Wartime demographic changes increased the number of Italian women in migrant marketplaces; Italian wives and daughters who either relocated to join their families in the United States and Argentina or were born abroad increasingly represented the "miss in America." Against the background of these transformations, women's war work helped to normalize consumption among a people who were more used to saving than spending and to link migrant marketplaces to both women and Italianità. These fund-raising activities demonstrate a transition in the gendering of consumption abroad, a transition that feminized postwar consumption of Italian imported foods.

Nation-specific contexts that differentiated migrants' discussions about race and about tipo italiano industries in the United States and Argentina also produced varying wartime experiences in le due Americhe. In both countries the war feminized postwar consumption. In Buenos Aires, however, migrants' transnational wartime experiences were mainly in connection with Italian imports and portrayed consumers of non-Italian items as traitors to their homeland. In the United States, conversely, migrants consumed for Italy by buying imported foodstuff as well as foods produced in the United States, especially tipo italiano goods, but also U.S. industrialized products. In both countries the war revealed migrant marketplaces as global and gendered sites where migrants crafted complex transnational identities through saving, buying, and eating.

"Blessed Are the Socks": Migrant Women's Pro-Wool Campaigns

It would be women's public association with a nonedible agricultural staple in their host countries that first opened the door to the feminization of migrant consumption during the interwar years. Shortly after Italy entered the war, migrant women, working in women's committees or female sections of various male-led wartime organizations, collected wool, yarn, and fabric—or money to buy these items—and turned them into mittens, sweaters, socks, scarves, face masks, and other clothing items for Italian troops on the frigid Alpine battlefront.[4] As "workers of the wool," female migrant women were catapulted onto the pages of New York's *Il Progresso* and Buenos Aires' *La Patria* in an unparalleled manner.[5] The newspapers repeatedly encouraged women as they labored over wool with knitting needles and sewing machines, celebrating their work by quantifying the colossal number of woolen items produced and sent back to Italy. In 1916 the Italian steamship *Tomaso di Savoia* departed for Italy from Buenos Aires with 3,480 pairs of socks, 301 scarves,

273 face masks, 131 sweaters, 69 pairs of woolen underwear, 28 pairs of gloves, 4 body belts, and 4 shoe insoles.[6] In October 1915 *Il Progresso* reported on a fourth shipment of clothing, on the Italian ship *Verona*, which included over twenty cases containing 5,700 pairs of socks.[7] The various woolen items, *La Patria* reminded its readers, "provide our brave soldiers with clothing that makes the winter days less severe on the mountains conquered by the enemy."[8]

Shifts in global migration patterns and the demographic changes in migrant communities they produced provide an important backdrop for understanding how wartime campaigns such as the pro-wool drives affected the gendering of consumption and national identities. With the outbreak of the war, overseas Italian migration decreased significantly. In 1910 a little over 104,000 Italians arrived in Argentina and just over 262,000 arrived in the United States; by 1918, however, only 640 Italians migrated to Argentina and only 2,793 migrated to the United States.[9] Furthermore, 51,774 Italian men from South America and 103,259 from North America repatriated during World War I, most of whom were recalled by the Italian government to fight for their country.[10] Italy's mobilization of its male population for military service reduced the number of men headed overseas and created a temporary rupture in the country's traditionally male-dominant migrations. In 1905 only 29 percent of Italians arriving in the United States and 23 percent of Italians arriving in Argentina had been female.[11] In 1917, however, 65 percent of Italians migrating to the United States and 49 percent of Italians to Argentina were female.[12] While the more gender-balanced and even female-dominant migrations to the United States and Argentina ended immediately after the war, these demographic changes increased the presence of women in migrant marketplaces during the very moment in which the war heightened feelings of Italianness relating to buying, spending, and saving.

Against the backdrop of these wartime demographic changes, migrant women—either newly arrived during the war or left in the United States and Argentina by their male relatives who returned to Italy—as well as the sizable, more gender-balanced second generation born abroad, attracted unprecedented attention by manufacturers, retailers, and the press. It is not a coincidence that while a short Sunday column titled "Nel Regno della Donna" (In the woman's realm) ran sporadically in New York's *Il Progresso* during the early twentieth century, during the war the paper inaugurated a regular column called "La Moda" (Fashion), in which *Il Progresso* advertised and sold patterns for women's clothing.[13] The paper also increased the number of articles and columns devoted to cooking, hygiene, fashion, and the home. Similarly, while in Buenos Aires' *La Patria* a lengthy column titled "Vita Sociale" (Social life) started in the early twentieth century and included articles covering women's association meetings, fashion, food, and beauty advice, in 1915 the paper began an additional column specifically aimed at women called

"Cronache femminile" (Feminine chronicle).[14] The press's new concern for migrant women during World War I would help produce a postwar print culture that paid an increasing amount of attention to women as readers and as consumers.

In their coverage and support of the pro-wool campaigns, the migrant press in both countries positioned women's work as "the duty of Italian women," a patriotic obligation that linked together women of every social class and rank. The press implored its readers to unite across divides in migrant communities—especially class and regional divides—as Italians. In 1915 *Il Progresso* urged "every woman, whether patrician or plebeian, supreme artist or modest worker, wife or young girl," to collect money for the campaign at work, with friends, at association meetings, and at family gatherings.[15] Similarly, *La Patria* wrote that wool and clothing campaigns demonstrated "Italian women in marvelous solidarity who have provided an example that will remain in history."[16] The wool drive, the paper proclaimed, joined poor and rich migrant women in cities and rural areas, across class and geographical lines.[17]

The press also portrayed pro-wool campaigns as unifying Italian women generationally and transnationally. Pro-wool initiatives strengthened generational relationships between Italian migrant mothers and their Argentine- and U.S. American–born children. The press actively encouraged young girls to participate in the wool drive along with their mothers. In 1915 *La Patria* reported on a girls' school run by Colonia Italiana, a prominent Italian fraternal organization, where the school's young students had knit two hundred scarves for Italian soldiers. The paper applauded the students: "How much tenderness and how much patriotism do these little hearts express for the homeland of their parents!!!"[18] The pro-wool campaign provided migrants the chance to stake claims on a growing second generation, despite Argentine and U.S. citizenship laws that legally declared such children as their own. The press also depicted the wool initiatives as joining migrant women transnationally to their female counterparts in Italy. Italian women in Italy and migrant women abroad were "linked in this hour of our nation."[19] *La Patria* detailed the pro-wool campaign in Italy, noting that all women—old, young, middle-class, uneducated, and professional—had dedicated themselves to buying and producing clothing for Italian soldiers. "Blessed are the socks!" the article concluded. "May Italian women in Argentina follow their example!" The paper published patterns and sewing and knitting instructions for the fabrication of socks, mittens, and face coverings, handed down from Italian consulates in Argentina, and informed its readers that Italians back home were begging their *connazionali* (co-nationals) across the ocean to send wool clothing or raw wool.[20] Pro-wool initiatives, the Italian-language press in both countries suggested, bound together women in Italy, Buenos Aires, and New York in their specifically feminine obligations as both women and Italians.[21] The wool drives represent the first major event during which migrant communities in the Americas employed women to forge a sense of national identity that transcended regional, class, generational, and national boundaries.

These campaigns projected gendered images of national belonging by portraying entire migrant communities—men and women—uniting around female wool workers. As *La Patria* wrote, "The true greatness of a population—it has been written—is seen in the nobility of a woman's spirit." The article continued: "The true sentiments of a nation are often the sentiments inspired by mothers, by wives, by female friends."[22] These feminized versions of Italian patriotism and nationalism in coverage of women's wartime activities departed from earlier turn-of-the-century images linking Italianità abroad to masculine images of merchant explorers, commercial warriors, and male consumption. The press depicted migrant marketplaces as responding positively to women's work of raising and spending money on behalf of Italy. In 1915 *Il Progresso* singled out for special thanks Mrs. Elvira Giordano, Italian language instructor and member of a women's war committee, who collected over thirty dollars for the wool campaign from Italian business owners, including Italian banker Mr. Filomeno Pecoraro and Mr. Michele Gargiulo, proprietor of an Italian restaurant on Coney Island.[23]

The migrant press enthusiastically supported pro-wool drives in ways that recognized and lauded women's specific contributions to the war effort while using gendered language to describe them almost exclusively as mothers, wives, sisters, and daughters. In a September 1915 article, *Il Progresso* urged women to think of their "sons, brothers, spouses" in the wintery Alpine trenches. Understanding caregiving as an innate female trait, the paper told women, "We must dress them and keep them warm; we need to give them the comforts of materials that have always been made by mothers, by sisters and by wives. . . . The wool that they receive from us, worked by the gentle hands of our women, will have a little family tenderness in them, as if a perfume."[24] The press depicted sewing and knitting as part of a woman's natural skill set, a traditionally female task, which the war transformed from a somewhat trivial and even narcissistic feminine pastime into a serious and selfless activity. *La Patria* ended a 1915 article on the wool drive by reminding women, "Work for the soldier! Here is a hobby that no one will dare criticize, a pleasure that nobody will accuse of egoism, an ingenious female work of national unity, not suspected of invasion in the men's field."[25] Receiving wool clothing from women in New York and Buenos Aires allowed brothers, sons, and husbands in Italy to "turn their thoughts and hearts to that domestic nest where there was much warmth of affection, where there was domestic comfort."[26] The press assured readers that despite women's active involvement as "wool workers," gendered divisions in wartime contributions remained intact. It was precisely because the Italian community understood sewing as a fundamentally female occupation, often completed in the home, that the press could acclaim women's central role in one of the most popular war-related Italian diasporic movements without appearing to challenge traditional gender roles.

The pro-wool drive was one of a number of transnational initiatives declared appropriate for women by migrant communities. Given women's association with food provisioning and cooking, wartime fund-raisers that focused on the dietary needs of co-nationals in Italy and abroad also launched women into migrant print culture. Migrant women demonstrated their duty to Italy by raising money for and assembling *scaldaranci*, handmade torches made from old newspapers and wax, used by Italian soldiers to heat their meals and stay warm on the cold Alpine battlefront. "After a strenuous military operation," *La Patria* explained, "our soldier must eat a slice of preserved meat—excellent certainly, but cold—and quench his thirst with spring water—and often water from snow—that makes not only the teeth but the stomach run cold."[27] By the end of the war, migrants in Argentina sent almost 30 million scaldaranci back to Italy.[28] Similarly, in the United States the Italian-American Ladies Association in New York, made up of first- and second-generation Italians, called out to women to join their organization and help the National Association for the Soldiers' Scaldarancio in Milan, reminding readers that "all the Italian women of America" should contribute to the *scaldarancio* drive.[29]

The press further linked migrant women to food consumption through another campaign dubbed by the press as migrants' "greatest patriotic duty." That "duty of our colony" was to support *le famiglie dei richiamati*, migrant families whose male relatives had been recalled to fight in Italy.[30] "Wives whose husbands have re-sponded to the call of the homeland, children whose fathers went to fight and fall with the fateful name of Italy on their lips," *La Patria* wrote, "are without resources and without bread. . . . The babies must eat, they want to eat."[31] Illustrative of the way the press used the war and women to privilege national identities over those that were regionally based, the paper described migrant "heroines" as calling out to their community, "We are *Italian* women and our relatives, who are leaving, are *Italian*, rushing home to sacrifice themselves for its glory. We are proud but the sacrifice that we made should not harm the children and the elderly relatives, not fit to work."[32] *Il Progresso* called on "Italians living in the Great America" to help "those for whom the horrors of the war . . . have tossed and will toss into the most horrible poverty."[33] In their coverage of such campaigns, the press represented women left behind in the United States and Argentina exclusively as dependents, despite the large numbers of first- and second-generation Italian women who worked for wages. The majority of reservists, *La Patria* pointed out, were manual laborers "without money and without resources who leave here their parents, their wives, their young children without protection and without means."[34]

At the same time, however, the press portrayed migrant women participating in initiatives designed to meet the needs of these families and interacting with wealthy donors, merchants, and Italian fraternal organizations in order to do so.

"In homes, in factories, at parties, above all demand from everyone a donation for the unfortunate; be propagandists for this sublime charity," *Il Progresso* urged women.[35] In addition to raising money, which was paid out to families in monthly installments, women working for the Italian War Committee in Argentina visited families to determine the exact requirements of each household; they documented their visits, using such information to distribute milk, food, medicine, clothing, and linens to women and children.[36] On September 20, 1915, as part of migrants' annual festivities honoring Italian unification in 1870, migrants ran a special campaign for families of Italian reservists when they put together and distributed *cesti-regali* (gift bags) for families of the recalled, containing mainly foodstuff. Each of the one thousand cesti-regali carried a combination of imported foods as well as items produced in Argentina, including wine, panettoni, cookies, candies, milk, oil, pasta, coffee, sugar, grain, flour, meat, fruit, vegetables, beans, rice, cheese, cigars, and cigarettes.[37] Leading migrant importers, retailers, and industrialists such as wine importer Giovanni Narice, retailer and representative of San Pellegrino sparkling water Giuseppe Ferro, and Italian food importer Lorenzo Leveratto donated the edible items for the gift bags. The collection and dispersal of the gift bags served "to strengthen the bonds of solidarity among Italians who feel in this solemn hour more alive than ever in their soul the saintly love for the common country."[38]

The gendered language used by migrant newspapers to portray such public, transnational campaigns as rooted in women's long-standing duties as wives, mothers, and daughters in the domestic sphere belied women's increasing visibility in migrant marketplaces that wartime exigencies facilitated. These various campaigns involved migrant women, as Italians, interacting with and pressuring male prominenti businessmen and journalists. During but especially immediately after the war, *Il Progresso* and *La Patria* began devoting more space to articles geared toward a female readership and to advertisements featuring female consumers. At the same time, while lauding women's public work for their homeland, newspapers tethered feminine wartime spending, saving, and wool initiatives to women's responsibilities as wives and mothers and to their transnational duties as "Italians" rather than to individual consumerist desires. In an attempt to manage migrant women's new, very public presence in migrant marketplaces brought on by the war, the Italian-language press sometimes reminded women and girls to resist cravings for clothing, toys, and other consumer items.[39] An anecdotal exchange between a father and his daughter published in *La Patria* served to curtail the spending of money, especially by women and girls, on anything other than war-related activities:

Father, will you give me a little money?
No, little one: I bought you a toy a little while ago and now is not the time to spend much . . . another time.
But I don't want to buy a toy.

And then why do you want the money?

Because the teacher told me that the Italian soldiers must spend winter on the Alps and that good Italians should buy wool to send to them winter clothes . . . you know it's cold in the snow.

Take it, little one: take the money and a kiss.[40]

Despite prescriptive messages instructing migrant women to direct their consumer energies toward the Italian nation-state exclusively, changes in migration patterns, combined with wartime fund-raising campaigns, placed women in a position to assist their home country while publicly participating as buyers in the burgeoning consumer cultures of their host societies. Ironically, "Wool, Wool, Wool" articles in *La Patria,* exhorting women to save their money for wool, often ran next to large ads for Buenos Aires department stores like Gath & Chaves and Harrods featuring fashionably dressed women buying fabrics of many textures and colors.[41] During the war the migrant press presented paradoxical images of migrant women as they emerged with more force as readers, spenders, and savers, first as wartime fund-raisers, but after the war as the major buyers and consumers of imported Italian products.

Diasporic Differences in Migrant Wartime Campaigns

In 1915 the Buenos Aires–based Italian Chamber of Commerce sponsored the adoption of a propaganda stamp on its publications stating, "Italians! Prefer always the Italian national industry if you have at heart the glory and the prosperity of the homeland."[42] The stamp appeared in *La Patria* alongside an appeal to "Italians residing abroad." Migrants held the responsibility to fortify their homeland against its enemies during the war by keeping Italian goods competitive on the international market. "It is the duty of Italians abroad to protect and defend the consumption of Italian products," the announcement stated, citing as an example Marchese Boccanegra–brand olive oil from Genoa, sold by Bernasconi and Company of Buenos Aires, one of the largest importers of Italian foods in Argentina. Italian migrants who gave preference to the foods of other countries, the paper stated, were simply bad patriots.[43] While New York's *Il Progresso* and Italian Chamber of Commerce also worried about the war's effect on Italy's export market and encouraged migrants to consume imported foods, they did not initiate an official propaganda campaign in support of Italian products. Instead, wartime consumption and identity formation in the United States became affiliated as much with U.S.-produced goods as it did with Italian foodstuff.[44]

Migrant newspapers in New York and Buenos Aires used women's fund-raising activities, especially the pro-wool drive, to fuse migrant communities together on the basis of a united Italian identity. In both countries female migrants took on new public roles as patriots in migrant marketplaces, consuming, spending, and producing as a transnational duty to the homeland, roles that would help feminize migrant food consumption during the interwar years. In most other facets of wartime mobilization, however, national differences in the economies, societies, and geopolitical priorities of the United States and Argentina produced distinctive experiences for migrants in New York and Buenos Aires.

In the more import-dependent Argentina, migrants rallied more often and with more intensity around items from Italy than did Italians in the United States, who by World War I had a wider array of locally produced industrialized foods and other items upon which to conceive of themselves as Italians and as consumers. In Argentina fund-raising events called specific attention to migrants as donors, buyers, and consumers of Italian foodstuff. Italian merchants and companies donated Italian imports such as olive oil, wine and spirits, and textiles to be included in gift bags for families of the recalled and to be auctioned off at fund-raising galas. In December 1915, for example, *La Patria* reported on a benefit held by the Rosario branch of the Italian War Committee, for which a number of Italian merchants and companies supplied imported items, including the Society for the Introduction of Cinzano Products, which contributed one case of Cinzano Italian vermouth, and the import firm Boero, Napoli, and Company, which supplied over a dozen bottles of Italian sparkling water.[45] These numerous fund-raising festivities depicted migrant consumption of Italian foodstuff as an expression of support for the Italian war effort and for Italian-Argentine trade, which was suffering as a consequence of the war.

The very prominent place of Italian imports in wartime mobilization in Argentina explains the chamber's official propaganda campaign that encouraged migrants to "buy Italian" exclusively during the war. "The home country does not only need soldiers," the chamber announced. Migrants must "remain on guard against those who mask products from other provenance with Italian brands."[46] Since the late nineteenth century, merchants had attempted to discourage migrant consumption of tipo italiano Greek olive oil, French wine, Spanish fish, and Swiss cigars. More than any other previous event, the "buy Italian" campaign provided merchants the opportunity to draw distinctions between foodstuff coming from Italy and those arriving from other European countries. The chamber also utilized the global conflict to try to usurp its European competitors. As part of a larger campaign to keep Italian-Argentine commercial relations active, the chamber undertook an extensive drive to identify goods that before the war had been imported from European nations but could now be substituted with Italian goods. *La Patria* applauded the chamber, urging them to use the war to "purge" the Italian market of the many inefficiencies that made imports susceptible to fraud. Such initiatives brought together Italy's heterogeneous people as Italians around the defense of imported foods. "We love, protect and defend unanimously the 'Italian brand,'" proclaimed *La Patria*. "And we respect it, so that it is respected."[47]

Italian merchants exploited the chamber's "buy Italian" campaign by making patriotic appeals to consumers in publicity. They equated the purchase of Italian products to expressions of Italian nationalism and used the war to depict themselves as heroic supporters both of their home country and their loyal consumer base in Buenos Aires. In an ad in *La Patria* for San Pellegrino sparkling water, importer and retailer Giuseppe Ferro promised to absorb the extra costs and risks associated with the transport of Italian goods during the war to assure consumers access to the popular beverage.[48] A 1916 ad for Florio wines sold by Francesco Jannello featured an illustration of a uniform-clad solider writing home to his sweetheart from the trenches of Thessaloniki, the Greek capital of Macedonia. Referencing Italian soldiers stationed in Greece, the soldier's letter read, "The Italians, my Nell, carried with them their enthusiasm, born of the sun, but also enthusiasm pressed from golden grapes, a sweet liqueur that warms cold veins: Florio Marsala and Malvasia wine."[49] Unlike earlier late nineteenth-century trademarks that portrayed men as detached from faraway families, the Florio publicity commodified these affective ties for migrant consumers. Migrant merchants like Jannello and Ferro employed World War I to bring a new and heightened awareness of migrants' national and consumer identities in ways that politicized buying as a patriotic obligation.

While migrants honored their homeland by buying Italian foods, they also redirected Argentine agricultural staples back to Italy. In a country where domestic food manufacturing continued to remain relatively small-scale, migrants capitalized on their host country's profitable agro-export sector to send not only wool but also wheat and frozen meat to connazionali in Italy. In 1915 Italians in Buenos Aires established the Italian Agrarian Committee to help Italy acquire grain, meat, wool, and leather from Argentina.[50] By organizing to send home such materials, Italian farmers would be undertaking "a work of great moral and economic importance for the homeland and obtain the approval of the authority and of the Argentine people," *La Patria* explained.[51] The plan benefited both Argentina's place in Italy's agricultural import market and the postwar Italian export market, as Argentina would continue to exchange their agricultural goods for Italian merchandise. In 1916 migrants helped the Italian War Committee send seventy-five hundred pesos' worth of bulk agricultural goods to Italy.[52] At the end of the year *La Patria* documented with great fanfare the departure of the Italian ship *Cavour*, which left Buenos Aires for Italy stocked with both Italian reservists and Argentine wheat.[53]

In Argentina, Latinità, cultivated over decades of transnational migration, and in part through consumption, produced expressions of solidarity in migrant marketplaces between Argentines and Italians, expressions largely absent between migrants and U.S. Americans. Women's war work made them central to reinforcing ties of Latinity. The migrant press pointed to wartime collaborations between Argentine and Italian women as proof of Argentina's support of the Italian cause, despite Argentina's official commitment to neutrality. In 1915 *La Patria* reported on the private Italian-Argentine Sewing Club, formed by a group of Argentine and Italian women in Rosario, "where Italians and Argentines live in fraternal agreement." The initiative, through which women raised money and made clothing for Italian soldiers, demonstrated that Argentine women were "sisters in the pious labor and bequeath to their work all the noble spirit of the people of the Latin race, understanding the grand cause of Italy and following with hope the fate of our army."[54] Collaboration between Italian and Argentine women proved that "our saintly war does not only move and excite us Italians, but it makes everyone's heart beat who knows Italy and knows the spirit of justice that guides the conquest of the irredentist land."[55] The war encouraged Argentine women, migrant women, and their Argentine-born daughters to join in support of their "brothers in Latinity" across the Atlantic.[56] Leading department stores in Buenos Aires and Rosario, including Gath &Chaves, La Favorita, and Harrods, donated wool and clothing for such drives and hosted lavish fund-raisers in their stores.[57] In September 1915 a group of migrant women carried out a benefit for the Red Cross at Harrods in Buenos Aires. The event, asserted *La Patria*, "was an extraordinary festival, for the remarkable occasion decorated with the flags of the Allied Nations outside, while inside it took on the appearance of an immense luxurious evening in which the elegant flowers and feminine beauty produced a mark of indescribable charm." Argentine department stores, which had already appealed specifically to female migrant consumers through their ads in *La Patria*, connected migrant and Argentine women together through fund-raising and female consumption during the war.[58] Although the war stitched together a triangular web of women as Italians in Buenos Aires, New York, and Italy, especially as "wool workers," nation-specific differences generated connections between migrant and Argentine women but not between migrants and U.S. Americans. New York's *Il Progresso* did not report on nor praise similar coordinated efforts, even after the United States entered the war on the side of the Allies in April 1917.

Italian merchants were not the only ones using nationalist sentiment to sell their wares; domestic manufacturers of foodstuff established or run by Argentines also employed the Italian-language press to publicize their support for Italy and market their goods among the largest foreign-born consumer block. In 1915 Argentine cigarette manufacture Piccardo and Company ran an ad in Italian for their popular 43-brand cigarettes depicting the crowned figure Italia standing on a map of Italy with a sword in her hand and the shield of the House of Savoy at her feet (see fig. 14).[59] The ad read simply, "Our emblem is freedom," while reminding readers that the

Figure 14. Ad for Piccardo & Co. 43-brand cigarettes, *La Patria degli Italiani* (Buenos Aires), September 20, 1915. Courtesy of the Hemeroteca, Biblioteca Nacional de la República Argentina.

cigarettes were "genuinely Argentine made." Notions of Latinità and the dominant presence of Italian migrants allowed Argentine manufacturers to assert the Italianità of their products by capitalizing on consumers' emerging national identities during the war. While U.S. food industrialists and department stores placed ads in Italian in New York's *Il Progresso* starting in the early twentieth century, it would not be until the mid-1920s that U.S. food conglomerates began targeting migrants specifically as Italians by referring to migrants' transnational social relations.

As in Argentina, the war brought newfound attention to migrant consumers in New York; however, the United States' more developed industrial and consumer society created a different setting in which migrants formed wartime identities through trade and consumption. New York's Italian Chamber of Commerce was no less concerned than their counterpart in Buenos Aires about sustaining Italian commerce. Just after war broke out in 1914, but before Italy's entrance, the New York chamber anticipated an opportunity for Italian imports, especially wine, to replace products from France and Germany, which were already embroiled in the conflict. Given that the war had "wreaked havoc on the vineyards of Eastern France," migrant merchants hoped that U.S. consumers would turn to Italian wine instead of domestically produced California substitutes. Just as merchants in Buenos Aires expected the war to benefit Italian imports over tipo italiano foods from Europe, importers in New York believed it would accomplish their long-standing goal of moving beyond migrants to reach the larger U.S. consumer market. "Before Americans allow patriotism to have the best of their taste," the *Rivista* hoped that U.S. Americans would challenge sellers of California wines who claimed their wines were "'just as good' as the products of Europe." Italian wines, already in demand at cafes, restaurants, and hotels catering to the "finest tastes of this cosmopolitan population," would please consumers "not only provisionally, but permanently, as American connoisseurs will relish them certainly as much as, and perhaps more than, the wines that have held sway on this market until the present."[60] Wishing in particular that Italian bubbly would came to replace French Champagne, the *Rivista* celebrated the characteristics of Italy's various regional sparkling wines, such as Moscato and Asti Spumante, "a lady's wine par excellence, owing to its harmless effects, luscious taste and nourishing qualities." As before the war, merchants continued to target Anglo-American women specifically as consumers of Italian imports.[61]

While hoping that the war would give Italian imports an advantage over those from other European nations, unlike in Buenos Aires, migrant merchants in New York focused the bulk of their efforts on stemming the production and sale of tipo italiano goods. Already before the war, the cheaper prices of tipo italiano foods had made them powerful competitors to imports in migrant marketplaces dominated by mainly male laborers who were intent on saving. The attenuation of Italian trade to both the United States and Argentina provided a powerful boost to the tipo italiano business in both countries, but especially in the United States, where an already robust industry existed. From 1915 to 1919 Italy's export of edible olive oil to Argentina dropped from 34,868 to 195 quintals; tomato preserves went from 35,516 to 11,151 quintals; and hard cheeses went from 27,212 to 485 quintals.[62] During those same years, the United States saw similar vertiginous drops: Italy's export of edible olive oil went from 89,830 to 406 quintals; tomato preserves decreased from 154,260 to 11,587 quintals; and hard cheeses plummeted from 84,672 to 1,456 quintals.[63] After 1916 Italy stopped sending cured meats and rice to the United States and Argentina for the duration of the war, opting to preserve those foods for Italian soldiers and civilians.[64] In 1916 the New York, Chicago, and San Francisco

Italian chambers of commerce prepared a report urging the Italian government to lift the ban on certain Italian exports, arguing that Italian companies would lose their hold over migrant marketplaces as tipo italiano entrepreneurs stepped in to fill consumer demand.[65] Their predictions proved correct; the number and variety of medium- to large-scale food companies expanded during and immediately after the war, and businesses were formed by migrants such as Vincenzo La Rosa, a Sicilian olive oil merchant who opened his pasta business during the war; by the mid-1930s, under the leadership of his children, the firm became the largest pasta supplier in the Northeast.[66] During the interwar years the number of migrant entrepreneurs and their children producing pasta, cheese, wine, cured meats, and other Italian-style foods throughout the United States mushroomed.[67]

Ironically, despite New York merchants' fears about tipo italiano foods, and unlike their counterparts in Buenos Aires, they did not carry out a massive campaign to "buy Italian" in order to discredit local products. Rather, they chose to focus their efforts on lobbying the Italian government to reduce restrictions on Italian exports.[68] By World War I tipo italiano foods and the migrants who consumed them were already too powerful a presence in migrant marketplaces, and already associated increasingly with a unified "Italian" national identity, to be depicted as unpatriotic by merchants. Instead, goods made in the United States by migrant entrepreneurs, and increasingly non-Italian businesses as well, were incorporated into transnational wartime campaigns.

Wartime initiatives in New York embraced the consumption of all goods circulating in its migrant marketplace—regardless of their origin—to build Italian identities around buying and consuming. Starting in November 1915, *Il Progresso* began a drive to raise money for Italian aid organizations for which the paper printed coupons for readers to cut out and present to business owners in New York. Italian migrants owned the majority of such establishments—grocery and food stores, bakeries, pharmacies, restaurants, butcher shops, and barbershops—including Giuseppe Gandolfo's grocery store, Francesco Altadonna's Italian butcher shop, and Polito Vincenzo's pasta factory and retail outlet.[69] In return for the coupon, buyers spending more than ten cents received a receipt that could be used as a raffle ticket for various prizes donated by *Il Progresso*. For every coupon distributed, participating retail establishments sent a one-penny donation to *Il Progresso*. The paper contributed the accumulated money to help the families of recalled soldiers.[70] This "pro patria initiative" that called out to "store owners and consumers" nationalized everyday exchanges between male store owners and mainly female migrant consumers, who used cash to buy groceries for their families in the United States and to assist Italy. Such campaigns encouraged migrants to "buy from Italians" rather than to "buy Italian" exclusively, reflecting the variety of consumer products—both domestic and imported—in New York's migrant marketplace.

Unlike in Buenos Aires, where migrants dispatched Argentine agricultural goods to Italy, migrants in New York organized to send mass-produced U.S. consumer items, including tipo italiano goods. One of the most popular transnational campaigns organized by Il Progresso consisted of collecting and sending U.S.-produced cigars and cigarettes to Italian troops. A cigar, explained the paper, is a soldier's "best companion." "In the wet trenches, in the camps, in the tiring marches, under the tents, in the barracks, in the hospital beds, during the rest hour or in the anxious vigils, nothing is dearer to soldiers than to smoke a good cigar or puff on a cigarette."[71] Il Progresso suggested that the purchase and consumption of tobacco products made in the United States linked migrant consumers transatlantically to Italian soldiers in the Alps. When soldiers smoked tobacco products from their connazionali in the United States, "they will think of their brothers beyond the Ocean and realize that even from a far distance Italians are united in one thought of love, in one wish of victory and in one heartbeat of hope for the triumph of the beloved homeland."[72] Cigarettes produced by tipo italiano tobacco companies, especially De Nobili Cigar Company in Long Island, were the most common brands donated. As with other campaigns, Il Progresso published a daily tabulated list of donors' names and quantities offered.[73] Migrant women featured centrally in the tobacco purchases and donations. In September 1917, for example, Miss L. Michelangelo of Hoboken, New Jersey, donated one hundred Tuscan-style cigars, and Mrs. A. Zeppini of Brooklyn, New York, gave twenty packets of tobacco. When the campaign ended on October 14, migrants had sent $4,027.09 worth of tobacco back to Italy.[74]

As the tobacco drive suggests, migrants in New York introduced their co-nationals in Italy to U.S. industrialized foodstuff during World War I. Another Il Progresso campaign rallied migrants to construct and send Christmas gift boxes to Italian troops in Italy. The paper called "all Italians, of whatever class, whatever social rank, both men and women, workers, industrialists, importers, merchants, artists, professionals, ladies and gentlemen," to assemble Christmas boxes for Italians back home. Each box contained a can of pears or peaches, a half-pound can of "chop meat" to fare sandwiches [make sandwiches], a box of "sweet crackers filled with fruit conserves (Fig Newton, fig bars, etc.)," a can of sardines, two Italian cigars, and a package of De Nobili tobacco.[75] As with the tobacco drive, Italian merchants and importers contributed large quantities of boxes. For example, Il Progresso thanked Antonio Zucca, former president of the Italian Chamber of Commerce in New York, for his 20-box donation, and Pasquale Pantano, New York importer, for his 10-box contribution.[76] When the drive closed on November 15, 1917, Il Progresso had collected 26,093 Christmas boxes.[77] In Buenos Aires migrants focused their efforts on sending unfinished agricultural staples such as meat, wheat, and wool to Italy, reserving gift boxes of foodstuff for the families left behind by their reservist husbands and fathers. In the United States, however, the war convinced increasing numbers of migrant consumers, who were especially skeptical of industrialized foods produced by non-Italians, to buy them not only for themselves but for con-nazionali in Italy as well.

Il Progresso portrayed campaigns involving U.S.-made foods as equally patriotic and "Italian" as *La Patria*'s coverage of fund-raisers and initiatives centered on Ital-ian imports. "All Italians must enthusiastically support our initiative," *Il Progresso* wrote, urging readers to buy goods and services from Italian-owned stores par-ticipating in the coupon drive.[78] "How can we prove that our hearts beat in unison with our brave soldiers if we do not satisfy their every desire?" asked *Il Progresso*, goading migrants to buy U.S.-made cigars as evidence they had "done their duty" as Italians.[79] The United States' more industrialized, consumer-oriented economy allowed migrants in New York to experiment with a wider variety of available goods in the construction of wartime identities than in Buenos Aires. Buying and consuming U.S. products may have taken on increasing symbolic weight once the United States entered the war on the side of the Allies in April 1917, after which the consumption, and later rationing, of U.S. goods, especially food, became a way for migrants to display their national identity as Italians and their dual loyalty to both Italy and the United States. This was especially crucial within the context of rising xenophobic and nationalist sentiments during and immediately after the war, when calls for immigration restriction intensified and migrants experienced pressure to prove their "100 percent Americanism" by renouncing homeland ties.[80] Starting in 1917 *Il Progresso* and the Italian Chamber of Commerce in New York exhorted Italians to buy U.S. as well as Italian war bonds, and the press reported with pride the number of first- and second-generation Italians fighting in the U.S. Army.[81] Migrants in the United States expressed their identity as Italians and their alle-giance to both their home and host nations by spending money on industrialized foodstuff made in the United States by Italian entrepreneurs and, increasingly, by large U.S. food corporations such as the National Biscuit Company, producers of the Fig Newton cookie.

While national contexts differentiated migrants' wartime experiences in Bue-nos Aires and New York, migrant print culture in both countries portrayed spend-ing, consuming, and redirecting goods to Italy as part of migrants' duty to their homeland. The Italian-language press described migrants not only as transna-tional laborers, fixated on saving for families back home, but also as transnational consumers, united around a common national identity and financially capable of caring for Italians in Italy and in their communities abroad. In ways that re-vealed their middle-class status in migrant marketplaces, prominenti journalists hesitated to label migrants' donations to the wool drive a sacrifice: "In America, for even the most modest of workers, ten cents does not damage his savings even when he wants to throw it to the wind; therefore, we cannot call it a sacrifice."[82] In their coverage of wartime campaigns, the press often made comparisons between the cost of living and the quality of life for migrants abroad and Italians in Italy. *Il Progresso* explained that Italians in New York were better off than Italians in Italy, where "there is no work, no money, no resources; there in this moment there is only misery and grief, lessened only to the hope of better fortunes." Sending food and clothing to Italians offered migrants a vehicle for expressing their Italianness as well as their ability to consume in ways their co-nationals back home could not. The paper asked, "What will all those poor women, children and elderly in Italy do?"[83] While heightened sentiments of Italianità connected migrants to Italians across the ocean, the war called attention to differences in lifestyles, and especially consumer opportunities, between migrants and co-nationals in Italy. And while campaigns may have portrayed women in Italy as impoverished, migrant women abroad, as major protagonists in wartime saving, spending, and consuming initiatives, feminized migrant marketplaces in the immediate postwar years.

The Feminization of Migrant Marketplaces in the Interwar Period

A series of ads for Cinzano, the famed Italian vermouth, shows how gendered links between migration and trade crafted during the war strengthened postwar connections between women and migrant marketplaces. The ads in Buenos Aires' *La Patria* in 1915 featured silhouettes of people relaxing and eating at home, chatting at parties, and participating in sporting and recreational activities.[84] One of the many ads depicts a woman in elegant horse-riding attire galloping on her steed; another ad shows a playful scene between a man and a woman with a cocktail glass in her hand (see figs. 15 and 16).

These wartime Cinzano ads differed greatly from their prewar predecessors. Prior to World War I, Cinzano publicity called attention to the enormous quantities of vermouth entering the country. A 1905 ad bragged that during the previous year, 161,000 cases of the vermouth were sold in Argentina; five years later another emphasized that in 1909 Cinzano had imported to Argentina 517,000 cases.[85] This prominence given to international trade faded during and after the war in favor of publicity that focused on consumers and consumption. The 1915 Cinzano ads also contrasted sharply with the focus on Italy's industrial capabilities and male migrant heroics that were so prevalent in trademarks produced by Italian businesses in Italy in the late nineteenth and early twentieth centuries. While these trademarks had featured factories and military figures, advertising iconography in migrant newspapers after World War I was more likely to display people eating food and imbibing alcohol in festive, often opulent settings.

The female migrant consumer, emerging from women's war-related activities in migrant marketplaces during the war, led to a feminization of migrant food

Figure 15. Ad for Cinzano vermouth, *La Patria degli Italiani* (Buenos Aires), December 19, 1915. Courtesy of the Hemeroteca, Biblioteca Nacional de la República Argentina.

Figure 16. Ad for Cinzano vermouth, *La Patria degli Italiani* (Buenos Aires), November 23, 1915, 6. Courtesy of the Hemeroteca, Biblioteca Nacional de la República Argentina.

consumption in the postwar years. In publicity and discussion of Italian products, the post–World War I era witnessed a shift toward an emphasis on consumption that showcased ordinary people interacting with commodities. This new attention to consumption brought more women into ads as consumers of Italian products, making them, rather than male migrants abroad, the main receivers of Italian foods traveling along transatlantic commodity chains. By the late 1910s and 1920s, ads for imports targeted migrant women specifically and used them to generate transnational consumer identities.

This shift in gendered messages in the Italian-language press coincided with demographic trends that created more gender-balanced Italian communities in the United States and Argentina. The war had produced a temporary reversal in the gender ratios of Italian international migration. While male-predominant migrations resumed after the war, provisions for family unification in immigration legislation, increasingly restrictive immigration policy, and the global depression slowly increased the proportion of women to men in Italian migrant communities.[86] Immigration law in both countries conceived of women almost exclusively as dependents, as trailing mothers, wives, and daughters of male-headed households. These gendered conceptualizations of the family and women's and men's places within it made it extremely difficult for single females to migrate independently; women were considered morally and sexually suspect by Argentine and U.S. immigration officials and anti–white slavery societies.[87] By the 1920s migrants from Italy in the United States and Argentina increasingly took advantage of preferences for family reunification in immigration legislation to bring over female relatives, especially as more employment opportunities opened for migrant women and their daughters in light manufacturing, such as the textile and artificial flower industries, but also in tipo italiano sectors such as candy, tobacco, and vegetable and fruit canning. Indeed, relocation abroad became economically viable for Italian families as more wage-earning opportunities for women became available.[88] Furthermore, during the interwar years the now sizable second generation of Italians increased the number of women in migrant marketplaces. The consumer practices of second-generation Italians altered the global and gendered dynamics that defined migrant marketplaces as these new consumers brought their experiences growing up abroad to bear on their interactions with the foods and culinary traditions from their parents' homeland.

The war, combined with these demographic changes, proved instrumental in turning migrants toward consumption during the 1920s and 1930s. The transnational subsistence economies in which migrants were enmeshed had made Italians unreliable consumers of imports. Even among migrant families reunited abroad, low-wage jobs and suspicion of unfamiliar industrialized food products made most migrants conservative consumers. Already by the early twentieth century, Italian government representatives and migrant *prominenti* in the diasporas observed migrants' reluctance to spend money. One 1906 *Bollettino* report discussed the "sad and distressing fact" that every dollar remitted home "almost always represents the most humiliating subtraction of the most essential life needs" of migrants overseas. Suggestive of the way food was linked to notions of the body and racial fitness, the report highlighted how remittances affected the racial stock of Italians abroad: "Every dollar sent corresponds to a privation of food," leading to "a weakening of the race and a deterioration of an entire population."[89] Ironically, as Italian trade and migration promoters touted male migrant consumption as being key to Italian commercial success, they also sometimes joined U.S. American and Argentine elites in chastising migrants for their "stingy and self-abnegating" ways. The *Bollettino* reported on an unnamed U.S. congressman who described Italians as "birds of passage" who "scarcely spend one cent in our market, and hate all that is America except for the gold they take with them."[90] Similarly, José María Ramos Mejía, a leading Argentine physician and politician, denounced male migrants' reluctance to spend; after a full day of hard labor, "he returns straightaway to the stand or dwelling where he has wasted no time in hiding away his savings in some safe spot."[91]

Officials reporting from abroad saw in consumption a salvo for ameliorating anti-migrant prejudice, urging migrants to live among native-born workers "without stinginess and deprivation."[92] Gerolamo Naselli, from the Italian consulate in Philadelphia, contended in 1903, "The excessive love of savings is the only reason, I believe, that has blocked Italians from becoming popular in this country." He continued: "It is not, as some believe, job competition or other reasons that cause Americans to resist opening the doors to our emigration, but the fear of parsimony and the spirit of economy that distinguishes our emigrants." Unlike German and Irish immigrants who spent money in the United States, Italians sent it home to their families. "The American wants money earned in this country to be consumed here." He concluded, "There is not a doubt that if the emigrant, once here, settled for good and consumes all his earnings here, all the restrictive emigration legislation will lessen."[93]

While Naselli's optimistic predictions about immigration policy proved wrong, he anticipated correctly that if male migrants "settled for good" abroad—with their wives and children beside them—it would change Italians' spending and saving practices. Women's increased visibility during World War I made them a lucrative target market for the Italian-language press and for Italian companies and merchants, who began featuring female consumers regularly in their ads for imports and in discussion about spending and shopping more generally. The interwar feminization of consumption was not unique to Italy or Italian migrants, for it reflected a more global process during which women became gradually associated with consumerism.[94] Nineteenth-century industrialization had gendered consequences for women and men; production moved outside of the home and became linked to mainly male wage earners, whereas women became increasingly moored to the domestic sphere, where they engaged in unpaid reproductive labor and consumption for the household.[95] In the late nineteenth and early twentieth centuries, middle-class white women expressed their class and racial status through engaging in the public marketplace as buyers of industrialized goods.[96] While more a model than a reality for minorities and working-class households, by the 1920s the white, middle-class female consumer had become a generalized ideal in popular culture throughout cities in Europe and in industrialized and industrializing nations, including the United States and Argentina, where her presence simultaneously ignited debates about gender roles and the construction of national identities.[97] Women's magazines, in-house corporate advertising departments, and gradually more independent advertising agencies assisted in the construction of the female consumer, whose main contributions to the household economy were portrayed as rational spending on behalf of the family.[98] Also important in wedding women to consumption was the burgeoning field of home economics, which professionalized women's special role as efficient household managers whose purview included nutrition and cooking, child rearing, and cleanliness.[99]

Middle-class and affluent white women in industrialized countries remain the focus of research on the history of modern consumerism, a history that has linked women's buying and spending activities to the formation and consolidation of national identities.[100] And yet migrant women were also affected by the broader gendering of consumption; their marketplace interactions, however, reflected their experiences as transnational people whose consumer desires and identities transcended national borders while being affected by them.[101] Focusing on migrant marketplaces as global arenas complicates historical research that portrays consumption as a generally straightforward path toward nation building and migrant assimilation.[102] Unlike her Anglo-American and Argentine counterparts, however, the female Italian migrant consumer emerged out of transnational linkages to the Italian state during World War I. Supporting the homeland valorized overseas consumption of Italian products in ways that strengthened migrants' sense of Italianità during the interwar years while fostering a more distinct ethnic identity in their host countries.

During the interwar years, Italian companies and merchants capitalized on the increasingly powerful connection between women and consumption and on migrants' transnational ties. After World War I, ads in the Italian-language press portrayed women as the principal buyers of Italian imports and, through their consumer preferences, the main generators and sustainers of Italian identities among migrants in New York and Buenos Aires. Ads like the Cinzano publicity moved from the public, male-oriented working world of factories and exhibitions to more private scenes centered on the home. In 1927 an ad for Banfi Products Corporation, an Italian food-importing firm in New York, suggested that the consumption of Italian spirits preserved the Italianità of special holidays. "How difficult to pass another Christmas far from the land that nourished us as infants!" the ad began. "But—thank goodness—this year, at my house, there will be a purely Italian atmosphere . . . One hundred percent. Italian friends, Italian food, and, on the table, for the benefit of the stomach and for my delight, will shine five magnificent products from our Italy: Marsala Florio, Ramazzotti, Strega, Vermouth Cora, Fernet de Vecchi." Such publicity brought products into domestic arenas associated with family, merriment, and leisure in order to reaffirm the Italianness of consumption in migrant marketplaces. While by the early twentieth century tipo italiano manufacturers in the United States and Argentina had led the way in shedding regional distinctions in product labeling, after World War I growing numbers of merchants followed their lead by downplaying regional distinctions in the descriptions of imported foodstuff. As the Banfi ad illustrated, consuming imported liqueurs over the Christmas holiday kept both eaters ("*Italian* friends") and their meals ("*Italian* food") linked to an image of a unified homeland.[103]

Rather than highlighting Italy's production capabilities, many ads after World War I emphasized the importance of Italian consumers abroad in driving Italian trade. A 1925 Spanish-language ad for Cirio-brand canned tomatoes in *La Patria* shuffled viewers along the entire transatlantic commodity circuit, beginning with tomatoes from the "best lands in Italy" and ending around a dinner table where families "enjoy perfect health because they always use in their kitchens Cirio-brand tomato extract" (see fig. 17).[104] Publicity like Cirio's redirected attention from the starting point of the commodity chain, Italian factories and laborers in Italy, to the receiving end, migrant consumers abroad, while showing how diasporic eating bolstered the Italian food industry back home.[105] Similarly, an *Il Progresso* ad for Florio Marsala included photographs of male Italian workers attaching labels to bottles in the Florio plant in Sicily next to images of buxom peasant women harvesting grapes. The ad instructed readers that buying Florio Marsala not only conserved the Italianness of migrant's dining practices abroad but also sustained commodity chains that supported Italian workers in Italy.[106]

By the 1920s female consumers in migrant marketplaces—rather than the exclusively male jury of political and business leaders at international exhibitions suggested in turn-of-the-century trademarks—judged the quality of Italian imports while serving as Italian cultural envoys abroad. As gatekeepers of links between migration and trade, ads depicted women as possessing the instinct and authority to choose authentic, high-quality Italian imports over inferior substitute brands. A 1932 ad for Bertolli olive oil in Chicago's Italian-language *L'Italia* used a discussion

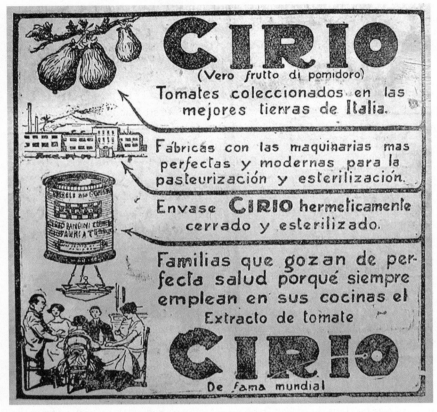

Figure 17. Ad for Cirio tomato extract, *La Patria degli Italiani* (Buenos Aires), September 3, 1925, 3. Courtesy of the Hemeroteca, Biblioteca Nacional de la República Argentina.

between two housewives, one knowledgeable and one inexperienced, to portray women as judicious custodians of Italian commerce while warning them against deception by dishonest retailers. The expert housewife scolds her friend, pointing to the English writing on the can indicating only a minimal amount of real olive oil. She asks, "You didn't realize that the grocer played a joke on you in that he sold you sesame seed oil flavored with the addition of the smallest amount of olive oil?"[107] She reminds her friend to demand only pure Italian olive oil from Italy. In contrast to early twentieth-century trademarks, which presented "Italia"—the embodiment of the Italian nation—guarding and facilitating Italian commerce, often from a celestial space above the Atlantic, these post–World War I ads depicted women protecting Italian trade and migration routes through their individual consumer preferences. As shown in an ad for Sasso-brand olive oil, publicity domesticated Italia, and the transnational economic spaces she oversaw, by reinventing her as a shopper, mother, and wife in stores and kitchens abroad. While the original Sasso trademark depicting the olive-harvesting woman in classical robes appears in small print on the can (see ch. 1, fig. 11), this postwar iteration presents a mob of female shoppers examining an oversized canister of Sasso oil (see fig. 18). Commercial iconography connected migrant women's everyday purchases—often represented as integral to the maintenance of Italian family traditions in the private domestic realm—to the very public sphere of transnational commerce and trade.[108] Women often symbolized the key and final point on an Italian commodity chain in which Italian laborers in Italy produced goods purchased by consumption-savvy migrant mothers and wives abroad.

While pre–World War I trademarks had created manly markets of emigration and trade by using male politicians, revolutionary heroes, and explorers in Italy and the Americas to condense time and space, interwar ads in the migrant press collapsed temporal and geographical divides through women consumers in homes and grocery stores. They showed migrant consumers actively engaged in

Figure 18. Ad for Sasso olive oil, *La Patria degli Italiani* (Buenos Aires), April 27, 1925, 4. Courtesy of the Hemeroteca, Biblioteca Nacional de la República Argentina.

transnational kin work: their purchases not only represented connections across Italian households in New York and Buenos Aires but also revealed generational links to families in Italy, where women used the same products.[109] Publicity for Bertolli olive oil, for example, implied that while women situated abroad could not physically participate in kin work across the Atlantic, they made imagined exchanges with extended family in Italy by consuming Italian brands. In a 1932 ad in Chicago's *L'Italia*, a woman buying olive oil from a grocer professes to always ask for Bertolli, "the purest, unsurpassed, made-in-Italy olive oil that my grandmother and mother used before me."[110] A 1916 ad for Sasso olive oil in *La Patria* called out to women, "Ladies! In Italy no food goods store lacks Sasso oil."[111] In ways that echoed the transatlantic solidarities between Italian women during wartime fund-raisers, postwar ads for imported Italian foods connected migrant households in the Americas to the kitchens and markets of their female relatives in Italy. Moreover, by identifying imports with Italian mothers, grandmothers, and sisters back home, ads constructed Italy as a consuming rather than exclusively producing economy. Migrant consumers saw in these ads not only male laborers working in Italy's industrial food sectors but also an increasingly consumer-oriented Italy of female buyers and food preparers who used the same ingredients and brands to build Italianità. This reflected actual changes in the eating habits of an expanding group of middle- and working-class consumers, mainly in northern cities, where industrialization, rising employment rates, and emigrant remittances boosted the standard of living, giving Italian consumers the means to spend more money on larger varieties and quantities of food.[112] Publicity for imports that portrayed Italian women in Italy with products and consumer expertise suggested that for both migrant women and women left behind, links between migration and commerce transformed women's position in a growing global consumer economy.[113]

Promotional material portrayed women using consumption not only to solidify transnational familial and commercial bonds but also to perpetuate distinctly Italian family structures revolving around women's domestic roles as mothers and wives. These ads resembled those for food products in English- and Spanish-language papers and magazines in the United States and Argentina, which frequently presented women using their consumerist skills to keep their families happy and healthy.[114] Like this mainstream literature, ads for Italian imports sometimes prescribed wives' agency in migrant marketplaces within the confines of husbands' palates, as in a 1915 Sasso ad that called out, "Mrs! Buy! Convince yourself that Sasso oil owes its taste to the best quality. . . . Prepare a meal with another oil that you have used and one with Sasso's. Your husband will tell you which is better."[115] Many ads targeted migrant mothers specifically, declaring that the purchase and use of Italian imported edibles allowed women to pass on generationally acquired nutritional and culinary knowledge originating in Italy. Brioschi Effervescent, a powdered Italian digestive aid, stated in its ad, "We believe that it is convenient to remain faithful to the discovery made by your grandmother and approved by your mother: when you need an antacid, or a refreshing thirst quencher, remember Brioschi Effervescent."[116] Italian companies capitalized on networks of food knowledge passed between generations of women to sell their products.[117]

Female migrant consumers began to replace the merchant explorers, military heroes, and notable men in turn-of-the-century export iconography. But they also began to take the place of migrant merchants and retailers themselves as custodians of migrant marketplaces. Earlier publicity in *La Patria* and *Il Progresso* spotlighted the names of merchants just as prominently, if not more so, than the brands of the Italian foods they sold. Italian businesses dealt with the complexities and financial risks involved in transatlantic commerce by giving exclusive import and distribution rights to individual merchants whose names became associated with the brand and its reputation abroad. This name recognition assisted companies to control and protect their merchandise as it passed through multiple hands and locations along international trade routes while helping guard against imitation, adulteration, and fraud. But the pairing of merchant and brand names also served an important cultural and economic function that facilitated migrant consumption in that it provided cautious migrant consumers a sense—however fictitious—of being shielded from the unfamiliar and sometimes hostile world of capitalist exchange and mass-produced foodstuff.[118] Migrant merchants as well as tipo italiano entrepreneurs employed their ethnic backgrounds as cultural and social capital to capture and sustain loyal consumers and labor markets, and migrants trusted them to help navigate novelties in migrant marketplaces. However, after World War I, well-known Italian imported brands became progressively unhinged from specific migrant sellers, as suggested by the Sasso, Cirio, and Cinzano ads. Merchants took a backseat while manufacturers made the brand name itself the publicity's main feature, tying these brands to images of consumers who were increasingly depicted as female. The advertising industry, still in its infancy in the early twentieth century, helped businesses speak directly to consumers by creating brand names accompanied by flashy imagery and persuasive messages aimed to both shape and reflect buyers' desires and feelings.[119]

While in both countries ads described women using foods from Italy to perpetuate transnational consumer patterns and identities, they also demonstrated differences in the way migrants used food consumption to express their incorporation into U.S. and Argentine societies. During the interwar years, publicity in *Il Progresso* began regularly referring to migrants' hyphenated identities as ethnic Americans. An ad directed at migrant mothers for Locatelli-brand cheeses in *Il Progresso* urged consumers to buy imported pecorino romano "so that a new Italian-American generation is able to perpetuate the tradition of taste, health, and nutrients."[120]

Similarly, a Caffè Pastene ad for imported Italian coffee, featuring a smiling young girl, read, "The good taste of eating, in dressing, and even in thinking is handed down from mother to daughter. The young girls of today—who will be the mothers of tomorrow—know that Caffè Pastene is good coffee—she acquires the taste of the mother, who after having tried many brands, comes to the conclusion that the most fresh and aromatic, the most exquisite is of course Caffè Pastene—an Italian type that is American."[121] Reflecting in part the growing second generation of Italian women who themselves were responding to Americanizing influences, merchants in the United States increasingly employed hyphenated monikers to describe Italians and the imported products they ate. Conversely, this hyphenization of Italian people and products in Buenos Aires was conspicuously absent in ads for Italian imports during the interwar years, notwithstanding the large second generation of Italians in Argentina by the 1920s. There, consumption kept female consumers, their families, and the cuisines they cooked Italian but rarely, if ever, "Italian-Argentine," demonstrating how differences in migrant incorporation and ethno-racial landscapes manifested in representations of identity making in the context of food consumption. Over the course of the twentieth century, both countries witnessed the slow evolution from regional to national designations of Italian people and products in migrant marketplaces; in both, sellers of imports continued to employ both national and regional labels to appeal to lingering local identities and migrants' rising awareness of a shared nationality to market their wares.[122] However, in the United States, but not in Argentina, the consumption of imports turned migrants into hyphenated ethnics during the interwar years.

*   *   *

World War I was a global event with long-lasting consequences for trade and migration patterns and for the consumer practices and identities of migrants abroad. Since the late nineteenth century, Italian leaders in Italy and migrant prominenti strove to wrench migrants from their village and regional ties and from the transnational family economies in which these ties were embedded in order to transform migrants into patriotic "Italian" consumers. However, it took Italy's entrance into the war to turn increasing numbers of migrants toward their homeland, culturally and commercially. Italian migrant communities organized and executed numerous campaigns to maintain international trade, collect and export monetary and material resources back to soldiers in Italy, and provide for their precariously positioned connazionali in the United States, Argentina, and Italy left behind by reservist husbands, brothers, and fathers.

During campaigns to help their homeland in need, migrants in Buenos Aires rallied more often and with more intensity around Italian imports than did migrants in New York. The wartime consumer identities they generated remained deeply linked to Italian-Argentine trade in Italian foods and other exports, and bulk agricultural goods such as wheat and wool that migrants sent home to Italy. In New York migrants used the more diverse resources at their disposal, which included some Italian imports but more frequently consumer items produced in the United States—including tipo italiano goods—to influence trade and consumption patterns. Migrants' wartime experiences did not completely unmoor migrants from their regional identities and transnational family economies, but neither did they foster complete incorporation into U.S. and Argentine society. Rather, consumption abroad—even of non-Italian products—in some cases strengthened migrants' commercial and cultural ties to their homeland while turning them into consumers of U.S. and Argentine goods.

These various transnational campaigns helped legitimize migrant consumption in the postwar years. By organizing, carrying out, and publicizing such campaigns, *La Patria* and *Il Progresso* defined Italians in Buenos Aires and New York as consumers whose monetary donations and purchases contained the power to influence international events. Women featured centrally in such initiatives, setting the stage for the feminization of consumption in migrant marketplaces after the war. World War I changed women's relationship with the migrant press when wartime campaigns launched women onto its pages as readers, workers, and consumers. Ads for Italian goods in newspapers during the interwar years connected migrant women's ordinary consumer choices to the preservation of Italian trade networks and to the maintenance of Italianità in grocery stores, around dinner tables, and at festive parties. Publicity for Italian products, as well as the identities they generated, became increasingly anchored simultaneously to consumption and to women.

The weakening of east-west transatlantic flows between Europe and the Americas during the war allowed for the strengthening not only of tipo italiano industries abroad but also of north-south hemispheric commercial ties between North and South America as U.S. politicians and industrialists hoped to fill in a gap left by Europeans in Latin America. During the interwar years, these ties between North and South America became more visible, especially in the Italian-language press in Buenos Aires, where savvy U.S. companies, having finally discovered migrant consumers in New York, began reaching out to Italians in Argentina.

CHAPTER 5

Reorienting Migrant Marketplaces in *le due Americhe* during the Interwar Years

During World War I, as geopolitical alliances shifted global associations among nation-states, Buenos Aires' *La Patria* debated whether Argentina should pursue *panispanesimo* by aligning with its former colonizer, Spain, or instead accept *panamericanismo*, led by its northern neighbor, the United States. Argentina, the paper argued in July 1917, should choose Spain as its ally. Not only had Spain remained neutral during the war—whereas the United States had entered on the side of the Allies by April—but U.S.-controlled Pan-Americanism increasingly threatened Argentine economic, political, and cultural independence. Comparing the Monroe Doctrine to German imperialist aims in Europe that had instigated the global war, the article concluded, "Panispanesimo means frankly neutrality, in opposition to panamericanismo that rings out—and how powerful a sound—intervention."[1] The Italian Chamber of Commerce in Buenos Aires agreed. While their counterpart in New York had worried that Italy's wartime moratorium on exports would advantage migrant manufacturers of tipo italiano foodstuff to the detriment of Italian trade, in Buenos Aires merchants feared that such prohibitions fostered panamericanismo. In the absence of Italian imports, U.S. companies would step in to conquer South American markets.[2] Simply put, panamericanismo threatened the consumption of Italian foods in Buenos Aires' migrant marketplace.

World War I, especially women's war-related work, helped normalize consumption and cultivate a more united national identity among migrants in New York and Buenos Aires as a transnational duty to Italy. While ushering in the Italian female consumer in migrant marketplaces overseas, the war also intensified a global reorientation in trade and migration patterns that affected migrants' consumer options and solidarities. As the *La Patria* editorial suggests, the war escalated long-standing discussions among migrants in Buenos Aires about U.S. expansion in Latin America and its influence on transatlantic connections between Italian people and products. For decades, migrants in the United States and Argentina had formed connections to each other and to Italy through Italian foods. But they also generated alternative subjectivities based on experiences and items particular to the western hemisphere. This included not only tipo italiano foodstuff but, increasingly, foods and other consumer goods produced by multinational U.S. firms. During the interwar years, U.S. food companies—which had previously disregarded migrants as a specific market within the larger U.S. consumer society—discovered Italians in New York's migrant marketplace as potential buyers of factory foods. After the war these mass-produced goods—processed meat, canned vegetables and fruits, tobacco products, pasta, liqueurs, sweets, and other industrialized edibles—appeared more frequently in New York's *Il Progresso* and other Italian-language papers in the United States. But they also emerged in Buenos Aires as U.S. industrialists, trade promoters, and investors turned with unprecedented enthusiasm to Latin American countries as importers and consumers of U.S. merchandise. As these U.S. enterprises moved their markets and factories south to Argentina, they too targeted Italians as consumers.

During the interwar years, the United States' increasing interest in Latin America as a receiver of U.S. exports and capital investment, a worldwide depression, intensifying restrictions against mobile people and goods, and rising nationalism changed the global geography of marketplace connections. To the consternation of Italian prominenti elites in Buenos Aires, continued Italian migration to Argentina collided with escalating north-south incursions of U.S. consumer products.[3] This collision, they feared, compromised the historic ties between Italian people and products that constituted migrant marketplaces and that had kept them critical sites for Italian nation and empire building. As they suspected, panamericanismo after the war signified U.S. unilateral intervention rather than equitable economic and political cooperation among countries of the western hemisphere. Pan-Americanism arrived in the form of U.S. imported foods and other consumer items in Argentina, which, while deepening hemispheric ties between migrant marketplaces of le due Americhe, simultaneously jeopardized the bonds between Italian migrants and trade products that had been fortified during the war.

Combating Yankee Imperialism: Migrants' Reactions to U.S. Expansion in Latin America during the Interwar Years

Well before World War I, when consumer items produced in the United States increasingly joined together Italians in New York and Buenos Aires, migrants fash-

Figure 19. Ad for Pineral *aperitivo*, *La Patria degli Italiani* (Buenos Aires),
September 20, 1905. Courtesy of the Hemeroteca, Biblioteca Nacional de la
República Argentina.

ioned diasporic connections linking consumers in the United States, Argentina,
and Italy. A 1905 advertisement in *La Patria* for Pineral-brand aperitivo made by
the Pini brothers, migrants from Lombardy, commodified hemispheric ties produced by the past migrations of famous Italian men (see fig. 19). The ad depicted
a toga-clad Italia against the backdrop of a city skyline with her arms around an
oversize bottle of Pineral liqueur. The right-hand corner features a scene at the
candle factory in Staten Island in New York City where Italian nationalist leader
and political exile Giuseppe Garibaldi worked for the Italian inventor Antonio
Meucci in the early 1850s. The image of the candle factory was one of sixty-four
illustrations in an album given to the Pini brothers' customers in honor of Italy's
Venti Settembre holiday, commemorating Italian unification.

The Pineral ad sheds light on the global context within which prominenti journalists, advertisers, and businesses in Buenos Aires portrayed migrant consumers in the early twentieth century. Garibaldi's own worldwide peregrinations made him an especially powerful symbolic vehicle for connecting Italians in Argentina both to their homeland and to Italians in the United States. Garibaldi, "the hero of two worlds," led the Italian legion during post-independence civil wars in South American countries during the early nineteenth century. After returning to Italy and leading an unsuccessful republican defense of the Papal States against French forces, Garibaldi went abroad as a political exile in New York, where he worked with Meucci. From New York he traveled again to Latin America, eventually ending up in Peru, where he took command of a merchant ship that sailed from South America across the Pacific and Indian oceans to the Philippines, southeastern China, Australia, and then back to the U.S. East Coast, after which he returned home to lead the Second Italian War of Independence.[4] The ad featuring Garibaldi and Meucci, another Italian nationalist sympathizer settled abroad, used migrant consumption of a tipo italiano beverage—made in Argentina but with ingredients imported from Italy—to link migrant marketplaces in Buenos Aires to both Italy and New York.

While the Pini brothers celebrated connections between the United States and Argentina produced by migration, as the twentieth century progressed, Italians in Argentina increasingly condemned relations between the United States and Argentina brought on by U.S. economic expansion. Until World War I, migrant prominenti in Buenos Aires had directed most of their concern toward European countries as probable obstructions to Italian migration and trade. In 1901 the Buenos Aires–based Italian Chamber of Commerce expressed angst that Spain, having lost its colonies in the Caribbean and Pacific to the United States after 1898, would refocus its efforts on strengthening commercial bonds to Argentina.[5] As seen in debates over tipo italiano foods arriving from Europe in the early twentieth century, migrants viewed Spain as a particularly menacing competitor; Spain's long-standing imperial connections to Latin America, the large number of Spanish migrants that continued to enter Argentina, and Spain's export market, which sent abroad foods similar to those produced in Italy, made Spain's rival migrant marketplaces especially alarming. However, by the eve of World War I Italians in Argentina had gradually turned away from Spain and other European countries and toward the United States in their efforts to protect linkages between Italian trade and migration.

Already by the turn of the century, journalists writing for *La Patria*, as well as migrant merchants and businessmen associated with the Italian Chamber of Commerce, looked with skepticism at the expanding presence of U.S. investment, consumer goods, and other cultural products in Argentina. The Monroe Doctrine, declared by President James Monroe in 1823 to protect both the newly independent countries of Latin America from European meddling and U.S. political and economic interests in the western hemisphere, received special criticism by Italians in Argentina. This was especially the case as Theodore Roosevelt and subsequent U.S. presidents employed the doctrine to justify increased U.S. activity south of its borders.[6] *La Patria* reminded its readers that the Monroe Doctrine encouraged Argentina to cut cultural and economic ties with Europe, essentially characterizing bonds between Italian migration and commerce as a danger rather than an aid to Argentine nation building.[7] In its coverage of Pan-American conferences held in the early twentieth century, *La Patria* criticized what it viewed as the United States' veiled acquisitive aims. At the fourth Pan-American Conference in Buenos Aires in 1910, *La Patria* argued that the "American spirit, American ideal" that the United States professed to cultivate through these meetings was in reality an "insidious movement" to discipline Central and South American countries into resisting European influence and therefore eliminating commercial competition in Latin America. The Monroe Doctrine, "waved around at every occasion," lined up the Americas against the "old world" and at the sole command of the United States, a reality that European countries, too distracted over fighting among themselves, did not understand.[8] The paper described U.S. goals in Latin America as "essentially imperialistic, occupying, assimilating, aggressive," citing Cuba and the Panama Canal as telling examples. Pan-American conferences had "become for the United States a means of propaganda and predominance," and other Latin American nations needed "to keep their eyes open," cautioned the paper.[9] *La Patria* praised articles in *La Nación* and *La Prensa* that confronted claims by the United States that Europe and Europeans, including Italy and Italians, symbolized threats to the integrity of Latin America.[10]

Swelling xenophobic sentiment in the United States gave Italians in Buenos Aires a platform for highlighting differences between the United States and Argentina that challenged notions of solidarity upon which panamericanismo rested. An editorial titled "The Lacuna of the Pan-American Conference" identified migration as conspicuously absent from the themes discussed at the 1910 meeting. The United States, believing their country did not need anymore migrants, increasingly looked to prohibit them. Echoing claims made by many Argentine statesmen, *La Patria* asserted that Latin America continued to consider migration from Europe "the natural foundation of prosperity and economic, political, and moral progress of America in general." In a manner that completely excised non-European migrants from discussions of nation building in either North or South America, the paper concluded that Argentina, unlike the United States, understood that regular European migration safeguarded the "American spirit" by neutralizing "every sentiment, be it Anglo-Saxon, Germanic, or Latin."[11] Nativist attitudes toward

European migrants allowed *La Patria* to differentiate rather than unite the United States and Argentina, calling into question whether U.S.-style panamericanismo advanced Argentine interests.

Visits by Italian and U.S. leaders provided *La Patria* occasions to rebuke U.S. commercial designs in Argentina and reminded readers of the demographic, commercial, and moral clout Italians held in their adopted country. In 1910 *La Patria* praised a speech given by the Italian criminologist Enrico Ferri at the Teatro Odeón in Buenos Aires in which he asserted that panamericanismo was inseparable from "North-American hegemony" and "North-American imperialism."[12] That same year, a trip by U.S. politician William Jennings Bryan elicited criticism from the paper, which claimed that while Bryan spoke publicly about cooperation, "in reality his was a trip of commercial exploration" for the exclusive benefit of the United States: "Until now the United States has neglected the markets of Latin America. Now it has decided to conquer, with its industrial production, this southern part of the continent." *La Patria* interpreted Bryan's visit as the beginning of a dangerous episode in Argentine history in which commercial relations with the United States would take precedence over those with Europe. The editorial concluded, "If European industrialists—and signally our Italians—will not know with all the means possible to beat in quality and price the terrible North American competition, they will be subjected to many bitter delusions in America."[13] The United States, *La Patria* asserted, used the "imaginary danger" of European intervention in South America to strengthen its hold on the continent and to "avert attention from that which is the true danger, the invasion of North America that threatens these Republics."[14]

While denouncing U.S. economic presence in Argentina, *La Patria* confidently pointed to Italian dominance in Argentine trade and industry. The paper reminded readers of Italians' great contribution to Argentina's national progress, a fact mentioned by many foreign visitors to Argentina, including a Russian who asserted, "If we could calculate all that Italian hands have turned out, regarding products, to the markets of the world, we would understand what enormous debt of gratitude European civilization owes to these audacious and valorous pioneers."[15] On the occasion of Argentina's centennial celebrations, *La Patria* proudly insisted that recent attempts by U.S. Americans, French, English, and Germans to monopolize Argentine commerce amounted to imitations of what Italy had already accomplished in its commercial relations with Argentina.[16] The Italian-language press used Pan-American conferences and the Argentine centennial to draw attention to the "intimate relations of interests and sentiments that unite Italy to the great country where its children find, as is said, a second homeland, and carry in exchange a continuous, precious contribution of the vigorous and refined Latin blood, of commercial and industrial genius and of honest work."[17]

"Latin blood," shored up by decades of recurring Italian migration, functioned as a stopgap measure against U.S. imperialism. A 1906 article in *La Patria* lauded a publication by Enrico Piccione, editor of *El Pensamiento Latino* in Santiago, Chile, in which he argued for a "Latin alliance" based on "blood ties" to stop U.S. encroachment. The strengthening of emigration and commercial bonds between Italy and other "Latin countries of Europe" would fend off German, but especially U.S., imperialism in Latin America, considered uniquely nefarious for its less overt qualities.[18] Latinità served as a means through which migrants manufactured ties between Argentines and Italians around food consumption, but it also offered a conduit for binding the United States and Germany together as a racialized Other—Anglo-Saxon and "Yankee"—who endangered Argentina racially and culturally. In 1925 *La Patria* covered the travels of Dr. Guglielmo di Palma Castiglione, Italian emigration administrator and senior officer of the International Labor Organization, who described the important protective "mission" Italians undertook in "young Argentina" besieged by "the invading Britannic, Teutonic and Slavic races." Employing patronizing and patriarchal language to describe Argentina as requiring safekeeping and tutelage, he added, "It is impossible that Argentines, intelligent and nobly ambitious as they are, would not appreciate the beauty of a mission so civil, a mission to help them realize their potential as youngsters, guided by us elders, to carry them toward peace, toward wealth, toward happiness." He assured readers that "Italians are embraced like siblings by the Argentines," which is why Italians preferred Argentina to the United States, even if they made less money in South America. Unlike the United States, Argentina "speaks to his [the Italian emigrant's] heart and adjusts to his spirit."[19] Notions of race, family, and patriarchy blended in discussions about the role Italian migrants played in containing U.S. commercial power in the western hemisphere. Italians' continued celebration of Latinity appeared as more Argentine thinkers began amending and even repudiating Europe as a racial and cultural yardstick for Argentine nation building; they championed Argentina's "Latin" heritage of racial hybridity as a contrast to North American racism, without, however, fully embracing *mestizaje* as official state doctrine.[20]

While migrants condemned the United States for jeopardizing Italy's stronghold in Argentina, they simultaneously and paradoxically expressed a sense of curiosity and even desire for U.S. consumer products and the modernity and affluence they symbolized. *La Patria* characterized consumerism in the United States—"the land of the dollar," where "the greed for money affects everyone"—as exerting a corrupting influence on Latin America, but it also included articles that praised the variety and quality of items available for purchase.[21] For example, after a visit to the United States, a *La Patria* journalist wrote glowingly about the wide array of goods—from ice cream sodas to sweets to medicines—that were obtainable at U.S. pharmacies, goods representing abundance, choice, and prosperity.[22]

These mixed sentiments paralleled debates among Latin American statesmen who, in their struggles to define themselves individually as nations and collectively as a continent, produced varied and shifting reactions toward enlarging U.S. investment and political sway in the western hemisphere.[23] By the turn of the century, a number of Argentines—particularly the growing middle classes at the helm of commerce and industry—sought to associate themselves not only with Europe but also with the increasingly powerful United States. In 1888 a group of industrialists in Argentina described Argentines as the "Yankees of South America" and U.S. Americans as Argentines' "big brothers," indexing how the country followed the United States in its "tireless work of progress."[24] Furthermore, to some nationalists hoping to diversify the Argentine economy and make it more self-sufficient, U.S. investment strategies and tariff policy offered productive industrial models.[25] At the same time, however, rising numbers of Argentine politicians expressed concern about U.S. hegemony in discussions over Argentine political and economic autonomy. In 1902 Argentine jurists passed the Drago Doctrine, which declared that foreign nations could not employ military force for debt collection against Latin America countries. Written mainly in response to the 1902 British, German, and Italian blockade and seizure of Venezuelan ports, the proclamation also functioned as a response to the Monroe Doctrine and as a stance against U.S. hemispheric dominance.[26] Incongruous images of the United States as a paragon of industrial progress and as a nefarious hemispheric bully circulated in Argentina among Argentines and Italians.

These condemnatory but often ambivalent attitudes increased as shifts in global trade made Argentina and other countries of the western hemisphere increasingly lucrative trade partners of the United States. In 1900 the United States had done most of its trade with Europe. On the eve of World War I, however, the United States had shifted its commercial gaze from Europe to the Americas and to Asia, receiving half of its imports from the western hemisphere and Asia and exporting many of its manufactured products and agricultural staples to these same areas.[27] Wartime slowdowns in investment and commodity flows between Europe and Latin America also intensified this shift. Before the war, Argentina had received most of its manufactured goods from Britain and other European countries in exchange for Argentine beef, wheat, wool, and other agricultural products.[28] World War I, however, dealt a heavy blow to European trade and investment capacities. This included the transatlantic trade in Italian foods and beverages, which slowed during the war, in some cases quite dramatically, as the Italian government redirected foods previously produced for export toward the home front. For example, Italy sent one-seventh the amount of wine to Argentina in 1919 as it did in 1915, and by the end of the war Italian wine imports to the United States had dropped by almost half.[29] This attenuation in transatlantic commerce fostered stronger economic partnerships between the United States and Latin America countries. During the war the value of Argentina's total exports to the United States quadrupled while the value of U.S. exports to Argentina experienced an almost sixfold increase.[30]

During the interwar years the increasing north-south orientation of trade patterns continued, with North and South America, as well as Asia, gaining ground on Europe as the United States' most important trade partner. Increasing numbers of U.S. companies looked for alternatives to the already saturated European consumer market, turning toward the less industrialized countries of Latin America and Asia as sites for consumption of U.S. products and capital investment. Latin American nations slowly incorporated their economies into North American commodity circuits as nations south of the U.S. border swapped raw materials for U.S. manufactured goods. By the end of the 1920s the United States received more unprocessed agricultural staples from South America than it did from anywhere else in the world.[31] In return, Latin America countries purchased U.S. machinery, industrial products, and foodstuff; by 1925 U.S. finished manufactured goods made up 76.8 percent of all U.S. exports to the region.[32] Argentina received the largest share of the United States' total exports to the continent, at 37 percent by the end of the 1920s, with Brazil next in line at just 20 percent.[33]

U.S. manufacturers, in their yearning for new markets, facilitated these transformations in geographies of trade. Leading U.S. industrial and business promoters championed Latin America as the United States' new commercial frontier. In 1938 James Farrell, past president of U.S. Steel and chairman of the National Foreign Trade Council, an organization formed in 1914 to promote U.S. foreign trade, advocated for a stronger commercial relationship among countries of the western hemisphere. Encouraging U.S. business leaders to turn their attention away from Europe, Farrell told U.S. industrialists, "We must pause in our gazing from East to West and follow instead the magnetic course of North and South."[34] While many U.S. companies exported their products to Latin America, other U.S. businesses established manufacturing branches there to take advantage of cheaper labor, to gain access to raw materials, and to avoid high tariffs against imported items. Professor Dudley Maynard Phelps's 1936 study on the "industrial migration" of North American manufacturing subsidiaries to Latin America shows that Argentina received by the far the majority of capital by U.S. firms after World War I. By the mid-1930s there were thirty-one branch plants of North American companies in Argentina as compared to nineteen in Brazil, the second most popular Latin American location for U.S. investment. Phelps estimated that by 1936 the total capital invested in U.S. manufacturing subsidiaries totaled $164,721,000 in Argentina and $47,165,000 in Brazil.[35] These companies represented a variety of industries that produced goods for domestic consumption within Argentina and for exportation abroad, such as automobiles and tires, construction materials and equipment, food and meat products, petroleum and pharmaceuticals, and phono-graph and radio equipment. Ford Motor Company, for example, opened a subsidiary in Argentina in 1913, and in 1915 Goodyear Tire Company founded a branch in Argentina and established a manufacturing plant there in 1930.[36] The United Shoe Machinery Corporation installed a factory in Argentina in 1903, and three years later the Singer Sewing Machine Company also opened a branch.[37]

U.S. food, beverage, and tobacco corporations counted among some of the largest retail outlets and subsidiaries in Argentina. Chief among them were two leading U.S. meatpacking houses: Chicago-based Swift and Company and Armour and Company. Swift purchased the largest meatpacking plant in Argentina in 1907, and a couple years later Amour, Swift, and Morris and Company combined to buy out another major Argentine processing plant.[38] By the interwar years, U.S. and British meatpacking conglomerates battled against each other for control of the Argentine beef industry and against a number of Argentine interests, especially ranchers, who pressed the Argentine government to regulate the foreign-owned packers.[39] Meatpacking firms in and around Buenos Aires employed a large number of Italian workers and administrators in their slaughterhouses and processing plants, such as Swift as well as Armour's large firm in the La Plata neighborhood of Berisso.[40]

Against the background of such changes in global trade and investment patterns, migrants' earlier twentieth-century concerns about panamericanismo took on new urgency during the interwar years. Italians in Buenos Aires discussed the rising presence of U.S. consumer goods, factories, retail outlets, and banks in Argentina as threats to migrant marketplaces. And yet if reorientations in commerce worried migrants, reorientations in transatlantic migration patterns, which after more than thirty years made Argentina again the number one receiver of Italian migrants in the western hemisphere, gave trade promoters hope for strengthening links between migrants and food exports. While sustained migration excited Italian trade promoters in Buenos Aires, it also gained the attention of U.S. companies interested in enlarging their markets. After discovering eager migrant consumers in New York, they too would look southward and see Italians, as consumers and producers, in Buenos Aires' migrant marketplace.

Shifting Migration Flows to *le due Americhe* during the Interwar Years

During the interwar years the strengthening of trade and consumption patterns between the United States and Argentina combined with changes in transatlantic migration flows to transform migrants' options for identity making relative to consumption in migrant marketplaces. U.S. "gatekeeping" policy, a process that had begun in the late nineteenth century with the passage of the Chinese Exclusion

Act, intensified after and as a result of World War I, when nationalist and xenophobic sentiments reached new heights. Nativist legislators passed a number of restrictive immigration laws during the war that culminated in the Immigration Act of 1924, which perfected Asian exclusion and radically reduced the number of Southern and Eastern Europeans through a racially discriminatory quota system.[41] As a result of the act, in 1925 only 29,723 Italians entered the United States, down from 349,042 in 1910.[42] Simultaneously, however, the act instigated a move toward more gender-balanced migrations to the United States by allowing women and children, as dependents of male migrants, entry outside of the quota system.[43]

As had earlier restrictive immigration legislation, the passage of the 1924 act reverberated globally to affect other migrant-receiving nations in the western hemisphere.[44] Already in the late nineteenth century the United States had pressured Canada and Mexico to enact racist immigration laws modeled after U.S. policy in an effort to prevent Chinese migrants from entering the country through its northern and southern borders. During the 1920s and 1930s South American countries such as Peru and Brazil passed laws against Asian migrants while reaffirming the whiteness of Europeans by continuing to keep its doors relatively open to them.[45] Argentina begin enforcing restrictive administrative measures—but not formal exclusionary policy—directed at particular ethnic groups, first in the 1920s against *gitanos*, a group associated mainly with the itinerant Roma people from Central and Eastern Europe, and then in the late 1930s against Jewish refugees. However, unlike in the United States, organized labor in Argentina, made up mainly of Southern European migrants, remained relatively weak and collectively did not advocate for ethnic restriction against their continuously arriving co-nationals. Argentine politicians' insistence on its nation's racial whiteness, its long-standing history of and preference for European migrants, and the country's geographical distance from the United States made racial selection in immigrant policy less pressing, and the country kept its doors open to migrants during the interwar years.[46] Migration statistics suggest that Italians responded to the closing of U.S. borders by redirecting their paths southward. In 1922 Argentina overtook the United States as the most popular destination for western hemisphere–bound Italians. In 1923, two years after the passage of the Immigration Restriction Act of 1921, which first established the quota system as a temporary measure, more than twice as many Italians migrated to Argentina as to the United States. Argentina would continue to receive annually about double the number of Italians than the United States for almost a decade.[47]

This shift in Italian migration from the United States to Argentina in the post–World War I decades combined with two events to reduce Italian migration globally, especially after 1930. Starting in the mid-1920s, Italian prime minister Benito Mussolini and his nationalist supporters discouraged Italian migration while expressing interest in how Italians who were already abroad might assist in Italy's larger imperial plans.[48] Second, the 1930s depression curtailed international migration as employment opportunities dwindled abroad and as countries instituted more restrictive migration procedures, as well as higher tariffs, to protect domestic labor and industry against foreign threats in the form of cheap labor and commodities.[49] The early 1920s, therefore, witnessed an almost decade-long shift in transatlantic Italian migration from North to South America and then, especially after 1930, an attenuation in transatlantic Italian migration and trade to both countries.

Trade promoters in the United States after World War I saw connections between ongoing migration to the Americas and increasing U.S. investment abroad. Dudley Phelps, identifying conditions that either promoted or hindered U.S. economic growth in South America, argued that business achievements depended in part on each country's history of migration. He pointed to Argentina and Brazil—the two most important receivers of U.S. capital in South America—as foils to make his point. In Argentina, where by the mid-1930s U.S. firms had found the most success, racial uniformity, he mistakenly believed, had been achieved by generations of white European arrivals and mixing between migrant and indigenous groups. Disregarding Argentina's history of extermination and subjugation campaigns against native and mixed-race peoples, Phelps asserted that the country's racial homogeneity created a level of political stability that was necessary for U.S. investment. Brazil, on the other hand, was a problematic "racial melting pot" of Europeans, Asians, blacks, and indigenous people, a pot made particularly "interesting" due to its large Japanese population.[50] Similarly, William Ricketts, an executive with J. Walter Thompson Company—one of the first and largest advertising agencies in the United States—also looked with suspicion on Brazil, where the majority of the population consisted of "Portuguese, Negro, and Indian extraction" whom he described as "poor, ignorant, and lazy." Still, he depicted the cities of Rio de Janeiro and São Paulo as particularly promising locations for advertising work because of the large number of "Italian and German colonists."[51] Phelps and Ricketts implied that if Brazil had done a better job regulating its borders and the distribution of migrants within those borders, as had Argentina, the country would have made a better environment for U.S. capital and commodities.[52]

To Phelps and Ricketts, then, the performance of U.S. enterprises in South American nations largely depended on the racial "quality" of migrant and native populations. Echoing eugenicists in the early twentieth century, such business leaders viewed migrants in countries south of the U.S. border through a hierarchy of desirability that was based principally on race and through their assumptions about and experiences with migrants in the United States. Referring to South American countries, Phelps wrote, "Each country presents a composite of races and nationalities, much like in the United States, but is more truly a composite, for there has been less racial segregation and color discrimination, and the blending process has been carried much further."[53] He described the makeup of employees at U.S. manufacturing branches in Argentina, including one factory where 20 percent of laborers were Italian; another 20 percent German, Lithuanian, and Polish; and a smaller number Russian, Scandinavian, Spanish and Argentine, as proof that U.S. businesses could profit from a multinational workforce dominated by Europeans whom they considered white.[54] Countries like Argentina, he argued, which contained a higher percentage of Europeans in the nation's overall foreign-born population, increased the likelihood of industrial success. This was partly because U.S. firms preferred to employ European migrants as overseers, executive personnel, and salespeople over native-born South Americans, especially in countries with significant black and indigenous populations. Since the early twentieth century, as historians such as Julie Greene and John Soluri have shown, U.S. economic ventures in Latin America—especially banana production in Honduras and Ecuador and the building of the Panama Canal—depended on a large multinational labor force of Latin American, indigenous, West Indian, European, and U.S. American workers, whose jobs, pay scales, and lifestyles were determined through an inequitable racial system.[55]

Although Phelps considered Italians to be of "supervisory caliber" in Argentina, higher-paying management positions in urban factories of the United States were most often reserved for native-born white workers, including the descendants of Northern European migrants.[56] This incongruity was not lost on Italians in Buenos Aires, who during the interwar years discussed U.S. immigration legislation, racism, and job discrimination against "Latin emigrants" like themselves with disgust.[57] Even while companies touted European migrants—even Southern and Eastern European workers—as ideal laborers in South America, calls for restriction against these very groups resulted in discriminatory immigration legislation that limited their numbers in the United States and propelled migrants southward to countries like Argentina. In the mid-1920s restrictive laws in the United States and continued migration to South America became an opportunity for Italians in Argentina to reassert their commercial and cultural importance while reinforcing cultural and racial ties of Latinità between Italians and Argentines. *La Patria* and the Italian Chamber of Commerce employed Latinità mainly as an integrative force for producing similarities in identities and consumer practices between Italians and Argentines; conversely, in their attempts to discern what racial amalgamations translated best to U.S. commercial development in South America, U.S. business leaders dissociated Italians, as Europeans, from South Americans, Asian migrants, and indigenous workers, who were considered inferior. In fact, promoters of U.S. trade and business sometimes referred to Italians, but not Asians, in South America as "colonists" rather than "immigrants," perhaps because "immigrant" carried a negative connotation in the United States, employed by nativists to advocate for the exclusion of Asians and, eventually, Southern and Eastern Europeans.[58]

In their attempts to describe and evaluate the racial makeup of South American countries, U.S. business leaders exposed their confusion over how to make sense of their southern neighbors' complex demographic landscapes and their consequences for U.S. business endeavors in the region. They required a certain terminological flexibility as they tried to reconcile their own understandings and experiences of migration with a different pattern in countries like Argentina and Brazil. During the mid-1920s and 1930s, as U.S. companies turned their attention toward Argentina, migrants, products, and capital converged to connect migrant marketplaces in New York and Buenos Aires.

Targeting Migrant Consumers: U.S. Commodities in the Italian-Language Press

J. Walter Thompson's Russell Pierce, writing from Argentina in 1929, noted that despite Argentina's continued mix of "modern" and "primitive" peoples, the country was a "market that takes one's breath away." Pierce, director of the agency's Buenos Aires office, described that market: "Almost 11,000,000 souls now. A decade and a half ago there were 7,800,000. And each day a European boat brings in the hardy immigrants from Southeastern Europe who are now moving out into the farm lands to build homes, raise families, crops, and to *stay in the country*."[59] Pierce's special emphasis on the permanency of migrant communities in Argentina suggests an implicit critique of labor migrants in the United States whose high return rates and even higher remittance rates signaled to many an unwillingness to assimilate as consumers and future citizens. Pierce believed that European migrants in Argentina were more likely to remain in the country and to therefore serve as a trustier and more stable consumer base, even though return rates for Southern and Eastern European migrants in Argentina were about the same as those to the United States in the early twentieth century.[60]

It is not surprising that Pierce viewed "hardy migrants" in both Argentina and the United States as business assets during the interwar years. Sellers of Italian imports and tipo italiano foodstuff had been targeting Italian migrants in the Italian-language press since the late nineteenth century. And yet until the 1920s U.S. businesses largely ignored migrant consumers in New York; while they sometimes publicized in the Italian-language press, U.S. companies often advertised in English rather than Italian, and they tended to present images of white, middle-class consumers for all buyers—migrant and native-born. By the late 1920s, however, business and advertising firms like J. Walter Thompson had discovered Italians in U.S. cities such as New York, Chicago, and San Francisco. They began viewing such migrant marketplaces as lucrative consumer markets, different from Anglo-American markets yet equally accessible if the right techniques were employed.

Already by 1914 the advertising industry journal *Printers' Ink* reported that 20 percent of all advertising appeared in foreign-language newspapers.[61] In the early 1920s J. Walter Thompson began instructing its employees on strategies for reaching migrant buyers. A number of articles ran in the company's monthly newsletter under the umbrella title "Unrecognized Cities in the United States." The series began in 1924 when the agency reprinted a translated article from New York's *Il Progresso* titled "The Italian City Larger Than Rome." The article argued that even though U.S. exporters looked to Italy for consumers and business opportunities, "right here in America, before our very eyes, within easy reach of many metropolitan sales forces, there is an Italian city larger than Rome. It is the Italian section of New York City." Insisting on the slow, if gradual, upward mobility of Italian migrants and their children, which made them "a tremendous consuming market" by the 1920s, the article continued:

> It is more than an Italian City because it combines all the buying power and tastes of the Italian plus the greater average wealth and ability to spend money which favors the Italian in New York. . . . The Italian father is generally the father of a good sized family. He takes pride in his children. He and his family love music. They love nice things to wear. They take delight in a well set table. Their hospitality is proverbial. They not only live—they live well. This is a splendid market; a market in which the necessities of life find a ready sale and in which the luxuries, too, find quick and ready sale. While the frugality of the Italian shopper is too well known to require discussion, that frugality only tends to make it possible for the Italians to spread out his purchases and acquire much more than the bare needs.[62]

The characterization of Italians who "live well" was a far cry from earlier condemnations of excessively stingy, savings-oriented labor migrants by U.S. politicians and some Italian *prominenti*. By the interwar years, J. Walter Thompson had reevaluated migrants as consumers, consumers whose frugality was reimagined as giving U.S. industry an advantage in the long run. After the *Il Progresso* reprint, each month the newsletter ran an article on an "unrecognized city" in the United States such as "The Jewish city of New York" and the "Polish city of Chicago"— each a "worth-while market"—and provided its employees with cultural, religious, economic, and racial "facts" about the communities for businesses interested in attracting migrant consumers. As they had with Italians, J. Walter Thompson characterized migrants as passionate and well-equipped consumers, even insisting that in New York and other cities foreigners were better consumers than native-born U.S. Americans.[63] The newsletter noted that "Chicago Poles are heavy buyers" and that in Milwaukee and Detroit a person of "Polish extraction rapidly acquires substance and becomes a liberal consumer of everything the market offers"; the Jewish in New York represented a "rich market" with the "power of

tremendous sales"; the Swedes in Chicago "have the incomes to gratify their desires"; and the "Czechs of Chicago represent a real purchasing power."[64] This image
of migrants consuming with abandon, wholeheartedly embracing U.S. consumer
culture, represented an advertising ideal rather than the actual lifestyles of many
working-class migrants. While many Italians in New York found themselves in
less precarious financial positions, especially as their U.S.-born children found
jobs in low-skilled industrial work and, increasingly, in semi-skilled and white-
collar positions, their consumer habits remained constrained by the economic
needs of the working-class family, slowly rising wages, and high unemployment
rates.[65] For many migrants, economic goals continued to be oriented eastward,
toward family and relatives in Italy, even while the war, restrictive immigration
legislation, and the global depression curbed people and capital flows after 1925.
Italians certainly expressed their aspirations for social mobility in part through
participation in the 1920s consumer revolution, but their involvement did not
signify a wholehearted embrace of Anglo-American, middle-class culture or a
complete disappearance of ethnic traditions; instead they accepted industrialized, mass-produced items, including foodstuff, in ways that meshed with their
everyday material and symbolic needs as transnational working-class people.[66]
Furthermore, as Italians' experiences during World War I indicate, migrants expressed their duty to Italy by consuming foods and other products made and sold
by Italian companies, migrant entrepreneurs, and U.S. firms, all of which fostered
among migrants a more united identity as "Italians."

Following the publication of the *Il Progresso* article, J. Walter Thompson looked
specifically to migrant newspapers both for information on these "unrecognized
markets" and as the critical vehicle for reaching foreign-born consumers.[67] The
newsletter noted that in the German section of Philadelphia, stores selling goods
and services of all kinds advertised in the German press. "The German market
is clearly recognized locally as a rich field inaccessible except through the paper
which talks to these people in their native tongue."[68] The agency went so far as
to seek out ethnic journalists to provide input on these articles. For example, the
agency enlisted Israel Friedkin, publisher of the Yiddish-language *Jewish Morning
Journal*, to write on the "Jewish City of New York."[69] Overall, J. Walter Thompson
expressed a fervent, newfound interest in uncovering, describing, and exploiting migrant consumers and in employing foreign-language newspapers to target
ethnic buyers.

Advertisements for industrialized foodstuff and other consumer goods in *Il Progresso* shows that by the interwar years, U.S. businesses followed advertisers' lead
in targeting consumers specifically as migrants rather than as Anglo-Americans.
In November 1924 Helmar-brand cigarettes, manufactured by the American Tobacco Company, placed an ad in *Il Progresso* for their Turkish-style cigarettes. The

ad depicted an uncle gleefully embracing his newly arrived, luggage-laden nephew. The young man proclaimed, "Fellow citizens, listen. When I came to America for the first time and debarked in New York, my uncle took me to his house. There he offered me a Helmar cigarette. I will never forget the first impression I had from Helmar's."[70] American Tobacco commodified the migration narrative, associating U.S.-made cigarettes with positive portrayals of a successful migration story. The company had been advertising in *Il Progresso* starting in the early twentieth century, but it was not until after World War I that it began treating readers of *Il Progresso* as a distinct consumer market with cultural ties that extended across the Atlantic.[71] Ironically, the publicity ran the same year as the Immigration Act of 1924, which severely curbed the number of Italians who could enter the United States; fewer foreign-born consumers of Helmar cigarettes would experience the migration tale represented in the ad.

Ads for foodstuff often focused on consumers not only as migrants but as Italians by advertising in Italian and by tying products to Italians' transnational culinary cultures. In 1935 an ad for Heckers-brand flour presented a large picture of a smiling man leaning over a plate of cannoli made from Heckers "infallible" flour. The man declared, "My wife is a marvel! All her cannoli are exquisite."[72] Rather than reference white bread or other more typical Anglo-American baked goods, Heckers depicted Italian wives making a specifically Italian dessert while simultaneously affirming women's role as generators and guardians of their family's transnational identities. The ad also mimicked others in depicting the feminization of migrant marketplaces after World War I as part of a larger gendered process that linked women from different ethnic, class, and nationality backgrounds to consumption. This role afforded migrant women, like their native-born counterparts, a degree of authority and respect within the domestic realm while further marginalizing them from political and economic participation in the public sphere.[73]

Similarly, Armour and Company capitalized on connections between women, food, and ethnicity to emphasize the Italianness of both their meat products and their consumers. Armour's 1937 ad in *Il Progresso* depicted an older woman in an apron, happily displaying a platter of sliced La Stella–brand prosciutto. She testified in Italian, "When I serve Armour prosciutto, I know that dinner will be a great success!" (see fig. 20). The ad continued: "La Stella Armour has that delicious taste, that fragrance, that aroma, characteristic of the old country, that Italians love so much." In its use of signs and symbols comprehensible to consumers who were oriented gastronomically to tastes, ingredients, preparation styles, and models of commensality in the "old country," the ad echoed those for Italian imports and *tipo italiano* foods that had appeared in *Il Progresso* already. As had publicity for these products, the Armour ad linked production to consumption to assure readers that Armour, "the largest manufacturer in the world of Italian style dried

Figure 20. Ad for Armour La Stella–brand prosciutto, *Il Progresso Italo-Americano* (New York), December 6, 1937, 3.

sausage," employed expert Italian workers with "long-standing experience."[74] The female Italian consumer, the ad intimated, did not have to purchase imported dried sausage and cured prosciutto in order to guarantee the happiness and Italianità of her family; buying and consuming Armour-brand meat products—produced in the United States using Italian labor and preparation methods—reproduced Italian identities in New York's migrant marketplace.

Already by the late 1910s, Armour and Company produced meats prepared in the styles of various European national and regional specialties. A 1916 company catalog featured "Milan Salami," "Salami di Genoa," "Bari Salami," and "Caserta Pepperoni," all dried or smoked sausages seasoned with various "Italian spices," such as garlic and red pepper, and "popular with the Italian trade."[75] Paralleling the assertions of migrant entrepreneurs who had professed their products' superiority over imports by pointing to the lower costs of their tipo italiano foodstuff, Armour and Company suggested that migrant marketplaces democratized as consumers became less attached to costly imported foods from their homes. "The excessive cost of importation," the catalog declared, placed imported meats among "luxuries" until U.S. meatpacking plants like Armour and Company, "perceiving the great possibilities of the product," used "modern" methods of production and distribution and "brought it within the reach of all."[76] By the interwar years, firms like Armour and Company followed the lead of migrant entrepreneurs in producing *tipo italiano* foods using U.S. technology and distribution networks, and often low-wage migrant labor, in employing the foreign-language press to emphasize the Italianness of their products and, finally, in appealing specifically to migrant women as transnational consumers and keepers of Italian food traditions.[77]

U.S. business interest in foreign-born consumers extended to migrants outside U.S. borders after World War I. By the late 1920s, Armour and Company and other firms transferred their experience targeting migrants in the United States to South American countries with large migrant populations. The conviction that migrants were valuable not only as workers but also as consumers played a role in J. Walter Thompson's own expansionist strategies. Already by 1909 the company claimed that they placed 80 percent of all advertising for U.S. companies in South America.[78] The firm—whose accounts included such U.S. multinationals as Swift and Company, Ford Motor Company, General Motors, Frigidaire, Ponds, and National City Bank—opened branches in Buenos Aires, Argentina; São Paulo, Brazil; and Montevideo, Uruguay, in 1929.[79] Such companies, and the advertising companies that assisted them, were smart to take note of Italians in Argentina during the interwar years. Unlike in the United States, where Italians comprised a small proportion of the total foreign-born population and of the total U.S. population, Italians and their descendants in Argentina made up a significantly higher proportion of the total Argentine population and hence a formidable consumer market that U.S. companies could not afford to ignore. After the passage of U.S. immigration laws in the 1920s, the migrant marketplaces that some firms hoped to exploit in the United States literally migrated south as Italians during the 1920s redirected their travels to Argentina. Furthermore, the withdrawal of European capital from countries like Argentina during World War I presented new opportunities for U.S. firms, and European nations, slowly recovering from the war, could absorb only so many of the United States' manufactured products in the immediate postwar years. Argentina continued to remain a society dominated by an influential landed elite and a large, urban, mainly migrant working class, but by the 1920s the middle classes had expanded to support a rapidly maturing consumer society. By 1913 Fernando Rocchi estimated that Argentina's consumer market was nine times larger than that of 1873 (during these same years the U.S. consumer market, while overall much larger, grew by only five times).[80] Ongoing migration, rising incomes, urban growth, transformations in advertising and marketing strategies, shifting notions of femininity and masculinity, and, more generally, a reshaping of people's perspective toward consumption accompanied the growth of Argentina's consumer society.[81] More than any other Latin American country by the 1920s, Argentina offered a promising environment for U.S. firms hoping to reach consumers with money and a desire for imported products.

While guided by a basic assumption that consumer desire was universal, as U.S. businesses moved into Latin American markets, new strategies for reaching a diverse consumer community guided their marketing approaches. Who better prepared than U.S. business leaders—well versed by the 1920s in exploiting racially and ethnically distinct labor and consumer markets within its own borders—to begin doing the same in Latin America? "Markets are People—Not Places" became J. Walter Thompson's motto for work outside the United States. The export problem, agency executive Clement Watson declared in 1938, was "one fundamentally human."[82] Cultivating successful consumer markets abroad, he wrote, required "first-hand knowledge of the habits, customs, traditions, and living conditions of the people to whom the merchandise is to be sold." He urged U.S. businesses to understand the "factors of history, race, politics, geography, religion and economics" that determine whether a product would be accepted or rejected by consumers.[83] In Argentina this approach appears to have included an awareness of the large Italian-speaking population. U.S. companies' treatment of consumers as migrants in Argentina in the 1920s and 1930s paralleled strategies that had been relied upon by such businesses to appeal to migrants in the United States. Just as they had in New York's *Il Progresso*, ads in Buenos Aires' migrant newspapers for food and other commodities produced by U.S. firms often targeted its readers specifically as Italians by advertising in Italian, by stressing the Italianità of their products, and by alluding to migrants' ties to Italy.

U.S. companies began advertising in Buenos Aires' *La Patria* in the early twentieth century. At this time U.S. wares were largely limited to agricultural equipment, rubber products, and small domestic and electrical appliances, especially sewing machines, typewriters, and phonographs.[84] These early ads were in either Italian or Spanish and consisted of short informative phrases describing the function of the product. After the war, as U.S. firms increasingly shifted their commercial interests southward, a larger number and wider variety of U.S. consumer items began appearing in the paper alongside Italian imports and Argentine-produced goods. By 1920 *La Patria* ran advertisements for cars and motors made by Harley-Davidson, Oldsmobile, Saxon, Ford Motors, Overland, and Studebaker; tires manufactured by Goodyear, Michelin, and the United States Rubber Export Company; and tractors and milling machines produced by International Harvester Corporation; J. I. Case; and Fairbank, Morse, and Company.[85] Smaller consumer items produced by U.S. firms also appeared, such as Kodak cameras, Bayer aspirin, Keds shoes, B.V.D. men's underwear, and Westinghouse Electric International electrical appliances.[86]

Promotional material for these products developed stylistically, often including elaborate graphics of consumers interacting with them, as well as testimonials and text declaring a product's ability to satisfy a range of physical and psychological needs.[87] Comparing the Italian-language press in New York and Buenos Aires indicates that U.S. economic and cultural expansion into Latin America increasingly connected migrant marketplaces.

Armour and Company led the way in employing the Italian-language press to reach migrant consumers in Argentina. By the end of World War I, Armour had meatpacking plants in the United States, Argentina, Brazil, Canada, and New Zealand, and while most meat produced in Argentina during and immediately after the conflict fed hungry consumers in war-torn Europe, during the interwar years, as European demand slowed, Armour directed its focus on building domestic and regional consumer bases. By 1920 their largest plant globally was in Buenos Aires, a plant with the capacity to process 2,500 cattle, 1,500 hogs, and 5,000 sheep per day.[88] An ad for Armour's "Genoa-style tripe" in the Buenos Aires–based Italian-language *Il Mattino d'Italia* stressed the Italianness of its product by making favorable, romanticized references to Italian history and Italy's emigrants (see fig. 21). The 1935 ad featured an illustration of medieval Genoa and a text in Spanish that began,

Figure 21. Ad for Armour Genoa-style tripe, *Il Mattino d'Italia* (Buenos Aires), November 10, 1935, 5. Courtesy of the Hemeroteca, Biblioteca Nacional de la República Argentina.

"The Genoese, who today are many in this welcoming land, brought us something other than their proverbial industriousness and aptitude for work. They also brought their flavorful regional dishes and, of course, the most exquisite of all—Genoese-style tripe—that now Armour gives you ready to serve."[89] Armour disclosed their awareness of Argentina's own migration history, in which Italians loomed large, by praising Italian labor migrants and the regional foods they brought with them.

U.S. companies selling nonedible consumer items also frequently spoke to readers' specific experiences as migrants with continuing transoceanic ties to Italy by tying their products to Italian notables, and even Italian commodities. In 1925 the New York–based firm Tide Water Oil Company featured the testimonials of Italian race-car drivers in ads for their Veedol-brand car lubricant. Pietro Bordino, who competed in a number of U.S. car races and won the Italian Grand Prix in 1922, testified, "I learned about 'Veedol' in 1921 during my first trip to the Unites States of America, where this valuable lubricant produced by Tide Water Oil Company of New York is used by the majority of automobile drivers." Italian sports celebrities figured centrally in the Veedol advertisements, but so too did Italian Fiat cars, which competed with Ford and Oldsmobile for the attention of consumers in Argentina. In his testimonial, Bordino indicated that he had broken a record at the Italian Grand Prix in his Fiat car using Veedol-brand Gear Compound oil, while Felice Nazzaro, another Italian race-car driver, lauded both U.S.-owned Veedol and Italian-owned Fiat, a company that created "a perfect gem of a car, an envied global masterpiece of automobile construction."[90] By highlighting Fiat automobiles and the Italian sports stars who drove them, the U.S. Tide Water Oil Company Italianized their product for migrant consumers while simultaneously forging symbolic connections between Italians in the United States, Argentina, and Italy. Headline slogans such as "Another link between Italy and Argentina is Veedol oil" and "Soon Veedol will be as well known in Argentina as it is in Italy" played down the products' U.S. identity by giving readers the impression that the lubricant was a widely popular commodity in Italy.[91]

Nation-specific differences in the two countries' paths toward industrialization and in Italian migrants' occupational options allowed U.S. companies to employ not only food consumption but also food production to generate transatlantic cultural ties between Italians in Argentina and Italy. In both countries Italians overwhelmingly opted to work as manual laborers in urban areas rather than as farmers in the countryside. Still, in Argentina, whose economy continued to rely heavily on the lucrative agro-export sector, a significant number worked in agriculture on the vast Argentine pampas plains as farmers, sharecroppers, and rural wage workers.[92] This explains in part why ads for agricultural equipment proliferated in Buenos Aires' *La Patria* but not in New York's *Il Progresso*. In 1920 J. I. Case Threshing Machine Co., a Wisconsin firm specializing in agricultural machinery and construction equipment, ran an ad in *La Patria* that capitalized on migrants' drive to collect money and other resources to help Italy pay off its foreign debts and rebuild after the war. The ad featured an illustration of a man tilling a field in Argentina on a Case tractor adjacent to a contrasting poster for the Consolidated Italian Loan, which showed a similar scene but with a man in Europe laboring with difficulty behind a set of oxen. "Everyone wins with the work of repairing the ravages of war," the ad began. "It is the patriotic and humane work of every farmer of good will to produce as much as possible, because Europe needs cereals and will pay a good price." The Case ad played on the sympathies of Italians concerned with famished connazionali in Italy. And yet it also juxtaposed the two images to link Italians in Argentina with the "modern mechanical drive that had worked so effectively to help the Allies during the war," and Italians at home with the "old custom of using horses and oxen for plowing."[93] Purchasing a Case tractor allowed Italians in Argentina to produce wheat needed by relatives back home while reaffirming their own ability to buy "modern" food-producing equipment, which was unavailable in the war-torn "old world." Conversely, in the United States merchants encouraged consumers to help pay off Italy's war debts by buying Italian imports; such purchases would help resolve Italy's negative balance of payments while creating employment opportunities for Italian workers in Italy's food industries.[94] Joseph Personeni, seller of Italian foods in New York, instructed buyers in 1935 that it was their "duty" to help Italy pay its war debt by buying Italian specialties and promoting their use among both Italians and U.S. Americans.[95] In both New York and Buenos Aires, migrant newspapers encouraged Italians to aid Italy fiscally by keeping transnational food chains active. In Argentina, however, they were also invited to buy U.S. agriculture equipment to dispatch foodstuff in the other direction, across the Atlantic, to needy Italians back home as they had during the war.

Migrant consumption in New York and Buenos Aires constructed and reflected the different processes of migrant incorporation. Already at the turn of the century, Argentine companies had targeted Italian consumers specifically as Italians in ways that reflected Italians' powerful demographic presence as the largest foreign-born population. Argentine beverage, food, and cigarette companies, such as Quilmes beer and Piccardo and Company cigarettes, reached out to readers of *La Patria* as migrants by placing ads in Italian and by referencing Italian traditions, holidays, and notable persons. During this time, conversely, U.S. companies largely disregarded migrants as transnational consumers. In this much more populous and diverse country, where Italians accounted for only one of many foreign-born communities, U.S. companies considered Italians too small a market, and a weak, racially problematic market to boot. In short, Italians in Buenos Aires, but not in New York, were a "worthy market"—the term used to describe Italians in New York by J. Walter Thompson only in the mid-1920s.

By that time U.S. and Argentine companies had reversed their approach toward Italian consumers. Ads for Argentine consumer goods on the whole stopped speaking to readers and consumers as a distinct Italian market within the larger Argentine consumer economy.[96] So too did ads for Italian-style foods made by migrant entrepreneurs, which by the interwar years rarely made reference to Italy or homeland culinary ties and instead sometimes described their products and their prospective consumers simply as "Argentine."[97] By the late 1920s, while migrants continued to pour into Argentina, a substantial group of second-generation Italians had grown up in a country that had absorbed them as "Argentines" rather than as hyphenated people. Aiding in this process was Argentina's historic partiality to European migrants, including Italians, who were considered ultimately, if not without controversy, white, as well as almost four decades of interaction between Italians and Argentines surrounding Italian imports, which helped produce Latinità and justified linkages between Italian migration and exportation. As Argentine food producers and sellers deemphasized the Italianità of their products and consumers in the Italian-language press, U.S. companies looking for migrant consumers in both the United States and Argentina began conceiving of Italians as a distinct target market.

Therefore, it took until the mid-1920s for U.S. companies to pay as close attention to Italians (in both the United States and Argentina) as Argentine companies already had done in the early twentieth century. Only after World War I did U.S. businesses made a conscious effort to reach Italian consumers; they purchased a plethora of advertising space in the Italian-language press, where their publicity most often appeared in Italian, even in the 1930s, when in Argentina many if not most ads for Argentine goods appeared in Spanish. That ads for U.S. goods remained in Italian rather than Spanish suggests that U.S. firms thought of Italians in Argentina more as "foreigners" in Argentine society than did Argentine and even Italian companies, who had been marketing in Spanish in *La Patria* for over three decades. Only during the interwar years, when immigration policy decreased the number of Italians entering the United States by tens of thousands annually, did U.S. companies celebrate and commodify Italians' transnational links to tastes, experiences, and family back home, links perceived as less threatening and potentially profitable only after Italian migration slowed. Confident in their assumptions about migrant consumers in large metropolitan cities and about Latin America as a future site of U.S. economic and cultural domination, U.S. business promoters turned with ambition and excitement to migrants in Argentina.

* * *

The cities and neighborhoods described by J. Walter Thompson in the mid-1920s were "unrecognized" only to U.S. advertising executives and business leaders; to migrant merchants, entrepreneurs, and consumers these sites were visible and vibrant migrant marketplaces—locations where Italians' consumer patterns and identities shaped and were shaped by the economic and cultural ties migrants maintained to Italy. Rather than neighborhoods made meaningful only after U.S.-owned businesses discovered them, they had been furnishing sellers and buyers with foods and other consumer goods upon which Italians created meaning in their lives as transnational people.

Migrant marketplaces of mobile people and mobile goods played an important but overlooked role in the relocating of trade and migration paths that increasingly made north-south, rather than exclusively east-west, orientations central to the history of globalization as the twentieth century progressed. Starting in the mid-1920s, commercial flows between the United States and Argentina intensified while the migration patterns that so dominated the political economy of the late nineteenth and early twentieth centuries declined. U.S. business leaders labored hard, and with much success, to export consumer goods and capital outside U.S. borders toward Latin American countries; at the same time, U.S. legislators labored hard, and also with success, to close U.S. borders to Italians and other migrant groups. The confluence of changes in people and trade flows toward Latin America after World War I generated new opportunities for migrant consumers and U.S. exporters who were interested in expanding their markets abroad.

Cultural historians of U.S.–Latin American relations have argued that U.S. economic, cultural, and military expansion into Latin America in the first three decades of the twentieth century triggered, as historian Ricardo Salvatore wrote, "a new imagined scenario where the possibility of cultural assimilation of South Americans depended on the diffusion of U.S. products."[98] How transnational migrants in Latin America figured into the history of U.S. empire-building projects—as workers and consumers—however, is still relatively unknown. Even before World War I, Italians expressed varied but overwhelmingly skeptical sentiments toward the United States. *La Patria* and the Italian Chamber of Commerce in Buenos Aires saw in U.S. products and capital a major threat to Argentina's migrant marketplaces and claimed that the presence of Italian people and products protected Argentina from the United States' ever increasing hegemonic influence. By the interwar years, however, as suggested by the large number of ads for U.S. foodstuff, automobiles, agricultural machinery, beauty products, clothing items, and banking services in the Italian-language press, the U.S. industrial and consumer revolutions that had influenced New York's migrant marketplace were also transforming that of Buenos Aires. U.S. businesses sought to reach not only migrants in the United States but also migrants in other countries to which U.S. capital and commodities moved. By the 1920s and 1930s, migrants had a variety of "Italian" goods at their disposal—imports, tipo italiano, U.S., and Argentine—to invent and perpetuate transnational identities as people situated in the cultures and economies of both their home and host countries.

Over the course of the twentieth century, Italian migrants in le due Americhe reinvented their transatlantic subjectivities and buying patterns within the context of hemispheric flows of capital, consumer values, and imperial campaigns. They would continue to do so in the late 1920s and 1930s, when Mussolini's Fascist government endeavored to fortify Italy's relationship with migrants abroad. In Mussolini's paradoxical quest to both profit from migrant consumption and dissociate it from U.S.-style consumption—in which the female consumer commanded center stage—Fascist Italy faced a tough battle. The female Italian consumer, materializing during wartime fund-raising campaigns to spend money and send goods to Italy, had become stubbornly ubiquitous in ads for Italian, U.S., and Argentine consumer products. By the 1930s, Italy, the United States, and Argentina all vied for Italian consumers, especially women, who continued to serve as symbols through which migrants formed national and consumer identities.

CHAPTER 6

Fascism and the Competition for Migrant Consumers, 1922–1940

In the late 1930s Italian-language newspapers in New York and Buenos Aires so-licited migrants to treat their relatives back home to a panettone, the traditional sweet bread enjoyed by Italians during the Christmas holiday. Advertisements for Motta-brand panettone in New York's *Il Progresso* publicized the company's special Christmas service that enabled Italians in New York to have panettoni sent to rela-tives and friends in Italy directly from the Motta factory in Milan.[1] In Argentina's *Il Mattino d'Italia* (hereafter *Il Mattino*), the Confetería del Molino, a Buenos Aires bakery run by Italian migrants, entreated readers to dispatch its panettone across the Atlantic to loved ones back home.[2] While the commodity chains along which these panettoni traveled originated in fields and factories separated by thousands of miles, both of them allowed migrants to forge a transnational consumer culture rooted in circulating networks of people and foods.

The two panettoni—one produced in Italy, the other in the diaspora—emerged out of enduring cultural and economic links between Italians abroad and their homeland established through decades of transatlantic migration. It built particu-larly on Italians' World War I experiences, during which migrants generated new identities as consumers and as Italians, in part by sending home agricultural staples like wheat, beef, and wool, and industrialized foodstuff like cigarettes, wine, and cookies. As they mobilized for their homeland in need, migrants coalesced around spending and saving in ways that regularized consumption as a duty to Italy while fostering a more intense sense of Italianità. Shifting gender ratios in international migration and in ethnic communities, combined with women's participation in fund-raising campaigns, gave women a new visibility in the Italian-language press as consumers of Italian foods and as guardians of Italian trade paths and culinary and familial traditions.

By the late 1930s Prime Minister Benito Mussolini's Partito Nazionale Fascista (National Fascist Party, or PNF), founded after his March on Rome in October 1922, endeavored to take advantage of Italian consumers in the transformed migrant marketplaces of New York and Buenos Aires. This proved especially the case in 1935 and 1936, when the League of Nations placed economic sanctions on Italy in response to that country's invasion of Ethiopia. However, by the mid-1930s Mussolini and his supporters faced a group of consuming connazionali abroad whose buying and eating practices—while still very much tied to products and traditions from back home—became less fixed to notions of duty to la patria. Migrants and their children after World War I had a surplus of foodstuff and other items upon which they developed consumer experiences as Italians but also as U.S. Americans and as Argentines. Much to Mussolini's chagrin, during the 1930s migrant marketplaces overwhelmingly featured female consumers making purchases in order to produce Italian identities even while in Italy he attempted to detach women from U.S.- and Western-style consumption.

The Global Depression, the Rise of Fascism, and Mussolini's Interest in Migrant Marketplaces

By the late 1930s the economic and geopolitical contexts in which transnational movements of people and products operated had drastically transformed. The Great Depression, and the nationalist economic policies it helped to produce, brought global trade to a standstill. In the United States panicked politicians passed the Smoot-Hawley Tariff Act, which increased trade barriers to new levels. Legislators had hoped that tariff hikes would protect U.S. jobs and manufacturing, but instead they largely exacerbated financial problems, as the legislation helped ignite a global trade war that stifled commerce worldwide.[3] The turn toward protectionism kept industrial and agricultural production levels low in the United States during the first five years of the Depression. Argentina too was hit hard, especially as the global prices for its agro-export commodities plummeted. During the 1930s Argentina experimented with an import substitution policy in order to advance domestic production, increase job opportunities, and diversify the economy to make it less dependent on fluctuating international markets, a policy that would intensify under nationalist Juan Domingo Perón in the 1940s and 1950s.[4] During and immediately after World War I, the Argentine legislature increased the tariff valuation upon which duties were based, giving manufacturers added protection from imports.[5] While commercial agriculture continued to serve as the primary engine of the nation's economic growth, manufacturing went from 15 percent of the gross national product on the eve of World War I to 21 percent by 1940.[6]

Coming to power amid the financial turmoil of the postwar years, Mussolini deepened his commitment to economic nationalism during the Depression. As part of his larger vision of an autarkic Italy, Mussolini limited trade, discouraged the consumption of foreign goods, and bolstered domestic manufacturing, including increased food production through agricultural land reclamation projects.[7] Italian exports to the western hemisphere began a slow decline after 1926 as Mussolini intensified trade relationships with fascist regimes in Europe and directed exports to Italy's colonies in North and East Africa. By 1934 the value of Italy's total exports to Argentina and the United States had decreased by about a fourth of their 1929 levels.[8] From the standpoint of the majority of Italians, Mussolini's austere trade and economic policies were largely unsuccessful; historians point to low consumption levels, especially among the working class, as evidence of autarky's inability to provide for its people and of the regime's willingness to prioritize state concerns over the basic needs of the Italian population.[9]

The rise and consolidation of the fascist state had major ramifications for Italy's migrants. Mussolini directed migrants to Italy's formal African colonies and re-conceptualized all Italian migration, even voluntary labor movements, as forms of Italian imperial expansion. While striving to curtail emigration and exportation to North and South America, he took an active interest in Italians abroad, especially in the United States and Argentina, where large populations of Italians and their descendants resided. By 1923 Mussolini had begun coordinating the activities of fascist supporters outside of Italy and limiting migrants' participation in the domestic politics of their host countries.[10] Fascists sought to tie Italian communities across the Atlantic to Italy through cultural-based propaganda campaigns organized by migrant organizations, including pro-Mussolini Italian-language newspapers and Italian chambers of commerce.[11] Mussolini hoped—as had his liberal predecessors—that rallying migrants in support of Italy would transfer into monetary support in the form of remittances and purchases of Italian goods abroad. Despite Mussolini's move to restrict Italy's trade relationship with the United States and Argentina at the diplomatic level, he encouraged migrant consumer demand for Italian commodities such as vegetable and fruit preserves because they were profitable and because most Italians in Italy could not afford such expensive, domestically produced items.[12]

While Mussolini looked to Italians in both the United States and Argentina as vital resources, fascists viewed Argentina as holding unique potential for amplifying Italian nation and empire building.[13] The United States' mature industrial sector, higher tariffs, and restrictive immigration legislation made it an increasingly inhospitable place for Italian people and products. Despite a shift toward economic self-sufficiency and import substitution, Argentina continued to require exports from abroad and the country kept its doors open to Italian migrants. Fascist supporters pointed to the powerful presence Italian migrants and their children continued to have in the Argentine economy. The 1935 Argentine industrial census established that of all foreign-born groups, Italians owned the largest number of factories, and their calculations did not include factories owned by second-generation Italians, who were counted as Argentine by census takers.[14] Italy also had a relatively large amount of fixed capital in Argentina by the 1930s. Like their U.S. counterparts, several major Italian companies, such as Cinzano, a vermouth producer; Fiat, a manufacturer of automobiles and agricultural machinery; Pirelli Tire and Company; and Gio. Ansaldo and Company, a producer of metallurgical goods, opened branches in Argentina during the interwar years.[15]

Furthermore, after 1930, when General José Félix Uriburu overthrew the democratically elected president Hipólito Yrigoyen of the Unión Cívica Radical (Radical Civic Union), Argentina appeared to be an even more favorable environment for the transfer of fascist political ideology. While Uriburu's dictatorship lasted only two years, historian Federico Finchelstein has suggested that Uriburu based his plans for Argentine national renewal on the Italian fascist model and that his military rule cultivated the presence of powerful right-wing nationalists, some of whom drew inspiration from Mussolini.[16] This ideological milieu blended with Mussolini's aggressive revitalization of Latinità to make Argentina a particularly fruitful site for expanding fascist economic and cultural influence. Already by the late nineteenth century, Italian leaders in both Argentina and Italy had celebrated Latinity to legitimatize Italian migration and trade. Mussolini built on these earlier racialized visions in the hopes that shared notions of Latinità between Italians and Argentines would result in support not only from Italians and their children but also from influential Argentine leaders.[17]

Mussolini found some level of backing from Italy's migrants in le due Americhe. Fascism drew support from many Italian nationalist prominenti in the United States and Argentina, especially members of Italian chambers of commerce but also elites in control of the Italian-language commercial press. Construction tycoon Generoso Pope, who assumed control of New York's *Il Progresso* in 1927, became outspokenly pro-Mussolini and reported favorably on fascist activities in Italy and abroad.[18] *La Patria*, which until 1930 had been the largest Italian-language newspaper in Argentina, shifted its politics toward a critical anti-Mussolini stance, reflecting many migrants' distrust or disinterest in fascism as an organized political party. By the end of the 1930s, the paper, which had reinvented itself as *La Nuova Patria degli Italiani*, had collapsed, dwindling from over fifteen pages of articles and ads in each edition to four or six pages by the end of the decade. The collapse was not accidental. After being named the Fascist Party delegate in Argentina, Vittorio

Valdani, an affluent industrialist who had migrated to Argentina in 1899, bought out *La Patria* only to kill it and divert remaining funds to the fascist daily *Il Mattino d'Italia*. Fascist supporter Piero Parini established the Buenos Aires *Il Mattino* in 1930, and under editor Michele Intaglietta's guidance, the paper's materials, aesthetics, and politics soon paralleled *Il Progresso*'s pro-Mussolini posturing.[19]

It would be shortsighted to characterize all Italians abroad who conveyed a sense of admiration for Mussolini during the 1930s as unequivocal fascists. Historians of fascism have acknowledged how little support the system actually enjoyed among Italians living in the United States and Argentina. The *Fasci all'estero* (Italian Fasci abroad), organizations established by the National Fascist Party to spread support for fascism and promote Italianità in migrant communities, were plagued with internal divisions and lacked widespread approval among migrants.[20] Fascists abroad also faced vocal anti-fascist organizations, mainly run by migrant socialist leaders, labor organizers, and anarchist groups.[21] Furthermore, scholars such as Matteo Pretelli and Stefano Luconi have asserted that prominenti at the helms of various migrant institutions tended to depoliticize fascist attitudes among migrants and their children by promoting an Italian identity rooted in love and respect for the customs, natural beauty, and rich history of their homeland.[22] Nevertheless, this culturally based understanding of Italianità promoted by fascist supporters came to influence migrants' consumer options and identities in migrant marketplaces. Despite pervasive indifference to fascism among migrants and their descendants, Italians abroad used and were used by fascism, and prominenti merchants, business leaders, and journalists achieved some success in cultivating an identity abroad anchored in a newfound Italian nationalism.[23] World War I first produced the formation of a more cohesive national identity among migrants who were drawn into transnational fund-raising drives to spend, save, and consume for the homeland. However, by the 1930s the end of mass migration, combined with an expanded second generation of "Italian Americans" and "Argentines" with more Americanized and Argentized palates, threatened Italian food trade, already weakened by the Depression. Against the background of global slowdowns in migration and trade and of rising nationalisms, fascists in Italy and abroad attempted to shore up their relationships with consumers in Buenos Aires and New York.

Debating Consumption in Migrant Marketplaces during the League of Nations' Boycott

Mussolini looked especially to migrant consumers in the wake of Italy's invasion and defeat of Ethiopia in 1935, an imperial campaign designed to expand Italy's colonial foothold in Africa. The League of Nations responded by instituting economic sanctions against Italy in November 1935. Lasting until July 1936, the sanctions included an arms and financial embargo and boycott against Italian trade goods. During the boycott Mussolini hoped that migrant demand for Italian goods would compensate for the decrease in Italian trade to the fifty-eight member countries in the League of Nations. Italians in the United States served as an especially critical outlet for Italian commodities; despite the U.S. government's increasing disapproval of Mussolini's imperial aims, the United States was not a member of the League of Nations and did not officially join the boycott.[24] Argentina, on the other hand, was a member of the league and formally instituted the ban, although historians have questioned the extent to which Argentina adhered to the sanctions, especially as the country grew irritated at the league's unwillingness to take the recommendations of Latin American countries seriously.[25]

Nation-based differences and changes in the ideological and political positioning of *Il Progresso* and *La Patria*—the two largest circulating Italian-language papers since the late nineteenth century—produced a diversity of migrant responses to Mussolini's overtures. In the early 1930s *La Patria*, now *La Nuova Patria*, became anti-Mussolini, expressing condemnatory attitudes toward the PNF but without embracing communist and socialist stances. Instead, both New York's *Il Progresso* and Buenos Aires' *Il Mattino* received direct financial assistance from the fascist regime in Italy through Italian consulates and embassies abroad. Coverage of the league's boycott therefore reflected the divergent ideological paths followed by the two migrant newspapers. Despite their contrasting political outlooks, both of these papers objected to the league's sanctions; their objections, however, were based on conflicting assumptions about Italy's commercial and export capacities, about Italian consumers in Italy, and about migrants' responsibilities as consumers to their homeland.

New York's pro-Mussolini *Il Progresso* positioned Italy as a powerful consumer and producer to argue that the boycott would severely disrupt international trade to all countries' disadvantage. By purchasing goods from abroad, Italy served as many nations' "best client," absorbing many international products. The paper even pointed to Italy's trade deficit, often viewed as an economic weakness, as evidence of Italy's ability as a powerful buyer to affect global trade.[26] Instead of harming Italy, *Il Progresso* predicted that the league's actions would prove disastrous to sanctioning countries like France and England, which would lose out on Italy's lucrative consumer market. *Il Progresso*'s Angelo Flavio Guidi wrote, "The day will come—not far from now—when the countries that wanted to apply the sanctions against Italy will understand that they have thrown a 'boomerang' that, without having touched its target, returned to hit he who threw it."[27] *Il Progresso* portrayed Italy as one of the United States' great trade partners and discouraged their host country from yielding to British pressure to apply the sanctions. The paper urged U.S. politicians to respect the Act of Neutrality, passed by Congress, under which the United States could legally prohibit the sale of arms and munitions to Italy but not the sale of primary materials such as the oil, cotton, steel, and iron that Italy greatly depended on. Articles often lauded the United States' right and necessity to remain independent of the league, especially of England, which the press consistently demonized.[28] Sanctions violated previous commercial pacts between Italy and the United States and denied U.S. businesses the Italian consumers in Italy on which their trade relied. *Il Progresso* calculated that, if applied, the sanctions would cost the United States $60 million per year in trade.[29] If the United States joined the sanctions, the paper threatened, Italy might retaliate in self-defense by refusing to buy U.S. goods in the future. The press argued that migrants had the support of the U.S. public, of English-language newspapers like the *Sun* and the *New York Herald*, and of U.S. industrialists and manufacturers, all of which backed Italy and migrants' calls for neutrality.[30] The paper's haughty depictions of the United States and Italy as commercially codependent masked the actual unequal commercial relationship between the two nations. While U.S. goods constituted 30 percent of all Italian imports, making the United States Italy's second most important trade partner behind France, Italian goods represented less than 2 percent of the total value of all U.S. imports and only 6.5 percent of the total European imports to the United States in 1935, the year the sanctions began.[31]

As it had during debates over tariffs in the early twentieth century, in objecting to the sanctions and encouraging U.S. neutrality in the 1930s, *Il Progresso* depicted migrants as an influential voice with the ability to affect international trade and diplomacy. *Il Progresso* editor Generoso Pope argued, "The Italians of America, because they are united, represent a large force, which the government and Congress cannot fail to take into account." Pope encouraged readers to send letters to their congressmen, suggesting that migrant protests kept the United States neutral.[32] The paper even insinuated that President Franklin D. Roosevelt would lose the Italian American vote in his 1936 bid for reelection if he supported the sanctions.[33] Naturalized Italians, but, more importantly, the large number of second-generation Italians born in the United States, would exercise their disapproval at the voting booth.

The anti-Mussolini *La Nuova Patria* in Buenos Aires also objected to the league's boycott, questioning the practicability and effectiveness of the sanctions. Like *Il Progresso*, the paper doubted that sanctioning countries would sacrifice the interests of big business to the league's authority and noted the boycott's potentially injurious consequences for smaller nations like Yugoslavia, whose economy depended on trade with Italy.[34] While condemning the sanctions, *La Nuova Patria* argued that migrants' delicate position in Argentina, a sanctioning country, precluded them from actively protesting the league's decision. The responsibility of Italians in Argentina regarding the sanctions, *La Nuova Patria* wrote, is, "in our humble opinion, nothing or very little."[35] When *Il Mattino* called on migrants to boycott products arriving in Argentina from sanctioning countries, *La Nuova Patria* pointed to the absurdity of doing so in such countries, where British-owned firms could "launch any day thousands of Italian workers on the streets."[36] The continued presence of British-owned businesses in Argentina turned battles between pro-Mussolini supporters and British capital in Argentina into one "between fleas and elephants." "Can you imagine an Italian who does not travel by train, tram, metro in order to damage British interests, who rejects the products of the British meat houses, who demands that his tailor is certain that the fabric he is using is not British, and who deserts the cinema?" asked the paper.[37] It was unreasonable for pro-Mussolini crusaders to ask migrants to sacrifice their consumer desires and needs, including their daily bread, in support of Italy's imperial ambitions.

Furthermore, Argentina's history of migration, *La Nuova Patria* implied, inhibited migrants as well as Argentines from applying the sanctions. A month before the boycott began, the paper praised an article by Rodolfo Rivarola, former president of the National University of La Plata, in the Argentine popular daily *La Nación*. Rivarola argued that Argentina's large Italian population made the application of sanctions impossible. He implied that breaking commercial ties with Italy would damage not only the relationship between Argentines and Italians within Argentina but also the relationship between Italians and the numerous other migrant groups in Argentina. Argentina's multinational society, composed of people with different economic priorities and national loyalties, excused the country from enacting the sanctions. The paper suggested that promoting harmonious relations among Argentina's diverse population took priority over the league's trade dictates, which, the paper predicted, would spark animosity among the country's many migrant and ethnic groups.[38]

Unlike discussion of economic protectionism at the turn of the century, which focused almost exclusively on migrant consumption, in their objections to the League of Nations both *Il Progresso* and *La Nuova Patria* concentrated on how the sanctions would affect Italian consumers in Italy. *La Nuova Patria* constructed Italian consumers as deprived and suffering, first, because of fascism's misguided economic policies, and, second, as guiltless victims of the league's actions. The paper pointed to the exorbitant cost of living in Italy, rising prices for food and other consumer items, reduced salaries, and the poverty under which most Italians lived; under fascism, the paper maintained, Italians "suffer and say nothing, fearing the worst."[39] The sanctions would not affect the Italian government, but rather the Italian people, especially women, children, and the elderly, "innocent victims" of hunger and malnutrition. The paper reminded readers, "Fascism is not Italy," observing that the Italian working class, not the fascist state, bore the material and spiritual effects of the sanctions.[40]

New York's pro-Mussolini *Il Progresso* painted an opposite picture of Italians' quality of life during the boycott. While representing the sanctions as "barbaric," the paper depicted Italians as prepared to face them "without a complaint, without a protest, without a defection," because Italians knew how to "live well on little."[41] Italians in Italy committed as consumers to fascism, willing to abandon "luxury and the whim of the palate, the flashy and unnecessary, without a drop of regret," and extolled Italian women specifically, who "protect the battle for the austere life."[42] Even after renouncing luxury goods, Italians actually saw their quality of life increase under fascism, the paper claimed. Italians profited from fascist economic policies; increases in the number of livestock per person and in the quantity of wheat per hectare boosted Italians' consumption levels of meat and bread. Any food restrictions on meat under the boycott, the paper added, would be compensated with increased cultivation and consumption of fish, game, fruits, and vegetables.[43] Even while the pro- and anti-Mussolini newspapers both disapproved of the sanctions, the league's boycott produced strikingly different opinions about Italians' ability to consume and live comfortably under fascism. And both made the Italian consumer in Italy a pivot around which diasporic debates concerning the sanctions turned.

As in migrant discussions about World War I, those about the league's sanctions underscored migrants' consuming and spending responsibilities vis-à-vis Italy. In response to the sanctions, Mussolini backers affiliated with the Italian-language press, and Italian chambers of commerce in both countries carried out campaigns to sustain Italian trade by encouraging migrants to buy goods from Italy.[44] While these drives were largely unsuccessful, they illustrate how the fascist state and its supporters in the United States and Argentina during the 1930s, like their liberal predecessors during World War I, sought to incorporate migrant marketplaces into transnational nation- and empire-building projects.

Unlike during World War I, when Buenos Aires' chamber of commerce ran an aggressive "buy Italian" campaign urging migrants to purchase Italian goods, during the sanctions New York's chamber instead joined its Argentine counterpart to rally migrants around Italian imports. *Il Progresso* covered with fanfare a series of radio addresses sponsored by the chamber, during which Italian *prominenti* in charge of key immigrant institutions pressured migrants to buy Italian goods.[45] The paper reported with praise a speech on the Italian radio station WOV New York by Antonio Corigliano, vice president of the Bank of Italy in New York, during which he pushed for the "defense and diffusion of Italian products in the United States."[46] Later that month, *Il Progresso* reported parts of another speech, by Vincenzo Vedovi, head of the Federation of Italian Veterans, in which Vedovi proclaimed, "Italians abroad have at their disposal a valid weapon for breaking the Geneva sanctions and for helping our Italy in this historic moment, which is the most difficult that has been seen since Italian unification was accomplished." That weapon, Vedovi insisted, was consumer choice. Italians should opt to buy all of Italy's exports, he instructed, not only food goods—the most popular Italian trade items—but other Italian products, such as hemp, raincoats, hats, and marble.[47]

Vedovi spoke specifically to women in migrant marketplaces. Echoing the paper's treatment of women during World War I campaigns, Vedovi suggested that women's purchases of Italian textiles and their domestic roles as housewives connected women of Italian descent across transatlantic spaces and generational lines:

> All of our housewives aspire to have a beautiful bed covering, whether of silk, cotton, or lace: Italy also makes these fabrics, and the difference from others is that they have great honor to have been made in a way that makes us remember a similar blanket seen one day, over a bed in a house far away, perhaps smaller, but so very special: the house where we spent the first years of our life, in the house of our beloved mother. Why shouldn't a similar blanket also adorn our house in this land where the events of life have carried us and give us a little Italian feel, the feel of our first years? With the Italian blanket that you bought, you will carry to your house an object that when you will see it, you will think of the faraway homeland, and you will have done something that gives back to the benefit to our country, during a moment in which it especially has needs.[48]

As buyers and preparers of food, migrant women also held the power to strengthen Italian commodity chains through the pressure they applied to sellers. Italians should always ask retailers for Italian goods, and "if he does not have them, when he is convinced that you want exclusively those goods, he will be obligated to procure them."[49] *Il Progresso* pressured its readers to purchase Italian imports in order to boost Italian commerce, but it also goaded readers to boycott goods from sanctioning countries like England and France. The paper guided migrants' purchases by publishing a list of countries, under the headline "Do not forget," divided into categories according to nations that adhered to the sanctions without reservations, those that adhered to the sanctions with reservations, and those that refused to adhere to the sanctions.[50] By channeling migrant consumption toward Italian merchandise, *Il Progresso* and the Italian Chamber of Commerce strove to keep migrants in line with fascist trade objectives.

Italian merchants used the sanctions, and growing nationalist sentiment more broadly, to reaffirm the Italianness of their products and to depict the purchase of food imports as acts of patriotism. An ad for Negroni-brand dried salami assured buyers that "the name NEGRONI is guaranteed to be an ITALIAN product," while food merchant Luigi Vitelli called out to buyers, "Italians! Prefer imported products from Italy."[51] Migrant entrepreneurs producing Italian-style foodstuff also saw the boycott as an opportunity to portray their products as genuinely Italian.

De Nobili and Company, the tobacco firm in Long Island City that had sent so many tipo italiano tobacco products to Italian troops during World War I, ran an ad reminding readers that for twenty-nine years the company had been "always entirely owned by Italians," even while De Nobili's tobacco products competed directly with those arriving from Italy.[52] Planter's Edible Oil Company, founded by Amedeo Obici from Venice, announced that the company's "Wings of Italy" peanut oil was the most popular cooking oil among Italian families in New York.[53] Migrants selling imported and tipo italiano foodstuff had been emphasizing the Italianità of themselves, as well as their products, employees, and consumers, since the early twentieth century; in most ways ads during the sanctions differed little from this earlier publicity in appealing to migrants as transnational consumers. However, the heightened sense of Italianità during the boycott gave makers and sellers of Italian foods an occasion to market their wares at a time when increasing numbers of migrants identified consumers in migrant marketplaces as "Italian," and when fewer goods and migrants were crossing the Atlantic.

Like their counterpart in New York, the Italian Chamber of Commerce in Buenos Aires ran a campaign in conjunction with the pro-Mussolini *Il Mattino* encouraging readers to consume Italian products and to avoid purchasing foods, beverages, and other items arriving from sanctioning countries, especially England.[54] The chamber formed a "blacklist" of British commercial houses and products and called for an "absolute boycott of all products originating from countries hostile to Italy in any way."[55] As in New York, fascist sympathizers in Buenos Aires politicized the consumption of imported foodstuff as a symbol of resistance to the league's "heinous" sanctions against Italy.[56] Supporting Italy meant not only preferring Italian imports but also rejecting and condemning imported English foods such as roast beef and whiskey. "All Italians worthy of their name," *Il Mattino* pronounced, "know very well that to drink a 'wisky' [*sic*] beyond ruining the stomach will give to England a bullet that tomorrow may strike an Italian chest." Genuine Italian patriots, the paper stated explicitly, abandoned whiskey and embraced *grappa*, a traditional alcoholic drink made from fermented grape pomace.[57] On the day the sanctions began, *Il Mattino* entreated Italians in Argentina to "consider all that emanates from Great Britain . . . whether products or traditions, merchandise or sports, poisonous alcohol or literature, the devil's excrement."[58] During the sanctions the criticism against U.S. economic and cultural hegemony in Argentina that was so prevalent in *La Patria* in the 1920s softened as migrant business authorities—particularly the pro-Mussolini supporters among them—branded England, rather than the United States, as the most malignant threat to migrant marketplaces.

Lest there be any confusion over where to shop, *Il Mattino* published lists of "Italian stores" where migrants were guaranteed to find imports from Italy. The paper assured readers that "the Italian trade in Argentina is perfectly equipped to respond to all the demands of the Italian consumer." The paper exhorted readers to "take up your role in the great Italian anti-sanctions battle by consuming exclusively Italian and Argentine products or products from non-sanctioning countries and renounce all others."[59] That the paper included Argentine as well as Italian products in their list of acceptable goods suggests that there were limits to the paper's nationalist stance; notwithstanding its patriotic appeals, the paper had to navigate its awkward position in a sanctioning country while acquiescing to the changing tastes and consumer options of Italians and their children.

As with New York's *Il Progresso*, *Il Mattino* characterized migrant consumption as a duty to the homeland, often singling out women specifically as it had during World War I. The paper described Italy's resistance to the sanctions as a transnational movement linking Italian women in the United States and Argentina. It ran articles about Italian women in Italy who were organizing to resist the boycott, and it printed Mussolini's special messages directed at Italian women during the sanctions. As migrants in various Argentine cities formed all-female "Pro Patria" groups to fund-raise for Italy, *Il Mattino* cheered them on, often sharing the amount of money or gold donated by women themselves or by the organizations and businesses they solicited for funds.[60]

Italian merchants, like their counterparts in the United States, exploited the national sentiment the boycott inspired to boost Italian trade and depict migrants' purchases as patriotic gestures. The Italian Tobacco Corporation in Buenos Aires prodded readers, "Italians! Prefer Italian products!"[61] Ads for Italian imports during the sanctions forged not only transnational links between Italians in Italy and those abroad but also imperial connections between Italians in the Americas and those in Italy's African empire. After Italy's declaration of victory over Ethiopia, an ad for Martini & Rossi announced, "Martini vermouth takes part in the jubilation of the Italian people for the victory achieved by its glorious army that, as a symbolic vessel, a messenger of strength, justice and civilization, reaches the port victorious with its sails fully unfurled."[62] Publicity for Italian imports associated Italian foodstuff and their consumers with Western imperialism and the racial assumptions it supported, inviting migrants to participate in and celebrate Italy's imperial triumphs.

In Argentina the "buy Italian" drive championed by *Il Mattino* and the Italian Chamber of Commerce inspired a vociferous defense in the anti-Mussolini *La Nuova Patria* of migrant entrepreneurs in Argentina, the tipo italiano foods they produced, and the consumers who bought them. In New York the pervasive, long-standing presence of tipo italiano foodstuff by the 1930s seems to have precluded criticism of migrant entrepreneurs in the United States by even by the most fervent pro-Mussolini apologists.[63] In Argentina, however, migrant entrepreneurs had been disadvantaged by a less industrially mature, import-dependent economy that delayed the development of the tipo italiano sector. And yet Argentine industrialization intensified after World War I, especially in the food sector, which by 1935 made up 47 percent of all domestic manufacturing.[64] The war had helped strengthen migrants' links to their homeland as Italians and as consumers of imports, but it also jump-started Argentine policies that supported a manufacturing sector producing a wider array of cheese, pasta, cigars, baked goods, and canned vegetables—many of them made by Italians.[65]

By the mid-1930s *La Patria* had moved far from the stance it had taken during World War I, when the paper commanded its readers to buy only Italian products. In response to the sanctions, *La Nuova Patria*, in its reincarnated anti-Mussolini form, printed a series of articles in 1936 under the headline "The Right to Make Italian Products Abroad" by Giuseppe Chiummiento, an anti-fascist Italian journalist and political exile.[66] In these articles Chiummiento objected to the Italian chamber's accusations that migrant makers and consumers of tipo italiano foods were unpatriotic and even traitorous. The paper framed its defense of migrant entrepreneurs within the context of Argentine economic development. In contrast to the predominantly agricultural nation of the early twentieth century, Argentina was as industrialized as the most advanced cities of Europe.[67] Chiummiento noted the "miracle of progress" in Buenos Aires over the previous twenty years, describing "the luxury of so many public places and of the accelerated pace of life."[68] Argentine industrial growth was "inevitable" and "natural" yet hastened by World War I, protectionist legislation, and Argentina's abundance of raw materials. In the early twentieth century *La Patria* had lobbied hard against high tariffs; by 1935 the paper claimed indifference to protectionism, a "product of an evolutionary process," and asserted that Argentina had the right to liberate itself from foreign imports, which it considered a form of "economic slavery."[69] Chiummiento's tone matched that of Argentine nationalists promoting industrialization and tariffs in the 1930s as a way to secure the nation's sovereignty.[70] Italians who made and consumed tipo italiano goods, the paper argued, were expressing their right to contribute to the industrial development and economic emancipation of Argentina.[71]

Just as migrants and their children had the right to employment in tipo italiano establishments, they were also entitled, as consumers, to reasonably priced food goods. "No one betrays one's country of origin: the immigrant producer, nor the one who consumes. As the descendants of the first, nor the second," Chiummiento wrote. The paper defended working-class migrant consumers against protectionist policies that put imported foods out of their reach. Who would buy imported Italian salami costing at least four times more than locally produced mortadella and prosciutto? the paper wondered. "Those who cannot buy a quarter pound of genuine parmesan cheese, because the family budget will not allow it, have at least the possibility . . . to eat spaghetti or ravioli with locally produced parmesan cheese," Chiummiento noted.[72] *La Nuova Patria* singled out for particular criticism affluent Mussolini supporters in Argentina, who could afford the more expensive Italian imports and who led the charge against poorer migrant manufacturers and consumers of Italian-style foods. These fascist supporters, while purporting to represent the Italian proletariat class, sought to prohibit working-class migrants' access to cheaper Argentine versions of Italian foodstuff and paper products.[73] While *Il Mattino* and the Italian Chamber of Commerce, like Mussolini's backers in New York, suggested that pro-Mussolini migrant supporters could commit equally to consumerism and to fascism, *La Nuova Patria* suggested that migrants' everyday consumer needs should trump fascist dictates.

Il Mattino's "buy Italian" campaign during the League of Nations' boycott pushed its readers to secure Italy's transnational trade routes by preferring Italian imports. However, in a somewhat paradoxical fashion, *Il Mattino* also advertised a number of Argentine commodities, including the tipo italiano foods that directly competed with Italian imports. During the sanctions, for example, *Il Mattino* advertised Mendoza wines as "The wines most similar to Italian wines," and "Italian-style *torroni*," a dense holiday cake made with honey, sugar, egg whites, and nuts.[74] As had migrant entrepreneurs in New York, those in Buenos Aires capitalized on the nationalism prompted by the boycott to sell their products and market them as "Italian." In 1935, Gaetano Graziosi, producer of Fox-brand prosciutto in Buenos Aires, ran an ad expressing New Year and Christmas wishes "to the Italian soldiers, to the Italian people, to its great conductor, the Duce, to the Italian colony in Argentina."[75] Despite admonishing readers to "Prefer Italian products," *Il Mattino* even used foods produced by U.S. corporations in campaigns to support Italy.[76] Starting in November 1935, the paper initiated a drive that prompted Italians in Argentina to "contribute with a material gesture of valor to the internal resistance of our people." As part of the drive, migrants purchased five- or ten-kilo packages filled with consumer goods of the "highest necessity" that had been reduced in Italy because of the sanctions and sent them to Italy. The chief items in the *pacchi tricolori* (three-color packages)—which suggested the red, white, and green Italian flag—included meat products made by the "renown North American Swift and Armour Meat Packing plants, products well known for their goodness and quality." *Il Mattino* reported that its readers had sent over six thousand packages on Italian steamships back to Italy only one month after the campaign began. After purchasing some ten tons of prosciutto for their homeland, *Il Mattino* bragged that Italian buyers had completely exhausted the annual stock of Armour and Swift meat products in Argentina.[77]

During the sanctions, *Il Mattino* characterized Armour and Swift not as U.S. American but as both Argentine and Italian, a strategy that had been employed by Armour itself starting in the 1920s, when it began targeting migrant consumers in Argentina. During the drive, *Il Mattino* pointed to the predominance of Italian migrant workers in Argentina's meat packaging plants while insisting that the packages were "composed solely of the products of the soil and of the Argentine industry, so closely connected to Italy by links of blood and labor."[78] By the late 1930s a convergence of global economic and geopolitical forces—protectionist economic policies, reorientations of trade and migration, and rising nationalisms—made possible the consumption of Swift and Armour meat products in the United States, Argentina, and Italy. If Armour joined other U.S. firms with an increasingly powerful presence in Argentina in deploying forms of U.S. imperialism in the 1920s and 1930s, the campaign also demonstrated how "on the ground" imperial exchanges could be absorbed and redeployed by locals. That Italian migrants incorporated the products of U.S. meatpacking plants into transnational campaigns to send food to Italy and to generate fascist support in migrant marketplaces suggests the "contact zone" quality of U.S. empire in Latin America defined not only by hegemony and unipolarity but also, as Gilbert Joseph writes, "of negotiation, borrowing, and exchange; and of redeployment and reversal."[79]

Furthermore, that *Il Mattino* employed Armour meat products to manufacture "links of blood" between Argentines and Italians signals not only how Italians co-opted the fruits of U.S. economic expansion to forge racial alliances in migrant marketplaces but also how the ethno-racial terrains of the United States and Argentina differentiated the way Italians generated identities based on buying and selling. Italian fascist supporters in Argentina, but not the United States, had at their disposal Latinità, which was cited during the sanctions to praise Italians' contributions to Argentine nation building, to spark pride in Italy and Italy's "civilizing mission" among Italians and their children in Argentina, and to once again justify Italian migration and trade.[80] During the League of Nations' boycott, pro-Mussolini trade promoters employed with fervor the discourse of Latinità to promote Italian-Argentine trade relations, the consumption of Italian products, and the boycott of British goods. Reminding readers of *Il Mattino* that Italy, "the great Latin Mother," "gave the world the highest and most enduring contribution to civilization throughout history," the paper regularly declared Italy's important role in civilization building worldwide but specifically in Argentina.[81] This heightened emphasis on race reflected Mussolini's preoccupation with protecting *la razza Italiana* (the Italian race) or *la stirpe* (race) at home and abroad through a variety of reproductive, imperial, and racial policies; in Latinità Mussolini saw a productive tool for building diplomatic and commercial bridges between Italy and Argentina that he hoped would serve as a transatlantic conduit for fascist propaganda.[82]

During the boycott, *Il Mattino* covered with great fanfare the arrival and activities of the Italian Commercial Mission to Argentina, sent by Mussolini to promote commercial relations between the two nations and to counteract Argentine enforcement of the sanctions. The mission was headed by fascist parliamentary member and commercial law expert S. E. Alberto Asquini and led by members of the Italian Chamber of Commerce in Buenos Aires. Asquini made much publicized visits not only to large, influential Italian firms and commercial establishments such as Cinzano, the Italian Tobacco Corporation, and Pirelli but also to major Argentine business, financial, and manufacturing institutions ranging from the Rotary Club to the Unión Industrial Argentina (UIA), Argentina's chief industrial association. In their coverage of these visits, *Il Mattino* called attention to the history of exchanges—cultural, commercial, and migratory—between Italy and Argentina that bound the two nations together. [83] The paper printed a speech by Davide Spinetto, president of the Rotary Club in Buenos Aires, who praised the Italian in Argentina as the "ideal migrant." He told members of the mission that the history of Italian migration in Argentina "created new bonds, and, with the related commercial trade that reached a remarkable figure, tightened always more the relations of cordial friendship between the two governments." The fact that Argentines and Italians were both "branches of the European civilization" and that Italians represented the most robust "graft" of that civilization in Argentine society explained the strong economic relationship between Italy and Argentina.[84] Ads for imported Italian foodstuff reinforced this message by suggesting that consumption united Italians and Argentines together in support of Italy during the sanctions. A Martini & Rossi ad in *Il Mattino* depicted a group of men and women raising glasses of vermouth with the headline "Greetings Argentina! With this exquisite vermouth let us commemorate magnificent Italy." While asking Argentines to honor Italy, the ad also toasted "the great Argentine nation." That the publicity invited Argentines and Italians to enjoy Martini & Rossi as a "symbol of brotherhood between the two powerful countries" shows that Latinità, forged over decades of migration, trade, and consumption, integrated both Argentines and Italians into campaigns to support Italy politically.[85]

The paper labored diligently to employ Latinità in various initiatives to garner the aid of Argentines, especially the sons and daughters of Italians. *Il Mattino* argued that the "legitimate relationship" between Italy and Argentina, both "Latin and Catholic" and evidenced by the some two million Italians and children of Italians in Argentina, made it "absurd" for Argentina to enforce the sanctions with vigor.[86] That Argentina joined the sanctions, even with reserve, was particularly appalling because Argentina was "a friendly nation, a sister nation, the only nation in the world through whose veins flow half-Italian blood."[87] The paper helped form the Comité Argentino Pro Italia, an Italian patriotic organization comprised of three hundred thousand second-generation Italians, and published the weekly column "La página de los hijos de italianos" (The children of Italy publication) in Spanish, aimed at cultivating their loyalty.[88] *Il Mattino* covered "Italy's Week" in mid-December 1935 to drum up wide-scale support for Italy during the sanctions, citing Latinità as justification. The paper called out in Spanish to "Italians! Argentine children of Italians! Latins!" to participate.[89] During "Italy's Week," *Il Mattino* asked all stores in downtown Buenos Aires to fly an Italian flag as proof of retailers' "faith in the fated destiny of Latin civilization, that is the Italian civilization, that is Argentine civilization." These bonds of amicable fraternity went only so far; the paper threatened violent reprisal against noncompliant Argentine-owned business owners who failed to fly the flag: "Our co-nationals take note of those stores and won't forget them. Remember the old Italian saying: 'eye for an eye, tooth for a tooth.'"[90]

The League of Nations' sanctions against Italy in the mid-1930s provoked discussion and debate in migrant marketplaces over Italy, the Italian people, and Italians abroad as global food consumers. While both pro- and anti-Mussolini leaders objected to the boycott, they presented contrasting images of Italians under fascism. New York's *Il Progresso* depicted Italy as able to meet the basic consumer and nutritional needs of its people and, paradoxically, represented Italians as prepared and committed to living an austere life. Buenos Aires' anti-Mussolini *La Nuova Patria* instead emphasized Fascist Italy's failure to feed its people while portraying Italians as deprived and hungry. Pro-Mussolini supporters in both countries pressured Italians to support Italy from afar during the sanctions by preferring Italian imports and by rejecting goods from sanctioning countries. In Argentina—a sanctioning country—*Il Mattino* softened its rhetoric against Argentine manufactures and even co-opted Argentine producers and consumers, as well as U.S. manufacturers, into their initiatives. As during World War I, migrants called on one another to consume and produce for their homeland in need, but by the late 1930s fascists faced two migrant marketplaces that had been much transformed by trade and migration and by the politics, economics, and cultures of their host countries. A close look at the Italian-language press suggests that despite intensified efforts by Fascist Italy and Italian trade promoters to nationalize migrant marketplaces and bring migrant consumption in line with fascist goals, the competition for migrant consumers was fierce; migrant entrepreneurs as well as U.S. and Argentine companies all competed for the dollars and pesos of Italians and their children in le due Americhe. In this battle over migrants' consumer loyalties, women, so visible in ads for Italian, Argentine, and U.S. foodstuff by the 1930s, exposed the limits of transnational nation and empire building through consumption.

Fascism, Gender, and Consumption: The Competition for Female Migrant Consumers

During the League of Nations' sanctions against Italy, San Pellegrino ran an ad in *Il Mattino* featuring a woman who, having partied too hard, required immediate digestive relief (see fig. 22). The ad depicted a scene from a festive costume ball; a

Figure 22. Ad for San Pellegrino sparkling water, *Il Mattino d'Italia* (Buenos Aires), February 26, 1936, 1. Courtesy of the Hemeroteca, Biblioteca Nacional de la República Argentina.

woman in the foreground adjusts her mask while behind her couples dance beneath balloons. "After the party if you ate or drank too much," the publicity instructs readers, "regulate your digestive system by drinking San Pellegrino."[91]

While the ad portrayed immoderate food and beverage consumption tying migrants to Italian imports, in Italy Mussolini condemned displays of decadence suggested in the ad and demanded that Italians, women in particular, subordinate their consumer desires to the needs of the autarkic state. Appearing in *Il Mattino*, which received financial support from Fascist Italy, the ad is particularly ironic because it shows Italian women abroad engaging in the type of overindulgent material and bodily consumption associated with the United States and Western Europe but reviled by fascists in Italy. By the 1930s the pro-Mussolini migrant press in both Argentina and the United States used female consumption to generate Italian identities; at home fascists instead attempted to separate Italian women from U.S.- and Western-style consumption. The disconnect between messages about femininity and consumption abroad and at home reveals the peculiar position female consumers held in migrant marketplaces as generators of national identities under fascism.[92]

As advertising became more omnipresent in Italian-language newspapers in New York and Buenos Aires in the late 1920s and 1930s, women took an increasingly prominent place in promotional material for a large variety of consumer items, especially industrialized foodstuff, but also nonedible products such as automobiles, clothing, and beauty products. The press's interest in mobilizing migrant women during World War I as transnational producers, savers, and spenders had launched women onto the pages of the migrant press; the war brought about a new set of regular columns, articles, and entire pages directed specifically at female readers. During the interwar years, this space devoted to women enlarged; Buenos Aires' *La Patria* ran a regular column called "Vita Femminile" (Feminine life), and by 1925 an entire women's page called "La Donna in Casa e Fuori" (The woman inside and outside the home) appeared, devoted to fashion, housekeeping, cooking, and motherhood.[93] In New York's *Il Progresso*, "Per Voi, Signore" (For you, ladies), which began as a column in the early 1920s, expanded to an entire women's page in the Sunday section by 1927, covering, like its Buenos Aires counterpart, topics related to food, fashion, and homemaking.[94] The paper also published a shortened version of "Per Voi, Signore" called "Vita Femminile"; this column, while running sporadically since the early 1920s, became a daily column by 1937.[95] This increased attention to women reflected growing literacy rates among women migrants and their daughters as well as changing gender ratios in migrant communities during the interwar years, when more women entered the country and as a more gender-balanced second generation of Italians came of age in the United States and Argentina.[96] By the mid-1920s women had gained a new visibility in Italian-language newspapers, as readers and consumers.

As discussed in chapter 4, merchants after World War I began featuring women in ads using imports to sustain and guard transnational trade routes and to reinforce the Italianità of migrant households. The migrant marketplaces of New York and Buenos Aires during the 1920s and 1930s became feminized as women, rather than men, became the main conduits for generating Italian national identities and consumer patterns around food. And yet by the mid-1920s, Argentine and U.S. companies too sought to capitalize on intensifying linkages between femininity and consumption to sell their products in the Italian-language press. Already in the early twentieth century, companies in Argentina, especially large department stores like British-owned Harrods and Gath y Chaves, ran ads in *La Patria* that marketed foodstuff, fabrics, clothing, and home furnishings specifically to women.[97] After World War I, as Argentina's manufacturing sector grew, greater numbers of Argentine food, beverage, and cigarette manufacturers, such as Piccardo company's 43-brand cigarettes and Diadema cooking oil, also gave prominence to women in ads appearing in *La Patria* and, later, *La Nuova Patria*.[98] Similarly, New York department stores, such as Alexander's, Wanamaker's, and May's, advertised their clothing and furniture to female readers of *Il Progresso*.[99] Furthermore, by the interwar years a wide variety of U.S. companies, such as Heckers flour, Armour meat products, and American Tobacco, began speaking specifically to women, with some passing their products off as "Italian."[100]

It is not surprising that for a regime that was preoccupied with masculinity, male-centered ads for Italian imports emerged in the early 1930s. In many ways these ads resembled trademarks from the late nineteenth and early twentieth centuries that portrayed manly markets of merchant explorers, warriors, and prized symbols of Italian industrial, technological, and cultural genius.[101] Fascists in the 1920s and 1930s, like nationalists in the late nineteenth century, would again resurrect the image of imperial Rome as the central vision for a "New Italy." Italy's defeat of Ethiopia actualized Francesco Crispi's late nineteenth-century failed colonial attempts in East Africa. Mussolini crafted and represented a new fascist model of masculinity grounded in aggressive virility and a strict division of gender roles.[102] However, by the 1920s, as a powerful symbol of transnational relationships between migration and trade, Italian women had indelibly shaped migrant food consumption in ways that U.S. and Argentine companies, and even pro-Mussolini businesses and migrants abroad, could not ignore. In New York's *Il Progresso* and Chicago's *L'Italia*, for example, ads for Bertolli olive oil, Buitoni pasta, Pastene coffee, and Florio Marsala all gave special prominence to women.[103] Similarly, in Argentina's *La Patria*, ads featuring women ran for Cirio canned tomatoes and sauces, Cinzano vermouth, and Sasso olive oil.[104]

The feminization of consumption became particularly visible and politicized with the rise of fascism in Italy when Mussolini attempted to strengthen Italy's relationship to migrant marketplaces in the United States and Argentina—in part by supporting the Italian-language press and Italian chambers of commerce abroad—while disassociating consumption from womanhood in Italy. Economically, the female consumer assisted Italy as the money from purchases of Italian canned tomatoes, boxed pastas, cheeses, and bottled wines fortified Italian companies and the Italian economy more generally. Politically and culturally, however, she represented a paradox. For while in New York and Buenos Aires the pro-Mussolini Italian-language press depicted the female consumer as producing Italian identities linked to Fascist Italy, Mussolini curbed female consumption at home while co-opting it to advance the interests and policies of the fascist state.

Ads for Italian foodstuff during the late 1920s and 1930s created transnational and generational ties by picturing Italian women in the United States and Argentina using the same wide variety of brand-name products that mothers and grandmothers cooked with back home. However, fascist food and trade policy demanded that women in Italy make do by feeding themselves and their families monotonous meals with little nutritional value. Carol Helstosky explains how fascists built a national cuisine based on austerity. As part of Mussolini's larger, inward-looking, autarkic aspirations, the fascist state managed the purchase, preparation, and consumption of food; limited imports; and increased wheat and cattle production. These policies, rather than providing adequately for Italy's people, led to major agricultural and industrial food shortfalls. Food shortages especially intensified during the League of Nations' boycott, forcing most Italians to do without flour, cornmeal, and other basic staples.[105] State-sponsored cookbooks, home economics literature, and magazines aimed at middle-class women promoted a diet that reflected the national imperative of feeding Italians with simple and cheap dishes; women were encouraged to prepare meals that relied heavily on carbohydrates, domestically grown produce, and very little meat and imported ingredients. This literature celebrated Italian women's thriftiness and sobriety while critiquing female consumers in the United States and Western Europe, women portrayed as immorally materialist, greedily individualistic, and insalubriously skinny.[106] Mussolini's food policies aimed at women buttressed his parallel battle against foreign beauty, body, and fashion models. As Victoria de Grazia has shown, fascists juxtaposed the Italian "authentic woman"—a wholesome, fecund, full-figured woman, eager to procreate for the state—against the image of the thin U.S. woman, the *donna crisi*, or crisis woman, who was genderless and sterile, a deprived boy-like waif subsisting mainly on cigarettes, cocktails, and canned goods.[107] Mussolini attempted to control women's identities, labor, spending habits, and reproductive choices as part of his larger aim to nationalize women as self-sacrificing mothers and wives rather than as consumers of U.S. industrialized foods, leisure, and cultural products.[108]

Ads for foodstuff in the pro-Mussolini Italian-language press abroad in some ways substantiated gendered imagery emanating from Italy. In these ads women supported transatlantic commodity chains by buying Italian products, which they used to maintain and police the Italianità of their families, themselves, and the dishes they served at the dinner table. Other times, however, publicity advanced messages about femininity and Italianità that directly contradicted fashion and food directives aimed at women in Italy. Like the woman soothing her dyspeptic stomach with San Pellegrino mineral water at a festive soirée, these ads associated Italian women with overconsumption and with bodily ideas directly at odds with the *Nuova Italiana*, the New Italian woman of Fascist Italy. In an ad for Florio Marsala in *Il Progresso* in the mid-1930s, a group of men stare open-mouthed at a modish, slender woman in lingerie. A man poses a question to the nearly nude svelte lady: "At this age how do you conserve the beautiful complexion of a young girl?" She maintains her diaphanous shape, she tells her admirers, by drinking eggnog made with Florio Marsala every morning, "which nourishes me, without making me gain weight, and keeps my body slim and my spirit awakened."[109] The ad encouraged women to purchase the Italian beverage as a device for achieving a particular form of fashion—and especially weight-conscious femininity rejected by fascists in Italy. Similarly, an ad in Buenos Aires' *Il Mattino* for Pirelli-brand shoes marketed a number of styles for women, including the "Alicia," the "Lavinia," and the "Anita," as well as others made especially for yachting. Pirelli's ads for shoes made with Pirelli rubber heels—"il taco degli Italiani" (the heels of Italians)—suggested that female identities, rather than being fixed within the confines of the Italian nation-state, or any nation-state for that matter, were forged by the changing preferences of the female migrant consumer.[110] Ads for Italian imported foods and other products depicted women buying Italian goods and using them to maintain a distinctly Italian household that revolved around women's roles as mothers, wives, and food preparers, images that complemented fascist ideals of domesticity. But they also showed women using imports to achieve identities and bodily standards in contrast to fascist dictates while drawing on ideas about consumption and femininity circulating in the United States, Argentina, and other countries with mature and burgeoning consumer societies.[111]

Furthermore, the larger culinary landscapes within which migrants and their children consumed imports differed from Italian food culture in Italy. For over three decades, migrants and their children had been experimenting with new ingredients in the United States and Argentina, integrating them into regional traditions from back home.[112] The integration of these novel foods into migrants' everyday eating patterns is visible in recipes on women's pages and columns in the Italian-language press during the 1920s and 1930s. Not only did newspapers include recipes for dishes that added new foods, especially meat and fish, into Italian regional specialties, but they also included recipes and ads for dishes and beverages associated with typical U.S. and Argentine food cultures, such as Thanksgiving Day turkeys and apple pies in the United States and empanadas and yerba mate in Argentina.[113] While ads for Italian imports portrayed Italian women in Italy and those in the United States and Argentina eating the same meals, the food practices of migrants and their children abroad—and into which Italian imports were incorporated—differed from those in Italy. Access to novel and cheap ingredients, new culinary experiences, and economic and familial imperatives differentiated migrant cuisines in the United States and Argentina from Italy and from each other. Moreover, by the late 1930s fascist food policies deprived Italians of the varied meals and of the expensive imported Italian coffee, pasta, wine, canned tomatoes, and cheeses portrayed in migrant newspapers and used to generate Italian identities.

That migrants associated women with the consumption of Italian and U.S. goods in order to generate Italian identities in Argentina must have been particularly frustrating for fascists who saw in Argentina the most promising location for strengthening economic, political, and cultural ties to Italians abroad. Mussolini and his fascist supporters both in Italy and Argentina stressed the shared racial and cultural bonds that united Argentines and Italians to encourage Argentine support for the "New Italy" and to compel migrants and their children to favor fascist policies.[114] The proliferation of U.S. consumer items in Argentina, as well as their accompanying messages about womanhood, however, challenged Mussolini's visions of Argentina as the most favorable overseas Italian "colony" for the transfer of fascist ideologies. By the 1930s fascists encountered an Italian-language press in Buenos Aires that was saturated with U.S. consumer goods. Already in the early twentieth century Argentina's increasingly consumer-oriented society began associating women, especially upper-class and middle-class women, with the nation's inchoate consumer society.[115] Once U.S. companies began marketing heavily in the Italian-language press in Argentina, women's presence in *La Patria*, and later *La Nuova Patria* and *Il Mattino*, rose exponentially. As more U.S. firms moved south to seek markets in South America, so too did the ties between femininity and consumer culture that were becoming so prevalent in U.S. print cultures. Because portrayals of U.S.-style feminization of leisure, consumption, and beauty so contrasted the ideals of the fascist *Nuova Italiana*, and because Argentina held a prominent place in the fascist imaginary, Argentina serves as a particularly unique location for exploring triangular interactions between consumption and gender amid the intense nationalism characterizing the interwar years.

By the early 1920s New York's *Il Progresso* discussed U.S. consumer goods in the context of institutions, styles of consumption, and female bodily standards that were popular in the early twentieth century United States. Articles and ads on "Per Voi, Signore" pages, especially those related to clothing and beauty products, were tied to images and discussions of college campuses, sporting events, and especially Hollywood stars. These articles connected migrant women's purchases to ideas about modernity and individuality circulating in larger U.S. society and, in particular, in women's magazines designed for middle-class white audiences.[116] By late 1920s and 1930s these links between femininity, consumption, and U.S. cultural products became increasingly prominent in Buenos Aires' *La Patria*. In the mid-1920s, for example, the newspaper began to regularly cover articles about Hollywood actresses and actors, U.S. fashion and beauty icons, and jazz music, often in a regularly published page titled "Tra cinematografi e 'films'" (Between cinema and "films").[117] Ads for U.S. goods in *La Patria* and *Il Mattino*, everything from foods to electrical appliances to beauty products, overwhelmingly portrayed women buying in ways that suggested affluent leisure patterns, progressive gender arrangements, and consumer abundance.[118] As explained in chapter 5, at times these companies treated readers as migrants by Italianizing their products. Other ads for U.S. goods in the Buenos Aires' Italian-language press—like their counterparts in New York—presented homogenous images of white middle- or upper-class lifestyles, especially in ads for U.S. automobiles, which depicted affluent women tooling around town in their cars, often unaccompanied by men.[119]

The omnipresence of U.S.-style models of womanhood and consumption in Buenos Aires' migrant marketplace made images of Italian women especially contradictory in the pro-Mussolini *Il Mattino*. While the paper ran a women's page expressly for female readers in the early 1930s, by 1935 it had removed almost all columns and material about fashion, consumption, and, in particular, Hollywood and other trappings of U.S. culture that had previously prevailed in *La Patria*. Instead, *Il Mattino* mentioned women in articles almost exclusively as they related to larger transnational fascist campaigns.[120] During the League of Nations' boycott, *Il Mattino* covered the fund-raising activities of female auxiliaries of various "Pro Patria" organizations. As with *Il Progresso* in New York, *Il Mattino* extolled migrant women during "Day of Faith" ceremonies, during which women donated wedding rings, gold jewelry, and other precious metals to the fascist cause.[121] In 1935 *Il Mattino* reprinted fascist and futurist leader Filippo Tommaso Marinetti's "ten commandments for Italian women during the Africa war." The commandments asked women "to practice a rigid discipline and severe economy" and "to live a simple and austere life."[122] A visit by Marinetti to Argentina during the sanctions served as a particularly opportune moment to urge women in Argentina toward fascist ideas of domesticity, cuisine, and consumption and away from the U.S.-inspired models. Marinetti hoped to use food to generate a more modern Italian identity under fascism, a goal concretized with the publication in 1932 of *La cucina futurista*, a culinary treatise that, quite controversially, denounced pasta for lighter, more creative dishes.[123] His travels through Argentina began with an enthusiastic reception and breakfast hosted by *El Hogar*, Argentina's most popular women's magazine.[124] In *El Hogar*'s salon, Marinetti prepared futurist dishes for the female director of the magazine along with a group of Argentine and Italian women and notable Italian businessmen. Marinetti even invented a dish in honor of the occasion: a meat roll stuffed with oranges called "Da mangiare a cavallo" (food for horse riding) and dedicated especially to gauchos, the cowboy figure once spurned by elites as barbaric and provincial but by the 1930s resurrected as a proud symbol of Argentine national identity.[125] Marinetti's visit to *El Hogar* and his fascisization of an Argentine culture figure promoted pride in fascist-inspired foodways among Italian and Argentine women while forging bonds between them.

Even while the paper encouraged values of patriotism and frugality among Italian migrant women, it continued to run ads for numerous U.S. products that linked migrant consumption to messages that were at odds with *Il Mattino*'s official treatment of women. Publicity in *Il Mattino* for Kent cigarettes, owned by the American Tobacco Company, featured four provocatively dressed, slender blonde women, one for each of the four letters making up the "Kent" brand name. The ad played on the word *bionda* (light) to describe both the hair color and complexion of the women and the bionda cigarettes sold by Kent. In what amounted to a confusing sensory and sensual overload, the ad invited readers to "conquer," "possess," and "please" themselves, the cigarettes, and the four women the cigarettes embodied by purchasing the "American cigarettes of superlative quality."[126] Similarly, an ad for Armour pasta sauce depicted a happy housewife preparing to serve her husband an enormous dish of steaming pasta. The ad tells readers that the canned sauce "requires no work, because it comes properly prepared."[127] This modern, fashionably dressed, slender housewife, released from the time-consuming burden of preparing foods from scratch by using a costly, canned meaty tomato sauce—"hot and ready to serve in only two minutes"—suggested a model of domesticity, consumption, and womanhood that fascists at home found threatening. Ads such as these for U.S. items, running in the pro-Mussolini migrant press, appeared incongruous next to articles touting the official party line. Argentina proved not to be the ideal location for building the *Nuova Italiana* of Fascist Italy. The extension of U.S. commercial influence into Argentina, and the overwhelming visibility of women in ads for all consumer goods, created expressions of womanhood and Italianità in New York and Buenos Aires that resembled each other much more than those of Fascist Italy.

In the 1930s, Italy, the United States, and Argentina all battled for the attention of the migrant consumer, especially the female migrant consumer, who after World War I became ubiquitous in ads for Italian imports and domestically produced foodstuff and other goods in Argentina and the United States. Women's overwhelming presence in ads made female migrants important vehicles for mobilizing Italians abroad in relation to imports. And yet ties between consumption and femininity in migrant marketplaces of the Americas posed a problem for Mussolini, as he was attempting to break associations between consumption and womanhood at home. Fascist Italy restricted the consumption of consumer goods—especially liqueurs, coffees, fashionable clothing, and other lavish items—and denounced U.S. forms of entertainment and leisure pursuits among women in Italy. Migrant newspapers, even those receiving financial backing from the fascist state, however, encouraged the consumption of these items and experiences among migrants. In presenting women buying imported and domestically made consumer luxuries rejected by fascists and unavailable in Italy, the female consumer in the pro-Mussolini Italian-language press was indeed a paradoxical creature.

*   *   *

Some expressions of fascism kept their ideological and organizational form as they moved from Italy to the Americas and emerged in pro-Mussolini migrant newspapers. During the League of Nations' boycott, *Il Progresso* and *Il Mattino* portrayed migrants answering fascist calls to oppose the sanctions by buying Italian imports, by spurning and even demonizing products from sanctioning countries, and by putting pressure on U.S. and Argentine politicians to maintain favorable trade policies with Italy. However, Mussolini struggled to transplant intact across the Atlantic fascist discourses about women and food consumption. Women's increasingly prominent role in ads for and discussion about imports during the 1920s and 1930s discloses the importance of female consumers in sustaining a transatlantic network of Italian trade and consumer behavior, even after the rise of fascism, when economic and political ties between Italy and the Americas became increasingly restricted and when fascists attempted to disrupt ties between women and consumption both in Italy and abroad. While rejecting images of U.S. and Western European–style consumption and beauty ideals among Italians, Mussolini helped expand these very images by supporting migrant newspapers like *Il Progresso* and *Il Mattino*. These papers employed the consumption of both Italian and non-Italian goods by migrant women to generate Italian identities. This transatlantic disconnect reveals mixed messages about womanhood, consumption, and nationhood in migrant newspapers.

During the 1930s, migrant newspapers depicted Italians in the United States, Argentina, and Italy all buying and eating Armour meat products. That ads for Armour prosciutto appeared in New York's *Il Progresso* and in Buenos Aires' *La Patria* and *Il Mattino* points to how U.S. goods increasingly linked Italian diasporas in North and South America to each other, as well as to Italy. Furthermore, pro-Mussolini Italians in Buenos Aires sent more than ten tons of Armour-brand meat on steamships to Italy at the exact period when Mussolini himself strove to make the country economically independent by limiting the importation of foreign goods and Italians' consumption of meat. Despite fascists' endeavors to monopolize migrants' interactions in migrant marketplaces, by the 1930s Italian, U.S., and Argentine companies all jockeyed, with growing success, for the attention of migrant consumers. Fascist Italy strove to turn migrants' heads with pride toward a new imperialist and economically formidable homeland; however, campaigns such as the "*pacchi tricolori*" drive reveal that Italy remained a diasporic nation as it had at the turn of the twentieth century, a nation that was dependent on support from its peoples abroad.

Epilogue

Sugary, slightly effervescent, licorice-flavored mouthwash. Both indelicate and desirable, Fernet con Coca has a taste that is difficult to describe. The cheerful sweetness of the carbonated Coca-Cola cuts the sharp bitterness of the seriously herbal fernet, producing a surprisingly balanced libation. A sip of the frothy Fernet con Coca, also known as a "Fernandito," conjures up images of Julie Andrews as Mary Poppins crooning to the impressionable Jane and Michael Banks, "Just a spoonful of sugar makes the medicine go down . . . in the most delightful way."[1] By the early 1990s Fernet con Coca had taken on the status of Argentina's national beverage and an emblem of Argentine pop culture. Ubiquitous in bars, clubs, and restaurants in cities throughout the nation, Fernet con Coca even served as the name of a 1994 music hit by the neo-folk Argentine band Vilma Palma e Vampiros.[2]

The Fernandito's standing as the national drink of Argentina, however, belies its more global origins in the country's migrant marketplaces of traveling people and trade goods in the early twentieth century. As its name implies, the drink is traditionally made from two products that were initially imported into Argentina: fernet, introduced to Argentina by migrants, and Coca-Cola, the bubbly soft drink from the United States. The beverage—with its bizarre hybrid flavor—divulges much about how the historic movements of products and people have shaped the eating and drinking habits, food cultures, and identities of migrants and nonmigrants alike.

Fernet's widespread popularity in Argentina originated in the demand for such homeland tastes by Italian migrants in Argentina starting in the early twentieth century. By this time advertisements for Fernet-Branca—which today remains the most popular brand of imported fernet in Argentina—appeared on the pages of both the Italian-language *La Patria* and the Spanish-language dailies. Ads lauded Fernet-Branca as an excellent appetite stimulant and digestive aid, perfect for calming nerves and dyspeptic stomachs. Publicity for the product resembled advertisements for other imported Italian foodstuff, such as pasta, olive oil, and canned tomatoes, in presenting the *digestivo* as a "grand Italian specialty" and celebrating migrant consumers' transatlantic cultural ties to the homeland they left behind.[3] Yet the fact that publicity for Fernet-Branca materialized in the mainstream Spanish-language press also shows the permeability of Buenos Aires' migrant marketplace as a space that brought Italian and Argentine consumers into liquor shops run by migrant merchants.[4] This same permeability was less prevalent in New York, where racial and cultural differences thwarted migrants' attempts to build shared consumer experiences with Anglo-Americans around imports like fernet.

Throughout most of the twentieth century, consumers in Argentina, like those in Italy, enjoyed fernet as a postprandial digestivo. It would not be until the 1980s, however, that fernet transformed into a symbol of *argentinidad* when it was combined with another imported beverage—Coca-Cola. Unlike fernet, Coca-Cola traveled to Argentina independent of labor migrants and their consumer preferences. During World War II the Coca-Cola Company, looking to expand its markets globally, turned to Argentina and other Latin American countries.[5] They followed the well-trodden footsteps of Armour, American Tobacco, and other U.S. companies who, during the interwar years, targeted migrant and native-born consumers in Latin America and opened manufacturing plants there. Indeed, Fernet con Coca aptly embodies the historic reorientations of trade and migration after World War I that were brought on by responses to progressively protectionist policies against mobile people, capital, and goods. Restrictive immigration legislation in the United States redirected western hemisphere–bound Italians and other migrant groups to Argentina at the same time as increasing numbers of multinational companies saw in Latin America a source of cheap labor and a burgeoning consumer market. In the 1940s the Coca-Cola Company established its first bottling plants in Buenos Aires and Córdoba, and by the 1970s the soft drink had gained widespread popularity across Argentina.[6]

Italian companies also continued their expansionist efforts in Latin America during the postwar years. Capitalizing on the robust consumer demand for the herbal digestivo fostered through decades of transnational migration, the Milan-based Fernet-Branca, founded in the mid-nineteenth century, established a distillery near Buenos Aires in 1941, making it the first branch established by Branca Brothers Distillery.[7] Branca trailed Italian companies like vermouth maker Cinzano

and the Pirelli Tire Company, both of which had established manufacturing subsidiaries in the early twentieth century. Both Fernet-Branca and Coca-Cola arrived as
Argentina embraced state-directed import substitution industrialization, a nationalist economic policy designed to decrease foreign dependency through domestic
production and high tariffs. As part of this plan, Argentina encouraged foreign investment by companies like Fernet-Branca and Coca-Cola, whose manufacturing
outlets helped industrialize the country while bolstering nationalist movements
under populist president Juan Domingo Perón.[8] These historic collisions of mobile
consumers, products, and capital marking twentieth-century globalization merged
in the 1980s, when, as the legend goes, bartenders in Córdoba first began mixing
fernet and Coca-Cola, thus igniting a national fad.[9]

Despite their humble beginnings in the migrant marketplaces of New York
and Buenos Aires, Fernet con Coca, pasta, pizza, and other foodstuff have been
mainstreamed as typical Argentine and U.S. family foods and identified with high-
end gustatory Italianità worldwide. That they did so only decades after mass Italian migration ended suggests that migrant marketplaces of mobile Italians and
foods today exist more in the imaginary and in commodified form than in the
actual, embodied movements of people and foods from Italy. While Italian migration to Argentina saw a return to prewar levels immediately after the war, by
the mid-1950s the age of Italian proletariat migration to the Americas had come
to an end.[10] Two decades of fascist rule and the ravages of World War II produced
new economic migrants from Italy, but they traveled to different places. In cities
like Toronto, Berlin, and Melbourne, Italians forged new migrant marketplaces.
As they had almost a century before in New York and Buenos Aires, Italian labor
migrants in these cities opened up trade routes in wines, pastas, cheeses, canned
tomatoes, and other homeland foods. Gender ratios in these postwar Italian diasporas gradually began to equalize, especially among transoceanic migrants to
Canada and Australia. Like their pre–World War II predecessors in New York and
Buenos Aires, the presence of wives and families transformed the way migrants
and their children shopped, ate, and identified.[11]

In the two decades following the end of the war, Italy experienced an economic
boom characterized by industrialization, job growth, and expanded welfare services and access to education, consumerism, and rising standards of living.[12] By
the late 1950s increased job opportunities in northern and central Italy during
Italy's "economic miracle" transformed international emigration into internal,
rural-to-urban and south-to-north migrations.[13] In cities such as Turin, Milan,
and Genoa, Italians from different regions met, as they had in Buenos Aires and
New York years before; they visited each other's market stalls, peered into each
other's cooking pots, and sampled each other's street foods, often in mistrust. Over
time, these sometimes fractious culinary interactions aided in nationalizing Italy's

people and a distinctive "Italian" cuisine for domestic consumption and export while solemnizing localism as the hallmark of "authentic" Italian cookery.[14]

As more and more Italians found *pane e lavoro* (bread and work) at home rather than in le due Americhe, the migrant marketplaces forged decades ago by mobile, hungry laborers became unmoored from their original geographies and social relations. In 1905 Italian American journalist and lawyer Gino C. Speranza, writing for New York's *Rivista*, had proclaimed, "For Italy, at the present moment, the most important export to the U.S. is the emigrant, infinitely more important than oil, wine, and macaroni."[15] Over a century later, as emigration slowed, and as second- and third-generation Italians moved solidly into the middle classes and out of their grandparents' tenement buildings and *conventillos*, that order of importance has been reversed.[16] Today it is generally middle-class and affluent consumers in the Americas and globally who drive the transnational trade in Italian foods associated with high culture and refined consumption: award-winning *piemontese* wines, herb-infused olive oils, San Marzano canned tomatoes, syrupy balsamic vinegars from Modena, and pungent slabs of aged *parmigiano* cheese.[17] These culinary and cultural goods are a postwar product of Italian economic success, the "discovery" of the healthful Mediterranean diet, and Italian food revolutionaries like Carlo Petrini. Petrini's slow food movement has championed, with much success, locally sourced ingredients and home-cooked meals as the antithesis of corporate factory foods and the loss of commensality, tradition, and the food diversity they represent.[18]

The mass popularity of Italian foodstuff today suggests, perhaps, that only once foods are divorced from the mass labor migrations they originally trailed, and the diasporic nations from which they left, do migrant-sending countries' foods gain elite status.[19] Slow food advocate Oscar Farinetti established the first Eataly store in Turin in 2007. This mammoth Italian food emporium, which sells Italian food specialties made by small- and medium-size artisanal producers—producers often protected by hard-to-get Italian and European Union certifications guaranteeing their products' place of origin and quality—now has locations in New York, Chicago, São Paulo, Munich, Istanbul, Dubai, Seoul, and Tokyo. It is easy to forget that in some of the cities decades ago, Italians, their foods, and the culinary traditions they brought with them were stigmatized as undesirable symbols of working-class culture.[20]

Nevertheless, imagined migrant marketplaces continue to play a critical role in the performance of ethnicity for the descendants of Italians and in the consumption of Italianità for Argentines and U.S. Americans. While some items like Fernet con Coca and pizza have been naturalized into Argentine and U.S. culinary landscapes, third- and fourth-generation Italians have sought to rediscover their roots in part by buying and cooking with imported ingredients from their great-grandparents' birthplaces. Ironically, those kinfolk may have been too poor to eat such specialties both before and after migration, relying instead on the cheaper tipo italiano substitutes.[21] Since the 1980s these now middle-class consumers of Italian heritage, as well as consumers with no family connection to Italy, have celebrated the hybrid migrant creations that emerged out of New York's and Buenos Aires' migrant marketplaces earlier in the century—classic meat, tomato, and cheese-based dishes like veal parmigiana in the United States and *milanesa napolitana* in Argentina.[22] For others, however, consuming Italian imports offers an alternative to those down-market culinary amalgamations invented by migrants, which they perceive as "not real Italian." Their cultural and economic capital lies in the knowledge they possess about imported wines, cheeses, and pastas from Italy's various regions; their ability to purchase them; and their patronage of restaurants in Buenos Aires and New York that have disassociated their fare from its modest migrant beginnings in favor of the "authentic" dishes of Italian regional cuisines.[23]

In their pursuit of true Italian eating experiences, consumers have the help of a host of first-, second-, and third-generation Italian celebrity chefs, restaurateurs, cookbook authors, and owners of upscale grocery stores, many of whom, including Mario Batali, have procured their cultural capital through tourism back to Italy. And today, as in the past, Italian food production and consumption in imagined migrant marketplaces of New York and Buenos Aires are not wholly gender-neutral. Smaller mom-and-pop Italian eateries and corporate giants like Olive Garden deliberately craft an atmosphere of ethnic domesticity, a largely feminized space where the food, décor, and music conjure up warm images of informal Sunday dinners prepared by a skillful *mamma* and where family, tradition, and nostalgia for the "old country" endure.[24] Since the 1980s, however, notwithstanding the presence of Italian female culinary personalities such as Marcella Hazan and Lidia Bastianich, the transplantation and commercialization of "authentic" regional ingredients and dishes, and their modernized cutting-edge reinterpretations, are dominated by professional male chefs, restaurateurs, and cookbook authors like Batali in New York and Donato De Santis in Buenos Aires.

Because the current passion for Italian food in the United States and Argentina emerged out of past migrant marketplaces, the Italian nation continues to capitalize on global connections between Italian people and goods, although they are detached from Italy's imperial ambitions of the early twentieth century. Back then, Italian labor migrants in le due Americhe helped create a *più grande Italia*, a nation whose emigrants pushed the geographical and cultural borders of the nation-state, building it from without by buying Italian products, sending home remittances, and returning to their home villages.[25] Italy's foods have now achieved the prestige status so desired by Italian economic and political elites on both sides of the Atlantic who desperately sought to portray Italian foodstuff as emblems of European civilization.

Today Italy and Italian food is being remade again from without, and not only by its citizens and their descendants dispersed throughout the world. Since the 1980s Italy has transformed from a migrant-sending to a migrant-receiving country.[26] Labor migrants from Eastern Europe, North Africa, and Asia, and, most recently, refugees from the Middle East, have created vibrant migrant marketplaces in small and large cities throughout Italy. Among these new arrivals are the ancestors of Italians born in Argentina, who have acquired Italian citizenship by descent and a European Union passport in the hopes of better prospects in Europe after Argentina's economic depression and currency collapse in 1998.[27] Just as homeland foods helped Italian construction workers and factory hands in New York and Buenos Aires create value in their lives as transnational people, so too have such foods for Filipino nurses in Rome, Chinese textile workers in Prato, and Tunisian street traders in Palermo today. These newcomers bring with them foods and traditions, they experiment with Italian foodways, and they introduce Italians to multinational eating experiences. Chinese restaurants run by migrants, with their Italianized versions of traditional fare and modest prices, are now commonplace in large cities and small towns throughout Italy.[28]

Migrants' visibility (and often invisibility) in the nation's food industries as agricultural workers, grocery store and restaurant owners, chefs and kitchen staff has provoked both curiosity and discomfort among Italians. Italy's multicultural eaters do not always support multicultural policies related to migration and naturalization. Migrants have been met with xenophobic and racist sentiments and calls for the restriction of immigration, residency permits, and work visas.[29] Unsurprisingly, fear of the perceived economic, political, and social menace posed by migrants finds expression in food politics. In 2004, for example, the Lega Nord, the right-wing, anti-immigrant regional party, staged a polenta protest in Como, Lombardy, during which some eighty pounds of polenta were handed out to bystanders as a defensive stance against exogenous threats to traditional regional foodways. Similarly, in 2009 the Tuscan town of Lucca banned kebabs and other foods considered non-Italian from the historic city center.[30] A century ago foods like polenta marked Italians as impoverished "others" abroad; today such foods are used in the othering of foreigners and their foods in Italy. Like they were in New York and Buenos Aires years ago, migrant marketplaces in Italy today are sites where racial differences are articulated to justify exclusion and celebrate pluralism.

Today's food fights point to the danger that lurks behind imagined migrant marketplaces detached from their embodied, material, and territorialized past. The risk lies in a historical amnesia that uncouples food commodities from the actual cross-border movements of the people who facilitate them, movements achieved against the backdrop of global, gendered, and often inequitable processes. The popularity of Fernet con Coca in Buenos Aires and pizza globally is not the simple outcome of Italian food culture's "expansion" or "spread" throughout the world. Histories of culinary globalization that rely on abstract diffusionist theories tend to divorce cuisines from the political, legal, and economic policies that allow for or discourage the mobility of food producers and consumers and to ignore the food hybridity and experimentation such mobility creates.[31] As this book argues, Italian migrants' choices and strategies drove the history of Italian food in the Americas, and they did so within large structures in Italy, Argentina, and the United States— labor demands, gendered assumptions about production and consumption, trade and migration policies, and racial hierarchies—that constrained and guided what, where, and how people ate. As in the past, today's mobile people and products, and impediments to such mobility, change the way migrants and nonmigrants eat, the identities forged by migrant eaters and inscribed upon them, and, ultimately, the larger culinary infrastructures in which they are enmeshed.

The history of Italian migration, trade, and consumption in North and South America suggests that there is much to learn about globalization and its consequences for food cultures by focusing on migrant marketplaces. The interconnections between people and products on the move that so shaped global integration in the late nineteenth and early twentieth centuries are just as important to twenty-first-century globalization, despite the reluctance of policy makers and multicultural eaters to see these connections. Several binational or multinational accords passed over the last thirty years have secured rights for products to enter and exit borders. Lower trade barriers, the foremost goal of these trade agreements, and other neoliberal economic policies aim to simultaneously promote national development and global economic integration. And they have given products (commodities, capital, services, technologies, and information) more freedom to traverse national boundaries than the people, particularly the low-wage workers, whose labor remains instrumental to the global economy. Furthermore, the planners of such accords have largely failed to anticipate or have remained indifferent to the consequences these trade partnerships have had on migration patterns as roadblocks to products, services, and capital lessen while barriers to mobile people remain unchanged.[32]

The North American Free Trade Agreement (NAFTA), passed in 1994 by the United States, Canada, and Mexico, serves as a telling example of this failure. While NAFTA generated hundreds of thousands of mainly low-paying jobs in *maquiladora* factories along the U.S.-Mexican border and in big retail stores like Wal-Mart in cities across Mexico, migration to the United States since 1994 has expanded. The opening of borders to commodities and investment made it increasingly impossible for small and medium-size Mexican farms and factories to compete, displacing large numbers of laborers hungry for work. Many Mexicans responded to economic changes brought on by NAFTA by migrating to the United States, where their labor continues to be in high demand, particularly in low-paying, seasonal agricultural work—including work in Midwestern corn fields that make possible the mass production of industrialized corn flour used in Mexican-style fast-food eateries like Taco Bell—even while obstacles to migration and U.S. citizenship have become more arduous. International Studies scholar Peter Andreas points to the challenges posed to countries like the United States and Mexico, which promote neoliberal initiatives to advance economic flows while intensifying law-enforcement policies to protect their nations from illicit movements of people and goods, especially drugs. Because neoliberal globalization itself promotes undocumented migration and illegal drugs, the state's border policing is more performative and symbolic, designed to assuage anxious citizens by projecting images of sovereignty and control, than it is an effective strategy for upholding the state's territorial rule.[33] Unable to see international trade and migration patterns as connected, or simply unmoved by NAFTA's effects on low-wage migrant laborers, its architects have all but guaranteed that migration will remain an unresolved, contentious topic in United States, Mexico, and Canada for decades to come.

European regional accords on trade and migration have raised similar debates over globalization and national sovereignty. The legal building blocks upon which the EU was established, the 1985 Schengen Agreement and the 1986 Single European Act, eliminated many of the region's internal borders to people, capital, and goods. These treaties and their amended versions, while allowing for increased mobility of products, including food and agricultural exports, have intensified both the migration incentives for non-EU labor migrants and refugees and the surveillance of the bloc's external borders.[34] The historical formation of New York's and Buenos Aires' migrant marketplaces, emerging from connections between people and commerce and obstructions to these connections, suggests that solutions depend on studying these inextricable links between migration and trade, and by recognizing both, together, as crucial value- and wealth-generating facets of globalization and nation building, whether in the nineteenth or twenty-first century.

Notes

Introduction

1. Ad for Cella's, *Il Progresso Italo-Americano* (New York), November 29, 1925 (hereafter *Il Progresso*).

2. Ad for Cella's, *Il Progresso*, December 13, 1925.

3. On the global scattering of Italy's people, see especially Donna R. Gabaccia, *Italy's Many Diasporas* (Seattle: University of Washington Press, 2000).

4. Gianfausto Rosoli, ed., *Un secolo di emigrazione italiana, 1876–1976* (Rome: Centro Studi Emigrazione, 1978), 353–55.

5. This percentage is based on trade statistics from several Italian government sources. For the years 1880–1902, see *Movimento commerciale del Regno d'Italia*, issued by the Ministero delle Finanze, Direzione Generale delle Gabelle; for the years 1903–1933, see *Annuario statistico italiano*, issued by Direzione Generale della Statistica e del Lavoro (1911–1915), issued by Ufficio Centrale di Statistica (1916–1918), issued by Direzione Generale della Statistica (1919–1921), issued by Istituto Centrale di Statistica del Regno d'Italia (1927–1943); for the years 1934–1938, see Istituto Centrale di Statistica, *Commercio di importazione e di esportazione del Regno d'Italia* (Rome: Tipografia Failli, 1939), 638, 640.

6. While historians of migration have long been aware of such cross-border processes, the pioneering work of anthropologists during the early 1990s ignited a multidisciplinary torrent of studies on transnational migration. See Nina Glick Schiller, Linda Basch, and Christina Blanc-Szanton, "Towards a Definition of Transnationalism: Introductory Remarks and Research Questions," *Annals of the New York Academy of Sciences* 645 (July 1992): ix–xiv; Nina Glick Schiller, Linda Basch, and Christina Blanc-Szanton, "From Immigrant to Transmigrant: Theorizing Transnational Migration," *Anthropological Quarterly* 68, no. 1

(1995): 48–63. Earlier work on Italian and European migration from a transnational perspective include Robert F. Foerster, *The Italian Emigration of Our Times* (Cambridge: Harvard University Press, 1919); Frank Thistlethwaite, "Migration from Europe Overseas in the Nineteenth and Twentieth Centuries," in *A Century of European Migrations, 1830–1930*, ed. Rudolph J. Vecoli and Suzanne Sinke (Urbana: University of Illinois Press, 1991), 17–57; and Ernesto Ragionieri, "Italiani all'estero ed emigrazione di lavoratori italiani: Un tema di storia del movimento operaio," *Belfagor, Rassegna di varia umanità* 17, no. 6 (1962): 640–69.

7. A short list on Italian migration to the United States and Argentina includes Virginia Yans-McLaughlin, *Family and Community: Italian Immigrants in Buffalo, 1880–1930* (Ithaca, NY: Cornell University Press, 1977); John W. Briggs, *An Italian Passage: Immigrants to Three American Cities, 1890–1930* (New Haven, CT: Yale University Press, 1978); Dino Cinel, *From Italy to San Francisco: The Immigrant Experience* (Stanford, CA: Stanford University Press, 1982); Donna R. Gabaccia, *From Sicily to Elizabeth Street: Housing and Social Change among Italian Immigrants, 1880–1930* (Albany: State University of New York Press, 1984); Donna R. Gabaccia, *Militants and Migrants: Rural Sicilians Become American Workers* (New Brunswick, NJ: Rutgers University Press 1988); Carol Lynn McKibben, *Beyond Cannery Row: Sicilian Women, Immigration, and Community in Monterey, California, 1915–99* (Urbana: University of Illinois Press, 2006); Piero Bevilacqua, Andreina De Clementi, and Emilio Franzina, eds., *Storia dell'emigrazione italiana. Partenze* (Rome: Donzelli, 2001); Piero Bevilacqua, Andreina De Clementi, and Emilio Franzina, eds., *Storia dell'emigrazione italiana. Arrivi* (Rome: Donzelli, 2002); Donna R. Gabaccia and Fraser M. Ottanelli, eds., *Italian Workers of the World: Labor Migration and the Formation of Multiethnic States* (Urbana: University of Illinois Press, 2001); Donna R. Gabaccia and Franca Iacovetta, eds., *Women, Gender, and Transnational Lives: Italian Workers of the World* (Toronto: University of Toronto Press, 2002); Fernando J. Devoto, *Historia de los italianos en la Argentina* (Buenos Aires: Editorial Biblos, 2006); Gianfausto Rosoli, ed., *Identità degli italiani in Argentina: Reti sociali, famiglia, lavoro* (Rome: Edizioni Studium, 1993); Fernando J. Devoto and Gianfausto Rosoli, eds., *L'Italia nella società argentina: Contributi sull'emigrazione italiana in Argentina* (Rome: Centro Studi Emigrazione, 1988).

8. Christiane Harzig and Dirk Hoerder, with Donna Gabaccia, *What Is Migration History?* (Cambridge, MA: Polity Press, 2009), 3.

9. On regionalism in Italy, see Carl Levy, ed., *Italian Regionalism: History, Identity, and Politics* (Oxford: Berg, 1996); John E. Zucchi, "Paesani or Italiani? Local and National Loyalties in an Italian Immigrant Community," in *The Family and Community Life of Italian Americans*, ed. Richard Juliani (New York: American-Italian Historical Association, 1983), 147–60; *Estudios Migratorios Latinoamericanos*, Special Issue: *Las cadenas migratorias italianas a la Argentina* 3, no. 8 (1988).

10. By focusing on the role of gender in organizing links between trade, migration, and consumption in New York and Buenos Aires, this book builds off of but moves well beyond Mark Choate's *Emigrant Nation: The Making of Italy Abroad*. Choate's study examines Italy's attempts to nation- and empire-build through governmental and nongovernmental programs, including Italian chambers of commerce abroad, that linked emigration and colonialism. Choate, however, is largely unconcerned with gender and with the large literature on consumer culture and food studies. He also favors a global approach rather

than the in-depth place-based comparative perspective privileged in *Migrant Marketplaces*. See Mark I. Choate, *Emigrant Nation: The Making of Italy Abroad* (Cambridge: Harvard University Press, 2008).

11. This book was in part inspired by Samuel Baily's comparative work on Italians in New York and Buenos Aires. I depart from Baily by shifting attention to identity formation and consumer practices around food exports in migrant marketplaces. Samuel L. Baily, *Immigrants in the Lands of Promise: Italians in Buenos Aires and New York City, 1870–1914* (Ithaca, NY: Cornell University Press, 1999); Gabaccia, *Italy's Many Diasporas*.

12. I follow the lead of Lok Siu, who has studied Chinese migrants in Panama within the context of both migrants' ongoing ties to their homeland and to the history of U.S. economic expansion in Panama. Lok C. D. Siu, *Memories of a Future Home: Diasporic Citizenship of Chinese in Panama* (Stanford, CA: Stanford University Press, 2005). On the integration of hemispheric and transnational approaches, see Sandhya Shukla and Heidi Tinsman, eds., *Imagining Our Americas: Toward a Transnational Frame* (Durham, NC: Duke University Press, 2007); Erika Lee, "Orientalisms in the Americas: A Hemispheric Approach to Asian American History," *Journal of Asian American Studies* 8, no. 3 (2005): 235–56.

13. Very few scholars have made connections between the historic movements of labor migrants and trade goods their central concern. Important exceptions include Kevin H. O'Rourke and Jeffrey G. Williamson, *Globalization and History: The Evolution of a Nineteenth-Century Atlantic Economy* (Cambridge: MIT Press, 1999); Donna R. Gabaccia, *Foreign Relations: American Immigration in Global Perspective* (Princeton, NJ: Princeton University Press, 2012); Alejandro Fernández, *Un "mercado étnico" en la Plata: Emigración y exportaciones españolas a la Argentina, 1880–1935* (Madrid: Consejo Superior de Investigaciones Científicas, 2004); Hasia R. Diner, *Roads Taken: The Great Jewish Migrations to the New World and the Peddlers Who Forged the Way* (New Haven, CT: Yale University Press, 2015).

14. See, for example, Patrick Manning, *Migration in World History*, 2nd ed. (New York: Routledge, 2013); Dirk Hoerder, *Cultures in Contact: World Migrations in the Second Millennium* (Durham, NC: Duke University Press, 2002); Jeffry A. Frieden, *Global Capitalism: Its Fall and Rise in the Twentieth Century* (New York: Norton, 2006).

15. A good introduction to sociological perspectives on immigrant enclaves and entrepreneurship is Alejandro Portes, ed., *The Economic Sociology of Immigration: Essays on Networks, Ethnicity, and Entrepreneurship* (New York: Russell Sage Foundation, 1995); Roger Waldinger, Howard Aldrich, and Robin Ward, *Ethnic Entrepreneurs: Immigrant Businesses in Industrial Societies* (Newbury Park, CA: Sage, 1990). More recent transnational approaches have challenged previous depictions of ethnic enclaves as closed economies by showing how migrant businesses facilitate global flows of workers, capital, and products. See Min Zhou, "Revisiting Ethnic Entrepreneurship: Convergencies, Controversies, and Conceptual Advancements," *International Migration Review* 38, no. 3 (2004): 1040–74; Alejandro Portes, Luis Eduardo Guarnizo, and William J. Haller, "Transnational Entrepreneurs: An Alternative Form of Immigration Economic Adaption," *American Sociological Review* 67, no. 2 (2002): 278–98.

16. Mary Douglass and Baron Isherwood, *The World of Goods: Towards an Anthropology of Consumption* (London: A. Lane, 1979).

17. See, for example, Yong Chen, *Chop Suey USA: The Story of Chinese Food in America* (New York: Columbia University Press, 2014); Donna R. Gabaccia, *We Are What We Eat: Ethnic Food and the Making of Americans* (Cambridge: Harvard University Press, 1998); Hasia R. Diner, *Hungering for America: Italian, Irish, and Jewish Foodways in the Age of Migration* (Cambridge: Harvard University Press, 2001); Robert Ji-Song Ku, Martin F. Manalansan IV, and Anita Mannur, eds., *Eating Asian America: A Food Studies Reader* (New York: New York University Press, 2013). Some important exceptions include Richard Wilk, *Home Cooking in the Global Village: Caribbean Food from Buccaneers to Ecotourists* (New York: Berg, 2006); Jeffrey M. Pilcher, *Planet Taco: A Global History of Mexican Food* (New York: Oxford University Press, 2012).

18. For an introduction to this literature, see Katharine M. Donato et al., "A Glass Half Full? Gender in Migration Studies," *International Migration Review* 40, no. 1 (2006): 3–26; Sarah J. Mahler and Patricia R. Pessar, "Gendered Geographies of Power: Analyzing Gender across Transnational Spaces," *Identities* 7, no. 4 (2001): 441–59; Donna Gabaccia, *From the Other Side: Women, Gender, and Immigrant Life in the U.S., 1820–1990* (Bloomington: Indiana University Press, 1994).

19. An important exception is Diane C. Vecchio, *Merchants, Midwives, and Laboring Women: Italian Migrants in Urban America* (Urbana: University of Illinois Press, 2006). See the work of Saskia Sassen for an example of how social scientists have more recently used gender and feminist perspectives to explore migrants in urban informal economies and in the wider global economy. Saskia Sassen, *Globalization and Its Discontents: Essays on the New Mobility of People and Money* (New York: New Press, 1998).

20. Leonore Davidoff and Catherine Hall, *Family Fortunes: Men and Women of the English Middle Class, 1780–1850* (Chicago: University of Chicago Press, 1987); Erika Diane Rappaport, *Shopping for Pleasure: Women in the Making of London's West End* (Princeton, NJ: Princeton University Press, 2000); Lisa Tiersten, *Marianne in the Market: Envisioning Consumer Society in Fin-de-Siècle France* (Berkeley: University of California Press, 2001); Kristin L. Hoganson, *Consumers' Imperium: The Global Production of American Domesticity, 1865–1920* (Chapel Hill: University of North Carolina Press, 2007).

21. Simone Cinotto, ed., *Making Italian America: Consumer Culture and the Production of Ethnic Identities* (New York: Fordham University Press, 2014); Nan Enstad, *Ladies of Labor, Girls of Adventure: Working Women, Popular Culture, and Labor Politics at the Turn of the Twentieth Century* (New York: Columbia University Press, 1999); Kathy Peiss, *Cheap Amusements: Working Women and Leisure in Turn-of-the-Century New York* (Philadelphia: Temple University Press, 1986); Elizabeth Ewen, *Immigrant Women in the Land of Dollars: Life and Culture on the Lower East Side, 1890–1925* (New York: Monthly Review Press, 1985); Andrew R. Heinze, *Adapting to Abundance: Jewish Immigrants, Mass Consumption, and the Search for American Identity* (New York: Columbia University Press, 1990); George J. Sanchez, *Becoming Mexican American: Ethnicity, Culture, and Identity in Chicano Los Angeles, 1900–1945* (New York: Oxford University Press, 1993); Krishnendu Ray, *The Ethnic Restaurateur* (New York: Bloomsbury Academic, 2016).

Important new work on consumption in Argentina has focused almost exclusively on the post–World War II years and pays little attention to migration. See Eduardo Elena, *Dignifying Argentina: Peronism, Citizenship, and Mass Consumption* (Pittsburgh: University of

Pittsburgh Press, 2011); Natalia Milanesio, *Workers Go Shopping in Argentina: The Rise of Popular Consumer Culture* (Albuquerque: University of New Mexico Press, 2013); Rebekah E. Pite, *Creating a Common Table in Twentieth-Century Argentina: Doña Petrona, Women, and Food* (Chapel Hill: University of North Carolina Press, 2013).

22. Victoria de Grazia, with Ellen Furlough, eds., *The Sex of Things: Gender and Consumption in Historical Perspective* (Berkeley: University of California Press, 1996).

23. "L'emigrazione transoceanica, le correnti commerciali, e i servizi marittimi," *Bollettino dell'emigrazione* 11 (1904): 109.

24. On the heuristic quality of food, readers might begin with foundational texts in food studies by cultural theorists in anthropology, sociology, geography, and semiotics. See Roland Barthes, "Toward a Psychosociology of Contemporary Food Consumption," in *Food and Culture: A Reader*, 3rd ed., eds. Carole Counihan and Penny Van Esterik (New York: Routledge, 2013), 23–30; Pierre Bourdieu, *Distinction: A Social Critique of the Judgment of Taste*, trans. Richard Nice (Cambridge: Harvard University Press, 1984); Claude Lévi-Strauss, "The Culinary Triangle," in Counihan and Van Esterik, *Food and Culture*, 40–47; Jack Goody, *Cooking, Cuisine, and Class: A Study in Comparative Sociology* (Cambridge: Cambridge University Press, 1982); Mary Douglas, "Deciphering a Meal," *Daedalus* 101, no. 1 (1971): 61–81.

While not about food specifically, *The Social Life of Things* offers a productive reflection on the cultural and symbolic value of commodities, reminding us that the value of food extends beyond the sum of labor required to produce it, and that commodity exchange involving food is not neutral but rather embedded in particular social relations and cultural contexts. Arjun Appadurai, *The Social Life of Things: Commodities in Cultural Perspective* (Cambridge: Cambridge University Press, 1988).

25. Simone Cinotto, *The Italian American Table: Food, Family, and Community in New York City* (Urbana: University of Illinois Press, 2013); Simone Cinotto, *Soft Soil, Black Grapes: The Birth of Italian Winemaking in California*, trans. Michelle Tarnopoloski (New York: New York University Press, 2012); Diner, *Hungering for America*; Gabaccia, *We Are What We Eat*; Vito Teti, "Emigrazione, alimentazione, culture popolari," in *Storia dell'emigrazione Italiana. Partenze*, ed. Piero Bevilacqua, Andreina De Clementi, and Emilio Franzina (Rome: Donzelli Editore, 2001), 575–600. On Italians' changing food habits in the United States and Argentina, see also Tracy N. Poe, "The Labour and Leisure of Food Production as a Mode of Ethnic Identity Building among Italians in Chicago, 1890–1940," *Rethinking History* 5, no. 1 (2001): 131–48; Paola Corti, "Emigrazione e consuetudini alimentari. L'esperienza di una catena migratoria," in *Storia d'Italia*, Annali 13. *L'alimentazione nella storia dell'Italia contemporanea*, ed. Alberto Capatti, Albero De Bernardi, and Angelo Varni (Turin: Einaudi, 1998), 683–719.

26. Peter H. Smith, *Politics and Beef in Argentina: Patterns of Conflict and Change* (New York: Columbia University Press, 1969); Roger Horowitz, *Putting Meat on the American Table: Taste, Technology, Transformation* (Baltimore: Johns Hopkins University Press, 2006); Jimmy M. Skaggs, *Prime Cut: Livestock Raising and Meatpacking in the United States, 1607–1983* (College Station: Texas A&M University Press, 1986).

27. On gendered food practices among Italians and other migrant groups, see Cinotto, *Italian American Table*, 47–71; Suzanne M. Sinke, *Dutch Immigrant Women in the United States,*

1880–1920 (Urbana: University of Illinois Press, 2002), 64–95; Valerie J. Matsumoto, "Apple Pie and *Makizushi*: Japanese American Women Sustaining Family and Community," in *Eating Asian America: A Food Studies Reader*, ed. Robert Ji-Song Ku, Martin F. Manalansan IV, and Anita Mannur (New York: New York University Press, 2013), 255–73; Sonia Cancian, "'Tutti a Tavola!' Feeding the Family in Two Generations of Italian Immigrant Households in Montreal," in *Edible Histories, Cultural Politics: Towards a Canadian Food History*, ed. Franca Iacovetta, Valerie J. Korinek, and Marlene Epp (Toronto: University of Toronto Press, 2012), 209–21; Meredith E. Abarca, *Voices in the Kitchen: Views of Food and the World from Working-Class Mexican and Mexican American Women* (College Station: Texas A&M University Press, 2006).

28. Rudolph J. Vecoli, "The Immigrant Press and the Construction of Social Reality, 1850–1920," in *Print Culture in a Diverse America*, ed. James P. Danky and Wayne A. Wiegand (Urbana: University of Illinois Press, 1998), 17–33.

29. On the Italian-language press in the United States, see Peter G. Vellon, *A Great Conspiracy against Our Race: Italian Immigrant Newspapers and the Construction of Whiteness in the Early 20th Century* (New York: New York University Press, 2014); Nancy C. Carnevale, *A New Language, A New World: Italian Immigrants in the United States, 1890–1945* (Urbana: University of Illinois Press, 2009); George E. Pozzetta, "The Italian Immigrant Press of New York City: The Early Years, 1880–1915," *Journal of Ethnic Studies* 1 (Fall 1973): 32–46; Philip V. Cannistraro, "Generoso Pope and the Rise of Italian-American Politics, 1925–1936," in *Italian Americans: New Perspectives in Italian Immigration and Ethnicity*, ed. Lydio F. Tomasi (Staten Island: Center for Migration Studies of New York Inc., 1985), 265–88. On Argentina, see Ronald C. Newton, "Ducini, Prominenti, Antifascisti: Italian Fascism and the Italo-Argentine Collectivity, 1922–1945," *Americas* 51, no. 1 (1994): 41–66; Mirta Zaida Lobato, "*La Patria degli Italiani* and Social Conflict in Early Twentieth-Century Argentina," trans. Amy Ferlazzo, in *Italian Workers of the World: Labor Migration and the Formation of Multiethnic States*, ed. Donna R. Gabaccia and Fraser M. Ottanelli (Urbana: University of Illinois Press, 2001), 63–78. For this book, I look exclusively at the mainstream commercial press. Italian-language print culture was also a key voice for anarchists, socialists, syndicalists, and radicals. This study does not include a consideration of the *sovversivi*, or leftist, press because as anticapitalist outlets, these newspapers less frequently discussed the experiences of Italian migrants as consumers.

30. In 1908 *Bollettino Mensile* became *Bollettino Ufficiale Mensile*. For an overview of Italian chambers of commerce abroad, see Giovanni Luigi Fontana and Emilio Franzina, eds., *Profili di Camere di commercio italiane all'estero*, vol. 1 (Soveria Mannelli, Italy: Rubbettino Editore, 2001); and Giulio Sapelli, ed., *Tra identità culturale e sviluppo di reti. Storia delle Camere di commercio italiane all'estero* (Soveria Mannelli, Italy: Rubbettino Editore, 2000).

Chapter 1. Manly Markets in *le due Americhe*, 1880–1914

1. *Dall'Italia all'Argentina: Guida practica per gli italiani che si recano nell'Argentina* (Genoa: Libreria R. Istituto Sordo-Muti, 1888), 119.

2. Luigi Tonissi, "Progetto per un banco del commercio italo-americano," in *L'esplorazione commerciale e L'esploratore* (Milan: Premiato stabilimento tipografico P. B. Bellini, 1896),

386. For migration, see Dirección General de Inmigración, *Resumen estadistico del movimiento migratorio en la Republica Argentina, años 1857–1924* (Buenos Aires: Talleres Gráficos del Ministerio de Agricultura de la Nación, 1925), 5.

3. Luigi Einaudi, *Un principe mercante: Studio sulla espansione coloniale italiana* (Turin: Fratelli Bocca, 1900), 86–87.

4. Ibid., 127–38.

5. Mark Choate skillfully describes these debates between nationalists and liberals over Italy's "emigrant colonialism." Mark I. Choate, *Emigrant Nation: The Making of Italy Abroad* (Cambridge: Harvard University Press, 2008), 21–56.

6. Einaudi, *Un principe mercante,* 23.

7. On the 1901 emigration law, see Choate, *Emigrant Nation,* 59–62; Mark I. Choate, "Sending States' Transnational Interventions in Politics, Culture, and Economics: The Historical Example of Italy," *International Migration Review* 41, no. 3 (2007): 728–68; Caroline Douki, "The Liberal Italian State and Mass Emigration, 1860–1914," in *Citizenship and Those Who Leave: The Politics of Emigration and Expatriation,* ed. Nancy L. Green and François Weil (Urbana: University of Illinois Press, 2007), 91–113.

8. Frank J. Coppa, *Planning, Protectionism, and Politics in Liberal Italy: Economics and Politics in the Giolittian Age* (Washington, DC: Catholic University of America Press, 1971); Alexander De Grand, *The Hunchback's Tailor: Giovanni Giolitti and Liberal Italy from the Challenge of Mass Politics to the Rise of Fascism, 1882–1922* (Westport, CT: Praeger, 2001).

9. On the Emigration Commissariat and the *Bollettino dell'emigrazione,* see Choate, *Emigrant Nation,* 59–62; 75; Douki, "Liberal Italian State," 91–113.

10. "L'emigrazione transoceanica, le correnti commerciali, e i servizi marittimi," *Bollettino dell'emigrazione* (hereafter *Bollettino*) 11 (1904): 107, 109.

11. Giovanni Luigi Fontana and Emilio Franzina, eds., *Profili di Camere di commercio italiane all'estero,* vol. 1 (Soveria Mannelli, Italy: Rubbettino Editore, 2001), and Giulio Sapelli, *Tra identità culturale e sviluppo di reti. Storia delle Camere di commercio italiane all'estero* (Soveria Mannelli, Italy: Rubbettino Editore, 2000) are two recent edited collections arguing for the centrality of Italian chambers of commerce abroad to the history of Italian global expansion.

12. Choate, *Emigrant Nation,* 82–89.

13. Guglielmo Godio, *L'America ne' suoi primi fattori: La colonizzazione e l'emigrazione* (Florence: Tipografia di G. Barbèra, 1893), 11, 17–18.

14. Ibid., 140.

15. Aldo Visconti, *Emigrazione ed esportazione: Studio dei rapporti che intercedono fra l'emigrazione e le esportazioni italiane per gli Stati Uniti del Nord America e per la Repubblica Argentina* (Turin: Tipografia Baravalle e Falconieri, 1912), 25.

16. Luigi Fontana-Russo, "Emigrazione d'uomini ed esportazione di merci," *Rivista coloniale* (1906), 30.

17. Torsten Feys, *The Battle for the Migrants: The Introduction of Steamshipping on the North Atlantic and Its Impact on the European Exodus* (St. John's, Nfld: International Maritime Economic History Association, 2013); Drew Keeling, *The Business of Transatlantic Migration between Europe and the United States, 1900–1914* (Zurich: Chronos, 2012).

18. Kevin H. O'Rourke and Jeffrey G. Williamson, *Globalization and History: The Evolution of a Nineteenth-Century Atlantic Economy* (Cambridge: MIT Press, 1999), 145–66; Dirk Hoerder, ed., *Labor Migration in the Atlantic Economies: The European and North American Working Classes during the Period of Industrialization* (Westport, CT: Greenwood Press, 1985).

19. "L'emigrazione transoceanica," 109.

20. Ministero delle Finanze, *Movimento commerciale del Regno d'Italia nell'anno 1907*, vol. 2 (Rome: Stabilimento tipografico G. Civelli, 1909), xxxi.

21. Vera Zamagni, *The Economic History of Italy, 1860–1990* (Oxford: Oxford University Press, 1993), 35. On the history of industrial food production in Italy, see Silvano Serventi and Françoise Sabban, *Pasta: The Story of a Universal Food* (New York: Columbia University Press, 2002); Francesco Chiapparino, "Industrialization and Food Consumption in United Italy," in *Food Technology, Science and Marketing: European Diet in the Twentieth Century*, ed. Adel P. den Hartog (East Linton, Scotland: Tuckwell Press, 1995), 139–55; David Gentilcore, *Pomodoro!: A History of the Tomato in Italy* (New York: Columbia University Press, 2010), 109–115, 136–42; Giorgio Pedrocco, "La conservazione del cibo: Dal sale all'industria agro-alimentare," in *Storia d'Italia, Annali 13, L'alimentazione*, ed. Alberto Capatti, Albero De Bernardi, and Angelo Varni (Turin: Einaudi, 1998), 419–52.

22. On Italian chambers of commerce in Argentina and the United States, see Fernando J. Devoto, *Historia de los italianos en la Argentina* (Buenos Aires: Editorial Biblos, 2006), 218–31; Mil Vassanelli, "La Camera di commercio italiana di San Francisco," in *Profili di Camere di commercio italiane all'estero*, vol. 1, ed. Giovanni Luigi Fontana and Emilio Franzina (Soveria Mannelli, Italy: Rubbettino Editore, 2001), 123–48; Sergio Bugiardini, "La Camera di commercio italiani di New York," in *Profili di Camera di commercio italiane all'estero*, vol. 1, ed. Giovanni Luigi Fontana and Emilio Franzina (Soveria Manelli, Italy: Rubbettino Editore, 2001), 105–121.

23. Guido Rossati, "La vendemmia in Italia ed il commercio dei vini italiani cogli S.U. nel 1905," *Rivista Commerciale* (New York) (hereafter *Rivista*), December 1905, 43.

24. Fontana-Russo, "Emigrazione d'uomini ed esportazione di merci," 26.

25. Italian American Directory Co., *Gli italiani negli Stati Uniti d'America* (New York: Andrew H. Kellogg Co., 1906), 158.

26. See, for example, Visconti, *Emigrazione ed esportazione*, 32, 48, 52; and "L'emigrazione transoceanica," 107.

27. Amy A. Bernardy, "L'etnografia della 'piccole italie,'" in *Atti del primo congresso di etnografia italiana*, ed. Società di Etnografia Italiana (Perugia, Italy: Unione Tipografica Cooperativa, 1912), 175. On Bernardy, see Amy Allemand Bernardy and Maddalena Tirabassi, *Ripensare la patria grande: Gli scritti di Amy Allemand Bernardy sulle migrazioni italiane* (Isernia, Italy: C. Iannone, 2005).

28. Fontana-Russo, "Emigrazione d'uomini ed esportazione di merci," 30.

29. Visconti, *Emigrazione ed esportazione*, 5.

30. Godio, *L'America ne' suoi primi fattori*, 122.

31. "Statistica degli emigranti curati durante l'anno 1906 nelle inferie di bordo ed appunti sul servizio dell'emigrazione," *Bollettino* 2 (1908): 182.

32. *L'Italia nell' America Latina: Per l'incremento dei rapporti industriali e commerciali fra l'Italia e l'America del Sud* (Milan: Società Tipografica Editrice Popolare, 1906), viii. On the im-

proved diets of peasants in Calabria due to migration, see Piero Bevilacqua, "Emigrazione transoceanica e mutamenti dell'alimentazione contadina calabrese fra Otto e Novecento," *Quaderni storici* 47 (August 1981): 520–55.

33. Cesare Jarach, *Inchiesta parlamentare sulle condizioni dei contadini nelle provincie meridionali e nella Sicilia*, vol. 2, *Abruzzi e Molise*, Tomo I (Rome: Tipografia nazionale di Giovanni Bertero e C., 1909), 264; Oreste Bordiga, *Inchiesta parlamentare sulle condizioni dei contadini nelle provincie meridionali e nella Sicilia*, vol. 4, *Campania*, Tomo I (Rome: Tipografia nazionale di Giovanni Bertero e C., 1909), 612.

34. Adolfo Rossi, "Vantaggi e danni dell'emigrazione nel mezzogiorno d'Italia," *Bollettino* 13 (1908): 6.

35. Giovanni Lorenzoni, *Inchiesta parlamentare sulle condizione dei contadini nelle provincie meridionali e nella Sicilia*, vol. 6, *Sicilia*, Tomo I (Rome: Tipografia nazionale di Giovanni Bertero e C., 1910), 705–706.

36. Fontana-Russo, "Emigrazione d'uomini ed esportazione di merci," 40.

37. On the development of Italy's consumer society, see Emanuela Scarpellini, *Material Nation: A Consumer's History of Modern Italy*, trans. Daphne Hughes and Andrew Newton (New York: Oxford University Press, 2011).

38. Einaudi, *Un principe mercante*, 10.

39. Visconti, *Emigrazione ed esportazione*, 5.

40. "Relazione sulla convenienza morale finanziaria che le camere all'estero accentrino ogni manifestazione economica, sia ufficiale che non ufficiale," *Rivista*, November 1911, 6.

41. Camera di Commercio Italiana in New York, *Nel cinquantenario della Camera di Commercio Italiana in New York, 1887–1937* (New York, 1937), 65.

42. I deliberately use the terms "U.S. American" rather than "American," and "United States" rather than "America," throughout the book to acknowledge that "America" and "American" are contested designations among scholars of the western hemisphere. In this I follow Mary Renda's lead in her work on the U.S. occupation of Haiti to remind readers of the hegemonic and imperialist assumptions underpinning the term "America" and "American." In the sources explored for this study, Italians in Argentina sometimes described Argentines and themselves as "American" as do some Argentines and Latin Americans today. See Mary A. Renda, *Taking Haiti: Military Occupation and the Culture of U.S. Imperialism, 1915–1940* (Chapel Hill: University of North Carolina Press, 2001), xvii.

43. On Candiani, see *L'Italia nell' America Latina: Per l'incremento dei rapporti industriali e commerciali fra l'Italia e l'America del Sud* (Milan: Società Tipografica Editrice Popolare, 1906), 131–34.

44. On "Italia," see Stephen Gundle, *Bellissima: Feminine Beauty and the Idea of Italy* (New Haven, CT: Yale University Press, 2007), 19–20, 28–29.

45. Einaudi, *Un principe mercante*, 23.

46. The government passed the first law regulating and protecting trademarks in 1868 and revised them in 1913. Leggi 30 agosto, 1868, n. 4577; Leggi 20 marzo 1913, n. 526. Applications for trademark registration were required to include reproductions of the actual trademark, a detailed description of the trademark's distinctive qualities (colors, form, language, etc.), and an indication of the intended mode of application.

47. Gian Paolo Ceserani, *Storia della pubblicità in Italia* (Rome: Laterza, 1988), 28, 32. In the late nineteenth century, before advertising emerged as a specialized field, business owners themselves maintained a considerable amount of control over the creation and content of their publicity. See also Pamela Walker Laird, *Advertising Progress: American Business and the Rise of Consumer Marketing* (Baltimore: Johns Hopkins University Press, 1998), 38–44.

48. Serventi and Sabban, *Pasta*, 159.

49. Trademark for Giacomo Costa Dante-brand olive oil, Archivio Centrale dello Stato, Ministero dell'Industria, del Commercio e dell'Artigianato, Ufficio Italiano Brevetti e Marchi (hereafter ACS, UIBM), fasc. 8415, 1907. For another example, see trademark for G. B. Martino Dante-brand olive oil, ACS, UIBM, fasc. 8618, 1908.

50. For trademarks featuring Mercury, see Luigi Parpaglioni olive oil, ACS, UIBM, fasc. 4964, 1901; Amoruso & Co. olive oil, ACS, UIBM, fasc. 4906, 1901; Franco & Lamb, Carroni "Cotone Mercurio" fabrics, ACS, UIBM, fasc. 8487, 1907.

51. Alfonso Scirocco, *Garibaldi: Citizen of the World*, trans. Allan Cameron (Princeton, NJ: Princeton University Press, 2007), 99–103, 122–37; Lucy Riall, *Garibaldi: Invention of a Hero* (New Haven, CT: Yale University Press, 2007), 41–56.

52. See, for example, trademark for Fratelli Branca e C. Fernet-Branca, ACS, UIMB, fasc. 3946, 1898.

53. Edoardo Pantano, "Conclusione," *Bollettino* 11 (1904): 119.

54. "Parte prima. Condizioni presenti dell'emigrazione italiana," *Bollettino* 11 (1904): 13.

55. *L'Italia nell'America Latina*, 37–43.

56. On Luigi Amedeo and his expedition, see Luigi Amedeo and Umberto Cagni, *On the Polar Star in the Arctic Sea*, trans. William Le Queux (London: Hutchinson & Co., 1903).

57. Trademark for Fratelli Branca e C. Fernet-Branca, ACS, UIMB, fasc. 5636, 1902.

58. On Latin American independence movements, see Jeremy Adelman, *Sovereignty and Revolution in the Iberian Atlantic* (Princeton, NJ: Princeton University Press, 2006); Jay Kinsbruner, *Independence in Spanish America: Civil Wars, Revolutions, and Underdevelopment*, 2nd rev. (Albuquerque: University of New Mexico Press, 2000).

59. The *fasce*—a bundle of sticks joined with an axe blade—was a symbol of republicanism during the Roman Republic, and of peasant cooperatives and working-class solidarity during the nineteenth and twentieth centuries. In the 1920s the Italian Fascist Party exploited the fasce as its chief symbol. Simonetta Falasca-Zamponi, *Fascist Spectacle: The Aesthetics of Power in Mussolini's Italy* (Berkeley: University of California Press, 1997), 95–99.

60. New technologies in printing, transportation, and distribution methods, as well as changes in business organization and culture, helped universalize progress discourse in advertising material. Laird, *Advertising Progress*, 101–151; Jackson Lears, *Fables of Abundance: A Cultural History of Advertising in America* (New York: Basic Books, 1994), 102–133.

61. On world expositions, see, for example, Peter H. Hoffenberg, *An Empire on Display: English, Indian, and Australian Exhibitions from the Crystal Palace to the Great War* (Berkeley: University of California Press, 2001); Robert W. Rydell, *All the World's a Fair: Visions of Empire at American International Expositions, 1876–1916* (Chicago: University of Chicago Press, 1984); Robert W. Rydell, *World of Fairs: The Century-of-Progress Expositions* (Chicago: University of Chicago Press, 1993).

62. Choate, *Emigrant Nation*, 87, 104–105; Einaudi, *Un principe mercante*, 3, 10.

63. "Esposizione internazionale di Torino 1911," *Bollettino Ufficiale Mensile della Camera Italiana di Commercio in Buenos Aires* (Buenos Aires, Argentina) (hereafter *Bollettino Mensile*), December 1910, 11.

64. Donna Gabaccia, "In the Shadows of the Periphery: Italian Women in the Nineteenth Century," in *Connecting Spheres: Women in the Western World, 1500 to Present*, ed. Marilyn J. Boxer and Jean H. Quataert (New York: Oxford University Press, 1987), 166–76.

65. Lears, *Fables of Abundance*, 17–39; Gundle, *Bellissima*, 48–54.

66. For examples of women as agricultural workers, see trademarks for V. del Gaizo tomato extract, ACS, UIBM, fasc. 6982, 1905; Muratorio & Martino olive oil, ACS, UIBM, fasc. 2904, 1895; Modesto Gallone butter, ACS, UIBM, fasc. 2932, 1894. Trademark for Poirè & Balletto "la Perfetta" pasta, ACS, UIBM, fasc. 8437, 1907.

67. Choate, *Emigrant Nation*, 50–51.

68. *L'Italia nell'America Latina*, 235–38.

69. Trademark for Raffaello & Pietro Fortuna olive oil, ACS, UIBM, fasc. 8384, 1907. For an overview of the history and historiography of the Risorgimento, see Lucy Riall, *Risorgimento: The History of Italy from Napoleon to Nation-state* (New York: Palgrave Macmillan, 2009).

70. *L'Italia nell'America Latina*, xxxi.

71. Einaudi, *Un principe mercante*, 7, 14, 16–18.

72. Visconti, *Emigrazione ed esportazione*, 7, 40.

73. "Assemblea Ordinaria del 15 Luglio 1900," *Bollettino Mensile*, August 1900, 2.

74. Richard J. Bosworth, *Italy, the Least of the Great Powers: Italian Foreign Policy before the First World War* (New York: Cambridge University Press, 1979), 1–38.

75. Ibid.

76. As part of the 1901 emigration law, the Italian state contracted the Bank of Naples to establish branches abroad and to transmit economic remittances from the Americas back to Italy at low costs. On remittances and the Bank of Naples, see Francesco Balletta, *Il Banco di Napoli e le rimesse degli emigrati (1914–1925)* (Naples: ISTOB, 1972); Dino Cinel, *National Integration of Italian Return Migration, 1870–1929* (New York: Cambridge University Press, 1991), 122–49.

77. Zamagni, *Economic History of Italy*, 38.

78. Loretta Baldassar and Donna R. Gabaccia, "Home, Family, and the Italian Nation in a Mobile World: The Domestic and the National among Italy's Migrants," in *Intimacy and Italian Migration: Gender and Domestic Lives in a Mobile World*, ed. Loretta Baldassar and Donna R. Gabaccia (New York: Fordham University Press, 2011), 21; Bosworth, *Italy, the Least of the Great Powers*, 6–7.

79. Lorenzoni, *Inchiesta parlamentare*, 514.

80. Linda Reeder, *Widows in White: Migration and the Transformation of Rural Italian Women, Sicily, 1880–1920* (Toronto: University of Toronto Press, 2003), 56.

81. Victoria de Grazia, with Ellen Furlough, eds., *The Sex of Things: Gender and Consumption in Historical Perspective* (Berkeley: University of California Press, 1996); Leonore Davidoff and Catherine Hall, *Family Fortunes: Men and Women of the English Middle Class, 1780–1850* (Chicago: University of Chicago Press, 1987); Erika D. Rappaport, *Shopping for Pleasure:*

Women in the Making of London's West End (Princeton, NJ: Princeton University Press, 2000); Lisa Tiersten, *Marianne in the Market: Envisioning Consumer Society in Fin-de-Siècle France* (Berkeley: University of California Press, 2001).

82. Scarpellini, *Material Nation*, 67–80.

83. Walter F. Willcox and Imre Ferenczi, *International Migrations*, vol. 1 (New York: Gordon and Breach Science Publishers, 1969), 820–21, 835.

84. Samuel L. Baily, *Immigrants in the Lands of Promise: Italians in Buenos Aires and New York City, 1870–1914* (Ithaca, NY: Cornell University Press, 1999), 64.

85. On family economies in late-nineteenth and early-twentieth century Italy, see especially David I. Kertzer, *Family Life in Central Italy, 1880–1910: Sharecropping, Wage Labor, and Coresidence* (New Brunswick, NJ: Rutgers University Press, 1984); Jane Schneider and Peter Schneider, *Culture and Political Economy in Western Sicily* (New York: Academic Press, 1976). On late nineteenth-century living conditions in rural Italy, see the Italian government's voluminous parliamentary inquest *Atti della giunta per la inchiesta agraria e sulle condizioni della classe agricola*, 15 vols. (Rome: Forzani e C., 1881–1886).

86. Gabaccia, "In the Shadows of the Periphery," 166–76.

87. Lorenzoni, *Inchiesta parlamentare*, 469–70; Ernesto Marenghi, *Inchiesta parlamentare sulle condizioni dei contadini nelle provincie meridionali e nella Sicilia*, vol. 5. Basilicata e Calabrie, Tomo II Calabrie (Rome: Tipografia nazionale di Giovanni Bertero e C., 1909), 592–602.

88. On the use of remittances by Italian migrants and returnees, see Cinel, *National Integration of Italian Return Migration*, 122–176.

89. Hasia R. Diner, *Hungering for America: Italian, Irish, and Jewish Foodways in the Age of Migration* (Cambridge: Harvard University Press, 2001), 61–77; Simone Cinotto, *The Italian American Table: Food, Family, and Community in New York City* (Urbana: University of Illinois Press, 2013); Donna R. Gabaccia and Jeffrey M. Pilcher, "'Chili Queens' and Checkered Tablecloths: Public Dining Cultures of Italians in New York City and Mexicans in San Antonio, Texas, 1870s–1940s," *Radical History Review* 110 (Spring 2011): 109–126; Vito Teti, "Emigrazione, alimentazione, culture popolari," in *Storia dell'emigrazione Italiana. Partenze*, ed. Piero Bevilacqua, Andreina De Clementi, and Emilio Franzina (Rome: Donzelli Editore, 2001), 575–600.

90. Samuel L. Baily and Franco Ramella, eds., *One Family, Two Worlds: An Italian Family's Correspondence across the Atlantic, 1901–1922*, trans. John Lenaghan (New Brunswick, NJ: Rutgers University Press, 1988), 44–45.

91. Reeder, *Widows in White*, 142–67. On Italian women in transnational family economies, see especially Donna R. Gabaccia, "When the Migrants Are Men: Italy's Women and Transnationalism as a Working-Class Way of Life," in *American Dreaming, Global Realities: Rethinking U.S. Immigration History*, ed. Donna R. Gabaccia and Vicki L. Ruiz (Urbana: University of Illinois Press, 2006), 190–206.

92. Jarach, *Inchiesta parlamentare*, 258. Italian migrants in the Americas or those who returned from the Americas to Italy were often called *americani* by locals.

93. Jarach, *Inchiesta parlamentare*, 159; quoted in Gabaccia, "When the Migrants Are Men," 199.

94. Bordiga, *Inchiesta parlamentare*, 612–13.

95. On women's role in fostering consumption in Italy, see Reeder, *Widows in White*, 142–67.

96. Historians have rejected simplified and homogenized depictions of the Italian south as economically, politically, and culturally backward, instead arguing for the existence of an emerging commercial economy alongside the continuation of subsistence agriculture. While economically the south lagged behind the north, capitalist and commodity markets touched Southern Europe and the South of Italy. John Davis, "Changing Perspectives on Italy's 'Southern Problem,'" in *Italian Regionalism: History, Identity, and Politics*, ed. Carl Levy (Oxford: Berg, 1996), 53–68; Robert Lumley and Jonathan Morris, *The New History of the Italian South: The Mezzogiorno Revisited* (Exeter: University of Exeter Press, 1997). On Italy's incipient consumer society, see Scarpellini, *Material Nation*, 3–80; Reeder, *Widows in White*, 223–31.

97. Quoted in Choate, *Emigrant Nation*, 73; and Richard Bosworth, *Italy, the Least of the Great Powers*, 422.

Chapter 2. Race and Trade Policies in Migrant Marketplaces, 1880–1914

1. C. A. Mariani, "Tariff Revision and the Italians in America," *Rivista Commerciale* (hereafter *Rivista*), December 1911, 44–45.

2. Ad for Luigi Bosca & Figli, *La Patria degli Italiani* (Buenos Aires, Argentina) (hereafter *La Patria*), May 25, 1910, 12.

3. Historians of Italian migration to Argentina have recognized Argentina's heavy dependence on Italian laborers as compared to other migrant groups. See Fernando J. Devoto, *Historia de los italianos en la Argentina* (Buenos Aires: Editorial Biblos, 2006); Fernando J. Devoto and Gianfausto Rosoli, eds., *L'Italia nella società argentina: Contributi sull'emigrazione italiana in Argentina* (Rome: Centro Studi Emigrazione, 1988); Eugenia Scarzanella, *Italiani d'Argentina: Storie di contadini, industriali e missionari italiani in Argentina, 1850–1912* (Venice: Marsilio, 1983).

4. Samuel L. Baily, *Immigrants in the Lands of Promise: Italians in Buenos Aires and New York City, 1870–1914* (Ithaca, NY: Cornell University Press, 1999), 54, 58–59.

5. Gianfausto Rosoli, ed., *Un secolo di emigrazione italiana, 1876–1976* (Rome: Centro Studi Emigrazione, 1978), 353; Scarzanella, *Italiani d'Argentina*, 25–30; Fernando J. Devoto, "Programs and Politics of the First Italian Elite of Buenos Aires, 1852–80," in *Italian Workers of the World: Labor Migration and the Formation of Multiethnic States*, ed. Donna R. Gabaccia and Fraser M. Ottanelli (Urbana: University of Illinois Press, 2001), 41–59.

6. "Atti della camera," *Bollettino Mensile della Camera di Commercio in Buenos Aires* (hereafter *Bollettino Mensile*), July (1901): 2.

7. Comitato della Camera Italiana di Commercio ed Arti, *Gli italiani nella Repubblica Argentina* (Buenos Aires, 1898), 17.

8. República Argentina, *Tercer Censo Nacional,* Tomo 8, *Censo del Comercio* (Buenos Aires: Talleres Gráficos de L. J. Rosso y Cía., 1917), 132, 135–36.

9. On Italians in Argentina's class system and the growing middle class, see Baily, *Immigrants in the Lands of Promise*, 73–75; Scarzanella, *Italiani d'Argentina*, 25–69; Eugenia Scarzanella, "L'industria argentina e gli immigrati italiani: Nascita della borghesia industriale

bonaerense," in *Gli italiani fuori d'Italia: Gli emigrati italiani nei movimenti operai dei paesi d'adozione, 1880–1940*, ed. B. Bezza (Milan: F. Angeli, 1983), 583–633; Devoto, *Historia de los italianos en la Argentina*, 204–230, 283–291.

10. Ad for Florio, *La Patria,* April 5, 1895, 3; ad for Florio, *La Patria*, January 21, 1905, 2; ad for Florio, *La Patria*, January 1910, 17.

11. On Jannello, see Comitato della Camera Italiana di Commercio ed Arti, *Gli italiani nella Repubblica Argentina* (1898), 303. See also *L'Italia nell' America Latina: Per l'incremento dei rapporti industriali e commerciali fra l'Italia e l'America del Sud* (Milan: Società Tipografica Editrice Popolare, 1906), 57; Comitato della Camera Italiana di Commercio ed Arti, "La Casa di Rappresentanze Francesco Jannello," *Gli italiani nella Repubblica Argentina all'Esposizione di Torino 1911* (Buenos Aires: Stabilimento Grafico della Compañia General de Fósforos, 1911).

12. On the working-class experiences of Italian urban laborers in the United States, see especially Jennifer Guglielmo, *Living the Revolution: Italian Women's Resistance and Radicalism in New York City, 1880–1945* (Chapel Hill: University of North Carolina Press, 2010); Donna R. Gabaccia, *Militants and Migrants: Rural Sicilians Become American Workers* (New Brunswick, NJ: Rutgers University Press 1988); Dino Cinel, *From Italy to San Francisco: The Immigrant Experience* (Stanford, CA: Stanford University Press, 1982); Virginia Yans-McLaughlin, *Family and Community: Italian Immigrants in Buffalo, 1880–1930* (Ithaca, NY: Cornell University Press, 1977); Robert F. Foerster, *The Italian Emigration of Our Times* (Cambridge: Harvard University Press, 1919), 342–62.

13. Baily, *Immigrants in the Lands of Promise*, 102.

14. For Italians in agricultural importing and wholesale businesses, see Donna R. Gabaccia, *We Are What We Eat: Ethnic Food and the Making of Americans* (Cambridge: Harvard University Press, 1998), 65–73. On Italian food businesses in New York, see especially Simone Cinotto, *The Italian American Table: Food, Family, and Community in New York City* (Urbana: University of Illinois Press, 2013).

15. Louise Odencrantz, *Italian Women in Industry* (New York: Russell Sage Foundation, 1919), 12.

16. On L. Gandolfi & Co., see Italian American Directory Co., *Gli italiani negli Stati Uniti d'America* (New York: Andrew H. Kellogg Co., 1906), 292–95. See also ad for L. Gandolfi & Co., *Rivista*, December 1905, 8.

17. Ad for Cora vermouth and Fernet-Branca amaro, *La Nación*, September 20, 1901, 6; ad for Felsina Buton amaro, *La Prensa*, December 2, 1900, 8; ad for Nocera Umbra mineral water, *La Prensa*, December, 1900, 7.

18. Ad for Jannello, *Caras y Caretas*, January 1, 1910.

19. Giuseppe Peretti was a member of the Italian Chamber of Commerce in Buenos Aires. Ad for Cora vermouth, *Caras y Caretas*, January 8, 1910.

20. Ad for La Gran Ciudad de Chicago, *La Patria*, January 1, 1910, 4–5.

21. William Leach, *Land of Desire: Merchants, Power and the Rise of a New American Culture* (New York: Pantheon Books, 1993). On Argentine department stores, see Fernando Rocchi, *Chimneys in the Desert: Industrialization in Argentina during the Export Boom Years, 1870–1930* (Stanford, CA: Stanford University Press, 2006), 71–72, 77, 83.

22. See, for example, "Vida Italiana," *La Nación*, September 4, 1901, 2; "Vida Italiana," *La Nación*, September 4, 1901, 2; "Notas Sociales, Circolo Italiano," *La Nacion*, September 23, 1901, 3.

23. For examples of advertisements for Italian exports in Spanish in *La Patria*, see ad for Fernet-Branca, *La Patria*, January 1, 1910, 6; ad for Malvasia Florio, *La Patria*, January 2, 1900, 7; ad for San Pellegrino, *La Patria*, January 7, 1905, 7; ad for Nocera Umbra, *La Patria*, January 11, 1910, 8.

24. For examples of manifesti in Spanish in *La Patria*, see "Manifesti: Città di Milano," *La Patria*, June 29, 1900, 6; "Manifesto d'arrivo: Italie," *La Patria*, January 6, 1905, 7; "Manifesti d'arrivo: Siena," *La Patria*, January 1, 1910, 5; "Manifesti: Brasile, Principe Umberto," *La Patria*, January 9, 1915, 9; "Manifesto d'arrivo: Tomaso di Savoia," *La Patria*, April 22, 1920, 11; "Manifesto d'arrivo: Ansaldo Savoia I," *La Patria*, February 14, 1925, 10. By 1910, all manifesti in *La Patria* appeared in Spanish rather than in Italian.

25. See, for example, "Bollettino Commerciale," *Il Progresso Italo-Americano* (hereafter *Il Progresso*), September 13, 1900, 2.

26. Alessandro Durante, ed., *A Companion to Linguistic Anthropology* (Malden, MA: Blackwell, 2004). Linguistic anthropologists interested in links between language, identity, and social action have discussed bilingualism and code switching (when two or more languages are employed during the same speech event) as two possible outcomes of language contact between speakers.

27. F. A., "Snazionalizzazione," *Rivista*, November 1909, 10.

28. "Nel nome di Colombo," *La Patria*, April 17, 1910, 7.

29. "Emigrazione," *Bollettino Mensile*, December 1910, 2.

30. Peter D'Agostino, "Craniums, Criminals, and the 'Cursed Race': Italian Anthropology in American Racial Thought, 1861–1924," *Comparative Studies in Society and History* 44, no. 2 (2002): 319–43.

31. Ibid.

32. For an excellent comparative study of racially based immigration policies of countries in the western hemisphere, see David Scott FitzGerald and David Cook-Martín, *Culling the Masses: The Democratic Origins of Racist Immigration Policy in the Americas* (Cambridge: Harvard University Press, 2014).

33. For a sweeping overview of Argentine history, see David Rock, *Argentina, 1516–1987: From Spanish Colonization to Alfonsín* (Berkeley: University of California Press, 1985). *Criollo* was a flexible catagory that changed over time and was shaped by factors such as region and class. For a discussion of the term *criollo* as it relates to Argentine food and identity see Rebekah E. Pite, "*La cocina criolla*: A History of Food and Race in Twentieth-Century Argentina," in *Rethinking Race in Modern Argentina*, ed. Paulina L. Alberto and Eduardo Elena (New York: Cambridge University Press, 2016), 99–125.

34. George Reid Andrews, *The Afro-Argentines of Buenos Aires, 1800–1900* (Madison: University of Wisconsin Press, 1980).

35. In the book, Sarmiento proposed a dichotomy between "barbarianism" embodied by *caudillos* such as the Argentine dictator Juan Manuel de Rosas and "civilization" represented by urban life, European migration, and North America. Domingo F.

Sarmiento, *Facundo; or, Civilization and Barbarism*, trans. Mary Mann (New York: Penguin Books, 1998).

36. Samuel L. Baily, "Sarmiento and Immigration: Changing Views on the Role of Immigration in the Development of Argentina," in *Sarmiento and His Argentina*, ed. Joseph T. Criscenti (Boulder, CO: L. Rienner Publishers, 1993), 131–42. See also Jose C. Moya, *Cousins and Strangers: Spanish Immigrants in Buenos Aires, 1850–1930* (Berkeley: University of California Press, 1998), 48–52.

37. Julia Rodriguez, *Civilizing Argentina: Science, Medicine, and the Modern State* (Chapel Hill: University of North Carolina Press, 2006), 16–18.

38. On scientific racism and immigration in Argentina, see Rodriguez, *Civilizing Argentina*; Eugenia Scarzanella, *Italiani malagente: Immigrazione, criminalità, razzismo in Argentina, 1890–1940* (Milan: F. Angeli, 1999).

39. Baily, *Immigrants in the Lands of Promise*, 80; Scarzanella, *Italiani malagente*.

40. Nancy Leys Stepan, *The Hour of Eugenics: Race, Gender, and Nation in Latin America* (Ithaca, NY: Cornell University Press, 1991), 139–45.

41. Donna R. Gabaccia, "Race, Nation, Hyphen: Italian-American Multiculturalism in Comparative Perspective," in *Are Italians White? How Race Is Made in America*, ed. Jennifer Guglielmo and Salvatore Salerno (New York: Routledge, 2003), 44–59. For a comparative study of racial selection in immigration policy for countries of the western hemisphere, see FitzGerald and Cook-Martín, *Culling the Masses*.

42. Paul R. Spickard, *Almost All Aliens: Immigration, Race, and Colonialism in American History and Identity* (New York: Routledge, 2007); Gary Gerstle, *American Crucible: Race and Nation in the Twentieth Century* (Princeton, NJ: Princeton University Press, 2001).

43. On the racial status of Italians in the United States, see Matthew Frye Jacobson, *Whiteness of a Different Color: European Immigrants and the Alchemy of Race* (Cambridge: Harvard University Press, 1999); James R. Barrett and David Roediger, "Inbetween Peoples: Race, Nationality, and the 'New Immigrant' Working Class," *Journal of American Ethnic History* 16, no. 3 (1997): 3–44; Thomas A. Guglielmo, *White on Arrival: Italians, Race, Color, and Power in Chicago, 1890–1945* (Oxford: Oxford University Press, 2003); Jennifer Guglielmo and Salvatore Salerno, eds., *Are Italians White?: How Race Is Made in America* (New York: Routledge, 2003).

44. Erika Lee, *At America's Gates: Chinese Immigration during the Exclusion Era, 1882–1942* (Chapel Hill: University of North Carolina Press, 2003).

45. On the history of nativism, see John Higham, *Strangers in the Land: Patterns of American Nativism, 1860–1925* (New Brunswick, NJ: Rutgers University Press, 1955). On the Immigration Act of 1924, see Mae M. Ngai, *Impossible Subjects: Illegal Aliens and the Making of Modern America* (Princeton, NJ: Princeton University Press, 2004), 21–55.

46. Gabaccia, "Race, Nation, Hyphen," 56.

47. Over the last two decades, food studies scholars and migration historians have moved beyond exploring food as a means through which migrants forge and sustain ethnic group identity to food as a site for producing racial demarcation and exclusion. This group of scholars, focused mainly on migrants of color in the United States, has provided an important corrective to apolitical and celebratory images of the United States

as "melting pot" of tolerant, multicultural eaters. See especially Anita Mannur, "Asian American Food-Scapes," *Amerasia Journal* 32, no. 2 (2006): 1–5; Robert Ji-Song Ku, Martin F. Manalansan IV, and Anita Mannur, eds., *Eating Asian America: A Food Studies Reader* (New York: New York University Press, 2013); Tanachai Mark Padoongpatt, "Too Hot to Handle: Food, Empire, and Race in Thai Los Angeles," *Radical History Review* 110 (Spring 2011): 83–108; Simone Cinotto, *Soft Soil, Black Grapes: The Birth of Italian Winemaking in California*, trans. Michelle Tarnopoloski (New York: New York University Press, 2012).

48. Istituto Coloniale Italiano, *Italia e Argentina* (Bergamo: Officine dell'Istituto Italiano d'Arti Grafiche, 1910), 9.

49. As Michel Gobat explains, Latin American elites in the mid-nineteenth century used the term "Latin race" to distinguish themselves from U.S. Americans, Europeans, and the masses of racially mixed residents of Latin American countries. Historians interested in "Latin America" as a continental historical invention have pointed to a number of historical actors who contributed to its emergence: French imperialists interested in Mexico; Latin American expats who popularized the term in Europe; and Latin America elites, who invoked the term to unite countries south of the Rio Grande against U.S. and European imperialism while justifying their political, economic, and racial superiority over indigenous and mixed race peoples. Less explored, however, are Italians and other migrant groups who harnessed notions of Latinness and Latin America to build and conserve economic and cultural bridges between themselves and Latin American consumers around global goods. Michel Gobat, "The Invention of Latin America: A Transnational History of Anti-Imperialism, Democracy, and Race," *American Historical Review* 118, no. 5 (2013): 1345–75.

50. "Il Centenario Argentino," *La Patria*, June 22, 1910, 7.

51. M. Gravina, ed., *Almanacco dell'italiano nell'Argentina* (Buenos Aires, 1918), 86.

52. "Solidarietà italo-argentina," *La Patria*, September 16, 1915, 6; "La formazione della razza argentina," *La Patria*, September 3, 1915, 4.

53. "Situazione generale," *Bollettino Mensile*, April 29, 1910, 5.

54. Ibid.; "Il centenario dell'independenza Argentina a Roma," *La Patria*, May 23, 1910, 3.

55. "Voci affettuose," *La Patria*, February 20, 1910, 5.

56. Luigi Einaudi, *Un principe mercante: Studio sulla espansione coloniale italiana* (Turin: Fratelli Bocca, 1900), 11.

57. "L'emigrazione italiana nel 1 semestre 1908," *Bollettino Mensile*, October 15, 1908, 6.

58. Bernardino Frescura, "La Mostra degli Italiani all'Estero, all'Esposizione Internazionale di Milano nel 1906," *Bollettino dell'emigrazione* 18 (1907): 79.

59. "Sull'America Latina," *La Patria*, April 14, 1910, 5.

60. Aldo Visconti, *Emigrazione ed esportazione: Studio dei rapporti che intercedono fra l'emigrazione e le esportazioni italiane per gli Stati Uniti del Nord America e per la Repubblica Argentina* (Turin: Tipografia Baravalle e Falconieri, 1912), 29, 40.

61. Ibid., 16.

62. Emilio Zuccarini, *Il lavoro degli italiani nella Repubblica Argentina dal 1516 al 1910* (Buenos Aires, 1910), 109.

63. Baily, *Immigrants in the Lands of Promise*, 151. On marriage patterns, see Eduardo José Míguez, "Il comportamento matrimoniale degli italiani in Argentina. Un bilancio," in *Identità degli italiani in Argentina: Reti sociali, famiglia, lavoro*, ed. Gianfausto Rosoli (Rome: Edizioni Studium, 1993), 81–105.

64. Conversely, it was not until after World War I that Italians in New York begin to produce a community that included a sizable aging and more gender-balanced population as well as a large second generation of Italian Americans. Baily, *Immigrants in the Lands of Promise*, 63–65.

65. Samuel L. Baily, "Marriage Patterns and Immigrant Assimilation in Buenos Aires, 1882–1923," *Hispanic American Historical Review* 60, no. 1 (1980): 32–48.

66. On eugenics and race in Argentina, see Stepan, *Hour of Eugenics*. For the United States, see Alan M. Kraut, *Silent Travelers: Germs, Genes, and the "Immigrant Menace"* (New York: BasicBooks, 1994); Alexandra Minna Stern, *Eugenic Nation: Faults and Frontiers of Better Breeding in Modern America* (Berkeley: University of California Press, 2005).

67. Comitato della Camera Italiana di Commercio ed Arti, *Gli italiani nella Repubblica Argentina*, 61.

68. "L'espansione italiana," *La Patria*, April 15, 1910, 7.

69. Ad for Luigi Bosca & Sons wines, *La Patria*, May 25, 1910, 12.

70. Ad for Florio Marsala, *La Patria*, April 29, 1911, 13.

71. Comitato della Camera Italiana di Commercio ed Arti, "La Casa di Rappresentanze Francesco Jannello," *Gli italiani nella Repubblica Argentina all'Esposizione di Torino 1911*.

72. Fabio Parasecoli, *Al Dente: A History of Food in Italy* (London: Reaktion Books, 2014), 136–37, 144–45; David Gentilcore, *Pomodoro!: A History of the Tomato in Italy* (New York: Columbia University Press, 2010), 45–68; Vito Teti, *Storia del peperoncino: Un protagonista delle culture mediterranee* (Rome: Donzelli Editore, 2007), 41–57, 83–119.

73. Donna R. Gabaccia, "Making Foods Italian in the Hispanic Atlantic" (unpublished paper, University of Minnesota, November 1, 2006).

74. On the history of Argentina cuisine, see Rebekah E. Pite, *Creating a Common Table in Twentieth-Century Argentina: Doña Petrona, Women, and Food* (Chapel Hill: University of North Carolina Press, 2013); Aníbal B. Arcondo, *Historia de la alimentación en Argentina: Desde los orígenes hasta 1920* (Córdoba: Ferreyra Editor, 2002); Eduardo P. Archetti, "Hibración, pertenencia y localidad en la construcción de una cocina nacional," in *La Argentina en el siglo XX*, ed. Carlos Altamirano (Buenos Aires: Universidad Nacional de Quilmes, 1999), 217–36.

75. Carols M. Urien and Ezio Colombo, *La República Argentina en 1910* (Buenos Aires: Maucci Hermanos, 1910), 63–65. On food's role in shaping ideas about race in colonial Latin America see Rebecca Earle, *The Body of the Conquistador: Food, Race, and the Colonial Experience in Spanish America, 1942–1700* (New York: Cambridge University Press, 2012).

76. On the different meanings of *criolla* in Mexican, Argentine, and Cuban culinary literature, see Jeffrey M. Pilcher, "Eating à la Criolla: Global and Local Foods in Argentina, Cuba, and Mexico," *IdeAs* 3 (Winter 2012): 3–16, and Pite, "*La cocina criolla.*" On food policy and eating under Perón, see Natalia Milanesio, "Food Politics and Consumption in Peronist Argentina," *Hispanic American Historical Review* 90, no. 1 (2010): 75–108.

77. Arcondo, *Historia de la alimentación en Argentina*, 25–26.

78. "N. y A. Canale y Ca.," *La Nación*, Numero del centenario, 1810–1910, 1910, 123; "Gran Hotel Italia (Rosario)," *La Nación*, Numero del centenario, 1810–1910, 1910, 150. On La Sonambula, opened by Nicolas Canale in 1863, see Arcondo, *Historia de la alimentación en Argentina*, 280.

79. Pite, *Creating a Common Table*, 72.

80. Quotes come from "Situazione generale," *Bollettino Mensile*, April 1910, 5, and Visconti, *Emigrazione ed esportazione*, 29, 40.

81. E. Mayor des Planches, "Gli Stati Uniti e l'emigrazione italiana," *Rivista Coloniale* (Rome, Italy) 1 (May–August 1906): 75.

82. "Perché gli americani cercano l'amicizia degli italiani," *Il Progresso*, November 8, 1906, 1; "I desiderabili," *Il Progresso,* May 26, 1905, 1.

83. Peter G. Vellon, *A Great Conspiracy against Our Race: Italian Immigrant Newspapers and the Construction of Whiteness in the Early 20th Century* (New York: New York University Press, 2014), 8.

84. Gabaccia, *We Are What We Eat*, 93.

85. Harvey Levenstein, "The American Response to Italian Food, 1880–1930," *Food and Foodways* 1 (1985): 1–24. On the stigmatization of Italian wine-makers and drinkers, see Cinotto, *Soft Soil, Black Grapes*.

86. Robert A. Woods, "Notes on the Italians in Boston," *Charities* 12 (1904): 451.

87. "Chicken with Macaroni," *New York Times,* August 16, 1888, 8.

88. Antonio Mangano, "The Italian Colonies of New York City," MA thesis, Columbia University, 1903, repr. *Italians in the City: Health and Related Social Needs*, ed. Francesco Cordasco (New York: Arno Press, 1975), 51.

89. It would be groups of bohemian writers, artists, and intellectuals in the early twentieth century who would initially explore Italian restaurants in migrant enclaves of cities like New York and San Francisco, seeing in them both tasty food and an exotic "Latin" culture of pleasure seeking and entertainment. Gabaccia, *We Are What We Eat*, 95–102.

90. Levenstein, "American Response to Italian Food," 4–5. Paul Freedman found that macaroni was the most common offered entrée in mid-nineteenth-century upscale restaurants. See Paul Freedman, "American Restaurants and Cuisine in the Mid-Nineteenth Century," *New England Quarterly* 84, no. 1 (2011): 5–59.

91. Emilio Perera, "Pro importazione italiana negli Stati Uniti," *Rivista*, September 1910, 7.

92. "Pure Food Exposition," *Rivista*, September 1911, 14–15; Guido Rossati, "La vendemmia in Italia ed il commercio dei vini italiani cogli S.U. nel 1905," *Rivista*, December, 1905, 41–51.

93. Luigi Solari, "Come sorse, che cosa é e ció che potrebbe essere la Camera di Commercio Italiana in New York," *Rivista,* September 1912, 7.

94. "Pure Food Exposition," 14.

95. "Parte ufficiale," *Rivista*, February 1910, 7; "Pure Food Law," *Rivista*, April 1909, 7.

96. Rossati, "La vendemmia in Italia," 41.

97. "A Few Hints to American Retailers and Consumers of Italian Articles of Food," *Rivista*, February 1911, 15.

98. Guido Rossati, "Olive verdi," *Rivista*, May 1912, 7.

99. "Per l'alimentazione pura," *Rivista*, March 1910, 8.

100. "A Few Hints," 15.

101. The act was part of a nationwide movement by Progressive reformers to protect consumers' safety and health and to enforce labor legislation. On the act, see James Harvey Young, *Pure Food: Securing the Federal Food and Drugs Act of 1906* (Princeton, NJ: Princeton University Press, 1989); Mitchell Okun, *Fair Play in the Marketplace: The First Battle for Pure Food and Drugs* (DeKalb: Northern Illinois University Press, 1986).

102. "Purity of Italian Food Articles," *Rivista*, March 1912, 23.

103. "Condemnations under the Pure Food Law," *Rivista*, September 1912, 23.

104. Italian American Directory Co., *Gli italiani negli Stati Uniti d'America*, 66.

105. "Pure Food Exposition,"14; Gustavo Porges, "'Quality Trust,'" *Rivista*, December 1911, 32.

106. "Prodotti alimentari italiani a Chicago," *Rivista*, February 1911, 13.

107. Perera, "Pro Importazione Italiana negli Stati Uniti," 7.

108. Emilio Longhi, "Italian Products on the Chicago Market," *Italian Chamber of Commerce Bulletin*, May 1908, 73–75.

109. Ibid.

110. Gustavo Porges, "Qualità il segreto del successo," *Rivista*, December 1912, 29.

111. Baily, *Immigrants in the Lands of Promise*, 150–52.

112. John F. Mariani, "Everybody Likes Italian Food," *American Heritage* 40, no. 8 (1989): 127.

113. Velma Phillips and Laura Howell, "Racial and Other Differences in Dietary Customs," *Journal of Home Economics* 12, no. 9 (1920): 411.

114. Gabaccia, *We Are What We Eat*, 122–31; Levenstein, "American Response," 7–10; Stephanie J. Jass, "Recipes for Reform: Americanization and Foodways in Chicago Settlement Houses, 1890–1920," PhD diss., Western Michigan University, 2004; Michael J. Eula, "Failure of American Food Reformers among Italian Immigrants in New York City, 1891–1897," *Italian Americana* 18 (Winter 2000): 86–99; Cinotto, *Italian American Table*, 55, 108–109.

115. Solari, "Come sorse, che cosa é e ció che potrebbe essere la Camera di Commercio Italiana in New York," 7.

116. "Importazione negli Stati Uniti di olio d'oliva dall'Italia," *Rivista*, August 1909, 13.

117. Longhi, "Italian Products on the Chicago Market," 73–75.

118. Gabaccia, *We Are What We Eat*, 99–102; Cinotto, *Italian American Table*, 180–209; Levenstein, "American Response."

119. "Importazione di commestibili e bibite," *Bollettino Mensile,* February 1902, 7.

120. "Importazione di commestibili e bibite," *Bollettino Mensile*, January 1904, 6; "Importazione di commestibili e bibite," *Bollettino Mensile*, February 1904, 6.

121. Donna R. Gabaccia, *Foreign Relations: American Immigration in Global Perspective* (Princeton, NJ: Princeton University Press, 2012), 54–55.

122. Kevin H. O'Rourke and Jeffrey G. Williamson, *Globalization and History: The Evolution of a Nineteenth-Century Atlantic Economy* (Cambridge: MIT Press, 1999), 185, 196.

123. Jeffry A. Frieden, *Global Capitalism: Its Fall and Rise in the Twentieth Century* (New York: Norton, 2006), 64–68. On the history of trusts in the United States, see Naomi R. Lamoreaux, *The Great Merger Movement in American Business, 1895–1904* (New York: Cambridge University Press, 1985); on Argentina, see Yovanna Pineda, *Industrial Development in a Frontier Economy: The Industrialization of Argentina, 1890–1930* (Stanford, CA: Stanford University Press, 2009), 18–39.

124. "Parte ufficiale," *Rivista,* July 1911, 8.

125. Qualcuno, "A chi giova il protezionismo?," *La Patria,* January 15, 1900, 3.

126. "L'immigrazione in pericolo," *La Patria,* March 7, 1900, 4.

127. "Il disagio presente," *La Patria,* April 7, 1900, 3.

128. "Emigrazione," *Bollettino Mensile,* December 5, 1901, 1.

129. "Iniquità fiscali," *La Patria,* June 28, 1900, 3; "La libertá del giuoco," *La Patria,* September 4, 1900, 3.

130. "Un pauroso fenomeno," *La Patria,* April 10, 1900, 3.

131. "Ci danno ragione," *La Patria,* July 17, 1900, 3.

132. "A proposito dello sciopero dei cappellai," *La Patria,* March 3, 1900, 5.

133. "Il plebiscito della Società Rurale," *La Patria,* January 16, 1900, 3.

134. "La conferenza sul regime degli zuccheri," *Bollettino Mensile,* April 5, 1902, 1.

135. "Ci danno ragione," 3.

136. Scholars continue to argue over the extent to which Argentine tariff policy in the late nineteenth and early twentieth centuries protected Argentine industry. Until recently, scholars have blamed the Argentine government not only for favoring agro-export sectors over industry but also for being actively antagonist toward it, pointing to low tariffs as a prime example of Congress' failure to support Argentina's industrialization. Other scholars, however, have argued that tariffs were more effective in encouraging industry than Structuralists writing mainly in the post–World War II era have acknowledged. On these evolving debates, see Carlos F. Díaz Alejandro, *Essays on the Economic History of the Argentine Republic* (New Haven, CT: Yale University Press, 1970), 277–308; María Inés Barbero and Fernando Rocchi, "Industry," in *The New Economic History of Argentina,* ed. Gerardo della Paolera and Alan Taylor (Cambridge: Cambridge University Press, 2003), 261–94.

137. Rocchi, *Chimneys in the Desert,* 204–236; Pineda, *Industrial Development,* 108–123.

138. Carlos F. Díaz Alejandro, "The Argentine Tariff, 1906–1940," *Oxford Economic Papers* 19, no. 1 (1967): 75–98; Carl Solberg, "The Tariff and Politics in Argentina, 1916–1930," *Hispanic American Historical Review* 53, no. 2 (1973): 260–84.

139. "Tariffa doganale argentina," *Bollettino Mensile,* November 1899, 4–6; "La revisione delle tariffe doganali argentine," *Bollettino Mensile,* August 1910, 12.

140. "La 'Liga de Defensa Comercial' e la legge di dogana," *La Patria,* September 9, 1905, 6.

141. "Politica doganale Italo-Argentina," *Bollettino Mensile,* July 1908, 7.

142. "Atti della camera," *Bollettino Mensile,* December 1, 1906, 1–2.

143. "Capitali italiani," *Bollettino Mensile,* January 5, 1901, 1.

144. Gabaccia, *Foreign Relations,* 122–32; Tom E. Terrill, *The Tariff, Politics, and American Foreign Policy, 1874–1901* (Westport, CT: Greenwood Press, 1973); Alfred E. Eckes, *Opening*

America's Market: U.S. Foreign Trade Policy since 1776 (Chapel Hill: University of North Carolina Press, 1995).

145. Mariani, "Tariff Revision," 44.

146. "Tentativo per abrogare la legge Payne-Aldrich fallito," *Il Progresso,* April 3, 1910, 1.

147. "Il discorso del Cav. Uff. L. Solari, presidente della camera," *Rivista,* February 1910, 11.

148. "Condemnations under the Pure Food Law," *Rivista,* September 1912, 23.

149. Gino C. Speranza, "La necessità di un accordo internazionale in riguardo agli emigranti," *Rivista,* December 1905, 21. On the interesting life of Italian American Gino Speranza and his eventual support for immigration restriction and Americanization programs, see Aldo E. Salerno, "America for Americans Only: Gino C. Speranza and the Immigrant Experience," *Italian Americana* 14, no. 2 (1996): 133–47.

150. Mariani, "Tariff Revision," 44.

151. "Per I venditori ambulanti," *Il Progresso,* February 25, 1905, 1; "Imperialismo e monopolismo," *Supplemento al Progresso-Italo-Americano,* October 7, 1900, 3.

152. Francesco Pisani, "Verso l'imperialismo o verso il lavoro?," *Supplemento al Progresso Italo-Americano,* May 7, 1905, 1; "L'America e gli americani giudicati da un europeo," *Il Progresso,* May 11, 1905, 1.

153. "I 'trusts' in America," *Rivista,* December 1905, 38.

154. "Il boicottaggio della carne," *Il Progresso,* April 7, 1910, 1.

155. For example, the paper supported the unsuccessful Democratic candidate William Jennings Bryan in the 1900 presidential election. "Italiani, tutti per Bryan!," *Il Progresso,* October 27, 1900, 1; "Gli italiani sono per Bryan. Il colossale meeting democratico," *Il Progresso,* October 28, 1900, 1.

156. "Ancora le cooperative," *La Patria,* May 7, 1906, 6; "Il rincaro della carne," *La Patria,* July 3, 1906, 6; "Il pane rincara," *La Patria,* May 12, 1906, 6.

157. Rocchi, *Chimneys in the Desert,* 103–115; Pineda, *Industrial Development,* 33–36.

Chapter 3. *Tipo Italiano*: The Production and Sale of Italian-Style Goods, 1880–1914

1. A. Dall'Aste Brandolini, "L'immigrazione e le colonie italiane nella Pennsylvania," *Bollettino dell'emigrazione* (hereafter *Bollettino*) 4 (1902): 57–58.

2. F. A., "Una visita alla Manifattura de Nobili," *Rivista Commerciale* (hereafter *Rivista*), December 1909, 41.

3. Ibid., 37.

4. Luigi Einaudi, *Un principe mercante: Studio sulla espansione coloniale italiana* (Turin: Fratelli Bocca, 1900), 23.

5. Aldo Visconti, *Emigrazione ed esportazione: Studio dei rapporti che intercedono fra l'emigrazione e le esportazioni italiane per gli Stati Uniti del Nord America e per la Repubblica Argentina* (Turin: Tipografia Baravalle e Falconieri, 1912), 30.

6. "L'emigrazione transoceanica, le correnti commerciali, e i servizi marittimi," *Bollettino* 11 (1904): 107.

7. See, for example, F. Prat, "Gli italiani negli Stati Uniti e specialmente nello Stato di New York," *Bollettino* 2 (1902): 26; Obizzo Luigi Maria Orazio Colombano Malaspina, "L'immigrazione nella Repubblica Argentina," *Bollettino* 3 (1902): 16–17.

8. On the wheat and cattle industries in Argentina, see James R. Scobie, *Revolution on the Pampas: A Social History of Argentine Wheat, 1860–1910* (Austin: University of Texas Press, 1964); Peter H. Smith, *Politics and Beef in Argentina: Patterns of Conflict and Change* (New York: Columbia University Press, 1969). For the United States, see William Cronon, *Nature's Metropolis: Chicago and the Great West* (New York: W. W. Norton, 1991), and Jimmy M. Skaggs, *Prime Cut: Livestock Raising and Meatpacking in the United States, 1607–1983* (College Station: Texas A&M University Press, 1986).

9. Silvano Serventi and Françoise Sabban, *Pasta: The Story of a Universal Food* (New York: Columbia University Press, 2002), 3, 192; Scobie, *Revolution on the Pampas*, 87.

10. F. Prat, "Gli italiani negli Stati Uniti e specialmente nello Stato di New York," 26.

11. Ad for Ernesto Bisi, *Il Progresso Italo-Americano* (hereafter *Il Progresso*), December 1, 1905, 3.

12. Ad for Tomba wines, *La Patria degli Italiani* (hereafter *La Patria*), September 29, 2.

13. See, for example, Diane C. Vecchio, *Merchants, Midwives, and Laboring Women: Italian Migrants in Urban America* (Urbana: University of Illinois Press, 2006); S .P. Breckinridge, *New Homes for Old* (New York: Harper & Brothers Publishing, 1921), 58–60; Mary Sherman, "Manufacturing of Foods in the Tenements," *Charities and the Commons* 15 (1906): 669–73.

14. Simone Cinotto, *Soft Soil, Black Grapes: The Birth of Italian Winemaking in California*, trans. Michelle Tarnopoloski (New York: New York University Press, 2012), 107–113; see also Simone Cinotto, *The Italian American Table: Food, Family, and Community in New York City* (Urbana: University of Illinois Press, 2013), 107–108; see also Hasia R. Diner, *Hungering for America: Italian, Irish, and Jewish Foodways in the Age of Migration* (Cambridge: Harvard University Press, 2001), 69–70.

15. At the "Italians Abroad" exhibit during the 1906 Milan International exhibition, the jury awarded prizes to many tipo italiano companies for the large number of Italian workers they employed. Bernardino Frescura, "La Mostra degli Italiani all'Estero, all'Esposizione Internazionale di Milano nel 1906," *Bollettino* 18 (1907): 219.

16. Comitato della Camera Italiana di Commercio ed Arti, *Gli italiani nell'Repubblica Argentina* (Buenos Aires: Compañia Sud-Americana de Billetes de Banco, 1898), 453.

17. Ettore Patrizi, *Gl'italiani in California, Stati Uniti d'America* (San Francisco: Stabilimento Tipo-Litografico, 1911), 53; Italian American Directory Co., *Gli italiani negli Stati Uniti d'America* (New York: Andrew H. Kellogg Co., 1906), 287.

18. Jennifer Guglielmo, *Living the Revolution: Italian Women's Resistance and Radicalism in New York City, 1880–1945* (Chapel Hill: University of North Carolina Press, 2010), 60–64, 139–75; José Moya, "Italians in Buenos Aires's Anarchist Movement: Gender Ideology and Women's Participation, 1890–1910," in *Women, Gender, and Transnational Lives: Italian Workers of the World*, ed. Donna R. Gabaccia and Franca Iacovetta (Toronto: University of Toronto Press, 2002), 189–216.

19. United States Immigration Commission, *Immigrants in Cities*, vol. 1 (Washington, DC: U.S. Government Printing Office, 1911), 176, 220.

20. Donna J. Guy, "Women, Peonage, and Industrialization: Argentina, 1810–1914," *Latin American Research Review* 16, no. 3 (1981): 78–80.

21. Louise Odencrantz, *Italian Women in Industry* (New York: Russell Sage Foundation, 1919), 17, 48–50. See also Miriam Cohen, *Workshop to Office: Two Generations of Italian Women in New York City, 1900–1950* (Ithaca, NY: Cornell University Press, 1993).

22. Patrizi, *Gl'italiani in California*, 46.

23. Italian American Directory Co., *Gli italiani negli Stati Uniti d'America*, 398–400.

24. Guglielmo, *Living the Revolution*, 69–72.

25. Ibid, 58. See also Donna R. Gabaccia, *From Sicily to Elizabeth Street: Housing and Social Change among Italian Immigrants, 1880–1930* (Albany: State University of New York Press, 1984), 64, 92, 94; Virginia Yans-McLaughlin, *Family and Community: Italian Immigrants in Buffalo, 1880–1930* (Ithaca, NY: Cornell University Press, 1977), 51–53.

26. Frescura, "La Mostra degli Italiani all'Estero," 75–81.

27. Ibid., 219; Lorenzo Faleni and Amedeo Serafini, eds., *La Repubblica Argentina all'Esposizione internazionale di Milano 1906* (Buenos Aires, 1906), 43–47.

28. "Panatteria e fabbrica a vapore di biscotti della Vedova Canale," in Faleni and Serafini, *La Repubblica Argentina*.

29. Italian American Directory Co., *Gli italiani negli Stati Uniti d'America*, 398–400.

30. Guido Rossati, "La nuova tariffa doganale degli Stati Uniti rispetto all'importazione italiana," *Rivista*, August 1909, 10–13; Comitato della Camera Italiana di Commercio ed Arti, *Gli italiani nell'Argentina*, 303.

31. Ad for Ernesto Petrucci, *Il Progresso*, August 23, 1900, 4.

32. Ad for Emilio Longhi & Co., *Italian Chamber of Commerce Bulletin* (Chicago), October 1908, 6.

33. Ad for Francesco Jannello, *La Patria*, April 23, 1905, 4.

34. Samuel L. Baily and Franco Ramella, eds., *One Family, Two Worlds: An Italian Family's Correspondence across the Atlantic, 1901–1922*, trans. John Lenaghan (New Brunswick, NJ: Rutgers University Press, 1988), 90, 157–58.

35. Frescura, "La Mostra degli Italiani all'Estero," 227.

36. Ibid., 227, 229.

37. Italian American Directory Co., *Gli iItaliani negli Stati Uniti d'America*, 264–67.

38. Ibid., 293.

39. "Il commesso viaggiatore," *Bollettino Mensile della Camera Italiana di Commercio in Buenos Aires* (hereafter *Bollettino Mensile*), March 5, 1900, 1.

40. "Progetto di nuova legge sui vini," *Bollettino Mensile*, July 1908, 12.

41. "More about Paste," Italian Chamber of Commerce Bulletin (Chicago), January–February 1909, 15, 17.

42. Ad for United States Macaroni Factory, *Il Progresso*, January 13, 1900, 1.

43. Ad for United States Macaroni Factory, *Il Progresso*, December 1, 1905, 3.

44. Ibid.

45. For example, see ad for Grandolini and Company's pasta machine, *La Patria*, July 9, 1910, 4; ad for Grandolini and Company's pasta machine, *Il Progresso*, April 1, 1905, 7.

46. On the industrialization of food production, see Harvey A. Levenstein, *Revolution at the Table: The Transformation of the American Diet* (New York: Oxford University Press, 1988); Amy Bentley, *Inventing Baby Food: Taste, Health, and the Industrialization of the American Diet*

(Berkeley: University of California Press, 2014); Susan Strasser, *Satisfaction Guaranteed: The Making of the American Mass Market* (New York: Pantheon Books, 1989); Helen Zoe Veit, *Modern Food, Moral Food: Self-Control, Science, and the Rise of Modern American Eating in the Early Twentieth Century* (Chapel Hill: University of North Carolina Press, 2013); Roger Horowitz, *Putting Meat on the American Table: Taste, Technology, Transformation* (Baltimore: Johns Hopkins University Press, 2006).

47. Cinotto, *Italian American Table*, 115–30.

48. Donna R. Gabaccia, *We Are What We Eat: Ethnic Food and the Making of Americans* (Cambridge: Harvard University Press, 1998), 55–63, 65–73.

49. Eugenia Scarzanella, *Italiani d'Argentina: Storie di contadini, industriali e missionari italiani in Argentina, 1850–1912* (Venice: Marsilio, 1983), 30–70.

50. Fernando Rocchi, *Chimneys in the Desert: Industrialization in Argentina during the Export Boom Years, 1870–1930* (Stanford, CA: Stanford University Press, 2006), 28–33, 96–115; Yovanna Pineda, *Industrial Development in a Frontier Economy: The Industrialization of Argentina, 1890–1930* (Stanford, CA: Stanford University Press, 2009), especially chapters 4 and 5.

51. Faleni and Serafini, *La Repubblica Argentina*, 92.

52. Rocchi, *Chimneys in the Desert*, 89.

53. Camera di Commercio Italiana in New York, *Nel cinquantenario della Camera di Commercio Italiana in New York, 1887–1937* (New York, 1937), 66–67.

54. "Vino di California," *Rivista*, April 1909, 30.

55. Pineda, *Industrial Development in a Frontier Economy*, 110–15. Oscar Cornblit, "Inmigrantes y empresarios en la politica argentina," *Desarrollo Económico* 6, no. 24 (1967): 641–91.

56. "Pure Food Law," *Rivista*, April 1909, 7.

57. Camera di Commercio Italiana in New York, *Nel cinquantenario della Camera di Commercio Italiana in New York*, 66–67, 132.

58. Frank R. Rutter, *Tariff Systems of South American Countries* (Washington, DC: U.S. Government Printing Office, 1916), 89–90.

59. See, for example, "Atti della camera," *Bollettino Mensile,* April 29, 1910, 3; "Raccomandazioni ai nostri speditori di formaggi," *Bollettino Mensile*, August, 1908, 6.

60. Italian American Directory Co., *Gli italiani negli Stati Uniti d'America*, 67.

61. Visconti, *Emigrazione ed esportazione*, 52.

62. G. Saint-Martin, "Gli italiani nel distretto consolare di Nuova Orleans," *Bollettino* 1 (1903): 16–17.

63. Ads for Castruccio & Sons pasta and B. Piccardo pasta, *Il Progresso*, April 1, 1905, 6.

64. Frescura, "La Mostra degli Italiani all'Estero," 79–80; Cinotto, *Italian American Table*, 135–36.

65. "Il Commercio Italo-Americano," *Rivista*, February 1912, 14–15; "Per le paste alimentari," *Rivista*, May 1906, 4.

66. Leonard Covello, *The Social Background of the Italo-American School Child: A Study of the Southern Italian Family Mores and Their Effect on the School Situation in Italy and America* (Leiden: E. J. Brill, 1967), 295, quoted in Diner, *Hungering for America*, 58.

67. Ministerio de Agricultura, Dirección de Comercio e Industria, *Censo Industrial de la República* (Buenos Aires, Talleres de Publicaciones de la Oficina Meteorológica Argentina, 1910), 12–13.

68. Comitato della Camera Italiana di Commercio ed Arti, *Gli italiani nella Repubblica Argentina*, 169–170.

69. Frescura, "La Mostra degli Italiani all'Estero," 220.

70. Trade statistics for 1916 came from Ufficio Centrale di Stastica, *Annuario statistico italiano* (1917–1918), 247. Trade statistics for 1909 came from Visconti, *Emigrazione ed esportazione*, 51.

71. Ad for United States Macaroni Factory, *Il Progresso*, January 13, 1900, 1.

72. Ad for Italian Cigar & Tobacco Company, *Il Progresso*, June 29, 1900, 3.

73. Elizabeth Zanoni, "'In Italy everyone enjoys it. Why not in America?': Italian Americans and Consumption in Transnational Perspective during the Early Twentieth Century," in *Making Italian America: Consumer Culture and the Production of Ethnic Identities*, ed. Simone Cinotto (New York: Fordham University Press, 2014), 71–82. On the history of marketing and mass adverting, see Strasser, *Satisfaction Guaranteed*; Jackson Lears, *Fables of Abundance: A Cultural History of Advertising in America* (New York: Basic Books, 1994); Stuart Ewen and Elizabeth Ewen, *Channels of Desire: Mass Images and the Shaping of American Consciousness* (New York: McGraw-Hill, 1982).

74. Ad for Razzetti Brothers, *Il Progresso*, December 16, 1910, 8; ad for G. B. Lobravico, *Il Progresso*, April 3, 1910, 3.

75. Ad for American Chianti Wine Company, *Il Progresso*, December 16, 4.

76. Ad for De Nobili, *Il Progresso,* September 2, 1915, 7; ad for De Nobili, *Rivista*, December 1911, 49.

77. John E. Zucchi, "Paesani or Italiani? Local and National Loyalties in an Italian Immigrant Community," in *The Family and Community Life of Italian Americans*, ed. Richard Juliani (New York: American-Italian Historical Association, 1983), 147–60.

78. Zanoni, "In Italy everyone enjoys it," 73–77.

79. Cinotto, *Italian American Table,* 172–76.

80. See, for example, Visconti, *Emigrazione ed esportazione*, 6–7.

81. Frescura, "La Mostra degli Italiani all'Estero," 220–21.

82. Luigi Solari, "Tutela d'interessi legittimi," *Rivista*, September 1909, 7.

83. "Per l'alimentazione pura contro le frodi sugli olii d'oliva," *Rivista*, March 1910, 7.

84. Ramon Ramon-Muñoz, "Modernizing the Mediterranean Olive-Oil Industry," in *The Food Industries of Europe in the Nineteenth and Twentieth Centuries*, ed. Derek J. Oddy and Alain Drouard (Burlington, VT: Ashgate, 2013), 71–88; Leo A. Loubère, *The Red and the White: A History of Wine in France and Italy in the Nineteenth Century* (Albany: State University of New York Press, 1978).

85. See, for example, "Atti della camera," *Rivista*, October 1909, 1; "Atti della camera," *Rivista*, February 1910, 9; "Atti della camera," *Rivista,* May 1910, 1; Solari, "Tutela d'interessi legittimi," 7.

86. "Frode in commercio contraffazione di marche," *Rivista*, October 1910, 6; "Sentenze commerciali," *Rivista*, February 1911, 19.

87. "Sentenze commerciali," *Rivista*, August 1911, 39; "Sentenze commerciali," *Rivista*, July 1911, 16.

88. See, for example, "Frodi e manipolazioni di prodotti italiani," *Bollettino Mensile*, August 31, 1908, 6; "Atti della camera," *Bollettino Mensile*, September 1908, 1.

89. "Assemblea Ordinaria del 15 Luglio 1900," *Bollettino Mensile*, August 5, 1900, 2.

90. "Ai produttori d'Italia," *Bollettino Mensile*, April 5, 1900, 1; "Atti della camera," *Bollettino Mensile*, January 5, 1901, 2; "Il Congresso Ispano-Americano," *Bollettino Mensile*, February 5, 1901.

91. Rocchi, *Chimneys in the Desert*, 90.

92. Comitato della Camera Italiana di Commercio ed Arti, *Gli italiani nella Repubblica Argentina all'Esposizione di Torino 1911* (Buenos Aires: Stabilimento Grafico della Compañia General de Fósforos, 1911), 67–69.

93. "Raccomandazioni ai nostri speditori di formaggi," *Bollettino Mensile*, August 1908, 6.

94. Comitato della Camera Italiana di Commercio ed Arti, *Gli italiani nella Repubblica Argentina all'Esposizione di Torino 1911*.

95. "Concorrenza," *Bollettino Mensile*, April 5, 1901, 1.

96. "Atti della camera," *Bollettino Mensile*, November 1899, 2.

97. "Atti della camera," *Bollettino Mensile*, April 1901, 2.

98. "Frodi e manipolazioni di prodotti italiani,", 6.

99. "Importazione di commestibili e bibite," *Bollettino Mensile*, July 1902, 7; "Importazione di commestibili e bibite," *Bollettino Mensile*, August, 1902, 7; "Notizie varie," *Bollettino Mensile*, February 1904, 5.

100. "Atti della camera," *Bollettino Mensile*, September 30, 1908, 2.

101. "Esportazione vinicola," *Bollettino Mensile*, September 5, 1900, 1–2.

102. "Ministero di Agricoltura, Industria e Commercio, Legge concernente disposizioni per combattere le frodi nella preparazione e nel commercio dei vini," *Bollettino Mensile*, May 5, 1901, 4–5.

103. "Importazione di commestibili e bibite," *Bollettino Mensile*, July 1902, 2; "Importazione di commestibili e bibite," *Bollettino Mensile*, August 1902, 7; "Notizie varie," *Bollettino Mensile*, February 1904, 5.

104. "Atti della camera," *Bollettino Mensile*, April 1901, 2; "Atti della camera," *Bollettino Mensile*, September 1901, 2.

105. "Atti della camera," *Bollettino Mensile*, August 1904, 3; "Atti della camera," *Bollettino Mensile*, January 1, 1905, 1.

106. "Rapporto del R. Enotecnico Italiano al R. Ministero di Agricoltura Industria e Commercio," *Rivista*, January 1909, 7–9.

107. "Concorrenza," 1.

108. "Il Congresso Ispano-Americano," 1–2.

109. Dirección General de Inmigración, *Resumen estadistico del movimiento migratorio en la Republica Argentina, años 1857–1924* (Buenos Aires: Talleres Gráficos del Ministerio de Agricultura de la Nación, 1925), 8–9.

110. "L'emigrazione italiana nel 1 semestre 1908," *Bollettino Mensile*, October 15, 1908, 5–6.

111. Comitato della Camera Italiana di Commercio ed Arti, *Gli italiani nella Repubblica Argentina all'Esposizione di Torino 1911*. On the competition between Spanish and Italian migrants in Buenos Aires, see Jose C. Moya, *Cousins and Strangers: Spanish Immigrants in Buenos Aires, 1850–1930* (Berkeley: University of California Press, 1998), especially chapter 7.

112. "Il Congresso Ispano-Americano," 1–2.

113. Donna R. Gabaccia, "Making Foods Italian in the Hispanic Atlantic" (unpublished paper, University of Minnesota, November 1, 2006); Vito Teti, ed., *Mangiare meridiano: Culture alimentari del Mediterraneo* (Traversa Cassiodoro, Italy: Abramo, 2002).

114. Visconti, *Emigrazione ed esportazione*, 17–18.

115. "Atto della camera," *Bollettino Mensile*, July 1904, 2–3; "Atto della camera," *Bollettino Mensile*, October 1904, 1.

116. Frescura, "La Mostra degli Italiani all'Estero," 81–86.

117. "Atti della camera," *Bollettino Mensile*, May, 1910, 3.

118. "Atti della camera," *Bollettino Mensile*, June, 1910, 4.

119. Ad for Confiteria los dos Chinos, *La Prensa*, December 16, 1900, 8; ad for Confiteria los dos Chinos, *La Patria*, December 22, 1905, 10.

120. Fabio Parasecoli, *Food Culture in Italy* (Westport, CT: Greenwood Press, 2004), 47.

121. On Mexican foodways, see Jeffrey M. Pilcher, *Que vivan los tamales!: Food and the Making of Mexican Identity* (Albuquerque: University of New Mexico Press, 1998).

122. Rebekah E. Pite discusses a recipe for *pan dulce de Navidad* from Doña Patrona's 1934 cookbook, *El libro de Doña Patrona*. See Rebekah E. Pite, *Creating a Common Table in Twentieth-Century Argentina: Doña Petrona, Women, and Food* (Chapel Hill: University of North Carolina Press, 2013), 91.

123. On Italians in the history of Argentine wine making, see Scarzanella, *Italiani d'Argentina*, 44–45. Aníbal B. Arcondo, *Historia de la alimentación en Argentina: Desde los orígienes hasta 1920* (Córdoba: Ferreyra Editor, 2002), 245–48. On the United States, see Cinotto, *Soft Soil, Black Grapes*; Donna R. Gabaccia, "Ethnicity in the Business World: Italians in American Food Industries," *Italian American Review* 6, no. 2 (1997/1998): 1–19.

124. On Tomba, see Comitato della Camera Italiana di Commercio ed Arti, *Gli italiani nella Repubblica Argentina,* 204–214; "Establecimiento vitivínicola Domingo Tomba, *La Nación*, Numero del centenario, 1810–1910, 1910, 241–43.

125. On the Italian-Swiss Colony, see Patrizi, *Gl'italiani in California,* 35–37; Cinotto, *Soft Soil, Black Grapes*, 4, 19; Gabaccia, *We Are What We Eat*, 73, 87.

126. Comitato della Camera Italiana di Commercio ed Arti, *Gli italiani nella Repubblica Argentina*, 213.

127. "Crisi vinicola," *Bollettino Mensile*, March 1902, 1–2.

128. Ad for Tomba wine, *La Patria*, September 20, 1910, 2.

129. "Establecimiento vitivícola Domingo Tomba," 241.

130. Ad for Tomba wine, *La Patria,* September 29, 1905, 2.

131. Marni Davis, *Jews and Booze: Becoming American in the Age of Prohibition* (New York: New York University Press, 2012).

132. Cinotto, *Soft Soil, Black Grapes.*

133. Patrizi, *Gl'italiani in California*, 35–37.

134. "Vino di California," *Rivista*, April 1909, 29–30; Rossati, "La vendammia in Italia ed il commercio dei vini italiani cogli S.U. nel 1905," 41.

135. "Perche non progredisce l'esportazione dei vini italiani," *La Patria*, January 20, 1910, 7.

136. Eugenia Scarzanella, *Italiani malagente: Immigrazione, criminalità, razzismo in Argentina, 1890–1940* (Milan: F. Angeli, 1999), 25; Arcondo, *Historia de la alimentación en Argentina*, 100–105.

Chapter 4. "Pro Patria": Women and the Normalization of Migrant Consumption during World War I

1. B. A., "Quel che insegna il presente dissidio tra l'Argentina e l'Italia," *Rivista Commerciale* (hereafter *Rivista*), October 1911, 6.

2. *Gli italiani nel Sud America ed il loro contributo alla guerra: 1915–1918* (Buenos Aires: Arigoni & Barbieri, 1922), 21–53; "Comitato Generale Italiano di Soccorso Pro Croce Rossa e famiglie dei richiamati," *Il Progresso Italo-Americano* (hereafter *Il Progresso*), September 8, 1915, 2; "Pro patria," *Il Progresso*, November 9, 1915, 1; E. Zuccarini, "Virtù italica," *La Patria degli* Italiani (hereafter *La Patria*), September 18, 1915, 4. On Italians' war efforts in Buenos Aires and Montevideo, see John Starosta Galante, "The 'Great War' in *Il Plata*: Italian Immigrants in Buenos Aires and Montevideo during the First World War," *Journal of Migration History* 2, no. 1 (2016): 57–92.

3. See, for example, "Vita sociale," *La Patria*, September 26, 1915, 5; "Vita sociale," *La Patria*, October 6, 1915, 5; *Gli italiani nel Sud America*, 199; "Sottocomitato della Boca," *La Patria*, September 15, 1915, 5; "Il gran concerto al Century per le famiglie dei richiamati," *Il Progresso*, July 29, 1915, 2.

4. For Argentina, see "Pro patria, la festa pro lana," *La Patria*, January 6, 1916, 5; "L'iniziativa della 'Patria degli Italiani,'" *La Patria*, September 1, 1915, 6; Un italiano, "Per il freddo dei nostri soldati," *La Patria*, September 4, 1915, 4; "Vita sociale," *La Patria*, October 8, 1915, 4. For the United States, see, "Il cuore delle nostre colonie per i prodi soldati d'Italia," *Il Progresso*, September 9, 1915, 1; "Proteggiamo i nostri soldati," *Il Progresso*, September 12, 1915, 1.

5. "Cronaca rosarino," *La Patria,* September 6, 1915, 7.

6. "Sezione Femminile del Comitato di Guerra," *La Patria*, January 8, 1916, 5.

7. "Per i nostri combattenti," *Il Progresso*, October 19, 1915, 2.

8. "Vita sociale," *La Patria*, September 2, 1915, 5.

9. Gianfausto Rosoli, ed., *Un secolo di emigrazione italiana, 1876–1976* (Rome: Centro Studi Emigrazione, 1978), 354.

10. Mark I. Choate, *Emigrant Nation: The Making of Italy Abroad* (Cambridge: Harvard University Press, 2008), 208.

11. For Argentina, see "Notizie statistiche sui movimenti migratori," *Bollettino dell'emigrazione* (hereafter *Bollettino*) 1 (1910): 77. For the United States, see "Emigrazione dall'Europa e immigrazione in America e in Australia," *Bollettino* 14 (1907): 127.

12. Commissariato Generale dell'Emigrazione, *Annuario statistico della emigrazione italiana dal 1876 al 1925* (Rome: Edizione del Commissariato Generale dell'Emigrazione, 1926), 432.

13. See, for example, "La moda," *Il Progresso*, November 3, 1915, 5; "Per le signore," *Il Progresso*, November 10, 1915, 9.

14. Examples include "Cronache femminile," *La Patria*, April 14, 1915, 4; "Cronache femminile," *La Patria*, May 23, 1915, 4. By the end of World War I the column had expanded slightly and changed its name to "Vita femminile" (feminine life). "Vita femminile," *La Patria*, June 1, 1917, 4; "Vita femminile," *La Patria*, January 1, 1920, 8.

15. "Per i nostri soldati," *Il Progresso*, September 4, 1915, 1.

16. "L'offerta del 'Costurero Italo-Argentino,'" *La Patria*, September 18, 1915, 5.

17. "Appunti. . . . lana, lana, lana!," *La Patria*, August 29, 1915, 4.

18. "Sezione Femminile del Comitato Italiano di Guerra," *La Patria,* August 15, 1915, 7.

19. S. Magnani-Tedeschi, "La donna italiana e la guerra," *La Patria*, September 21, 1915, 3.

20. "Appunti. . . . lana, lana, lana!," 4; "Date lana," *La Patria*, November 10, 1915, 4.

21. Magnani-Tedeschi, "La donna italiana e la guerra."

22. "L'offerta del 'Costurero Italo-Argentino,'" *La Patria*, September 18, 1915, 5.

23. "La raccolta per la lana del Comitato delle Donne Italiane sotto gli auspicii del Progresso Italo-Americano," *Il Progresso*, September 17, 1915, 2.

24. "Proteggiamo i nostri soldati," *Il Progresso*, September 12, 1915, 1.

25. "Date lana," *La Patria*, 4.

26. "Pro patria," *La Patria*, January 6, 1916, 5.

27. Ibid., 6.

28. *Gli italiani nel sud America*, 38.

29. "Italian-American Ladies Association for Italian Soldiers Relief Fund," *Rivista*, January 17, 1916, 1.

30. "Il fascio delle forze italiane," *La Patria*, July 13, 1915, 3. For the United States, see Camera di Commercio Italiana in New York, *Nel cinquantenario della Camera di Commercio Italiana in New York, 1887–1937* (New York, 1937), 142.

31. "Il dovere della nostra colonia," *Rivista*, July 19, 1915, 1.

32. Luigi Solari, "Appello ai soci," *Rivista*, August 23, 1915, 1. Emphasis is in the original.

33. "Comitato Generale Italiano di Soccorso pro Croce Rossa e famiglie dei richiamati," *Il Progresso*, July 10, 1915, 2.

34. "Agli abbonati, ai lettori, agli amici," *La Patria*, May 24, 1915, 5.

35. "Per l'album al Principe di Udine," *Il Progresso*, June 7, 1917, 2.

36. *Gli italiani nel Sud America*, 32, 199.

37. "Per la celebrazione del XX Settembre," *La Patria*, September 18, 1915, 5; "Attraverso i rioni della città durante la distribuzione dei cesti-regalo," *La Patria*, September 24, 1915, 4. See also M. Gravina, *Almanacco dell'Italiano nell'Argentina (Buenos Aires, 1918)*, 189; *Gli italiani nel Sud America*, 34–35.

38. "Per la celebrazione del XX Settembre," *La Patria*, September 18, 1915, 5.

39. "Appunti. . . . lana, lana, lana!," *La Patria*, August 29, 1915, 4.

40. "Vita sociale," *La patria*, September 7, 1916, 5.

41. See ad for Gath & Chaves, *La Patria*, September 10, 1915, 6; ad for Gath & Chaves, *La Patria*, August 13, 1915.

42. "Le assemblee della Camera Italiana di Commercio," *La Patria*, September 12, 1915, 6.

43. "Agli italiani residenti all'estero," *La Patria*, September 20, 1916, 27.

44. Camera di Commercio Italiana in New York, *Nel cinquantenario della Camera di Commercio Italiana in New York*, 142.

45. "Cronaca rosarina," *La Patria*, December 15, 1915, 6.

46. "Agli italiani residenti all'estero," 27.

47. "Un grande dovere patriottico," *La Patria*, September 26, 1915, 7.

48. Ad for San Pellegrino sparking water, *La Patria*, September 20, 1917.

49. Ad for Florio Marsala and Malvasia, *La Patria*, July 8, 1917, 7.

50. D. Bórea, "Comitato Agrario Italiano nell'Argentina," *La Patria*, September 5, 1915, 6.

51. Ibid.

52. *Gli italiani nel Sud America*, 39–40.

53. "Pro patria," *La Patria*, January 13, 1916, 7.

54. "L'offerta del 'Costurero Italo-Argentino,'" *La Patria*, September 18, 1915, 5. See also "Solidarietà italo-argentina," *La Patria*, September 16, 1915.

55. "Costurero Privado Italo-Argentino," *La Patria*, September 12, 1915, 6.

56. *Gli italiani nel Sud America*, 252–53.

57. See, for example, "Vita sociale," *La Patria*, September 26, 1915, 5; "Per la Croce Rossa Alleata," *La Patria*, September 26, 1915, 8.

58. Ad for Harrods, *La Patria,* September 26, 1915, 8.

59. On Piccardo, see Fernando Rocchi, *Chimneys in the Desert: Industrialization in Argentina during the Export Boom Years, 1870–1930* (Stanford, CA: Stanford University Press, 2006), 55, 79–81.

60. "Italian Wines in Competition with French and German Wines," *Rivista*, October 5, 1914, 1–2.

61. "Italian Sparkling Wines Successfully Competing with the Best Champagne Brands," *Rivista*, October 12, 1914, 1–2.

62. Ministero delle Finanze, *Movimento commerciale del Regno d'Italia nell'anno 1919*, Parte Seconda (Rome: Stabilimento Poligrafico per l'Amministrazione della Guerra, 1921), 1046, 1065. A quintal is one hundred kilograms.

63. Ibid., 1288, 1301, 1302.

64. Ibid., 1064, 1065, 1301.

65. Camera di Commercio Italiana in New York, *Nel cinquantenario della Camera di Commercia Italiana in New York*, 141–43. In response to the chambers' pleas, Italy allowed Italian ships to devote a higher quantity of tonnage to the transport of Italian merchandise to the United States. For a list of items banned from exportation by the Italian government, see "Elenco completo delle merci delle quali il governo italiano ha vietata l'esportazione," *Rivista*, March 15, 1915, 1.

66. On La Rosa, see Simone Cinotto, *The Italian American Table: Food, Family, and Community in New York City* (Urbana: University of Illinois Press, 2013), 137.

67. Ibid., 130–41.

68. Camera di Commercio Italiana in New York, *Nel cinquantenario della Camera di Commercio Italiana in New York*, 142.

69. "Una nostra nuova iniziativa pro patria," *Il Progresso*, November 20, 1915, 1. See also "Pro patria," *Il Progresso*, November 21, 1915, 2.

70. "Per la patria," *Il Progresso*, November 25, 1915, 3.

71. "Sigari per i nostri soldati!," *Il Progresso*, September 2, 1917, 3.

72. Ibid.

73. Ibid. See ad for De Nobili cigars, *Il Progresso*, September 2, 1915, 7.

74. See, for example, "Per la salute dei nostri soldati," *Il Progresso*, October 15, 1917, 3.

75. "La cassetta di Natale per i nostri trionfatori sulle Alpi," *Il Progresso*, September 2, 1917, 2; emphasis is mine.

76. "La cassetta di Natale per i nostri trionfatori sulle Alpi," *Il Progresso*, September 3, 1917, 2.

77. "La casette di Natale per i nostri trionfatori sulle Alpi," *Il Progresso*, November 15, 1917, 3.

78. "Una nostra nuova iniziativa pro patria," 1.

79. "Sigari e sigarette pei nostri combattenti," *Il Progresso*, September 1, 1917, 3.

80. Gary Gerstle, *American Crucible: Race and Nation in the Twentieth Century* (Princeton, NJ: Princeton University Press, 2001), 81–127; John Higham, *Strangers in the Land: Patterns of American Nativism, 1860–1925* (New Brunswick, NJ: Rutgers University Press, 1955), 194–221; Donna R. Gabaccia, *Foreign Relations: American Immigration in Global Perspective* (Princeton, NJ: Princeton University Press, 2012), 122–25.

81. Camera di Commercio Italiana in New York, *Nel cinquantenario della Camera di Commercio Italiana in New York*, 142; "Prestito del Governo Italiano negli Stati Uniti," *Il Progresso*, October 30, 1915, 9; "Gli italiani nell'esercito dei Uncle Sam," *Il Progresso*, September 18, 1917, 1; "Il secondo prestito della libertà," *Il Progresso*, October 5, 1917, 2; "Il Progresso a disposizione dei suoi lettori per l'acquisto dei liberty-bonds," *Il Progresso*, October 5, 1917, 2. On foreign-born soldiers in the U.S. military, see Nancy Gentile Ford, *Americans All!: Foreign-Born Soldiers in World War I* (College Station: Texas A&M University Press, 2001).

82. "La raccolta per la lana e la nostra iniziativa," *Il Progresso*, October 16, 1915, 2.

83. Gravina, *Almanacco dell'italiano nell'Argentina*, 190; "Per le desolate famiglie dei nostri combattenti," *Il Progresso*, November 7, 1915, 2.

84. For additional examples, see ads for Cinzano, *La Patria*, December 11, 1915, 6; *La Patria*, December 15, 1915, 6; *La Patria*, December 17, 1915, 6; *La Patria*, November 27, 1915, 6.

85. Ad for Cinzano vermouth, *La Patria*, February 4, 1905, 3; ad for Cinzano, *La Patria*, January 23, 1910, 4.

86. Donna R. Gabaccia, "Women of the Mass Migrations: From Minority to Majority, 1820–1930," in *European Migrants: Global and Local Perspectives*, ed. Dirk Hoerder and Leslie Page Moch (Boston: Northeastern University Press, 1996), 90–111.

87. David Cook-Martín, "Soldiers and Wayward Women: Gendered Citizenship, and Migration Policy in Argentina, Italy, and Spain since 1850," *Citizenship Studies* 10, no. 5 (2006): 571–90; Donna J. Guy, *Sex and Danger in Buenos Aires: Prostitution, Family, and Nation in Argentina* (Lincoln: University of Nebraska Press, 1991), 16–35; Martha Gardner, *The Qualities of a Citizen: Women, Immigration, and Citizenship, 1870–1965* (Princeton, NJ: Prince-

ton University Press, 2005); Eithne Luibhéid, *Entry Denied: Controlling Sexuality at the Border* (Minneapolis: University of Minnesota Press, 2002).

88. Donna R. Gabaccia, "When the Migrants Are Men: Italy's Women and Transnationalism as a Working-Class Way of Life," in *American Dreaming, Global Realities: Rethinking U.S. Immigration History*, ed. Donna R. Gabaccia and Vicki L. Ruiz (Urbana: University of Illinois Press, 2006), 199.

89. Bernardino Frescura, "La Mostra degli Italiani all'Estero, all'Esposizione Internazionale di Milano nel 1906," *Bollettino* 18 (1907): 171.

90. Leopoldo Corinaldi, "L'emigrazione italiana negli Stati Uniti," *Bollettino* 2 (1902): 5.

91. José María Ramos Mejía, *The Argentine Masses* (1899), in *Darwinism in Argentina: Major Texts, 1845–1909*, ed. Leila Gómez, trans. Nicholas Ford Callaway (Lanham, MD: Bucknell University Press), 209–210.

92. "Instruzioni per chi emigra negli Stati Uniti dell'America del Nord," *Bollettino* 15 (1904): 52.

93. G. Naselli, "Gli Italiani nel distretto consolare di Filadelfia," *Bollettino* 10 (1903): 33.

94. On the gendering of consumption globally, see especially Victoria de Grazia, with Ellen Furlough, eds., *The Sex of Things: Gender and Consumption in Historical Perspective* (Berkeley: University of California Press, 1996).

95. For classic treatment of this gendered process, see Louise A. Tilly and Joan W. Scott, *Women, Work, and Family* (New York: Holt, Rinehart, and Winston, 1978).

96. Leonore Davidoff and Catherine Hall, *Family Fortunes: Men and Women of the English Middle Class, 1780–1850* (Chicago: University of Chicago Press, 1987); Erika D. Rappaport, *Shopping for Pleasure: Women in the Making of London's West End* (Princeton, NJ: Princeton University Press, 2000); Lisa Tiersten, *Marianne in the Market: Envisioning Consumer Society in Fin-de-Siècle France* (Berkeley: University of California Press, 2001).

97. For the United States, see Kristin L. Hoganson, *Consumers' Imperium: The Global Production of American Domesticity, 1865–1920* (Chapel Hill: University of North Carolina Press, 2007). For Argentina, see Cecilia Tossounian, "Images of the Modern Girl: From the Flapper to the Joven Moderna (Buenos Aires, 1920–1940)," *Forum for Inter-American Research* 6, no. 2 (2013): 41–70.

98. Jennifer Scanlon, *Inarticulate Longings: The* Ladies' Home Journal, *Gender, and the Promises of Consumer Culture* (New York: Routledge, 1995).

99. Carolyn M. Goldstein, *Creating Consumers: Home Economists in Twentieth-Century America* (Chapel Hill: University of North Carolina Press, 2012); Rebekah E. Pite, *Creating a Common Table in Twentieth-Century Argentina: Doña Petrona, Women, and Food* (Chapel Hill: University of North Carolina Press, 2013), 27–29.

100. For an overview of this literature, see de Grazia and Furlough, *Sex of Things*.

101. Elizabeth Zanoni, "'Per Voi, Signore': Gendered Representations of Fashion, Food, and Fascism in *Il Progresso Italo-Americano* during the 1930s," *Journal of American Ethnic History* 31, no. 3 (2012): 33–71; Simone Cinotto, "All Things Italian: Italian American Consumers, the Transnational Formation of Taste, and the Commodification of Difference," in *Making Italian America: Consumer Culture and the Production of Ethnic Identities*, ed. Simone Cinotto (New York: Fordham University Press, 2014), 1–31.

102. For the United States, see Lizabeth Cohen, *Making a New Deal: Industrial Workers in Chicago, 1919–1939*, 2nd ed. (Cambridge: Cambridge University Press, 2008); Meg Jacobs, *Pocketbook Politics: Economic Citizenship in Twentieth-American America* (Princeton, NJ: Princeton University Press, 2005). For Argentina, see Eduardo Elena, *Dignifying Argentina: Peronism, Citizenship, and Mass Consumption* (Pittsburgh: University of Pittsburgh Press, 2011); Natalia Milanesio, *Workers Go Shopping in Argentina: The Rise of Popular Consumer Culture* (Albuquerque: University of New Mexico Press, 2013).

103. Ad for Banfi Products Co., *Il Progresso*, December 21, 1927, 2; emphasis is mine.

104. Ad for Cirio tomato extract, *La Patria*, September 4, 1925, 3. On Cirio and the early development of the Italian tomato production, see David Gentilcore, *Pomodoro!: A History of the Tomato in Italy* (New York: Columbia University Press, 2010), 83–89, 109–115, 136–42.

105. On migration's influence on the tomato industry in Italy, see Gentilcore, *Pomodoro!*, 109–119.

106. Ad for Florio Marsala, *Il Progresso*, November 21, 1937, 9.

107. Ad for Bertolli olive oil, *L'Italia* (Chicago), August 14, 1932.

108. Notice the only man in the ad is in a chef outfit, showing continued gendered divisions between the informal, non-remunerative food work done by women in the domestic realm and the professional, paid work of male chefs in restaurants and public eating cultures.

109. Elizabeth Zanoni, "'In Italy everyone enjoys it. Why not in America?': Italian Americans and Consumption in Transnational Perspective during the Early Twentieth Century," in Cinotto, *Making Italian America*, 79–81.

110. Ad for Bertolli, *L'Italia* (Chicago), August 14, 1932.

111. Ad for Sasso, *La Patria*, January 3, 1916, 2.

112. On the rising standards of living in Italy, see Emanuela Scarpellini, *Material Nation: A Consumer's History of Modern Italy*, trans. Daphne Hughes and Andrew Newton (New York: Oxford University Press, 2011); Francesco Chiapparino, Renato Covino, and Gianni Bovini, *Consumi e industria alimentare in Italia dall'unità a oggi: Lineamenti per una storia*, 2nd ed. (Narni, Italy: Giada, 2002), 81–90.

113. Linda Reeder, *Widows in White: Migration and the Transformation of Rural Italian Women, Sicily, 1880–1920* (Toronto: University of Toronto Press, 2003), 14.

114. On gendered messages about food and domesticity intended for middle-class, female readers in the United States, see Scanlon, *Inarticulate Longings*; Laura Shapiro, *Perfection Salad: Women and Cooking at the Turn of the Century* (New York: Farrar, Straus, and Giroux, 1986); Amy Bentley, *Inventing Baby Food: Taste, Health, and the Industrialization of the American Diet* (Berkeley: University of California Press, 2014). For Argentina, see Pite, *Creating a Common Table*, 45–52, 58–65, 76–84. See also Sherrie A. Inness, ed., *Kitchen Culture in America: Popular Representations of Food, Gender, and Race* (Philadelphia: University of Pennsylvania Press, 2001); Sherrie A. Inness, *Cooking Lessons: The Politics of Gender and Food* (Lanham, MD: Rowman & Littlefield, 2001).

115. Ad for Sasso olive oil, *La Patria*, November 29, 1915, 2.

116. Ad for Brioschi digestive aid, *Il Progresso*, February 9, 1936, illustrated section.

117. Hasia Diner, among others, discusses these generational networks of food culture within the Italian American context. Hasia R. Diner, *Hungering for America: Italian, Irish, and Jewish Foodways in the Age of Migration* (Cambridge: Harvard University Press, 2001), 79.

118. Cohen, *Making a New Deal*, 110–16; Donna R. Gabaccia, *We Are What We Eat: Ethnic Food and the Making of Americans* (Cambridge: Harvard University Press, 1998), 45–63.

119. For the history of advertising, see Pamela Walker Laird, *Advertising Progress: American Business and the Rise of Consumer Marketing* (Baltimore: Johns Hopkins University Press, 1998); Jackson Lears, *Fables of Abundance: A Cultural History of Advertising in America* (New York: Basic Books, 1994); Roland Marchand, *Advertising the American Dream: Making Way for Modernity, 1920–1940* (Berkeley: University of California Press, 1985); Stuart Ewen, *Captains of Consciousness: Advertising and the Social Roots of the Consumer Culture* (New York: McGraw-Hill, 1976). For Argentina, see Rocchi, *Chimneys in the Desert*, 77–85; Milanesio, *Workers Go Shopping in Argentina*, 83–122. This trend also coincided with the slow move away from selling food in bulk, instigated in part by food safety laws requiring the labeling of foods by origin, weight, and contents; the smaller food units sold in boxes, cans, jars, and bottles were more easily branded than foodstuff transported and sold in bulk. Susan Strasser, *Satisfaction Guaranteed: The Making of the American Mass Market* (New York: Pantheon Books, 1989); Aníbal B. Arcondo, *Historia de la alimentación en Argentina: Desde los orígienes hasta 1920* (Córdoba, Argentina: Ferreyra Editor, 2002).

120. Ad for Locatelli cheese, *Il Progresso*, December 16, 1934, 14.

121. Ad for Pastene coffee, *Il Progresso*, October 29, 1939, illustrated section.

122. Tracy N. Poe, "The Labour and Leisure of Food Production as a Mode of Ethnic Identity Building among Italians in Chicago, 1890–1940," *Rethinking History* 5, no. 1 (2001): 131–48; John E. Zucchi, "Paesani or Italiani? Local and National Loyalties in an Italian Immigrant Community," in *The Family and Community Life of Italian Americans*, ed. Richard Juliani (New York: American-Italian Historical Association, 1983), 147–60.

Chapter 5. Reorienting Migrant Marketplaces in *le due Americhe* during the Interwar Years

1. "Commentarii," *La Patria degli Italiani* (hereafter *La Patria*), July 4, 1917, 3.

2. F. Filippini, "Camera Italo-Argentina di Industria e Commercio di Genova," *La Patria*, May 12, 1915, 6.

3. I follow the lead of Lok Siu, who argues that the migration of Chinese to Latin America should be understood within the context of migrants' enduring ties to their homeland and to the larger history of U.S. economic, political, and military interventions in Latin America. Lok C. D. Siu, *Memories of a Future Home: Diasporic Citizenship of Chinese in Panama* (Stanford, CA: Stanford University Press, 2005).

4. On Garibaldi, see especially Lucy Riall, *Garibaldi: Invention of a Hero* (New Haven, CT: Yale University Press, 2007); Alfonso Scirocco, *Garibaldi: Citizen of the World*, trans. Allan Cameron (Princeton, NJ: Princeton University Press, 2007).

5. "Il Congresso ispano-americano," *Bollettino Mensile della Camera Italiana di Commercio in Buenos Aires*, February 5, 1901, 1–2.

6. On U.S. economic and cultural expansion in Latin America, see especially Emily S. Rosenberg, *Financial Missionaries to the World: The Politics and Culture of Dollar Diplomacy, 1900–1930* (Cambridge: Harvard University Press, 1999); María I. Barbero and Andrés M. Regalsky, eds. *Americanización: Estados Unidos y América Latina en el siglo XX. Transferencias económicas, tecnológicas y culturales* (Buenos Aires: EDUNTREF, 2014); Gilbert M. Joseph, Catherine C. LeGrand, and Ricardo D. Salvatore, eds., *Close Encounters of Empire: Writing the Cultural History of U.S.-Latin American Relations* (Durham, NC: Duke University Press, 1998).

7. "Lotta fra due mondi," *La Patria,* January 26, 1910, 5; "La crisi del Monroismo," *La Patria*, April 8, 1906, 3.

8. "Psicologia Pan-americana," *La Patria*, July 17, 1910, 5.

9. "La politica yankee," *La Patria,* July 21, 1910, 6.

10. "Lo spauracchio yankee," *La Patria*, July 24, 1910, 5.

11. "La lacuna del Congresso Pan-americano," *La Patria*, July 19, 1910, 5.

12. "Panamericanismo," *La Patria*, October 18, 1910, 7.

13. "Tocchi in penna," *La Patria*, March 3, 1910, 5.

14. Vico Mantegazza, "Italia e Argentina," *La Patria*, May 16, 1910, 3.

15. "Il verbo della disillusione," *La Patria*, June 8, 1910, 5.

16. "Italia e Argentina," *La Patria*, July 9, 1910, 7.

17. "Il Centenario Argentino," *La Patria*, June 22, 1910, 7.

18. "L'America Latina per Enrico Piccione," *La Patria*, August 3, 1906, 3.

19. S. Magnani Tedeschi, "Argentini e Italiani per il trionfo della latinità," *La Patria*, August 18, 1925, 4.

20. Paulina L. Alberto and Eduardo Elena, "Introduction: Shades of the Nation," in *Rethinking Race in Modern Argentina*, eds. Paulina L. Alberto and Eduardo Elena (New York: Cambridge University Press, 2016), 1–22.

21. "Sull'America Latina," *La Patria*, April 14 1910, 4.

22. R. Lucente, "Vita americana," *La Patria*, May 2, 1906, 4.

23. Michel Gobat, "The Invention of Latin America: A Transnational History of Anti-Imperialism, Democracy, and Race," *American Historical Review* 118, no. 5 (2013): 1345–75.

24. Alfredo Malaurie and Juan M. Gazzano, *La Industria Argentina y la Exposición del Paraná* (Buenos Aires: De Juan M. Gazzano y Cia., 1888), 9, 64, 145.

25. Andrés Regalsky and Aníbal Jáuregui, "Americanización, proyecto económico y las ideas de Alejandro Bunge en la década de 1920," in Barbero and Regalsky, *Americanización*, 85–117.

26. Samuel Flagg Bemis, *The Latin American Policy of the United States* (New York: Harcourt, Brace and Co., 1943), 147, 230.

27. Donna R. Gabaccia, *Foreign Relations: American Immigration in Global Perspective* (Princeton, NJ: Princeton University Press, 2012), 84.

28. From the mid-nineteenth century to World War I, the British invested heavily in Argentina's agro-export industries and in railroads, ports, and communication networks. Donna J. Guy, "Dependency, the Credit Market, and Argentine Industrialization, 1860–1940," *Business History Review* 58, no. 4 (1984): 532–61.

29. Direzione Generale di Statistica e del Lavoro, *Annuario statistico italiano* (Rome, 1915), 178; Direzione Generale di Statistica, *Annuario statistico italiano* (Rome, 1919–1921), 268.

30. Department of Commerce, Bureau of Foreign and Domestic Commerce, *Statistical Abstract of the United States: 1920* (Washington, DC: U.S. Government Printing Office, 1921), 411.

31. Department of Commerce, Bureau of Foreign and Domestic Commerce, *Statistical Abstract of the United States: 1931* (Washington, DC: U.S. Government Printing Office, 1931), 503.

32. Ibid., 504.

33. Department of Commerce, Bureau of Foreign and Domestic Commerce, *Statistical Abstract of the United States: 1929* (Washington, DC: U.S. Government Printing Office, 1929), 487.

34. James A. Farrell, "South Americans Can Gain by Use of Own Money Locally," National Foreign Trade Council Bulletin #55 (1938), box 25, folder bulletins B-1B-68 1938, National Foreign Trade Council Records, Hagley Museum and Library, Wilmington, Delaware (hereafter Hagley).

35. Dudley Maynard Phelps, *Migration of Industry to South America* (New York: McGraw-Hill, 1936), 13, 15, 18–21.

36. Ibid., 128. M. J. French, "The Emergence of a U.S. Multinational Enterprise: The Goodyear Tire and Rubber Company, 1910–1939," *Economic History Review* 40, no. 1 (1987): 69, 72.

37. Phelps, *Migration of Industry*, 11.

38. Ibid., 46–47. On Armour, see "L'inaugurazione del frigorifico Armour," *La Patria*, July 3, 1915, 6. See also Swift's biography: Louis F. Swift and Arthur Van Vlissingen Jr., *The Yankee of the Yards: The Biography of Gustavus Franklin Swift* (Chicago: A. W. Shaw, 1927).

39. On the history of the meatpacking industry, see especially Peter H. Smith, *Politics and Beef in Argentina: Patterns of Conflict and Change* (New York: Columbia University Press, 1969). See also Pepé Treviño, *La carne podrida: El caso Swift-Deltec*, 2nd ed. (Buenos Aires: A. Peña Lillo, 1972); Diego P. Roldán, *Chimeneas de carne: Una historia del frigorífico Swift de Rosario, 1907–1943* (Rosario, Argentina: Prohistoria Ediciones, 2008).

40. Samuel L. Baily and Franco Ramella, eds., *One Family, Two Worlds: An Italian Family's Correspondence across the Atlantic, 1901–1922*, trans. John Lenaghan (New Brunswick, NJ: Rutgers University Press, 1988), 195,198; Daniel James, *Doña Maria's Story: Life History, Memory, and Political Identity* (Durham, NC: Duke University Press, 2000).

41. Erika Lee, *At America's Gates: Chinese Immigration during the Exclusion Era, 1882–1943* (Chapel Hill: University of North Carolina, 2003); Robert F. Zeidel, *Immigrants, Progressives, and Exclusion Politics: The Dillingham Commission, 1900–1927* (DeKalb: Northern Illinois University Press, 2004); Aristide R. Zolberg, *A Nation by Design: Immigration Policy in the Fashioning of America* (New York: Russell Sage Foundation, 2006).

42. Gianfausto Rosoli, ed., *Un secolo di emigrazione italiana, 1876–1976* (Rome: Centro Studi Emigrazione, 1978), 354.

43. Gardner, *The Qualities of a Citizen: Women, Immigration, and Citizenship, 1870–1965* (Princeton, NJ: Princeton University Press, 2005).

44. See Eduardo José Míguez, "Introduction: Foreign Mass Migration to Latin America in the Nineteenth and Twentieth Centuries—an Overview," in *Mass Migration to Modern Latin America*, ed. by Samuel Baily and Eduardo José Míguez (Wilmington, DE: Scholarly Resources, 2003), xiii.

45. Erika Lee, "Orientalisms in the Americas: A Hemispheric Approach to Asian American History," *Journal of Asian American Studies* 8, no. 3 (2005): 235–65. The United States pressured countries in the western hemisphere to enact harsh immigration laws, especially Canada and Mexico. See Adam M. McKeown, *Melancholy Order: Asian Migration and the Globalization of Borders* (New York: Columbia University Press, 2008); Erika Lee, "Enforcing the Borders: Chinese Exclusion along the U.S. Borders with Canada and Mexico, 1882–1924," *Journal of American History* 89, no. 1 (2002): 54–86.

46. David Scott FitzGerald and David Cook-Martín, *Culling the Masses: The Democratic Origins of Racist Immigration Policy in the Americas* (Cambridge: Harvard University Press, 2014), 299–332; Samuel L. Baily and Eduardo José Míguez, ed., *Mass Migration to Modern Latin America* (Wilmington, DE: SR Books, 2003).

47. After about 1930 the U.S. would again become the more popular destination for western hemisphere–bound Italians but only by a couple thousand migrants annually. Rosoli, *Un secolo di emigrazione italiana*, 353–54.

48. Donna R. Gabaccia, *Italy's Many Diasporas* (Seattle: University of Washington Press, 2000), 129–52; Philip V. Cannistraro and Gianfausto Rosoli, "Fascist Emigration Policy in the 1920s: An Interpretive Framework," *International Migration Review* 13, no. 4 (1979): 673–92.

49. Kevin H. O'Rourke and Jeffrey G. Williamson, *Globalization and History: The Evolution of a Nineteenth-Century Atlantic Economy* (Cambridge: MIT Press, 1999), 186–206.

50. On immigration and ethnicity in Brazil, see Jeffrey Lesser, *Immigration, Ethnicity, and National Identity in Brazil, 1808 to the Present* (Cambridge: Cambridge University Press, 2013).

51. William Ricketts, "What Does South America Offer the American Advertiser," 31–37, box MN5, folder 1928, March-1929, Dec., JWT Newsletter Collection, 1910–1986, J. Walter Thompson Company Collections, Hartman Center for Sales, Advertising and Marketing History, David. M. Rubenstein Rare Book & Manuscript Library, Duke University, Durham, North Carolina (hereafter JWT Collections).

52. Phelps, *Migration of Industry*, 104–106.

53. Ibid., 239.

54. Ibid., 241.

55. Julie Greene, *The Canal Builders: Making America's Empire at the Panama Canal* (New York: Penguin Press, 2009); John Soluri, *Banana Cultures: Agriculture, Consumption, and Environmental Change in Honduras and the United States* (Austin: University of Texas Press, 2005); Steve Striffler and Mark Moberg, *Banana Wars: Power, Production, and History in the Americas* (Durham, NC: Duke University Press, 2003).

56. Phelps, *Migration of Industry*, 243. On U.S. racial attitudes toward Italian and other working-class migrant groups, see Matthew Frye Jacobson, *Whiteness of a Different Color: European Immigrants and the Alchemy of Race* (Cambridge: Harvard University Press, 1999);

James R. Barrett and David Roediger, "Inbetween Peoples: Race, Nationality, and the 'New Immigrant' Working Class," *Journal of American Ethnic History* 16, no. 3 (1997): 3–44.

57. "Le correnti di emigrazione latina negli Stati Uniti e le restrizioni legali nordamericane," *La Patria*, February 6, 1925, 1.

58. Donna R. Gabaccia, "Nations of Immigrants: Do Words Matter?," *Pluralist* 5, no. 3 (2010): 5–31.

59. Russell Pierce, "See How We've Grown in South America!," *News Letter*, September 15, 1929; 3–4, box MN8, folder 1929 Jan. 1–Dec. 15, JWT Newsletter Collection, 1910–1986, JWT Collections; emphasis in the original.

60. Mark I. Choate, *Emigrant Nation: The Making of Italy Abroad* (Cambridge: Harvard University Press, 2008), 92–97.

61. *Printers' Ink*, June 5, 1914, cited in Stuart Ewen, *Captains of Consciousness: Advertising and the Social Roots of the Consumer Culture* (New York: McGraw-Hill, 1976), 65.

62. "Cities within a City—And Each One a Worth-While Market," *JWT News Letter* no. 13, February 7, 1924, 4, box MN6, folder 1924, Jan. 3–Feb. 28 Newsletters, JWT Newsletter Collection, 1910–1986, JWT Collections.

63. *JWT News Letter* no. 19, March 20, 1924, 6, box MN6, folder 1924, Mar. 6–April 7 Newsletters, JWT Newsletter Collection, 1910–1986, JWT Collections.

64. "Unrecognized Cities in the United States, No. 4: The Czechoslovak City of Chicago," *News Letter*, no. 28, May 2, 1924, 3, box MN6, folder 1924, May 22–June 24, JWT Newsletter Collection, 1910–1986, JWT Collections; "Unrecognized Cities in the United States, No. 7: The Swedish City of Chicago," *News Letter*, no. 45, September 16, 1924, box MN6, folder 1924 Aug.–Oct. 9, JWT Newsletter Collection, 1910–1986, JWT Collections; "Unrecognized Cities in the United States, No. 9: The Polish City of Milwaukee," *News Letter*, no. 50, October 13, 1924, 3, box MN6, folder 1924, Oct. 16–Nov. 13, JWT Newsletter Collection, 1910–1986, JWT Collections; "Unrecognized Cities in the United States: The Policy City of Chicago," *News Letter*, no. 75, April 9, 1925, 2, box MN6, folder 1925 March 26–May 7, JWT Newsletter Collection, 1910–1986, JWT Collections.

65. Lizabeth Cohen, *Making a New Deal: Industrial Workers in Chicago, 1919–1939*, 2nd ed. (Cambridge: Cambridge University Press, 2008), 99–203.

66. Ibid., 100–158; Simone Cinotto, *The Italian American Table: Food, Family, and Community in New York City* (Urbana: University of Illinois Press, 2013); Hasia R. Diner, *Hungering for America: Italian, Irish, and Jewish Foodways in the Age of Migration* (Cambridge: Harvard University Press, 2001).

67. "Jewish Papers and New York Coverage," News Letter, no. 192, Nov. 15, 1927, 485, box MN8, folder 1927: Nov. 1–Dec. 15, JWT Newsletter Collection, 1910–1986, JWT Collections.

68. "Unrecognized Cities in the United States, No. 5: The German City of Philadelphia," *News Letter*, no. 31, June 12, 1924, box MN6, folder 1924, May 22–June 24, JWT Newsletter Collection, 1910–1986, JWT Collections.

69. "Unrecognized Cities in the United States, No. 3: The Jewish City of New York," *News Letter*, no. 24, April 24, 1924, 6, box MN6, folder 1924, April 17–May 15, JWT Newsletter Collection, 1910–1986, JWT Collections.

70. Ad for Helmar cigarettes, *Il Progresso Italo-Americano* (hereafter *Il Progresso*), November 4, 1924, 8.

71. See, for example, ad for Helmar cigarettes, *Il Progresso*, April 10, 1917, 7.

72. Ad for Heckers flour, *Il Progresso*, January 8, 1935, 5.

73. Cinotto, *Italian American Table*, 57–58, 64–69; Sherrie A. Inness, ed., *Kitchen Culture in America: Popular Representations of Food, Gender, and Race* (Philadelphia: University of Pennsylvania Press, 2001); Laura Shapiro, *Perfection Salad: Women and Cooking at the Turn of the Century* (New York: Farrar, Straus, and Giroux, 1986).

74. Ad for Armour prosciutto, *Il Progresso*, December 6, 1937, 3.

75. Armour and Company, *Catalogue of Products Manufactured by Armour and Company* (Chicago: Armour and Company, 1916), 64–69.

76. Ibid., 56.

77. Similarly, in the 1930s U.S. food companies such as Quaker Oats, Hershey's, and Procter and Gamble sold kosher pancake mix, chocolate, and Crisco to Jewish consumers. Jenna Weissman Joselit, *The Wonders of America: Reinventing Jewish Culture 1880–1950* (New York: Henry Holt, 1994), 171–218; Roger Horowitz, *Kosher USA: How Coke Became Kosher and Other Tales of Modern Food* (New York: Columbia University Press, 2016).

78. "Spanish Advertising Department," in *A Series of Talks on Advertising* (New York, 1909), box DG6, folder 1909, Publications Collection, 1887–2005, Domestic Publications Series, JWT Collections.

79. A second Brazil branch opened in Rio de Janeiro in 1931. The Montevideo office closed in 1930 but reopened again in 1937. See "Our South American Forces," *News Letter*, March 15, 1929, 3, box MN8, folder 1929 Jan. 1–Dec. 15, JWT Newsletter Collection, 1910–1986, JWT Collections; Arthur Farlow, "J.W.T. Pioneers in South America," *News Letter*, July 1, 1929, box MN8, folder 1929 Jan. 1–Dec. 15, JWT Newsletter Collection, 1910–1986, JWT Collections; Pierce, "See How We've Grown in South America!"

80. There has been debate over the size of Argentina's middle class and, relatedly, the extent to which working-class Argentines could participate in a national consumer culture before World War II. Fernando Rocchi sees a rising middle class assisting in the large-scale formation of a consumer society already in the early twentieth century. Natalia Milanesio argues that it was not until the mid-nineteenth century, after Juan Domingo Perón's government took power, that most lower-income Argentines could fully participate in mass consumption. Fernando Rocchi, *Chimneys in the Desert: Industrialization in Argentina during the Export Boom Years, 1870–1930* (Stanford, CA: Stanford University Press, 2006), 51, 61–62. Natalia Milanesio, *Workers Go Shopping in Argentina: The Rise of Popular Consumer Culture* (Albuquerque: University of New Mexico Press, 2013), 2.

81. Rocchi, *Chimneys in the Desert*, 49–85.

82. Clement H. Watson, "Markets Are People—Not Places," JWT *News Bulletin*, July 1938, 3–4, JWT Newsletter Collections, 1910–1986, box MN5, JWT Newsletter Collection, 1910–1986, JWT Collection.

83. Ibid., 6. On J. Walter Thompson and advertising in South America, see Jennifer Scanlon, "Mediators in the International Marketplace: U.S. Advertising in Latin America in the Early Twentieth Century," *Business History Review* 77, no. 3 (2003): 387–415; Ricardo

D. Salvatore, "Yankee Advertising in Buenos Aires: Reflections on Americanization," *Interventions* 7, no. 2 (2005): 216–35; Milanesio, *Workers Go Shopping*, 54–60, 115.

84. See, for example, ad for Remington typewriter, *La Patria*, January 18, 1900, 7; ad for American Light Company, *La Patria*, April 20, 1905, 2; ad for Victor phonograph, *La Patria*, June 15, 1911, 4; ad for Singer sewing machines, *La Patria*, March 4, 1900, 2.

85. See, for example, ad for Michelin, *La Patria*, September 20, 1917; ad for United States Rubber Export Co., *La Patria*, January 8, 1920, 6; ad for Overland, *La Patria*, May 9, 1920, 12; ad for Studebaker Corporation of America, *La Patria*, September 20, 1920, 106; ad for Harley-Davidson, *La Patria*, September 20, 1920, 8; ad for Goodyear, *La Patria*, September 8, 1925, 3; ad for Ford Motor Co., *La Patria*, August 17, 1930, 11; ad for Chevrolet, *La Patria*, January 26, 1930, 11; ad for Case, *La Patria*, September 3, 1930, 8; ad for International Harvester Corporation, *La Patria*, January 1, 1920, 11; ad for Fairbanks, Morse & Co., *La Patria*, April 1, 1920, 7.

86. Ad for Kodak, *La Patria*, May 15, 1920, 6; ad for Frederick Gee Watches Company, *La Patria*, January 9, 1915, 1; ad for Westinghouse Electric International, *La Patria*, December 20, 1920, 7; ad for B.V.D. Company, *La Patria*, November 18, 1920, 9; ad for Keds shoes, *La Patria*, November 4, 1925, 4; ad for Bayer, *La Patria*, January 4, 1925, 6.

87. On the evolution of advertising in the U.S., see Jackson Lears, *Fables of Abundance: A Cultural History of Advertising in America* (New York: Basic Books, 1994); Pamela Walker Laird, *Advertising Progress: American Business and the Rise of Consumer Marketing* (Baltimore: Johns Hopkins University Press, 1998). For Argentina, see Rocchi, *Chimneys in the Desert*, 77–85; Milanesio, *Workers Go Shopping*, 83–122; Noemí M. Girbal-Blacha and María Silvia Ospital, "'Vivir con lo nuestro': Publicidad y política en la Argentina de los años 1930," *European Review of Latin American and Caribbean Studies* 78 (April 2005): 49–66.

88. *Armour and Company: Containing Facts about Business and Organization* (Armour & Company, 1917).

89. Ad for Armour tripe, *Il Mattino d'Italia* (Buenos Aires, Argentina; hereafter *Il Mattino*), November 10, 1935, 5.

90. Ad for Veedol oil, *La Patria*, August 5, 1925, 2.

91. Ad for Veedol oil, *La Patria*, August 6, 1925, 2; ad for Veedol, *La Patria*, August 5, 1925, 2.

92. Carina Frid de Silberstein, "Migrants, Farmers, and Workers: Italians in the Land of Ceres," in *Italian Workers of the World: Labor Migration and the Formation of Multiethnic States*, ed. Donna R. Gabaccia and Fraser M. Ottanelli, 79–101 (Urbana: University of Illinois Press, 2001).

93. Ad for Case threshing machine, *La Patria*, January 29, 1920, 8.

94. See, for example, ad for Elvea, Vitelli & Company canned tomatoes, *Il Progresso*, March 3, 1935, 3; and ad for L. Gandolfi & Company, *Il Progresso*, December 5, 1926, 9.

95. Ad for Joseph Personeni Inc., *Il Progresso,* December 1, 1925, 12.

96. Ad for Aguila Saint chocolate, *La Patria*, September 20, 1917; ad for Barilá Turrochole, *Il Mattino*, July 7, 1936, 3; ad for Quilmes beer, *Il Mattino*, July 7, 1936, 4.

97. See, for example, ad for Terrabussi cookies, *Il Mattino*, December 15, 1935, 7; ad for Confetteria del gas, *Il Mattino*, December 25, 1935, 9. Confetteria del gas, while calling out to connazionali, also described its baked goods as an "Argentine tradition."

98. Ricardo D. Salvatore, "The Enterprise of Knowledge: Representational Machines of Informal Empire," in *Close Encounters of Empire: Writing the History of U.S.–Latin American Culture Relations*, ed. Gilbert M. Joseph, Catherine C. LeGrand, and Ricardo D. Salvatore (Durham, NC: Duke University Press, 1998), 94.

Chapter 6. Fascism and the Competition for Migrant Consumers, 1922–1940

1. Ad for Motta panettone, *Il Progresso Italo-Americano* (hereafter *Il Progresso*), November 28, 1937, 8.

2. Ad for Confetería del Molino panettone, *Il Mattino*, November 7, 1936, 3.

3. Jeffry A. Frieden, *Global Capitalism: Its Fall and Rise in the Twentieth Century* (New York: Norton, 2006), 177–81.

4. Yovanna Pineda, *Industrial Development in a Frontier Economy: The Industrialization of Argentina, 1890–1930* (Stanford, CA: Stanford University Press, 2009), 115–23; María Inés Barbero and Fernando Rocchi, "Industry," in *The New Economic History of Argentina*, ed. Gerardo della Paolera and Alan Taylor (Cambridge: Cambridge University Press, 2003), 261–94.

5. Fernando Rocchi, *Chimneys in the Desert: Industrialization in Argentina during the Export Boom Years, 1870–1930* (Stanford, CA: Stanford University Press, 2006), 204–207.

6. Peter H. Smith, *Politics and Beef in Argentina: Patterns of Conflict and Change* (New York: Columbia University Press, 1969), 16.

7. Vera Zamagni, *The Economic History of Italy, 1860–1990* (Oxford: Oxford University Press, 1993), 243–71.

8. Istituto Centrale di Statistica del Regno d'Italia, *Annuario statistico italiano* (1931, publisher varies), 271; Istituto Nazionale di Statistica, *Commercio di importazione e di esportazione del Regno d'Italia* (1939, publisher varies), 638, 640.

9. Carol Helstosky, *Garlic and Oil: Politics and Food in Italy* (Oxford: Berg, 2004), 63–126.

10. Donna R. Gabaccia, *Italy's Many Diasporas* (Seattle: University of Washington Press, 2000), 136, 141–44; Philip V. Cannistraro and Gianfausto Rosoli, "Fascist Emigration Policy in the 1920s: An Interpretive Framework," *International Migration Review* 13, no. 4 (1979): 673–92.

11. Matteo Pretelli, "Culture or Propaganda? Fascism and Italian Culture in the United States," *Studi Emigrazione* 43, no. 161 (2006): 171–92; Stefano Luconi and Guido Tintori, *L'ombra lunga del fascio: Canali di propaganda fascista per gli "italiani d'America"* (Milan: M&B Publishing, 2004); Stefano Luconi, *La "diplomazia parallela": Il regime fascista e la mobilitazione politica degli italo-americani* (Milan: F. Angeli, 2000).

12. Stefano Luconi, "Etnia e patriottismo nella pubblicità per gli italo-americani durante la guerra d'Etiopia," *Italia Contemporanea* 241 (2005): 514–22; Simone Cinotto, "'Buy Italiano!': Italian American Food Importers and Ethnic Consumption in 1930s New York," in *Italian Americans: A Retrospective on the Twentieth Century*, edited by Paola A. Sensi-Isolani and Anthony Julian Tamburri (Chicago Heights, IL: American Italian Historical Association, 2001), 167–78.

13. Federico Finchelstein, *Transatlantic Fascism: Ideology, Violence, and the Sacred in Argentina and Italy, 1919–1945* (Durham, NC: Duke University Press, 2010), 35–41; Vanni Blengino and Eugenia Scarzanella, ed., *Fascisti in Sud America* (Florence: Le Lettere, 2005).

14. República Argentina, *Censo Industrial de 1935* (Buenos Aires: Ministerio de Hacienda, 1938), 35.

15. María Inés Barbero, "Empresas y empresarios Italianos en la Argentina (1900–30)," in *Studi sull'emigrazione: Un'analisi comparata*. Atti del Convegno storico internazionale sull'emigrazione, ed. Maria Rosaria Ostuni (Biella, Italy: Fondazione Sella, 1989), 303–313. On Pirelli, see María Inés Barbero, "Grupos empresarios, intercambio commercial e inversiones italianas en la Argentina. El caso de Pirelli (1910–1920)," *Estudios Migratorios Latinoamericanos* 5, nos. 15–16 (1990): 311–41.

16. Federico Finchelstein, *Fascismo, liturgia e imaginario. El mito del General Uriburu y la Argentina nacionalista* (Buenos Aires: Fondo de Cultura Económica, 2002).

17. Finchelstein, *Transatlantic Fascism*, 80–89, 104–107.

18. On Pope and pro-Mussolini support, see Philip V. Cannistraro, "The Duce and the Prominenti: Fascism and the Crisis of Italian American Leadership," *Altreitalie* 31 (July–December, 2005): 82–83; Philip V. Cannistraro, "Generoso Pope and the Rise of Italian-American Politics, 1925–1936," in *Italian Americans: New Perspectives in Italian Immigration and Ethnicity*, ed. Lydio F. Tomasi (Staten Island: Center for Migration Studies of New York Inc., 1985), 265–88.

19. David Aliano, *Mussolini's National Project in Argentina* (Madison, WI: Fairleigh Dickinson University Press, 2012), 64–71, 120; Ronald C. Newton, "Ducini, Prominenti, Antifascisti: Italian Fascism and the Italo-Argentine Collectivity, 1922–1945," *Americas* 51, no. 1 (1994): 48–49; Pantaleone Sergi, "Fascismo e antifascismo nella stampa italiana in Argentina: così fu spenta 'La Patria degli Italiani,'" *Altreitalie* 35 (July–December 2007): 4–43.

20. Luca de Caprariis, "'Fascism for Export'? The Rise and Eclipse of the Fasci Italiani all'Estero," *Journal of Contemporary History* 35, no. 2 (2000): 151–183; Emilio Gentile, "La politica estera del partito fascista: Ideologia e organizzazione dei fasci italiani all'estero (1920–1930)," *Storia Contemporanea* 26, no. 2 (1995): 897–956.

21. Two good places to start for antifascist activities of Italians in the United States and Argentina are Pietro Rinaldo Fanesi, "Italian Antifascism and the Garibaldine Tradition in Latin America," trans. Michael Rocke, and Fraser M. Ottanelli, "'If Fascism Comes to America We Will Push It Back into the Ocean': Italian American Antifascism in the 1920s and 1930s," both in *Italian Workers of the World: Labor Migration and the Formation of Multiethnic States*, ed. Donna R. Gabaccia and Fraser M. Ottanelli (Urbana: University of Illinois Press, 2001), 163–77 and 178–95 respectively.

22. Pretelli, "Culture or Propaganda?"; Matteo Pretelli, "Tra estremismo e moderazione. Il ruolo dei circoli fascisti italo-americani nella politica estera italiana degli anni Trenta," *Studi Emigrazione* 40, no. 150 (2003): 315–23; Luconi, *La "diplomazia parallela"*; Stefano Luconi, "The Italian-Language Press, Italian American Voters, and Political Intermediation in Pennsylvania in the Interwar Years," *International Migration Review* 33, no. 4 (1999): 1031–61.

23. Cannistraro, "The Duce and the Prominenti," 77–78.

24. Leo V. Kanawada Jr., *Franklin D. Roosevelt's Diplomacy and American Catholics, Italians, and Jews* (Ann Arbor, MI: UMI Research Press, 1982), 75–89.

25. Finchelstein, *Transatlantic Fascism*, 53–57.

26. "Il peso attivo dell'Italia nella bilancia del commercio mondiale," *Il Progresso*, November 29, 1935, 6.

27. Angelo Flavio Guidi, "Italia e le sanzioni," *Il Progresso*, November 28, 1935, 6.

28. Generoso Pope, "Gli Stati Uniti e le sanzioni," *Il Progresso*, November 26, 1935, 1; Generoso Pope, "Rispettare la neutralità," *Il Progresso*, November 27, 1935, 1; "Note del giorno," *Il Progresso*, November 6, 1935, 6. On the pressure applied to Congress to stay neutral by Italian migrants in Philadelphia, see Stefano Luconi, *From Paesani to White Ethnics: The Italian Experience in Philadelphia* (Albany: State University of New York Press, 2001), 87–89.

29. I. C. Fablo, "L'embargo alle materie prime," *Il Progresso*, November 23, 1935, 6; I. C. Falbo, "Stati Uniti e Italia," *Il Progresso*, November 20, 1935, 6.

30. "Autorevoli voci contro la politica sanzionista," *Il Progresso*, November 2, 1935, 2; I. C. Falbo, "La neutralità americana," *Il Progresso*, November 2, 1935, 6.

31. Department of Commerce, Bureau of Foreign and Domestic Commerce, *Statistical Abstract of the United States 1937*, no. 59 (Washington, D.C.: U.S. Government Printing Office, 1938), 455, 457.

32. Generoso Pope, "Vigili e attivi," *Il Progresso*, December 7, 1935, 1.

33. Falbo, "Stati Uniti e Italia," 6. On Italians and the New Deal, see Stefano Luconi, "Italian Americans, the New Deal State, and the Making of Citizen Consumers," in *Making Italian America: Consumer Culture and the Production of Ethnic Identities*, ed. Simone Cinotto (New York: Fordham University Press, 2014), 137–47.

34. "Il problema delle sanzioni," *La Nuova Patria degli Italiani* (hereafter *La Nuova Patria*), October 6, 1935, 2.

35. "I doveri degli italiani in Argentina," *La Nuova Patria*, December 15, 1935, 1.

36. "Nervi a posto, connazionali!," *La Nuova Patria*, October 20, 1935, 1.

37. "Il boicottaggio agli inglesi," *La Nuova Patria*, August 25, 1935, 1.

38. "L'Argentina e le sanzioni," *La Nuova Patria*, October 13, 1935, 1.

39. "Dati e impressioni dall'italia alla vigilia della guerra in Africa," *La Nuova Patria*, August 18, 1935, 3.

40. G. Chiummiento, "Di fronte alle sanzioni," *La Nuova Patria*, November 24, 1935, 1.

41. Generoso Pope, "L'aggressione economica," *Il Progresso*, November 19, 1935, 1; I. C. Falbo, "Fronte e retrofronte," *Il Progresso*, November 10, 1935, 6.

42. "Note del giorno," *Il Progresso*, November 23, 1935, 6.

43. "Il malvagio esperimento," *Il Progresso*, November 24, 1935, 6.

44. Luconi, "Etnia e patriottismo nella pubblicità per gli italo-americani durante la guerra d'Etiopia."

45. Simone Cinotto, *The Italian American Table: Food, Family, and Community in New York City* (Urbana: University of Illinois Press, 2013), 168.

46. Ad for WOV radio, "Per la diffusione dei prodotti italiani," *Il Progresso*, November 24, 1935, 2.

47. "'Comprate prodotti italiani,'" *Il Progresso*, December 6, 1935, 11.

48. Ibid.

49. Ibid.

50. "Non dimenticate," *Il Progresso*, December 8, 1935, 6.

51. Ad for Negroni salami, *Il Progresso*, December 12, 1935, 10; ad for Luigi Vitelli–Elvea, *Il Progresso*, November 10, 1935, 3.

52. Ad for De Nobili, *Il Progresso*, November 17, 1935, 3.

53. Ad for Planters Edible Oil Company, *Il Progresso*, November 3, 1935, illustrated section; Cinotto, *Italian American Table*, 166.

54. "Le sanzioni dell'Italia," *Il Mattino*, November, 14, 1935, 1; "Ricordate," *Il Mattino*, December 11, 1935, 3.

55. "Nervi a posto, connazionali!," *La Nuova Patria*, October 20, 1935, 1.

56. "L'accademia d'Italia contro le infami sanzioni," *Il Mattino*, November 19, 1935, 1.

57. "Il mirabile slancio della collettivitá per l'assistenza ai volontari e la solidarietá nazionale," *Il Mattino*, November 10, 1935, 3. On roast beef, see "Spaghetti o roastbeef," *Il Mattino*, December 24, 1935, 2.

58. "La data dell'iniquitá e dell'ignominia nella storia del mondo," *Il Mattino*, November 18, 1935, 1.

59. "Il rassegna del 'Commercio Italiano' in Argentina," *Il Mattino*, November 18, 1935, 5.

60. "Le donne italiane contro le sanzioni," *Il Mattino*, November 2, 1935, 1; "La parola del Duce alle donne italiane," *Il Mattino*, December 2, 1935, 1; "Costituzione del Comitato Femminile 'Pro Patria,'" *Il Mattino*, November 14, 1935, 5.

61. Ad for Società Anonima Tabacchi Italiani, *Il Mattino*, November 11, 1935, 5.

62. Ad for Martini & Rossi, *Il Mattino*, April 26, 1936, 28. See also ad for Ferro China Bisleri, *Il Mattino*, May 6, 1936, 2. For the United States, see ad for Fernet-Branca amaro, *Il Progresso*, January 12, 1936, illustrated section.

63. Cinotto discusses the accelerated growth of the tipo italiano food industry in the United States after, and as a result of, World War I. Cinotto, *Italian American Table*, 105–148.

64. Smith, *Politics and Beef in Argentina*, 16–17.

65. For examples of tipo italiano businesses, see ad for Fraschini tobacco, *La Patria degli Italiani* (hereafter *La Patria*), September 20, 1916, 16; ad for Alfredo Canonico's pasta factory, *Il Progresso*, September 20, 1930, 30.

66. On Chiummiento and *La Patria*, see Sergi, "Fascismo e antifascismo nella stampa italiana in Argentina."

67. G. Chiummiento, "Dove entrano in scena perfino i salami, con rispetto parlando," *La Nuova Patria*, September 13, 1936, 1.

68. G. Chiummiento, "Dove si parla di presunti anti italiani fabbricanti di formaggio," *La Nuova Patria*, September 6, 1936, 1.

69. G. Chiummiento, "Dove si parla anche di traditori fabbricanti di carta," *La Nuova Patria*, August 30, 1936, 1, 2.

70. Girbal-Blacha, Noemí M., and María Silvia Ospital. "'Vivir con lo nuestro': Publicidad y política en la Argentina de los años 1930." *European Review of Latin American and Caribbean Studies* 78 (April 2005): 49–66.

71. Chiummiento, "Dove entrano in scena perfino i salami, con rispetto parlando," 1; Chiummiento, "Dove si parla anche di traditori fabbricanti di carta," 1, 2.

72. Chiummiento, "Dove si parla di presunti anti italiani fabbricanti di formaggio," 1.

73. G. Chiummiento, "Il diritto di fabbricare prodotti italiani all'estero," *La Nuova Patria*, August 23, 1936, 1; Chiummiento, "Dove si parla anche di traditori fabbricanti di carta," 1, 2.

74. Ad for Vinos Ruiseñor, *Il Mattino*, December 8, 1935, 7. See also, for example, ad for Vino de Calidad, *Il Mattino*, November 2, 1935, 6; ad for Tampieri & Cia. pasta, *Il Mattino*, February 16, 1936, 12; ad for prodotti Barilà, *Il Mattino*, November 15, 1935, 17.

75. Ad for Fox ham, *Il Mattino*, December 25, 1935, 15; ad for Fox ham, *Il Mattino*, January 1, 1931, 12, 14.

76. Ad for Società Anonima Tabacchi Italiani, *Il Mattino*, November 11, 1935, 5.

77. "Una grande iniziativa del 'Mattino d'Italia' per la resistenza interna," *Il Mattino*, November 18, 1935, 3. See also "Il grandioso successo del 'pacco tricolore,'" *Il Mattino*, November 19, 1935, 3; "I pacchi tricolori per le nostre famiglie," *Il Mattino*, December 12, 1935, 9.

78. "Una grande iniziativa del 'Mattino d'Italia' per la resistenza interna," 3. On packing house workers before 1940, see Smith, *Politics and Beef*, 52–53, 233–36. Daniel James presents the life story of Doña María, a meatpacking worker from Berisso, Argentina. Daniel James, *Doña Maria's Story: Life History, Memory, and Political Identity* (Durham, NC: Duke University Press, 2000).

79. Gilbert M. Joseph, "Close Encounters: Toward a New Cultural History of U.S.–Latin American Relations," in *Close Encounters of Empire: Writing the Cultural History of U.S.–Latin American Relations*, ed. Gilbert M. Joseph, Catherine C. LeGrand, and Ricardo D. Salvatore (Durham, NC: Duke University Press, 1998), 5.

80. "Il mirabile slancio della collettivitá per l'assistenza ai volontari e la solidarietá nazionale," 3.

81. "Nobile incitamento agli italiani d'America," *Il Mattino*, November 4, 1935, 5.

82. Finchelstein, *Transatlantic Fascism*, 40–41, 86–90.

83. On the Italian Commercial Mission, see "Il ricevimento di S. E. Asquini alla Camera di Commercio Italiana," *Il Mattino*, November 7, 1935, 5; "S. E. Asquini e i membri della missione hanno visitato gli stabilimenti del CIAE e della Pirelli," *Il Mattino*, November 21, 1935, 5; "La missione commerciale italiana accompagnata da S. E. l'Ambasciatore visita lo stabilimento della S.A.T.I.," *Il Mattino*, November 22, 1935, 4; "S. E. Asquini e i membri della missione commerciale hanno visitato la 'Cinzano,'" *Il Mattino*, December 20, 1935, 5.

84. "Cerimonie in onore della missione commerciale italiana," *Il Mattino*, November 14, 1935, 5.

85. Ad for Martini vermouth, *Il Mattino*, May 25, 1936, 2.

86. "L'Argentina e le sanzioni," *Il Mattino*, December 13, 1935, 1.

87. Michele Intaglietta, "Italia e Argentina," *Il Mattino*, May 25, 1936, 2.

88. Michele Intaglietta, "Amici lettori," *Il Mattino*, December 1, 1935, 1.

89. "Semana de Italia" propaganda, *Il Mattino*, December 15, 1935, 9.

90. T.S., "Bandiere! Bandiere! Bandiere!," *Il Mattino*, December 15 1935, 9; "Fraternitá italo-argentina," *Il Mattino*, December 16, 1935, 1.

91. For another example, see ad for Ferro-Quina Bisleri, *Il Mattino*, October 18, 1936, 7.

92. This section builds off a previous article on portrayals of gendered consumption under fascism in *Il Progresso*. See Elizabeth Zanoni, "'Per Voi Signore': Gendered Representations of Fashion, Food, and Fascism in *Il Progresso Italo-Americano* during the 1930s," *Journal of American Ethnic History* 31, no. 3 (Spring 2012): 33–71.

93. Examples include "Vita femminile," *La Patria*, January 4, 1920, 6; "Vita femminile," *La Patria*, February 1, 1920, 4; "La donna in casa e fuori," *La Patria*, March 1925, 9; "La donna in casa e fuori," *La Patria*, May 10, 1925, 9.

94. Examples include "Per voi, signore," *Il Progresso*, January 16, 1925; "Per voi, signore," *Il Progresso*, July 31, 1932, 6-S. In 1933 the column changed to "Per voi, signore e signorine" (For you ladies and misses), reflecting the paper's growing interest in targeting a younger group of second-generation Italians.

95. See, for example, "Vita femminile," *Il Progresso*, October 9, 1937, 9.

96. Nancy C. Carnevale, *A New Language, A New World: Italian Immigrants in the United States, 1890–1945* (Urbana: University of Illinois Press, 2009); Donna Gabaccia, *From the Other Side: Women, Gender, and Immigrant Life in the U.S., 1820–1990* (Bloomington: Indiana University Press, 1994), 27–41; Samuel L. Baily, *Immigrants in the Lands of Promise: Italians in Buenos Aires and New York City, 1870–1914* (Ithaca, NY: Cornell University Press, 1999), 63–66.

97. Ad for Gath y Chaves, *La Patria*, January 20, 1910, 8; ad for Gath y Chaves, *La Patria*, April 18, 1915, 7; ad for Harrods, *La Patria*, January 4, 1920, 11; ad for Gath y Chaves, *La Patria*, August 30, 1925, 10; ad for Harrods, *La Patria*, March 16, 1930, 4.

98. Ad for 43-brand cigarettes, *La Patria*, September 20, 1920, 6; ad for Diadema cooking oil, *Il Mattino*, December 6, 1936, 5.

99. Ad for Alexander's, *Il Progresso*, March 31, 1935, 4; ad for May's, *Il Progresso*, March 3, 1935, 4; ad for May's, *Il Progresso*, October 8, 1939, 2; ad for Kaye's Studio Shop, *Il Progresso*, October 11, 1939, 3.

100. See, for example, ad for General Electric, *Il Progresso*, November 7, 1937, 21; ad for Lucky Strike, *Il Progresso*, June 19, 1932, illustrated section; ad for Pontiac, *Il Progresso*, October 31, 1937, 4-S; ad for Ford, *Il Mattino*, September 6, 1935, 9; ad for Armour, *Il Mattino*, November 24, 1935, 5.

101. Ad for Florio Marsala, *Il Progresso*, December 21, 1924, 9-S; ad for Fernet-Branca amaro, *Il Progresso*, January 12, 1926, illustrated section; ad for Fiat cars, *Il Mattino*, July 15, 1936, 2.

102. On Mussolini and masculinity, see Gigliola Gori, "Model of Masculinity: Mussolini, the 'New Italian' of the Fascist Era," in *Superman Supreme: Fascist Body as Political Icon—Global Fascism*, ed. J. A. Mangan (London: Frank Cass Publishers, 1999), 27–61; Sandro Bellassai, "The Masculine Mystique: Anti-Modernism and Virility in Fascist Italy," *Journal of Modern Italian Studies* 10, no. 3 (September 2005): 314–35.

103. Ad for Florio Marsala, *Il Progresso*, April 21, 1935, 3; ad for Buitoni pasta, *Il Progresso*, December 3, 1926; ad for Caffè Pastene, *Il Progresso*, October 15, 1939, illustrated section; ad for Caffè Pastene, *Il Progresso*, October 29, 1939, illustrated section; ad for Bertolli olive oil, *L'Italia*, August 14, 1932.

104. Ad for Ferro-China, *Il Mattino*, January 11, 1931, 13; ad for Olio Sasso, *La Patria*, April 27, 1924, 4; ad for Cirio, *La Patria,* November 12, 1925, 3; ad for Cinzano, *La Patria*, November 12, 1925, 4; ad for Spumante Margherita, *La Patria*, December 5, 1925, 4; ad for Toscano cigarettes, *Il Mattino*, December 27, 1935, 5.

105. Helstosky, *Garlic and Oil*, 63–89.

106. Ibid., 81–85.

107. Victoria de Grazia, *How Fascism Ruled Women, Italy, 1922–1945* (Berkeley: University of California Press, 1992), 211–24. On femininity, beauty, and consumption under fascism, see also Stephen Gundle, *Bellissima: Feminine Beauty and the Idea of Italy* (New Haven, CT: Yale University Press, 2007), 80–106; Eugenia Paulicelli, *Fashion under Fascism: Beyond the Black Shirt* (Oxford: Berg, 2004).

108. On fascism's treatment of Italian women, see Perry Willson, *Peasant Women and Politics in Fascist Italy: The Massaie Rurali* (New York: Routledge, 2002); Perry Willson, *The Clockwork Factory: Women and Work in Fascist Italy* (New York: Oxford University Press, 1993); Piero Meldini, *Sposa e madre esemplare: Ideologia e politica della donna e della famiglia durante il fascismo* (Rimini, Italy: Guaraldi, 1975); Robin Pickering-Iazzi, ed., *Mothers of Invention: Women, Italian Fascism, and Culture* (Minneapolis: University of Minneapolis Press, 1995); Maura E. Hametz, *In the Name of Italy: Nation, Family, and Patriotism in a Fascist Court* (New York: Fordham University Press, 2012).

109. Ad for Florio Marsala, *Il Progresso*, April 21, 1935, 3.

110. Ad for Pirelli shoes, *Il Mattino*, October 28, 1936, 19. Kathy Peiss, "Making Up, Making Over: Cosmetics, Consumer Culture, and Women's Identity," in *The Sex of Things: Gender and Consumption in Historical Perspective*, ed. Victoria de Grazia, with Ellen Furlough (Berkeley: University of California Press, 1996), 311–36.

111. Ad for Pirelli tires, *La Patria*, August 29, 1920, back page; ad for Ferro-China liqueur, *Il Mattino*, January 11, 1931, 13.

112. Hasia R. Diner, *Hungering for America: Italian, Irish, and Jewish Foodways in the Age of Migration* (Cambridge: Harvard University Press, 2001), 20–35; Cinotto, *Italian American Table*; Vito Teti, "Emigrazione, alimentazione, culture popolari," in *Storia dell'emigrazione Italiana. Partenze*, ed. Piero Bevilacqua, Andrina De Clementi, and Emilio Franzina (Rome: Donzelli Editore, 2001), 575–600; Paola Corti, "Emigrazione e consuetudini alimentari. L'esperienza di una catena migratoria," in *Storia d'Italia*, Annali 13. *L'alimentazione nella storia dell'Italia contemporanea*, ed. Alberto Capatti, Albero De Bernardi, and Angelo Varni (Turin, Italy: Einaudi, 1998), 683–719.

113. For a discussion of recipes on women's pages in *Il Progresso*, see Zanoni, "'Per Voi, Signore,'" 50–52. For Thanksgiving dinner, see "Pel pranzo di Thanksgiving," *Il Progresso,* November 19, 1939, 7-S. For empanadas, see ad for Confetería del Molino empanadas, *Il Mattino*, April 5, 1936, 12. For yerba mate, see ad for Carbador yerba, *La Patria*, January 15, 1910, 4. Yerba is the plant from which *mate* tea is made; the tea is a staple in many South American countries. For examples of recipes from *Il Mattino* that incorporate animal proteins into traditional foods from Italy, see "La ricetta gastronomica: Pizza rustica," *Il Mattino*, February 10, 1931, 8; "La ricetta gastronomica: Tagliatelle alla messinese," *Il Mattino*, January 24, 1931, 8; "La ricetta gastronomica: Agnello alla cacciatora," *Il Mattino*, January 20, 1931, 6.

114. Finchelstein, *Transatlantic Fascism*, 50–52, 70–78.

115. On the birth and growth of the Argentine female consumer, as well as on Argentines' embrace of and challenge to U.S. consumer models, see Cecilia Tossounian, "Images of the Modern Girl: From the Flapper to the Joven Moderna (Buenos Aires, 1920–1940)," *Forum for Inter-American Research* 6, no. 2 (2013): 41–70. See also Fernando Rocchi, "La americanización del consumo: Las batallas por el mercado argentino, 1920–1945," in *Americanización: Estados Unidos y América Latina en el siglo XX*, ed. María Barbero and Andrés Regalsky (Buenos Aires: EDUNTREF, 2014), 150–216; Fernando Rocchi, "Inventando la soberanía del consumidor," in *Historia de la vida privada en la Argentina: La Argentina plural 1870–1930*, ed. Fernando Devoto and Marta Madero (Buenos Aires: Taurus, 1999), 301–321; Natalia Milanesio, *Workers Go Shopping in Argentina: The Rise of Popular Consumer Culture* (Albuquerque: University of New Mexico Press, 2013), 70–71, 101–109, 177–78.

116. On sporting events and college life, see, for example, "Ragazze di collegio," *Il Progresso*, September 3, 1939, 7-S; "Lavori estivi," *Il Progresso*, July 31, 1932, 6-3. For suggestions on clothing for automobile rides, see "Per voi, signore e signorine," *Il Progresso*, April 21, 1935, 7-S. On Hollywood, see "Quel che si porta ad Hollywood," *Il Progresso*, October 19, 1937, 9; "Le sosia delle stelle del cinema," *Il Progresso*, June 26, 1932, 4; "Illusioni del trucco," *Il Progresso*, March 31, 1935, 7-S. On ideas of individuality and modernity in mainstream U.S. women's fashion literature, see Kathy Peiss, *Hope in a Jar: The Making of America's Beauty Industry* (Philadelphia: University of Pennsylvania Press, 2011).

117. See, for example, "Tra cinematografi e 'films,'" *La Patria*, July 14, 1925, 5; "Tra cinematografi e films," *La Patria*, January 2, 1930, 12; "Il cinematografo," *Il Mattino*, January 1, 1931, 17; "Il cinematografo," *Il Mattino*, January 9, 1931, 12. On cinema in Argentina, see Matthew B. Karush, *Culture of Class: Radio and Cinema in the Making of a Divided Argentina, 1920–1946* (Durham, NC: Duke University Press, 2012).

118. Ad for Coleman lamps, *La Patria*, September 20, 1920, 12; ad for Kent cigarettes, *Il Mattino*, December 14, 1925, 7; ad for General Electric vacuum, *La Patria*, May 16, 1930, 5; ad for DUO electric water heater, *La Patria*, July 15, 1930, 4.

119. Ad for United States Rubber Company, *La Patria*, January 22, 1920, 8; ad for Ford, *Il Mattino*, September 6, 1936, 9. On women, femininity, and the development of the U.S. automobile industry, see Virginia Scharff, *Taking the Wheel: Women and the Coming of the Motor Age* (Albuquerque: University of New Mexico Press, 1992).

120. "Donne dell'Italia fascista," *Il Mattino*, February 23, 1936, 1.

121. See, for example, "Comitato Femminile Italiano Pro-patria. Raccolta dell'oro," *Il Mattino*, December 5, 1935, 10; "La 'Giornata della Fede' e la raccolta dell'oro," *Il Mattino*, December 19, 1935, 4; "L'imponente celebrazione del 'Giorno della Fede,'" *Il Mattino*, December 19, 1935, 6; "Benefica attività del fascio femminile," *Il Mattino,* July 18, 1936, 5.

122. The commandments were originally published in the Italian daily *Il Giornale d'Italia.* "I diece comandamenti per le donne italiane durante la guerra d'Africa," *Il Mattino*, November 3, 1935, 9. See also "Le donne italiane contro le sanzioni," *Il Mattino*, November 2, 1935, 1.

123. Filippo Tommaso Marinetti, *The Futurist Cookbook* (1932; repr., San Francisco: Bedford Arts, 1989). On futurist cooking, see Carol Helstosky, "Recipe for the Nation:

Reading Italian History through *La scienza in cucina* and *La cucina futurista*," *Food and Food-ways* 11, nos. 2/3 (2003): 113–40.

124. On *El Hogar* and Argentine cuisine, see Rebekah E. Pite, *Creating a Common Table in Twentieth-Century Argentina: Doña Petrona, Women, and Food* (Chapel Hill: University of North Carolina Press, 2013), 58–64, 76–79.

125. "Marinetti cuoco futurista," *Il Mattino*, September 2, 1936, 3.

126. Ad for Kent cigarettes, *Il Mattino*, December 13, 1925, 3.

127. Ad for Armour pasta sauce, *Il Mattino*, November 17, 1935, 5.

Epilogue

1. Robert B. Sherman and Richard M. Sherman, "A Spoonful of Sugar," performed by Julie Andrews, *Mary Poppins*, Walt Disney Productions, 1964, CD.

2. Mario "Pájaro" Gomez and Jorge Risso, "Fernet con coca," performed by Vilma Palma e Vampiros, *Fondo Profundo*, Barca Discos, 1994, CD. The best popular piece I have found on Fernet con Coca is Diego Vecino, "Fernet: Una historia de amor argentina," *Brando*, http://www.conexionbrando.com/1387961-fernet-una-historia-de-amor-argentina. See also Jonathan Gilbert, "How One Company Turned Grandpa's Booze into Argentina's National Drink, *Fortune*, March 18, 2016, http://fortune.com/2016/03/18/fernet-branca-argentina.

3. For example, see ad for Fernet-Branca, *La Patria*, January 15, 1900, 7; ad for Fernet-Branca, *La Patria*, April 2, 1905, 2; ad for Fernet-Branca, *La Patria*, January 19, 1910, 16; ad for Fernet-Branca, *La Patria*, December 8, 1915, 10; ad for Fernet-Branca, *La Patria*, January 20, 1920, 8. See also "Che cosa é il Fernet-Branca," *La Patria*, September 20, 1911.

4. For example, see ad for Fernet-Branca, *La Nación*, September 22, 1901, 8; ad for Fernet-Branca, *La Prensa*, December 9, 1915, 15.

5. Mark Pendergrast, *For God, Country, and Coca-Cola: The Unauthorized History of the Great American Soft Drink and the Company that Makes It* (New York: Scribner's, 1993), 230.

6. Coca-Cola Argentina, "Nuestra historia," http://www.cocacoladeargentina.com.ar/nuestra-compania/nuestra-historia.

7. F.lli Branca Destilerias S.A., Branca International S.p.A., http://www.brancainternational.com/en/THEGROUP/companies/Distillerie/Destilerias/index.html.

8. Paul H. Lewis, *The Crisis of Argentine Capitalism* (Chapel Hill: University of North Carolina Press, 1990), 289–328.

9. Vecino, "Fernet." Fernet has followers in the United States as well, especially among Californians, where in San Francisco, fernet is often followed by a chaser of ginger ale. Nate Cavalleri, "The Myth of Fernet," *SF Weekly*, December 7, 2005, http://archives.sfweekly.com/sanfrancisco/the-myth-of-fernet/Content?oid=2158526.

10. By 1959 only 10,806 Italians entered the United States and only 7,549 entered Argentina. Gianfausto Rosoli, ed., *Un secolo di emigrazione italiana, 1876–1976* (Rome: Centro Studi Emigrazione, 1978), 355.

11. On postwar Italian emigration, see Donna R. Gabaccia, *Italy's Many Diasporas* (Seattle: University of Washington Press, 2000), 153–73.

12. Andrea Leonardi, Alberto Cova, and Pasquale Galea, *Il Novecento economico italiano: Dalla grande guerra al "miracolo economico" (1914–1962)* (Bologna, Italy: Monduzzi, 1997); Guido Crainz, *Storia del miracolo italiano: Culture, identità, trasformazioni fra anni cinquanta e sessanta* (Roma: Donzelli, 1996).

13. Ugo Ascoli, *Movimenti migratori in Italia* (Bologna, Italy: Il Mulino, 1979); Giovanni Pellicciari and Gianfranco Albertelli, ed., *L'immigrazione nel triangolo industriale* (Milan: Angeli, 1970); Gabaccia, *Italy's Many Diasporas*, 168–70.

14. Fabio Parasecoli, *Al Dente: A History of Food in Italy* (London: Reaktion Books, 2014), 271.

15. Gino C. Speranza, "La necessità di un accordo internazionale in riguardo agli emigranti," *Rivista Commerciale*, December 1905, 21.

16. Silvia Lepore, "Economic Profile of Italian Argentines in the 1980s," in *The Columbus People: Perspectives in Italian Immigration to the Americas and Australia*, ed. Lydio F. Tomasi, Piero Gastaldo, and Thomas Row (New York: Center for Migration Studies, 1994), 125–51; Joel Perlmann, *Italians Then, Mexicans Now: Immigrant Origins and Second-Generation Progress, 1890 to 2000* (New York: Russell Sage Foundation, 2007).

17. On the globalization of Italian cuisines, see especially Parasecoli, *Al Dente*, 225–47; John F. Mariani, *How Italian Food Conquered the World* (New York: Palgrave Macmillian, 2011).

18. Carlo Petrini, *Slow Food: The Case for Taste*, trans. William McCuaig (New York: Columbia University Press, 2003).

19. Jeffrey M. Pilcher, "'Old Stock' Tamales and Migrant Tacos: Taste, Authenticity, and the Naturalization of Mexican Food," *Social Research* 81, no. 2 (2014): 441–62; Krishnendu Ray, *The Ethnic Restaurateur* (New York: Bloomsbury Academic, 2016).

20. Eataly, "Stores," https://www.eataly.com/us_en/stores. On geographical indicators, see Parasecoli, *Al Dente*, 253–59.

21. Marilyn Halter, *Shopping for Identity: The Marketing of Ethnicity* (New York: Schocken Books, 2000); Matthew Frye Jacobson, *Roots Too: White Ethnic Revival in Post–Civil Rights America* (Cambridge: Harvard University Press, 2006).

22. David Gentilcore, *Pomodoro!: A History of the Tomato in Italy* (New York: Columbia University Press, 2010),130.

23. Simone Cinotto, *The Italian American Table: Food, Family, and Community in New York City* (Urbana: University of Illinois Press, 2013), 211–17.

24. Fabio Parasecoli, "We Are Family: Ethnic Food Marketing and the Consumption of Authenticity in Italian-Themed Chain Restaurants," *Making Italian America: Consumer Culture and the Production of Ethnic Identities,* ed. Simone Cinotto (New York: Fordham University Press, 2014), 244–55; Davide Girardelli, "Commodified Identities: The Myth of Italian Food in the United States," *Journal of Communication Inquiry* 28, no. 4 (2004): 307–324.

25. Mark I. Choate, *Emigrant Nation: The Making of Italy Abroad* (Cambridge: Harvard University Press, 2008).

26. On migration to Italy, see, for example, Russell King, "Recent Immigration to Italy: Character, Causes and Consequences," *GeoJournal* 30, no. 3 (July 1993): 283–92; Paul M. Sniderman et al., *The Outsider: Prejudice and Politics in Italy* (Princeton, NJ: Princeton

University Press, 2000); Graziella Parati, *Migration Italy: The Art of Talking Back in a Destination Culture* (Toronto: University of Toronto Press, 2005); Hans Lucht, *Darkness before Daybreak: African Migrants Living on the Margins in Southern Italy Today* (Berkeley: University of California Press, 2012); Elisabetta Zontini, *Transnational Families, Migration and Gender: Moroccan and Filipino Women in Bologna and Barcelona* (New York: Berghahn Books, 2010).

27. Over 450,000 Argentines with Italian ancestry acquired Italian citizenship from 1998 to 2010. See Guido Tintori, "More than One Million Individuals Got Italian Citizenship Abroad in Twelve Years (1998–2010)," European Union Democracy, November 21, 2012, http://eudo-citizenship.eu/news/citizenship-news/748-more-than-one-million-individuals-got-italian-citizenship-abroad-in-the-twelve-years-1998-2010%3E. On Italian-Argentines and dual nationality, see David Cook-Martín, *The Scramble for Citizens: Dual Nationality and State Competition for Immigrants* (Stanford, CA: Stanford University Press, 2012).

28. Parasecoli, *Al Dente*, 246–47.

29. Kitty Calavita, *Immigrants at the Margins: Law, Race, and Exclusion in Southern Europe* (New York: Cambridge University Press, 2005); Demetrios G. Papademetriou and Kimberly A. Hamilton, *Converging Paths to Restriction: French, Italian, and British Responses to Immigration* (Washington, DC: Carnegie Endowment for International Peace, 1996).

30. Parasecoli, *Al Dente*, 238–40.

31. Donna R. Gabaccia, "Food, Mobility, and World History," in *The Oxford Handbook of Food History*, ed. Jeffrey M. Pilcher (New York: Oxford University Press, 2012), 305–323.

32. Jeffrey M. Pilcher, *Planet Taco: A Global History of Mexican Food* (New York: Oxford University Press, 2012), 211–20. On NAFTA and Mexican migration, see Alejandro Portes, "NAFTA and Mexican Immigration," Border Battles: The U.S. Immigration Debates, Social Science Research Council, 2006, http://borderbattles.ssrc.org/Portes; Deborah Barndt, *Women Working the NAFTA Food Chain: Women, Food, and Globalization* (Toronto: Second Story Press, 1999); Douglas S. Massey, Jorge Durand and Nolan J. Malone, *Beyond Smoke and Mirrors: Mexican Immigration in an Era of Economic Integration* (New York: Russell Sage Foundation, 2002).

33. Peter Andreas, *Border Games: Policing the U.S.-Mexico Divide* (Ithaca, NY: Cornell University Press, 2000).

34. Ibid., 115–39. See also Christina Boswell and Andrew Geddes, *Migration and Mobility in the European Union* (New York: Palgrave Macmillan, 2011).

Bibliography

Archives

ITALY

Archivio Centrale dello Stato, Rome
Biblioteca Nazionale Centrale di Roma, Rome
Biblioteca Storica Nazionale dell'Agricoltura, Rome
Istituto Nazionale di Statistica, Rome

ARGENTINA

Biblioteca Nacional de la República Argentina, Buenos Aires
Centro de Documentación e Información, Ministerio de Hacienda y Finanzas Públicas,
    Buenos Aires
Centro de Estudios Migratorios Latinoamericanos, Buenos Aires

UNITED STATES

David M. Rubenstein Rare Book and Manuscript Library, Duke University, Durham, North
    Carolina
Hagley Museum and Library, Wilmington, Delaware
Immigration History Research Center, University of Minnesota
New York Public Library, New York

Newspapers and Journals

Bollettino Mensile della Camera Italiana di Commercio in Buenos Aires (Buenos Aires)
Il Mattino d'Italia (Buenos Aires)

Il Progresso Italo-Americano (New York)
Italian Chamber of Commerce Bulletin (Chicago)
L'Italia (Chicago)
La Nación (Buenos Aires, Argentina)
La Nuova Patria degli Italiani (Buenos Aires)
La Patria degli Italiani (Buenos Aires)
La Prensa (Buenos Aires)
New York Times (New York)
Rivista Commerciale (New York)

Government Publications

ITALY

Atti della giunta per la inchiesta agraria e sulle condizioni della classe agricola. 15 vols. Rome: Forzani e C., 1881–1886.

Bordiga, Oreste. *Inchiesta parlamentare sulle condizioni dei contadini nelle provincie meridionali e nella Sicilia.* Vol. 4. *Campania,* Tomo 1. Rome: Tipografia nazionale di Giovanni Bertero e C., 1909.

Commissariato Generale dell'Emigrazione. *Annuario statistico della emigrazione italiana dal 1876 al 1925.* Rome: Edizione del Commissariato Generale dell'Emigrazione, 1926.

———. *Bollettino dell'emigrazione.* Rome: Tipografia Società Cartiere Centrali, 1902–1927.

Direzione della Statistica Generale (1881–1885); Direzione Generale della Statistica (1886–1907; 1919–1921); Direzione Generale della Statistica e del Lavoro (1911–1915); Ufficio Centrale di Statistica (1916–1918); Istituto Centrale di Statistica del Regno d'Italia (1927–1943). *Annuario statistico italiano.* Publisher varies.

Istituto Centrale di Statistica. *Commercio di importazione e di esportazione del Regno d'Italia.* Publisher varies,1934–1951.

Jarach, Cesare. *Inchiesta parlamentare sulle condizioni dei contadini nelle provincie meridionali e nella Sicilia.* Vol. 2. *Abruzzi e Molise,* Tomo 1. Rome: Tipografia nazionale di Giovanni Bertero e C., 1909.

Lorenzoni, Giovanni. *Inchiesta parlamentare sulle condizione dei contadini nelle provincie meridionali e nella Sicilia.* Vol. 6. *Sicilia,* Tomo 1. Rome: Tipografia nazionale di Giovanni Bertero e C., 1910.

Marenghi, Ernesto. *Inchiesta parlamentare sulle condizioni dei contadini nelle provincie meridionali e nella Sicilia.* Vol. 5. *Basilicata e Calabrie,* Tomo 2 Calabrie. Rome: Tipografia nazionale di Giovanni Bertero e C., 1909.

Ministero delle Finanze. Direzione Generale della Gabelle. *Movimento commerciale del Regno d'Italia.* Publisher varies,1880–1904.

ARGENTINA

Dirección General de Inmigración. *Resumen estadistico del movimiento migratorio en la Republica Argentina, años 1857–1924.* Buenos Aires: Talleres Gráficos del Ministerio de Agricultura de la Nación, 1925.

Ministerio de Agricultura, Dirección de Comercio e Industria. *Censo Industrial de la República*. Buenos Aires, Talleres de Publicaciones de la Oficina Meteorológica Argentina, 1910.

República Argentina. *Censo Industrial de 1935*. Buenos Aires: Ministerio de Hacienda, 1938.

República Argentina. *Tercer Censo Nacional*, Tomo 8, *Censo del Comercio*. Buenos Aires: Talleres Gráficos de L. J. Rosso y Cía., 1917.

UNITED STATES

Department of Commerce. Bureau of Foreign and Domestic Commerce. *Statistical Abstract of the United States*. Washington, DC: U.S. Government Printing Office, 1921–1938.

United States Immigration Commission. *Immigrants in Cities*. Vol. 1. Washington, DC: U.S. Government Printing Office, 1911.

Willcox, Walter F., and Imre Ferenczi. *International Migrations*. Vol. 1. New York: Gordon and Breach Science Publishers, 1969.

Additional Primary Sources

Amedeo, Luigi and Umberto Cagni. *On the* Polar Star *in the Arctic Sea*. Translated by William Le Queux. London: Hutchinson & Co., 1903.

Armour and Company. *Catalogue of Products Manufactured by Armour and Company*. Chicago: Armour & Company, 1916.

Armour and Company: Containing Facts about Business and Organization. Armour & Company, 1917.

Bernardy, Amy A. "L'etnografia della 'piccole italie.'" In *Atti del primo congresso di etnografia italiana*, edited by Società di Etnografia Italiana, 173–79. Perugia, Italy: Unione Tipografica Cooperativa, 1912.

Breckinridge, S. P. *New Homes for Old*. New York: Harper & Brothers Publishing, 1921.

Camera di Commercio Italiana in New York. *Nel cinquantenario della Camera di Commercio Italiana in New York, 1887–1937*. New York, 1937.

Comitato della Camera Italiana di Commercio ed Arti. *Gli italiani nella Repubblica Argentina*. Buenos Aires: Compañia Sud-Americana de Billetes de Banco, 1898.

———. *Gli italiani nella Repubblica Argentina all'Esposizione di Torino 1911*. Buenos Aires: Stabilimento Grafico della Compañia General de Fósforos, 1911.

Covello, Leonard. *The Social Background of the Italo-American School Child: A Study of the Southern Italian Family Mores and Their Effect on the School Situation in Italy and America*. Leiden, Netherlands: E. J. Brill, 1967.

Dall'Italia all'Argentina: Guida pratica per gli italiani che si recano nell'Argentina. Genoa: Libreria R. Istituto Sordo-Muti, 1888.

Einaudi, Luigi. *Un principe mercante: Studio sulla espansione coloniale italiana*. Turin: Fratelli Bocca, 1900.

Faleni, Lorenzo, and Amedeo Serafini, eds. *La Repubblica Argentina all'Esposizione internazionale di Milano 1906*. Buenos Aires, 1906.

Fontana-Russo, Luigi. "Emigrazione d'uomini ed esportazione di merci." *Rivista Coloniale* (1906): 26–40.

Gli italiani nel Sud America ed il loro contributo alla guerra: 1915–1918. Buenos Aires: Arigoni & Barbieri, 1922.

Godio, Guglielmo. *L'America ne' suoi primi fattori: La colonizzazione e l'emigrazione*. Florence: Tipografia di G. Barbèra, 1893.

Gravina, M. ed. *Almanacco dell'italiano nell'Argentina*. Buenos Aires, 1918.

Istituto Coloniale Italiano. *Italia e Argentina*. Bergamo, Italy: Officine dell'Istituto Italiano d'Arti Grafiche, 1910.

L'Italia nell'America Latina: Per l'incremento dei rapporti industriali e commerciali fra l'Italia e l'America del Sud. Milan: Società Tipografica Editrice Popolare, 1906.

Italian American Directory Co. *Gli italiani negli Stati Uniti d'America*. New York: Andrew H. Kellogg Co., 1906.

Malaurie, Alfredo, and Juan M. Gazzano. *La Industria Argentina y la Exposición del Paraná*. Buenos Aires: De Juan M. Gazzano y Cia., 1888.

Mangano, Antonio. "The Italian Colonies of New York City." MA thesis, Columbia University, 1903. Reprint, *Italians in the City: Health and Related Social Needs*, edited by Francesco Cordasco, 1–57. New York: Arno Press, 1975.

Marinetti, Filippo Tommaso. *The Futurist Cookbook*. 1932. Reprint, San Francisco: Bedford Arts, 1989.

Mayor des Planches, E. "Gli Stati Uniti e l'emigrazione italiana." *Rivista Coloniale* 1 (May–August 1906).

Odencrantz, Louise. *Italian Women in Industry*. New York: Russell Sage Foundation, 1919.

Patrizi, Ettore. *Gl'italiani in California, Stati Uniti d'America*. San Francisco: Stabilimento Tipo-Litografico, 1911.

Phelps, Dudley Maynard. *Migration of Industry to South America*. New York: McGraw-Hill, 1936.

Phillips, Velma, and Laura Howell. "Racial and Other Differences in Dietary Customs." *Journal of Home Economics* 12, no. 9 (1920): 396–411.

Rutter, Frank R. *Tariff Systems of South American Countries*. Washington, DC: U.S. Government Printing Office, 1916.

Sarmiento, Domingo F. *Facundo; or, Civilization and Barbarism*. Translated by Mary Mann. New York: Penguin Books, 1998.

Sherman, Mary. "Manufacturing of Foods in the Tenements." *Charities and the Commons* 15 (1906): 669–73.

Swift, Louis F., and Arthur Van Vlissingen Jr. *The Yankee of the Yards: The Biography of Gustavus Franklin Swift*. Chicago: A. W. Shaw, 1927.

Tonissi, Luigi. "Progetto per un banco del commercio italo-americano." In *L'esplorazione commerciale e L'esploratore*, 383–401. Milan: Premiato stabilimento tipografico P. B. Bellini, 1896.

Urien, Carols M., and Ezio Colombo. *La República Argentina en 1910*. Buenos Aires: Maucci Hermanos, 1910.

Visconti, Aldo. *Emigrazione ed esportazione: Studio dei rapporti che intercedono fra l'emigrazione e le esportazioni italiane per gli Stati Uniti del Nord America e per la Repubblica Argentina*. Turin: Tipografia Baravalle e Falconieri, 1912.

Woods, Robert A. "Notes on the Italians in Boston." *Charities* 12 (1904): 451–52.

Zuccarini, Emilio. *Il lavoro degli italiani nella Repubblica Argentina dal 1516 al 1910*. Buenos Aires, 1910.

Scholarly Books and Articles

Abarca, Meredith E. *Voices in the Kitchen: Views of Food and the World from Working-Class Mexican and Mexican American Women*. College Station: Texas A&M University Press, 2006.

Adelman, Jeremy. *Sovereignty and Revolution in the Iberian Atlantic*. Princeton, NJ: Princeton University Press, 2006.

Alberto, Paulina L., and Eduardo Elena. "Introduction: Shades of the Nation." In *Rethinking Race in Modern Argentina*, edited by Paulina L. Alberto and Eduardo Elena, 1–21. New York: Cambridge University Press, 2016.

Aliano, David. *Mussolini's National Project in Argentina*. Madison, WI: Fairleigh Dickinson University Press, 2012.

Andreas, Peter. *Border Games: Policing the U.S.-Mexico Divide*. Ithaca, NY: Cornell University Press, 2000.

Andrews, George Reid. *The Afro-Argentines of Buenos Aires, 1800–1900*. Madison: University of Wisconsin Press, 1980.

Appadurai, Arjun. *The Social Life of Things: Commodities in Cultural Perspective*. Cambridge: Cambridge University Press, 1988.

Archetti, Eduardo P. "Hibración, pertenencia y localidad en la construcción de una cocina nacional." In *La Argentina en el siglo XX*, edited by Carlos Altamirano, 217–36. Buenos Aires: Universidad Nacional de Quilmes, 1999.

Arcondo, Aníbal B. *Historia de la alimentación en Argentina: Desde los orígienes hasta 1920*. Córdoba, Argentina: Ferreyra Editor, 2002.

Ascoli, Ugo. *Movimenti migratori in Italia*. Bologna, Italy: Il Mulino, 1979.

Baily, Samuel L. *Immigrants in the Lands of Promise: Italians in Buenos Aires and New York City, 1870–1914*. Ithaca, NY: Cornell University Press, 1999.

———. "Marriage Patterns and Immigrant Assimilation in Buenos Aires, 1882–1923." *Hispanic American Historical Review* 60, no. 1 (1980): 32–48.

———. "Sarmiento and Immigration: Changing Views on the Role of Immigration in the Development of Argentina." In *Sarmiento and His Argentina*, edited by Joseph T. Criscenti, 131–42. Boulder, CO: L. Rienner Publishers, 1993.

Baily, Samuel L., and Eduardo José Míguez, eds. *Mass Migration to Modern Latin America*. Wilmington, DE: SR Books, 2003.

Baily, Samuel L., and Franco Ramella, eds. *One Family, Two Worlds: An Italian Family's Correspondence across the Atlantic, 1901–1922*. Translated by John Lenaghan. New Brunswick, NJ: Rutgers University Press, 1988.

Baldassar, Loretta, and Donna R. Gabaccia. "Home, Family, and the Italian Nation in a Mobile World: The Domestic and the National among Italy's Migrants." In *Intimacy and Italian Migration: Gender and Domestic Lives in a Mobile World*, edited by Loretta Baldassar and Donna R. Gabaccia, 1–24. New York: Fordham University Press, 2011.

Balletta, Francesco. *Il Banco di Napoli e le rimesse degli emigrati (1914–1925)*. Naples: ISTOB, 1972.

Barbero, María Inés. "Empresas y empresarios Italianos en la Argentina (1900–30)." In *Studi sull'emigrazione: Un'analisi comparata*. Atti del Convegno storico internazionale sull'emigrazione, ed. Maria Rosaria Ostuni, 303–313. Biella, Italy: Fondazione Sella, 1989.

———. "Grupos empresarios, intercambio commercial e inversiones italianas en la Argentina. El caso de Pirelli (1910–1920)." *Estudios Migratorios Latinoamericanos* 5, nos. 15–16 (1990): 311–41.

Barbero, María I., and Andrés M. Regalsky, eds. *Americanización: Estados Unidos y América Latina en el siglo XX. Transferencias económicas, tecnológicas y culturales*. Buenos Aires: EDUNTREF, 2014.

Barbero, María Inés, and Fernando Rocchi. "Industry." In *The New Economic History of Argentina*, edited by Gerardo della Paolera and Alan Taylor, 261–94. Cambridge: Cambridge University Press, 2003.

Barndt, Deborah. *Women Working the NAFTA Food Chain: Women, Food, and Globalization*. Toronto: Second Story Press, 1999.

Barrett, James R., and David Roediger. "Inbetween Peoples: Race, Nationality, and the 'New Immigrant' Working Class." *Journal of American Ethnic History* 16, no. 3 (1997): 3–44.

Barthes, Roland. "Toward a Psychosociology of Contemporary Food Consumption." In *Food and Culture: A Reader*, 3rd ed., edited by Carole Counihan and Penny Van Esterik, 23–30. New York: Routledge, 2013.

Bellassai, Sandro. "The Masculine Mystique: Anti-Modernism and Virility in Fascist Italy." *Journal of Modern Italian Studies* 10, no. 3 (2005): 314–35.

Bemis, Samuel Flagg. *The Latin American Policy of the United States*. New York: Harcourt, Brace and Co., 1943.

Bentley, Amy. *Inventing Baby Food: Taste, Health, and the Industrialization of the American Diet*. Berkeley: University of California Press, 2014.

Bernardy, Amy Allemand, and Maddalena Tirabassi. *Ripensare la patria grande: Gli scritti di Amy Allemand Bernardy sulle migrazioni italiane*. Isernia, Italy: C. Iannone, 2005.

Bevilacqua, Piero. "Emigrazione transoceanica e mutamenti dell'alimentazione contadina calabrese fra Otto e Novecento." *Quaderni storici* 47 (August 1981): 520–55.

Bevilacqua, Piero, Andreina De Clementi, and Emilio Franzina, eds. *Storia dell'emigrazione italiana. Arrivi*. Rome: Donzelli, 2002.

———. *Storia dell'emigrazione italiana. Partenze*. Rome: Donzelli, 2001.

Blengino, Vanni, and Eugenia Scarzanella, eds. *Fascisti in Sud America*. Florence: Le Lettere, 2005.

Boswell, Christina, and Andrew Geddes. *Migration and Mobility in the European Union*. New York: Palgrave Macmillan, 2011.

Bosworth, Richard J. *Italy, the Least of the Great Powers: Italian Foreign Policy before the First World War*. New York: Cambridge University Press, 1979.

Bourdieu, Pierre. *Distinction: A Social Critique of the Judgment of Taste*. Translated by Richard Nice. Cambridge: Harvard University Press, 1984.

Briggs, John W. *An Italian Passage: Immigrants to Three American Cities, 1890–1930.* New Haven, CT: Yale University Press, 1978.

Bugiardini, Sergio. "La Camera di commercio italiani di New York." In *Profili di Camera di Commercio Italiane all'estero*, vol. 1, edited by Giovanni Luigi Fontana and Emilio Franzina, 105–121. Soveria Manelli, Italy: Rubbettino Editore, 2001.

Calavita, Kitty. *Immigrants at the Margins: Law, Race, and Exclusion in Southern Europe.* New York: Cambridge University Press, 2005.

Cancian, Sonia. "'Tutti a Tavola!' Feeding the Family in Two Generations of Italian Immigrant Households in Montreal." In *Edible Histories, Cultural Politics: Towards a Canadian Food History*, edited by Franca Iacovetta, Valerie J. Korinek, and Marlene Epp, 209–221. Toronto: University of Toronto Press, 2012.

Cannistraro, Philip V. "The Duce and the Prominenti: Fascism and the Crisis of Italian American Leadership." *Altreitalie* 31 (July–December, 2005): 76–86.

———. "Generoso Pope and the Rise of Italian-American Politics, 1925–1936." In *Italian Americans: New Perspectives in Italian Immigration and Ethnicity*, edited by Lydio F. Tomasi, 265–88. Staten Island: Center for Migration Studies of New York Inc., 1985.

Cannistraro, Philip V., and Gianfausto Rosoli. "Fascist Emigration Policy in the 1920s: An Interpretive Framework." *International Migration Review* 13, no. 4 (1979): 673–92.

Carnevale, Nancy C. *A New Language, A New World: Italian Immigrants in the United States, 1890–1945.* Urbana: University of Illinois Press, 2009.

Cavalleri, Nate. "The Myth of Fernet." *SF Weekly*, December 7, 2005. http://archives.sf weekly.com/sanfrancisco/the-myth-of-fernet/Content?oid=2158526.

Ceserani, Gian Paolo. *Storia della pubblicità in Italia.* Rome: Laterza, 1988.

Chen, Yong. *Chop Suey USA: The Story of Chinese Food in America.* New York: Columbia University Press, 2014.

Chiapparino, Francesco. "Industrialization and Food Consumption in United Italy." In *Food Technology, Science, and Marketing: European Diet in the Twentieth Century*, edited by Adel P. den Hartog, 139–55. East Linton, Scotland: Tuckwell Press, 1995.

Chiapparino, Francesco, Renato Covino, and Gianni Bovini. *Consumi e industria alimentare in Italia dall'unità a oggi: Lineamenti per una storia.* 2nd ed. Narni, Italy: Giada, 2002.

Choate, Mark I. *Emigrant Nation: The Making of Italy Abroad.* Cambridge: Harvard University Press, 2008.

———. "Sending States' Transnational Interventions in Politics, Culture, and Economics: The Historical Example of Italy." *International Migration Review* 41, no. 3 (2007): 728–68.

Cinel, Dino. *From Italy to San Francisco: The Immigrant Experience.* Stanford, CA: Stanford University Press, 1982.

———. *National Integration of Italian Return Migration, 1870–1929.* New York: Cambridge University Press, 1991.

Cinotto, Simone. "All Things Italian: Italian American Consumers, the Transnational Formation of Taste, and the Commodification of Difference." In *Making Italian America: Consumer Culture and the Production of Ethnic Identities*, edited by Simone Cinotto, 1–31. New York: Fordham University Press, 2014.

———. "'Buy Italiano!': Italian American Food Importers and Ethnic Consumption in 1930s New York." In *Italian Americans: A Retrospective on the Twentieth Century*, edited by Paola A. Sensi-Isolani and Anthony Julian Tamburri, 167–78. Chicago Heights, IL: American Italian Historical Association, 2001.

———. *The Italian American Table: Food, Family, and Community in New York City*. Urbana: University of Illinois Press, 2013.

———, ed., *Making Italian America: Consumer Culture and the Production of Ethnic Identities*. New York: Fordham University Press, 2014.

———. *Soft Soil, Black Grapes: The Birth of Italian Winemaking in California*. Translated by Michelle Tarnopoloski. New York: New York University Press, 2012.

Cohen, Lizabeth. *Making a New Deal: Industrial Workers in Chicago, 1919–1939*. 2nd ed. Cambridge: Cambridge University Press, 2008.

Cohen, Miriam. *Workshop to Office: Two Generations of Italian Women in New York City, 1900–1950*. Ithaca, NY: Cornell University Press, 1993.

Cook-Martín, David. *The Scramble for Citizens: Dual Nationality and State Competition for Immigrants*. Stanford, CA: Stanford University Press, 2012.

———. "Soldiers and Wayward Women: Gendered Citizenship, and Migration Policy in Argentina, Italy, and Spain since 1850." *Citizenship Studies* 10, no. 5 (2006): 571–90.

Coppa, Frank J. *Planning, Protectionism, and Politics in Liberal Italy: Economics and Politics in the Giolittian Age*. Washington, DC: Catholic University of America Press, 1971.

Cornblit, Oscar. "Inmigrantes y empresarios en la política argentina." *Desarrollo Económico* 6, no. 24 (1967): 641–91.

Corti, Paola. "Emigrazione e consuetudini alimentari. L'esperienza di una catena migratoria." In *Storia d'Italia*, Annali 13. *L'alimentazione nella storia dell'Italia contemporanea*, edited by Alberto Capatti, Albero De Bernardi, and Angelo Varni, 683–719. Turin: Einaudi, 1998.

Crainz, Guido. *Storia del miracolo italiano: Culture, identità, trasformazioni fra anni cinquanta e sessanta*. Roma: Donzelli, 1996.

Cronon, William. *Nature's Metropolis: Chicago and the Great West*. New York: W. W. Norton, 1991.

D'Agostino, Peter. "Craniums, Criminals, and the 'Cursed Race': Italian Anthropology in American Racial Thought, 1861–1924." *Comparative Studies in Society and History* 44, no. 2 (2002): 319–43.

Davidoff, Leonore, and Catherine Hall. *Family Fortunes: Men and Women of the English Middle Class, 1780–1850*. Chicago: University of Chicago Press, 1987.

Davis, John. "Changing Perspectives on Italy's 'Southern Problem.'" In *Italian Regionalism: History, Identity, and Politics*, edited by Carl Levy, 53–68. Oxford: Berg, 1996.

Davis, Marni. *Jews and Booze: Becoming American in the Age of Prohibition*. New York: New York University Press, 2012.

de Caprariis, Luca. "'Fascism for Export'? The Rise and Eclipse of the Fasci Italiani all'Estero." *Journal of Contemporary History* 35, no. 2 (2000): 151–83.

De Grand, Alexander. *The Hunchback's Tailor: Giovanni Giolitti and Liberal Italy from the Challenge of Mass Politics to the Rise of Fascism, 1882–1922*. Westport, CT: Praeger, 2001.

de Grazia, Victoria. *How Fascism Ruled Women, Italy, 1922–1945*. Berkeley: University of California Press, 1992.

de Grazia, Victoria, with Ellen Furlough, eds. *The Sex of Things: Gender and Consumption in Historical Perspective*. Berkeley: University of California Press, 1996.

Devoto, Fernando J. *Historia de los italianos en la Argentina*. Buenos Aires: Editorial Biblos, 2006.

——. "Programs and Politics of the First Italian Elite of Buenos Aires, 1852–80." In *Italian Workers of the World: Labor Migration and the Formation of Multiethnic States*, edited by Donna R. Gabaccia and Fraser M. Ottanelli, 41–59. Urbana: University of Illinois Press, 2001.

Devoto, Fernando J., and Gianfausto Rosoli, eds. *L'Italia nella società argentina: Contributi sull'emigrazione italiana in Argentina*. Rome: Centro Studi Emigrazione, 1988.

Díaz Alejandro, Carlos F. "The Argentine Tariff, 1906–1940." *Oxford Economic Papers* 19, no. 1 (1967): 75–98.

——. *Essays on the Economic History of the Argentine Republic*. New Haven, CT: Yale University Press, 1970.

Diner, Hasia R. *Hungering for America: Italian, Irish, and Jewish Foodways in the Age of Migration*. Cambridge: Harvard University Press, 2001.

——. *Roads Taken: The Great Jewish Migrations to the New World and the Peddlers Who Forged the Way*. New Haven, CT: Yale University Press, 2015.

Donato, Katharine M., Donna Gabaccia, Jennifer Holdaway, Martin Manalansan, and Patricia R. Pessar. "A Glass Half Full? Gender in Migration Studies." *International Migration Review* 40, no. 1 (2006): 3–26.

Douglas, Mary. "Deciphering a Meal." *Daedalus* 101, no. 1 (1971): 61–81.

Douglas, Mary, and Baron Isherwood. *The World of Goods: Towards an Anthropology of Consumption*. London: A. Lane, 1979.

Douki, Caroline. "The Liberal Italian State and Mass Emigration, 1860–1914." In *Citizenship and Those Who Leave: The Politics of Emigration and Expatriation*, edited by Nancy L. Green and François Weil, 91–113. Urbana: University of Illinois Press, 2007.

Durante, Alessandro, ed., *A Companion to Linguistic Anthropology*. Malden, MA: Blackwell, 2004.

Earle, Rebecca. *The Body of the Conquistador: Food, Race, and the Colonial Experience in Spanish America, 1942–1700*. New York: Cambridge University Press, 2012.

Eckes, Alfred E. *Opening America's Market: U.S. Foreign Trade Policy since 1776*. Chapel Hill: University of North Carolina Press, 1995.

Elena, Eduardo. *Dignifying Argentina: Peronism, Citizenship, and Mass Consumption*. Pittsburgh: University of Pittsburgh Press, 2011.

Enstad, Nan. *Ladies of Labor, Girls of Adventure: Working Women, Popular Culture, and Labor Politics at the Turn of the Twentieth Century*. New York: Columbia University Press, 1999.

Estudios Migratorios Latinoamericanos. Special Issue: *Las cadenas migratorias italianas a la Argentina* 3, no. 8 (1988).

Eula, Michael J. "Failure of American Food Reformers among Italian Immigrants in New York City, 1891–1897." *Italian Americana* 18 (Winter 2000): 86–99.

Ewen, Elizabeth. *Immigrant Women in the Land of Dollars: Life and Culture on the Lower East Side, 1890–1925*. New York: Monthly Review Press, 1985.

Ewen, Stuart. *Captains of Consciousness: Advertising and the Social Roots of the Consumer Culture*. New York: McGraw-Hill, 1976.

Ewen, Stuart, and Elizabeth Ewen. *Channels of Desire: Mass Images and the Shaping of American Consciousness*. New York: McGraw-Hill, 1982.

Falasca-Zamponi, Simonetta. *Fascist Spectacle: The Aesthetics of Power in Mussolini's Italy*. Berkeley: University of California Press, 1997.

Fanesi, Pietro Rinaldo. "Italian Antifascism and the Garibaldine Tradition in Latin America." In *Italian Workers of the World: Labor Migration and the Formation of Multiethnic States*, translated by Michael Rocke, edited by Donna R. Gabaccia and Fraser M. Ottanelli, 163–77. Urbana: University of Illinois Press, 2001.

Fernández, Alejandro. *Un "mercado étnico" en la Plata: Emigración y exportaciones españolas a la Argentina, 1880–1935*. Madrid: Consejo Superior de Investigaciones Científicas, 2004.

Feys, Torsten. *The Battle for the Migrants: The Introduction of Steamshipping on the North Atlantic and Its Impact on the European Exodus*. St. John's, Newfoundland: International Maritime Economic History Association, 2013.

Finchelstein, Federico. *Fascismo, liturgia e imaginario. El mito del General Uriburu y la Argentina nacionalista*. Buenos Aires: Fondo de Cultura Económica, 2002.

———. *Transatlantic Fascism: Ideology, Violence, and the Sacred in Argentina and Italy, 1919–1945*. Durham, NC: Duke University Press, 2010.

FitzGerald, David Scott, and David Cook-Martín. *Culling the Masses: The Democratic Origins of Racist Immigration Policy in the Americas*. Cambridge: Harvard University Press, 2014.

Foerster, Robert F. *The Italian Emigration of Our Times*. Cambridge: Harvard University Press, 1919.

Fontana, Giovanni Luigi, and Emilio Franzina, eds. *Profili di Camere di commercio italiane all'estero*. Vol. 1. Soveria Mannelli, Italy: Rubbettino Editore, 2001.

Ford, Nancy Gentile. *Americans All!: Foreign-Born Soldiers in World War I*. College Station: Texas A&M University Press, 2001.

Freedman, Paul. "American Restaurants and Cuisine in the Mid-Nineteenth Century." *New England Quarterly* 84, no. 1 (2011): 5–59.

French, M. J. "The Emergence of a U.S. Multinational Enterprise: The Goodyear Tire and Rubber Company, 1910–1939." *Economic History Review* 40, no. 1 (1987): 64–79.

Frid de Silberstein, Carina. "Migrants, Farmers, and Workers: Italians in the Land of Ceres." In *Italian Workers of the World: Labor Migration and the Formation of Multiethnic States*, edited by Donna R. Gabaccia and Fraser M. Ottanelli, 79–101. Urbana: University of Illinois Press, 2001.

Frieden, Jeffry A. *Global Capitalism: Its Fall and Rise in the Twentieth Century*. New York: Norton, 2006.

Gabaccia, Donna R. "Ethnicity in the Business World: Italians in American Food Industries." *Italian American Review* 6, no. 2 (1997/1998): 1–19.

———. "Food, Mobility, and World History." In *The Oxford Handbook of Food History*, edited by Jeffrey M. Pilcher, 305–323. New York: Oxford University Press, 2012.

———. *Foreign Relations: American Immigration in Global Perspective*. Princeton, NJ: Princeton University Press, 2012.

———. *From Sicily to Elizabeth Street: Housing and Social Change among Italian Immigrants, 1880–1930*. Albany: State University of New York Press, 1984.

——. *From the Other Side: Women, Gender, and Immigrant Life in the U.S., 1820–1990*. Bloomington: Indiana University Press, 1994.

——. "In the Shadows of the Periphery: Italian Women in the Nineteenth Century." In *Connecting Spheres: Women in the Western World, 1500 to Present*, edited by Marilyn J. Boxer and Jean H. Quataert, 166–76. New York: Oxford University Press, 1987.

——. *Italy's Many Diasporas*. Seattle: University of Washington Press, 2000.

——. "Making Foods Italian in the Hispanic Atlantic." Unpublished paper, University of Minnesota, November 1, 2006.

——. *Militants and Migrants: Rural Sicilians Become American Workers*. New Brunswick, NJ: Rutgers University Press 1988.

——. "Nations of Immigrants: Do Words Matter?" *Pluralist* 5, no. 3 (2010): 5–31.

——. "Race, Nation, Hyphen: Italian-American Multiculturalism in Comparative Perspective." In *Are Italians White? How Race Is Made in America*, edited by Jennifer Guglielmo and Salvatore Salerno, 44–59. New York: Routledge, 2003.

——. *We Are What We Eat: Ethnic Food and the Making of Americans*. Cambridge: Harvard University Press, 1998.

——. "When the Migrants Are Men: Italy's Women and Transnationalism as a Working-Class Way of Life." In *American Dreaming, Global Realities: Rethinking U.S. Immigration History*, edited by Donna R. Gabaccia and Vicki L. Ruiz, 190–206. Urbana: University of Illinois Press, 2006.

——. "Women of the Mass Migrations: From Minority to Majority, 1820–1930." In *European Migrants: Global and Local Perspectives*, edited by Dirk Hoerder and Leslie Page Moch, 91–111. Boston: Northeastern University Press, 1996.

Gabaccia, Donna R., and Franca Iacovetta, eds. *Women, Gender, and Transnational Lives: Italian Workers of the World*. Toronto: University of Toronto Press, 2002.

Gabaccia, Donna R., and Fraser M. Ottanelli, eds. *Italian Workers of the World: Labor Migration and the Formation of Multiethnic States*. Urbana: University of Illinois Press, 2001.

Gabaccia, Donna R., and Jeffrey M. Pilcher. "'Chili Queens' and Checkered Tablecloths: Public Dining Cultures of Italians in New York City and Mexicans in San Antonio, Texas, 1870s–1940s." *Radical History Review* 110 (Spring 2011): 109–126.

Galante, John Starosta. "The 'Great War' in *Il Plata*: Italian Immigrants in Buenos Aires and Montevideo during the First World War." *Journal of Migration History* 2, no. 1 (2016): 57–92.

Gardner, Martha. *The Qualities of a Citizen: Women, Immigration, and Citizenship, 1870–1965*. Princeton, NJ: Princeton University Press, 2005.

Gentilcore, David. *Pomodoro!: A History of the Tomato in Italy*. New York: Columbia University Press, 2010.

Gentile, Emilio. "La politica estera del partito fascista: Ideologia e organizzazione dei fasci italiani all'estero (1920–1930)." *Storia Contemporanea* 26, no. 2 (1995): 897–956.

Gerstle, Gary. *American Crucible: Race and Nation in the Twentieth Century*. Princeton, NJ: Princeton University Press, 2001.

Gilbert, Jonathan. "How One Company Turned Grandpa's Booze into Argentina's National Drink." *Fortune*, March 18, 2016. http://fortune.com/2016/03/18/fernet-branca -argentina.

Girardelli, Davide. "Commodified Identities: The Myth of Italian Food in the United States." *Journal of Communication Inquiry* 28, no. 4 (2004): 307–324.

Girbal-Blacha, Noemí M., and María Silvia Ospital. "'Vivir con lo nuestro': Publicidad y política en la Argentina de los años 1930." *European Review of Latin American and Caribbean Studies* 78 (April 2005): 49–66.

Gobat, Michel. "The Invention of Latin America: A Transnational History of Anti-Imperialism, Democracy, and Race." *American Historical Review* 118, no. 5 (2013): 1345–75.

Goldstein, Carolyn M. *Creating Consumers: Home Economists in Twentieth-Century America*. Chapel Hill: University of North Carolina Press, 2012.

Gomez, Mario, and Jorge Risso. "Fernet con Coca." Performed by Vilma Palma e Vampiros. *Fondo Profundo*. Barca Discos, 1994. CD.

Goody, Jack. *Cooking, Cuisine, and Class: A Study in Comparative Sociology*. Cambridge: Cambridge University Press, 1982.

Gori, Gigliola. "Model of Masculinity: Mussolini, the 'New Italian' of the Fascist Era." In *Superman Supreme: Fascist Body as Political Icon—Global Fascism*, edited by J. A. Mangan, 27–61. London: Frank Cass Publishers, 1999.

Greene, Julie. *The Canal Builders: Making America's Empire at the Panama Canal*. New York: Penguin Press, 2009.

Guglielmo, Jennifer. *Living the Revolution: Italian Women's Resistance and Radicalism in New York City, 1880–1945*. Chapel Hill: University of North Carolina Press, 2010.

Guglielmo, Jennifer, and Salvatore Salerno, eds. *Are Italians White?: How Race Is Made in America*. New York: Routledge, 2003.

Guglielmo, Thomas A. *White on Arrival: Italians, Race, Color, and Power in Chicago, 1890–1945*. Oxford: Oxford University Press, 2003.

Gundle, Stephen. *Bellissima: Feminine Beauty and the Idea of Italy*. New Haven, CT: Yale University Press, 2007.

Guy, Donna J. "Dependency, the Credit Market, and Argentine Industrialization, 1860–1940." *Business History Review* 58, no. 4 (1984): 532–61.

———. *Sex and Danger in Buenos Aires: Prostitution, Family, and Nation in Argentina*. Lincoln: University of Nebraska Press, 1991.

———. "Women, Peonage, and Industrialization: Argentina, 1810–1914." *Latin American Research Review* 16, no. 3 (1981): 65–89.

Halter, Marilyn. *Shopping for Identity: The Marketing of Ethnicity*. New York: Schocken Books, 2000.

Hametz, Maura E. *In the Name of Italy: Nation, Family, and Patriotism in a Fascist Court*. New York: Fordham University Press, 2012.

Harzig, Christiane, and Dirk Hoerder, with Donna Gabaccia. *What Is Migration History?* Cambridge, MA: Polity Press, 2009.

Heinze, Andrew R. *Adapting to Abundance: Jewish Immigrants, Mass Consumption, and the Search for American Identity*. New York: Columbia University Press, 1990.

Helstosky, Carol. *Garlic and Oil: Politics and Food in Italy*. Oxford: Berg, 2004.

———. "Recipe for the Nation: Reading Italian History through *La scienza in cucina* and *La cucina futurista*." *Food and Foodways* 11, nos. 2/3 (2003): 113–40.

Higham, John. *Strangers in the Land: Patterns of American Nativism, 1860–1925*. New Brunswick, NJ: Rutgers University Press, 1955.

Hoerder, Dirk. *Cultures in Contact: World Migrations in the Second Millennium*. Durham, NC: Duke University Press, 2002.

———, ed. *Labor Migration in the Atlantic Economies: The European and North American Working Classes during the Period of Industrialization*. Westport, CT: Greenwood Press, 1985.

Hoffenberg, Peter H. *An Empire on Display: English, Indian, and Australian Exhibitions from the Crystal Palace to the Great War*. Berkeley: University of California Press, 2001.

Hoganson, Kristin L. *Consumers' Imperium: The Global Production of American Domesticity, 1865–1920*. Chapel Hill: University of North Carolina Press, 2007.

Horowitz, Roger. *Kosher USA: How Coke Became Kosher and Other Tales of Modern Food*. New York: Columbia University Press, 2016.

———. *Putting Meat on the American Table: Taste, Technology, Transformation*. Baltimore: Johns Hopkins University Press, 2006.

Inness, Sherrie A., ed. *Cooking Lessons: The Politics of Gender and Food*. Lanham, MD: Rowman & Littlefield, 2001.

———. *Kitchen Culture in America: Popular Representations of Food, Gender, and Race*. Philadelphia: University of Pennsylvania Press, 2001.

Jacobs, Meg. *Pocketbook Politics: Economic Citizenship in Twentieth-American America*. Princeton, NJ: Princeton University Press, 2005.

Jacobson, Matthew Frye. *Roots Too: White Ethnic Revival in Post–Civil Rights America*. Cambridge: Harvard University Press, 2006.

———. *Whiteness of a Different Color: European Immigrants and the Alchemy of Race*. Cambridge: Harvard University Press, 1999.

James, Daniel. *Doña Maria's Story: Life History, Memory, and Political Identity*. Durham, NC: Duke University Press, 2000.

Jass, Stephanie J. "Recipes for Reform: Americanization and Foodways in Chicago Settlement Houses, 1890–1920." PhD diss., Western Michigan University, 2004.

Jones, Jennifer. "*Coquettes* and *Grisettes*: Women Buying and Selling in Ancien Régime Paris." In *The Sex of Things: Gender and Consumption in Historical Perspective*, edited by Victoria de Grazia, with Ellen Furlough, 25–53. Berkeley: University of California Press, 1996.

Joselit, Jenna Weissman. *The Wonders of America: Reinventing Jewish Culture 1880–1950*. New York: Henry Holt, 1994.

Joseph, Gilbert M. "Close Encounters: Toward a New Cultural History of U.S.–Latin American Relations." In *Close Encounters of Empire: Writing the Cultural History of U.S.–Latin American Relations*, edited by Gilbert M. Joseph, Catherine C. LeGrand, and Ricardo D. Salvatore, 3–46. Durham, NC: Duke University Press, 1998.

Joseph, Gilbert M., Catherine C. LeGrand, and Ricardo D. Salvatore, eds. *Close Encounters of Empire: Writing the Cultural History of U.S.–Latin American Relations*. Durham, NC: Duke University Press, 1998.

Kanawada, Leo V., Jr. *Franklin D. Roosevelt's Diplomacy and American Catholics, Italians, and Jews*. Ann Arbor, MI: UMI Research Press, 1982.

Karush, Matthew B. *Culture of Class: Radio and Cinema in the Making of a Divided Argentina, 1920–1946*. Durham, NC: Duke University Press, 2012.

Keeling, Drew. *The Business of Transatlantic Migration between Europe and the United States, 1900–1914*. Zurich: Chronos, 2012.

Kertzer, David I. *Family Life in Central Italy, 1880–1910: Sharecropping, Wage Labor, and Coresidence*. New Brunswick, NJ: Rutgers University Press, 1984.

King, Russell. "Recent Immigration to Italy: Character, Causes and Consequences." *GeoJournal* 30, no. 3 (1993): 283–92.

Kinsbruner, Jay. *Independence in Spanish America: Civil Wars, Revolutions, and Underdevelopment*, 2nd rev. ed. Albuquerque: University of New Mexico Press, 2000.

Kraut, Alan M. *Silent Travelers: Germs, Genes, and the "Immigrant Menace."* New York: Basic-Books, 1994.

Ku, Robert Ji-Song, Martin F. Manalansan IV, and Anita Mannur, eds., *Eating Asian America: A Food Studies Reader*. New York: New York University Press, 2013.

Laird, Pamela Walker. *Advertising Progress: American Business and the Rise of Consumer Marketing*. Baltimore: Johns Hopkins University Press, 1998.

Lamoreaux, Naomi R. *The Great Merger Movement in American Business, 1895–1904*. New York: Cambridge University Press, 1985.

Leach, William. *Land of Desire: Merchants, Power and the Rise of a New American Culture*. New York: Pantheon Books, 1993.

Lears, Jackson. *Fables of Abundance: A Cultural History of Advertising in America*. New York: Basic Books, 1994.

Lee, Erika. *At America's Gates: Chinese Immigration during the Exclusion Era, 1882–1943*. Chapel Hill: University of North Carolina, 2003.

———. "Enforcing the Borders: Chinese Exclusion along the U.S. Borders with Canada and Mexico, 1882–1924." *Journal of American History* 89, no. 1 (2002): 54–86.

———. "Orientalisms in the Americas: A Hemispheric Approach to Asian American History." *Journal of Asian American Studies* 8, no. 3 (2005): 235–56.

Leonardi, Andrea, Alberto Cova, and Pasquale Galea. *Il Novecento economico italiano: Dalla grande guerra al "miracolo economico" (1914–1962)*. Bologna, Italy: Monduzzi, 1997.

Lepore, Silvia. "Economic Profile of Italian Argentines in the 1980s." In *The Columbus People: Perspectives in Italian Immigration to the Americas and Australia*, edited by Lydio F. Tomasi, Piero Gastaldo, and Thomas Row, 125–51. New York: Center for Migration Studies, 1994.

Lesser, Jeffrey. *Immigration, Ethnicity, and National Identity in Brazil, 1808 to the Present*. Cambridge: Cambridge University Press, 2013.

Levenstein, Harvey. "The American Response to Italian Food, 1880–1930." *Food and Foodways* 1 (1985): 1–24.

———. *Revolution at the Table: The Transformation of the American Diet*. New York: Oxford University Press, 1988.

Lévi-Strauss, Claude. "The Culinary Triangle." In *Food and Culture: A Reader*. 3rd ed., edited by Carole Counihan and Penny Van Esterik, 40–47. New York: Routledge, 2013.

Levy, Carl, ed. *Italian Regionalism: History, Identity, and Politics*. Oxford: Berg, 1996.

Lewis, Paul H. *The Crisis of Argentine Capitalism*. Chapel Hill: University of North Carolina Press, 1990.

Lobato, Mirta Zaida. "*La Patria degli Italiani* and Social Conflict in Early Twentieth-Century Argentina," translated by Amy Ferlazzo. In *Italian Workers of the World: Labor Migration and the Formation of Multiethnic States*, edited by Donna R. Gabaccia and Fraser M. Ottanelli, 63–78. Urbana: University of Illinois Press, 2001.

Loubère, Leo A. *The Red and the White: A History of Wine in France and Italy in the Nineteenth Century*. Albany: State University of New York Press, 1978.

Lucht, Hans. *Darkness before Daybreak: African Migrants Living on the Margins in Southern Italy Today*. Berkeley: University of California Press, 2012.

Luconi, Stefano. *La 'diplomazia parallela': Il regime fascista e la mobilitazione politica degli italo-americani*. Milan: F. Angeli, 2000.

——. "Etnia e patriottismo nella pubblicità per gli italo-americani durante la guerra d'Etiopia." *Italia Contemporanea* 241 (2005): 514–22.

——. *From* Paesani *to* White Ethnics: The Italian Experience in Philadelphia. Albany: State University of New York Press, 2001.

——. "Italian Americans, the New Deal State, and the Making of Citizen Consumers." In *Making Italian America: Consumer Culture and the Production of Ethnic Identities*, edited by Simone Cinotto, 137–47. New York: Fordham University Press, 2014.

——. "The Italian-Language Press, Italian American Voters, and Political Intermediation in Pennsylvania in the Interwar Years." *International Migration Review* 33, no. 4 (1999): 1031–61.

Luconi, Stefano, and Guido Tintori. *L'ombra lunga del fascio: Canali di propaganda fascista per gli "italiani d'America."* Milan: M&B Publishing, 2004.

Luibhéid, Eithne. *Entry Denied: Controlling Sexuality at the Border*. Minneapolis: University of Minnesota Press, 2002.

Lumley, Robert, and Jonathan Morris. *The New History of the Italian South: The Mezzogiorno Revisited*. Exeter: University of Exeter Press, 1997.

Mahler, Sarah J., and Patricia R. Pessar. "Gendered Geographies of Power: Analyzing Gender across Transnational Spaces." *Identities* 7, no. 4 (2001): 441–59.

Manning, Patrick. *Migration in World History*, 2nd ed. New York: Routledge, 2013.

Mannur, Anita. "Asian American Food-Scapes." *Amerasia Journal* 32, no. 2 (2006): 1–5.

Marchand, Roland. *Advertising the American Dream: Making Way for Modernity, 1920–1940*. Berkeley: University of California Press, 1985.

Mariani, John F. "Everybody Likes Italian Food." *American Heritage* 40, no. 8 (1989): 122–131.

——. *How Italian Food Conquered the World*. New York: Palgrave Macmillian, 2011.

Massey, Douglas S., Jorge Durand, and Nolan J. Malone. *Beyond Smoke and Mirrors: Mexican Immigration in an Era of Economic Integration*. New York: Russell Sage Foundation, 2002.

Matsumoto, Valerie J. "Apple Pie and *Makizushi*: Japanese American Women Sustaining Family and Community." In *Eating Asian America: A Food Studies Reader*, edited by Robert Ji-Song Ku, Martin F. Manalansan IV, and Anita Mannur, 255–73. New York: New York University Press, 2013.

McKeown, Adam M. *Melancholy Order: Asian Migration and the Globalization of Borders*. New York: Columbia University Press, 2008.

McKibben, Carol Lynn. *Beyond Cannery Row: Sicilian Women, Immigration, and Community in Monterey, California, 1915–99*. Urbana: University of Illinois Press, 2006.

Meldini, Piero. *Sposa e madre esemplare: Ideologia e politica della donna e della famiglia durante il fascismo*. Rimini, Italy: Guaraldi, 1975.

Míguez, Eduardo José. "Il comportamento matrimoniale degli italiani in Argentina. Un bilancio." In *Identità degli italiani in Argentina: Reti sociali, famiglia, lavoro*, edited by Gianfausto Rosoli, 81–105. Rome: Edizioni Studium, 1993.

——. "Introduction: Foreign Mass Migration to Latin America in the Nineteenth and Twentieth Centuries—an Overview." In *Mass Migration to Modern Latin America*, edited by Samuel Baily and Eduardo José Míguez, xiii–xxv. Wilmington, DE: Scholarly Resources, 2003.

Milanesio, Natalia. "Food Politics and Consumption in Peronist Argentina." *Hispanic American Historical Review* 90, no. 1 (2010): 75–108.

——. *Workers Go Shopping in Argentina: The Rise of Popular Consumer Culture*. Albuquerque: University of New Mexico Press, 2013.

Moya, Jose C. *Cousins and Strangers: Spanish Immigrants in Buenos Aires, 1850–1930*. Berkeley: University of California Press, 1998.

——. "Italians in Buenos Aires's Anarchist Movement: Gender Ideology and Women's Participation, 1890–1910." In *Women, Gender, and Transnational Lives: Italian Workers of the World*, edited by Donna R. Gabaccia and Franca Iacovetta, 189–216. Toronto: University of Toronto Press, 2002.

Newton, Ronald C. "Ducini, Prominenti, Antifascisti: Italian Fascism and the Italo-Argentine Collectivity, 1922–1945." *Americas* 51, no. 1 (1994): 41–66.

Ngai, Mae M. *Impossible Subjects: Illegal Aliens and the Making of Modern America*. Princeton, NJ: Princeton University Press, 2004.

Okun, Mitchell. *Fair Play in the Marketplace: The First Battle for Pure Food and Drugs*. DeKalb: Northern Illinois University Press, 1986.

O'Rourke, Kevin H., and Jeffrey G. Williamson. *Globalization and History: The Evolution of a Nineteenth-Century Atlantic Economy*. Cambridge: MIT Press, 1999.

Ottanelli, Fraser M. "'If Fascism Comes to America We Will Push It Back into the Ocean': Italian American Antifascism in the 1920s and 1930s." In *Italian Workers of the World: Labor Migration and the Formation of Multiethnic States*, edited by Donna R. Gabaccia and Fraser M. Ottanelli, 178–95. Urbana: University of Illinois Press, 2001.

Padoongpatt, Tanachai Mark. "Too Hot to Handle: Food, Empire, and Race in Thai Los Angeles." *Radical History Review* 110 (Spring 2011): 83–108.

Papademetriou, Demetrios G., and Kimberly A. Hamilton. *Converging Paths to Restriction: French, Italian, and British Responses to Immigration*. Washington, DC: Carnegie Endowment for International Peace, 1996.

Parasecoli, Fabio. *Al Dente: A History of Food in Italy*. London: Reaktion Books, 2014.

——. *Food Culture in Italy*. Westport, CT: Greenwood Press, 2004.

——. "We Are Family: Ethnic Food Marketing and the Consumption of Authenticity in Italian-Themed Chain Restaurants." In *Making Italian America: Consumer Culture and the*

Production of Ethnic Identities, edited by Simone Cinotto, 244–55. New York: Fordham University Press, 2014.

Parati, Graziella. *Migration Italy: The Art of Talking Back in a Destination Culture*. Toronto: University of Toronto Press, 2005.

Paulicelli, Eugenia. *Fashion under Fascism: Beyond the Black Shirt*. Oxford: Berg, 2004.

Pedrocco, Giorgio. "La conservazione del cibo: Dal sale all'industria agro-alimentare." In *Storia d'Italia, Annali 13, L'alimentazione*, edited by Alberto Capatti, Albero De Bernardi, and Angelo Varni, 419–52. Turin: Einaudi, 1998.

Peiss, Kathy. *Cheap Amusements: Working Women and Leisure in Turn-of-the-Century New York*. Philadelphia: Temple University Press, 1986.

———. *Hope in a Jar: The Making of America's Beauty Industry*. Philadelphia: University of Pennsylvania Press, 2011.

———. "Making Up, Making Over: Cosmetics, Consumer Culture, and Women's Identity." In *The Sex of Things: Gender and Consumption in Historical Perspective*, edited by Victoria de Grazia, with Ellen Furlough, 311–36. Berkeley: University of California Press, 1996.

Pellicciari, Giovanni, and Gianfranco Albertelli, ed. *L'immigrazione nel triangolo industriale*. Milan: Angeli, 1970.

Pendergrast, Mark. *For God, Country, and Coca-Cola: The Unauthorized History of the Great American Soft Drink and the Company That Makes It*. New York: Scribner's, 1993.

Perlmann, Joel. *Italians Then, Mexicans Now: Immigrant Origins and Second-Generation Progress, 1890 to 2000*. New York: Russell Sage Foundation, 2007.

Petrini, Carlo. *Slow Food: The Case for Taste*. Translated by William McCuaig. New York: Columbia University Press, 2003.

Pickering-Iazzi, Robin, ed. *Mothers of Invention: Women, Italian Fascism, and Culture*. Minneapolis: University of Minneapolis Press, 1995.

Pilcher, Jeffrey M. "Eating à la Criolla: Global and Local Foods in Argentina, Cuba, and Mexico." *IdeAs* 3 (Winter 2012): 3–16.

———. "'Old Stock' Tamales and Migrant Tacos: Taste, Authenticity, and the Naturalization of Mexican Food." *Social Research* 81, no. 2 (2014): 441–62.

———. *Planet Taco: A Global History of Mexican Food*. New York: Oxford University Press, 2012.

———. *Que vivan los tamales!: Food and the Making of Mexican Identity*. Albuquerque: University of New Mexico Press, 1998.

Pineda, Yovanna. *Industrial Development in a Frontier Economy: The Industrialization of Argentina, 1890–1930*. Stanford, CA: Stanford University Press, 2009.

Pite, Rebekah E. "*La cocina criolla*: A History of Food and Race in Twentieth-Century Argentina." In *Rethinking Race in Modern Argentina*, edited by Paulina L. Alberto and Eduardo Elena, 99–125. New York: Cambridge University Press, 2016.

———. *Creating a Common Table in Twentieth-Century Argentina: Doña Petrona, Women, and Food*. Chapel Hill: University of North Carolina Press, 2013.

Poe, Tracy N. "The Labour and Leisure of Food Production as a Mode of Ethnic Identity Building among Italians in Chicago, 1890–1940." *Rethinking History* 5, no. 1 (2001): 131–48.

Portes, Alejandro, ed. *The Economic Sociology of Immigration: Essays on Networks, Ethnicity, and Entrepreneurship*. New York: Russell Sage Foundation, 1995.

———. "NAFTA and Mexican Immigration." Border Battles: The U.S. Immigration Debates. Social Science Research Council, 2006. http://borderbattles.ssrc.org/Portes.

Portes, Alejandro, Luis Eduardo Guarnizo, and William J. Haller. "Transnational Entrepreneurs: An Alternative Form of Immigration Economic Adaption." *American Sociological Review* 67, no. 2 (2002): 278–98.

Pozzetta, George E. "The Italian Immigrant Press of New York City: The Early Years, 1880–1915." *Journal of Ethnic Studies* 1 (Fall 1973): 32–46.

Pretelli, Matteo. "Culture or Propaganda? Fascism and Italian Culture in the United States." *Studi Emigrazione* 43, no. 161 (2006): 171–92.

———. "Tra estremismo e moderazione. Il ruolo dei circoli fascisti italo-americani nella politica estera italiana degli anni Trenta." *Studi Emigrazione* 40, no. 150 (2003): 315–23.

Ragionieri, Ernesto. "Italiani all'estero ed emigrazione di lavoratori italiani: Un tema di storia del movimento operaio." *Belfagor, Rassegna di varia umanità* 17, no. 6 (1962): 640–69.

Ramon-Muñoz, Ramon. "Modernizing the Mediterranean Olive-Oil Industry." In *The Food Industries of Europe in the Nineteenth and Twentieth Centuries*, edited by Derek J. Oddy and Alain Drouard, 71–88. Burlington, VT: Ashgate, 2013.

Ramos Mejía, José María. *The Argentine Masses* (1899). In *Darwinism in Argentina: Major Texts, 1845–1909*, edited by Leila Gómez, translated by Nicholas Ford Callaway, 207–216. Lanham, MD: Bucknell University Press.

Rappaport, Erika. "'A Husband and His Wife's Dresses': Consumer Credit and the Debtor Family in England, 1864–1914." In *The Sex of Things: Gender and Consumption in Historical Perspective*, edited by Victoria de Grazia, with Ellen Furlough, 163–87. Berkeley: University of California Press, 1996.

———. *Shopping for Pleasure: Women in the Making of London's West End*. Princeton, NJ: Princeton University Press, 2000.

Ray, Krishnendu. *The Ethnic Restaurateur*. New York: Bloomsbury Academic, 2016.

Reeder, Linda. *Widows in White: Migration and the Transformation of Rural Italian Women, Sicily, 1880–1920*. Toronto: University of Toronto Press, 2003.

Regalsky, Andrés, and Aníbal Jáuregui. "Americanización, proyecto económico y las ideas de Alejandro Bunge en la décade de 1920." In *Americanización: Estados Unidos y América Latina en el siglo XX. Transferencias económicas, tecnológicas y culturales*, edited by María I. Barbero and Andrés M. Regalsky, 85–117. Buenos Aires: EDUNTREF, 2014.

Renda, Mary A. *Taking Haiti: Military Occupation and the Culture of U.S. Imperialism, 1915–1940*. Chapel Hill: University of North Carolina Press, 2001.

Riall, Lucy. *Garibaldi: Invention of a Hero*. New Haven, CT: Yale University Press, 2007.

———. *Risorgimento: The History of Italy from Napoleon to Nation-state*. New York: Palgrave Macmillan, 2009.

Rocchi, Fernando. "La americanización del consumo: Las batallas por el mercado argentino, 1920–1945." In *Americanización: Estados Unidos y América Latina en el siglo XX*, edited by María Barbero and Andrés Regalsky, 150–216. Buenos Aires: EDUNTREF, 2014.

———. *Chimneys in the Desert: Industrialization in Argentina during the Export Boom Years, 1870–1930*. Stanford, CA: Stanford University Press, 2006.

———. "Inventando la soberanía del consumidor." In *Historia de la vida privada en la Argentina: La Argentina plural 1870–1930*, edited by Fernando Devoto and Marta Madero, 301–321. Buenos Aires: Taurus, 1999.

Rock, David. *Argentina, 1516–1987: From Spanish Colonization to Alfonsín*. Berkeley: University of California Press, 1985.

Rodriguez, Julia. *Civilizing Argentina: Science, Medicine, and the Modern State*. Chapel Hill: University of North Carolina Press, 2006.

Roldán, Diego P. *Chimeneas de carne: Una historia del frigorífico Swift de Rosario, 1907–1943*. Rosario, Argentina: Prohistoria Ediciones, 2008.

Rosenberg, Emily S. *Financial Missionaries to the World: The Politics and Culture of Dollar Diplomacy, 1900–1930*. Cambridge: Harvard University Press, 1999.

Rosoli, Gianfausto, ed. *Identità degli italiani in Argentina: Reti sociali, famiglia, lavoro*. Rome: Edizioni Studium, 1993.

———. *Un secolo di emigrazione italiana, 1876–1976*. Rome: Centro Studi Emigrazione, 1978.

Rydell, Robert W. *All the World's a Fair: Visions of Empire at American International Expositions, 1876–1916*. Chicago: University of Chicago Press, 1984.

———. *World of Fairs: The Century-of-Progress Expositions*. Chicago: University of Chicago Press, 1993.

Salerno, Aldo E. "America for Americans Only: Gino C. Speranza and the Immigrant Experience." *Italian Americana* 14, no. 2 (1996): 133–47.

Salvatore, Ricardo D. "The Enterprise of Knowledge: Representational Machines of Informal Empire." In *Close Encounters of Empire: Writing the History of U.S.–Latin American Culture Relations*, edited by Gilbert M. Joseph, Catherine C. LeGrand, and Ricardo D. Salvatore, 69–104. Durham, NC: Duke University Press, 1998.

———. "Yankee Advertising in Buenos Aires: Reflections on Americanization." *Interventions* 7, no. 2 (2005): 216–35.

Sanchez, George J. *Becoming Mexican American: Ethnicity, Culture, and Identity in Chicano Los Angeles, 1900–1945*. New York: Oxford University Press, 1993.

Sapelli, Giulio, ed. *Tra identità culturale e sviluppo di reti. Storia delle Camere di commercio italiane all'estero*. Soveria Mannelli, Italy: Rubbettino Editore, 2000.

Sassen, Saskia. *Globalization and Its Discontents: Essays on the New Mobility of People and Money*. New York: New Press, 1998.

Scanlon, Jennifer. *Inarticulate Longings: The* Ladies' Home Journal, *Gender, and the Promises of Consumer Culture*. New York: Routledge, 1995.

———. "Mediators in the International Marketplace: U.S. Advertising in Latin America in the Early Twentieth Century." *Business History Review* 77, no. 3 (2003): 387–415.

Scarpellini, Emanuela. *Material Nation: A Consumer's History of Modern Italy*. Translated by Daphne Hughes and Andrew Newton. New York: Oxford University Press, 2011.

Scarzanella, Eugenia. "L'industria argentina e gli immigrati italiani: Nascita della borghesia industriale bonaerense." In *Gli italiani fuori d'Italia: Gli emigrati italiani nei movimenti operai dei paesi d'adozione, 1880–1940*, edited by B. Bezza, 585–633. Milan: F. Angeli, 1983.

———. *Italiani d'Argentina: Storie di contadini, industriali e missionari italiani in Argentina, 1850–1912*. Venice: Marsilio, 1983.

——. *Italiani malagente: Immigrazione, criminalità, razzismo in Argentina, 1890–1940*. Milan: F. Angeli, 1999.

Scharff, Virginia. *Taking the Wheel: Women and the Coming of the Motor Age*. Albuquerque: University of New Mexico Press, 1992.

Schiller, Nina Glick, Linda Basch, and Christina Blanc-Szanton. "From Immigrant to Transmigrant: Theorizing Transnational Migration." *Anthropological Quarterly* 68, no. 1 (1995): 48–63.

——. "Towards a Definition of Transnationalism: Introductory Remarks and Research Questions." *Annals of the New York Academy of Sciences* 645 (July 1992): ix–xiv.

Schneider, Jane, and Peter Schneider. *Culture and Political Economy in Western Sicily*. New York: Academic Press, 1976.

Scirocco, Alfonso. *Garibaldi: Citizen of the World*. Translated by Allan Cameron. Princeton, NJ: Princeton University Press, 2007.

Scobie, James R. *Revolution on the Pampas: A Social History of Argentine Wheat, 1860–1910*. Austin: University of Texas Press, 1964.

Sergi, Pantaleone. "Fascismo e antifascismo nella stampa italiana in Argentina: Così fu spenta 'La Patria degli Italiani.'" *Altreitalie* 35 (July–December 2007): 4–43.

Serventi, Silvano, and Françoise Sabban. *Pasta: The Story of a Universal Food*. New York: Columbia University Press, 2002.

Shapiro, Laura. *Perfection Salad: Women and Cooking at the Turn of the Century*. New York: Farrar, Straus, and Giroux, 1986.

Sherman, Robert B., and Richard M. Sherman. "A Spoonful of Sugar." Performed by Julie Andrews. *Mary Poppins*. Walt Disney Productions, 1964.

Shukla, Sandhya, and Heidi Tinsman, eds. *Imagining Our Americas: Toward a Transnational Frame*. Durham, NC: Duke University Press, 2007.

Sinke, Suzanne M. *Dutch Immigrant Women in the United States, 1880–1920*. Urbana: University of Illinois Press, 2002.

Siu, Lok C. D. *Memories of a Future Home: Diasporic Citizenship of Chinese in Panama*. Stanford, CA: Stanford University Press, 2005.

Skaggs, Jimmy M. *Prime Cut: Livestock Raising and Meatpacking in the United States, 1607–1983*. College Station: Texas A&M University Press, 1986.

Smith, Peter H. *Politics and Beef in Argentina: Patterns of Conflict and Change*. New York: Columbia University Press, 1969.

Sniderman, Paul M, Pierangelo Peri, Rui J.P. de Figueiredo Jr., and Thomas Piazza. *The Outsider: Prejudice and Politics in Italy*. Princeton, NJ: Princeton University Press, 2000.

Solberg, Carl. "The Tariff and Politics in Argentina, 1916–1930." *Hispanic American Historical Review* 53, no. 2 (1973): 260–84.

Soluri, John. *Banana Cultures: Agriculture, Consumption, and Environmental Change in Honduras and the United States*. Austin: University of Texas Press, 2005.

Spickard, Paul R. *Almost All Aliens: Immigration, Race, and Colonialism in American History and Identity*. New York: Routledge, 2007.

Stepan, Nancy Leys. *The Hour of Eugenics: Race, Gender, and Nation in Latin America*. Ithaca, NY: Cornell University Press, 1991.

Stern, Alexandra Minna. *Eugenic Nation: Faults and Frontiers of Better Breeding in Modern America*. Berkeley: University of California Press, 2005.

Strasser, Susan. *Satisfaction Guaranteed: The Making of the American Mass Market*. New York: Pantheon Books, 1989.

Striffler, Steve, and Mark Moberg. *Banana Wars: Power, Production, and History in the Americas*. Durham, NC: Duke University Press, 2003.

Terrill, Tom E. *The Tariff, Politics, and American Foreign Policy, 1874–1901*. Westport, CT: Greenwood Press, 1973.

Teti, Vito. "Emigrazione, alimentazione, culture popolari." In *Storia dell'emigrazione Italiana. Partenze*, edited by Piero Bevilacqua, Andreina De Clementi, and Emilio Franzina, 575–600. Rome: Donzelli Editore, 2001.

——, ed. *Mangiare meridiano: Culture alimentari del Mediterraneo*. Traversa Cassiodoro, Italy: Abramo, 2002.

——. *Storia del peperoncino: Un protagonista delle culture mediterranee*. Rome: Donzelli Editore, 2007.

Thistlethwaite, Frank. "Migration from Europe Overseas in the Nineteenth and Twentieth Centuries." In *A Century of European Migrations, 1830–1930*, edited by Rudolph J. Vecoli and Suzanne Sinke, 17–57. Urbana: University of Illinois Press, 1991.

Tiersten, Lisa. *Marianne in the Market: Envisioning Consumer Society in Fin-de-Siècle France*. Berkeley: University of California Press, 2001.

Tilly, Louise A., and Joan W. Scott. *Women, Work, and Family*. New York: Holt, Rinehart, and Winston, 1978.

Tintori, Guido. "More Than One Million Individuals Got Italian Citizenship Abroad in Twelve Years (1998–2010)." European Union Democracy, November 21, 2012. http://eudo-citizenship.eu/news/citizenship-news/748-more-than-one-million-individuals-got-italian-citizenship-abroad-in-the-twelve-years-1998-2010%3E.

Tossounian, Cecilia. "Images of the Modern Girl: From the Flapper to the Joven Moderna (Buenos Aires, 1920–1940)." *Forum for Inter-American Research* 6, no. 2 (2013): 41–70.

Treviño, Pepé. *La carne podrida: El caso Swift-Deltec*, 2nd ed. Buenos Aires: A. Peña Lillo, 1972.

Vassanelli, Mil. "La Camera di commercio italiana di San Francisco." In *Profili di Camere di Commercio Italiane all'estero*, vol. 1, edited by Giovanni Luigi Fontana and Emilio Franzina, 123–48. Soveria Mannelli, Italy: Rubbettino Editore, 2001.

Vecchio, Diane C. *Merchants, Midwives, and Laboring Women: Italian Migrants in Urban America*. Urbana: University of Illinois Press, 2006.

Vecino, Diego. "Fernet: Una historia de amor argentina." *Brando*. http://www.conexion brando.com/1387961-fernet-una-historia-de-amor-argentina.

Vecoli, Rudolph J. "The Immigrant Press and the Construction of Social Reality, 1850–1920." In *Print Culture in a Diverse America*, edited by James P. Danky and Wayne A. Wiegand, 17–33. Urbana: University of Illinois Press, 1998.

Veit, Helen Zoe. *Modern Food, Moral Food: Self-Control, Science, and the Rise of Modern American Eating in the Early Twentieth Century*. Chapel Hill: University of North Carolina Press, 2013.

Vellon, Peter G. *A Great Conspiracy against Our Race: Italian Immigrant Newspapers and the Construction of Whiteness in the Early 20th Century*. New York: New York University Press, 2014.

Waldinger, Roger, Howard Aldrich, and Robin Ward. *Ethnic Entrepreneurs: Immigrant Businesses in Industrial Societies*. Newbury Park, CA: Sage, 1990.

Wilk, Richard. *Home Cooking in the Global Village: Caribbean Food from Buccaneers to Ecotourists*. New York: Berg, 2006.

Willson, Perry. *The Clockwork Factory: Women and Work in Fascist Italy*. New York: Oxford University Press, 1993.

———. *Peasant Women and Politics in Fascist Italy: The Massaie Rurali*. New York: Routledge, 2002.

Yans-McLaughlin, Virginia. *Family and Community: Italian Immigrants in Buffalo, 1880–1930*. Ithaca, NY: Cornell University Press, 1977.

Young, James Harvey. *Pure Food: Securing the Federal Food and Drugs Act of 1906*. Princeton, NJ: Princeton University Press, 1989.

Zamagni, Vera. *The Economic History of Italy, 1860–1990*. Oxford: Oxford University Press, 1993.

Zanoni, Elizabeth. "'In Italy everyone enjoys it. Why not in America?': Italian Americans and Consumption in Transnational Perspective during the Early Twentieth Century." In *Making Italian America: Consumer Culture and the Production of Ethnic Identities*, edited by Simone Cinotto, 71–82. New York: Fordham University Press, 2014.

———. "'Per Voi Signore': Gendered Representations of Fashion, Food, and Fascism in *Il Progresso Italo-Ameriano* during the 1930s." *Journal of American Ethnic History* 31, no. 3 (2012): 33–71.

Zeidel, Robert F. *Immigrants, Progressives, and Exclusion Politics: The Dillingham Commission, 1900–1927*. DeKalb: Northern Illinois University Press, 2004.

Zhou, Min. "Revisiting Ethnic Entrepreneurship: Convergencies, Controversies, and Conceptual Advancements." *International Migration Review* 38, no. 3 (2004): 1040–1074.

Zolberg, Aristide R. *A Nation by Design: Immigration Policy in the Fashioning of America*. New York: Russell Sage Foundation, 2006.

Zontini, Elisabetta. *Transnational Families, Migration and Gender: Moroccan and Filipino Women in Bologna and Barcelona*. New York: Berghahn Books, 2010.

Zucchi, John E. "Paesani or Italiani? Local and National Loyalties in an Italian Immigrant Community." In *The Family and Community Life of Italian Americans*, edited by Richard Juliani, 147–60. New York: American-Italian Historical Association, 1983.

Index

A. Castruccio and Sons, 86
advertisements: feminization of, 118–20, 122–28, 174–76; history of, 122, 127, 225n119; for Italian imports during the League of Nations' boycott, 165, 167–68; for Italian imports during World War I, 111, 118–19; for Italian imports in the Argentine press, 48, 184; for Italian imports in the U.S. press, 48; for Italian imports under fascism, 147, 165–66, 167–69, 173–74, 177–78; and *Latinità*, 56; as a source, 7–9; in Spanish, 49, 154; for *tipo italiano* goods, 81, 83–84, 88–89, 113, 133, 166–67, 170; for U.S. goods in the Italian-language press, 147–54, 170, 175–76, 179, 180–81
Aeneid, 44
A. Fiore & Company, 90
agriculture: commercial, 20, 32–33, 37–38, 47, 90, 158, 160; and exports, 6, 35, 69, 139; under fascism, 159, 177; gendered transformations of, 32–33; and machinery for, 152–53, 155; and pro-wool campaigns, 103–9; and *tipo italiano* industries, 77, 85, 97, 99; work in, 38, 49, 188, 189–90; and World War I fund-raising campaigns, 111
Alighieri, Dante, 26–27
Amedeo, Luigi (Duke of Abruzzi), 28

America. *See* United States
American Chianti Wine Company, 88
American Tobacco Company, 146–47, 176, 180
Andreas, Peter, 190
Andrews, Julie, 183
Anglo Americans: and consumption, 36–37; 121–22, 146; and Italian foods, 44, 52, 59–60, 61–64, 90; and perceived differences from Italians, 52, 59–60, 96, 184; and U.S. food traditions, 59; and women, 36–37, 62–63, 74, 114
Appadurai, Arjun, 195n24
Arcondo, Aníbal, 58
Argentina: and fascism, 159–60; and food traditions in, 57–58, 183–85, 187; Italian population in, 45–46; Italians and class in, 45–46, 230n80; Italians and race in, 51, 53–59; as member of League of Nations, 162, 164–64; as receiver of migrants and exports, 2–3, 18–19, 141; *tipo italiano* industries in, 85, 86–88; and trade policy, 65, 68, 158–59
Armour and Company: in Argentina, 140, 151–52, 170–71, 181, 182; in the United States, 71, 147–49, 182
Artusi, Pellegrino, 58

ELIZABETH ZANONI is an assistant professor of history at Old Dominion University.

The University of Illinois Press
is a founding member of the
Association of American University Presses.

University of Illinois Press
1325 South Oak Street
Champaign, IL 61820-6903
www.press.uillinois.edu